Timber
Design and Construction
Handbook

Timber Design and Construction Handbook

Prepared by

Timber Engineering Company

An affiliate of the National Lumber Manufacturers Association

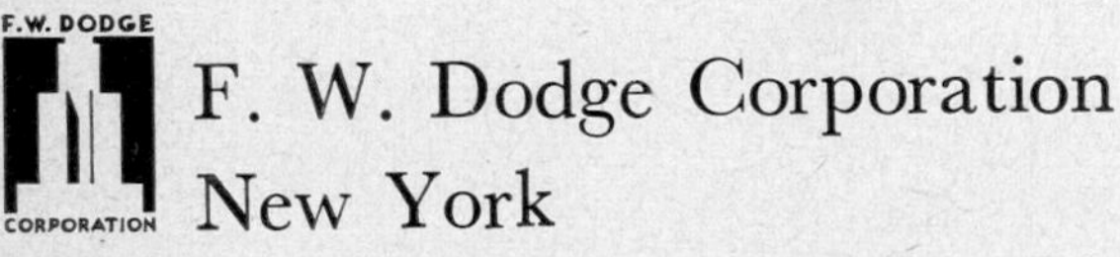

F. W. Dodge Corporation
New York

Printed and bound in U.S.A.

Library of Congress Catalog Card No. 56-10879

PREFACE

Design procedure and construction practice—in applying engineering principles to wood—have been improved significantly in recent years.

The improvements are more the result of experimentation and experience of individual designers and builders, than of ordained results flowing inevitably from theory. Consequently, much of the information on design and construction, and their interrelation, has been accumulated only by those who have specialized in timber construction for many years.

The benefits of these specialists' experience have not been generally available to architects, engineers, and students. Considerable data on basic structural design exist, but in fragmentary form scattered throughout innumerable publications, making timber design a tedious and time-consuming task.

To bring the benefits of this experience to professional and student designers, and to concentrate essential structural data in one source for easy reference, this book has been developed by Timber Engineering Company, the research and engineering affiliate of the National Lumber Manufacturers Association. The first of its kind, this work has been accomplished with the cooperation of leading technical men of the lumber, wood products, and allied industries, who served as authors, advisers, and editors.

These recognized authorities, some of them pioneers in their fields, bring to the work an abundance of practical experience of inestimable value to the architect, engineer, and student. By covering the fundamentals and the practical aspects of designing in timber, these authorities have made the book equally useful as a design reference, a practical field manual, and a textbook.

Recognizing the broad scope and intricate details of a technical publication of this type, the editors have sought to simplify and facilitate the use of the material by presenting it in three general sections.

Preface

The first section, Basic Properties (Chapters 1 and 2), deals with the fundamental structure and characteristics of wood, its species and grades, preservation, types of fastenings, and related topics that will help the designer make use of wood wisely and economically.

The second section, Design (Chapters 3 through 10), treats of preliminary considerations, general design procedure, design details, fabrication, and erection. This is the "experience" section, of which little has ever appeared before in print. Particular emphasis is placed on the more frequent problems in design, especially those common to building design. Designs of basic members and joints that have often been troublesome are illustrated by examples. In addition, the authors have dealt with many special problems and structures less frequently encountered in daily practice; constructive evaluation and outline of design procedures are included.

The design information in the second section is augmented by discussions of fabrication, assembly, erection, maintenance, and related subjects that may affect the general and the detailed design approach.

The third section, Design Standards (Chapters 11 through 13), contains specifications and tabular data. These have been conveniently grouped to provide quick reference. The tabular data are presented in simplified form so that, by interpolation, they may be easily converted to apply to a particular grade and species. Thus, the user has a concise tabular reference without the great detail, otherwise necessary, to fit the many combinations of grade, span, and loading.

The Timber Engineering Company is appreciative of the time, thought, and efforts of the men who cooperated so generously in the development and preparation of this book, among whom are:

A. S. Boisfontaine, Southern Pine Inspection Bureau
R. R. Cahal, Southern Pine Inspection Bureau
J. H. Carr, Jr., James H. Carr, Inc.
D. R. Countryman, Douglas Fir Plywood Association
*W. R. Ganser, Jr., American Institute of Timber Construction
*Ralph H. Gloss, Timber Engineering Company
*F. J. Hanrahan, American Institute of Timber Construction
A. C. Horner, Timber Engineering Company of California
Stuart Huckins, Timber Engineering Company of New England
A. C. Hutson, formerly of National Board of Fire Underwriters
R. P. A. Johnson, and staff of U.S. Forest Products Laboratory
W. D. Keeney, Service Bureau, American Wood Preservers Institute
*Verne Ketchum, Timber Structures, Inc.

*Active in the work of the Editorial Committee.

G. R. Kiewitt, Roof Structures, Inc.
*R. G. Kimbell, National Lumber Manufacturers Association
R. E. Mahaffay, West Coast Lumbermen's Association
R. W. Mann, Service Bureau, American Wood Preservers Institute
*T. K. May, West Coast Lumbermen's Association
Ward Mayer, Timber Structures, Inc.
*W. H. O'Brien, Southern Pine Association
N. S. Perkins, Douglas Fir Plywood Association
*C. A. Rasmussen, Western Pine Association
*W. H. Scales, National Lumber Manufacturers Association
H. V. Simpson, West Coast Lumbermen's Association
J. C. Van Dyke, Unit Structures, Inc.
C. H. Woodworth, Timber Structures, Inc.

Acknowledgment is also made to the many others, too numerous to list, whose counsel was most helpful during the more than four years this work was under way.

The Timber Engineering Company is especially grateful to those active in the work of the Editorial Committee, and particularly to its senior engineer, Ralph H. Gloss, who served as a member and secretary of the Editorial Committee, as an author, and as coordinator of the entire work.

HARRY G. UHL

President
Timber Engineering Company

Washington, D.C.
November 1956

FOREWORD

IF wood were discovered today it would startle the world. Mankind has lived with this "discovery" so long that it is too often taken for granted.

Assume for a moment that wood, instead of having been used since the dawn of mankind, had never existed. Plenty of stone and clay products, plenty of metal, plenty of glass—but no wood.

Suddenly, out of the research laboratories comes an amazing new product.

This "new" material is available in vast quantities. The supply renews itself so the product will always be available. It is strongly competitive in cost. It will not shatter when struck; its resilience permits it to absorb shocks that would rupture or break other material. It has fine natural insulating qualities. It can be produced in large sizes; it can readily be worked into items of exceptional delicacy. It stands up ruggedly under abuse. When properly used it will last indefinitely. Left in its natural state, it offers an infinite variety of beautiful patterns. Painted, it presents a smooth, attractive, enduring surface. It responds to manipulation with the simplest of tools and may be employed repeatedly. It is relatively light in weight, yet possessed of great strength.

There is a reason why wood has remained a primary construction material for thousands of years. The reason is simply that no competitive material has *all* the advantages of wood.

One may equal it in stiffness but lack its insulating quality. Another may rival it in strength but fail on the point of workability. A third may rank with it in workability but fail to measure up in ruggedness.

Amazing progress has been made in this generation in transforming wood from a material of craftmanship to one of engineering. Reliable structural grading, improved fastenings, efficient fabrication, and glue laminating have all contributed to making wood a truly modern engineering material.

Timber connectors and other improvements in fastenings have meant that small members could be used for larger spans. The giant blimp and dirigible hangars erected during World War II are examples of this application, and 100- to 250-ft. clear-span timber trusses are becoming common sights in our new structures. And yet the strength was always in the pieces. Who is to say that even better methods of fastening will not be developed?

There is a wide spread of strength in each classification, or grade, of lumber. Therefore, a design in wood is based on the weakest piece that may be found in a specified grade. This means that much strength is not fully used. One day there will be found a practical yet accurate way of determining the strength in lumber —and the result will be an even more efficient and economical use of wood than is possible today.

The increase in use of glued-laminated lumber has been little short of spectacular. For all practical purposes its commercial birth in this country occurred with the use of glued-laminated members at the Forest Products Laboratory in 1935. By now, interior use has become widespread and, of late, there have even been exterior and waterproof applications in such structures as bridges and ships.

The laminated arches used in churches and other buildings are among the most beautiful structures ever created from wood. A laminated beam has greater strength than a solid sawed member of the same size. It is the same lumber with which everyone is familiar, but new and improved.

Where today's combination of lumber and glue will lead, no one knows. One can only be certain that the engineers and the technicians have by no means reached the end of the possibilities.

The use of preservatively treated lumber has tripled since 1900. It is a beginning, no more. Developing fast, for example, are rigid pillar structures, the basis of which is treated poles and timbers.

As important as any factor is the growing tendency to judge lumber on the basis of the function it performs rather than on its appearance alone. Excellent service is realized today from lumber which five years ago would have gone to the mill burner or would never have been taken out of the woods. Only a start has been made along the road of differentiating between the appearance of a piece of lumber and its utility. The ultimate goal is a more efficient use of the product and therefore a more extensive application.

A great many good things are happening with wood, and the end is not yet in sight. Architects, engineers, and designers with imagination and a fresh approach will find a modern wood technology is available to help them rediscover wood's utility, beauty, and economy in construction, as well as to develop new uses for the better service of mankind.

Contents

Contents

1

Wood Properties

PHYSICAL AND NONSTRUCTURAL PROPERTIES

1.1 Cell formation A tree grows by the formation of new cells—myriads of new cells—under the bark and at the tips of the branches and roots. The growing region just under the bark is known as the cambium. If the cambium is severed by girdling, the tree will soon die. Tree growth year by year hence consists in the addition of a new and complete layer or envelope over the entire tree structure, the thickness of the growth layer depending on the growth conditions, the species, and many other factors.

Most of the cells are oriented vertically in the tree, and because they are longer than they are wide, they are called fibers.

The fibers as a rule comprise the major part of the wood. In the hardwoods, the fibers serve simply as structural elements in the tree, but in the softwoods they function also in the conduction of sap.

1.2 Hardwoods and softwoods The terms "hardwood" and "softwood" are often confusing to those not familiar with the lumber industry. Instead of indicating the hardness or softness of wood, these terms are simply popular descriptive names for two great groups known as "trees with broad leaves" and as "evergreens" or "conifers." Although the terms "hardwoods" and "softwoods" are the most generally accepted popular names for the two classes of trees, they are the most misleading. Oak, birch, and basswood are common "hardwood" species, whereas longleaf pine, spruce, and cypress are "softwoods." Although it is true that many "hardwoods," such as oak, are really hard, others, such as basswood, are softer than many "softwoods." In fact, one of the softest woods in the world, balsa, is a broadleaved species, and falls in the so-called "hardwood" group.

1.3 Annual rings In climates where temperatures limit tree growth to the summer months, each year's growth increment is usually readily distinguishable and is called an annual ring (Fig. 1.1). In

Courtesy Forest Products Laboratory

Fig. 1.1 Log cross sections

In the log at left, the denser summerwood rings are plainly darker than the springwood growth. In the log at right, the more durable heartwood appears darker than the outer sapwood.

tropical climates, growth is more or less continuous but concentric demarcations still occur as a result of fluctuations in growth activity; such demarcations should not be confused with the annual rings.

1.4 Springwood and summerwood In many trees, cells formed in the spring, when growth is most active, are comparatively large and thin-walled, whereas those formed later in the year are smaller and relatively thick-walled. The fast growth areas constitute the springwood, and the slower growth the summerwood. Obviously the thin-walled cells are weaker than the thick-walled cells, and hence summerwood is, in general, denser and stronger than springwood. In woods that exhibit a marked contrast in springwood and summerwood, such as Douglas fir and southern yellow pine, the proportion of summerwood offers a visual basis for estimating density and strength.

1.5 Sapwood and heartwood In the tree, certain of the wood elements function as living cells for a time, but eventually become inactive. As the tree increases in age and size, an increasing portion of the cells from the center of the tree outward cease to function, except as mechanical support. This inner, and usually darker, portion of the tree is called the heartwood. The outer layers of growth, which contain the only living elements of the wood, are called sapwood. The sapwood is light in color and varies greatly in thickness among species, in individual trees of the same species, and even in portions of the same tree. Sapwood is as strong as heartwood, but is not so resistant to decay.

1.6 Physical structure In physical structure, wood is made up of small, hollow fibers. The fibers in softwoods are about $\frac{1}{7}$ in. long and 0.07 in. thick; generally those in the hardwoods are much shorter. The length of the fibers, however, is not a criterion of the strength of the wood. The bond between fibers, regardless of length, is exceedingly strong, as evidenced by the fact that the fibers of wood tested in tension do not commonly separate from one another but rather tear apart.

1.7 Chemical composition Wood fibers, like those of cotton, are composed principally of cellulose and are cemented together with a substance called lignin. Cellulose comprises approximately 60 per cent of wood substance; lignin, 28 per cent; and sugars and extractives, the remaining 12 per cent. If wood chips are subjected to a chemical process, the lignin cementing material can be dissolved and the cellulose fibers freed. The fibers then become known as pulp, which, after further processing, can be made into diversified paper and paperboard products or converted to rayon and other cellulose derivatives.

It seems axiomatic that the mechanical properties of wood are dependent on physical structure and chemical composition, yet the chemistry of wood is so complex that no very definite relations have so far been established between its mechanical properties or utility and its chemical composition.

1.8 Moisture content All the functional development of the tree takes place in the presence of moisture, and throughout its life all the wood remains "green" or moist. The moist condition is hence the normal one for wood, whereas the dry condition is abnormal. On the other hand, most uses of wood require the dry condition, so that drying or seasoning is important.

The moisture content of wood is important to all commercial applications. Moisture content is the weight of the water contained in the wood, expressed as a percentage of the weight of oven-dry wood. The oven-drying method of determining moisture content usually requires one or two days. There are now available a number of electrical instruments for the instantaneous determination of moisture content, and these work on the principle of electrical resistance or of capacity. Such instruments have certain limitations of range and require calibration, but are nevertheless exceedingly useful.

The amount of moisture in the living tree varies widely among species, individual trees of the same species, different parts of the same tree, and between heartwood and sapwood.

Many coniferous species have a large proportion of moisture in the sapwood and much less in the heartwood. Most hardwoods, on the other hand, show more nearly the same moisture content in heartwood and sapwood. Extreme limits observed in the moisture content of green wood range from as low as 30 to 40 per cent in the heartwood for such species as black locust, white ash, Douglas fir, southern pine, and various cedars, to about 200 per cent (twice the weight of the oven-dry wood) in the sapwood of some coniferous species.

1.9 Fiber-saturation point Storage of moisture in green wood is partly by absorption by the cell walls, and partly by retention in the cell cavities as in a container. As wood dries, the cell walls do not give off moisture until the adjacent cavities are empty. The condition in which the cell walls are fully saturated and the cell cavities empty is known as the "fiber-saturation point." It varies from about 25 to 35 per cent moisture content for most of the commonly used species.

1.10 Moisture content and strength Increase in strength begins when the cell walls begin to lose moisture, that is, after the wood is dried to below the fiber-saturation point. From this point on, most strength properties increase rapidly as drying progresses. This increased strength of dry over green wood of the same dimensions is due to two causes: (1) actual strengthening and stiffening of the cell walls as they dry out, and (2) increase in the compactness or the amount of wood substance in a given volume because of the shrinkage that accompanies drying below the fiber-saturation point.

Drying wood to 5 per cent moisture content may add from about 2.5 to 20 per cent to its density, as a result of shrinkage; in small pieces, moreover, end-crushing strength and bending strength may easily be doubled and, in some woods, tripled. Thus the stiffening and strengthening of the cell walls is chiefly responsible for the increase in strength.

The increase in strength with seasoning is much greater in small, clear specimens of wood than in large timbers containing defects. In large members, the increase in strength is to a great extent offset by the influence of defects that develop in seasoning.

The various strength properties are not equally affected by changes in moisture content. Whereas some properties, such as crushing strength and bending strength, increase greatly with decrease in moisture content, others, such as stiffness, change only moderately; and still others, such as shock resistance, may even show a slight decrease.

Shock resistance is affected adversely because it depends upon pliability as well as strength, and although the drier wood will sustain a greater load, it will not bend so far as green wood before failure.

Table 1.1 shows the average variation of the strength properties of wood with change in moisture content.

TABLE 1.1 Effect of 1 per cent change in moisture content upon strength properties

Property affected	Average change [1] *per cent*
Static bending	
Fiber stress at proportional limit	5
Modulus of rupture, or cross-breaking strength	4
Modulus of elasticity, or stiffness	2
Work to proportional limit	8
Work to maximum load or shock-resisting ability	0.5
Impact bending	
Fiber stress at proportional limit	3
Work to proportional limit	4
Height of drop of hammer causing complete failure	0.5
Compression parallel to grain	
Fiber stress at proportional limit	5
Maximum crushing strength	6
Compression perpendicular to grain	
Fiber stress at proportional limit	5.5
Hardness, end grain	4
Hardness, side grain	2.5
Shearing strength parallel to grain	3
Tension perpendicular to grain	1.5

[1] Plus or minus.

1.11 Equilibrium moisture content Any piece of wood will give off or take on moisture from the surrounding atmosphere until the moisture in the wood has come to a balance with that in the atmosphere. The moisture in the wood at the point of balance is called the equilibrium moisture content. The actual amount of moisture in any piece of wood at "equilibrium" is always proportional to the amount indicated by the oven-dry weight of the piece of wood substance. The actual moisture in a dense piece of wood at equilibrium is hence much greater than that in a low-density piece of the same volume. Because the percentage of moisture—based on oven-dry weight—is correlated with the strength, the amount of shrinking and swelling, and other factors, a simple medium of dealing with moisture effects is established, independent of species and variations in density within a species.

Assuming constant temperatures, the ultimate moisture content that a given piece of wood will attain, expressed as a percentage of its oven-dry weight, depends entirely upon the relative humidity of the atmosphere surrounding it. This atmospheric relative humidity is the amount of water vapor in the air, expressed as a percentage of the amount air would hold at saturation. This relationship is illustrated by Fig. 1.2, which shows, for example, that wood kept in an atmosphere

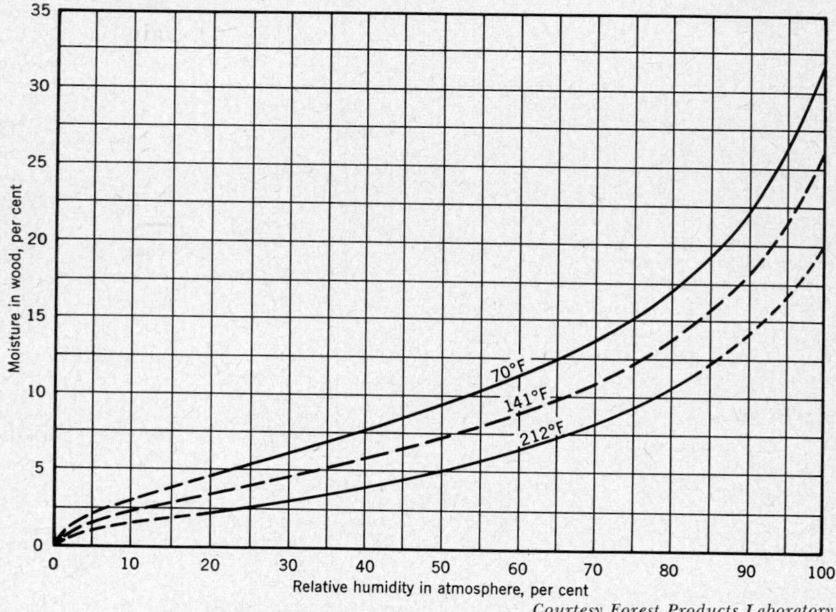

Courtesy Forest Products Laboratory

Fig. 1.2 Relation of equilibrium moisture content of wood to temperature and atmospheric humidity

constantly at 70°F and 60 per cent relative humidity will eventually come to a moisture content of about 11 per cent.

1.12 Shrinkage Shrinkage across the grain (in width and thickness) results when wood loses some of its absorbed moisture. Conversely, swelling occurs when dry or partially dry wood is soaked or absorbs moisture from the air or other source. Shrinkage and swelling in the direction of the grain (lengthwise) of normal wood is only a small fraction of 1 per cent and is not of practical importance in most applications.

Quartersawed (edge-grained or vertical-grain) boards shrink less in width but more in thickness than do flat-sawed boards. The greater the difference between radial and tangential shrinkage for a species, the greater is the advantage to be gained through minimizing shrinkage in width by using quartersawed wood. The less the difference between radial and tangential shrinkage, the less tendency there is for the wood to check in drying and to cup or warp (see Fig. 1.3) when its moisture content changes. Direction of sawing or grain is not controlled in construction lumber.

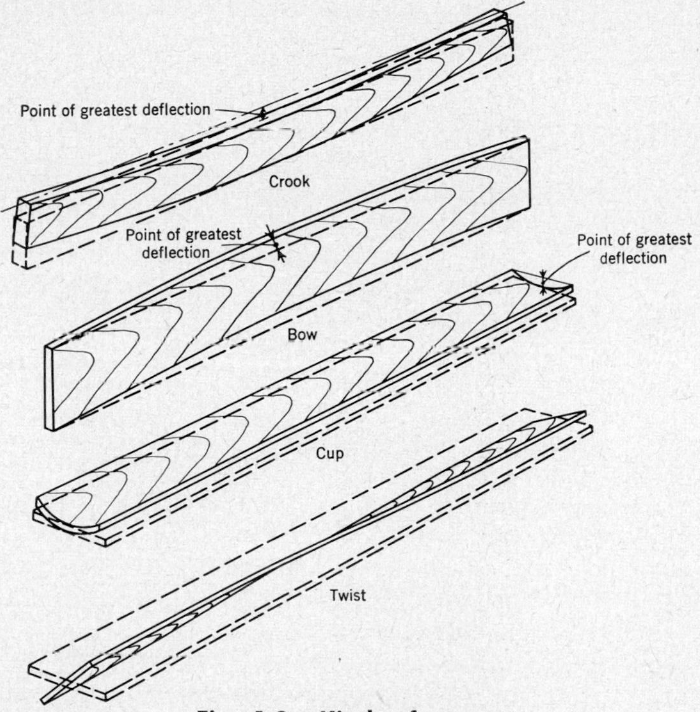

Fig. 1.3 Kinds of warp

In general, the heavier species of wood shrink more across the grain than the lighter ones. Heavier pieces also shrink more than lighter pieces of the same species.

The amount of shrinkage in drying is proportional to the moisture lost below the fiber-saturation point. Approximately ½ the total shrinkage possible will have occurred in wood seasoned to an air-dry condition (12 to 15 per cent moisture content) and about ¾ in lumber kiln-dried to a moisture content of about 7 per cent.

1.13 Effect of moisture content on fastenings Most published values for fastenings are based on the assumption that the lumber is seasoned at the time of fabrication and will remain seasoned in use. These values might be thought of as basic values for fastenings, and reductions are generally required for other conditions. In general, allowable working stresses for all fastenings are lower if unseasoned material is used. With some fastenings, the allowable loads recommended for lumber fabricated unseasoned but used seasoned are different from those for lumber fabricated unseasoned and used unseasoned or wet. Values for other fastenings depend only on the condition of lumber at the time of fabrication. Specific recommendations for the adjustment of allowable working stresses may be found in Sec. 3.17 (Table 3.1) and Chap. 13.

1.14 Thermal expansion Like most substances, wood expands when heated, although not to an extent that matters in most applications. Different investigators are not in close agreement in their values for this thermal expansion, although they do agree that the expansion across the grain is much greater than that along the grain for species on which data are available. Values of the coefficient of thermal expansion of wood per degree Fahrenheit at ordinary temperatures range from 0.0000011 for yellow birch to 0.0000036 for black walnut parallel to the length or direction of the fibers; and from 0.0000146 for yellow birch to 0.0000341 for American beech across the grain. These species, however, have little or no structural application.

1.15 Destructive agencies In any factual appraisal of engineering materials, it must be recognized that there is no such thing as absolute permanence under all conditions of service and use. The engineer must be constantly alert to improve the properties of materials in order to extend their useful life and meet special service requirements. Hence, there is naturally much concern over destructive agencies and their control, and such terms as rust, corrosion, electrolysis, embrittlement, spalling, decomposition, decay, and aging are in everyday use.

Wood too is vulnerable to attack, and must be protected from a group of destructive agencies largely peculiar to itself. The principal causes of the deterioration of wood, in their general order of importance, are: decay, fire, insects and marine borers, mechanical wear and breakage, weathering, and chemical decomposition.

1.16 Decay prevention Decay in wood is produced by organisms known as fungi, which live on the wood substance. Wood-destroying fungi require favorable conditions of moisture, temperature, and access to air; lack of any one of these essentials will inhibit the growth of fungi. Thus wood presents no decay hazard if it has less than a certain critical moisture content, or is maintained at extremely high or low temperatures, or is immersed in water to exclude air.

The one outstanding precaution that must usually be observed in preventing decay in untreated wood is to keep the wood dry, as air-dry wood does not contain enough moisture to permit the growth of wood-destroying fungi. Even the so-called "dry rot" fungi require more moisture than is found in air-dry wood. At moisture contents below the fiber-saturation point (25 to 30 per cent) decay is greatly retarded; below 20 per cent, fungus growth is completely inhibited.

Keeping wood saturated with water and thus excluding air will also prevent decay. The constantly submerged parts of pilings in fresh water, for example, have long life. Likewise, foundation piles under buildings and bridges do not decay if the ground water level is constantly higher than the top of the piles. Wood buried deeply in the soil, especially if the soil is nonporous, decays very slowly if at all, because air is largely excluded.

For use of wood under adverse conditions, two effective methods of decay prevention may be employed: (1) species of high natural decay resistance should be selected, or (2) preservative treatment should be used (see Sec. 3.18–3.25). A number of native species have heartwood of high natural decay resistance. It should be pointed out, however, that the sapwood of all species is low in decay resistance. In general, the decay-resistant species are those in which the heartwood contains an appreciable amount of toxic extractives that act as a natural preservative.

For many outdoor uses, especially if the wood is to be in contact with the ground, the life of untreated wood is too short, and preservative treatment must be resorted to for the sake of ultimate economy.

1.17 Protection from insects and borers Precautions effective against decay are, for the most part, effective also against insects. Preservative treatment, for example, protects against both insects and decay. Other protective methods, however, may require special precautions against insects.

In termite control, as in decay control, it is of primary importance to keep untreated wood dry, well ventilated, and removed from contact with the ground. If additional measures are required, mechanical barriers may be provided to keep the termites from entering the structure. Termites must maintain contact or passage to and from the ground, and barriers prevent their passage. Usually barriers take the form of metal shields that extend over the top of the foundation, beneath the sills, and outward and downward at an angle of 45 deg beyond the face of the foundation on both sides. Soil poisoning and treatment of the timber in place are also resorted to at times.

Lyctus powder-post beetles confine their activities mainly to the seasoned sapwood of lumber, furniture, flooring, interior trim, tool handles, and similar products. They seldom attack products that are constantly handled and moved about, but work mainly in material that is left undisturbed. Preventing their attack on woodwork is best accomplished by insuring that the lumber used is sound and free from attack.

Protection for uninfested wood can be provided by coating all surfaces with paint, varnish, linseed oil, or any other finishing material that fills the pores of the wood and prevents the adult beetles from depositing their eggs in it.

Protection against marine borers in waters where they are plentiful is an economic necessity. The most generally useful and practical protection is obtained by treating the piling with maximum absorptions of coal-tar creosote. Nothing less than the maximum amount of oil that can be injected into the wood should be used except in waters where the rate of attack is slow. Heavy creosote treatment is very effective against borers of the shipworm type, but Limnoria, Chelura, and Sphaeroma have been known to work even in creosoted wood. Depth of penetration, as well as high absorption of the creosote is essential, for the borers quickly detect any weaknesses in the treatment and get through to the untreated wood in the interior, where they can work unhindered. Care should be taken in handling treated wood to avoid cutting the surface or exposing areas that remain untreated.

1.18 Fire resistance For many years it has been recognized that time is a vital element in the destruction of buildings by fire. In the early history of America, the promptness with which water could be applied made the difference between a nominal loss and total destruction. In those days there were no water supply lines with nearby hydrants to furnish hundreds and thousands of gallons of water. If the few available buckets of water were not sufficient to control the fire, there was little or no hope of saving the structure.

The combustibility of the contents, then and now, was such that stone in the structure would spall, brick walls collapse, iron warp, and wood be consumed. It was generally thought that reduction of the combustibility of the structure itself was the acme of protection against fire.

Today it is recognized that noncombustibility of the building material is not the sole, or most important, factor to be considered in modern industrial and storage buildings, and even those for office use.

No fire in any building of appreciable size can be extinguished from the outside. Whether it is safe to make an entrance depends upon the evaluation or "size up" of the probable time the fire has been burning, the violence of the fire, the kind of occupancy, and the ability of the structural members to withstand heat without collapsing.

This last factor in the size up is most important to designers. The choice of unprotected steel of a minimum thickness to carry the load solely on the premise that it is not combustible certainly leads to false security. The danger of collapse is overlooked by many otherwise well-informed designers.

Unlike unprotected metal, "slow burning" or "heavy timber" construction does not collapse in the early stages of a fire. It can be expected to afford a high degree of safety to firemen.

Wood will burn, but it must be realized that heat is harmful to all other materials used in the erection of buildings. There is little difference, from an economic standpoint, between the destruction of a material and its being so damaged that it cannot be used.

Life hazard in fires is largely due to gases and fumes rather than flame, as witness the fireproof hotel disasters of the last decade. Many incombustible materials must be heatproofed (insulated or protected) to be fireproofed. To improve their natural slow-burning character, wood structures may be protected by sprinkler systems and other means as effectively and economically, measured in long-term cost, as other materials can be heatproofed.

Fire resistance can be imparted to wood by impregnating it with substantial quantities of suitable chemicals—notably the phosphates of ammonia, or mixtures of ammonium phosphate, ammonium sulfate, borax, and boric acid. Some degree of fire resistance can be provided by fire-resistant coatings, but unfortunately, despite the best efforts of investigators, effective coatings that are practical and that retain their effectiveness under exposure to the weather over a long period of time are still lacking. For interior use, there are several very efficient coatings.

An effective way to provide fire safety in wood structures is to design them to provide slow-burning construction, thus making it possible to confine fires to limited portions of structures, to prevent rapid spread of flames, and to facilitate the safe and prompt escape of the occupants. Fire stops in walls, for example, delay the spread of fire within the walls and greatly increase the opportunities to detect and extinguish the fire before it is out of control. Industrial structures properly designed and built with large timbers are slow burning and are safer from fire than some buildings built of so-called "incombustible" materials. The contents of the building are often more important from the fire standpoint than the materials of construction, for flammable contents can burn in any building.

1.19 Chemical resistance The chemical resistance of wood frequently makes it decidedly superior to other construction materials. In the chemical industry, wood is not only an important material for supports, roofing, and other structural uses, but also serves for piping, vats, tanks, and other containers. The resistance of wood to a wide variety of chemicals, including organic materials, hot or cold solutions of acid or neutral salts, and dilute acids makes it a valuable material in plant construction. The use of wood in direct contact with caustic is not recommended.

Wood is naturally resistant to rapid destruction by contact with most chemicals, but is destroyed in time by strong acids and alkalies and certain other materials. Impregnation of wood with paraffin or similar materials increases its resistance to chemical action to some extent, but has only limited effectiveness. Impregnating wood with a solution of resin-forming materials and inducing a resin-forming reaction offers promise of increased chemical resistance.

Although roof trusses, beams, and other structural members may be attacked by acid or other corrosive vapors and lose some of their strength, the extent of damage is slight in most ordinary industrial applications. The hazard is so much less with wood than with most metals that wood is the preferred material. Chemical vapor action on wood is generally limited in depth, and conservative design practice is recommended in order that the unaffected inner portion may be adequate to carry the load. The reduction in strength of wood in processing equipment is usually of little importance because the structural requirements are minor and replacement or repair can be easily made.

Wood also resists exposure to industrial stack gases, atmospheres of high relative humidity, and sea air. Sea air must be coped with by a considerable portion of the nation's industry situated on seaboards or near other navigable bodies of water. In such plants, wood is used advantageously in window framing, door sash and framing, walkways, and other construction items.

One great advantage wood offers in process equipment is that, if attack does occur, it seldom produces harmful effects. This property makes wood a superior material for textile dyeing vats, for example, because even the slightest corrosion of metal tanks may cause noticeable effects on the dye shade.

Wood trusses and framing are widely used as well in paper mills and other wet-process industries where any condensation on metal may produce undesirable discolorations in the product.

Four general types of action may affect the use of wood in chemical plants: (1) extraction of colored substances from the wood by water or other solvents, (2) swelling because of absorption of water or some organic liquids, (3) acid hydrolysis, and (4) delignification by aqueous alkali solutions.

The extraction of colored substances does not contribute to a decrease in strength of the wooden member, but would present a problem if the color contamination proved objectionable, as in washing tubs or drinking water. This objection can be reduced by selecting a wood of low water-soluble content, so that the water-soluble portion will be removed after a short period of use. Problems caused by extraction generally become more apparent with the use of hot water than with cold water. Also, extraction will decrease the natural durability of some species of wood by leaching some of the toxic materials contributing to durability. This deterioration may be prevented by treating the wood with fungicides that will not interfere with the process for which it is being used.

The second difficuly is the swelling of wood when brought into direct contact with aqueous solutions or some classes of organic compounds. An inverse relationship has been found between the swelling of wood due to organic liquids, chiefly alcohols, and its maximum crushing strength. For the same degree of swelling, however, test blocks in organic liquids are stronger than those swollen with water. Benzene does not cause swelling or affect appreciably the strength of oven-dry wood. The amount of swelling caused by concentrated solutions of inorganic salts is generally related to the solubility of the salts and the lyotropic series of ions. In any event, the wet strength generally will not fall below 60 to 70 per cent of the oven-dry strength.

Hydrolysis and delignification are the result of direct chemical action on wood and produce a permanent decrease in strength. Acids have the hydrolytic effect and alkalies appear to cause a weakening by a combination of softening, excessive swelling, and dissolving of lignin and hemicelluloses. In general, at room temperature or lower, wood will tolerate solutions in the pH range between 3 and 10 if exposure times are moderate. Hydrochloric acid up to 5 per cent strength, sulfuric acid up to 20 per cent, and dilute organic acids have little effect on wood. Tests on several species have shown that six months' exposure to 10 per cent and 60 per cent acetic acid, 10 per cent formic and propionic acids, and a concentrated water solution of phenol produce no appreciable decrease in the wood's strength. Care must be taken in using certain classes of metallic salts that are acidic; if wood is treated with the chlorides of zinc and iron in solutions more concentrated than 10 per cent, its impact strength tends to be reduced considerably. Apparently, there is a migration of the salt to the surface during the drying process, so that a concentration is built up strong enough to contribute to wood breakdown by hydrolysis. Chlorinated phenols and creosote have no apparent effect on wood.

For more detailed information the reader may consult:

1. *The Book of Tanks,* The Hauser-Stander Tank Co., Cincinnati, Ohio
2. *Wood Pipe Handbook,* National Tank & Pipe Co., Kenton Station, Portland, Ore.
3. *Wood Tanks* (cat. No. 37), National Tank & Pipe Co., Kenton Station, Portland, Ore.
4. *Chemistry of Wood,* Hagglund, E., Academic Press, Inc., New York (1951)
5. *Chemical Processing of Wood,* Stamm, A. J., and Harris, E. E., Chemical Publishing Co., Inc., New York (1953)
6. *Wood Chemistry* (2nd ed., Vol. II), Wise, L. E., and Ahn, John J., Reinhold Publishing Corporation, New York (1952)

Weathering can usually be neglected as a destroyer of wood, although for some applications the appearance of weathered wood is objectionable. Weathering is prevented by paint and other surface coatings.

1.20 Permanence Although wood, like all other materials, is subject to attack by various destructive agents, methods are available to prolong its life so that various practical service requirements can be met. There is ample historical evidence of its permanence when suitable protection is provided.

So far as is known, the lignin and cellulose that constitute the wood substance are not subject to chemical changes when kept dry, although the color of wood may be slightly changed by long-continued exposure to air. Possibly this change of color results from oxidation of substances that are not structural parts of the wood substance.

Literally hundreds of well-designed bridges made entirely or partly of wood have served satisfactorily, and with but little maintenance, for long periods. Many that are more than a century old are still in service, whereas others, although in satisfactory condition, have been altered or replaced to meet today's demands for greater width of roadway and higher load capacity.

In Europe, many centuries-old wood structures or structural units are still in existence. Perhaps the most notable are the trusses in the Basilica of St. Paul at Rome, part of which was constructed in 816. Certain such timber roof trusses are known to have given service for over 1,000 years. If years of satisfactory service are a measure of permanence, no other material is more permanent than timber. Practically speaking, there is no such thing as a permanent material; there are only materials that have a life expectancy greater than their assumed normal service life.

1.21 Electrical properties The most important electrical property of wood is its resistance (the reciprocal of conductance) to the passage of an electric current. This property forms the basis for one method for determining the moisture content of wood (see Sec. 1.8). It is what makes wood such a valuable material for high-voltage power line poles and cross arms, and also for the insulating handles on linemen's tools.

The direct-current electrical resistance of wood varies greatly with moisture content, especially below the fiber-saturation point of approximately 25 per cent, decreasing as the moisture content increases. It also varies with species, is greater across the grain than along it, and approximately doubles for each drop in temperature of 22.5°F. Electrical resistance also varies inversely with the density of the wood, but this effect is so slight that it does not significantly interfere with moisture content determinations by the resistivity method. The variation among species is probably caused by minerals or electrolytes in the wood itself, or dissolved in the water present in the wood.

Because a change in moisture content from 25 to 7 per cent may cause the electrical resistance to increase tenfold, moisture content is a vital factor in wood used as an insulator, as in power-line poles or tool handles. The leakage of current from power lines increases with increase in the moisture content of the cross arms and poles. Salt preservative treatments lower resistance. The average electrical resistance of some commercially important species is given in Table 1.2.

At a low moisture content, wood is normally classified as an electrical insulator, or dielectric, rather than as a conductor. A dielectric will be heated if it is subjected to a high-frequency electrical field, either by placing it between electrodes upon which are impressed the proper oscillating voltage, or by some other method. This property is utilized to heat-cure glued surfaces in wood.

1.22 Thermal insulation The rate of heat flow through a unit area of any homogeneous substance is referred to as its thermal conductivity. This property is symbolized by the letter k and is measured in British

TABLE 1.2 Electrical resistance of some commercially important woods

Species	Moisture content, *per cent*													
	7	8	9	10	11	12	13	14	15	16	17	18	19	20
	Resistance,[1] *megohms*													
Conifers														
Cypress, southern	12,600	3,980	1,410	630	265	120	60	33	18.6	11.2	7.1	4.6	3.09	1.78
Douglas fir (coast region)	22,400	4,780	1,660	630	265	120	60	33	18.6	11.2	7.1	4.6	3.09	2.14
Fir, white	57,600	15,850	3,980	1,120	415	180	83	46	26.9	16.6	11.0	6.6	4.47	3.02
Hemlock, western	22,900	5,620	2,040	850	400	185	98	51	28.2	16.2	10.0	6.0	3.89	2.52
Larch, western	39,800	11,200	3,980	1,445	560	250	120	63	33.9	19.9	12.3	7.6	5.02	3.39
Pine, longleaf	25,000	8,700	3,160	1,320	575	270	135	74	41.7	24.0	14.4	8.9	5.76	3.72
Pine, northern white	20,900	5,620	2,090	850	405	200	102	58	33.1	19.9	12.3	7.9	5.01	3.31
Pine, ponderosa	39,800	8,910	3,310	1,410	645	300	150	81	44.7	25.1	14.8	9.1	5.62	3.55
Pine, shortleaf	43,600	11,750	3,720	1,350	560	255	130	69	38.9	22.4	13.8	8.7	5.76	3.80
Redwood	22,400	4,680	1,550	615	250	100	45	22	12.6	7.2	4.7	3.2	2.29	1.74
Spruce, Sitka	22,400	5,890	2,140	830	365	165	83	44	25.1	15.5	9.8	6.3	4.27	3.02
Hardwoods														
Ash, commercial white	12,000	2,190	690	250	105	55	28	14	8.3	5.0	3.2	2.0	1.32	.89
Basswood	36,300	1,740	470	1[illegible]0	85	45	27	16	9.6	6.2	4.1	2.8	1.86	1.32
Birch	87,000	19,950	4,470	1,290	470	200	96	53	30.2	18.2	11.5	7.6	5.13	3.55
Elm, American	18,200	2,000	350	110	45	20	12	7	3.9	2.3	1.5	1.0	0.66	0.48
Gum, red	38,000	6,460	2,090	815	345	160	81	45	25.7	15.1	9.3	6.0	3.98	2.63
Hickory, true		31,600	2,190	340	115	50	21	11	6.3	3.7	2.3	1.5	1.00	0.71
Maple, sugar	72,400	13,800	3,160	690	250	105	53	29	16.6	10.2	6.8	4.5	3.16	2.24
Oak, commercial red	14,400	4,790	1,590	630	265	125	63	32	18.2	11.3	7.3	4.6	3.02	2.09
Oak, commercial white	17,400	3,550	1,100	415	170	80	42	22	12.6	7.2	4.3	2.7	1.70	1.15
Poplar, yellow	24,000	8,320	3,170	1,260	525	250	140	76	43.7	25.2	14.5	8.7	5.76	3.81
Walnut, black	51,300	9,770	2,630	890	355	155	78	41	22.4	12.9	7.8	4.9	3.16	2.14

[1] Average of measurements made along the grain between two pairs of needle electrodes 1¼ in. apart and driven to a depth of 5⁄16 in. Prevailing temperature was 80°F.

thermal units (Btu) per hour per square foot per inch of thickness per degree Fahrenheit change in temperature. Conversely, the value of a material as an insulator is the reciprocal ($1/k$) of the thermal conductivity. This quantity is called its thermal resistance and, measured in degrees Fahrenheit per British thermal unit per hour per square foot per inch of thickness, can give the required difference between the interior and exterior temperatures to effect a transmission of 1 Btu per hour per square foot for each inch of thickness.

The thermal conductivity of wood varies little with species. Such differences as do occur are caused by variations of (1) direction of grain; (2) specific gravity; (3) moisture content and distribution; (4) kind, quantity, and distribution of extractives; (5) proportion of springwood and summerwood; and (6) defects, such as checks, knots, and cross grain. In normal wood, the relative rate of heat flow is approximately the same in the radial and tangential directions, but thermal conductivity is generally 2¼ to 2¾ times faster along the grain than in the transverse directions. Since thermal conductivity increases with specific gravity, the lighter weight woods are the better insulators.

The relative effectiveness of various construction materials as insulators is presented in Table 1.3. From these data it can be observed that solid wood of the species used in construction is markedly superior to other materials in retarding heat transmission.

TABLE 1.3 Thermal properties of building materials used in wall construction

Material [1]	Thermal conductivity, k *Btu/hr/°F* [2]	Thermal resistance, $1/k$ *°F/Btu/hr* [3]	Relative efficiency *per cent* (wood = 100)
Air	0.168	5.95	476.0
Wood (avg. coniferous)	0.80	1.25	100.0
Clay brick	4.8	0.208	16.5
Limestone	6.5	0.154	12.3
Sandstone	12.0	0.083	6.6
Concrete (sand and gravel)	12.6	0.079	6.3
Steel	312.0	0.0032	0.25
Aluminum	1,416.0	0.000707	0.06

[1] A 1-sq ft panel 1 in. thick is assumed.

[2] Thermal conductivity is conventionally expressed as heat energy in British thermal units transmitted each hour through a panel of material 1 ft square and 1 in. thick for each 1°F temperature differential on opposite sides of the panel.

[3] Thermal resistance is conventionally expressed as the temperature differential in degrees Fahrenheit required to effect a transfer of 1 Btu per hour through a panel of material 1 ft square and 1 in. thick.

Not only is wood in the solid state an excellent insulator but, when fabricated to form a conventional 2 x 4-in. stud wall, it provides an additional 3⅝ in. of dead air space between the exterior sheathing and the interior plaster lath. This space can be left vacant, to utilize the effective insulating properties of dead air, or it can be filled with any of the excellent commercial wool or blanket insulating materials.

The concept of thermal conductivity can be applied only to homogeneous materials, like wood, clay, or aluminum. The heat-transmitting ability of composite materials—like frame or masonry walls—is a function of all the component materials, however, and is referred to as the coefficient of thermal transmission (U). The insulating function of such a composite wall is again called its thermal resistance, but it is computed as $1/U$, and is measured through the total thickness of the wall, rather than per inch of thickness.

Table 1.4 compares the coefficient of thermal transmission and also

TABLE 1.4 Thermal properties of conventional wall construction

Wall construction [1]	Coefficient of thermal transmission, U *Btu/hr/°F* [1]	Thermal resistance, $1/U$ *°F/Btu/hr* [1]	Relative insulating efficiency, *per cent* (wood frame = 100)
Frame wall, wood siding, wood sheathing, lath, plaster, 3⅝-in. wool insulation	0.07	14.3	357.5
Wood frame (as above), no insulation	0.25	4.0	100.0
8-in. plain brick	0.50	2.0	50.0
8-in. brick, ½-in. plaster	0.46	2.2	55.0
8-in. brick; lath, plaster, furred	0.32	3.1	77.5
8-in. hollow tile; stucco, ½-in. plaster	0.37	2.7	67.5
8-in. hollow tile; stucco, lath, plaster, furred	0.27	3.7	92.5
8-in. limestone or sandstone	0.70	1.4	35.0
8-in. limestone or sandstone, ½-in. plaster	0.64	1.6	40.0
8-in. concrete, ½-in. plaster	0.64	1.6	40.0
8-in. concrete; ½-in. plaster, furred	0.39	2.5	62.5
6-in. concrete, 4-in. brick, ½-in. plaster	0.54	1.8	45.0
6-in. concrete, 4-in. brick; plaster, furred	0.41	2.4	60.0
6-in. hollow tile, 4-in. cut stone, ½-in. plaster	0.35	2.9	72.5
6-in. concrete, 4-in. cut stone, ½-in. plaster	0.58	1.7	42.5
6-in. concrete block, 4-in. cut stone, ½-in. plaster	0.44	2.3	57.5

[1] Both U and $1/U$ are measured through the entire thickness of a section wall 1 ft square.

the thermal resistance of common types of wall construction. Again the superiority of wood as an insulator and the effectiveness of the 3⅝-in. space for additional insulation in wood-frame walls is evident.

The other types of wall construction are between 35.0 and 92.5 per cent as efficient as uninsulated wood frame in retarding heat passage. The wood frame wall is from 2⅝ to 4⅝ in. thinner than other walls, and yet has superior insulating qualities.

1.23 Acoustical properties To the structural engineer, the most important acoustical property of wood is its ability to dampen vibrations. Because of its high internal friction, wood has much more damping capacity than most other structural materials, particularly the metals. For structural components in which vibration is a hazard, therefore, wood is the preferred material.

In sound conditioning a room, both the sound-absorption coefficients and the sound-transmission coefficients of floor, wall, and ceiling materials have to be considered. For sounds emitted within a room, the objective is for the walls to absorb some of the sound waves. Considering the sound absorption of an open window 1 ft square to be 100 per cent, the absorption of unfinished wood is 6 per cent, and that of varnished wood is 3 per cent, the same as brick, glass, and plaster. These values are approximate, for the sound absorption of wood varies with species, moisture content, direction of grain, and density. However, wood may be patterned to improve its sound absorption. Carved paneling and etched or striated surfaces improve absorption properties.

For control of sounds emitted from a source outside of a room, the sound insulating properties of the walls, floor, and ceiling are called into play. The amount of energy transmitted through a wall depends on the amount of noise on the opposite face, the mass of the wall, its stiffness, and the nature of the fastenings. The insulating quality varies as the logarithms of the masses of the material. Massive barrier walls are not particularly effective, therefore, as a wall weighing 1,000 lb per cu ft is only 50 per cent more effective than one weighing 100 lb per cu ft. Generally speaking, the wall should be as stiff as possible to resist forced vibration. The addition of a spongy material between wall surfaces helps considerably.

An excellent wood-frame sound barrier consists of 2 x 6 sill and plates with 2 x 4 studs set in a staggered pattern so that alternate studs—being flush with one edge of the sill and plate—are in contact with one wall face, and the intermediate studs—being flush with the opposite edge—are in contact with the opposite wall face (see Fig. 1.4). Thus there can be no direct transmission except through the plates.

Occasionally a heavy paper is woven between the studs, or the void is filled with some spongy insulation material.

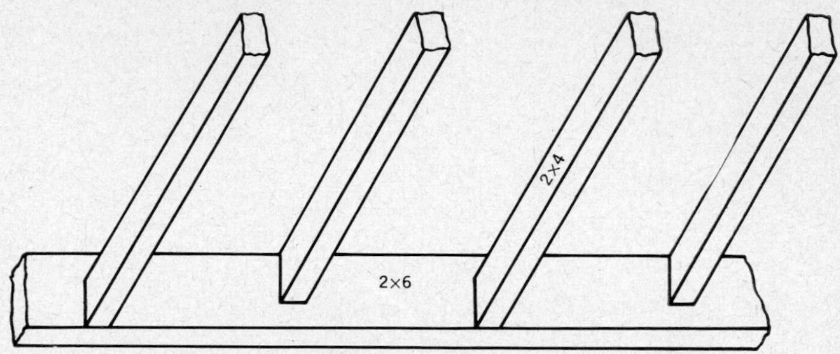

Fig. 1.4 Sound insulating stud wall

STRENGTH PROPERTIES

1.24 Directional properties Wood is a fibrous rather than a crystalline material, and the fibers are oriented so that their length essentially parallels the axis of the tree trunk. For this reason, the strength of wood parallel with the grain is quite different from its strength across the grain. Wood is 5 or 10 times as strong in compression parallel to the grain as it is perpendicular to the grain; the ratio is even higher in tension. The modulus of elasticity may be more than 100 times as great parallel to grain as perpendicular.

In the directions perpendicular to grain, there are only minor differences in the strength properties parallel (tangential) to and perpendicular (radial) to the direction of the annual rings (see Fig. 1.5). The property most affected by the direction of growth rings is compression

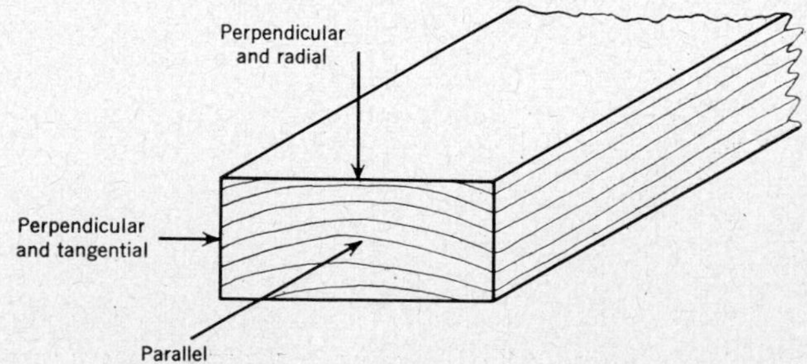

Fig. 1.5 Directions of compression relative to grain

perpendicular to grain; working stresses for design in compression perpendicular to grain take this fact into account and are applicable for any angle of rings.

1.25 Compression parallel to grain The crushing strength of wood in the direction parallel to grain depends upon the resistance of the tiny fibers that make up its structure. Each fiber is in itself a small hollow column receiving lateral support from and giving support to the adjacent fibers. If stressed to the point of failure, these tiny structural columns bend or buckle much the way larger columns do.

The strength of a wood column is affected by its length as well as by the size and shape of the cross section. Wood columns may theoretically be divided into three length classes characterized by their type of failure under load. If the length does not exceed about 10 times the least dimension, failure is by crushing and the full compressive strength of the wood is developed. For intermediate lengths ranging approximately from 10 to 25 times the least dimension, ultimate failure is theoretically a combination of crushing and lateral buckling. Longer columns generally fail by lateral deflection or buckling, and their strength is accurately estimated according to the well-known Euler or "long column" formula. The differences between the Euler formula and an "intermediate length" column formula are not great, and thus the Euler formula is used for all slenderness ratios.

The Euler formula is applicable if unit stresses do not exceed the proportional limit, and working stresses for short columns are well below this limit. As a result, the Euler long-column formula is used for all ratios of length to least dimension, provided that unit stress does not exceed tabulated unit stresses based on short columns (see Chap. 13, NDS).[1] Unless the type of end fastening of a column is such as to provide a positive degree of fixity, the Euler formula for pin-end conditions is used.

In calculating the compressive strength, it is necessary to take into account the extent to which the cross section is reduced by bolt holes, connectors, and other cuts. In longer columns, the compressive strength of the wood is reduced by the slenderness ratio, and the strength of the net cross section based on full compressive strength will rarely govern the design.

Tests have shown that for both long and short columns, it is the area of the cross section and not whether it is round or square that determines its load-bearing capacity. If a long round column has appreciable taper, the size requirement is determined at a point ⅓ of the

[1] "National Design Specification for Stress-Grade Lumber and Its Fastenings."

length from the small end. The unit compressive stress at the small end of the column should also be checked.

Butt or end-bearing joints in compression members should be accurately cut and closely fitted. In short posts, pieces butted end to end fail at 75 to 80 per cent of the crushing strength of the wood. If a butt joint has full lateral support and a metal plate not thinner than 20 gauge is tightly fitted between the butted pieces to prevent springwood from bearing on summerwood, the joint will sustain practically the full crushing strength of the wood.

Compression parallel to grain is one of the strength properties receiving considerable benefit from the drying of the wood substance. Small clear pieces of wood gain as much as 75 per cent in this strength property when dried from the green to a well-seasoned condition. Larger pieces receive less benefit, but an increase of working stress of about $\frac{3}{8}$ is assumed in stock for glued-laminated construction. In still larger structural timber, the strengthening and stiffening of the wood substance from drying is somewhat offset by the development of drying defects, but increases of strength ranging from 10 per cent in 12-in. columns up to 30 per cent in 4-in. columns are common.

1.26 Compression perpendicular to grain The ultimate strength of wood in compression perpendicular to grain is not known, but its value is very great. When wood is compressed to about $\frac{1}{3}$ of its original thickness, all of the cell cavities are filled. The wood is greatly densified and its compressive strength is many times the original value. Practically, however, the allowable deformations limit the loads or stresses allowable in compression perpendicular to grain. Working stresses for structural design are commonly based on a proportional limit stress, beyond which the crushing continues rapidly with little or no increase of load until the wood is reduced to about $\frac{1}{3}$ of the original thickness.

When a piece of wood is loaded in compression perpendicular to grain over a portion of its area, the fibers extending from adjacent unloaded areas give support to the loaded fibers. Thus small areas sustain considerably higher unit stresses than do large areas. Published working stresses for design in this property are for areas unlimited in size, and increases are provided for smaller areas, like those under plates or washers.

The stress in compression perpendicular to grain often enters into design of beams, especially short beams carrying heavy loads. In calculating bearing areas required at the ends of beams, no allowance need be made for the fact that as the beam bends, the pressure on the inside edge of the bearing is greater than that at the opposite edge; the wood yields enough under allowable working stresses so that the pressures become equalized. Larger bearing areas may be required for wood beams supported on columns; the areas may be increased by the use of a bolster of a species or grade having a higher allowable compression perpendicular value, by corbels, or by larger steel column caps or plates.

Strength in compression perpendicular to grain, like that parallel to grain, increases considerably with drying. In large timbers, the development of drying defects does not offset this increase, so that it is customary to increase working stresses for dry material 50 per cent above the level for green material. Conversely, a working stress suitable for dry conditions should be decreased by about ⅓ if bearing surfaces are likely to remain moist or wet.

1.27 Compression at angles to grain The compressive strength of wood at intermediate angles to the grain has an appropriately intermediate value between the strengths parallel and perpendicular to grain. Safe stress is commonly calculated by the Hankinson formula or may be taken from the Scholten nomograph based on the Hankinson formula (see Chap. 13, NDS).

1.28 Bending strength Wood develops high strengths in the extreme fiber in bending. A clear specimen of a number of common species is about 1/12 of the weight of an equal volume of structural steel but has about 1/10 of the strength. Pound for pound, wood is the stronger of the two.

Tests have shown that a somewhat lower unit bending strength is developed in deep beams than in shallow beams. This depth or form factor is taken into account in setting working stresses in bending that are applicable to solid sawed beams ranging in depth up to about 16 in. Special formulas are available for glued-laminated beams, but reductions are not generally necessary for depths less than 30 in.

Round beams have a form factor of 1.18; in other words, the unit bending stress developed is 1.18 times the bending stress developed in a rectangular section. Beams of square cross section placed with a diagonal of the square vertical have a similar form factor of 1.414. As the section moduli of these sections are less than that of a normally loaded square section of the same area, it can be shown from these form factors that a round beam, or a square beam with its diagonal vertical, has the same bending strength as a square beam of equal cross section placed in the conventional position.

The bending strength of wood increases by about ½ as the wood is dried from a green to a well-seasoned condition. In lumber of structural size, however, much of this gain in strength is offset by the development of drying defects, such as checks, shakes, or splits. Some net increase of strength with drying is recognized in joist and plank grades not more than 4 in. thick. Larger increases are used with stock not more than 2 in. thick for glued-laminated structural members that are fabricated dry and are to be used dry.

1.29 Modulus of elasticity Published values for modulus of elasticity of wood are obtained from the results of standard bending tests and are therefore directly applicable in calculating the deflections of members subject to bending, such as structural beams or joists. If service conditions require that beams be designed for stiffness, deflections are calculated by applying the conventional engineering formulas for the type of loading and support assumed.

Deflection of beams will usually increase slightly over long periods of time. If the timbers were unseasoned when installed and seasoned while under load, the increase in deflection will be greater than for timbers fully seasoned before loading.

The increase in deflection of a beam with time is sometimes thought of as indicating a decrease in the modulus of elasticity; tests have shown, however, that the beam is actually as stiff as it was before the load was applied. The relation of unit stress to unit strain for increments of load applied or removed is the same after long-time loading as it was before loading.

The slight normal increase of deflection in a wood beam under long-continued loading is usually imperceptible. The rate of deflection decreases and a condition of equilibrium is approached. If the beam is overloaded so that deflection continues at a uniform or at an increasing rate, failure may be imminent.

The stiffness of wood as expressed by the bending modulus of elasticity is little affected by drying. An increase of about 10 per cent is assumed for partially seasoned material—typical of that used in most construction—as compared to unseasoned or green timbers.

1.30 Axial tension Tensile strength parallel to the grain is the strongest property in wood. In practice, however, because of small irregularities of grain and the need to retain grading practice based on use primarily in bending, the full value is not used. It is common to use the same working stress in tension parallel to grain as in the extreme fiber in bending.

Structural lumber graded for bending strength may have larger knots or more slope of grain in the end portions than in the center portion of the length. If such members are used in tension—as in the lower chords of trusses—the grade requirements for the central portion of the length should be applied to the full length. Tensile strength is more sensitive than bending strength to the cumulative effects of two or more knots in the same cross section. It is good practice to restrict the sum of the sizes of all knots in a cross section to the size of the largest permissible single knot in bending (see Sec. 2.11).

The reduction of cross section from bolt holes or other cuts must be taken into account in structural design for tension. Although stress concentrations at the location of such cuts may reduce the tensile strength, the use of the safe bending stress as the safe tensile stress provides adequate allowance for the reduction.

1.31 Combined axial and bending stresses Design formulas for structural members subjected to combined bending and axial stresses are commonly based on keeping the algebraic sum of the two stresses in the extreme fiber within the allowable stress limit. This procedure is followed whether the axial stress is in tension or in compression. If axial compressive stresses are eccentrically applied or bending moment in long columns is involved, an eccentric column analysis is required (see Chap. 13, NDS).

1.32 Tension perpendicular to grain The strength of wood in tension perpendicular to grain rarely enters into structural design. On occasion, however—for example, in evaluating secondary stresses in curved members—it must be considered. This property is quite sensitive to stress concentration effects, and therefore reliable, safe values are difficult to determine. Best practice limits the working stress in tension perpendicular to grain to ⅓ the working stress in shear for softwoods and ⅜ the working stress in shear for hardwoods.

1.33 Shear Shearing stress is increased at certain locations in a wood beam by stress concentration effects. The most common concentration of stress is at the base of shakes, checks, or splits, where there is an abrupt change of cross section. As checking occurs to some extent in practically all structural beams, a suitable factor for stress concentration is introduced in setting the recommended working values in shear.

Another shear stress concentration may occur immediately adjacent to points of application of a concentrated load or reaction. Such a concentration is not usually critical because allowable bearing values in compression perpendicular to grain ordinarily require fairly large bearing areas. Special cases involving applications of load or reaction to areas $\frac{1}{2}$ in. or less in length along the grain may require analysis of the effect on shearing strength.

The conventional formula for shear in beams gives shear stress at the neutral axis. If a wood beam is checked near the neutral axis, the upper and lower portions act partly as two independent beams and partly as a unit. A portion of the external shear is resisted internally by each half of the beam acting independently; that portion, as shown by analysis and supported by strength tests results, increases rapidly as load approaches the support. The remaining portion of the external shear, which is resisted at the neutral plane, is correspondingly reduced. It reaches a maximum when the distance from the support to the load is about 3 times the depth of the beam, and becomes negligible when the distance from the support to the load is about equal to the depth of the beam. This condition is recognized in the calculation of shear stress at the neutral plane by the appropriate formula of Sec. 4.6.

Wood beams are sometimes notched at the ends, where shear stresses are high (see Fig. 1.6). Notches not only reduce the effective area resisting horizontal shear but also result in stress concentration. Formulas for design of notched beams are given in Sec. 4.8. Notches on the lower side are more serious than those on the upper side. Rounding the notch with a generous fillet gives substantially increased shear strength values.

As shear stress in beams is ordinarily not large in the central portion of the length, notches at or near the center of the length commonly have no effect on the design for shear. If it is necessary to have a notch at or near the center of length, the bending stress in the outer fiber at the bottom of the notch is calculated on the basis of the cross section as reduced by the notch.

Because defects of seasoning ordinarily have more effect on shear than on other strength properties, there is very little net increase in shearing strength of wood with drying. An increase of about $\frac{1}{8}$ is taken in stock for glued-laminated structural members that are to be fabricated and used dry.

1.34 Fatigue properties Fatigue properties are generally unimportant in the design of buildings but may be critical if wood is subjected to rapid cyclic stresses, as in the moving parts of machinery.

Tests to date indicate that wood, being a fibrous material, is less sensitive to repeated loads than are the more crystalline structural materials. Endurance limits are likely to be higher in proportion to the ultimate strength values for wood than for some of the metals. Fatigue

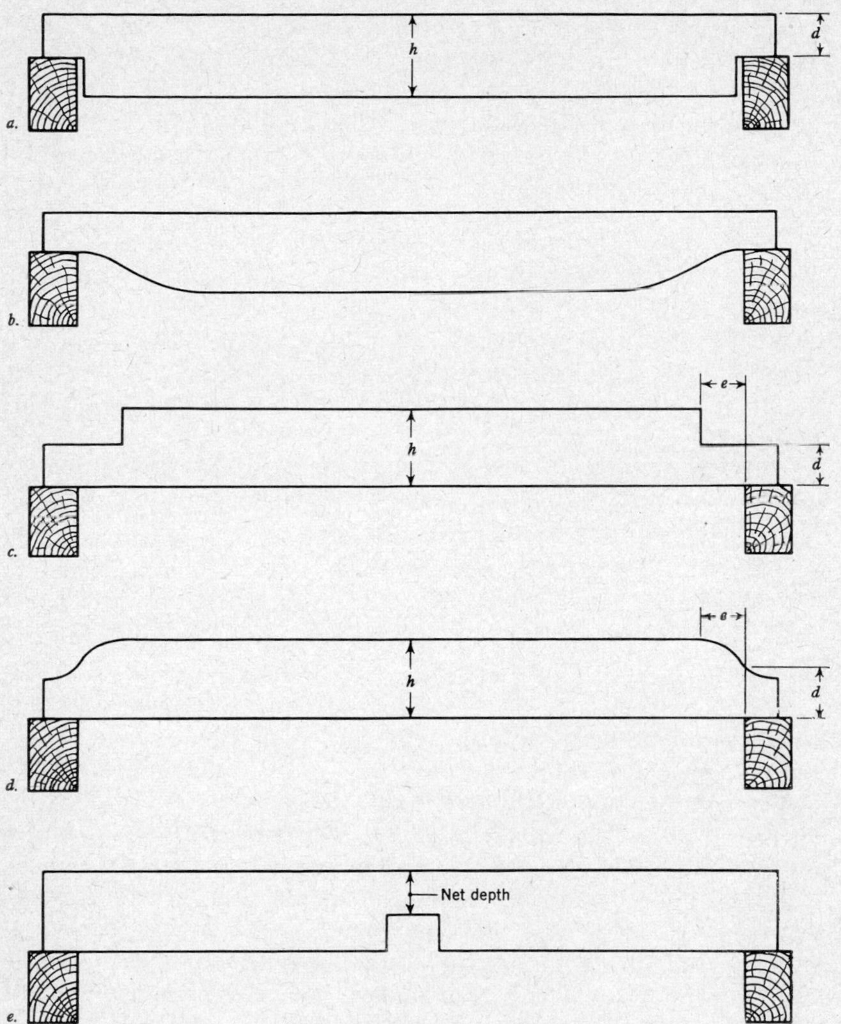

Fig. 1.6 Notched beams

a. Notched to ½ depth at ends
b. Depth changed gradually at ends to avoid concentration of stress
c. Upper side notched to ½ depth
d. Upper side beveled
e. Notched at center to ½ depth

tests in tension parallel to grain of dry wood indicate that the endurance load for 30 million cycles of stress is about 40 per cent of the static strength, as determined by a standard static test. Fatigue tests in repeated bending of green wood indicate that the endurance limit is about 60 per cent of the static bending strength.

For most structural designs with wood, safe working stresses for long-time loading are generally considered safe for fatigue effects from any number of stress repetitions that are likely to occur.

1.35 Torsional strength The torsional strength of wood is seldom needed in design but data are available that permit calculation of torsional properties if they are required. The torsional deformation of wood is related to the moduli of rigidity in the longitudinal-radial, longitudinal-tangential, and radial-tangential planes. These moduli of rigidity are commonly not published with recommended working stresses but can be found in publications such as the *Wood Handbook*.[1] Moduli of rigidity in the longitudinal-radial and longitudinal-tangential planes are often nearly the same and are sometimes taken as $\frac{1}{16}$ of the modulus of elasticity parallel to the grain.

For solid wood members, the allowable torsional shear stress may be taken as the recommended allowable stress in horizontal shear of beams.

1.36 Temperature Temperature affects the strength of wood, but the effects are not large in the ordinary temperature ranges. Recommended working stresses contain a factor of safety to provide for the effects of temperature ranges in ordinary construction, and usually no further consideration of temperature is necessary.

Tests of wood conducted at about —300°F show that the important strength properties of dry wood in bending and in compression, including stiffness and shock resistance, are much better at extremely low temperatures than at normal temperatures.

Exposure to high temperatures, on the other hand, can weaken wood in two ways. There is an immediate, temporary weakening while the fibers of the wood are at the high temperature. It should be observed, however, that the insulating properties of wood rapidly slow down the transfer of heat from the surroundings to the interior fibers so that these fibers remain at a comparatively low temperature. The temperature of the wood itself will usually be much lower than that of the surrounding air.

[1] *Wood Handbook* (Agriculture Handbook No. 72) Forest Products Laboratory, Forest Service, U.S. Dept. of Agriculture, Government Printing Office, Washington, D.C. (1955).

If exposure to temperatures of 150°F or higher is prolonged for extended periods, however, wood is not only temporarily but also permanently weakened. This permanent loss of strength depends upon a number of factors, including the moisture content of the wood, the heating medium, duration of exposure, and of course temperature, and also to some extent the species and size of the piece. Available data indicate that exposure of wet wood for a year to a temperature of 180°F will result in a substantial permanent loss in strength and that a significant strength loss may occur with a year's exposure at 150°F. Dry wood is damaged less than wet wood. Shock resistance is affected most, bending strength next, and stiffness the least. No practical protection has yet been found against the damage effected by continuous exposure to high temperatures, and conservatism in design for such conditions is recommended.

Working stresses ordinarily recommended for structural lumber are obtained from strength values at about 70°F, but contain a factor of safety to provide for the effects of a range of temperatures up to about 125°F in wood structures. If the design must provide for unusually high temperatures or an unusually long period of exposure, the stresses should be modified accordingly.

1.37 Preservative treatment The chemicals commonly used for preservative treatment of wood have little or no effect upon its strength. The pressures and temperatures of the treating process can have a weakening effect, however, and thus are limited by the treating firms as much as is consistent with the requirements for penetration and retention of the preservative.

As proper preservative treatment so effectively reduces the damage caused by decay, it is common practice to use the same allowable unit stresses as for untreated lumber and to neglect the small loss of strength from the treating process.

Treating conditions specified by the American Wood Preservers' Association should never be exceeded. Temperatures and treating periods permitted by those specifications are maximum values and proper treatment can often be obtained with a lower temperature or a shorter period.

Tests of treated timber show strength reduction in extreme fiber in bending and in compression perpendicular to grain. Compression parallel to grain is affected less and the modulus of elasticity very little. The effect on resistance to horizonal shear is dependent on the presence of checks and shakes after preservative treatment, just as in untreated lumber.

1.38 Working stresses Working stresses for structural design with wood are obtained by applying to the average strength values a number of factors that represent the characteristics of structural lumber and the conditions under which it is used. The most important of these factors are: (1) variability, (2) moisture content, (3) duration of load, (4) defects, and (5) factor of safety. The practice in the United States is to establish a "basic stress," which is a safe working stress for clear wood of a species and takes into account all the factors required in a safe design stress except the factor for growth characteristics. A working stress for a structural grade is obtained by modifying the basic stress by a strength ratio that is related to the size of knots or other characteristics permitted in that grade.

Individual specimens of clear wood within any species vary in strength through a range of values. For design safety, working stresses are related to the lower portion of that range as determined from examination of frequency distributions based on many hundreds of test values. In this way, the working stress is suitable for the full range of clear wood in the species.

Recommended working stresses assume a dry use condition such as prevails in most covered structures. Under continuously wet conditions, the working stresses in compression should be reduced by $\frac{1}{10}$ parallel to grain, and by $\frac{1}{3}$ perpendicular to grain, and the modulus of elasticity should be reduced by $\frac{1}{11}$.

Wood has the ability to absorb considerable overloads for short periods, or smaller overloads for long periods without damage. This fact is taken into account in structural design. In deriving working stresses from laboratory test strength values, a reduction factor is applied to allow for the reduction of strength under long-time loading conditions. Conversely, the safe working stress for long-time loading may be increased when loads are of shorter duration. Duration-of-load adjustments apply to all stresses except to modulus of elasticity in bending; adjustments do apply, however, to the modulus for column design.

The level of "normal loading" for which working stresses are recommended presumes that full maximum design load will be applied for not more than about 10 years during the anticipated life of a permanent structure. Stresses for this condition are about 10 per cent higher than those for long-time loading. Recommendations provide for 10 per cent reduction if long-time or permanent full load on the structure is expected. Increases are permissible for short-time loadings such as snow, wind, or earthquake.

Knots, cross grain, shakes, checks, and splits are commonly thought of as defects. They are, however, characteristic of all structural grades of lumber and are therefore more accurately defined as strength-reducing characteristics. Their effect upon strength has been evaluated from many tests of structural timbers and is fully taken into account in establishing working stresses for the standard structural grades.

1.39 Safety factor As the safe working stress in bending in a standard grade of structural lumber may be no more than $\frac{1}{5}$ of the average strength determined by standard laboratory tests, it might be assumed that that working stress has a factor of safety of 5. The allowance, however, is not this great. Much of the difference between the high laboratory test average values and accepted working stresses is applied to converting from the conditions of the laboratory to the conditions of use.

The true factor of safety in an individual timber depends upon the conditions of use as well as upon the strength and thus may vary over a rather wide range. Studies of this range have been made, and it has been estimated that the most probable value of the true factor of safety of a structural timber is about $2\frac{1}{2}$. Probably 99 per cent of strucural timbers have factors of safety of $1\frac{1}{4}$ or more, and a few have factors of safety as high as 5. Low values of the true factor of safety result if a piece of less than average strength is used under unfavorable conditions; the highest values may occur if a piece above average in strength is used under the most favorable conditions. A piece that is below average may be in service under such favorable conditions that its actual factor of safety is greater than that of a stronger piece used less favorably.

1.40 Fastenings Factors reducing laboratory test values for fastenings to safe working loads are comparable to those for structural timber. Allowable loads on nails may be $\frac{1}{6}$ to $\frac{1}{10}$ of the ultimate strength in test, as factors other than ultimate test load must be considered. Safe long-time withdrawal loads on lag screws may be about $\frac{1}{5}$ of the ultimate loads. Loads on bolts are in general based on proportional limit and are calculated from basic stresses that are very similar to the basic stresses used for structural lumber and contain comparable factors of safety. Similar reduction factors are used with other fastenings. For fastenings as for structural timbers, the difference between laboratory test values and safe design loads does not entirely represent a factor of safety but in part is required to convert from the conditions of the laboratory to the conditions of use.

1.41 Plywood More detailed discussion of plywood may be found in Chap. 9. The strength properties of plywood can be estimated quite satisfactorily in terms of the thickness and arrangement of the various plies and their strength and elastic properties. As wood has much greater strength parallel than perpendicular to grain, those plies with grain perpendicular to the direction of stress can often be entirely neglected in design without serious error. Working stresses for clear or practically clear grades of veneer are the same as the basic stresses for structural lumber. These are converted to working stresses for plywood by means of simplified formulas developed at the Forest Products Laboratory and discussed in the *Wood Handbook*.

Greater utilization of available veneer supplies has resulted in recent years in the use of plywoods with inner plies of lower grade. Studies of strength values in such veneers are needed, as it is not clear how much reduction of strength may be expected in comparison to the values in clear veneers. In general, it appears that defects have less effect than they do in structural lumber.

1.42 Glued-laminated lumber Glued-laminated timbers made with laminations of a certain lumber grade generally may be expected to have higher allowable unit stresses than solid timbers of the same grade. These higher stresses result from two factors—dispersion of defects in a laminated member, and the fact that advantage may be taken of the higher dry strength of wood in certain types of service.

A knot in a large solid timber is known to penetrate a considerable distance from the surface into the interior. In a laminated member, a knot penetrates only through the thickness of one lamination. The likelihood that there is a similar knot at the same location in the next lamination is extremely small. When the frequency of occurrence of knots within a grade is known, the probability of any given concentration of knots may be estimated. In practical terms, such concentrations are highly improbable.

Large sawed timbers are generally designed on the green strength of wood because of the difficulty of seasoning them to a low moisture content prior to service, and because of the strength-reducing effects of drying stresses. Laminated members, however, are commonly made from material of thicknesses that can be seasoned without damage before gluing. As the laminations must be seasoned to relatively low moisture contents because of gluing requirements, the member enters service at a low moisture content and, if it remains at that moisture level, the design may be based on the dry strength of wood.

Moreover, higher design stresses for beams or arches are possible if the outer groups of laminations are of high-grade material. This procedure takes full advantage of the higher strength of the high-grade material by using it in the regions of high stress.

High stresses in glued-laminated structural members require a high-quality product, made with adequate equipment by well-trained and supervised personnel. Many operations are involved in surfacing a large number of laminations, spreading and curing the glue, and fitting and positioning the joints. Each operation must be done properly if a satisfactory product is to result. The necessity for adequate control of these essentials generally means a carefully planned and well-operated laminating plant, and may preclude field gluing.

Many laminated members are curved. Obviously, in bending the laminations to curved form, stresses are set up in the individual laminations. Although it has been found that much of this stress is relieved in time, reduction of the design stress for this factor is necessary as provided in the specifications of Chap. 13 (NDS).

The choice of a type of adhesive is an important factor in providing a satisfactory laminated member. Casein glues are most often used for average covered structures and will give long service under conditions of average moisture content. Casein glues have limited durability, however, if moisture content in service is high. Phenol-formaldehyde, resorcinol-formaldehyde, or mixtures of the two will withstand severe moisture conditions without significant deterioration and are used for exterior or other applications requiring a waterproof glue.

2

Commercial Lumber Standards

2.1 History Historically, lumber manufacture and grading practices developed largely on a regional basis, with considerable variation between different regions and even between some individual producers in the same region. When these regional products began competing in the same markets by reason of expanding production and improved transportation facilities, national standards for sizing, grading, and inspecting them became imperative.

Although it was impractical to develop uniform working stresses or standards for end products—because of existing regional practice and natural variation in strength and growth characteristics of different species—it was possible to standardize the procedure by which value is measured in terms of size, strength, and appearance. Thus, American Lumber Standards are standards by which regional standards or commercial grades can be developed. Lumber is specified and purchased on the basis of the commercial grades.

2.2 American Lumber Standards The "American Lumber Standards for Softwood Lumber," originally adopted in 1924, are the result of a long-term program on the part of the lumber industry to simplify and make as uniform as possible the sizes, nomenclature, grades and inspection procedures of the various softwood species. Softwood Standards are issued in the form of a Simplified Practice Recommendation by the U.S. Department of Commerce, and as stated in the Standards provide "a standardized working basis for the coordination of the grades of the various species and for the preparation of grading rules applicable to each species."

Standards for hardwoods are not covered by the American Lumber Standards but have been developed along similar lines by the various hardwood industry groups such as the National Hardwood Lumber Association.

The American Lumber Standards are not intended for use either as grading rules or as purchase specifications and are not adaptable to such use because they do not include specific grade descriptions or the many other details that are required in grading classifications. Specifications and purchase should be based on the standard grades and grading rules for the various species as established by those agencies promulgating grading rules and maintaining inspection services. Lumber may be designated as American Standards Lumber when it meets the minimum size provisions of the ALS and has been graded under rules that have been approved by the Board of Review of the American Lumber Standards Committee as conforming to the basic requirements of the ALS.

The American Lumber Standards Committee, appointed by the Department of Commerce, is made up of representatives not only of all of the agencies that formulate and publish grading rules and maintain inspection facilities covering the various softwood lumber species, but of other inspection agencies, architects, engineers, contractors, railroads, wood-using industries, millwork manufacturers, and lumber retailers and wholesalers. This Committee is responsible for the revision of these standards from time to time. To carry out the judicial function of passing on the conformance of grading rules to basic ALS requirements and on the competence and reliability—as well as the adequacy of the facilities—of inspection agencies, the Committee has established a Board of Review.

2.3 Scope of basic provisions The American Lumber Standards apply to yard lumber, structural lumber, and factory and shop lumber. These classifications are defined as follows:

1. *Yard lumber* is lumber of those grades, sizes, and patterns that are generally intended for ordinary construction and general building purposes.
2. *Structural lumber* is lumber that is 2 in. or more in thickness and width for use where working stresses are required.
3. *Factory and shop lumber* is lumber that is produced or selected primarily for remanufacturing purposes.

Size standards are established in the form of tabulations showing the minimum dressed thickness and width of finish siding, flooring, ceiling, boards, dimension lumber, timbers, and other items of dressed and worked lumber. The minimum rough dry thickness and width of the various items likewise is specifically covered.

2.4 Structural lumber In the structural lumber section, the American Lumber Standards base the grading of structural lumber upon the applicable provisions of "Guide to the Grading of Structural Timbers," [1] including supplements thereto, but permit deviations if approved by the American Lumber Standards Committee.

The Guide establishes the relation of: size and location of knots; size of shakes, checks, and splits; amount of wane permitted; slope of grain restriction; and the like, to the strength of a piece. The characteristics permitted and limitations prescribed in each commercial stress-grade are based on the fundamentals established in the Guide to provide material of assured strength. Standard grades, as established in industry grading rules, provide a wide range of allowable working stresses.

2.5 Grading and inspection The lumber industry has long accepted responsibility for providing dependable grading and inspection service for the benefit of lumber consumers. In some areas, private grading and inspection agencies provide services comparable to those furnished by the industry groups. The distributing, specifying, and consuming groups look on the maintenance of this service for each species as being the responsibility of the agencies of the lumber industry that sponsor the grading rules for such species. Grading agencies or bureaus have been established in all important lumber producing areas in the United States. Some of these agencies are part of the trade association that serves the area, although usually the subscribers to the service of the grading agency need not be members of the trade association. All the grading agencies that are operated in conjunction with trade associations provide grading rules for species manufactured in their territory.

The grading and inspection service that the lumber industry provides for the benefit of its trade is of several kinds. One function is to coach and train mill graders to be proficient in applying the grading rules. Another is to provide, on request from buyers and sellers, capable inspectors who will certify to the quality of lumber—that is, its conformity to particular specifications.

2.6 Grade-marking and certificate of inspection There are usually two types of grade certification. The first general type is the grade-marking service (see Fig. 2.1). Most inspection agencies have their own employees provide grade-marking services for manufacturers. Others have licensing agreements permitting manufacturers to do their own

[1] Miscellaneous Publication 185, Forest Products Laboratory, U.S. Department of Agriculture.

Fig. 2.1 Typical grademarks (or grade stamps)

Such marks usually include abbreviations or symbols for grade, species, mill, and grading agency. Top, Southern Pine Inspection Bureau; left, West Coast Lumber Inspection Bureau; right, Western Pine Association.

grade-marking. Under these licensing arrangements, the inspection agency supervises the performance of the individual manufacturer and reserves the right to test his performance and to cancel the arrangement if inspection rules are not maintained. Grade-marking generally is available in all items covered by the grading rules.

Most agencies offer a certificate service in addition to the grade-marking. Any grade, whether special or in the grading rules, may be covered by a certificate that indicates the quality and quantity of the material and any other essential information. Lumber may be covered by certificate as well as grade-marked if it is a standard yard item. Generally, certificates are issued only by employees of the grading agencies.

2.7 Reinspection The grading agencies that are part of the trade associations offer a reinspection service that is available to both manufacturers and buyers for the settlement of grading disputes. This service is provided in all parts of the market in which a particular species is sold. A competent inspector in the employ of the agency regrades and retallies the lumber at destination and reports exactly what is found to all interested parties. This provides an independent evaluation that is generally accepted as final in the settlement of disputes. The charge made for reinspection varies with the species and the services performed and is usually payable by the party in error in the dispute. Reinspections are not common, but they are offered in order to enable a buyer who is concerned about a shipment to determine the correctness of the original grading.

2.8 Structural grades In structural grades, specific allowable stress values are assigned to lumber 2 in. and over in nominal thickness. If fiber stress values or compression values are assigned to a particular species and grade, these values are indicated in the grading rules. (See Chap. 11.)

The grading rules class structural lumber according to its size and use as follows:

Beam and stringer: Pieces of rectangular cross section, 5 by 8 in. and larger (nominal dimensions), graded primarily with respect to their strength in bending when loaded on the narrow face, but also suitable for axial tension or compression stresses.

Joist and plank: Pieces of rectangular cross section, 2 to 4 in. thick and 4 in. or more wide (nominal dimensions), graded primarily according to their strength in bending edgewise or flatwise, but also used where axial tensile or compressive strength is required.

Posts and timbers: Pieces of square or approximately square cross section, 5 by 5 in. and larger (nominal dimensions), graded primarily for use as posts or columns, but also suitable for uses in which strength in bending is of less importance.

The principles of stress-grading make possible the assignment of strength ratios in axial compression or tension to the joist and plank grades, in bending or axial tension to the post and timber grades, or in bending flatwise and axial compression and tension to the beam and stringer grades. The most common of such combinations is in the assignment of axial compression or tension values to joist and plank and to beam and stringer grades used in wood trusses.

2.9 Poles and piles Round timbers such as poles or piles are not generally graded to a specific strength rating, although their strength is affected by such characteristics as slope of grain and knots in much the same way as is the strength of sawed lumber. It is generally believed, however, that the effect of strength-reducing characteristics is somewhat less in round timbers than in sawed lumber. In some poles, the swell of the trunk at the location of a branch offsets the weakening effect of the knot, so that the timber may be fully as strong at the knot as in the clear portion of the tree away from the knot. This principle does not apply, of course, if the round timber is trimmed to remove the swell of the trunk. (See Chap. 13.)

2.10 Boards The increasing use of 1-in. boards in light-weight trusses or other structural elements, as well as in glued-laminated structural members, means that boards must frequently be stress-graded. The same principles as for joist and plank may be applied. Stress-grades for boards are not currently covered by most grading rules. The sum of sizes of knots is limited in the same way as in joist and plank grades.

Effects of slope of grain upon strength are about the same as in thicker lumber. As knots and other growth characteristics usually appear in one or both wide faces, the narrow faces, or edges, are seldom considered in stress grading of boards.

2.11 Axial stress Grading rules are largely based on the use of the entire member as a simple beam in bending or as a column. The grade limitations do, however, permit assignment of axial stress values for compression parallel to grain and for tension parallel to grain to joist and plank and to beam and stringer grades when the following additional provisions (or their equivalent) are applied to the grades:

> The sum of the sizes of all knots in any 6 in. of the length of the piece shall not exceed twice the maximum permissible size of knot. Two knots of maximum permissible size shall not be within the same 6 in. of length of any face.
>
> The slope of grain limitation applicable to the mid-portion of the length of the piece shall be applied to the full length of the piece when used in tension parallel to grain.

Some grading rules contain the foregoing or a similar statement as a standard provision; others include it only as a special grade provision. Some such provision must either be specified or covered by proper selection of material at time of fabrication when recommended axial stress values are used. The detailed application of this provision is covered further in Chap. 5 in the discussion on truss design.

2.12 Glued-laminated lumber Standard inspection procedures for glued-laminated lumber have been developed by the American Institute of Timber Construction. Standard sizes and standard grades and grade combinations are set forth in specifications for "Structural Glued-Laminated Southern Pine," "Hardwood Glued-Laminated Lumber," and "Structural Glued-Laminated Lumber" (see Chap. 13, NDS). Included in the specifications are some provisions for proper quality control. It is not possible to grade a glued-laminated member after fabrication. Assured quality or grade can only be guaranteed by proper quality control during lamination.

Although independent inspection on a continuous basis is frequently unavailable, or is furnished only at extra cost, the established fabricator and those having professional supervision can be relied upon to maintain control in quality of material and in the lamination process to guarantee the required quality of the assembly. To satisfy the infrequent requirements for inspection by an outside source, arrangement can usually be made with or by the fabricator, to obtain inspection by experienced professional engineers, or by established independent laboratories or inspection agencies.

3

Preliminary Design Considerations

DURATION OF LOAD

3.1 Duration of load Of all construction materials, only timber has the structural property of being able to sustain higher loads for short durations of time than for long durations. For example, timber will support twice as much load of extremely short duration—such as impact—as it will a load of 10 years' duration. Because many design loads are of intermittent application and intensity, this property may be utilized to advantage in design with timber.

Although design recommendations for other materials allow an increase in unit stresses for wind and earthquake loads combined with other loads, the increase merely represents taking a calculated risk that the maximum loading conditions for wind and earthquake will not occur at the same time as other maximum live loads; and in a sense, the increase represents a reduction in the factor of safety. There is no such reduction with timber, because it is an actual, physical property of the wood that permits it to carry greater loads for short periods.

3.2 Basic stresses In determining basic stresses for wood from laboratory test specimens, adjustment is made to compensate for the short duration of the tests, thus reducing short-time test values to safe, permanent-load values. For example, ultimate test values for extreme fiber stress in bending are reduced by $\frac{7}{16}$ to convert the short-time test loading to recommended values for expected permanent load, and corresponding reductions are made from basic test values for other stresses.

The ability of timber to sustain higher stresses for short durations is shown by the graph illustrating Appendix H of the "National Design

Specification for Stress-Grade Lumber and Its Fastenings" (Chap. 13). The adjustments apply to all tabulated unit stresses except modulus of elasticity, *E*, when used for determining deflection. Thus *E* is not adjusted for duration of load for beam or truss deflection computations, but is adjusted for compression member or column design.

3.3 Adjustment of stresses Adjustments in working stresses for duration of load do not reduce the factor of safety. Thus if the ultimate load for 10 years' durations were 3 times the normal load design value, the ultimate value for wind loading would be 4 times the normal load, and the factor of safety would be the same. Apparently there is also a relationship between duration of load and frequency of application, particularly for shorter-duration loads like impact, and this relationship is under study.

Recommended adjustments of tabulated normal load working stresses for other durations of load are the following:

Increase for two months' duration, as for snow	+15 per cent
Increase for seven days' duration	+25 per cent
Increase for wind or earthquake	+33⅓ per cent
Increase for impact	+100 per cent
Reduction for permanent loading	−10 per cent

These adjustments do not apply to *E* when used to determine deflections. The increases apply to a combination of dead load and any loads of the duration indicated; the increase for the shortest duration load in the combination is used. The resulting section must not be less than that required for permanent load or dead load alone, with any other combination of loads.

3.4 Normal load As a rule, most loads on structures other than dead loads do not stress members continuously and permanently to maximum allowable value. Tabulated allowable working stresses are based on "normal" loading, which contemplates that a member will not be stressed to maximum design load for a cumulative time of more than 10 years or that no more than 90 per cent of this load will be applied continuously throughout the remainder of the life of the structure without encroaching on the factor of safety. Floor loads are ordinarily considered normal loads.

3.5 Permanent load If cumulative duration of maximum permissible load is to exceed that contemplated for normal load, only 90 per cent of the tabulated working stresses are used. A dead storage warehouse might be designed on this basis, as might a structure supporting a permanent load alone, such as a storage vat or tank, or timber retaining walls.

3.6 Snow load All members or assemblies for which maximum stress occurs with snow load (that is, a load with a maximum cumulative duration of about two months in combination with other loads of longer duration), are designed on the basis of 15 per cent increase in tabulated working stresses. The resultant section must not be less than that required for the longer duration loads alone.

3.7 Wind and earthquake, seven-day loads, impact As with snow load, tabulated working stresses are increased for wind or earthquake (33⅓ per cent), for loads of seven days' duration (25 per cent), and for impact (100 per cent) when any of these is combined with other loads of longer duration.

3.8 Combination of loads If there are several durations of live loads and dead load to be considered, the percentage increase to be used is based on the shortest duration load of the combination (the one yielding the largest increase), provided the resulting section is adequate for a combination of other longer duration loads. An example would be a roof designed for dead load, snow, and wind or earthquake. Members would be designed on the basis of the total of stresses due to dead, snow, and wind loads, with a 33⅓ per cent increase in tabulated working values to accommodate the wind load—the shortest of the three. The section would then be checked for requirements based on dead and snow loads with a corresponding 15 per cent increase in values. Usually the critical combination can be determined by observation.

3.9 Deflection The recommended adjustments for duration of load do not apply to the tabulated modulus of elasticity, E, for design problems involving deflection. Thus where design is controlled by deflection, as in a beam or truss, no effect of duration of load is recognized.

3.10 Fastenings Duration of load adjustments for fastenings are similar, and usually equal, to those for lumber working stresses. The adjustments are equal if strength is dependent on the strength of the wood alone and not the strength of the material of the fastening. The adjustments are less than those for wood stresses if load value is determined both by the strength of the wood and the material of the fastening, such as in toothed rings. For shear plate timber connectors, which transfer the load from bolt to metal by metal bearing and shear on the bolt, the adjusted values for duration of load must not exceed the allowable bolt values based on metal working stresses. Tabulated allowable loads for fastenings are based on "normal" duration of load. (See Chap. 13, DM.[1])

SPECIES, GRADES, AND SIZES OF LUMBER

3.11 Availability Lumber is probably the most readily available of all building materials, as there are lumber dealer stocks in every community. Although the species, grades, sizes, and lengths vary geographically, the local supplier can advise what material and sizes are in stock or promptly obtainable, and the designer proceed accordingly.

3.12 Sawed lumber The average local lumber inventory will include stress grades in thicknesses from 2 to 4 in. and widths up to 12 in. The most common lengths do not exceed 20 to 24 ft. The usual stress grades will be from 1,100 to 1,700 psi for bending with the correspondingly appropriate working stresses for compression and shear. If a project requires large amounts—for example, a carload—of lumber, local stocks are of less import because shipments may be made from regional concentration yards or from the mills, and a wider range of grade, size, and length thus be obtained.

Frequently the choice of lumber species is only a question of availability, and usually there are several species that will serve equally well for the same design. All species may be structurally graded. Those species for which rules for stress-grades have been established are listed in the "National Design Specification" of Chap. 13.

The lower and medium stress grades are the most readily available. The higher grades, however, may permit the use of smaller member sizes, and such members may sometimes be more easily obtained than larger sizes of lower grades. As modulus of elasticity is the same for all grades of sawed lumber of the same species, medium or lower grades meet requirements for stiffness, rigidity, or deflection as well or better than the higher grades. Moreover, joint-area requirements for the installation of fastenings frequently favor the use of the average grades, because the slightly larger member sizes required with average grades furnish more joint area than do the higher grades. Conversely, the dense grades of some species sometimes require fewer fastenings because of their higher fastening values.

The present ratio of labor cost to material cost makes it preferable to use larger sizes and longer lengths whenever doing so permits a reduction in labor cost by eliminating joints. For example, it may be

[1] "Design Manual for Timber Connector Construction."

cheaper to substitute six panels in a truss for eight panels of smaller size timber, or to employ two chord splices in place of three. Too often the saving made in quantity of lumber through the use of smaller members is more than offset by the increased labor needed in framing. Thus, proportioning a frame or truss to use a 3 x 10 chord member in place of a 3 x 6 or 3 x 8 might be desirable (availability might rule out the use of a 3 x 14 in place of a 3 x 10 or a 3 x 12, however). It may be added that a minimum thickness of 4 in. instead of 2 or 3 in. would also improve the fire resistance.

3.13 Glued-laminated lumber Glued-laminated lumber is frequently used in place of sawed timber for truss members, beams, stringers, columns, and arches. It has the advantage of higher working stresses, of being available in larger sizes and longer lengths than sawed timber, and of reducing to a minimum the problems of shrinkage and the resultant secondary stresses in joints.

Standard specifications given in Chap. 13 (NDS) cover species, sizes, stress-grade combinations, and use conditions for glued-laminated members.

The average and lower grades and grade combinations are recommended for average conditions, but there are also savings in the higher grades if their higher working stresses for extreme fiber in bending and for compression parallel to grain can be fully utilized. There is no advantage in the higher bending grades if deflection, horizontal shear, or compression perpendicular to the grain are controlling factors, because these properties are not increased proportionally by the higher grade. The designer should specify the required allowable working stresses rather than any particular grade or grade combination, so that the fabricator may have freedom to furnish that combination which meets the requirement and which will be most economical in terms of fabricating procedure and available lumber supply.

Standard widths of members are based on the dressed widths obtainable from the commercial lumber sizes used in the laminating. If a width just larger than a standard is specified, the buyer will usually pay for the next larger standard width and thus not obtain the most for his money.

Lumber used in laminating is seasoned and accurately surfaced before being glued. Tabulated working stresses for glued-laminated members take into account dry conditions of use typical of most covered structures and wet conditions of use prevalent in exterior or submerged service.

Sizes and lengths of glued-laminated members sometimes are limited by shipping and handling problems. As size limitations vary widely for different methods of shipment and for different areas in the case of highway shipment, it is recommended that the designer ask timber fabricators to recommend maximum shipping sizes.

SEASONING AND USE CONDITIONS

3.14 Effect on working stresses An understanding of seasoning and use conditions is important to determine the appropriate working stresses for lumber and its fastenings. Significant change in moisture content after fabrication or assembly is particularly important to fastening values. Seasonal variations in moisture content are seldom of concern in most covered structures.

Chapter 1 discussed the effect of moisture content on working stresses for lumber. The specifications of Chap. 13 (NDS) include recommendations for adjustments in working stresses of both lumber and its fastenings under various seasoning and use conditions.

3.15 Lumber seasoning conditions The most desirable seasoning for lumber is that which reduces its moisture content approximately to the level it will reach in service. Such seasoning minimizes dimensional change in the lumber, eliminates need for reduction in design values of fastenings due to change in moisture content, and minimizes secondary stresses that may be set up due to shrinkage. However, seasoned lumber is not normally available from local suppliers in the 3-in. and larger thicknesses frequently required for structural use, and frequently even 2-in. seasoned material is not readily available.

Unseasoned lumber has a mositure content above the fiber-saturation point, which for commonly used species will vary from 24 to 30 per cent. There is no change in lumber dimension or appreciable change in strength properties as a result of change in moisture content above this fiber-saturation point. Seasoned lumber, on the other hand, has been dried to a moisture content substantially below fiber-saturation point but usually somewhat above the moisture content that the lumber will reach in normal covered use. This level represents an assumed moisture content of 12 to 15 per cent in the outer ½ in. of a member's thickness for average climatic conditions, although the final moisture content after years of service may be 8 to 10 per cent.

The moisture content of much of the lumber used in structural framing lies somewhere between the two extremes labeled seasoned and unseasoned. Seasoned lumber, particularly members of 3-in. nominal thickness and over, is generally available only on special order and will not be found in most commercial stocks unless the lumber has been air dried in storage for a period of time.

3.16 Lumber use conditions No adjustment in lumber working stresses for variation in moisture content is necessary for most structures, because allowable unit working stresses for sawed timber are based on unseasoned values. Credit for seasoning is taken in those strength properties only if a limited amount of seasoning has normally taken place before use. For average covered-use conditions, the standard recommended lumber working stresses are used.

Likewise, for exposed-use conditions in which the lumber is wet only for short periods and dry most of the time, no adjustment in working stresses is usually necessary. Bearing points that remain damp may warrant reduction in compression values parallel to grain, and of course decay is a hazard to exposed lumber.

Continuously damp or wet lumber that remains unseasoned in use requires reduction of compression stresses parallel and perpendicular to the grain and also of modulus of elasticity. Other primary working stresses remain the same as for seasoned lumber.

The designer will be concerned with moisture content primarily as it affects fastening values and joint details so that he may minimize secondary stresses due to shrinkage. Seasoning characteristics of the lumber itself are usually of concern only as they affect deflection and appearance. In arid regions or in highly heated buildings, the final moisture-content equilibrium may be substantially below the average. In such places, additional care is necessary to avoid or minimize the effect of the seasoning shrinkage.

3.17 Effect on fastening values Tabulated design values for fastenings are calculated in terms of lumber that is seasoned at the time of fabrication and that will remain seasoned or dry in use. Seasoned at fabrication means that under average conditions the outer ¾ in. of thickness has a moisture content of 12 to 15 per cent. Such seasoning is ideal because it permits the maximum values for fastenings. If unseasoned or partially seasoned lumber is employed, adjustments in fastening values are necessary regardless of its moisture content after fabrication.

Design specifications in Chap. 13 (NDS) include recommendations for reductions from tabulated (seasoned) fastening values both for unseasoned lumber that will become seasoned before or while in use, and for that which will remain or become unseasoned.

Seasoned lumber should be planned on and specified, if available, so that maximum values may be realized for the fastenings. Such lumber also lessens the need for bolt tightening—a particular advantage of glued-laminated members as they are made of seasoned stock. Joints sometimes loosen considerably when unseasoned lumber dries.

Unless the designer knows definitely that seasoned material is available, he should assume that he will be working with only partially seasoned lumber. Some seasoning will normally have taken place in the outer thickness of most members before fabrication. Naturally, should it be known that totally unseasoned, freshly cut lumber is to be used, the designer must be guided accordingly. The adjustments to apply to tabulated values for the various fastenings are given in Table 3.1.

TABLE 3.1 Allowable load adjustments for fastenings

(Italics indicate recommended assumptions for average dry-use conditions if exact original moisture condition is not known.)

Type of fastening	Condition of lumber		Percentage of tabulated allowable load
	At fabrication	In service	
Timber connectors	Seasoned	Seasoned	100
(Split rings, shear plates, toothed rings)	*Partially seasoned*	*Seasoned*	*90*
	Unseasoned	Seasoned	80
	Seasoned or unseasoned	Unseasoned or wet	67
Bolts and lag screws	Seasoned	Seasoned	100
(Lateral resistance)	*Partially seasoned*	*Seasoned*	*75*
	Unseasoned	Seasoned	40
		Exposed to weather	75
		Wet	67
Nails and spikes	Seasoned	Seasoned	100
(Lateral resistance)	*Partially seasoned*	*Seasoned*	*90*
	Unseasoned	Unseasoned or wet	75

PRESERVATIVES

3.18 Protective measures For exposed conditions in which lumber may attain a moisture content conducive to decay, or to insect attack, protective measures should be taken. Either the heartwood of a naturally resistant species should be used, or the wood should be treated with preservative chemicals, applied by a recognized and acceptable process, to give it the necessary degree of resistance. A variety of such chemicals is available.

3.19 Standard preservatives The following preservatives are recognized in the Standards of the American Wood Preservers' Association:

Preservative oils
- Creosote
- Creosote–coal tar solutions
- Creosote–petroleum solutions

Oil-borne preservatives
- Pentachlorophenol
- Copper naphthenate

Water-borne preservatives
- Chromated zinc chloride (CZC)
- Copperized chromated zinc chloride (CCZC)
- Tanalith (Wolman Salts)
- Celcure
- Chemonite
- Greensalt (Eradlith)
- Boliden salts

3.20 Treatment methods The selection of the proper method of treatment is as important as the selection of the proper preservative. The best preservative known will not increase the life of wood appreciably if it is not effectively injected into the wood. The increased life thereby obtained, moreover, is in direct proportion to the thoroughness with which the treatment has been carried out. Methods of treatment may be divided into two general classes: (1) pressure processes, and (2) nonpressure processes.

3.21 Pressure processes For maximum protection, pressure processes are the best because they permit the greatest penetration of preservative. Timber to be treated by a pressure process is loaded on tram cars (Fig. 3.1) and rolled into long steel cylinders. The cylinders are then sealed and filled with the preservative. Through established combinations of temperature, vacuum, and pressure, the preservative is injected into the wood. Two basic methods, known as the full-cell (Bethell) process and the empty-cell (Rueping or Lowry) process, are available.

Courtesy American Wood Preservers Institute

Fig. 3.1 Pressure processing

Lumber framed to specification and loaded on tram cars for preservative treatment.

Treatment by the full-cell process leaves the cells of the wood, within the depth of penetration, full of preservative. It is used in treating all material for marine construction and also if a specified retention is greater than that which can be obtained by the empty-cell process.

The empty-cell process leaves the cell walls saturated but with no free liquid preservative in the cell cavities. This process yields a drier product and permits maximum penetration for any specified weight of treatment.

Except for marine structures, the empty-cell process is generally specified for oil preservatives. Salt preservatives are usually injected by the full-cell process. Oil-borne pressure-treated material may be used without further seasoning immediately after it comes from the retort. Wood treated with salt preservatives, however, may require seasoning after treatment to a moisture content suitable for the intended end use of the material, should seasoning after fabrication be undesirable.

3.22 Nonpressure processes Nonpressure processes cover all modifications of immersion or dip treatments at atmospheric pressures. They range from the hot-and-cold bath, which essentially creates pressure differences by expelling some of the air in the wood, to the spray or brush treatment.

If the decay hazard is small or the application is not essential to building safety, protection by nonpressure processes may prove satisfactory even if not as effective as that by pressure processes, which can provide greater penetration and retention of chemicals. Effectiveness can usually be increased by a higher degree of seasoning of the wood, by lengthening the time of immersion, and by utilizing a natural vacuum such as in the hot-and-cold-bath process.

Spray and brush treatments should be used only for on-the-job localized care for areas that have been exposed by boring or grooving after original treatment by other methods.

3.23 Preparation for treatment Wood that is resistant to penetration by preservatives is sometimes incised before treatment to permit deeper and more uniform penetration. Sawed or hewed material is passed through a machine having horizontal and vertical rollers equipped with teeth that cut into the wood to a predetermined depth, usually ½ to ¾ in. The teeth are spaced to give the desired distribution of preservative with the minimum number of incisions. A machine of different design is required for incising the butts of poles. The effectiveness of incising is based on the fact that preservatives usually penetrate into wood much farther in a longitudinal direction than in a direction perpendicular to the face of the stock. By exposing end-grain surfaces, the incisions permit such penetration. They are especially effective in improving penetration in the heartwood portions of sawed or hewed surfaces.

All possible cutting, framing, and boring of holes should be done before treatment. Cutting into the wood in any way after treatment may expose the untreated or lesser treated portions of the timber and thus permit ready access to destructive fungi. When such cutting cannot be avoided, after-treatment of the area by soaking it with several applications of hot preservative is recommended. The end grain of wood, such as pile cutoffs, can be effectively treated by setting up a mud or sheet metal dam around the end and filling it several times with hot preservative. Holes can be treated by inserting a plug at one end and a pressure gun at the other to force the hot preservative into the wood. The after-treatment preservative should be the same as that originally used on the whole member.

3.24 Choice of preservation process Many factors must be considered in selecting the proper treatment process and chemical for a specific situation. The conditions of exposure, the after-treatment required (such as painting), the estimated useful life of the structure, the availability of special treating equipment, are but a few. Wood used in permanent structures in direct contact with the ground—such as piling, poles, or foundation timbers—requires the best treatment possible. Items that are protected from leaching by paint or other surface finish —such as window sashes and exterior trim—can be given sufficient protection with a dip treatment. The possibility of leaching, as well as of corrosion of metal fastenings, is a factor to be considered when salt-type preservatives are used. Salt treatment of wood that remains dry or is only occasionally wet in service causes no trouble. Under conditions of severe exposure to moisture, however, corrosion or leaching can be severe.

3.25 Specifications Federal Specification TT-W-571c presents a conservative guide for specifiers and users of pressure treated timber. Tables 3.2, 3.3, and 3.4, excerpted from this specification, recommend the types of preservatives applicable to different classes of material and varying locations of use. Minimum retention of preservative per cubic foot is stipulated, and the standard American Wood Preservers' Association (AWPA) specification for the applicable treating process is prescribed.

For millwork, containers, and other items suitably treated by the nonpressure process, Federal Specification TT-W-572 and the "Minimum Standards for Water Repellent Preservatives" prepared by the National Woodwork Manufacturers Association (NWMA) as a basis for their seal of approval define the various preservatives and their application.

The NWMA's "Minimum Standard for Preservative Treatment of Millwork at the Factory" requires complete immersion of stock in an approved treating solution for not less than 3 minutes, or comparable penetration obtained by vacuum or vacuum-pressure methods.

3.26 Fire-retardant treatments It is possible to make wood highly resistant to the spread of fire by impregnating it with one of the approved chemical formulations. Wood will char if exposed to fire or fire temperatures even if it is treated with a fire-retardant solution, but the rate of its destruction and transmission of heat can definitely be retarded by chemicals. The most significant contribution chemicals make, however, consists in checking the spread of the fire. Wood that has absorbed adequate amounts of one of the recognized compounds will not support combustion nor contribute fuel, and will cease to burn as soon as the source of ignition is removed. As some of the standard salts recommended for protecting wood from decay are also used in fire-

TABLE 3.2 Treatment of wood with creosote and solutions containing creosote

(Schedule of recommended practice in the treatment of timber in various forms)

Form of product and service conditions	Minimum net retention of preservative recommended [1]			Treating specification [3] (AWPA Spec. T1 and others listed below [4])
	Coal-tar creosote (Fed. Spec. TT–W–556 and AWPA Spec. P1)	Creosote-coal tar solutions (Fed. Spec. TT–W–566 and AWPA Spec. P2)	Creosote-petroleum solution [2] (Fed. Spec. TT–W–568 and AWPA Spec. P3)	
	lb per cu ft	*lb per cu ft*	*lb per cu ft*	
Ties [5]				T6
Crossties, switch ties, bridge ties	8	8	9	
Lumber and structural timber				T2
For use in coastal waters:				
Pacific Coast Douglas fir [6]	14	14	(7)	
Southern yellow pine	20	20	(7)	
For use in fresh water, in contact with the ground, or for important structural members not in contact with the ground or water [6]	10	10	12	
For other use not in contact with the ground nor in water	6	6	7	
Piles [8]				T3 [9]
For use in coastal waters:				
Pacific Coast Douglas fir	14	14	(7)	
Southern yellow pine	20	20	(7)	
For land or fresh-water use:				
Douglas fir; oak, red and white; pine, jack, lodgepole, ponderosa, red, and southern yellow	12	12	14	Until jack, lodge pole, ponderosa, and red pines are covered in T3, use T4
Poles [8]	8 [10 11 12]			T4 [9] and T8
Posts [13]	6 [14]	6 [14]	7 [14]	T5 [15]

[1] Where it is impractical to obtain retentions specified, treatment shall be to refusal.

[2] Petroleum meeting the requirements of American Wood Preservers' Association Specification P4 shall be used.

[3] When penetration is not otherwise specified, the penetration in the sapwood shall be not less than 2½ in. unless 85 per cent of the sapwood depth is penetrated.

[4] These specifications cover treatment of species most commonly treated. Specifications covering some other species are being developed.

[5] See current issue of Federal Specification MM–T–371 for species acceptable.

retardant treatments, such treatments may thereby serve a dual purpose.

The two general methods of improving the resistance of wood to fire are: (1) impregnation with an effective chemical, and (2) coating the surface with a layer of noncombustible paint. The first method is the more effective; for interiors or locations protected from the weather, impregnation treatments can be considered permanent. Some coatings and fire-resistant paints nevertheless have considerable value in preventing ignition. These surface applications offer the principal means of increasing the fire-retardant properties of existing structures. They may, however, require periodic renewal if an effective coating is to be maintained.

Because the effective chemicals are water soluble, fire-retardant treatments are not well adapted to weather exposure. In some out-of-door structures using lumber impregnated with fire-retardant salts, attempts have been made to retard leaching of the chemicals due to rain or other water by the application of ordinary paint. As yet, however, there is very little information on the effectiveness of the paint in preventing leaching or on the effect of the paint itself on fire performance. Some tests, however, have indicated that a second shallow impregnation with a fire-retardant, water-repellent sealer substantially retards leaching even under severe exposure.

Fire-retardant salts are injected into wood by the same pressure processes used in treatments to prevent decay. However, considerably heavier absorptions of preservative are necessary for fire retardance

---

[6] All Douglas fir 3 in. or more in thickness shall be incised on 4 sides except that, in fabricated material, incising may be omitted on any face or edge that would be seriously damaged thereby.

[7] Not recommended for use in coastal waters.

[8] Since difficulty may be encountered in securing the specified retention and penetration, piles and poles should be selected for treatment that have sufficient sapwood thickness and are sufficiently conditioned to permit obtaining the retention and penetration specified. For piles to be used in coastal waters, maximum possible retentions are recommended but in no case should the retention be less than the minimum indicated. Additional requirements of the physical characteristics of piles are covered in Federal Specification MM–P–371.

[9] In Douglas fir the penetration shall be not less than ¾ in.; at least 85 per cent of the sapwood depth shall be penetrated unless the penetration is 1⅝ in. or more.

[10] Where conditions do not favor rapid decay, a retention of 6 lb per cu ft is acceptable for Group A poles of jack and lodgepole pines and western larch whose circumference 6 ft from butt is less than 37.5 in., provided that the penetration specified for an 8 lb per cu ft treatment is met. For Group B poles of all acceptable species except cedar (see footnote 11), whose circumference 6 ft from butt is 37.5 in. or more, a minimum retention of 10 lb per cu ft is recommended.

[11] For full-length pressure-treated cedar poles this minimum retention may be decreased 50 per cent. Butt-treated cedar poles may be used where conditions do not favor decay or termite attack in the untreated part of the pole.

[12] This retention requirement may be waived in the case of cedar, Douglas fir, lodgepole pine, or western larch poles treated full length by the hot- and cold-bath process, provided that penetration requirements of American Wood Preservers' Association Specification T4 (see also footnote 9) are met.

[13] Rectangular posts shall be treated according to specifications for lumber and structural timber.

[14] For cedar posts these minimum retentions may be decreased by 1 lb per cu ft.

[15] In half-round or quarter-round posts, penetration measurements shall be made in the sapwood.

TABLE 3.3 Treatment of wood with water-borne preservatives [1, 2]

(Schedule of recommended practice in the treatment of timber in various forms)

Form of product and service conditions	Minimum net retention of preservative recommended [1]						Treating specification [3] (AWPA Spec. T1 and others listed below [4])
	Celcure (acid-cupric-chromate) (Fed. Spec. TT-W-546)	Chemonite (ammoniacal copper arsenite) (Fed. Spec. TT-W-549)	Chromated-zinc-chloride (Fed. Spec. TT-W-551 and AWPA Spec. P5)	Tanalith (Fed. Spec. TT-W-573 and AWPA Spec. P5)	Zinc-chloride (Fed. Spec. TT-W-576 and AWPA Spec. P5)	Zinc-meta-arsenite (Fed. Spec. TT-W-581 and AWPA Spec. P5)	
	lb per cu ft	*lb per cu ft*	*lb per cu ft*	*lb per cu ft*	*lb per cu ft*	*lb per cu ft*	
Lumber and structural timber [5, 6]							T2
For use under moderate leaching conditions [7]	0.75	0.45	1.15	0.55	1.50	0.55	
For use not in contact with the ground nor in water	0.50	0.30	0.75	0.35	1.00	0.35	
Posts [8]	0.75	0.45	1.15	0.55	1.50	0.55	T5 [9]

[1] The use of wood treated with other salts is permitted to a limited extent only and where service records are to be kept to determine their effectiveness. The minimum retention permitted for such preservatives shall be not less than the lowest minimum recommended in this table.

[2] Where maximum service life is of primary importance, these preservatives are not recommended for use under severe leaching conditions.

[3] When penetration is not otherwise specified, the penetration in the sapwood shall be not less than 2½ in., unless 85 per cent of the sapwood depth is penetrated.

[4] These specifications cover treatment of species most commonly treated. Specifications covering some other species are being developed.

[5] All Douglas fir 3 in. or more in thickness shall be incised on four sides except that in fabricated material, incising may be omitted on any face or edge that would be seriously damaged thereby.

[6] For Douglas fir timbers 12 in. or more in the smallest cross-section dimension, the retentions shall be reduced by 25 per cent.

[7] By "moderate leaching conditions" is meant occasional exposure to water or constant exposure to the ground in areas of moderate rainfall.

[8] Rectangular posts shall be treated according to specifications for lumber and structural timber.

[9] In half-round or quarter-round posts, penetration measurements shall be made in the sapwood.

TABLE 3.4 Treatment of wood with oil-borne preservatives [1]

(Schedule of recommended practice in the treatment of timber in various forms)

Form of product and service conditions	Minimum net retention of preservative recommended [2]		Treating specifications[4] (AWPA Spec. T1 and others listed below[5])
	Pentachlorophenol solution in petroleum[3] equivalent to 5 per cent pure pentachlorophenol (Fed. Spec. TT-W-570 and AWPA Spec. P8)	Copper naphthenate solution in petroleum[3] equivalent to 0.5 per cent copper (AWPA Spec. P8)	
	lb per cu ft	*lb per cu ft*	
Lumber and structural timber			T2
For use in contact with the ground [6]	10	10	
For use not in contact with the ground nor in water	6	6	
Poles [7]	8 [8 9 10]	8 [8 9 10]	T4 [11] and T8
Posts [12]	6 [13]	6 [13]	T5 [14]

[1] During the limited number of years these preservatives have been in commercial use, they have given favorable results but their effectiveness has not yet been fully evaluated. With properly selected solvents they are suitable for use where cleanliness is important. It is permissible to blend them with coal-tar creosote in any proportions where their use alone is approved. Methods of treatment recommended for creosote are also recommended for these preservatives.

[2] Where it is impractical to obtain retentions specified, treatment shall be to refusal.

[3] When a Federal specification for petroleum oils to be used in these solutions becomes available, it shall be used. Until then oils conforming to American Wood Preservers' Association Specification P9 may be used.

[4] When penetration is not otherwise specified, the penetration in the sapwood shall be not less than 2½ in. unless 85 per cent of the sapwood depth is penetrated.

[5] These specifications cover treatment of species most commonly treated. Specifications covering some other species are being prepared.

[6] All Douglas fir 3 in. or more in thickness shall be incised on four sides except that in fabricated material, incising may be omitted on any face or edge that would be seriously damaged thereby.

[7] Since difficulty may be encountered in securing the specified retention and penetration, poles should be selected for treatment that have sufficient sapwood thickness and are sufficiently conditioned to permit obtaining the retention and penetration specified.

[8] Where conditions do not favor rapid decay, a retention of 6 lb per cu ft is acceptable for Group A poles of jack and lodgepole pines and western larch whose circumference 6 ft from butt is less than 37.5 in., provided that the penetration specified for an 8 lb per cu ft treatment is met. For Group B poles of all acceptable species except cedar (see footnote 9) whose circumference 6 ft from butt is 37.5 in. or more, a minimum retention of 10 lb per cu ft is recommended.

[9] For full-length pressure-treated cedar poles this minimum retention may be decreased 50 per cent. Butt-treated cedar poles may be used where conditions do not favor decay or termite attack in the untreated part of the pole.

[10] This retention requirement may be waived in the case of cedar, Douglas fir, lodgepole pine, or western larch poles treated full-length by the hot- and cold-bath process, provided that penetration requirements of American Wood Preservers' Association Specification T4 (see also footnote 11) are met.

[11] In Douglas fir the penetration shall be not less than ¾ in.; at least 85 per cent of the sapwood depth shall be penetrated unless the penetration is 1⅝ in. or more.

than for protection from decay. Table 3.5 lists recommended retentions of such fire-retardant preservatives as Minalith, Pyresote, and chromated zinc chloride (FR), each described in AWPA Standard P10.

TABLE 3.5 Recommended minimum retention of fire-retardant salts

Thickness of lumber *in.*	Minimum retention, For moderate fire-retardance (*lb per cu ft*)	Minimum retention, For high fire-retardance (*lb per cu ft*)
Not over 2	2.5	5.0
Over 2 but not over 4	2.0	4.0
Over 4 but not over 6	1.75	3.5
Over 6 but not over 8	1.5	3.0
Over 8 but not over 12	1.25	2.5
Over 12 but not over 16	0.75	1.5
Over 16	0.5	1.0

FASTENINGS

3.27 Types of fastenings Improvements in fastenings and development of reliable design standards have contributed greatly to the increased use of timber construction. Joints are now designed with the same accuracy as other parts of a structural frame so that a balanced construction will result. Details should no longer be left to unqualified job-site judgment.

A wide variety of fastenings are available for timber: nails, spikes, screws, bolts, lag screws, driftpins, and a number of kinds of timber connectors. Each type of fastening has its own distinct advantages.

3.28 Nails and spikes Nails are the oldest and most common fastenings in use today (see Fig. 3.2). The design recommendations for allowable loads apply for bright, smooth, common steel wire nails driven into wood without splitting. For special nails, the allowable loads may be adjusted in accordance with the designer's judgment based on the manufacturer's recommendations and the type of construction.

Nails used structurally should be loaded laterally or in shear and not be subject to calculated withdrawal forces. For lateral forces under usual conditions, there is little advantage in the use of special nails, except for high-strength steel nails, because lateral resistance is primarily a function of nail diameter. Special nail shanks or specially

[12] Rectangular posts shall be treated according to specifications for lumber and structural timber.
[13] For cedar posts these retentions may be decreased by 1 lb per cu ft.
[14] In half-round or quarter-round posts, penetration measurements shall be made in the sapwood.

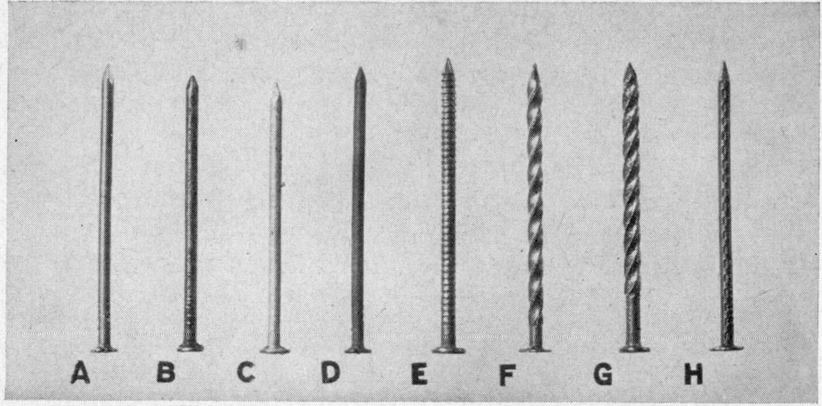

Courtesy Forest Products Laboratory

Fig. 3.2 Types of nails and spikes

A Standard wire nail or spike
B Cement-coated
C Zinc-coated or galvanized
D Chemically etched
E Annular grooved
F Spirally grooved
G Spirally grooved and barbed
H Barbed

treated shanks have little effect on lateral strength. Threaded-type shank nails or spikes are often recommended for use with preservative-treated timber, however, because the treating chemicals or carrier may have a lubricating effect, thus reducing both the lateral and withdrawal resistance of common nails or spikes.

Although comprehensive data are not available, special nails with improved withdrawal resistance also have a theoretical advantage in lateral resistance. Such advantage would accrue when normal penetration is not possible, when changes in moisture content is a factor, and when vibration might tend to loosen common nails. Specially hardened nails theoretically permit higher loads than common nails of the same diameter. Conversely, they also theoretically permit use of smaller diameters and thus reduce splitting. These advantages of special nails in lateral resistance have not been thoroughly proved by test or experience, however, and must be weighed against their higher cost.

Special nails can have shanks that have been treated to improve withdrawal resistance or special points that also improve it as well as possibly reduce splitting. Commercial types offer cement-coated surfaces, etched or roughened shank surfaces, barbed shanks, spirally grooved or twisted shanks, and annular grooved shanks. (Cement-coated nails are commonly used for box nails, and spirally grooved or annular grooved nails for flooring and shingles.)

Common nails and spikes are limited in construction use primarily by the size and number that can be driven without undue splitting of the wood. The tendency of lumber to split varies with the species and moisture content, so that no precise rules are possible. Offsetting adjacent nails from the same grain line minimizes the danger, however, as does blunting the point of a nail before driving. Some designers use an arbitrary rule for softwoods of $\frac{1}{2}$ nail length for spacing and end distance, and $\frac{1}{4}$ length for edge distance, but experience and trial remain the best guide. Obviously the quality of workmanship is a factor.

Nailing is primarily used for material 2 in. and thinner, although spikes up to 12 in. in length are available.

3.29 Allowable loads for nails and spikes Because no well-defined proportional limit is obtainable in tests, recommended design loads in lateral resistance for nails and spikes are based on test loads at deformation of about 0.01 in. The ratio of ultimate or failure load to design load is somewhat higher for nails and spikes than for some other fastenings, but the higher ratio is desirable because of the greater variation in strength due to moisture conditions, workmanship, and splitting. Nail values are predicated on a specified penetration of the point. In lieu of standard penetration, some designers accept clinching. No specifications presently cover nails or spikes in double shear, but some data indicate that the single shear value is doubled if nails are clinched or if equivalent withdrawal resistance is provided on the member receiving the point. Allowable loads for common nails and spikes are given in Chap. 13 (NDS).

If it becomes necessary to prebore nail or spike holes to prevent splitting and a large number of nails are required, another type of fastening of greater capacity may simplify fabrication.

3.30 Nailed gusset plates Frequently plywood or metal gusset plates are used to increase the joint area available for nailing, thus permitting greater capacity and reducing the possibility of splitting. They require twice the amount of nails and labor of a direct connection, however, not to mention the additional labor and material represented by the gusset plate itself.

3.31 Framing anchors Special metal fittings such as framing anchors are used to eliminate the difficulties and uncertainties of toenailing and withdrawal loads as well as to provide a stronger shear connection. One variety of 18 gauge is made in three styles, each with a right and left hand, and is therefore adaptable to innumerable connections in light frame or secondary structural connections (see Fig. 3.3). The anchors are $4\frac{7}{8}$ in. high, the rectangular flange is $1\frac{5}{8}$ in. wide, and the triangular flange is $2\frac{3}{8}$ in. wide at the base. If a portion of

Fig. 3.3 Framing anchors

the rectangular flange is bent, the bent portion is $1\frac{5}{8}$ in. long. Special nails, equivalent to approximately half-length eightpenny (8d) nails, are furnished by the manufacturer. Type "A" framing anchors are used where one member crosses another, such as in joist-to-beam or rafter-to-wall joints (Fig. 3.4); type "B" where one member butts against another, such as stud-to-plate or -sill or joist-to-header (Fig. 3.5). Type "C," with butting members, is used primarily as a joist hanger (Fig. 3.6). A number of other special light-gauge connections of this nature are available for special purposes, such as stud sockets and column caps. The manufacturers' recommendations for allowable loads for directions indicated in Figs. 3.4, 3.5, and 3.6 appear in Table 3.6.

3.32 Wood screws Wood screws are seldom used in structural work because their primary advantage over nails or spikes is in withdrawal resistance (such loading should be avoided if possible) and because other fastenings are more efficient for lateral resistance and require less installation labor. Allowable loads for wood screws are given in Chap. 13 (NDS).

3.33 Driftpins, driftbolts, lag screws If through bolts are undesirable or impractical, driftpins, driftbolts, lag screws, twisted dowels, and

Fig. 3.4 Type "A" anchor, installed

special twisted spikes may be used. They are installed in prebored holes and, except for lag screws, are driven into place. Thus they are usually not recommended if shrinkage or changes in moisture content would necessitate their being retightened. Lag screws, being turned into place, may be retightened, and are used most often if a through bolt is impractical. The lateral resistance is similar in all. Withdrawal resistance is provided either by twisted or threadlike shanks or by a tight fit in undersize holes. Driftpins and driftbolts are often used to anchor heavy caps to the tops of piles or columns, or stringers to tops of beams or caps. Such applications occur in heavy, site-built construction such as mining structures, railroad trestles, and piers and docks.

Lag screw design is complicated by the interrelation of thickness of

Fig. 3.5 Type "B" anchor, installed

Fig. 3.6 Type "C" anchors, installed

TABLE 3.6 Recommended allowable loads for framing anchors

Type of load	Allowable lcad, direc ions *A–F* *lb per anchor*					
	A	*B*	*C*	*D*	[illegible]	*F*
Short-term: wind and earthquake	450	825	420	300	450	675
Long-term: live and dead loads	300	530	[illegible]	[illegible]		450

side members and penetration with lag diameter and length. A simplified design approach is suggested in Chap. 12 (see Table 12.34) that will often be satisfactory. To obtain high efficiency under unusual conditions, it will be necessary to apply the specifications of Chap. 13 (NDS) in detail.

3.34 Bolts Bolts and bolts in conjunction with timber connectors are the two types of fastenings most commonly used in structural connections that must sustain sizeable computed loads. Bolts are simple to use, but as the allowable load per bolt is less than that for timber connectors, more bolts than connectors may be required. Because of spacing and edge distance requirements, it may sometimes be necessary to increase member sizes in order to accommodate the number needed. Timber connectors would then prove the preferable fastening if they permitted the use of smaller size members. For fabrication in place or fabrication with all members laid in position (assembly fabrication), bolts have the advantage as nothing more is required than the boring of a hole through two or more members and the insertion of the bolt. If members are prefabricated separately and then assembled, the labor advantage lies with the connectors because fewer units are required and the chance for misfits is thereby lessened.

Greater efficiency is obtained from large bolts than small ones. Sizes generally used range from $\frac{3}{8}$ to $1\frac{1}{2}$ in., the most common being $\frac{1}{2}$ to 1 in. Bolt holes are generally bored either $\frac{1}{32}$ or, more usually, $\frac{1}{16}$ in. oversize. Allowable loads for bolts are given in Chap. 13 (NDS).

3.35 Timber connectors Connectors are less widely known and used than bolts but are extensively employed by firms specializing in fabrication of timber structures, and in more recent years by contractors doing on-the-site fabrication.

Connectors are the most efficient of mechanical fastenings. Most other fastenings tend to deform irregularly under loads because of their ratio of length to diameter or minimum dimension. As a result, they develop higher bearing stresses near the surface of the wood than in the interior. Connectors, on the other hand, are installed only in the outer fibers and do not bend or deform materially. They therefore develop higher stresses per unit of bearing. The bearing area of 4-in. split rings in opposite faces of a member, for example, corresponds to that of a 1-in. bolt, and yet the design load is from 3 to 4 times as great. Connectors have done much to improve timber construction by improving joint efficiency and providing a system of fastening more applicable to efficient assembly line fabrication than do other fastenings.

3.36 Split rings The most popular timber connector for wood-to-wood connections is the split ring, available in 2½-in. and 4-in. diameters. Developing a higher efficiency than any other fastening, it is installed in precut conforming grooves (Fig. 3.7) made with a special

Fig. 3.7 Installing split rings

Wedge-shaped rings (TECO) furnish maximum joint efficiency and are easily, quickly installed in grooves by hand.

power-driven grooving tool (Fig. 3.8). The tongue and groove "split" in the ring permits simultaneous bearing of the inner surface of the ring against the core left by grooving and of the outer face of the ring against the outer wall of the groove. The special wedge shape of the ring section provides maximum tolerance for easy insertion but also a tight-fitting joint after the ring is fully seated in the conforming groove. Specifications and allowable loads for split rings are given in Chap. 13

Fig. 3.8 Split-ring grooving tool

(NDS, DM). Split rings and a companion type of fastening, shear plates, are the most desirable connectors for completely prefabricated assemblies.

3.37 Shear plates Shear plates in $2\frac{5}{8}$-in. and 4-in. diameters correspond in capacity to split rings and are used for steel-to-wood connections or for demountable wood-to-wood connections. Like the split rings, they are installed in conforming grooves but sit flush with the timber face once installed. Two shear plates make the equivalent of one split ring. The most common uses are for steel gusset-plate joints, field or erection joints with either metal or wood side plates, and column-to-foundation connections. Power tools are necessary for grooving. (See Fig. 3.9.)

The bolt in a shear-plate joint transfers the shear stress between shear plates or between a shear plate and a metal side member. Thus, joint strength may sometimes be limited by allowable bolt shear or bearing. Impact loads that are disregarded for most wood connections, and other short duration loads except wind and earthquake, must be taken into account if bolts are used in shear plate joints.

Specifications and allowable loads for shear plates are given in Chap. 13 (NDS, DM). The bolt limits assume no bearing on bolt threads, and reduction of maximum values by 11 per cent may be necessary if thread bearing occurs.

Fig. 3.9 Shear plate and grooving tool

3.38 Toothed rings Toothed rings in 2-in., 2⅝-in., 3⅜-in., and 4-in. diameters are recommended only whenever power tools are not available or it is impractical to install other types of connectors. Toothed rings provide wood-to-wood connections and are installed by pressure into lapping timbers. The most common installation process involves the use of a high-strength rod and ball bearing washer, which is removed and replaced with an ordinary bolt after the joint has been drawn tight. (See Fig. 3.11.) Care must be exercised to draw joints together slowly and evenly, in order to eliminate rod breakage and minimize possible splitting during installation, both of which can occur in the denser species of timber. Specifications and allowable loads for toothed rings are given in Chap. 13 (NDS, DM).

3.39 Spike grids Spike grids of flat, circular, and single-curve styles (Fig. 3.12) are similar to the toothed rings and are usually installed in the same manner. (See Figs. 3.13–3.15.) Their primary use is for wood-to-wood connections in the heavy framing typical of highway and railway trestle bents. Using smaller bolts, they provide a strong joint that is resistant to loosening due to vibration, impact, and reversible lateral loads. Flat spike grids are used in similar heavy structures when it is impractical to prefabricate (otherwise split rings would

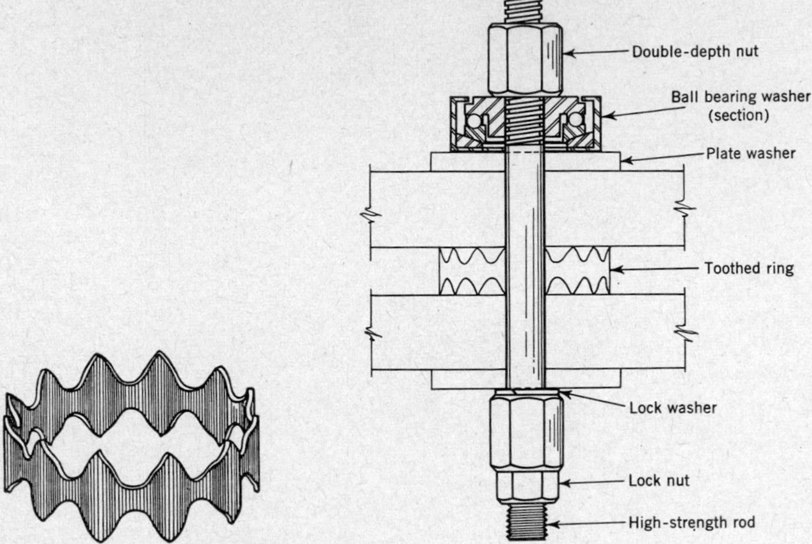

Fig. 3.10 Toothed ring

Fig. 3.11 Toothed-ring installation

be used). Single-curve grids are used to connect sawed timbers to round timbers.

Flat and single-curve grids are $4\frac{1}{8}$ in. square, and the curved side of the single-curve grid is curved for a 10-in.-diameter pile or pole. Circular grids are $3\frac{1}{4}$ in. in diameter and 1.2 in. wide. Additional specifications and allowable loads are given in Chap. 13 (NDS, DM).

3.40 Clamping plates Clamping plates (Fig. 3.16) are for wood-to-wood connections and are designed primarily for guard-timber-to-tie connections in open-deck railway trestles. Flat clamping plates are $5\frac{1}{4}$ in. square with teeth projecting from both sides to grip the guard timber and the tie. (See Fig. 3.17.) Flanged clamping plates, for use with sawed ties, are 8 in. wide and have teeth on only one face to grip

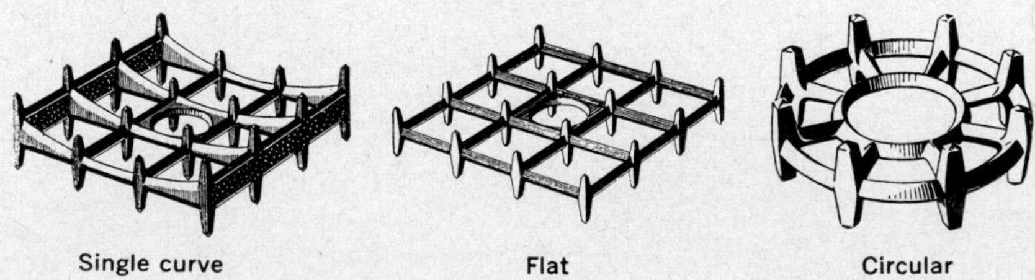

Fig. 3.12 Spike grids

Fig. 3.13 Spike-grid installation

Single curve grid is placed in position for joint between circular member and diagonal brace. High-strength rod is placed in previously bored bolt hole.

the guard timber. The flanges project down over the sides of the 8-in.-wide ties. (See Fig. 3.18.) The plates are installed by driving the teeth into the wood with a heavy ram or sledge, the plate or wood being protected by heavy metal driving plates.

3.41 Other connectors The timber connectors mentioned in Sec. 3.35–3.40 are those in most common use today. Many other styles have been used in the past, but most have been found less suitable for American practice than those described.

Fig. 3.14 Spike-grid installation (Cont.)

Grid is embedded into circular member and diagonal brace. Ball bearing thrust washer reduces friction.

Fig. 3.15 Spike-grid installation (Cont.)

High-strength rod is replaced by machine bolt to complete the joint.

3.42 Joint slip As bolt holes and grooves for split rings and shear plates must be somewhat oversize to provide installation clearance, there is both inelastic and elastic deformation of the joints under load. It is often necessary to know the approximate total deformation so that the proper camber may be given to roof trusses, concrete form supports, and other frames. Camber can often be satisfactorily estimated from the empirical formulas of Chap. 13 (NDS, DM) or by computing the deflection due to elasticity of the members and using from $1\frac{1}{2}$ to 2 times that amount to make allowance for joint deformation.

It is impossible to determine precise values for joint slip for average conditions because the slip is affected by many factors, such as duration and intensity of load, moisture content, rate of feed, sharpness of tools, fabrication accuracy, and species and density of the wood. Nevertheless, the approximate values for joint deformation, or slip, of Table 3.7 are suggested as satisfactory for the computation of average truss deflection under normal load conditions for seasoned lumber,

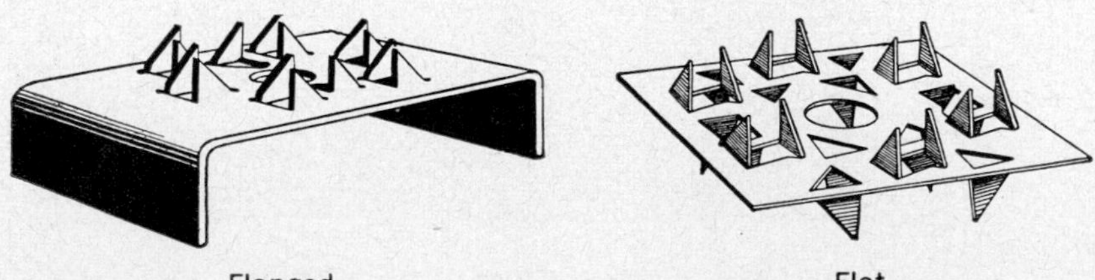

Fig. 3.16 Clamping plates

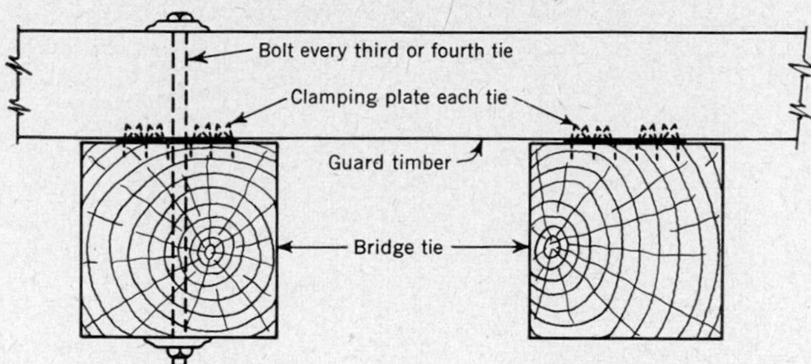

Fig. 3.17 Flat clamping-plate installation

provided a full live load is not permanently applied. Deformation of $1\frac{1}{2}$ to 2 times these amounts may be expected for live load conditions with unseasoned lumber and also with seasoned lumber if live loads are applied permanently over a period of many years. For the average proportions of dead to live load, the dead load deformation will probably equal $\frac{2}{3}$ to $\frac{3}{4}$ of the values in the table.

3.43 Fastenings for treated wood Fastenings relying directly or indirectly on withdrawal strength may be affected adversely by preservative or fire retardant treatments. These may tend either to lubricate the fastening, as has been noted, or, as with certain salt treatments, to combine with moisture in the wood and produce a chemical reaction with the metal. Under such conditions, corrosion-resistant hardware should be used.

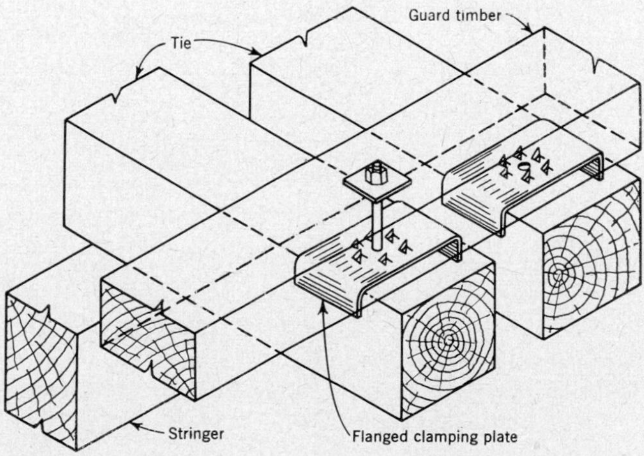

Fig. 3.18 Flanged clamping-plate installation

TABLE 3.7 Average joint deformation, or slip

Connection	Parallel to grain	Perpendicular to grain
	in.	
Bolts [1]	0.02 –0.04	0.04 –0.06
2½-in. Split ring	0.025–0.03	0.03 –0.04
4-in. Split ring	0.03 –0.04	0.035–0.04
2⅝-in. Shear plates, wood-to-wood [1]	0.02 –0.04	0.03 –0.04
2⅝-in. Shear plates, wood-to-steel [1]	0.02 –0.03	0.03 –0.04
4-in. Shear plates, wood-to-wood [1]	0.04 –0.06	0.05 –0.06
4-in. Shear plates, steel-to-wood [1]	0.03 –0.04	0.03 –0.05

[1] Plus theoretical bolt clearance, such as $1/16$ in.

CHOICE OF FASTENING

3.44 Structural considerations There are many interrelated factors that affect the choice of fastening for a particular project. For structural purposes, the main considerations are thickness of lumber, load-bearing capacity required, method of fabrication, type of loading, and assembly or erection problems.

3.45 Balanced deformation No two kinds of fastenings have the same deformation characteristics. The working strength of a nail or spike is determined empirically by the amount of deflection assumed to be reasonable under full load; there is no initial load-slip with nails or spikes. A reasonable deformation is also assumed in determining bolt capacity, but as bolts are installed in prebored holes, usually slightly larger than the bolt diameter, a varying amount of inelastic load-slip must be taken into account. It is not considered good design to mix connector sizes or types in the same joint, because one size or kind can be overloaded before the efficiency of the other is realized.

3.46 Thickness of lumber For lumber thicknesses most frequently used in structural work—2 in. and greater—nearly all of the common fastenings are suitable. Nails and spikes and other driven fastenings are seldom employed in framed assemblies of lumber thicker than 2 in., however, because nails long enough for proper penetration are also large enough to induce splitting. If it is necessary to prebore to prevent splitting, other fastenings usually prove more economical. For heavy framed assemblies, the choice of fastening will usually be either bolts or timber connectors, which are applicable to almost any thickness of lumber. Nails and spikes are widely used, however, for 3-in. and 4-in. laminated decks and similar solid lumber sections.

3.47 Number of fastenings In general, it may be said that the fewer fastenings required, the better, both from the standpoint of the labor required and of fabrication accuracy. Thus it is preferable to use a small number of large bolts rather than many small bolts, a few connectors in place of many bolts, and a large connector in place of several smaller ones, such as a 4-in. split ring in place of several $2\frac{1}{2}$-in. rings. Opinion is divided on whether different sizes of bolts or connectors should be used for different joints in the same frame, although there is agreement that different sizes or types should not be used in the same joint. Many designers feel that the small potential saving to be obtained from the use of different sizes is offset by the added labor of fabricating.

3.48 Method of fabrication The method of fabrication of itself may favor one fastening over another. (See Chap. 10.) If fabrication is by an assembly process in which the members are laid together before the holes are bored, bolts will have some advantage because the disassembly necessary for connectors will not be required. Additional bolts, however, will be needed to make the equivalent of a connector joint, and often the added quantity will necessitate the use of larger members. These two factors may outweigh the advantage of avoiding disassembly. The assembly method of fabrication is used primarily at the building site and has little if any advantage if the structure must be taken apart for shipment because each member must be accurately marked for reassembly in the same manner in which it was fabricated. Like members from different trusses, it may be noted, are usually not interchangeable.

If the structure is to be prefabricated piece by piece from templates for later assembly, timber connectors are preferable because fewer units are required. This reduction in fasteners means fewer boring and grooving operations, less chance for errors in hole locations, and simpler assembly. Prefabrication is usually the most economical system if more than a few units are needed, and it is the method used by most timber fabricators.

3.49 Type of loading The type of loading may be a factor in the choice of fastenings in so far as it affects increase in allowable loads for the duration of loading, the effect of which varies for different types of fastenings. Vibratory or reversal loads, which tend to loosen some fastenings, may also influence the choice of fastening. Timber connectors are usually considered better than bolts for vibration, load reversal, and impact loading, because they have less tendency to work or wear loose.

3.50 Assembly and erection problems If joints are to be made at the time of assembly or during erection, fastenings should be selected that can be fabricated and assembled with a minimum of effort. Bolted or shear-plate joints are desirable for erection joints, because it is not necessary to spread members for installation as it is for other types of connectors.

4

Post-and-Beam Construction

4.1 Components If span, spacing, and loading requirements permit the use of solid sawed members, post-and-beam construction usually provides the most economical framing system. However, structures with post-free floor areas or a minimum of posts often prove to be more efficient. Glued-laminated beams and arches, or timber trusses, are normally used only if sawed beams of the required sizes are not available, but the freedom of space they provide may justify their use even at higher construction cost (see Fig. 4.1). Post-and-beam construction is sometimes used for lower-story floor support in structures that use timber roof trusses for the sake of large, clear-span top-floor areas. Components of post-and-beam construction are posts or columns in conjunction with beams or beams and girders. The floor or roof framing may consist of joists or plank or laminated construction.

COLUMNS

4.2 Columns Timber columns may be divided into three general classes: simple solid columns, spaced columns (see Sec. 4.3), and built-up columns (see Sec. 4.19 and 4.20). Formulas for timber columns conservatively assume pin-end conditions, but no increase is recommended for square-end conditions, because minor eccentricities may exist even in theoretically perfect square-end columns.

As most wood columns are square or rectangular in section, the ratio of length to least dimension, the "slenderness ratio," is commonly expressed as l/d, in which l is the unsupported length in inches between points of lateral support and d the least dimension in inches.

Fig. 4.1 Laminated-beam construction

Simple solid wood columns can fail in one of several ways under test loads. Columns with low slenderness ratio fail in the crushing or buckling of individual wood fibers. As the slenderness ratio increases, failure may result from a combination of crushing of the fibers and buckling of the entire member, or from buckling alone, without fiber crushing. The strength of simple solid wood columns is satisfactorily represented by the Euler formula, provided the allowable unit compressive stress does not exceed the allowable c value for the grade of material specified:

$$P/A = \frac{\pi^2 E}{2.727(l/r)^2} = \frac{3.619E}{(l/r)^2}$$

For columns of square or rectangular cross section, this formula reduces to:

$$P/A = \frac{0.30E}{(l/d)^2}$$

in which:

P/A = allowable unit stress in compression, in pounds per square inch
E = modulus of elasticity, in pounds per square inch, adjusted as necessary for duration of load or seasoning conditions

l = unsupported over-all length, in inches, between points of lateral support of simple columns or from center to center of lateral supports of continuous or spaced columns

r = least radius of gyration of section, in inches

d = dimension, in inches, of the column parallel to the direction of lateral support; usually the least side of a simple solid column and the least side of individual members of a spaced column

The l/d ratio based on the width of a rectangular simple column or rectangular member of a spaced column may be the controlling factor if the spacing of lateral supports, l, in a direction parallel to the width, or wide face, is greater than the spacing of supports parallel to the thickness, or narrow face.

The Euler formula is applicable if the working stress is below the proportional limit of the wood when subjected to bending or compression. Because duration of load adjustment applies to the compression and bending stresses on which the strength of a Euler column depends, the column formulas may be adjusted for various durations of load as provided in Chap. 13 (NDS). Simple solid columns with a slenderness ratio greater than 50 should not be used.

4.3 Spaced columns Spaced columns consist essentially of two parallel members separated by one or more spacer blocks. These are located at the ends and at the center of the length and are usually joined through the end blocks with timber connectors. The individual column pieces are normally of the same thickness. The spaced column may be used for the direct support of vertical loads but often appears as a chord or other compression member in a wood truss.

The l/d ratio of a spaced column should not exceed 80. If it is less than $\sqrt{0.30E/c}$, there is no advantage to spaced column analysis because the allowable load or unit stress is limited by the tabulated allowable value for compression parallel to grain (see Chap. 13, NDS, par. 401-B-2). Load may be applied directly to the ends of the compression members, with the end spacer blocks not extending beyond the ends of the column. In trusses, however, the end spacer blocks may extend beyond the ends and the load applied through them and their connections to the compression members. Web members constitute the end spacer blocks in many trusses. The centroid of end connections to tension members is considered a point of lateral support for truss web members.

The spacer block connection should be of sufficient strength and rigidity to restrain differential movement between the compression members. As the forces causing differential movements are less in short than in long spaced columns, the connection requirements are correspondingly less. The capacity of connections required on each face of each end spacer block is determined by multiplying the required cross-sectional area in compression of one member by the constants given in Chap. 13 (NDS, par. 401-F-3).

Spacer blocks are required at both ends of the spaced column. A spacer block is also required at mid-length of such size and so fastened as to insure that the compression members will maintain their initial spacing under load. Spiking or bolting is generally adequate for joining the middle blocks to the compression members. If spacer blocks are less thick than the individual compression members, an additional length of spacer block will be required. Spacer blocks must not be less than ½ the thickness of the individual compression member.

If possible, the grain of the spacer blocks should be parallel to the length of the compression members. The minimum length of the end spacer blocks is determined by the end distances required for the timber connectors. Truss joints can take the place of end or middle spacer blocks if their members and connection capacity at the appropriate angle of load to grain meet the requirements for regular spacer blocks.

Simple solid columns of pin-end design have an elastic curve under load as indicated in Fig. 4.2a. If the ends of the column are restrained, the elastic curve is similar to that in Fig. 4.2b.

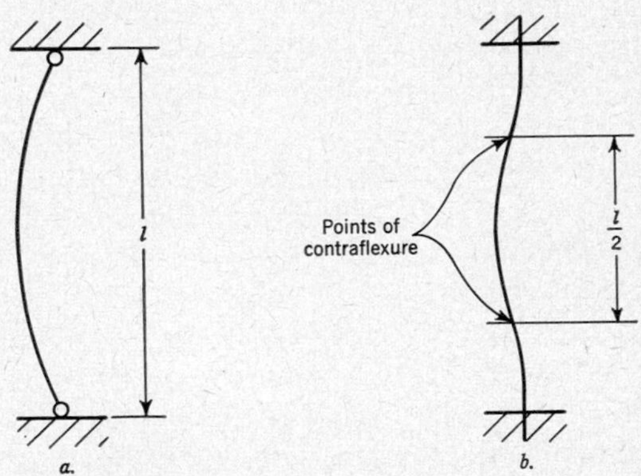

Fig. 4.2 Column elastic curves

a. Pin end *b. Fixed end*

The elastic curve of a spaced column lies somewhere between these two extremes. The connections in the end spacer blocks provide partial end restraint because the center spacer block insures that the members will act in the same direction, thus setting up shear forces at the end connections. Depending on the location of the timber connectors in the end spacer blocks with respect to the end of column, the allowable loads for spaced columns are 2½ or 3 times the values determined by the Euler formula for simple solid columns of the same slenderness ratio. If there were no mechanical or elastic slip in the end connection and full end fixity were provided by the spacer block fastening, the allowable loads would be 4 times that for simple solid column action, because the effective length would be only ½ in computations for the slenderness ratio.

Conservative specifications for spaced columns using two or more pieces of different thickness require d of the smallest member to be controlling. However, there is logic in using the average thickness of the members as the d in the column formula, provided the l/d ratio of the thinnest member does not exceed 80. Test data to substantiate this method, however, are not available.

BEAMS

4.4 Beams, joists, girders Structurally speaking, beams, joists, and girders are essentially the same. The distinction in use is that joists are normally employed for spacings up to 24 in. on centers and usually carry floor or roof sheathing, whereas beams and girders are spaced farther apart and support heavier floor or roof framing. Joists may be supported by walls, trusses, or girders. A girder may be supported by walls or columns and frequently supports joists or beams.

Structural beams are usually of rectangular section and of uniform depth throughout their span. Design guided by customary formulas is based on: (1) extreme fiber stress in bending; (2) horizontal shear stress; and (3) stress in compression perpendicular to the grain at end bearings or at loading points. Design may also be limited by deflection under load if deflection may affect appearance, choice of roofing or ceiling material, or operation of equipment, such as cranes or line shafts.

Both the ultimate bending strength and the safe load for a wood beam of rectangular cross section may be calculated from the formula:

$$M = Ffbd^2/6$$

in which:

M = bending moment, in inch-pounds
F = form or depth factor
f = unit flexural stress in the extreme fiber, in pounds per square inch
b = width of the beam
d = depth of the beam

If the ultimate bending strength is desired, f is the modulus of rupture. If the safe load is desired, f is the safe flexural stress for the species and grade of material used.

The depth factor, F, in the basic design formula for rectangular beams takes into account the somewhat lower unit strength developed in deep beams as compared to shallow beams. In arriving at the basic stress values for bending strength—from which allowable working stresses for various grades are derived—a depth factor is assumed that corresponds approximately to a 12-in. depth of beam. Form factor is not a design factor except for very deep beams (see Chap. 13, NDS Appendix D).

If flexural stress in the extreme fiber is combined with axial or direct stress resulting from the application of end compression or tension, the combined stress is determined by algebraic addition of the stresses. For example, compressive stress is added to bending stress in the upper fiber of a beam, and tensile stress is added to bending stress in the lower fiber of the beam. Stresses so combined should not exceed allowable values obtained by the formulas given in the following section.

4.5 Combined bending and axial loads If a beam loaded in bending is also under end compression and is stayed against lateral buckling, the allowable stress is such that:

$$\frac{P/A}{c} + \frac{M/S}{f} \leq 1$$

in which:

P/A = unit direct stress induced by axial load in compression parallel to grain (P is the axial compressive load and A is the area of the cross section)

M/S = flexural stress induced in bending (M is the bending moment and S is the section modulus, equal to $bd^2/6$)

c = allowable working stress in compression parallel to grain

f = allowable working stress in bending

As the end compression approaches zero, the term $\frac{P/A}{c}$ also approaches zero, and the preceding equation approaches:

$$\frac{M/S}{f} = 1$$

or:

$$M = fS = fbd^2/6$$

the basic formula for flexural stress. If the span-to-depth-of-member ratio is more than 11, the beam subject to combined bending and compression should be checked in the same manner as an eccentric column.

If a beam loaded in bending is also in axial tension, the allowable stress is such that:

$$\frac{P/A}{t} + \frac{M/S}{f} \leq 1$$

in which:

P/A = unit direct stress induced by axial load in tension
t = allowable working stress in tension parallel to grain
M/S and f are the quantities previously defined

Frequently t and f have the same value, and the equation can be stated:

$$P/A + M/S = t = f$$

4.6 Shear in beams The general formula for horizontal shear in beams is:

$$H = VQ/It$$

in which all units are in inches or pounds, and:

H = maximum horizontal shearing stress
Q = statical moment, about the neutral axis, of the area either above or below the axis at which the shear is desired (as used here, statical moment is a product of an area and the distance from the center of gravity of that area to an axis)
V = external or vertical shear
I = moment of inertia of the entire section about the neutral axis
t = width of the beam at the axis in question

For a rectangular beam b in. wide and d in. deep, the general formula for horizontal shear, at the neutral axis, reduces to:

$$H = 3V/2bd$$

Shearing stress is increased at certain locations in a beam because of stress concentration effects. The most common concentration of stress is at the base of horizontal shakes, checks, or splits, where there is an abrupt change of cross section. This concentration causes shear failures in beams at relatively low stress values, even if the beam has been calculated on the net cross section obtained after deduction of the area of actual opening. As checking occurs to some extent in practically all structural beams, a large factor for stress concentration has been introduced in the recommended shear stress values. Shakes, checks, or splits in a vertical plane are unimportant.

Another shear stress concentration may occur immediately adjacent to points of application of a concentrated load or reaction. Such a concentration seldom controls because allowable bearing values in compression perpendicular to grain ordinarily require fairly large bearing areas. Furthermore, building regulations usually specify lengths of bearing that prevent critical stress concentrations.

Because the upper and lower portions of a beam checked horizontally near the neutral axis act partly as two beams and partly as a unit, a portion of the end reaction is resisted internally by each half of the beam acting independently and consequently is not associated with shearing stress at the neutral plane. In using the basic formula for horizontal shear, in which b is the full width of the beam and H the allowable unit shear stress (based on the assumption that checks are present), allowance for two-beam action should be made in calculating the allowable vertical shear, V. The recommended procedure for calculating the horizontal shear on the neutral plane in checked beams is given in Chap. 13 (NDS, par. 400-D-2 and Appendix E).

4.7 Deflection of beams If service conditions require that beams be designed for stiffness, the dimensions are determined by applying the usual deflection formulas. The deflection taken into account is usually that due only to live load. It is often limited to $\frac{1}{360}$ of the span of framing over plastered ceilings, and over unplastered ceilings to $\frac{1}{240}$ of the span. A ratio of $\frac{1}{200}$ of the span has been used for highway bridges, but some engineers advocate a more severe limitation. A commonly recorded limitation for stringers in railroad bridges and trestles is $\frac{1}{300}$ of the span. For floors that support shafting, deflection limitations much more severe than the preceding are sometimes required to prevent vibration and misalignment.

The deflection of wood beams caused by permanently applied loads will increase beyond the deflection occurring immediately after the load was first applied. Because of the lower value for modulus of elasticity, this characteristic is particularly apparent in green timbers that are allowed to season under load, and also to a limited extent in partially seasoned material. In thoroughly seasoned beams, there is little permanent increase in deflection.

Deflection calculations using tabulated values for modulus of elasticity will give the initial deflection of a beam. If deflection under a long-time load is to be limited, it is customary to design for an initial deflection of about $\frac{1}{2}$ the value permitted for long-time deflection, either by doubling the amount of the long-time load in the calculation or by using ½ the tabulated values for modulus of elasticity.

4.8 Notched beams Joists and beams are sometimes notched at the ends, usually to make the top surfaces level with adjacent beams or girders and thus reduce over-all building height. Occasionally members are also notched at intermediate points, either bottom or top, in order to clear other parts of a structure or to receive other members.

If a short, relatively deep beam is notched on the lower side at the end, its strength is decreased by an amount that depends on the shape of the notch and on the relation of the depth of the notch to the depth of the beam. If the notch is to be square-cornered (see Fig. 4.3),

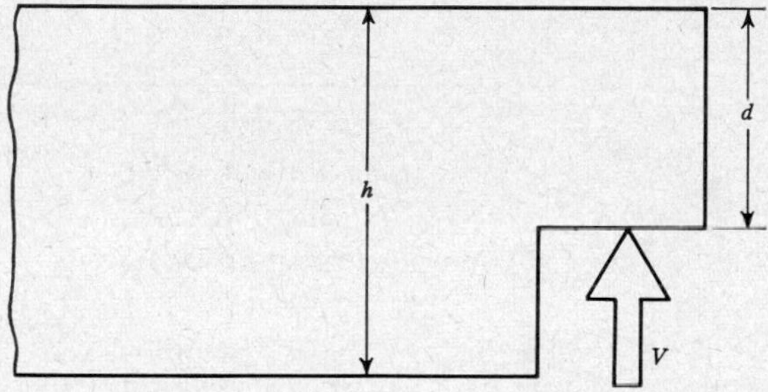

Fig. 4.3 Member notched at bottom

it is recommended that the desired bending load be checked against the load obtained by the following equation:

$$V = \frac{2Hbd}{3}\left(\frac{d}{h}\right)$$

in which:

V = the vertical shear
b = the width of the beam
d = the end depth above the notch
h = the total depth of the beam
H = the working stress in horizontal shear

In setting up this equation, only the end depth is used as the effective depth to resist shear. The safe shear stress is further reduced in that it is multiplied by the ratio of the actual depth to the total depth. A joist or beam notched to ½ depth thus has only ¼ the shear strength of the unnotched member.

If the end is notched by a gradual change in the cross section so that the notch is not square-cornered, the shearing strength approaches that computed for the net depth above the notch, d, and the d/h factor is eliminated.

Beams are occasionally notched or beveled on the upper side (see Fig. 4.4). These beams suffer less from stress concentration effects than

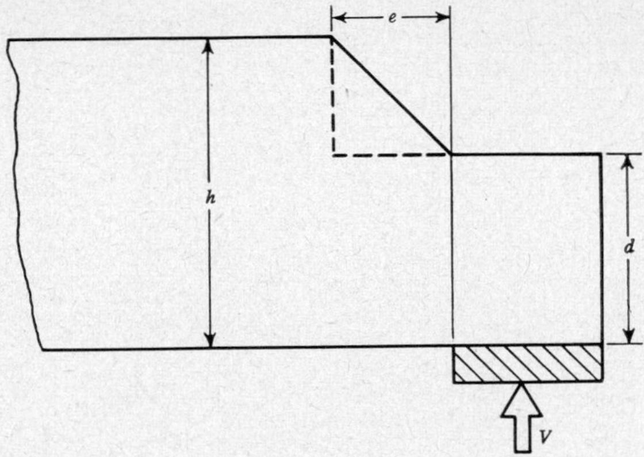

Fig. 4.4 Member notched at top

beams notched or beveled on the lower side. Experiments with notches in the upper side indicate that shear stress should be checked with the formula:

$$V = \frac{2}{3} Hb \left[h - \left(\frac{h - d}{d} \right) e \right]$$

in which:

V = the vertical or external shear
H = the working stress in shear
b = the width of the beam
h = the total depth of the beam
d = the depth below the notch
e = the distance that the notch extends inside the inner edge of the support

If e exceeds h, this formula is not used; rather, the shear strength is evaluated on the basis of the depth of the beam below the notch, d. For a beam with a bevel on the upper side instead of a square notch, d is taken as the height of the beam at the inner edge of the support, and e as the distance from the support to the start of the bevel. The depth of a notch on the upper side should not exceed 40 per cent of the depth h of the beam.

If notches are located either at or near the middle of the length of a beam, or in areas of high bending moment, the net depth should be used in determining the bending strength. Tests have shown that this rule is sufficiently conservative as far as breaking loads are concerned, provided there are no "maximum size" knots in the remaining area. The general tendency of a notch on the top or bottom of a beam and near the point of maximum moment, however, is to lower the proportional-limit load and to start compression or tension failure at lower loads than would be expected of an unnotched beam of a depth equal to the net depth of the notched beam. Tapered notches are desirable to lessen abrupt changes in cross section, both for bending and for shear. The stiffness or deflection of a beam is practically unaffected by notches of normal proportions.

4.9 Distribution of concentrated loads Tests at the Forest Products Laboratory indicate that loads up to 400 lb concentrated on an area of $\frac{1}{3}$ sq ft at midspan of a conventional dwelling floor system are distributed laterally for a considerable distance, with only 20 to 30 per cent carried by the joist directly under the load. The floor system in the tests consisted of joists, bridging, a diagonally laid subfloor, and a 1-in. finish floor normal to the joists.

The general problem of load distribution has been extensively investigated, particularly with reference to moving loads on bridge floor systems. Recommendations from those investigations indicate that about $\frac{1}{4}$ to $\frac{1}{2}$ of a concentrated load on a joisted floor may be carried by the joist under the load. The percentage is higher if the loaded joist is near the side of the floor system than if it is at the center. Plank floors on beams that are spaced 5 ft or more apart show little or no distribution of load to beams other than the one directly under the load (see Chap. 13, NDS Appendix A). The need for further study seems particularly desirable with respect to wheel load distribution on bridge decks and the horizontal shear forces that result. Some designers allow higher shear values on the basis that experience with bridge stringers, theoretically overstressed in shear, has been satisfactory.

4.10 Round and diagonally loaded square beams Common round members include piles, poles, and masts, which are subject to bending as well as compressive stresses. Such members may also be used as beams alone. To calculate their bending strength, it is necessary to include a form factor in the beam formula.

The design formula for a beam of round section is:

$$M = Ff\pi r^3/4$$

in which:

M = bending moment
F = form factor
f = unit flexural stress in the outer fiber
r = radius of the cross section

The form factor F for a round wood beam has a value of 1.18. For round beams, then, the formula becomes:

$$M = 1.18f\pi r^3/4 = 0.927fr^3$$

If round wood beams have an appreciable taper, the maximum value for stress in the outer fiber under uniformly distributed load—as in a joist or rafter—occurs toward the small end of the beam. The location of maximum stress varies with the taper, being at midspan if there is no taper. It occurs at a distance from the small end of 0.27 times the span if the small end has ½ the diameter of the large end.

The design formula for a beam of square cross section placed so that the diagonal of the section is vertical is:

$$M = Ffa^3/6\sqrt{2}$$

in which:

M = bending moment
F = form factor
f = unit flexural stress in the outer fiber
a = side of the square

The form factor F for a square beam with a diagonal vertical has a value of 1.414. The formula then becomes:

$$M = 1.414fa^3/6\sqrt{2} = fa^3/6$$

It can be shown from the preceding formulas that a beam of square cross section has the same bending strength whether placed in the usual manner or with a diagonal of the section vertical, and also that a round beam without taper has the same strength as a square beam of the same cross-sectional area.

4.11 Cantilevered and suspended-span beams and girders Cantilevered beams and suspended beams permit savings in multiple-span buildings by reducing the bending moment requirements for uniform loading to ½ to ⅔ of those for simply supported beams. They thus permit longer spans or larger loads for the same size member, provided size is not controlled by compression perpendicular to grain at the supports, or by horizontal shear. The most popular lumber for the purpose is the glued-laminated variety because larger sizes and longer lengths are available. The general advantages apply equally, however, to solid sawed timber. Figure 4.5 illustrates the various types of beams that may be used in a cantilevered system.

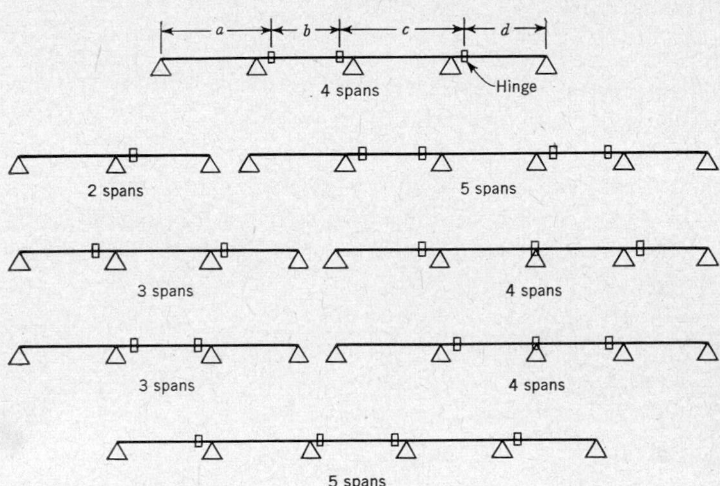

Fig. 4.5 Typical cantilevered systems

Beam "a" is a single cantilever, "b" a suspended beam, "c" a double cantilever, "d" a beam with one end suspended.

Various combinations of these types of cantilevered and suspended beams may be used. The relative economy of the single and the double cantilever depends on the exact span and loading conditions. For an even number of spans, at least one single cantilever is necessary unless one of the beams is continuous over three supports; if the building is to be symmetrical in cross section, two are required.

In the interests of economy, the negative bending moment at the supports of the cantilevered beam should equal the positive moment in the cantilever span. Thus for uniform balanced loading, the negative moment at the support of the single cantilevered beam should equal $wl^2/11.65$ and the negative moment at each support of a symmetrical double cantilevered beam should equal $wl^2/16$ (in which l represents the span or spacing of supports for the cantilever). With the length of adjacent spans known, the length of cantilever should be calculated to produce these bending moments. If the bending moment is either more or less than these amounts, a larger cantilever beam will be needed.

As an example, assume a building of 30-ft, 40-ft, and 30-ft spans. If single cantilevers are used for the side spans and a suspended beam over the center span (see Fig. 4.6a), the length of cantilever x is determined as follows:

$$\text{Reaction of suspended span at } P \text{ equals } w(40 - 2x)/2$$
$$M_2 = wx(40 - 2x)/2 + wx^2/2 = w(30)^2/11.65$$
$$20x - x^2 + x^2/2 = (30)^2/11.65$$
$$x = 4.3 \text{ ft}$$

A cantilever length of 4.3 ft will thus produce equal positive and negative bending moment in the cantilever. It will require a larger member for the center 31.4-ft span member, however. If the cantilever is lengthened, the bending moment in the cantilever at the support will increase in the same amount that the bending moment is reduced for the center section. Economically it would be better to use a larger member for the center span, which is only 31.4 ft long than to have to increase the size of the two side cantilevers, which have the combined length of 68.6 ft.

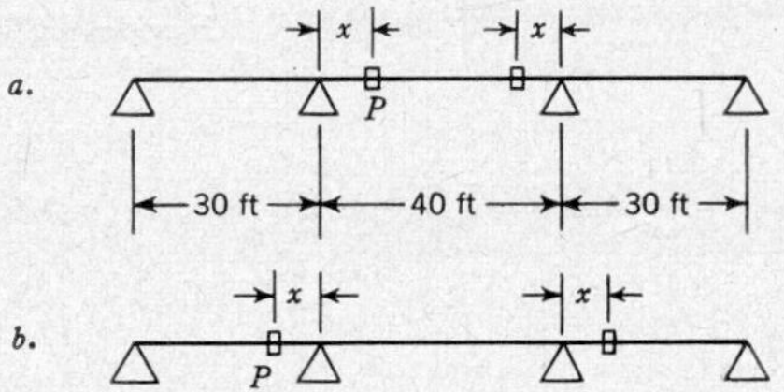

Fig. 4.6 Determining cantilever length

For the 4.3-ft cantilever, the maximum bending moment for uniform load is $76.8w$ ft-lb in the cantilever and $123.2w$ ft-lb in the center span. If the cantilever is lengthened (to 5.9 ft) so that the same size beam is required for both the center and the cantilever spans, the maximum bending moments will be $100.0w$ ft-lb, an alternative which will require 6 per cent more lumber than would the 4.3-ft cantilever, assuming the same width of members.

If a double cantilevered beam were used over the center span, on the other hand, and beams were suspended at one end on the end spans (see Fig. 4.6b), the length of cantilever x would be calculated as follows:

$$M_2 \text{ should equal } wl^2/16$$
$$\text{Reaction of suspended span at } P \text{ equals } w(30 - x)/2$$
$$M_2 = wx(30 - x)/2 + wx^2/2 = w(40)^2/16$$
$$15x - x^2/2 + x^2/2 = 40^2/16$$
$$x = 6.67 \text{ ft}$$

A cantilever length of 6.67 ft will thus produce equal positive and negative bending moments in the double cantilevered beam for uniform loading. The maximum bending moments would be $100w$ ft-lb in the center cantilever and $67.9w$ ft-lb in the end spans. There would be no theoretical advantage to lengthening or shortening the cantilever. Shortening it would increase requirements for both the center cantilever and the side spans. Lengthening it would increase requirements for the center cantilever proportionately more than it would reduce them for the side spans, and consequently the over-all requirements would be greater.

Assuming the same width of beams (so that their relative sizes may vary in proportion to the square root of the bending moments), the solution with the double cantilever center span will require 3 per cent less lumber than the 4.3-ft single cantilever side span and 8 per cent less lumber than the 5.9-ft single cantilever side span.

Detailed calculations such as these are necessary to determine whether the single or double cantilever will give the most economical solution. For nearly equal spans, the double cantilever usually has the advantage. For an odd number of spans, either the single or double cantilever is applicable. For an even number of spans, at least one single cantilever is required unless one of the beams is continuous over three supports.

Attention must be given to deflection in cantilevered multiple spans. Whenever feasible, roofs should be sloped sufficiently to eliminate water pockets caused by natural deflection. Otherwise roofs may be designed for a minimum depth of water, or interior drains may be provided.

Unbalanced loading conditions must be investigated for maximum bending moment, deflection, and stability. As a rule, there is little unbalanced roof load on relatively flat roofs, but concentrated loads—such as piles of material used during construction or suspended equipment or hoist loads—may have to be taken into account.

Suspended beam connections may be made in many ways, such as those shown in Fig. 4.7. The notches must not be reversed, or horizontal shear may become critical. Provisions for both vertical support and a horizontal tie are desirable. A special metal seat saves notching the ends of the beams or girders.

4.12 Sheathing, planking, and laminated deck Sheathing used in flooring or roofing generally consists of boards up to 1 in. in thickness, usually spanning between joists. It may be applied normal to the joists for greatest strength, or diagonally for rigidity and diaphragm action.

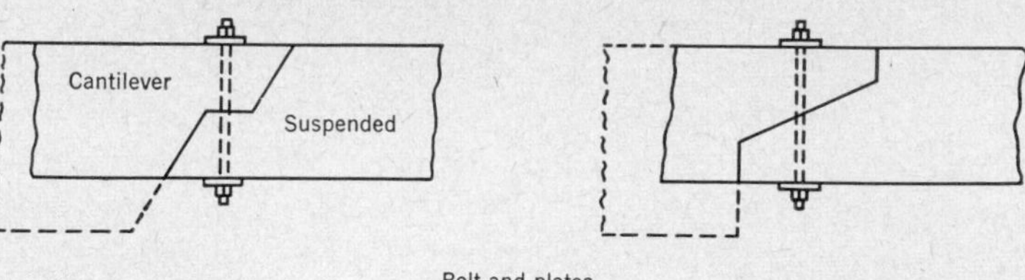

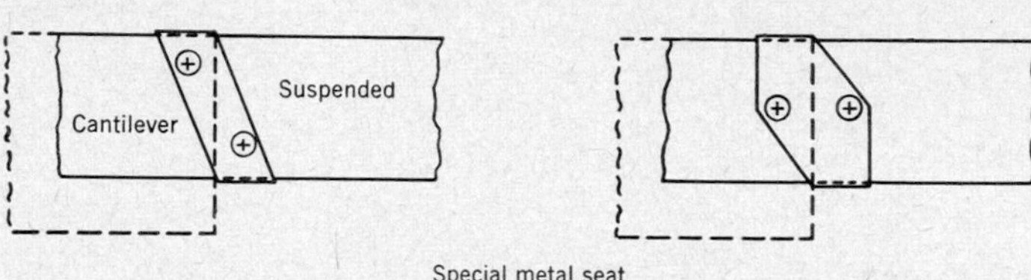

Fig. 4.7 Suspended-beam connections

Sheathing may be square-edged, shiplapped, or tongued and grooved.

Planking is generally 2, 3, or 4 in. thick. It is applied directly to beams or girders, usually normal to the supporting members but sometimes diagonally. Two-inch planking is usually tongued and grooved. Thicker planking is more often splined. It may often be obtained in either pattern, and no distinction is usually made in design.

Sheathing and planking used in floors or roofs have the effect of a shallow beam. The design procedure involving them is therefore similar to that applicable to beams with certain modifications. Whereas most timber beams are single span, sheathing and planking may be continuous over several spans (preferably with staggered joints to provide lateral tie and maximum continuity with patterned stock). Consequently, the designer should take into consideration the lower bending moment that is the result of such continuity. In beam design, moreover, deep, short-span beams may be limited by horizontal shear. Shear requirements, however, will very seldom control design of sheathing and planking except for heavy concentrated loads.

Deflection limitations on sheathing or planking are generally similar to those for the over-all framing system previously discussed. Deflection may be limited by ceiling, flooring, or roofing materials. In plank floors, creep under long-time loads may be a factor and should be considered in the design (see Sec. 1.29).

If design loads are heavy, floors are sometimes made from joists 4 in. or more in width and 2 to 3 in. in thickness. These are set on edge side by side and firmly nailed together at about 18-in. intervals with 20d or 30d nails spaced alternately near the top and bottom. Such a floor is known as a laminated floor and provides better distribution of concentrated loads than do plank floors. Provisions for expansion may be necessary with large areas (see Sec. 4.13).

Laminated floors are designed as if they were simple or continuous beams. Like beams, they should be checked for horizontal shear for deep short spans. Continuous beam action is possible on multiple spans with random length members if splices are well staggered so that no more than one of four adjacent laminations is spliced in the same 2 or 3 ft of length.

4.13 General framing For post-and-beam construction employing solid sawed members, maximum spans are generally no longer than 20 to 24 ft for joists or beams, and 12 to 16 ft for girders, which carry greater floor area. For average roof loads and the lighter floor loads, joists or beams with sheathing or planking generally prove to be the most economical solution. For heavy loadings, the best solution often is laminated decks or floors, spanning between either beams or girders. The girders carry the heaviest load, and available sizes and lengths control the spacing of columns in the direction of the girders. For uniform loading, minimum girder sizes are possible if beams are employed at the one-third span points.

Most codes require that joists framing against masonry walls have sloping fire cuts at the end bearing on the masonry wall so that the top end of the cut will be at the face of the masonry. Joisted floors and flat roofs used as decks should be cross bridged or solid blocked at the centerline or at a spacing of about 8 ft center to center, in order to stiffen the structure and distribute concentrated loads over several joists.

Several methods of framing joists to beams or girders are employed. The most common has the joist bear directly on the beam. The joists are then toenailed to the beam, or, if care must be taken against uplift due to wind—as in roof construction—special metal framing anchors may be used.

To reduce exterior wall height or to minimize the effects of seasoning, joists are often framed into the sides of beams or girders. One method is to fasten a ledger on the face of the beam to provide bearing for the joists. This method is used most often if the beam is deeper than the joist. If the beam depth is about the same as that of the joist, the ledger board method requires notching of the joists, a measure which reduces the shear strength (see Sec. 4.8). To avoid such notching, the ledger may be replaced by metal strap hangers or seats, or special metal framing anchors. If shrinkage might tend to lower the top of the joist with respect to the beam, as could happen with strap hangers or ledgers, the joist should be set proportionally above the beam at installation.

It is desirable to limit notching for ledger support to $\frac{1}{4}$ to $\frac{3}{8}$ of the joist depth. The ledger connection must be adequate for the joist reaction. It should not be used with other fastenings between the joist and the beam for purposes of vertical load transfer, because two different types of load transfer seldom work in unison.

"Heavy Timber Construction" utilizes combinations of planks or laminated floors supported by beams or girders. Exterior walls may be frame, masonry, or metal. The type of connection used in Heavy Timber Construction depends on such factors as efficiency, fire safety, availability and ease of erection. It should be remembered that connections with exposed metal parts are more vulnerable to fire than those without. Every type of connection, whether located at a masonry wall or at a steel column cap or base, should have some provision for ventilation; otherwise, if there is risk of decay due to trapped moisture, the lumber should be treated.

For Heavy Timber Construction to qualify as "Mill or Slow-Burning Construction," the exterior walls must be of masonry. The interior structural elements—including columns, floors, and roof construction—must consist of heavy timbers with smooth flat surfaces assembled to avoid thin sections, sharp projections, and concealed or inaccessible spaces. An abstract of the specification requirements as recommended by the National Board of Fire Underwriters follows, with editorial additions and provisions of other model codes italicized:

COLUMNS

(a) Wooden columns shall not be less than 8-in. nominal in any dimension. All corners shall be rounded or chamfered.

(b) Columns shall be superimposed throughout all stories on each other, on reinforced-concrete or metal post caps with brackets, or be connected by properly designed steel or iron caps, pintles and base plates, or by timber splice blocks affixed to the columns by means of devices or connectors housed within the contact faces. (*See Figs. 4.8–4.11.*)

(c) Columns shall not rest on floor timbers; nor shall they rest on masonry foundations unless stone, cast iron, or steel bases are used to transmit their loads. (*See Figs. 4.11 and 4.12.*)

BEAMS AND GIRDERS

(a) Beams and girders of wood shall be not less than 6-in. nominal in least dimension nor less than 10-in. nominal in depth. If built up of two or more pieces, they shall be properly glued- or bolted-laminated pieces; precaution

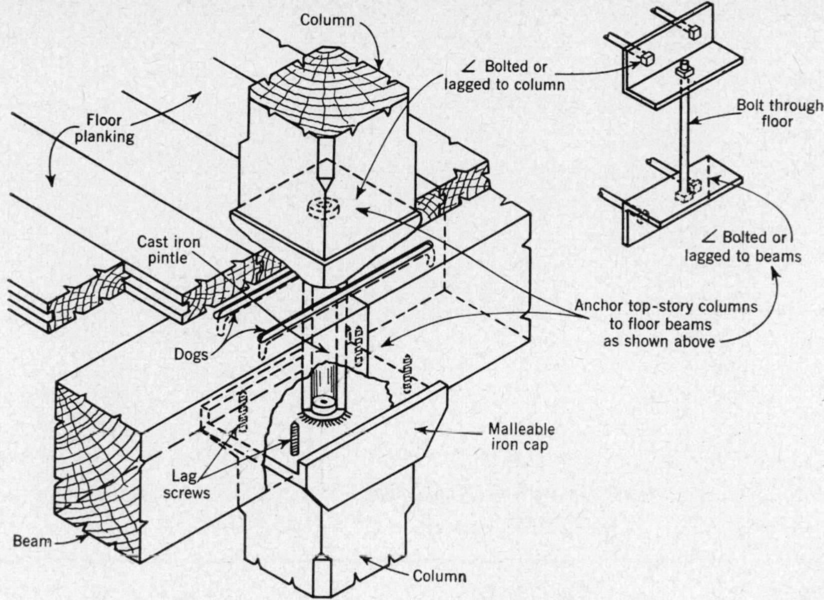

Fig. 4.8 Iron-cap column-to-column joint

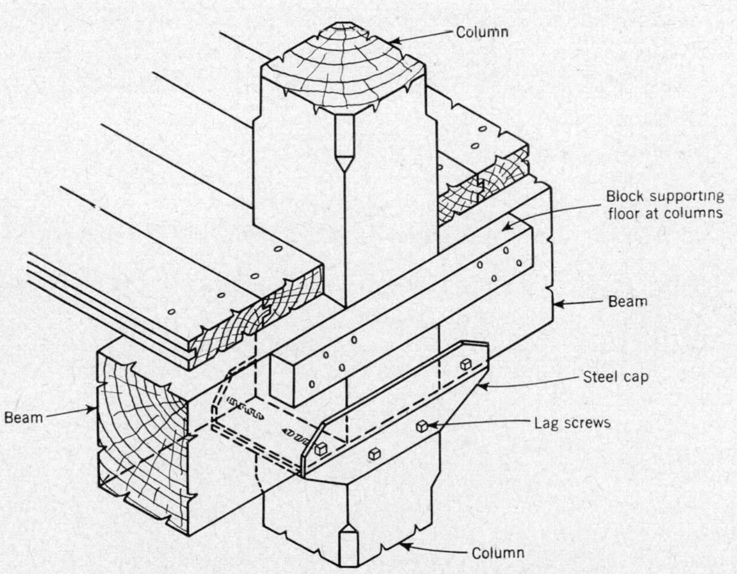

Fig. 4.9 Steel-cap column-to-column joint

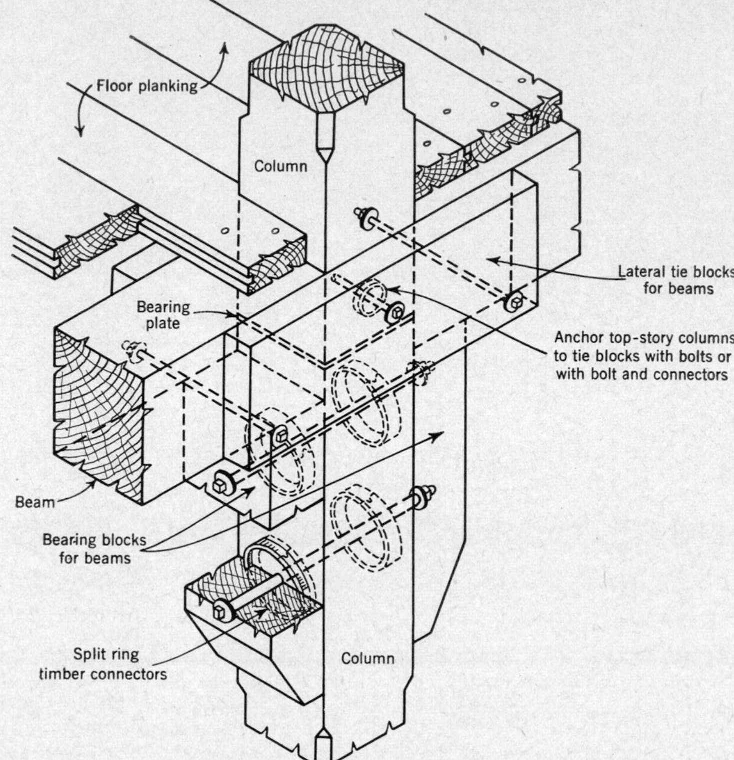

Fig. 4.10 Bearing-plate column-to-column joint

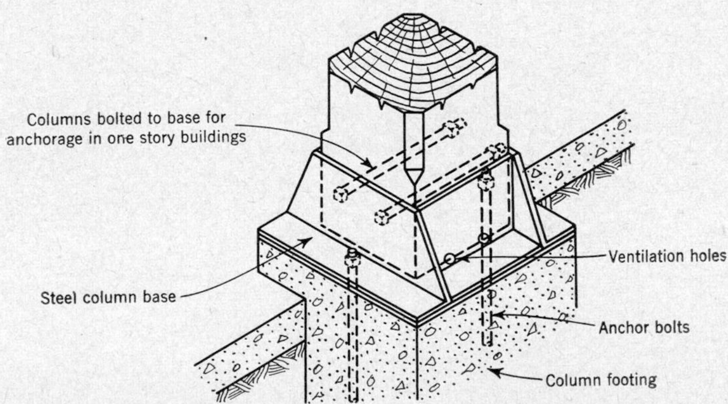

Fig. 4.11 Steel column base

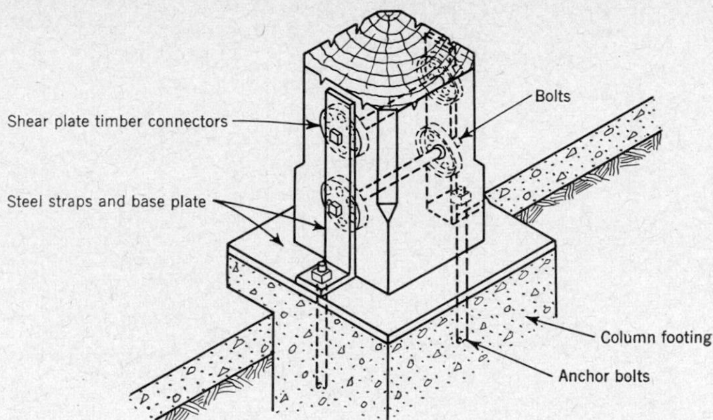

Fig. 4.12 Column base with steel straps and base plate

shall be taken to prevent decay of contact faces, *by means of mastic, or bituminous, or other approved sealers.*

(b) Wall plates, boxes of self-releasing type, or approved hangers shall be provided where beams or girders rest on walls. (*See Figs. 4.13–4.16.*)

(c) Where girders and beams meet columns, they shall be fitted around pintles and round columns or butted up close to rectangular columns. The adjoining ends of girders and beams shall be crosstied by approved reinforced-concrete, steel, or iron post caps or metal straps lag screwed or bolted to their sides, or shall be intertied to and with the columns by through-bolted corbel blocks, side bolsters, splice blocks and fillers so that the stresses are transferred by means of devices or metal connectors housed within the contacting faces of the members. (*See Figs. 4.8–4.11 and 4.17–4.20.*)

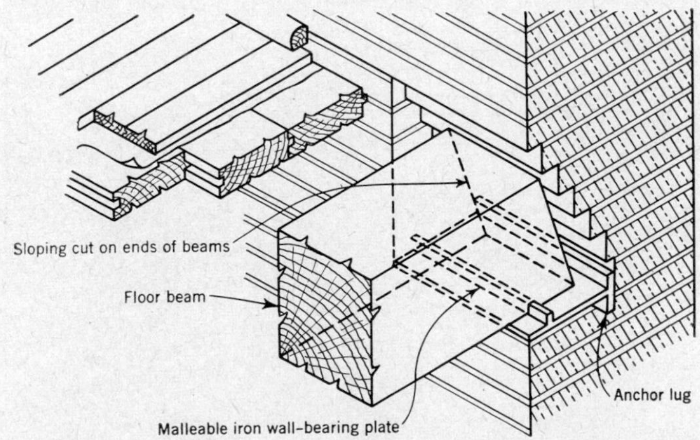

Fig. 4.13 Exterior-wall floor-framing detail

Floor beam notched over lug in malleable iron wall-bearing plate.

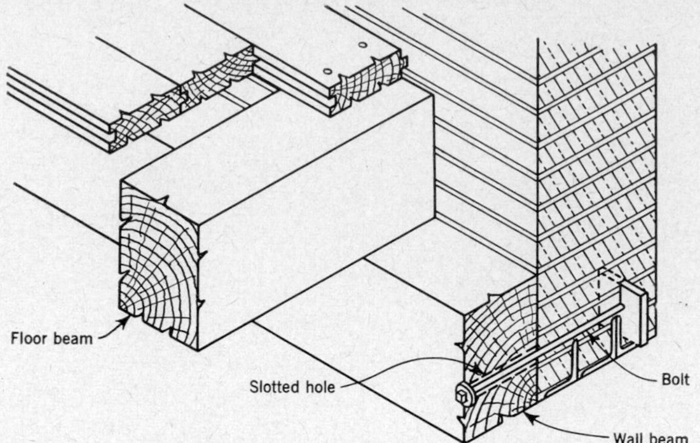

Fig. 4.14 Exterior-wall floor-framing detail

Floor beam supported on wall beam bolted to masonry and supported at piers.

(d) Where intermediate beams are found necessary for the support of a floor, they shall rest on top of the girders; or they may be supported by approved steel or iron hangers into which the ends of beams shall be closely fitted. Interstices between beams framed together shall be filled in with a preservative compound.

(e) Wooden beams and girders supported by walls shall have at least 8 in. of masonry between their ends and the outside face of the wall. Where beams enter walls from opposite sides, there shall be at least 8 in. of masonry between sides *or ends* of adjacent beams.

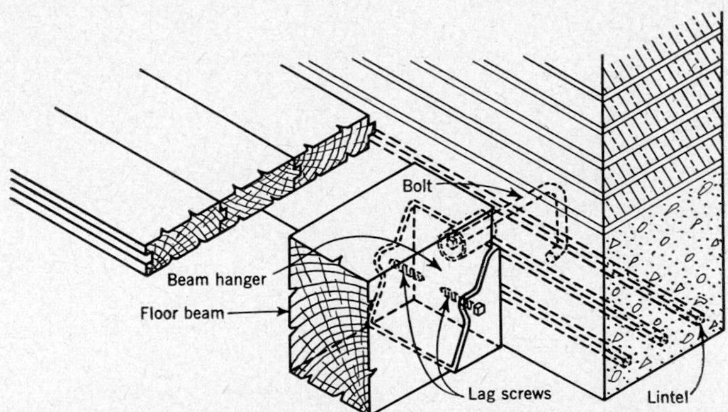

Fig. 4.15 Exterior-wall floor-framing detail

Floor beam supported by beam hanger bolted to lintel.

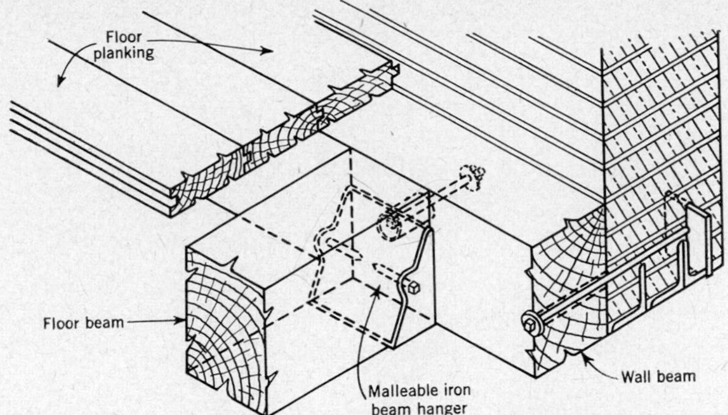

Fig. 4.16 Exterior-wall floor-framing detail

Floor beam supported by malleable iron beam hanger bolted to wall beam.

FLOORS

(a) Floors shall be constructed of splined or tongued and grooved plank not less than 3-in. nominal dimension in thickness, covered with a 1-in. flooring, nominal dimension, laid crosswise or diagonally; but this shall not preclude the use of laminated floors, consisting of planks not less than 4 in. wide, nominal dimension, set on edge close together, and spiked at intervals of 18 in. and covered with 1-in. nominal dimension flooring. In laminated floors, the planks shall be laid with broken joints so that no continuous line will occur across the floor. Laminated floors shall not be spiked to the sup-

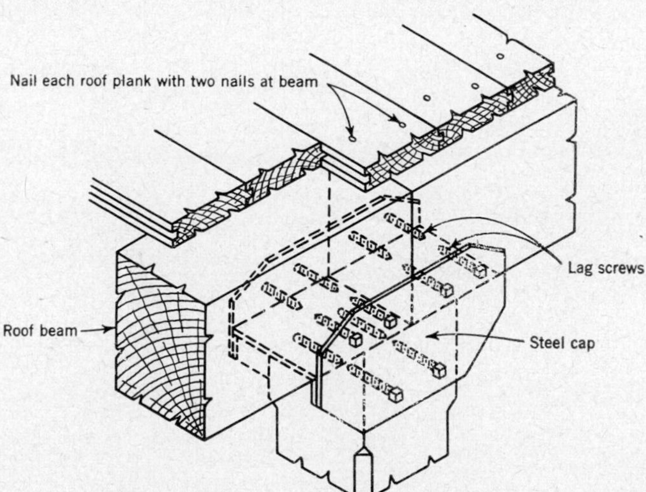

Fig. 4.17 Roof beam and column connection, with steel cap

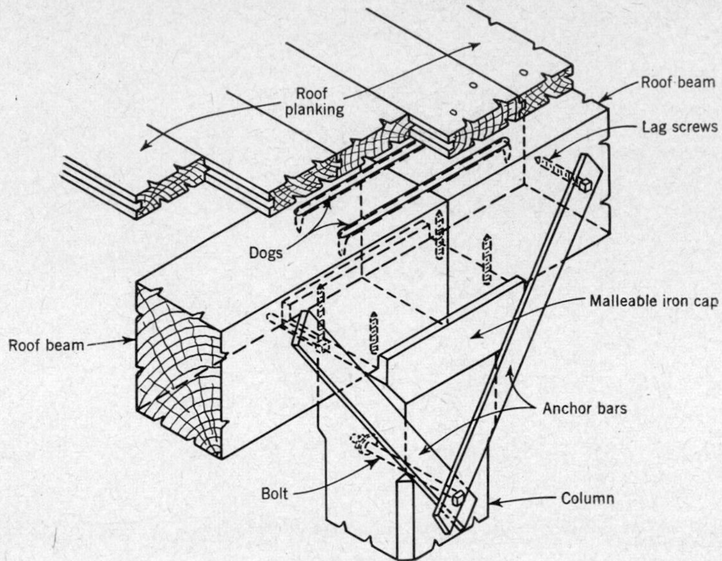

Fig. 4.18 Roof beam and column connection, with iron cap

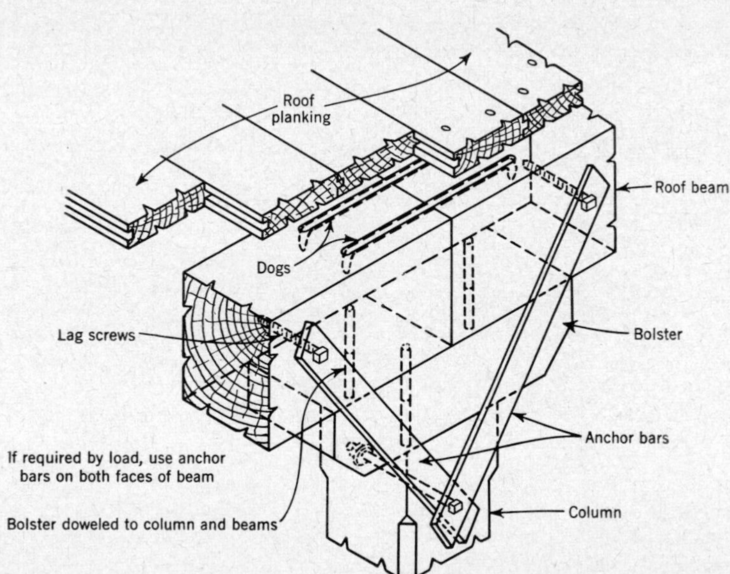

Fig. 4.19 Roof beam and column connection, with bolster

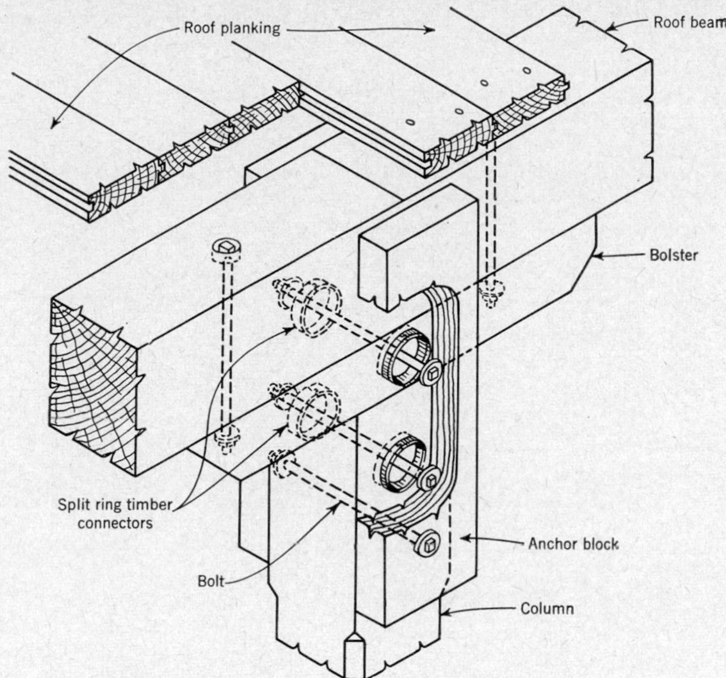

Fig. 4.20 Roof beam and column connection, with bolster and anchor block

porting girders *parallel to the laminations.* Joints of the planking shall be over supports or at the quarter-span points with no more than two-thirds of the joints at such quarter points. Joints beween planks shall be perfectly tight. (Note: It is recommended that the floors be given a pitch of about 1 in. in 20 ft. to points of discharge to relieve the floors of the weight of water from automatic sprinklers and hose, and avoid, as much as possible, water drainage to floors below.)

(b) *Finish* flooring *and plank or laminated subfloor* shall not extend closer than ½ in. to walls, and the space thus left shall be covered by a moulding which will not obstruct an expansive movement of the floor due to wetting; or the masonry may be corbeled under the floor planks to cover this space.

(c) Floors shall have the least possible number and amount of openings, and these shall in all cases be protected by shafts or in some other approved manner.

ROOFS

(a) Roof decks shall be of matched or splined plank of not less than 2½-in. nominal thickness (*other model codes permit a nominal 2-in. deck*), or of laminated planks not less than 3-in. nominal width, set on edge close together and laid as required for floors; and beams and girders supporting roof loads only shall be not less than 6-in. nominal in least dimension. When supporting roof loads only, wood bolsters intertieing adjoining girders or connecting roof trusses with columns may be used. Other forms of roof decks may be used if of noncombustible materials.

(b) Timber arches or trusses may be used to support roof loads. The framing members shall be not less than 4 x 6-in. nominal dimensions, except that spaced members may be composed of two or more pieces not less than 3-in. nominal thickness when blocked solidly throughout their intervening spaces, or when such spaces are tightly closed by a continuous wood plate of not less than 2-in. nominal thickness secured to the underside of the members. Splice scabs shall be not less than 3-in. nominal thickness. When protected by approved automatic sprinklers under the roof deck, the framing members may be reduced to not less than 3-in. nominal thickness.

In Heavy Timber Construction, every roof girder and every alternate roof beam shall be anchored to an exterior or interior wall or to an interior column; roof planking where supported by a wall shall be anchored to such wall at intervals not exceeding 20 ft; every monitor and every saw-tooth construction shall be anchored to the main roof construction. Such anchors shall consist of steel or iron bolts or straps of sufficient strength and ample anchorage to resist a net vertical uplift of the roof of not less than 20 psf.

BUILT-UP SECTIONS

4.14 Built-up sections The term "built-up" applies to members composed of two or more smaller members joined by nailing, bolting, or other mechanical fastenings. They are to be distinguished from glued-laminated members, which are also built up of small members but which do not require such fastenings because of the quality of their fabrication and gluing. Glue is also used in some built-up members on the assumption that mechanical fastenings will provide the pressure glue needs. The quality of such gluing, however, is less predictable. For average fabrication conditions, the contribution of the glue should not be considered and only the mechanical fastenings relied upon to develop the strength of the built-up section.

Structural members can be built up to desired size or shape with small pieces of lumber if solid sawed members are not available or practical. As smaller pieces can be obtained well-seasoned, members made of them are less vulnerable to the disadvantages of seasoning and of natural strength-reducing defects, such as knots. Compression members can be successfully built up for use with the lapped joint type of framing. Built-up sections are frequently used in the top-chord members of trusses and for segmental arches.

The general theory of built-up sections requires that the individual members be fastened together and loaded so as to act as a solid unit. As there is some movement or deformation in all mechanical fastenings, built-up sections are not generally as efficient as solid sawed sections of equivalent size if composite action depends on the action of the fastening.

Built-up beams are usually vertically laminated but may also be horizontally laminated. Several pieces of the same depth placed side by side and spiked, bolted, or otherwise joined together with the surfaces in a vertical plane are called vertically laminated. Two or more pieces of the same width placed on top of each other and fastened together with the surfaces in a horizontal plane are called horizontally laminated.

4.15 Vertically laminated beams Vertically laminated beams in which the length of all laminations is equal to the span are equal in strength and vertical stiffness to solid sawed sections of equal cross section. Actually, the built-up section will probably be somewhat better than a solid section of the same grade, because the better-than-average member of the built-up section assists the average members, and knots in adjacent laminations are not as likely to occur at the same location.

If some of the individual laminations are spliced rather than full span in length, the beam theoretically will not be equal to a solid section in strength or stiffness unless the splices have been properly scarfed and glued. Tests have shown that in a beam consisting of two full-length outside laminations and one equally wide center lamination butt-jointed at the center of the span, the butt-jointed lamination adds about $\frac{1}{2}$ as much strength and stiffness to the beam as a full-length lamination would add. If laminations are spliced within the span, it is preferable to use four or five laminations in place of two or three thicker ones. With many laminations and well-staggered splices, the assembly can equal a solid timber of the same grade if the larger knots permitted by the grade do not appear at the same cross section. In calculations for the strength of a section, conservative practice considers only the unspliced laminations occurring at the section.

The individual laminations of a vertically laminated beam must be well fastened to each other to prevent lateral or horizontal buckling. Spikes with bolts are recommended for beams more than 10 in. in depth. It is good practice to use bolts at the ends of the pieces, regardless of depth, if nails or spikes are the principal means of fastening elsewhere along the length.

Flitch beams, another type of vertically laminated beam, are built up of timbers that are set on edge with a steel plate between or with steel plates or shapes on both sides. Because they are uneconomical, such beams are seldom used for new construction. Their primary use is for the reinforcement of a wooden member to increase its allowable load. If the wood and steel are properly connected—as with bolts or lag screws—to prevent buckling of the steel, the wood may be assumed to provide lateral support for the steel. The flitch beam principle is also used for the reinforcement of damaged wood beams. The strength and stiffness of the damaged beam may then be estimated or neglected entirely. Flitch beams are designed so that the wood and steel carry the loads in proportion to their relative stiffness, which is dependent on modulus of elasticity and moment of inertia. For example, the general form of the equation for deflection is:

$$\Delta = KML^2/EI$$

in which:

Δ = deflection, in inches
K = constant depending on the type of loading and support conditions
L = span of the beam
M = bending moment
E = modulus of elasticity
I = moment of inertia

Because the deflections of the wood and steel are to be equal, the deflection of the wood beam may be equated with the deflection of the steel; and if the spans of wood and steel are equal, the term L drops out of the equation. It then becomes apparent that the ability of the wood and steel to resist the bending moment will vary as the ratio of EI of the two sections if the type of loading constant, K, is the same.

As an example, a 20-ft simply supported 4 x 12 beam with an f of 1,100 psi can carry a uniform load of 146 lb per lin ft, limited by bending. Assume that it is desired to provide 4 times this capacity and that space is limited so that additional wood beams are not possible. What size metal plates must be used to reinforce this beam?

If balanced design is desired, the EI ratio of wood to steel must be 1:3 provided both are loaded in the same manner.

$$EI \text{ of wood} = 1{,}600{,}000 \times 459.43 = 735{,}088{,}000$$
$$I \text{ of steel} = 3 \times 735{,}088{,}000/29{,}000{,}000 = 76.04$$

Therefore, the I of the individual plates must be 38.02. The I of two ½ x 10-in. plates equals 83.4. More accurately, using ½-in. plates:

$$I = bh^3/12$$
$$38.02 = 0.5(h)^3/12$$
$$h^3 = (12 \times 38.02)/0.5 = 913$$
$$h = 9.625 \text{ in.}$$

The steel plates must be located on the sides of the wood beam so that they are in bearing at the support points. This positioning is necessary to prevent the wood member from being overstressed in horizontal shear.

As the steel is to carry 438 lb per ft of the beam, and as 2⅝-in. shear plates have a value of 2,200 lb perpendicular to the grain, the number required equals (438 × 20)/2,200, or 3.98. Therefore, four shear plates should be used.

These connectors could be located at the third-points. The beam was assumed to be uniformly loaded, however, and if connectors are placed at the third-points, the steel plates will be loaded by concentrated loads at the third-points and will therefore not deflect with respect to the beam in the assumed proportion. Computations will also show that they will have to be laterally supported to prevent buckling.

The AISC recommends that the unsupported width of web for compression members should not exceed 40 times the thickness. Assuming that this specification applies here, the spacing of bolts along the top edge of the plates is found as follows:

$$L/t = 40; \qquad t = \tfrac{1}{2}\text{ in.}; \qquad \text{therefore, } L = 20\text{ in.}$$

Therefore the plates will be fastened to the wood beam with ½-in. bolts or lag screws spaced 20 in. apart on centers along the top edge of the plate. As sufficient edge distance must be provided, the gauge line of the bolts or lag screws should be a minimum of 1 in. from the top edge of the plate. However, a gauge of 2 in. will be preferable because the bolt holes will then be located closer to the center of the assembly where the unit bending stresses are lower. The lower side of the plates will be fastened to the wood beam with ½-in. bolts or lag screws on a 2-in. gauge line with a spacing of 40 in. These fastenings should be staggered below the bolts on the top row. Shear plates will not be necessary because the bolts alone will provide a connection that will be sufficient.

For this particular problem, a steel shape such as a channel or angle might have been chosen to provide its own lateral support. In that event, the steel would require connections only at the third-points. The *EI* relationship between the wood and steel, however, would then have to be computed with the steel subject to concentrated loads (the connectors) at the third-points and with the wood subject to uniform load.

Other types of flitch beams are constructed with a steel plate between two wood beams, or with two angles fitted around the bottom edge of the wood beam (see Fig. 4.21). For these types of flitch beams,

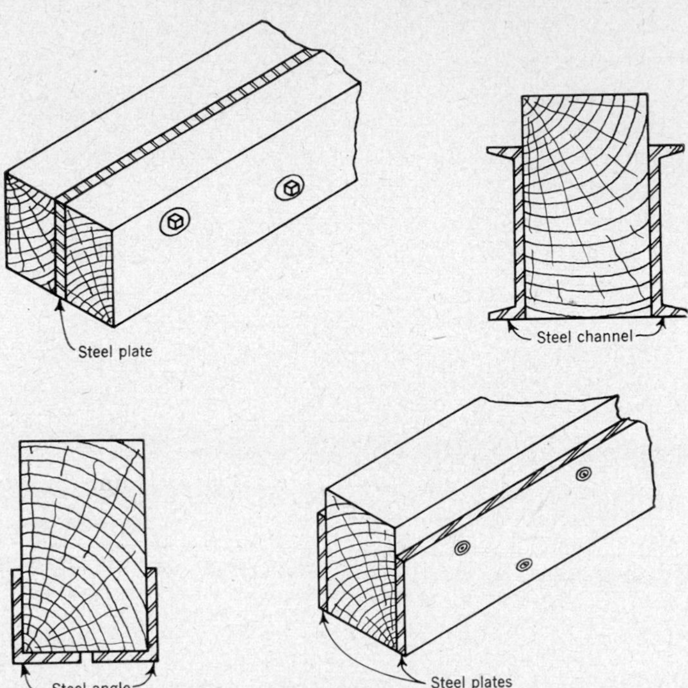

Fig. 4.21 Combination steel-wood beams

the lateral support of the metal plates or angles is not often a controlling factor in the design of the fastenings.

4.16 Horizontally laminated beams Typical horizontally laminated beams are sheathed and keyed beams (see Figs. 4.22 and 4.23). A sheathed beam may be built up of two or more pieces of the same width placed on top of each other and sheathed on the sides with diagonal boards at 45 deg. The diagonal sheathing often runs in opposite directions on the two sides of the beam. The side in tension should theoretically be the more efficient by creating friction between the laminations. Sheathing that runs parallel and in tension on both sides should also be satisfactory. Plywood is sometimes used in place of the diagonal sheathing. Tests have shown that sheathed beams with span-to-depth ratios of 12 are 70 per cent efficient compared to the strength of solid beams of the same size; with a span-to-depth ratio of 24, the efficiency is about 80 per cent. In both cases, however, deflections are about double those of the solid beams. If additional strength is required, a combination of sheathed and keyed beams is often used.

In keyed beams, the shear between adjacent timber is transmitted by

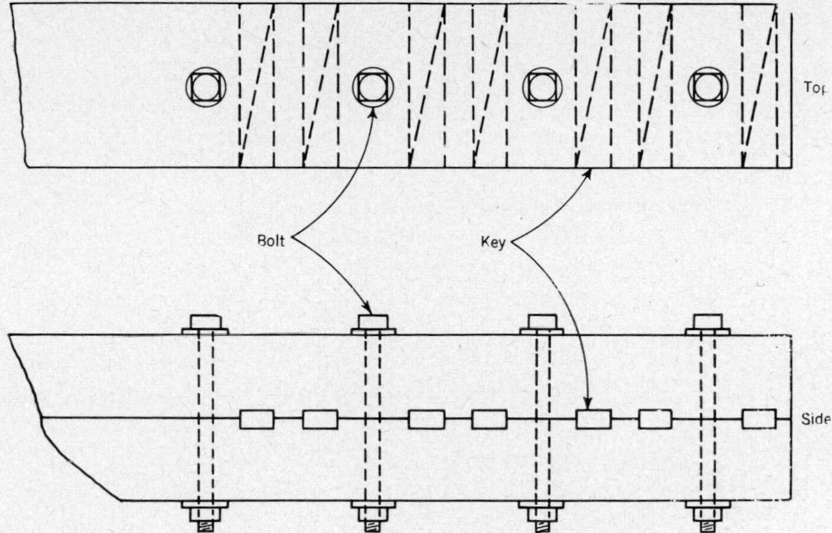

Fig. 4.22 Horizontally laminated beam, keyed

hardwood or metal keys and bolts, or by timber connectors. The keys are sometimes tapered like wedges to give a drive fit and reduce inelastic deformation. Well seasoned timber should be used in the construction of keyed beams and great care exercised to obtain a tight fit in framing.

The required capacity per inch of length for keys, bolts, or timber connectors is obtained by multiplying the computed horizontal shear stress by the width of the member at the point of connection. The spacing of connections can then easily be computed for the point of maximum shear, for a support or point of concentrated load, and for other points along the beam as the shear reduces. To lessen the effect of the elastic deformation of the fastenings, a more conservative or

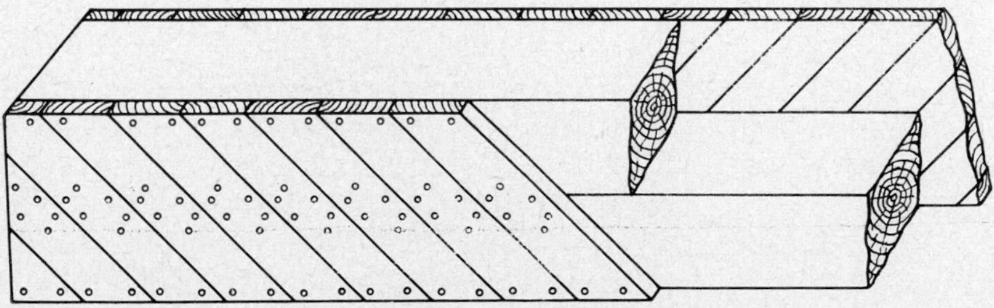

Fig. 4.23 Horizontally laminated beam, sheathed

closer spacing than the one computed is recommended. Such deformation in a keyed beam permits considerably more deflection than would occur in a solid beam.

If two 6 x 6-in. members are used in a horizontally laminated beam, for example, and if the computed maximum horizontal shear is 100 psi, the fastening required would be rated at 550 lb per lin in. (5.5-in. width $\times$ 100). Thus fastenings such as 4-in. split rings, of say, 5,500-lb capacity, might be spaced 10 in. apart. For a uniformly loaded simple span, the 10-in. spacing at the support could increase to 20 in. at the one-quarter span point, and even more near the center of the span where shear approaches zero. Usually a maximum spacing, say 24 in., would be used regardless of computed values. For a simple beam supporting a single concentrated load, the spacing of fastenings would remain constant along the length from the load to the support because the shear would remain the same.

As horizontal shear varies parabolically from the neutral axis for a rectangular beam, the horizontal shear requirement for fastenings in a horizontally laminated rectangular beam of three equal thicknesses would be 89 per cent of that for a two-member beam. For four equal laminations, the connection requirement between the outer and next inner lamination would be $\frac{3}{4}$ of that at the neutral axis.

4.17 Trussed beams Trussed beams can be economically used for long spans and large loads when headroom permits. The simplest forms of trussed beams are the king- and queen-post types (Fig. 4.24.)

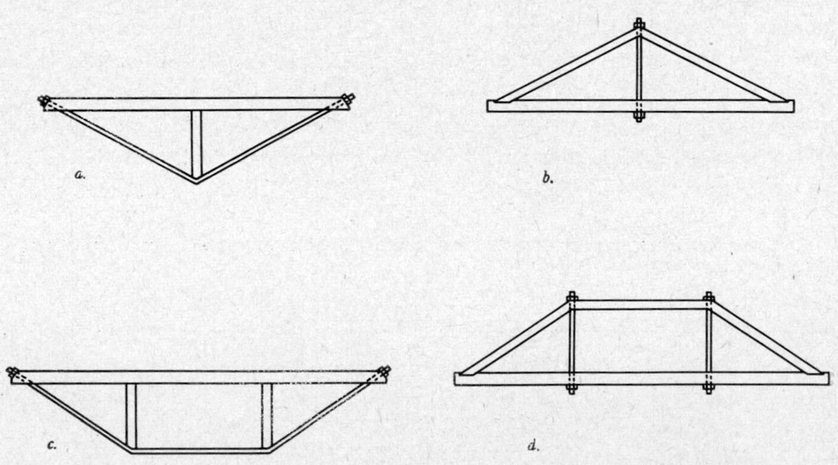

Fig. 4.24 Simple trussed beams

a., b. King-post types *c., d. Queen-post types*

If headroom is limited but adequate room is available above the beam, the king-post type is sometimes used in an inverted position with all the members made of wood except the steel rod hanger. For longer spans, or if headroom is limited, or if the principal loads on the beam are two concentrated ones, the queen-post type of trussed beam is used.

In general, trussed beams should have as much depth as conditions will permit in order to keep the stresses low. Greater stability is obtained if the beam is continuous for the full span than if it is spliced over the struts. Vertically laminated built-up members with splices well staggered in adjacent laminations are sometimes used for long-span trussed beams if full-length solid members are not available.

Exact analysis of trussed beams involves a knowledge of indeterminate stress analysis. One method often used is that of least work. A conservative approximation of the stresses, however, can usually be determined from the formulas for trussing below the beam found in Table 4.1. The formulas assume a continuous beam over equal spans.

TABLE 4.1 Stress formulas for trussed beams

Type of loading	Single strut [1]	Double strut [1]
Uniform loading		
Tension in diagonal rod	$0.312Wh/r$	$Wh/3r$
Compression in strut	$0.625W$	$W/3$
Compression in beam and tension in horizontal rod	$0.312WL/2r$	$WL/9r$
Bending moment in beam (at strut)	$-WL/32$	$-WL/90$
Concentrated load over struts		
Tension in diagonal rod	$Ph/2r$	Ph/r
Compression in strut	P	P
Compression in beam and tension in horizontal rod	$PL/4r$	$PL/3r$

[1] W = total load, in pounds; h = slope length of panel; r = depth of truss; L = span of truss; P = concentrated load, in pounds.

4.18 Glued-laminated beams Glued-laminated beams can be constructed in a wide variety of shapes and sizes. They have been built for clear spans of over 100 ft although the majority are for spans of less than 100 ft; they are most practical for spans of less than 80 ft. They can be designed with constant section, with taper in one or both directions from the centerline, with or without camber, and even split (to form a skylight arm). The possibilities are almost limitless.

Laminated beams have the advantage over sawed beams in strength and appearance. They can be cambered, moreover, to compensate for deflection. (Because the ratio of allowable bending stress to the modulus of elasticity is higher for such beams than for most grades of sawed timber, their deflection will be slightly larger.) As with sawed timber, only the live-load deflection is usually considered as affecting plaster (see Sec. 4.7).

There are no structural design rules for cambering because camber is solely a matter of appearance and has no effect on strength. Floor beams are not usually cambered; neither are roof beams unless the computed deflection exceeds ½ in. If necessary or desirable to camber, the common practice is to do so for twice the computed dead-load deflection. Camber should be very carefully used with beams on flat roofs unless it is meant to provide drainage to down-spouts. Simple spans over individual rooms may be cambered as much as several feet to produce the appearance of an arch. If beams are sawed to a peak on the upper surface and cambered on the lower face, roof pitches as great as 4:12 are possible without producing significant thrust at the supports. Experience has shown that the deflection of tapered and cambered beams will be approximately the same as for a straight beam if the design cross section determined as for a straight beam is used at a point 15 per cent of the span from the centerline and if the minimum section for shear is used at the ends.

The use of cantilevered beams for continuous spans results in controlled reduced moments in the beams and therefore in savings in size and cost. The possibility of unbalanced loads should be considered, that is, if bays are alternately loaded and unloaded or partially loaded. Cantilevered beams may be cambered for both positive and negative deflections. Horizontal shear is more likely to be critical with cantilevered beams. (See Sec. 4.11.)

4.19 Glued-laminated columns Glued-laminated columns have the same general advantages over sawed columns as laminated beams have over sawed beams, that is, higher allowable working stresses, improved appearance, and unusual shapes and sizes. If appearance is a factor, glued-laminated columns provide a nearly check-free surface. As an alternative, sawed timber columns can be encased for a good finished appearance. The checks in such columns are anticipated in establishing working stresses, moreover, and thus need cause no structural concern.

The cross section of a laminated column can be varied at any point to form tapers, corbels, or brackets at a saving both in hardware and maintenance. Columns may even be curved for any desired effect.

4.20 Built-up columns It is often desirable, particularly in truss design, to increase the stiffness of certain compression members in order to increase the allowable unit stress and thus keep member sizes reasonable. The most efficient solution is achieved by increasing the least dimension of the member. Sometimes, however, this method is not practical. For example, if the thickness of the simple compression web member of a truss is increased, either the ends of the member have to be scarfed or the thickness of all other members of the truss that lie in the same plane also have to be increased. To avoid this difficulty, many designers use a built-up "I" or "T" section, made by fastening an additional member or members to a single main member. Some situations may require "L" or "U" sections, but sections symmetrical about at least one axis of the main member are preferable (for spaced columns, see Sec. 4.3).

If the flanges of these built-up sections are properly glued, the standard properties of the section (moment of inertia and section modulus) can be computed and used in the design of the members. However, most members of this type are nailed together and therefore act in a manner neither completely composite nor independent. As conclusive test results are lacking, the designer must rely on his own judgment. One approach is to assume that the member, or members, added to the primary member stiffen it but do not provide composite action—that is, that the fastening is merely adequate to make the added members bend or deflect in the same direction as the main member.

A conservative theoretical least dimension, *d*, can be determined for the main member, assuming the width of member remains the same, so that the moment of inertia of the new theoretical main member equals the sum of the inertias of the actual two or more members considered to be bending independently in the same general direction. For example, a 2 x 8 compression member, 10 ft long, is to be strengthened by the addition of a 2 x 6 to form a "T" section. Assuming that the 2 x 6 cover plate will carry none of the direct stress, the allowable load on the "T" section can be determined as follows:

$$
\begin{aligned}
I_{yy} \text{ of } 2 \times 8 &= 2.68 \\
I_{xx} \text{ of } 2 \times 6 &= 24.10 \\
I_{yy} + I_{xx} &= 26.78 = d^3h/12 \\
h &= 7.5 \text{ in.} \\
d^3 &= (12 \times 26.78)/7.5 \\
d &= 3.5 \\
\therefore \quad l/d &= (10 \times 12)/3.5 = 34.3
\end{aligned}
$$

According to the column curve of Chap. 12 (Fig. 12.1) or the formulas of Chap. 13 (NDS), the allowable P/A for an l/d of 34.3 is 445 psi for a simple solid column. The area of the 2 x 8 equals 12.19 sq in.

Thus the "T" will carry 12.19 $\times$ 445, or 5,430 lb. The 2 x 8 member, moreover, cannot be used alone as its l/d is greater than 50.

The preceding computations are conservative. Many designers consider the d of a built-up section, particularly bracing members, equal to the width of the member added (5.625 in the above example).

A column may be elastically unstable if its cross section includes thin outstanding flanges or parts. It can fail—either by wrinkling of the outstanding part or by torsion of the whole section about its own axis—at loads less than those indicated by the column formulas for crushing or bending failure. These limitations seldom control the usual "T," "U," or "I" sections if the ratio of thickness to width of the individual members ranges from 1:3 to 1:4. For smaller ratios, however, the sections should be checked by the following approximate method, particularly if species of lower E value are used.

If an outstanding flange under a compressive load projects from a column section that is high in torsional stiffness, the wrinkling stress may be critical, that is, the outstanding part may wrinkle and make the remaining section unsafe. The stress at which wrinkling may occur is given by:

$$p = 0.07Eh^2/b^2$$

in which:

p = critical wrinkling stress
E = modulus of elasticity
h = thickness of the outstanding flange
b = width of the outstanding flange

If one or more relatively wide but thin parts project from a compression member that does not have great torsional stiffness, the member may twist about its own longitudinal axis. The critical stress for twisting is given by:

$$p = 0.044Eh^2/b^2$$

The coefficients of both preceding equations were obtained from tests of Sitka spruce, but they are applicable to other species of wood without appreciable error. The rigidity of the section may sometimes be such that the critical stress will occur at a value between the values given by the wrinkling and twisting formulas. For circumstances requiring precise design, reference should be made to a more comprehensive discussion of the subject.

The stresses given above are critical or failing stresses; the unit stress permitted on the compression member should normally be much lower. The factor of safety—the amount of reduction required from the critical value—is left for the structural designer to determine on the basis of the particular conditions under which the member is to be used.

No arrangement of pieces with any kind of mechanical fastenings will make a built-up column fully equal in strength to a one-piece column of comparable material and over-all dimensions. Arrangements with parallel planks and cover plates or with planks boxed around a solid core (Fig. 4.25) yield percentages of strength of an equivalent one-piece column as shown in Table 4.2. For l/d ratios of 10 or greater, these percentages apply to both built-up columns in which the individual pieces are full length and columns in which well fitted butt-jointed pieces are used.

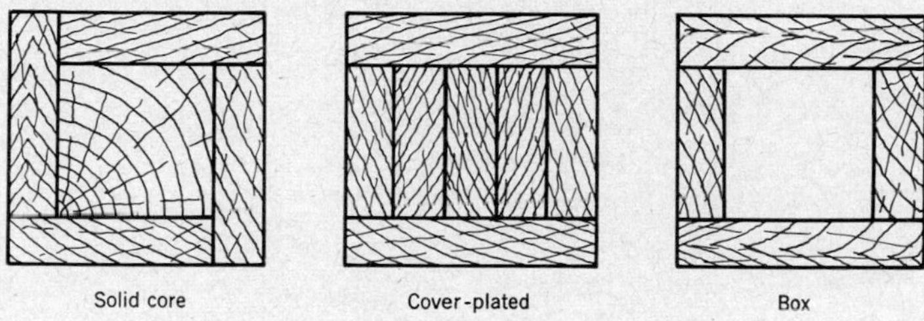

Fig. 4.25 Built-up columns

TABLE 4.2 Strength comparison of built-up and one-piece columns

L/d ratio	Strength *per cent* (one-piece column = 100)	L/d ratio	Strength *per cent* (one-piece column = 100)
6	82	18	65
10	77	22	74
14	71	26	82

Butt joints in compression members should be perpendicular to the direction of stress, accurately cut, and tightly fitted. In short posts, pieces butted end to end fail at 75 to 80 per cent of the crushing strength of full-length pieces. If the joint in a short column has full lateral support (such as in the compression members of trusses) and a metal plate not thinner than 20 gauge is tightly fitted between the butted pieces, no reduction of compressive strength need be assumed.

Tests for strength of box columns indicate that the design formulas for solid columns are applicable to box columns of square cross section. The d in the formulas for solid columns is replaced by $\sqrt{d_1^2 + d_2^2}$ for square box columns, in which d_1 equals the outside and d_2 the inside dimensions. It is recommended that the ratio of width to thickness of the side members of the box should not exceed 10. If the box column is of rectangular section or has adjacent sides of different thickness, it seems reasonable to apply the formula separately to the two axes and to use the lesser of the two d values thus determined.

4.21 Built-up arches Curved segmented rafters or roof arches (see Chap. 6) can be made by vertically laminating relatively short pieces of lumber with bolts or spikes and bandsawing their upper edges to a curved outline (see Fig. 4.26).

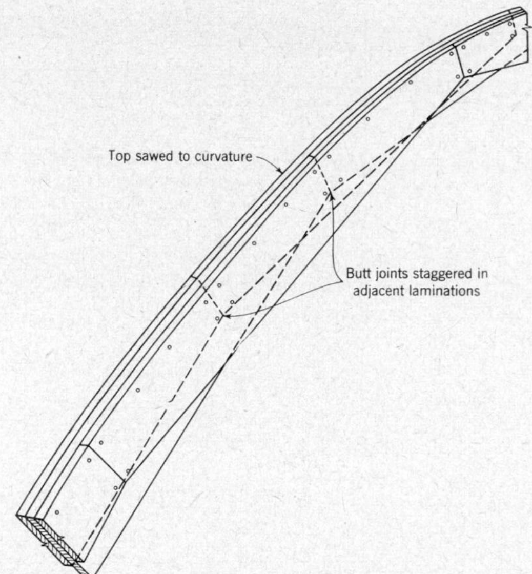

Fig. 4.26 Vertically laminated segmental arch

Butt joints at ends of the segments of vertically laminated and segmented arches transmit no bending stress and only limited compressive stress. Design for bending at the butt joints should be based on the unjointed section of the arch, and the butted segment should be adequate for a compression of ½ the total for two laminations, ⅓ for three laminations, and so forth. Working stresses suitable for the design of one-piece members of the same species and grade may be used with that net section. As all segments are not of the same depth at a cross section of the arch, the stiffness can only be estimated—usually on the basis of an average depth of section. Because of the curvature of the member, stresses at the ends of the segments are not parallel to the direction of grain. If the radius of curvature is short, this fact should be taken into account in determining the working stresses.

A segmented, laminated arch does not have a high degree of lateral stability. Coverplates nailed to the top surface help to counteract this weakness. If one of the edges of the arch is held firmly in line by the roof deck, the depth-to-thickness ratio of its cross section should not exceed 5.

5

Roof Trusses

TYPES OF ROOF TRUSSES

5.1 Selection of roof trusses Architectural style, types of roofing material, methods of support or column framing, and relative economy are the principal factors influencing a choice among the three basic types of trusses: bowstring, pitched, and flat. In addition, side- and end-wall height and type, roof shape, and bracing requirements must be considered.

Other factors being equal, economy is the prime consideration. Economy is dependent upon efficiency in use of material relative to truss type and proportions and to fabrication labor. Although the relative economy of the various types cannot be precisely ascertained, it is nevertheless possible to define the theoretical advantages of one truss over another in supporting loads. Theoretically, the three basic types in order of relative efficiency are bowstring, pitched, and flat.

The function of a truss is to transfer load from point of application to the supports as directly as possible. Thus for a concentrated load at the centerline of a span, a simple "A" frame is the most efficient. Likewise, if only two equal and symmetrically placed concentrated loads are involved, a truss similar to the queen-post type is the most efficient. In both trusses, the load is transferred to the support directly through the sloping top-chord members without the need for web members.

5.2 Bowstring trusses For more or less uniform loads, which are usually assumed in roof construction, an arch in the shape of a parabola is theoretically the most efficient because direct stress alone is developed in the arch and in the tie member. A parabolic arch has no need for a larger arch section to take care of bending moment, moreover, and no need to introduce web members to lessen the amount of bending. Because most structures must sustain some unbalanced load, however, web members are desirable, and a circular arc is simpler to fabricate than a parabolic one. Thus the widely used bowstring truss has a top chord in a circular arc and sufficient web members to keep top-chord sizes reasonable.

Bowstring trusses are usually analyzed for direct stress as though the top chord were in a straight line between panel points. Top chords may be glued-laminated (Fig. 5.1) to the curvature or may be solid timbers laid to the curved pattern with or without their top surfaces sawed to the curvature (Fig. 5.2). The bending moment due to eccentricity between panel points must be considered both for curved-laminated members and for members sawed to curvature if the center-line of the member does not coincide with the assumed direction of axial stress. If joists are spaced along the top chord, this secondary bending moment may permit the use of smaller member sizes than would a truly segmental, sawed timber top chord. In addition, because of their higher allowable unit stresses, glued-laminated top chords and other glued-laminated members normally permit the use of smaller sizes. They also eliminate or lessen the need for the seasoning maintenance required by some sawed members. Because of the extra labor involved in laminating, however, they may be more expensive than sawed members.

Fig. 5.1 Bowstring truss, glued-laminated

Eight 54-ft span trusses spaced 18 ft, 6 in. on centers.

Courtesy Cartwright & Morrison

Fig. 5.2 Bowstring truss, segmental

Sixteen 130-ft span trusses for a skating rink.

Top chords that have been mechanically laminated with nails, bolts, or both are sometimes used for bowstring trusses. Although their efficiency is less than that of a glued-laminated member or a sawed member of the same size, they are suitable for use if the amount of nailing has been designed or specified on the basis of experience to provide the required strength of the built-up section. The section will usually be larger than that needed for a glued-laminated member, but it will also be more suitable for field lamination.

The use of nails in place of clamps for gluing pressure in structural members is not recognized in U.S. standards. In Canada, however, much experimenting has been done with nail-pressure gluing, and tests indicate lower and more erratic results than those yielded by clamp-pressure products. The Canadian Standards Association specification lists the following requirements:

> Nailing shall not be used as a means of applying gluing pressure except for gap-filling glues such as casein. When used, flat-headed common nails or other nails of approved design shall be at least 2½ times the thickness of the lamination, and there shall be one nail for each 8 sq in. of glue area. Nails shall be driven home so that adequate glue squeeze-out is apparent.

Where nail pressure is used for gluing, longitudinal shear and radial tension stresses shall be 60 per cent of those used for clamp-pressure products. All other stresses shall be the same as for clamp-pressure methods.

Nail-pressure glued timbers should be used with a full consideration of their actual structural condition and not given undue merit nor used in lieu of standard structural glued-laminated work. In nail-pressure gluing, the nails are not considered as adding to the strength of the glue line but as applying the pressure to the glue line to obtain surface contact.

A bowstring truss may be built up to provide the appearance of either a flat or a pitched truss and thus is probably the most flexible of all truss types. For such constructions, proper lateral bracing should be provided for that portion of the curved top chord which lacks direct lateral support from the roof framing. (See Fig. 5.3.)

Fig. 5.3 Bowstring truss, built-up

Eighteen 76-ft span trusses, one 72-ft truss, one 68-ft truss.

5.3 Pitched trusses Pitched trusses (Fig. 5.4) have some of the theoretical advantages of bowstrings in that a portion of the load is transferred to the supports directly through the top-chord members and need not be carried through the web members. For average spans, the top chords of pitched trusses have the economic advantage of permitting the use of sawed timber without special sawing or fitting to

Fig. 5.4 Pitched truss

Eighteen 64-ft span Belgian trusses.

curvature, and of being simple to lay out and fabricate. Web-member and other connections are also simple, as a rule. Like those in a bowstring truss, they are much less complicated than flat-truss connections.

5.4 Flat trusses Flat trusses (Fig. 5.5) are less efficient than either the pitched or bowstring type. They are preferable only if a relatively flat roof surface, particularly one with multiple spans, is desired. For lateral-bracing and column connections, they have the advantage of providing a bracing effect, because both the top and bottom chords may be attached to the columns. For usual truss proportions, their web-member stresses will be considerably greater than those for pitched or bowstring trusses and their web connections more complicated and expensive.

Fig. 5.5 Flat Pratt truss

5.5 Raised-chord trusses Raised-chord trusses (Fig. 5.6) are trusses with the center portion of the bottom chords raised substantially above the level of supports. They are frequently used for reasons of appearance or added clearance. Typical examples are crescent trusses of a bowstring type, the so-called cambered or raised-bottom-chord pitched trusses employing Howe, Pratt, or Fink web systems, and scissors trusses. Unless these trusses are analyzed as arches and fixity or resistance to horizontal thrust provided accordingly at the support, the effective depth-to-span ratios of simple trusses should be maintained.

A raised-chord truss, particularly one with spans longer than 50 ft, should be analyzed for the thrust on the walls induced by deflection, and the walls or columns designed accordingly. Otherwise special bearing details or wall framing should be provided to relieve the thrust.

If a truss is supported by masonry, thrust due to deflection may be minimized by means of slotted anchorage connections. Roller supports at one bearing are not common except in large spans where more positive free movement is considered necessary. Provision for deflection thrust relief is most important at the time of erection; later the truss will have stabilized substantially. If maximum vertical live load and wind are assumed not to occur at the same time, moreover, the normal

Fig. 5.6 Scissors truss

Span of 33 ft, 6½ in.; 12-ft spacing; 45-deg roof slope; 30-deg bottom-chord slope.

provision for wind loads on the supports is often considered adequate for vertical-load deformation thrust. For trusses supported on free-standing columns with masonry side walls, it is well to allow clearance for lateral deflection between column and wall at the time of erection. After original lateral movement, the connections between column and wall may be tightened. Required clearance may be determined by deflection calculations, but it is frequently rather arbitrarily chosen on the basis of experience.

5.6 Special trusses There are many other types of trusses as well as combinations of the standard types that offer special advantages for special conditions. In general, the same recommendations for proportions, spacing, and other design details continue to apply. Typical combinations are bowstring-flat (Fig. 5.7a) and pitched-flat trusses (Fig. 5.7b) of a two-span width, which provide drainage to outside walls. Combinations of Pratt and Howe web systems are frequently used with flat trusses. Special types include the common saw-tooth truss, cantilevered trusses, and inverted trusses.

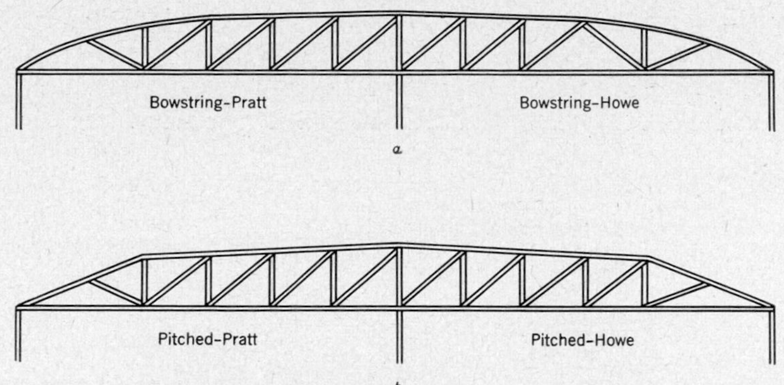

Fig. 5.7 Combinations of truss types

Indeterminate structures, such as rigid frames or continuous trusses, are not frequently used in timber. Such trusses frequently present erection problems that increase costs more than the savings made in materials. If conditions warrant consideration of this type of special framing, particular attention must be given in the design analysis to feasible methods of erection and to deformation in the timber joints, as well as to the elastic deformation of the members themselves.

MAXIMUM ROOF-TRUSS SPANS

5.7 Economic factors The maximum economical span of any given type of timber truss will vary with the material available, loading conditions, spacing, type of truss, ratio of labor to material cost, and fabrication methods. As all of these are interrelated factors, no specific conclusion can possibly cover the many variables.

5.8 Pitched and flat roof trusses Pitched and flat roof trusses with average loading and spacing of 15 to 20 ft are infrequently used for spans in excess of 80 ft. Economical spans are usually limited by the available sizes and lengths of solid sawed or glued-laminated timber and by the potential capacity of the web-member connections. If loading and spacing are smaller, larger spans may be constructed with the same relative member sizes and joint details.

5.9 Bowstring roof trusses Bowstring trusses are economical in spans up to 250 ft or more. Bowstring trusses using glued-laminated members are usually shop-fabricated and are not recommended for field fabrication unless competent supervision is provided and essentially the same quality control is exercised as required under shop conditions. As many fabricators have standardized on the bowstring type, it may profitably be considered as an alternative even though original designs may call for a flat or pitched type truss.

5.10 Light roof trusses Light trusses, such as trussed rafters of 2- to 4-ft spacing, are recommended for spans up to about 50 ft (see Fig. 5.8). They can be built for longer spans, but a heavy truss with

Fig. 5.8 Triangular trussed rafters

larger spacing may be more economical for this purpose and may even be so for spans under 50 ft. Trussed rafters are particularly suitable for contractor fabrication because they require small, readily available pieces of lumber, their joints are simple to fabricate, and completed units are light enough in weight to be handled and erected without special equipment.

TRUSS PROPORTIONS

5.11 Truss proportions If economy, deflection, and secondary stresses due to deflection are disregarded, trusses may theoretically be built to almost any proportions. An understanding of the interrelated factors that contribute to performance and economy will aid the designer in selecting the best system.

5.12 Depth-to-span ratio Certain ratios of effective depth to span are recommended as being satisfactory on the basis of experience. The larger the span, the more desirable it is to use deeper trusses. Although trusses of less depth than these may be acceptable, special attention should then be given to the possibility of greater deflection and secondary stresses. Deflection in trusses of less-than-average depth may be held to a minimum by the following practices: (1) conservative design, (2) the use of low or intermediate grades of material, (3) the use of a minimum number of chord splices (by employing the longest available lengths), (4) the use of fastenings with the smallest deformation, and (5) the use of as few panels as possible. As modulus of elasticity is the same for all grades of a given species, a lower ratio of allowable working stress to the species modulus can be obtained by using the low or intermediate grades. Stiffer members are also obtained, and therefore less deflection for a given load.

It is recommended that the top chord of a bowstring truss be fabricated with a radius about equal to the span. The suggested effective depth-to-span ratio is between 1:6 and 1:8. A radius equal to the span will give a ratio slightly larger than the suggested minimum.

For pitched trusses, an effective depth-to-span ratio between 1:5 and 1:6 is recommended, and a minimum of not less than 1:7 unless special consideration is given to deflection. Much deeper trusses may be used for the sake of appearance, such as for the steeply pitched roofs popular in churches.

For flat trusses, a minimum depth-to-span ratio between 1:8 and 1:10 is recommended, the deeper trusses being preferred for the longer spans. Roofs should have a minimum slope of ¼ in. per ft for proper drainage, although steeper slopes are often desirable. Flat roofs with no slope for drainage are not recommended unless provision is made in the design for possible accumulation of water due to a stopped drain or natural deflection. Drains on flat roofs should be located at the low points. These are at the center of the span if the truss is built flat.

In longer spans, secondary deflection stresses are probably more important. As these stresses are not capable of exact computation, the larger depth-to-span ratios should be used for trusses employing such spans. Deflection of free-span trusses is usually well within acceptable limits, even that for plaster, but care should be taken to see that the natural deflection does not interfere with auxiliary framing. Suspended ceilings are often desirable. Ample clearance should be provided between trusses and so-called nonbearing partitions or plate glass windows. Provision should also be made for adjustment in the level of the hangers if there is a possibility that deflection may interfere with the proper operation of truss-suspended doors or machinery.

5.13 Number of panels It is desirable to use as few truss panels as the use of reasonable member sizes will allow. This practice will mean fewer members to handle, fewer joints to fabricate and assemble, and theoretically improved performance. The number of panels usually should be determined by reasonable top-chord sizes rather than by any fixed formula. For material of 2- to 4-in. thickness, desirable panel length will usually be in the range of 6 to 10 ft. Thus, a symmetrical truss of 30-ft span would probably have four panels whereas a 40-ft truss might have either four or six, and an 80-ft truss eight or ten.

WEB-MEMBER SYSTEMS

5.14 Web-member systems Although there is not a great deal of difference in either theoretical performance or economy between the various web systems commonly used, certain systems are preferable for special conditions. Generally, web systems should be avoided that require more than two web members (a member may be composed of more than one piece) to frame to the same point on a chord. Exception may be made if design stresses are so light that the joints may be framed eccentrically or if wood or steel gusset plates are used.

5.15 Systems for bowstring trusses Besides systems of a tied-arch type—which merely provide vertical hangers between top and bottom chords—the web-member systems most often used in bowstring trusses are of the Warren type. One is for relatively small spans (see Fig. 5.9a), and a second, with vertical members added to keep the top chord panels to a reasonable length, is for longer spans (see Fig. 5.9b). As subdivided panels increase the number of joints and web members, they are not often used, although they do have the advantage of keeping the lengths of many of the compression web members to a minimum. Indeterminate, lattice-type web framing is seldom used, because of the greater amount of material and labor required.

5.16 Systems for pitched trusses Web systems commonly used with pitched trusses include Belgian (Fig. 5.9c), Fink (Fig. 5.9d), Pratt (Fig. 5.9e), and Howe (Fig. 5.9f). The advantage of one style over another may depend on either the auxiliary framing or the joint system em-

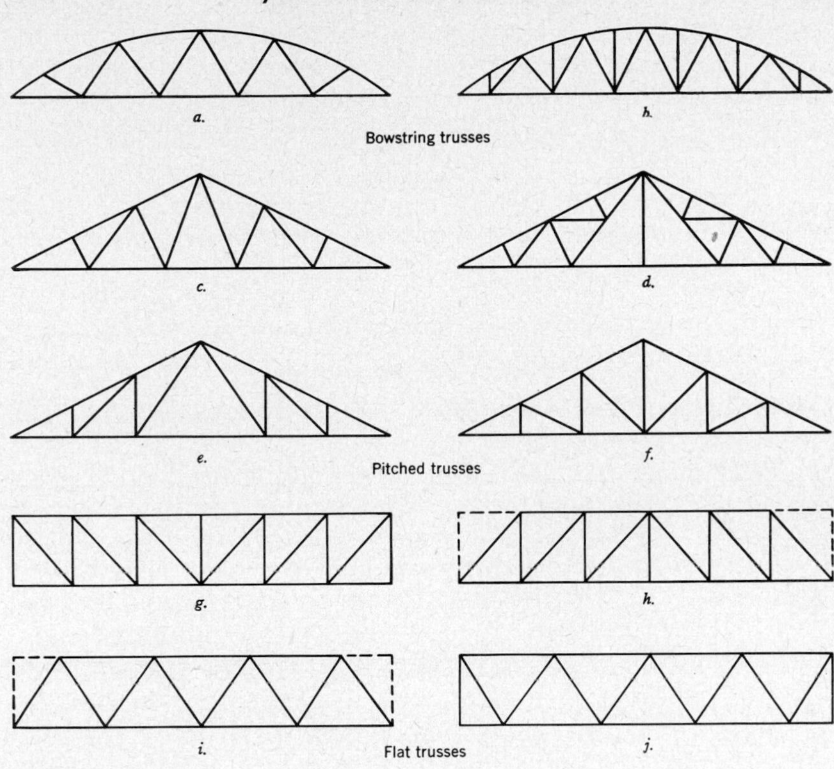

Fig. 5.9 Truss types and web-member systems

ployed. For normally proportioned trusses, the Belgian system will provide more nearly balanced web-member stresses than the other three. This attribute frequently simplifies joint details if gusset plates or the multiple-member style of joint is used. Depending on the arrangement of members in a multiple-member joint, the Pratt or Howe system may permit simpler details if the smaller stress in the vertical web member is the critical stress. The style of Belgian most often used with the multiple-member system places the web members perpendicular to the top chord. This arrangement provides a simple support and easy anchorage for purlins or joists by allowing the web members to be extended above the chord.

With multiple-member lapped joints, the Pratt or the Howe web system may have advantages if monitors or other special framing is installed above or below the truss, because the vertical web members can be extended to form an integral part of this framing. The Pratt system has shorter compression web members than the Howe or Belgian and may permit the use of smaller sizes. The Howe system is more suitable for the rod-and-block joint system (see Sec. 5.20) if steel rods are used for the vertical tension web members.

If the length of compression web members toward the centerline of the span is such that unreasonable member sizes would be required (usually long-span trusses or ones with a large depth-to-span ratio), the Fink truss may be used. The critical web-member stresses in the Fink system are higher than those in other systems, however, and one joint involves three web members at the same point. These two factors make connections more difficult, with the result that the Fink system is less desirable than the others.

5.17 Systems for flat trusses The web-member systems frequently used for flat trusses are the Pratt (Fig. 5.9g), Howe (Fig. 5.9h) and Warren (Figs. 5.9j and k). For flat as well as pitched trusses, the Pratt system has the advantage of keeping the length of compression web members to a minimum. If trusses are made up of a multiple number of members and if timber columns are built integral with the trusses, this system is desirable. If trusses are to be supported on walls or on corbels, however, the Howe system is preferable, provided its compression members do not require excessive sizes. The Howe system is the basis for the original rod-and-block type of framing, in which steel rods are used for the vertical tension web members. Flat trusses with multiple members, half Pratt and half Howe, simplify the joint at the centerline of the span, because the framing does not reverse direction.

For multiple-member lapped joints in smaller-span trusses where the depth of truss is considerably less than the panel length, the simple Warren web system is the most desirable because it provides the more nearly balanced web-member stresses. With vertical members added, it is also used for long-span flat trusses, although the concentric framing of three web members to the same point on the bottom chord may present a design problem if gusset plates are not used. The double Warren web system, which reduces the web stresses, is seldom employed because the other types are usually more economical.

GENERAL FRAMING SYSTEMS

5.18 Multiple-span simple trusses If multiple-span simple trusses are joined to common columns, details should be such that natural truss deflection after erection will not develop perpendicular to the grain stresses in the column; otherwise the column may be split. Connections from truss to truss preferably should permit some "give" to lessen the possibility of continuous truss action, and the column should not serve as the connecting piece.

To simplify column connections with two simple flat trusses, the Pratt type may be framed to the column top and the Howe type to a corbel or to the column at a lower point (see Fig. 5.10a). To balance

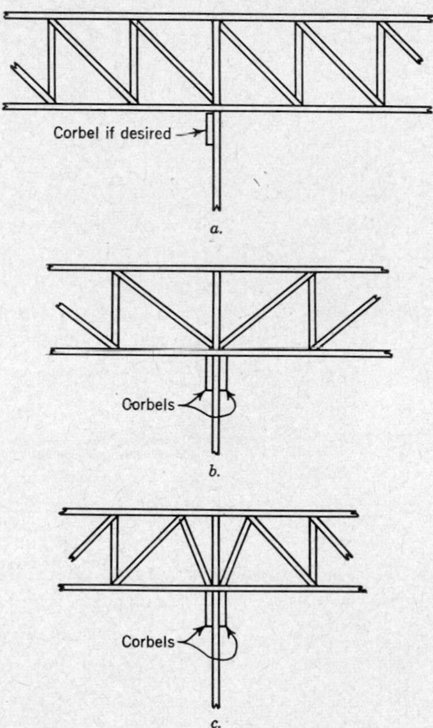

Fig. 5.10 Flat-truss column connections

a. Left, Howe; right, Pratt *c. Left and right, Pratt*
b. Left and right, Howe

the column loading better, corbels may be used at the bottom chord level to support two Howe trusses (Fig. 5.10b) or two modified Pratt trusses with slightly sloping end members (Fig. 5.10c). Metal straps or plates or wood splice plates should be used to join or tie the trusses across the column, frequently with bolted connections that permit "give" and reduce the chance of continuous truss action.

Steel gusset plates may be used for column-to-truss connections either with shear plates or with bolted joints. Both provide a slip joint for in-the-air connection during erection, although the shear plates, needing only a few bolts, may be easier to assemble "in place" than would a larger number of bolts alone. Corbels usually provide the simplest joint, because they lend the truss a support point prior to the placement of anchorage and horizontal-tie connections.

Columns with only one corbel must be analyzed for eccentric loading. Columns with two opposing corbels must also be analyzed for the possibility of such loading, which could be caused either by unequal spans to either side or by possible unbalanced loading.

5.19 Monochord trusses A truss using single solid members for the chords and web members all in one plane, sometimes referred to as a monochord type, requires gusset plates for the connections (Fig. 5.11).

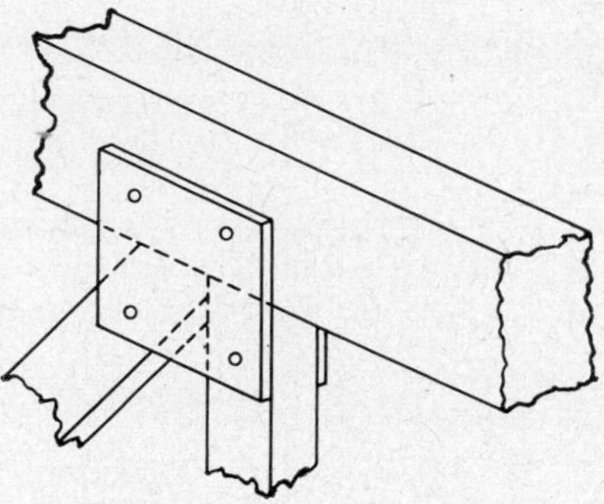

Fig. 5.11 Monochord gusset-plate joint

The system has an advantage in that all of its wood members are loaded substantially parallel to the grain, an arrangement that provides the highest connection value. It also offers improved fire resistance because of the thicker members required. The cost of custom-fabricated gusset plates may be high, however, and roughly double the normal amount of fasteners will be required because the stresses must be transferred from one member to the gusset plate and then from the gusset plate to the other member. The monochord type of truss, particularly the bowstring type in which the gusset plate connections are relatively simple, has become standard with some fabricators, and is competitive with the multiple-member type.

5.20 Rod-and-block framing Another general type of framing called rod-and-block uses steel rods for the tension web members (see Fig. 5.12). If web-member stresses are transferred by bearing perpendicular to the grain and by shear parallel to the chord members, the joints

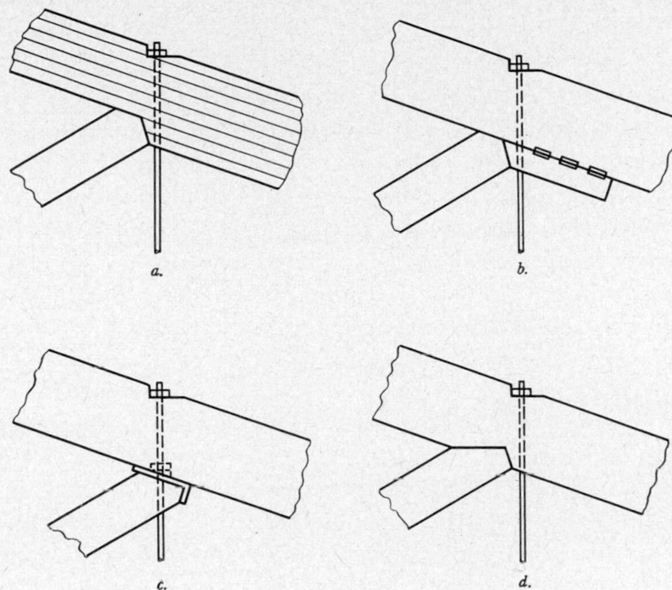

Fig. 5.12 Typical rod-and-block joints

a. Extra laminations
b. Shear block
c. Special metal fittings
d. Notching chord

and member sizes of rod-and-block framing are somewhat less efficient than either gusset-plate connections or multiple-member connections. Special metal fittings are often necessary at the joints. As these can be quite expensive on a special order basis, many fabricators standardize them to keep costs to a minimum. Rod-and-block trusses have the unique advantage of making re-cambering possible merely by a tightening of the rods.

The modern version of the rod-and-block style of truss uses glued-laminated lumber for the chord members and sometimes for the compression web members. Extra laminations may be added to the chords at the panel points to transfer the component of the load parallel to the chord (Fig. 5.12a), or bearing blocks may be fastened to the chord by connectors or other mechanical fastenings (Fig. 5.12b). Special details, such as combining the tension rod with a metal plate between the web and the chord, are sometimes used (Fig. 5.12c). This arrangement permits the component of the web-member stress perpendicular to the chord to be transferred directly to the rod through the metal plate instead of having to be carried by bearing on the side grain of the chord. The glued-laminated members, being of seasoned material, reduce to a minimum or eliminate the need for retightening of bolts due to shrinkage. Retightening may be necessary with unseasoned material.

5.21 Roof construction systems Only two basic systems of roof construction need be considered in truss design. One applies roof loads to the truss only at the panel points; the other applies them either continuously, as with plank roofing, or at intervals along the top, as with joists. The former system produces only direct stress in the chord member; the latter introduces bending as well as direct stress. It is usually not necessary to decide at the outset whether purlins are to be used only at the panel points or whether loads are to be applied along the chord. As loads along the chords must be translated to loading at panel points for the stress analysis, this question can be resolved in the design of the chord member, unless the general roof-framing system is determined by other factors.

In terms of lumber alone, joists closely spaced along the chords or purlins placed at and between panel points are more economical than purlins placed only at the panel points because the latter require heavier plank roofing or rafters and sheathing. However, labor costs are less if purlins and planking are used instead of closely spaced joists because there are fewer pieces to handle and fewer points at which the planking must be nailed. Thick planks of the lighter species of wood, with special tongues and grooves, are sometimes applied directly to the top chords in place of joists or purlins. They are probably the least expensive to install from a labor standpoint. Plank roofing and heavy purlins offer improved fire resistance, as do all heavy truss members compared to thinner or lighter members. Purlins used at panel points do not introduce appreciable bending in the top chord. They may therefore be desirable as a means of keeping chord sizes reasonable, particularly for larger spans, heavier loadings, and for flat, pitched, or other straight-chord trusses.

5.22 Roof-truss spacing There are no fixed rules for spacing trusses in buildings. Spacing may be affected by roof framing, wall construction, size of material available, loading conditions, and the column spacing desired for material handling or traffic. In general, the greater the spacing, the more economical the construction, and the longer the span, the more desirable the greater spacing. Spacing limits are set by the purlin or joist sizes available for framing between trusses. Spacing is often more or less arbitrarily chosen because of its suitability for a particular roof and wall construction or building function. For example, if masonry walls are used, a truss spacing is frequently selected that will fit the pilaster spacing required for the lateral support of the walls. If roof sheathing material is to be applied directly to the trusses without auxiliary framing—in order to save the labor of placing the purlins—the spacing might vary from, say, 2 ft with 1-in. sheathing, to 7 to 9 ft, with 2-in. plank, or to still greater dimensions with heavier plank. If joists or purlins are used between trusses, the spacing might be determined by economical and available joist sizes although common usage would probably call for a spacing in the range of 14 to 20 ft. If spacing exceeds 20 ft, the availability of required sizes and lengths should definitely be considered. If spacing is desired that is greater than that suitable for sawed purlins, either glued-laminated purlins or trussed purlins may be used instead.

In recent years there has been a trend away from the use of rafters with purlins in favor of plank with purlins or sheathing with closely spaced purlins (joists) along the top chord. The latter method reduces the cubage or space above the truss, gives better lateral support to the top chord, eliminates the extra labor of placing the rafters, and normally permits use of smaller joists or purlins.

5.23 Purlin trusses If the spacing of trusses requires longer purlins than are commercially available, purlin trusses are frequently used. Their design is similar to that of any simple truss. If purlin trusses are inclined from the vertical, that is, if they do not have their top and bottom chords in the same vertical plane, as when used on pitched trusses, it is important that bracing be provided to keep the bottom chords in proper position.

5.24 Roof-truss bracing and anchorage Bracing and anchorage is necessary to hold trusses and truss members in proper position so that they can resist vertical loads as well as lateral loads such as wind, impact, or earthquake. Although roof framing will usually serve as lateral bracing for the top-chord members, it is important that adequate lateral supports be provided for the bottom-chord members (see Fig. 5.13), and also that consideration be given to the possible need for vertical-sway bracing between top and bottom chords of adjacent trusses (see Fig. 5.14). Horizontal cross-bracing is sometimes required in the plane of either the top or the bottom chord, particularly in long buildings in which the diaphragm action of the roof framing is not adequate for end-wall forces, or in which side-wall loads are resisted by end walls or intermediate bracing such as cross walls. The latter situation arises if each truss and its support are not designed as a bent to resist the lateral load.

Trusses must be securely anchored to properly designed walls or

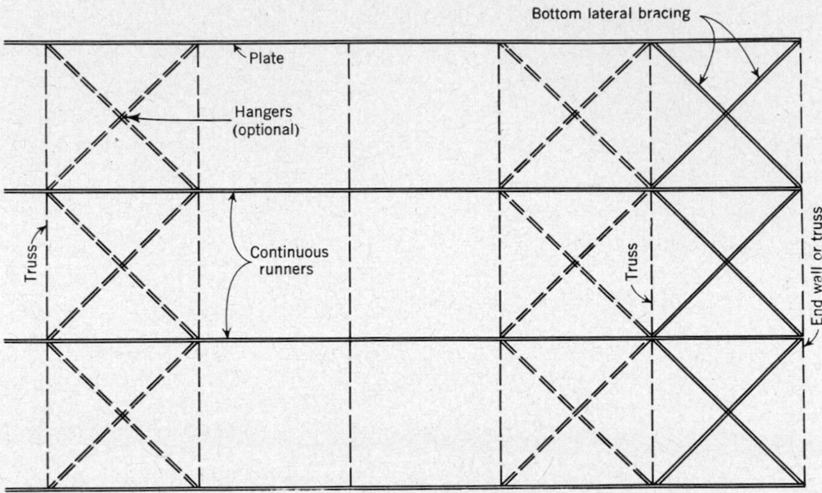

Fig. 5.13 Bottom lateral bracing

If required, bottom lateral bracing usually appears in same sections as vertical sway bracing. Members are fastened to truss or to horizontal runners and plate. Wood members may be used, or steel rods. Hangers *may be used from roof framing to eliminate sag in members.* Continuous runners *run full length of building. They may be nearly square, solid members or built up in "T," "U," or "I" shapes. They are fastened to bottom chord or web members near chord.* Built-up runners *should be spiked and bolted together. For* top lateral bracing, *diagonal roof sheathing well applied to joists or purlins—with these in turn securely fastened to the truss—is usually sufficient. Sometimes, however, bracing similar to bottom lateral bracing should be applied in the plane of the top chords.*

columns and columns in turn anchored to foundations. Unless some other provision is made for lateral loads on the side walls and on the vertical projection of the roof—such as for diaphragm action in walls and roof sheathing—lateral resistance should be provided in the column members by means of knee braces (Fig. 5.15) or fixity at the column base. The bracing should be designed and detailed with the same care as the truss itself and not left to the judgment of the contractor.

The bracing requirements here suggested are minimums, and are not dependent on actual lateral-load analysis or on local code requirements. Vertical cross-bracing should be installed at intervals along the span of not more than 35 ft and in every fourth bay between trusses. Horizontal struts should be installed at the bottom chord at the location of the vertical bracing and be continuous from end wall to end

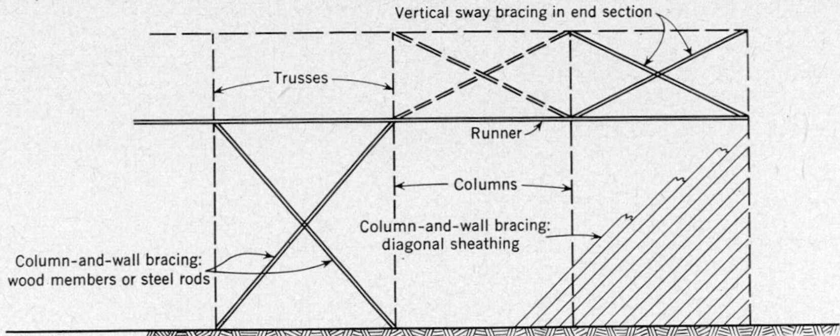

Fig. 5.14 Vertical sway bracing and wall-and-column bracing

Vertical sway bracing *is to be used in end section as a minimum, possibly two sections at each end and near midspan for long buildings. It consists of wood members or steel rods fastened to the truss, roof structure, or runners.* Column-and-wall bracing *should be used where possible. It may consist of diagonal sheathing with studs or girts, let-in bracing, or cross-bracing. Cross-bracing may be of wood members or steel rods.*

wall. Such struts and cross-bracing should be adequate for a minimum horizontal-compression load of 10 per cent of the bottom-chord stress. The 10 per cent may be distributed in ratio to the number of lines of cross-bracing and in proportion to the number of cross-braces in each line if additional bays in excess of the minimum are provided. Positive fastenings, such as bolts, lag screws, or timber connectors, should be provided. Special precautions should be taken to provide adequate bracing of trusses during and after erection and until the permanent bracing system and roof sheathing are installed.

A TYPICAL TRUSS AND BUILDING FRAME

5.25 Design conditions As an illustration of design methods and alternatives in design, the more important details of a 60 x 80-ft building with clear-span trusses will be developed in Sec. 5.25 to 5.34. The following conditions are assumed:

1. Fourteen-foot clearance under trusses
2. Trusses supported by columns with knee braces permissible

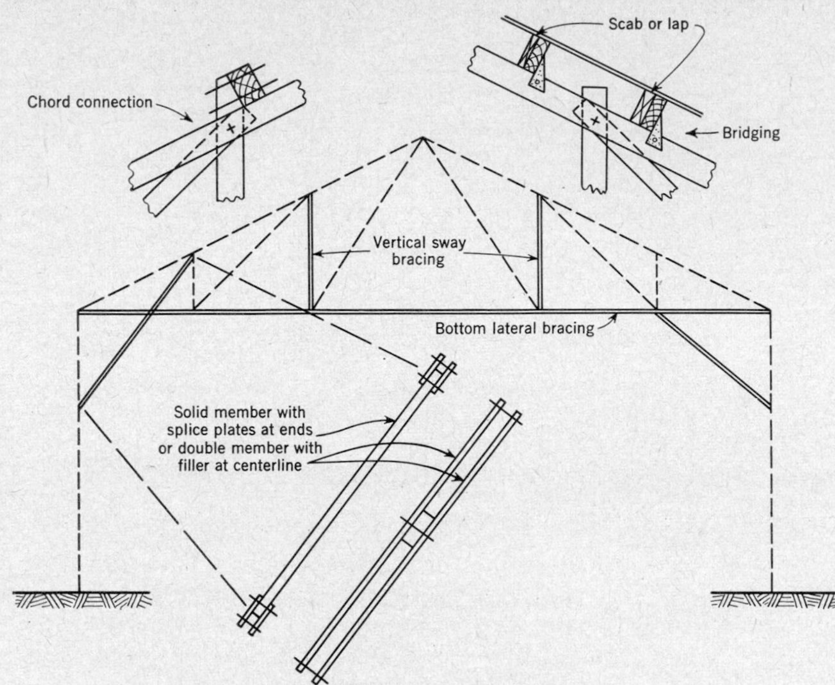

Fig. 5.15 Knee brace

Knee braces may connect at top- or bottom-chord panel point. Purlins or joists must be securely fastened to the chord. If possible, truss web members should be extended to make the connection. Bridging is to be applied as required. Purlins or joists should be lapped or joined bv scabs. Framing anchors may be used to fasten joists to chord.

3. Design loading of 30-psf live load and 15-psf dead load on the horizontal projection of the truss and walls
4. Bracing and column design loading of 20-psf horizontal wind load on the vertical projection

These are average design conditions. As noted in Chap. 12 (see Tables 12.40–12.45) live-load requirements vary considerably, and usually wind and other loads must also be considered in the design of the truss. Designers should make an estimate of dead load based on assumed methods of roof construction and on preliminary estimates of weight for the truss itself.

5.26 Selection of truss type As mentioned in Sec. 5.1, the three general types of truss that may be used are flat, pitched, and bowstring. A bowstring or pitched truss will be more efficient and economical than a flat truss for the structure in question, although all three types would be suitable. The roof framing cubage for heating will probably not vary more than 10 per cent between the three types if they are of usual proportions. The flat truss, unless it has a Howe end (sloping end post) requires higher side walls. All three may be adapted to a broached-end roof framing, similar to a hip-end, to save on end-wall height. The built-up roofing, such as tar and gravel surface, that is required for flat and bowstring trusses is more expensive than the shingle or roll roofing that can be used with the pitched type. Built-up roofs, however, may be used for pitched trusses as well. A pitched truss will be chosen for the primary analysis, but similar details will be developed for flat and bowstring trusses.

5.27 Selection of spacing As discussed in Sec. 5.22, many factors affect the choice of spacing of trusses. If considerations such as side-wall framing, spacing of side-wall supports for desired lateral clearance, type of roof framing, or available lengths and sizes of purlins or joists do not control, then the spacing may be chosen according to its suitability for the over-all building length. Other things being equal, trusses, columns, and foundations are more costly than framing between trusses. Therefore, the larger the spacing, the better—providing the dimensions do not complicate framing between trusses or require unduly heavy truss framing. For simple-span sawed purlins or joists between trusses, a 20-ft spacing is practical if 20-ft purlins in the required sizes are available. This spacing will require three trusses provided no trusses are assumed at the end walls. If 20-ft lengths are not available, the next shorter even spacing of 16 ft will require four trusses. The 16-ft spacing will be used for this problem as being more widely representative of available purlin lengths and sizes in many species of timber.

5.28 Selection of proportions The suggested minimum effective depth-to-span ratio for pitched trusses is between 1:5 and 1:6. (See discussion of truss proportions, Sec. 5.11–5.13.) The rise of a pitched truss with a 60-ft span would therefore be 10 to 12 ft. It is suggested that the lower rise be investigated first. If it should be found that stresses for the lower rise require substantially heavier members and connections than would those of a deeper truss, the designer may choose to increase the depth to improve the economy and perhaps to simplify construction details.

There are no rigid rules by which the most effective depth-to-span ratio can be assumed at the beginning. A slight change in the ratio can often bring considerable economy if the proportions originally assumed just exceed those which will permit the use of smaller members or simpler details. This possibility will be apparent to the designer after the stress analysis has been made and preliminary details worked out.

With a panel length of 6 to 10 ft, the top chord of this pitched truss might use from six to ten panels. The maximum chord and web stresses will not be altered substantially by the number of panels. For these particular span and loading conditions, experience shows that the assumption of six panels and joists along the top chord to introduce bending moment would result in excessive top-chord sizes unless high-stress-grade material were used. Eight panels will therefore be assumed for the top chord.

5.29 Selection of web system The discussion of web-member systems in Sec. 5.14–5.17 obviously could not cover the many factors involved in the selection of the best type of system for a particular truss. For normally proportioned pitched trusses, such as the one specified for this problem, either of the four basic web systems—Fink, Belgian, Pratt, or Howe—could be assumed.

The Fink type would be suggested only if there were reason to believe that the long length of compression web members near the center of the span would require unreasonable member sizes with the other types. No such difficulty is apparent in this example, and thus only the Pratt, Belgian, and Howe systems will be considered.

A study of web-member stresses for these three types shows that the Pratt system offers the shortest length compression web members but also the highest stressed tension web members. The Belgian system has the lowest stressed compression web members, although they are longer in length than those of the Pratt system; and stresses are relatively equal in its tension and compression web members. The Howe system has the longest compression web members and the largest compression stresses but also the lowest stressed tension members.

Given these relationships between stresses and lengths of web members, selection of a system frequently depends upon the possible presence of substantial differences among the three types not only in compression web-member sizes but also in their connections. The solution to these interrelated factors is dependent upon the general framing system, the thickness of material, and the type of connection assumed to be employed.

Assume that the truss will be of a multiple-member type that customarily uses timber connectors and frequently bolts as well; that the compression web members will be double members and the tension members single members; and that the relative positions of the members in the most highly stressed web-member joints will be as shown in Fig. 5.16. It will be found that the Howe-type web system requires

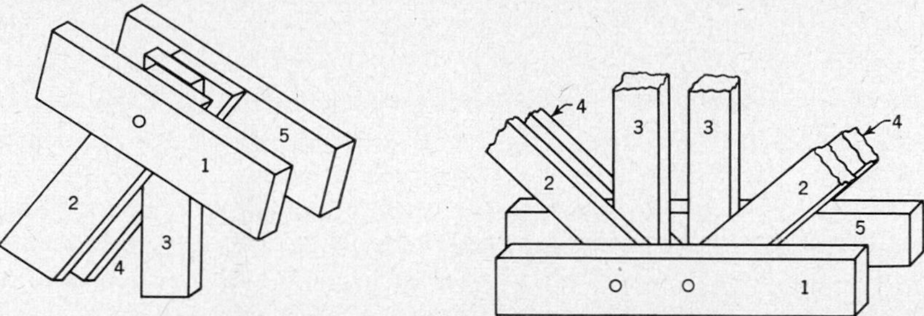

Fig. 5.16 Typical multiple-member truss joints

substantially the same size of material for the web members as the other types and offers the advantage of permitting single bolts with connectors at the connections to give a pin-joint effect. As the Belgian and Pratt systems would require two bolts with connectors for the web members near the centerline of the span, they would not be theoretically as desirable and would be somewhat more complicated and expensive to build. Even though pin- or single-bolted joints may require additional material, the savings in fabrication and improved theoretical action they obtain usually justify their use.

If the Belgian system permitted single-bolted joints with connectors, it would be preferable to the Howe not only because it requires somewhat less material—as a result of the shorter length of its double-compression web members—but also because it provides simple support and easy anchorage for joists or purlins at the top chord—by the extension of those web members that are perpendicular to the top chord. If the Pratt system permitted single-bolted connections, it would require the least amount of material of the three systems. As Pratt tension web members are more highly stressed than those of the other types, however, single connections with bolts and connectors are less likely to be sufficient.

For the truss in question, the assumed arrangement of members in the critical joint favors the Howe type of system with a two-piece vertical member at the centerline and the bottom-chord joint offset. Assume that the two-piece chord members will be lap-spliced at about the one-quarter span points and that they will be on the outside of the truss near the centerline and one member thickness apart near the ends of the truss. As will be explained in discussing angle of load to grain (see Sec. 5.49), the arrangement of members sometimes affects the number of connectors required in the joint. The arrangement of the compression web member near the centerline of this span, with a vertical member on one side and a chord member on the other, will permit the use of a single bolt with the connectors.

If the chord members are butt-spliced instead of lap-spliced, there will be no substantial difference in the connections required for the web members, and either the Pratt, Belgian, or Howe system could be used.

It should be noted that the use of fewer panels or a deeper truss would reduce the web-member stresses slightly; conversely, more panels and a shallower truss would increase them. These factors may also be considered in choosing or adjusting truss proportions for maximum economy. Such weighing of alternatives in choosing a web-member system and the arrangement of members in a multiple-member truss will result in the most economical, efficient, and practical solution.

5.30 Advantages of system selected The multiple-member system here chosen is probably the most widely used system for flat and pitched trusses. It provides sufficient room at the lap of the members for the installation of fastenings; permits the use of members of small thickness, which are generally more easily obtained and probably better seasoned than heavy timbers; frequently uses less material than solid-member trusses; and permits a direct transfer of stress from one primary member to another without their having to be joined by gusset plates or some other intermediate member. Generally speaking, shear connections are more efficient in relatively thin members than in heavy timber.

5.31 Stress analysis Figure 5.17a shows the stresses in a pitched truss for the conditions and proportions that have been assumed. These stresses are based on the vertical dead and live loads alone. (Only vertical loads are to be analyzed, as this book is not concerned with the details of building-frame stress analysis.) Also shown are stresses for a bowstring (Fig. 5.17b) and a flat truss (Fig. 5.17c) of normal proportions. It is obvious that the bowstring offers the greatest theoretical economy because its chord and web-member stresses are smaller than those for the pitched and flat trusses of the proportions indicated. If a deeper pitched truss were used, its chord stresses might be as low as those of the bowstring, but the web stresses would not change appreciably. The comparatively large web stresses for the flat truss make

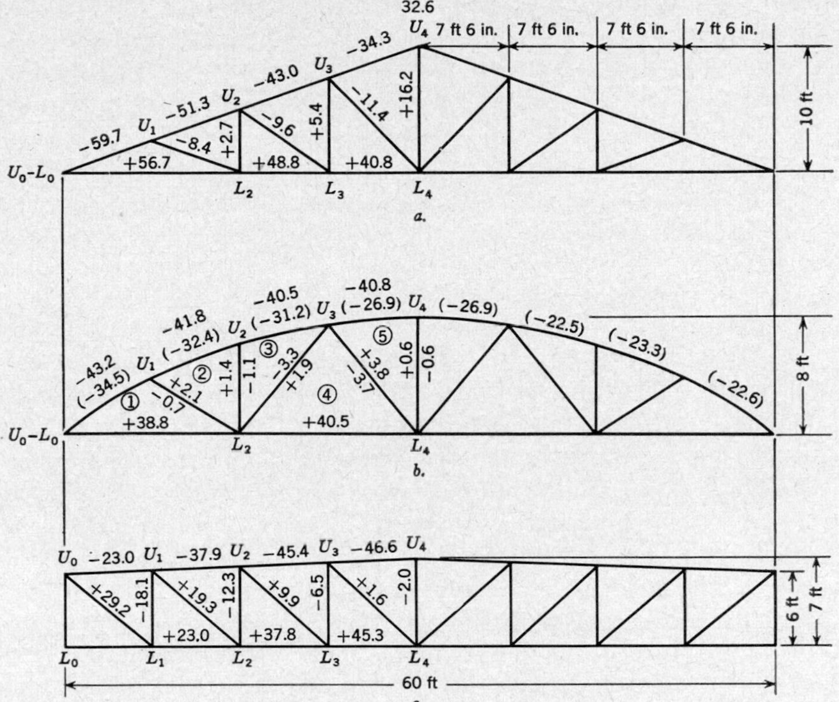

Fig. 5.17 Alternate truss types and design stresses

it the most expensive. The web-member stresses and the chord stresses of the bowstring (indicated in the diagram by parentheses) are for full load on the left half of the span and dead load on the right half. The other chord stresses shown on the left half are for full uniform load. Code requirements differ, and some permit design for only ½ the live load on one side and full live load or dead load on the other.

Vertical load requirements control for most pitched and flat trusses because wind load in combination with partial vertical live load will probably not require larger sections or connections than will vertical load alone. The designer, however, must satisfy himself that unbalanced loading or the combination of wind with other loading will not produce the critical condition. Wind will more likely be critical for roofs that are very steep, or, as in the South, that are designed for snow loads which are relatively light compared with wind load. The designer must also consider the stresses introduced in the truss by the column and knee-brace connections as a result of lateral loads such as wind or earthquake.

5.32 Stress-grade of material Allowable unit stresses in pounds per square inch for the truss and roof-framing material can be assumed as: 1,400 extreme fiber in bending, 1,200 compression parallel to grain, 120 horizontal shear, 390 compression perpendicular to grain, and 1,760,000 modulus of elasticity. Although these values do not correspond exactly to any one grade or species, the designer will note in NDS Table 1 of Chap. 13 that there are a number of grades and species that have values within the limits of these unit stresses. In practice, the designer may wish to assume an exact species and grade, depending on local availability.

5.33 Thickness of material For a multiple-member truss, thickness of material will generally be 2-, 3-, or 4-in. nominal. The exact choice of thickness will depend upon size requirements for the stresses involved, the type of fastening used, and the length of compression members (from the standpoint of slenderness ratio).

For the truss in question, 2- or 3-in. material will be adequate, although 4-in. material could also be used. The thinner members are more efficient in that they require a greater width and thus provide additional area for fastenings at the joints. If the system of framing were of the gusset plate or rod-and-block style, with single solid truss members, 4- or 6-in. thickness would be assumed.

5.34 Type of fastening Bolts and bolts with timber connectors are the most commonly used fastenings in timber trusses regardless of the type of framing. Both are designed in approximately the same manner. For the truss in question, it will be assumed that timber connectors are to be used, although a few bolt details will also be shown. Split rings will be chosen because they are the most efficient of the timber connectors for wood-to-wood connections and the most adaptable to prefabrication. It is desirable to have as few bolts with connectors at each joint as possible. Designers therefore prefer to use the 4-in.-diameter split ring because it has about double the capacity of the $2\frac{1}{2}$-in. size and thus permits fewer connectors and simpler details. Nominal surfaced 2-in. lumber is the minimum size that can take 4-in. split rings in opposite faces of the same number, but net section requirements and the higher allowable connector loads favor nominal 3-in. material. Therefore, assume that the members with connectors in opposite faces will be of 3-in. thickness, and that members on the outside—which have connectors in only one face—will be of 2-in. material. The minimum nominal width of members using 4-in. split rings is 6 in.; thus the minimum member sizes will be either 2 x 6 or 3 x 6.

DESIGN OF TRUSS COMPRESSION MEMBERS

5.35 General design procedure Deciding whether truss members or truss joints should be designed first is relatively unimportant. As web member sizes are frequently determined by minimum requirements for the connections, it is suggested that they be designed at the same time as the connections. Chord members are usually designed first and the web members and connections next.

Wider chord members are desirable because they provide the larger area for web member connections. A 3 x 8 provides about the same cross-sectional area as a 2 x 12, but the 2 x 12 may be better for connections and will be superior for bending stresses. If it is found later that a larger chord size is necessary to meet the connection requirements, consideration should then be given to changing truss proportions, such as the number of panels or depth of truss, in order to make fuller use of the larger chord section.

The discussions and computations presented here are intended to illustrate the design procedures usually followed, and to call attention to the possible variables or alternatives. Sometimes only the controlling stress conditions at a joint are considered, but it should be remembered that in practice a similar procedure is used for the analysis of other stresses as well.

5.36 Top-chord members In multiple-member trusses (see Fig. 5.17), the chord members are usually composed of two members separated by one or more web members, and the top chords are designed as spaced columns providing that lateral support is furnished by purlins at the panel points. For the special design problems presented by the top chords of bowstring trusses, see Sec. 5.39–5.43.

There are no universally accepted definitions of what constitutes adequate lateral support, although some building codes establish arbitrary standards. (See Chap. 13, NDS, par. 400-F-4.) It is suggested that purlins 3 in. or more in thickness and 4 ft or more on centers be firmly anchored to the truss by bolt or lag screws of not less than ⅜-in. diameter. This connection may be made by means of blocking or metal clips, extension of members, or special devices.

Joists spaced less than 4 ft apart are often accepted as lateral support if well toenailed to the top of the chord, or if nailed to blocking that in turn is nailed to the chord. Joists and purlins may also be notched slightly to fit tightly to the sides of the chord. Special metal clips for joists serve the dual purpose of giving better lateral support than is provided by toenailing and of improving resistance to roof uplift.

Plank or laminated deck spanning between trusses and spiked to the chords also is usually considered adequate for lateral support.

Tabulated working stresses should be adjusted for duration of load and for moisture content, if necessary, and the allowable load determined for the appropriate ratio of unsupported length to least dimension (see Chaps. 4 and 13). The end connection for truss members acting as spaced columns corresponds to condition "a" of Chap. 13 (NDS, par. 401-F-4), in which the connections are within $l/20$ from the end. In truss members, the connections are at the theoretical end of the column. Adjustment in allowable working stresses for duration of load in compression apply to E and to tabulated c values.

For the assumed grade of material and normal loading, the allowable compression parallel to grain, c, is 1,200 psi and the modulus of elasticity, E, 1,760,000 psi. As the maximum stress is caused by snow load combined with dead load, both c and P/A may be increased 15 per cent.

The allowable unit stress, P/A, for the top-chord section U_0–U_1 of Fig. 5.17a is determined by the spaced column formula (Chap. 13, NDS):

$$P/A = \frac{0.3E \times 2.5}{(l/d)^2}$$

in which l equals the length between lateral supports in inches, or panel length, here 95 in., and d equals the least dimension of member in inches, here 2⅝ in., assuming nominal 3-in. lumber. Thus:

$$l/d = 95/2.625 = 36.2$$

$$P/A = 0.3 \times \frac{1{,}760{,}000}{(36.2)^2} \times 2.5 = 1{,}010 \text{ psi normal load}$$

$$P/A = 1{,}010 \times 1.15 = 1{,}160 \text{ psi snow load}$$

The allowable working stress, P/A, must not exceed the appropriate allowable compression parallel to the grain. Computing the latter for snow load, we have:

$$c = 1{,}200 \times 1.15 = 1{,}380 \text{ psf}$$

If the spaced column curves of Chap. 12 (Fig. 12.1) had been used to determine the allowable P/A, it would have been obvious whether P/A exceeded the c value.

The required column (top-chord) area, A', is the axial stress in compression, P', divided by the allowable unit stress (either P/A or c, whichever is least). In this example:

$$A' = \frac{P'}{P/A} = \frac{59{,}700}{1{,}160} = 51.4 \text{ sq in. required}$$

This area will require two 3 x 12 members, providing 60.38 sq in.

The top-chord sizes determined by the spaced column design must be adequate to satisfy the simple column formula, using a greater dimension of 11.5 in. and a length between vertical supports of 95 in.:

$$P/A = \frac{0.3E}{(l/d)^2}$$

$$l/d = 95/11.5 = 8.25$$

$$P/A = \frac{0.3 \times 1{,}760{,}000 \times 1.15}{(8.25)^2} = 8{,}930 \text{ psi}$$

The allowable compression based on this analysis is greater than that for the spaced column analysis, which controls. This check of a spaced column as a simple column will not be necessary if the ratio of l/d of the spaced column, condition "a," is more than 1.6 times that for the simple column, or if condition "b" (Chap. 13, NDS, par. 401-F-4) is more than 1.75 times that for a simple column.

Required net section is determined from the National Design Specification (Chap. 13, par. 502-B-1) either on the basis of clear material with no knots in the net section, or on the more conservative basis of 87.5 per cent of the allowable unit stress in bending for the grade of lumber used. Assuming a Group B species, the net section constant for snow loading with lumber 4 in. or less thick is 2,300. For clear lumber, the axial stress, 59,700 lb, divided by the net-section constant, 2,300, equals the required net section, 25.9 sq in.

The conservative method gives a much higher requirement: 59,700 divided by $1{,}400 \times 1.15 \times 0.875$, or 42.3 sq in. However, unless designers make sure that knots will not occur at the joints–by specification provisions and competent inspection–this method is preferred for computing net-section requirements. Net-section and the end spacer-block requirements are frequently checked at the time joint details are determined.

The end spacer-block constant for an l/d ratio of 36.2 and Group B material is 205 (see Chap. 13, NDS Table 3). Therefore, the connections in the end spacer blocks between the chord members (in this truss the web members) must be adequate for 205×25.7 (required area of one member of the column) or 5,280 lb.

5.37 Web members It has already been assumed that the compression web members for the chosen truss are to be spaced double members 3 in. thick and therefore to be designed as spaced columns. The same procedure is followed for them as for the top-chord member. For web member U_3–L_4 of Fig. 5.17a, $l = 122$ in.; $d = 2.625$ in; $l/d = 46.5$; $E = 1{,}760{,}000$ psi; $c = 1{,}200 \times 1.15 = 1{,}380$ psi; $P' = 11{,}400$ lb. Thus:

$$P/A = \frac{0.3 \times 1{,}760{,}000 \times 2.5 \times 1.15}{(46.5)^2} = 700 \text{ psi (controls)}$$

$$\frac{P'}{P/A} = \frac{11{,}400}{700} = 16.3 \text{ sq in. required}$$

Although two 3 x 4 members will provide 19.04 sq in., the minimum face width for the 4-in. split rings previously assumed is 6 in. nominal. Thus two 3 x 6 members will be used for member U_3–L_4 instead.

Required net section should be checked as outlined for the top-chord member. Because 3 x 6 members are to be used where only 3 x 4 members are required, however, the net section will be much more than needed.

The end spacer-block constant equals 289. Therefore, the required connection in the end spacer blocks (in this example the tension web member) equals 8.15 (required area of one member of the column) multiplied by 289, or 2,360 lb.

5.38 Combined compression and bending The top chord of the pitched truss (Fig. 5.17a) may be designed for joists on 16- to 24-in. spacing along the length or for purlins between panel points. Either way, the member is designed for combined bending and axial (compression) stress. For closely spaced joists, the bending moment, M, is usually computed as for a simple beam with uniform loading. Assuming that each joist provides lateral restraint for the chord, the l/d ratio will be small, and usually the allowable c value will control rather than the column formula. (See Chap. 13, NDS, par. 400-F-4.) The chord is then designed as a simple column. Assume joists spaced 24 in. on centers, an l of 24 in., and a d of 2.625 in. (3-in. lumber). Then:

$$l/d = 9.2$$

$$P/A = \frac{0.3 \times 1{,}760{,}000 \times 1.15}{(9.2)^2} = 7{,}170 \text{ psi}$$

$$c = 1{,}200 \times 1.15 = 1{,}380 \text{ psi (controls)}$$

$$f = 1{,}400 \times 1.15 = 1{,}610 \text{ psi}$$

$$A' = \frac{P'}{c} = \frac{59{,}700}{1{,}380} = 43.2 \text{ sq in. required}$$

The bending moment, M, equals $Wl^2/8$ where W equals the load per linear foot and l equals the horizontal projection of panel length. If $W = 40 \times 16 = 640$ lb per lin ft (40 psf is assumed for dead and live loads on the roof, with 5 psf dead load assumed for the balance of the truss itself) and $l = 7.5$ ft, then:

$$M = \frac{640 \times (7.5)^2 \times 12}{8} = 54{,}000 \text{ in.-lb}$$

The section modulus required, S, equals M/f. Therefore:

$$S = 54{,}000/1{,}610 = 33.6$$

If two 3 x 12 members are used, they will furnish an area of 60.38 sq in. and a section modulus of 115.72. It is required that the sum of the two ratios—the area required to that furnished and the section modulus required to that furnished—must be equal to or less than 1 (See Chap. 13, NDS, par. 403-B-2). In this instance, the sum works out as follows:

$$43.2/60.38 + 33.6/115.72 = 0.715 + 0.291 = 1.006$$

Many designers would accept two 3 x 12 members as they are theoretically less than 1 per cent overstressed, and the simple beam bending moment is conservative. The size could be increased to either 3 x 14 or 4 x 10.

The top-chord size is determined for the most highly stressed panel, and frequently the same size is used throughout the length of the truss. Sometimes, however, the top chord is figured for the lower direct stress occurring near the center, and a smaller chord size may be spliced into that portion of the truss. In preliminary analysis, the top chord is generally assumed to be a simple beam between panels, although analysis of the chord as a continuous beam with a possibly somewhat smaller bending moment may sometimes be justified.

DESIGN OF BOWSTRING TOP CHORDS

5.39 Procedures according to chord type If the top chords of a bowstring truss are laminated or sawed to curvature, the design procedure differs from that for straight members because of the eccentricity of the member with regard to a straight line between panel points. For glued-laminated members, the procedure also differs because of the higher allowable working stresses.

If the bowstring top chord is truly segmental—not sawed to curvature—its design is similar to that of the top chord for a pitched truss. If it is a monochord with purlins only at the panel points, it is designed as a simple column. If sawed to curvature, a segmental split (two-member) chord is similar to the segmental monochord except that it may act as a spaced column.

5.40 Eccentricity Eccentricity in a bowstring top chord must be considered in so far as it affects secondary bending moment and possible reduction in allowable compression stress. (See Chap. 13, NDS, Appendix B.) There is no reduction in P/A due to bending moment or eccentricity unless the l/d ratio in the plane of the eccentricity, that is, the ratio of panel length to depth of member, exceeds 11.

5.41 Segmental sawed top chords For a segmental sawed top chord in the truss of Fig. 5.17b, the eccentricity would be 1 in. (see Fig. 5.18a). This produces a negative bending moment that will reduce the effect of positive bending introduced by loads along the chord.

The critical combination of live-load bending moment and direct-stress eccentric bending moment may be for either full uniform loading

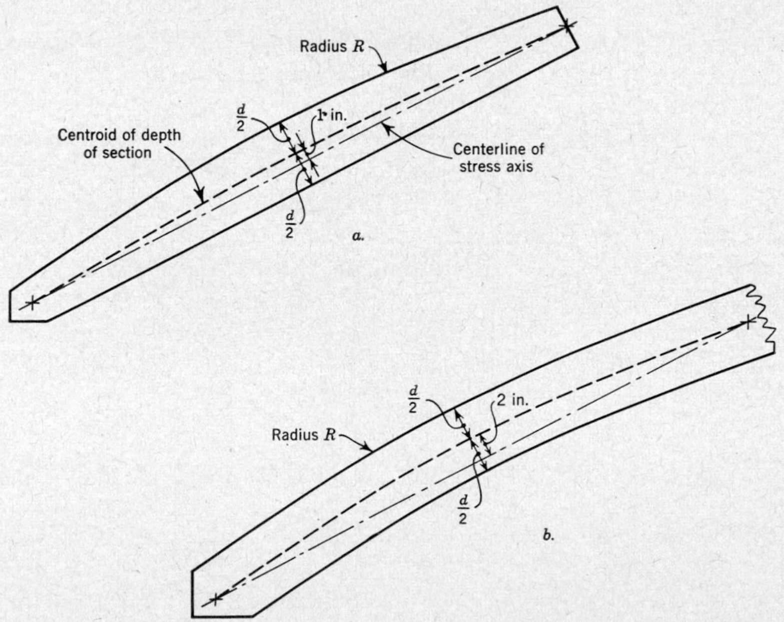

Fig. 5.18 Eccentricity in bowstring top chord

a. Segmental sawed chord *b. Laminated chord*

or unbalanced loading. With unbalanced loading, the critical or controlling panel may be either on the loaded or unloaded side. It is possible that the eccentric bending moment may add to the live-load moment if the chord segment is two panels long.

The requirements based on full uniform load and panel U_0–U_1 are nearly identical to requirements based on unbalanced loading and the same panel on the loaded side. Computations for full loading—assuming that joint spacing = 24 in.; $l = 24$ in.; $d = 2.625$ (3-in. lumber); and $P' = 43{,}200$ lb—follow:

$$l/d = 9.2$$
$$c = 1{,}200 \times 1.15 = 1{,}380 \text{ psi}$$
$$f = 1{,}400 \times 1.15 = 1{,}610 \text{ psi}$$
$$A' = P'/c = 43{,}200/1{,}380 = 31.3 \text{ sq in. required}$$
$$M = Wl^2/8 - P'e \quad \text{(where } W = 40 \times 16 = 640 \text{ lb per lin ft, as before, and } e = \text{eccentricity} = 1 \text{ in.)}$$
$$= \frac{640 \times (7.5)^2 \times 12}{8} - (43{,}200 \times 1) = -10{,}800 \text{ in.-lb}$$
$$S = M/f = 10{,}800/1{,}610 = 6.7 \text{ required}$$

Many alternatives will satisfy these A and S requirements, such as one 3 x 14 or 4 x 12 member, or two 3 x 8 or 4 x 6 members. If the 3 x 8 or 4 x 6 members are desired, however, analysis must be made of them as eccentric columns in a vertical plane. This will show that two 3 x 10 or 4 x 8 members are needed instead.

If purlins, instead of equally spaced joists, are used at the panel points, the bending moment will be restricted to that caused by the eccentricity of curvature. The chords should therefore not be sawed to curvature, because the centerline of the member may then coincide with the line of axial stress and thereby eliminate eccentricity.

The length of chord between panel points is 101 in. at the end panel. If the 3 x 8 or 4 x 6 members are chosen, the l/d ratio in a vertical plane will be 13.5 and 18.4 respectively, and the combined loading must be checked as for eccentric columns (see Chap. 13). Obviously, the deeper members are the more efficient.

Segmental split (two-member) chords that are sawed to curvature are frequently used with staggered splices in the two members. The members accordingly are not identical in size at the same section. The axial load may be assumed equally divided, because the two segments correspond to parallel arches, each spliced the same number of times. It is necessary to have a tight fit at the ends of the sections and desirable to use metal bearing plates of not less than 20 gauge. Such plates are mandatory for monochords as well as split chords and any other wood-to-wood end bearing if the end compression exceeds 75 per cent of the allowable parallel-to-grain compression value.

If a chord has staggered splices, bending moment occurs only in the unspliced member at the point of the splice in the other. Considering continuity, it is reasonable to design the member that is continuous through the splice for 80 per cent of the bending moment of a simple beam, less any negative moment due to eccentricity in the top chord.

5.42 Glued-laminated top chords For a glued-laminated top chord (Fig. 5.18b), the eccentricity will be 2 in., or double that for the segmental sawed chord. For laminated grades corresponding to those of solid sawed members, allowable normal load stresses in pounds per square inch might be: $c = 1{,}900$; $f = 2{,}000$; $c_{\perp} = 390$; $H = 165$ (see Chap. 13, NDS Table 20). These stresses are increased 15 per cent for snow loading.

If 2-in. nominal lumber is assumed for laminating, the f value is modified by a curvature factor that is dependent on the thickness of the laminations and the radius of curvature (equal to span in this example).

$$\text{Curvature factor} = 1 - 2{,}000\left(\frac{1{,}625}{60 \times 12}\right)^2 = 0.989$$

$$f = 2{,}000 \times 0.989 \times 1.15 = 2{,}270 \text{ psi}$$

$$A' = P'/c = 43{,}200/2{,}180 = 19.8 \text{ sq in. required}$$

$$M = \frac{640 \times 7.5 \times 7.5 \times 12}{10} - (43{,}200 \times 2) = -43{,}200 \text{ in.-lb}$$

$$S = M/f = \frac{43{,}200}{2{,}270} = 18.95 \text{ required}$$

A denominator of 10 was used in the bending formula because of the continuity of the glued-laminated chord. Some designers disregard continuity and use 8, but in this truss the value 10 gives a more conservative requirement. The conservative practice is to use a denominator of either 8 or 10 for bending moment, depending upon which gives the higher net requirement.

The higher allowable unit stresses of glued-laminated lumber permit the use of smaller member sizes. If 2 x 3 or 2 x 4 lumber is used in the lamination, the dressed width will be 2¼ and 3¼ in., respectively. The depth will be an even multiple of 1⅝ in. Several alternatives will satisfy the A and S requirements (such as one 3¼ x 9¾-member or two 2¼ x 8⅛-members) so that the ratios of area required to that furnished and of section modulus required to that furnished may have a sum equal to or less than 1.

The continuous glued-laminated chords are subject to a further check as eccentric columns in a vertical plane, but the slenderness ratio, l/d, is based on an assumed distance, l, between points of contraflexure in a continuous member. This distance may be assumed to be about 60 to 66 per cent of the panel length for interior unspliced panels and 75 per cent of the panel length for end panels. On this basis, the glued-laminated member sizes of the preceding example prove satisfactory, because the l/d ratio is less than 11 if $d = 8\frac{1}{8}$ in.

If the top chord of the bowstring is continuous, it must also be checked for bending moment at the panel points. An assumed bending moment that is 80 per cent of that of a simple span beam is suggested. If there is eccentricity of web-member connections, the bending moment resulting from the eccentricity is added to the moment due to continuity.

The bending moment due to joint eccentricity is equal to the component of the web-member stress normal to the top chord multiplied by the "offset," or distance between the web-member connections. If two web members are connected to a continuous chord, the designer may calculate the moment at each of the web-member connections due to the other web-member stress, and the moment due to the purlin or assumed panel-point load, and then average the two bending moments thus obtained. The average bending moment determined by this empirical method is assumed to be distributed as $\frac{1}{2}$ positive moment to one side of the joint and $\frac{1}{2}$ negative moment to the other side. The negative moment adds to the panel moment that is caused by continuity. For three eccentric web members, the moments due to joint eccentricity are calculated only at the outer connections, not at the center member (see Sec. 5.55).

The chosen size of the glued-laminated members must be checked for radial tension or radial compression due to the bending moment (see Chap. 13, NDS, par. 903-C-2). In the preceding example, the net negative bending moment induces radial compression, but its magnitude is very small. Radial forces will seldom be critical if members have little curvature or if the bending moment is not the primary design factor.

5.43 Nailed-laminated top chords Nailed-laminated top chords, like glued-laminated chords in bowstring trusses, must be designed for axial compressive stress, for bending moment due to joist loading and eccentricity, and for bending moment and shear due to eccentric web-member connections. Even though nailed-laminated chords may be continuous over several panels, the efficiency of the nailing and of staggered butt joints is not high enough to permit full continuity. For joist loading, most engineers design in terms of simple span bending moments. Figure 5.19 illustrates a section of a nail-laminated bowstring truss.

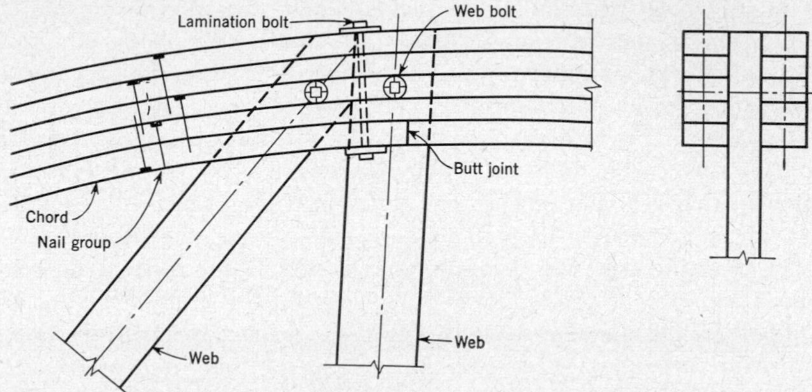

Fig. 5.19 Mechanically laminated truss chord

The butt end-bearing joints of individual laminations, if fabricated accurately, may be assumed to have full bearing, because the nails permit the slight slippage necessary for adjustment. Butt joints should not be assumed effective for bending stresses and should be so spaced that at any given section there are at least two unspliced laminations adjacent to a spliced lamination. Butt splices in interior laminations should not exceed ⅓ of the section. Splices in exterior laminations should not be closer than 36 in. and preferably should be in different panels. The fewer splices and the greater the spacing of splices, the better.

The nailing of mechanical, laminated top chords of bowstring trusses usually assumes a predetermined nailing pattern with nail size and spacings arbitrarily chosen. Generally, the allowable shear for the nails or spikes may be based on the number of shear planes penetrated. Thus a nail penetrating ½ the third lamination is considered effective in two shear planes, and a nail penetrating ½ the fourth lamination is considered effective in three shear planes. The largest diameter and longest length that can be driven without undue splitting should be selected.

The following nailing pattern has been used for average conditions. For 2-in. nominal-thickness laminations, the first two laminations are nailed with 16d nails and each additional lamination nailed to these laminations with 30d nails. For 3-in. nominal-thickness laminations, 30d and 50d nails are used. Nailing is started with inner laminations;

after the members are built up to full size, the first lamination is back-nailed with 30d or 50d nails depending on the thickness of individual laminations. Nails are generally spaced one to each lamination for 3- and 4-in. widths and are slightly staggered in order to miss the nails in the next lamination. They are driven nearly on top of one another so that they lie in groups from inner to outer lamination. These groups should be evenly spaced between panel points at intervals not exceeding 24 in. and so placed as to avoid lamination bolts and panel-point joints.

Bolts, generally of ⅝-in. diameter, are placed close to each panel point and extend through all laminations. The net-section area must be checked for axial and bending stresses.

Bolts with timber connectors used to join webs to chords may be installed without regard to the positioning of the bolt within the individual laminations of the chord. The action of the bolt is the same whether it falls within a lamination or in a joint between laminations. Connectors with bolts in the side of a nailed-laminated member are not so effective as in a solid member. Although no test data are available, it is recommended that loads not exceed 60 to 75 per cent of those for solid members. Under these conditions, designers may similarly reduce bolt values as well.

Tabulated allowable working stresses for nailed horizontally laminated chords are the same as those for the grade of lumber used. The primary question in design is the proper d to use to determine the l/d ratio for allowable compression parallel to grain with respect to column action in a vertical plane. The d for action in a generally horizontal plane is either the width of the lamination or the width of the coverplate or cap that may be used with a double-leaf chord. Such a cap is not considered as resisting axial or bending stress but only as stiffening the chords. (See Sec. 4.20.)

For column action in a vertical plane, the stiffness of the nailed horizontally laminated section is somewhat superior—because of friction and the shear resistance of the nails—to the stiffness of the individual laminations, but not greatly so. Designers experienced in this type of work have many different arbitrary rules for the determination of d; they include, if four or more laminations are involved:

1. A product ½ again as great as the thickness of the lamination.
2. An average of the thickness and the width of the lamination.
3. The width of the lamination, providing the P/A value thus determined is reduced in a straight-line manner, when l exceeds 60 in., from 0 per cent at 60 in. to 50 per cent at 96 in. and greater lengths.

Consider the design of the top chord of the bowstring truss of Fig. 5.17b as a nailed horizontally laminated member. The axial compression is 43,200 lb; the net bending moment due to simple beam bending and curvature, —32,400 in.-lb; the vertical shear (as simple beam), 2,700 lb; the length between panel points, 101 in. Assume 2 x 4 lumber for the laminations. The design for combined bending and compression in a vertical plane obviously controls because there is no bending in the horizontal plane and the slenderness ratio, l/d, is less in the horizontal plane.

Of the three methods given for determining *d,* the first would give an l/d of 41.4, the second of 38.5, and the third of 27.9. The appropriate normal-load allowable stress, P/A, would be 309 psi by the first method, 352 by the second, and 340 by the third. These values may be increased 15 per cent for snow loading, to 355, 405, and 391 psi, respectively. As the slenderness ratio in each method exceeds 11, the combined stress must be checked as for an eccentric column. (See Chap. 13, NDS Appendix B.) The allowable bending stress for the grade is modified for curvature.

Computations will show that two members, each built up of ten 2 x 4 pieces, are needed to satisfy the requirements. Each member will thus have a net size of $3\frac{5}{8}$ x $16\frac{1}{4}$ in. All ten pieces are assumed effective for compression, but the section modulus is based on only nine pieces as one outside lamination may be spliced at the point of maximum moment. If glued- instead of nailed-laminated chords were used, two $2\frac{1}{4}$ x $8\frac{1}{8}$ members would satisfy the requirements, as would two 3 x 10 or two 4 x 8 segmental sawed chords. Obviously the nailed-laminated chord is less economical.

The horizontal shear at the neutral axis of the nailed-laminated members will be about 125 lb per in. of length for 2,700 lb total vertical shear. The size and spacing of nails previously discussed are theoretically not adequate for this amount of shear. Thus, either the vertical shear is much less than the 2,700 lb based on simple beam action, or more likely, a substantial resistance to horizontal shear is provided by friction between laminations.

DESIGN OF TRUSS TENSION MEMBERS

5.44 Bottom chords Tension members are simple to design because the slenderness ratio is not a factor as it is in compression members. The required cross-sectional area is determined from the allowable axial tension stress, f (see Chap. 13, NDS Table 1), with adjustment for duration of load.

The bottom-chord stresses in Fig. 5.17 vary from 56,700 to 40,800 lb for the pitched truss, from 40,500 to 38,800 lb for the bowstring, and from 45,300 to 23,000 lb for the flat truss. Assume an allowable tensile stress of 1,400 $\times$ 1.15, or 1,610 psi. If the chords are built up of two members, member sizes for the pitched truss could thus be 2 x 12 or 3 x 8; for the bowstring truss, 2 x 10 or 3 x 6; and for the flat truss, 2 x 10 or 3 x 6 (assuming in each case that the joints will not require larger sizes). Net section is checked on the same basis as outlined for top chords (see Sec. 5.36).

The designer may tentatively select sizes based on about ⅔ of the usual stress and then check the net section after the joint details have been developed. On this conservative basis, the tentative member sizes would be 3 x 12 for the pitched-truss chord, 3 x 8 for the bowstring chord, and 3 x 10 for the flat-truss chord.

As no ceiling loads were assumed, the bottom chords are subject to direct axial tension only, not considering bending moment due to the dead weight of the members themselves. If ceiling or other loading introduces bending, computations are similar to those for combined loading on the top chord (see Sec. 5.38). Net section is less likely to control if there is combined axial and bending stress, because a larger section is required for the bending.

DESIGN OF SUPPLEMENTAL STRUCTURAL UNITS

5.45 Joists or purlins For the pitched truss of Fig. 5.17, assume a dead and live roof load of 40 psf. If wood sheathing is used, it is suggested that the vertical load ordinarily be considered as acting normal to the joists or purlins. Such analysis is conservative if the sheathing or rafters, in tension or compression, will carry the component parallel to the roof slope. The diaphragm action of the sheathing or rafters will aid in transferring the parallel component to the trusses, walls, or ridge. In unusually steep roofs, special consideration of normal and parallel components may be necessary—particularly at the peak where the parallel-to-slope components may introduce secondary loading on the joist or purlin.

If the members are computed as 16-ft simple beams (either independently or by means of the tables in Chap. 12) with an allowable bending stress, f, of 1,400 $\times$ 1.15, or 1,610 psi, it will be found that

2 x 10 joists spaced 24 in. on center are adequate. Moreover, 6 x 10 or 4 x 12 purlins at the panel points will also be found satisfactory. These sizes are based on bending alone, but deflection can be similarly checked if it is limited. For deflection computations, the tabulated modulus of elasticity is used without any increases for duration of loading, such as are used in column computations involving E values.

Joists along a top chord usually, but not always, require a larger size chord than is required by purlins at panel points. If purlins are used at panel points, the designer must provide spacer blocks at the mid-panel points on the top chord to give the spaced column action assumed. If joists are used along the top chord, the spacer block is not necessary, because the chords are designed as simple columns. However, if the joists are assumed in l/d computations to support the top chord laterally, they must be securely anchored to the chord. Anchoring can be accomplished by fastening short wood members between the chord members, by notching the joists partially down beside the top chord, by supporting the joists with a joist-hanger arrangement beside the chords, or by fastening metal clips or framing anchors to the chord and to the joists. If joists or purlins are on a slope, the wood sheathing or rafters usually give the required lateral support and resistance to the component of the load along the slope, provided the opposite sides of the roof are well joined over the center of the truss. Material that does not have the strength or stiffness of wood sheathing may have to be designed for sag rods—to eliminate the bending parallel to the slope—or for the installation of bridging—in order that the outer wall may resist the parallel component. Purlins can also be designed for loading about two axes, one parallel and one normal to the roof, for the appropriate components of the vertical load.

5.46 Sheathing and rafters If purlins are used with the pitched truss, plank spanning between purlins, or rafters along the slope, can be used. The tables of Chap. 12 or independent computations will show that 2-in. plank is sufficient, as are 2 x 6 rafters, 24 in. on center, or 2 x 4 rafters, 16 in. on center with 1-in. wood sheathing. Although rafters require less lumber, the extra labor they involve makes it more desirable to use plank.

One-inch sheathing supported by joists or rafters on spacing up to possibly 24 in. need not be computed as a rule. Recommendations for plywood sheathing are given in Chap. 9.

Frequently plank or laminated deck is applied directly to the top chords of trusses without the use of purlins or joists. This method requires more material than if joists or purlins are used but permits some savings in labor costs. It also provides a more finished appearance, better thermal insulation, and improved fire resistance. A 4-in. plank or laminated deck can be used for this 16-ft spacing of trusses.

5.47 Columns Figure 5.20 illustrates wind and vertical loads on the pitched-truss bent, assuming 26-ft over-all height, 16-ft spacing, knee brace 9 ft from column base, girts at one-third wall-height points, 20-lb horizontal wind forces divided either 1:1 or 3:2 between windward and leeward columns, 45 psf total vertical load on leeward slope, and 15 psf dead load on windward slope.

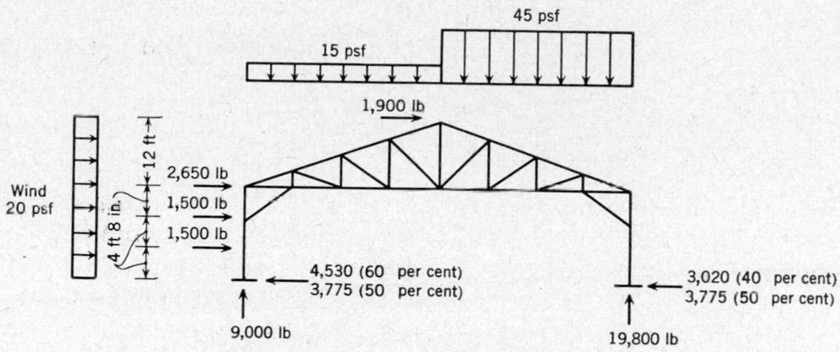

Fig. 5.20 Wind-load diagram for a pitched truss

Computations using a ⅓ increase in allowable stresses for combined bending and direct stress at the knee brace on the leeward column—which has the higher axial compression and bending moment—show that 10 x 14 or 12 x 12 columns are required for the 1:1 distribution, and 10 x 12 or 8 x 14 columns for the 3:2 distribution. These dimensions assume no fixity at the column base; the columns must be laterally braced along the wall by the girts or wall framing. The computations are as follows:

$f = 1{,}400 \times 1.33 = 1{,}860$ psi

$M = 3{,}775 \times 9 \times 12 = 408{,}000$ in.-lb

$S = M/f = 408{,}000/1{,}860 = 219$ cu in. required for 1:1 shear distribution

$M = 3{,}020 \times 9 \times 12 = 326{,}000$ in.-lb

$S = M/f = 326{,}000/1{,}860 = 175$ cu in. required for 3:2 shear distribution

$P' = 19{,}800$ lb

$c = 1{,}200 \times 1.33 = 1{,}600$ psi

$A = P/c = 19{,}800/1{,}600 = 12.38$ sq in. required

$$\frac{A \text{ required}}{A \text{ furnished}} + \frac{S \text{ required}}{S \text{ furnished}} \leq 1$$

For 1:1 shear distribution, try 10 x 14 and 12 x 12 columns:

$$12.38/128.25 + 219/288.6 = 0.10 + 0.76 = 0.86 < 1$$

Thus, 10 x 14 is sufficient

$$12.38/132.25 + 219/253.5 = 0.09 + 0.86 = 0.95 < 1$$

Thus, 12 x 12 is sufficient

For 3:2 shear distribution, try 10 x 12 and 8 x 14 columns:

$$12.38/109.25 + 175/209.4 = 0.113 + 0.837 = 0.950 < 1$$

Thus, 10 x 12 is sufficient

$$12.38/101.25 + 175/227.8 = 0.122 + 0.768 = 0.890 < 1$$

Thus, 8 x 14 is sufficient

If fixity to provide a point of contraflexure 4½ ft from the base is provided (a fixed-end condition), only ½ the section modulus is required, and 8 x 10 or 6 x 12 columns will be satisfactory. Base connections and foundation to develop a moment of 204,000 in.-lb will be necessary, however, assuming 1:1 shear distribution. Thus, if connection for base fixity is made on the inside and outside of a 12-in. nominal width member, the connection on each face must be adequate for 15,700-lb wind load (204,000 in.-lb divided by 11.5 in.).

This example assumes that the vertical live load on the column at the time of maximum wind loading will not exceed dead load plus full vertical live load on the leeward half. Frequently, only ½ the vertical live load on one-half of the truss is assumed to occur at the time of maximum wind loading.

The distribution of wind shear to the columns will depend on the method of sidewall construction and on the assumed action of the wind. Wind can be assumed to act as pressure on the windward wall alone or to exert suction on the leeward wall as well. Although there are many different standards for wind design, end results will probably be much the same regardless of the standard followed. If local codes exist, they naturally control.

Shear is often arbitrarily divided equally between columns. This distribution usually makes the leeward column the critical column for direct stress and bending moment, provided no suction on it is assumed. Theoretically, the shear should be divided between the columns in proportion to their relative stiffness, that is, with a distribution of about $\frac{2}{3}$ the shear to the windward column and $\frac{1}{3}$ to the leeward column, assuming uniform wind pressure on the former and no suction on the latter.

Resistance to lateral loads is provided at the top of the column by the connections of the truss and the knee brace, assumed to be 5 ft down on the column. The further down the column the knee brace can be attached, the stiffer the bent will be, the smaller the column size needed, and the smaller the connection requirements. The bending moment, M, at the knee brace on the leeward column, with no base fixity, is either 326,000 or 408,000 in.-lb, depending on whether the assumed distribution is 3:2 or 1:1. As the resisting-moment couple arm is 60 in. (distance of knee brace from top of column), the connection from truss to column must be adequate for either a 5,440- or 6,800-lb wind load (M divided by the resisting-moment arm). The knee-brace design stress must produce a horizontal component equal to the sum of the stress on the truss-to-column connection plus the shear at the column base. In this example, the horizontal component of the knee brace would be either 8,460 or 10,575 lb, and the actual stress in the knee brace considerably higher, depending on the angle the brace makes with the column. Knee-brace and truss-to-column requirements are proportionately reduced by the reduction in bending moment in the column caused by fixity at the base. The designer must consider the stresses applied to the truss by the column and knee-brace connections to make sure that those forces do not create critical stresses within the truss itself.

If column sizes are very large and lateral deflection is to be held to a minimum, it is particularly desirable to develop fixity at the connection of the column to the foundation (see Fig. 5.21). Full fixity may be assumed in wood column design if the anchorage details are able to eliminate that inelastic movement in the connections which could otherwise permit partial pin-ended action in the column before its assumed fixity comes into play. In order that elastic deformation may be held to a minimum, it is important that the connection to provide fixity at the base have as large a moment couple arm as possible.

A relatively long couple arm can be obtained by embedding a steel angle or member in the foundation and letting it extend several feet up beside the column. Fixity can also be obtained by making the connections on the inside and outside edges of the column with steel shapes or straps. These are detailed in such a manner that initial load or pre-stress can be applied to the fastenings to remove the inelastic deformation. The connections can be made by allowing clearance between the end of the steel member and the concrete in order that the

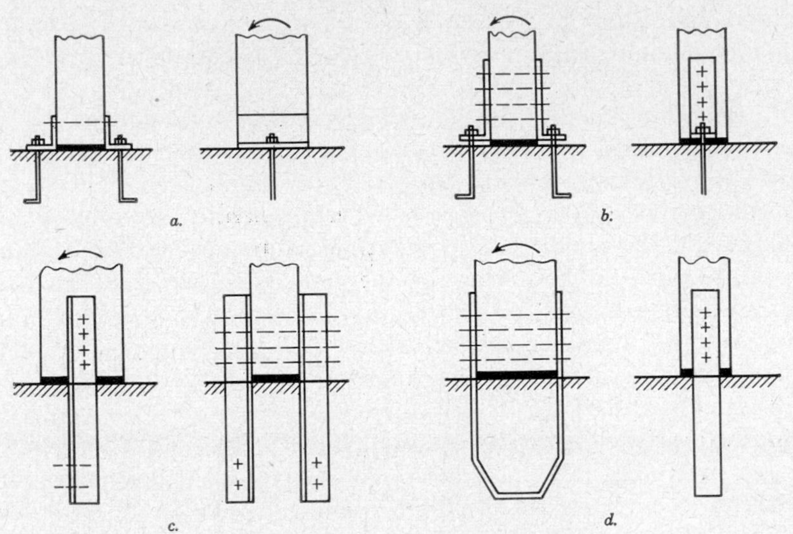

Fig. 5.21 Typical column anchorages

a. Simple or partial fixity
b. Full or partial fixity
c. Simple or partial fixity
d. Simple or partial fixity

anchor bolts can be tightened to draw the steel strap downward and thus prestress the fastenings in the column.

Wood columns can be embedded in masonry or the ground to provide end fixity, but such practice is satisfactory for heavy structural work only if the proper precaution is taken against decay. Columns, footings, or other wood members bearing on masonry should have a metal bearing plate or other moisture barrier and be detailed so as not to create a moisture trap or permit any damp condition at the bearing that might be conducive to decay.

Eccentrically loaded columns, or those having l/d ratios exceeding 11 and subject to combined bending and compression, are designed on the basis of the procedures outlined in Chap. 13 (NDS Appendix B). Wood columns, like columns of other materials, should not be eccentrically loaded whenever practicable not to do so.

5.48 Bracing The truss column and knee brace of the structure in question were designed to resist lateral wind loads and other lateral loads, such as earthquake. For buildings more than twice as long as they are wide, it may be desirable to use diagonal wood sheathing on the roof to improve the diaphragm action and to equalize sidewall loads among the various truss and column bents.

Other bracing that might be necessary includes (1) horizontal bracing in the plane of either the top or bottom chord, (2) vertical sway bracing between top and bottom chords of adjacent trusses, (3) horizontal struts or runners at the point of attachment of the vertical sway bracing to the bottom chord and running the entire length of the building, and (4) end and sidewall bracing.

The minimum truss bracing, apart from knee braces for the columns, would be comprised of horizontal runners the length of the building and vertical sway bracing installed between adjacent trusses in the end bays and in a minimum of one-quarter of the truss spaces. With this arrangement, no truss is further than one spacing from the vertical sway bracing. It is suggested that the horizontal runners be located on a spacing about $1\frac{1}{4}$ times the spacing of trusses, or not more than 35 ft. The runners are usually considered to act in compression only and are frequently made up of several built-up wood members to form a "T" or "I" section. Horizontal runners should be fastened so that they are continuous to one another, for example, placed above the bottom chord for a direct tie or joined across the truss with scabs.

Cross-bracing members are generally used for vertical sway bracing and are assumed to act in tension only. The stresses in these members should be computed on the basis of the lateral load on the end wall, and the remaining bracing down the length of the building should be made the same as that for the end wall or end trusses.

End wall and sidewalls must be properly braced for lateral forces either through diaphragm action of the wall construction itself or through introduction of compression or tension diagonals. For large buildings, introduction of separate members for bracing is recommended, although the end wall may be designed as a diaphragm. Frequently steel tension-rod cross bracing is used in the walls.

DESIGN OF JOINTS

5.49 Joint design considerations For heavy construction, timber connectors and bolts are the most commonly used fastenings. Design procedure is similar for each in that the factors to be considered include the moisture condition of the lumber before and after fabrication, duration of load, angle of load to grain, edge distance, end distance, and spacing of connections. If joints are not concentric, shear and secondary bending moment must also be considered.

The type of truss framing and the arrangement of members for a multiple-member truss can have an important effect on the joint details.

Gusset-plate connections provide angle of load parallel to the grain of the wood members and therefore develop the maximum fastening values.

In multiple-member trusses—which usually do not exceed five members in thickness—the arrangement of members influences the loads to be carried by the fastenings and determines the angle of load to grain. The thickness of members also affects the joint details, but is generally dictated, not by their requirements, but by the design of the members themselves.

5.50 Timber connectors Factors to be considered in determining the basic allowable load per connector include type and size of connector, species or connector-group classification of the lumber, moisture condition, duration of load, thickness of members, and angle of load to grain. In the following examples, split rings will be used for wood-to-wood connections and shear plates for steel-to-wood connections. If connectors of a small size require more than two bolts, it is usually desirable to use a larger size. As there are only two sizes of split rings ($2\frac{1}{2}$ in. and 4 in.) and of shear plates ($2\frac{5}{8}$ in. and 4 in.), the larger size will therefore be selected for the design analysis. Some designers and fabricators use different sizes in the same truss, but fabrication is simplified if only a single size is used throughout.

It will be assumed that the lumber is classified as Group B and that it is partially seasoned at time of fabrication and will become seasoned in service. Thus a seasoning factor of 90 per cent will be applied to tabulated connector values.

Assuming maximum load results from snow or two-months' duration load, a duration factor of 115 per cent will be applied to tabulated connector values. The combination of 90 per cent and 115 per cent gives a resultant factor of 103 per cent. A duration factor of 120 per cent (1.33×90) will be used for wind stress combined with other loads.

The thickness of members is usually chosen before joint details are considered. It must be decided, moreover, if there are to be connectors on only one side (one face) of the member or opposite on both sides (two faces). A member on the outside of a truss usually has connectors in only one face whereas an inside member usually has connectors in two faces.

The angle of load to grain depends on the arrangement of members and the presence or absence of exterior loads. Generally, for a five-thickness multiple-member truss in which two of the three members framing to a joint are double members and the other is a single piece, the connections to the outside members and to the single center member will be substantially parallel to the grain. The connectors in the two remaining members, which are between the outside member and the single center members, will be at an angle to the grain. For a seven-member joint, with three different web members framing to the same point on the chord, or four different members framing at a joint, the connections to the outside and to the center single members will usually be parallel to grain whereas the other four members will be loaded at an angle to the grain. The arrangement of members in a lapped-joint heavy truss should be balanced and symmetrical on each side of the centerline of the thickness of the truss. Thus multiple-member trusses will always have an odd number of members, usually five.

Factors or requirements governing edge distance, end distance, and spacing are determined after preliminary joint requirements are determined. If feasible, 100 per cent values are recommended even though lesser values may be permissible.

5.51 Bolts Factors to be considered in determining basic allowable load per bolt are identical to those for connectors, and similar comments apply. The factors include size, species of lumber, moisture condition, duration of load, thickness of members, and angle of load to grain.

For the design analysis, assume ¾-in. bolts, southern pine, Douglas fir, or comparable species, a seasoning factor of 75 per cent, a duration factor of 115 per cent (for snow load), or a combined factor of 86 per cent.

5.52 Member arrangement For a typical five-thickness multiple-member truss, there are two possible basic member arrangements, assuming the chord member is composed of two pieces. One arrangement places the chords on the outside and is most often used at the ends of flat trusses. The other places the chord members between the web members and is most often used at the ends of pitched trusses. In Fig. 5.22 the relative positions of the members are indicated by the numbers *1* through *5* or *7* (depending on the number of members across the truss), position *1* being on the near side of the truss and position *5* or *7* on the far side.

The arrangement with chords in positions *2* and *4* is most desirable at the end of a pitched truss in order that the heel joint may be made with splice plates in positions *1, 3,* and *5*. Toward the center of the span, the chord members may be lap-spliced to positions *1* and *5,* with the web members in positions *2, 3,* and *4*.

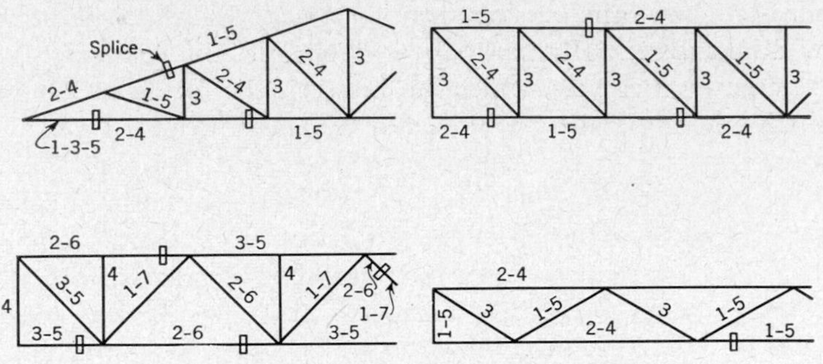

Fig. 5.22 Relative member positions

The arrangement with chords in positions *2* and *4* can also be used for flat Pratt or Howe trusses, but simpler joint details usually result if chords are in positions *1* and *5*. Chords in positions *2* and *4* are desirable for the flat Warren type of truss or other trusses in which the web members intersect the chord at about the same angle.

5.53 Chord splices Figure 5.23 shows the load conditions for top-chord member U_1–U_2 of the pitched truss in Fig. 5.17a. The chord sizes have been previously determined as two 3 x 12 members with joists along the chord or two 3 x 10 members with purlins at panel points. A chord splice in this panel may be designed as a lapped splice

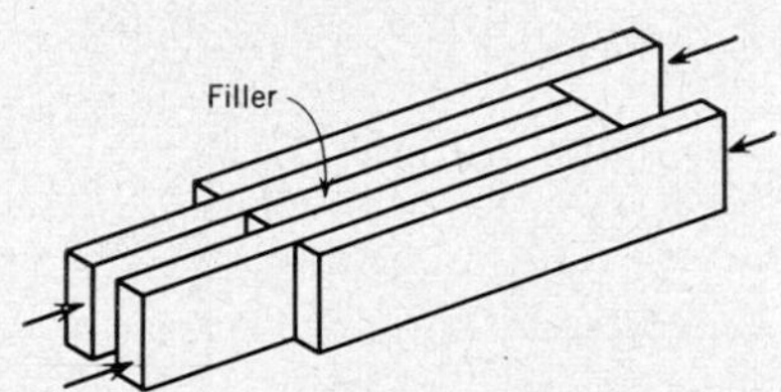

Fig 5.23 Load conditions in top-chord splice, member U_1–U_2 (Fig. 5.17a)

so that if the lower-section members are in positions *2* and *4*, the upper-section members will be in positions *1* and *5*. The splice may also be designed as a butt splice—with splice plates in positions *1*, *3*, and *5*—or as a butt end-bearing compression splice.

Assume a lapped splice, as shown in Fig. 5.23, 4-in. split rings, Group B lumber, 90 per cent moisture factor, 115 per cent duration-of-load factor, nominal 3-in. thickness (2.625 in.), and connectors in one face only. (See the Design Manual of Chap. 13 for connector design data.)

Angle of load to grain = 0° (parallel)
Tabulated value of one split ring = 5,740 lb
Adjusted value of one split ring = 5,740 × 0.90 × 1.15
= 5,950
Member stress = 51,300 lb
Number of split rings required = 51,300/5,950 = 8.6
Percentage of allowable value
used with ten split rings = 8.6/10 = 86 per cent

If the connectors are on the same gauge line parallel to the length of the member, 7-in. spacing is required for 86 per cent of value and 0-deg angle of load. If connectors are opposite each other on the parallel gauge lines—each an equal distance off the centerline of the piece in the same face—minimum spacing perpendicular to the grain is 5 in., a figure that permits 100 per cent of value for 0-deg angle of load.

End distance required in a compression member for 86 per cent of value and 0-deg angle of load is 4¾ in. Minimum edge distance required is 2¾ in., which permits 100 per cent of value for 0-deg angle of load.

Larger spacing and end distances than those required are recommended if they can be achieved without materially increasing costs (such as by requiring members of a longer standard length or a larger size). For this reason, a spacing parallel to grain of 9 in., a spacing perpendicular to grain of 6 in., and an end distance of 7 in. are desirable.

If 3 x 12 chord members are required for combined axial and bending stresses, the maximum values for spacing parallel and perpendicular to grain and for end distance may be used.

It is desirable to space the rings symmetrically across the width of the member. Thus two bolts can be placed on gauge lines 3 in. off the centerline and the fifth bolt placed on the centerline. The perpendicular spacing of the fifth bolt in relation to another bolt will then be 3 in., a distance that requires 5¼-in. spacing parallel to grain for 86 per cent of value, or 7¼-in. spacing for 100 per cent. The minimum and maximum spacings and end distances for 3 x 12 members are shown in Fig. 5.24.

If chord members subject to bending are continuous through two panel points, the chord members at the splice may act as cantilevers from the adjacent panel points. The chord size based on bending moment for a simple beam is usually adequate and splices should be as close to panel points as possible. Because of the slip or elastic deformation of the fastenings, it is not usually possible to develop complete

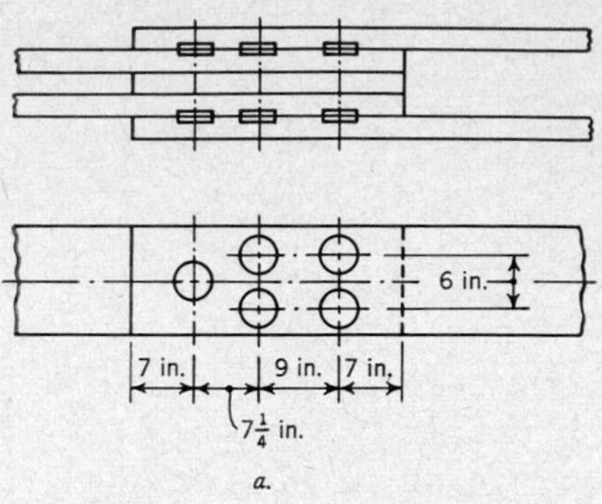

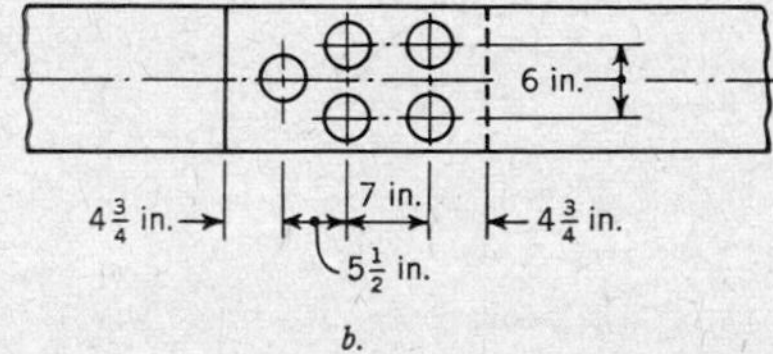

Fig. 5.24 Bolt spacing in splice

a. 100 per cent value *b. 86 per cent value*

continuity in a chord splice; hence the possible secondary stresses on the connections due to partial continuity are usually neglected. If it is desirable to reduce deflection of a chord member by developing continuity in the splice, then the initially determined connector spacing is analyzed as for a rivet group, because the individual connectors resist bending moment in direct proportion to their distance from the centroid of the group. Figure 5.25 illustrates the secondary stresses on the con-

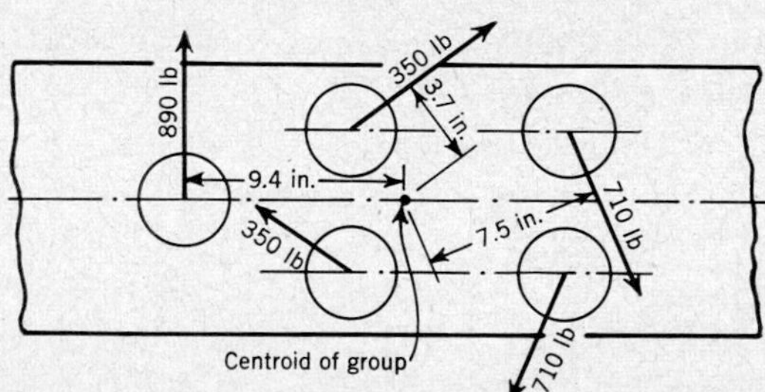

Fig. 5.25 Splice stresses due to bending

nectors of Fig. 5.24, assuming the splice must resist a bending moment of 43,000 in.-lb, or 80 per cent of that of a simple beam. If moment resistance is considered, these forces are added to the 5,130-lb force on the connectors due to axial load. The connectors must then be rechecked for the resultant total loads.

If the splice of Fig. 5.24 were a butt joint, either the pattern would be repeated for the other half of the splice, or the center filler could be considered as a splice plate and three bolts used, each with four split rings. The members on the outside would correspond to the adjacent chord section in a lapped splice and a filler without connectors would be used in the center. In chord members of unseasoned or partially seasoned lumber, end distances up to 12 in. are recommended for both bolts and connectors in order to minimize the possibility of seasoning checks extending from the end of the member into the joint area. End distance of 12 in. is required for unseasoned, short splice plates.

A lapped splice with ¾-in. bolts and the same member arrangement is designed as follows:

Angle of load to grain = 0 deg
Thickness of side plates = 2⅝ in.
Equivalent thickness of center member = 5¼ in. (twice thickness of side members)
Tabulated value of 1¾-in. bolt = 2,830 lb
Adjusted value of 1¾-in. bolt [1] = 2,830 × 0.75 × 1.15
= 2,450 lb
Stress = 51,300 lb
Number of bolts required = 51,300/2,450 = 21
Spacing parallel to grain = 3 in. (4 times bolt diameter)
Spacing perpendicular to grain = 4 in. (based on net section)
Edge distance = 2¾ in. (based on net section)
End distance = 3 in. (4 times diameter)

Seven bolts should thus be used in each of 3 rows (total 21), with a 4-in. spacing between rows. If the joint were a butt joint and the center filler used as a splice plate, the adjusted value per bolt would be 4,100 lb (twice the value for a 2⅝-in. center member) and 13 bolts would be required in each half, or 26 in all.

If fastenings are used to transfer the stress, the lapped splice is desirable as it requires only one-half as much hardware as the butted splice, saves the lumber required for splice plates, and provides a direct transfer of stress from one chord section to the other. It also lessens the possible need for maintenance caused by checking in relatively short splice plates.

If the compression chord members are in the same planes, the splice

[1] 75 per cent value is the assumed adjustment for partially seasoned lumber.

may be designed to transfer the load by end bearing between the two chord sections. This design demands close fabrication tolerances to provide a uniform bearing, but it substantially reduces the connections required. No more fastening is required than can keep the chord members in line and transfer a minimum amount of shear, due to unbalanced load, across the joint. If the unit compression stress parallel to the grain in end bearing exceeds 75 per cent of the allowable value, thin metal bearing plates of not less than 20 gauge should be installed between the ends of the chord members. The plates will minimize the effect of summerwood of one member bearing on springwood of the other.

To minimize the effect of seasoning shrinkage, split splice plates may be used for the butt splice and for the end-bearing splice. For the lapped splice, a saw kerf may be provided on the centerline of the chord member. Theoretically, there is little secondary stress set up by seasoning in a chord splice if the grain of the members is parallel, but it is good practice to make provision for such relief nevertheless. In the preceding examples, the use of saw kerfing will require an additional bolt and two connectors (see Fig. 5.26). Split splice plates will require an additonal two bolts and four connectors.

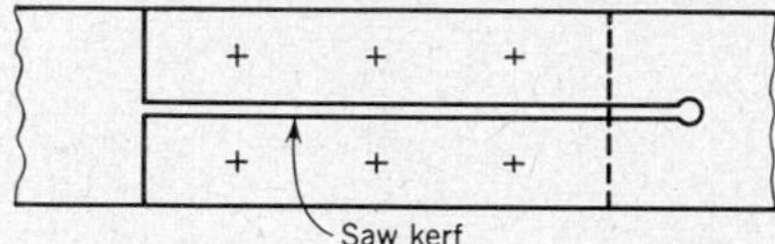

Fig. 5.26 Bolt spacing in splice with saw kerf

5.54 Web-member connections Consider the top-chord panel point U_3 in Fig. 5.17a. The stresses and assumed relative positions of the web members are shown in Fig. 5.27. Also shown is a stress diagram that can be drawn for any concentric joint. The diagram should help

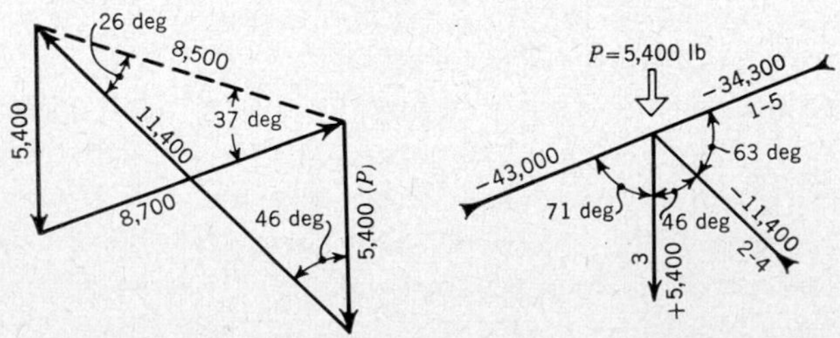

Fig. 5.27 Stress diagram for web-member joint U_3 (Fig. 5.17a)

to clarify the method of analysis used for determining the magnitude and direction of lapped-joint loads.

To begin on the outside, the connections between chords *1* and *5* and diagonal web members *2* and *4* must be adequate to resist the resultant (8,500 lb) of the chord stress differential (8,700 lb) and the panel point load (5,400 lb), assuming joists or purlins supported on the chords. This resultant is at an angle of 26 deg with the grain of the diagonals, and 37 deg with the grain of the chords.

Assume 3-in. nominal (2⅝-in. actual) lumber, Group B species, 90 per cent seasoning factor, 115 per cent duration-of-load (snow) factor and 4-in. split rings. (See Chap. 13, NDS and DM, for design data.) With connectors in opposite faces of the diagonal (one side connecting to the chord, the other side to the vertical), the tabulated allowable load per ring for 26-deg angle of load is 5,200 lb. For the connector in one face of the chords, the tabulated value at 37-deg angle of load is 4,950 lb. Tabulated values adjusted for seasoning and duration are 5,400 lb and 5,130 lb, respectively. The number of 4-in. split rings required in the diagonal is 1.57 (8,500 divided by 5,400), and in the chord 1.66 (8,500 divided by 5,130). Two rings will be used, therefore, one between members *1* and *2* and one between members *4* and *5*. Thus edge and end distance must be adequate for 78½ per cent of value in the diagonal, and edge distance for 83 per cent of value in the chord. As only a single bolt is needed, there is no spacing problem.

Connection between the vertical and the diagonals must be adequate for the stress in the vertical (5,400 lb) acting parallel (at 0 deg) to grain in the vertical and at 46 deg to grain in the diagonals. Tabulated value for one ring, parallel to grain, two faces, is 5,600 lb, and at 46 deg, 4,600 lb. Adjusted values are 5,800 lb and 4,760 lb, respectively. With two rings, edge and end distance in the diagonals must provide 57 per cent of value and in the vertical 47 per cent of value.

As requirements for the chord connections are greater, end and edge distances for the diagonals must be adequate for 78½ per cent of value, thus requiring a minimum width of member of 5½ in. and end distance of 4½ in. Full end distance of 7 in. is desirable. The chord must be a minimum of 5½ in. wide, but 3 x 12 or 3 x 10 members are needed for stress and bending requirements, as was previously determined.

The vertical may be a minimum size of 3 x 6 with required minimum end distance of 3½ in., although 7 in. is preferred. The completed joint is shown in Fig. 5.28. If the top chord acts as a spaced column, the one ring must satisfy requirements for end spacer-block connections, independently of the member stress analysis.

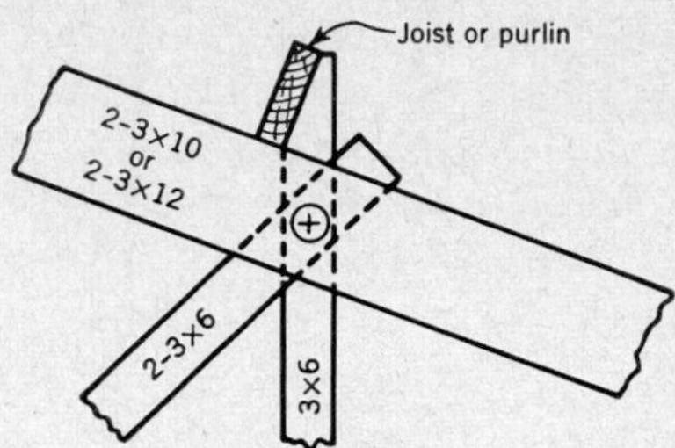

Fig. 5.28 Web-member joint U_3, chords 1–5

If the arrangement of members is changed so that the diagonal web members are placed on the outside of the chords, the connection between the diagonals and the chords must be adequate for 11,400 lb at 63 deg. to grain. Tabulated adjusted value of one ring will be only 4,450 lb, and two bolts with four rings will be required for the diagonal to chord connections. A possible solution for this arrangement is shown in Fig. 5.29. Here, the chords are in positions *2* and *4* at the ends of the truss and are butt spliced instead of lap spliced.

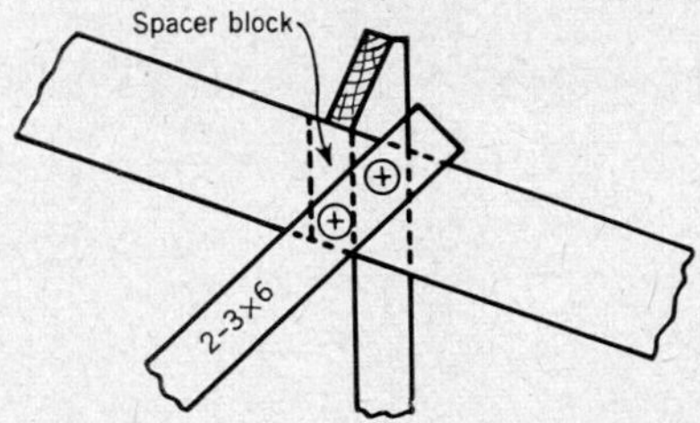

Fig. 5.29 Alternate web joint U_3, chords 2–4

It is apparent that an arrangement of members having the chords on the outside, the diagonal compression web members next inside, and the vertical tension web member in the center gives the simplest joint details. This arrangement works well with the lapped chord splice, because toward the ends of the truss, where the chords are between the web members, the web-member stresses are light enough for the use of single bolts with connectors.

This system of framing places the chords in positions *2* and *4* at the end of the truss and the web members in positions *1, 3,* and *5*. If the lap splice is toward the center of the truss, the chords are then in positions *1* and *5,* the diagonal web member in positions *2* and *4,* and the vertical web member in position *3*. The latter is a typical arrangement for a pitched-type truss in which the double web members act as the compression web members. To avoid splicing a web member in five-piece truss joints, the lap-splice locations on top and bottom chords should be such that a line joining them crosses a one-piece web member. Should the line cross a two-piece web member, that member must be lap spliced if it is to be in proper framing position at the joints.

A typical arrangement for a flat Pratt or Howe type truss is one with chord members in positions *1* and *5* at the ends of the truss, diagonals in positions *2* and *4*, and verticals in position *3*. This arrangement will usually permit the simplest joint details, although chord members may sometimes be switched to positions *2* and *4* without making a great deal of difference. The basic design principle stipulates that the member arrangement for the critical web-member stresses (stresses in web members near the center of span of a pitched truss or near the ends of a flat truss) shall be such that only the minimum stresses need be carried by the fastenings. Thus, where the web member stresses are highest, it is desirable to have the two-piece diagonal web member in positions *2* and *4* so that the fastenings need carry only the components of the total stress that are represented by the stress in the vertical, the panel-point load, and the chord differential stress. As a rule, design procedure based on minimum stress will also provide the smallest angle of load to grain for that stress.

5.55 Eccentric joints If the joint of the preceding examples is assumed to be eccentric, with one-piece diagonal and vertical web members framing between a two-piece chord, the connections are designed by a similar process. However, joint shear and bending moment must also be considered. Assuming an eccentricity of 8 in., the connections to the chord would be similar to those of Fig. 5.29 except for their being offset.

For maximum shear strength (see Chap. 13, NDS, par. 400-D-4), the rings must be located to give the maximum possible distance, h_e, between the connector and the edge toward which the stress acts (see Fig. 5.30). For 3 x 12 chord members, the maximum attainable h_e with

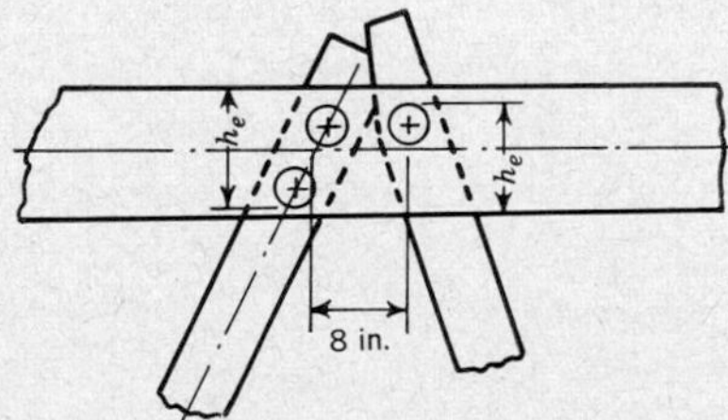

Fig. 5.30 Eccentric web joint U_3

4-in. rings would be 10¾ in. For a permissible allowable shear value of 120 psi, increased 50 per cent for shear in joint details and 15 per cent for duration of load, the maximum permissible vertical shear must not exceed 7,800 lb.

$$3/2H = 3V/2bh_e$$
$$V = Hbh_e$$
$$V = 120 \times 1.15 \times 2.625 \times 10.75 = 3{,}900 \text{ lb}$$

As there are two chord members to resist this shear, however, the total allowable vertical shear is 7,800 lb (3,900 × 2). With 3 x 10 chord members, the maximum vertical shear must not exceed 6,300 lb. Thus shear is satisfactory for the vertical web stress but too high for the normal-to-chord component of the diagonal stress unless the panel-point load represents only purlins at the panel point. In that case, the effective vertical shear is only that of the normal-to-chord component of the vertical web-member stress. If joists are used along the chord, deeper or wider chord members are needed to keep shear within allowable limits.

The bending moment introduced by the eccentricity must be used in computing required top-chord sizes (see Sec. 5.36). For this analysis, the bending moment equals the product of the normal-to-chord component of the vertical web-member stress times the eccentricity. The purlin or assumed panel-point load is subtracted from the normal-to-chord component of the diagonal so that the resultant equals the vertical member component. The assumed panel-point load for joists along the chord is assumed to be applied at the compression web-member connection for top-chord joints, or at the tension web-member connection for bottom-chord joints. Purlin loads at panel points are computed for the point at which they occur. This is an empirical method that ignores the effect of secondary bending moment in altering the distribution of bending loads to the various panel points.

If the chord is continuous in each panel to each side of the joint, and the panels are about equal in length, ½ the eccentric bending moment may be assumed as adding positive moment in the panel to one side, and ½ adding negative moment to the other side. If the chord is spliced in one panel and continuous in the adjacent panel, the eccentric moment is conservatively assumed to be resisted in the unspliced panel.

An eccentric joint analysis is necessary for the top- and bottom-chord joints in the bowstring truss of Fig. 5.17b if the joints are offset, as they usually are if two member chords are used. The maximum vertical shear will be the vertical component (2,500 lb) of member U_3–L_4.

5.56 Heel joint Consider the heel joint of the pitched truss of Fig. 5.17a. Previously it was determined that top chords could be two 3 x 10 or two 3 x 12 members for bending and that bottom chords could range from two 3 x 8 to two 3 x 12 members, depending on net section criteria. The chords were assumed to be in positions *2* and *4*.

Either the top chords or the bottom chords may be in bearing on the support. The allowable bearing is higher on the partial end grain of the top chord than on the side grain of the bottom chord, and the joint requirement is less if the top chord is in bearing. Thus assume that the top chord bears, the bottom chord is cut short of the support, and the splice plates are in positions *1, 3,* and *5*. Assume, moreover, that top chords will be 3 x 12, the center splice plate 3 x 8, outside splice plates 2 x 8, and bottom chords 3 x 8. The member arrangement and stress diagram for the joint is shown in Fig. 5.31.

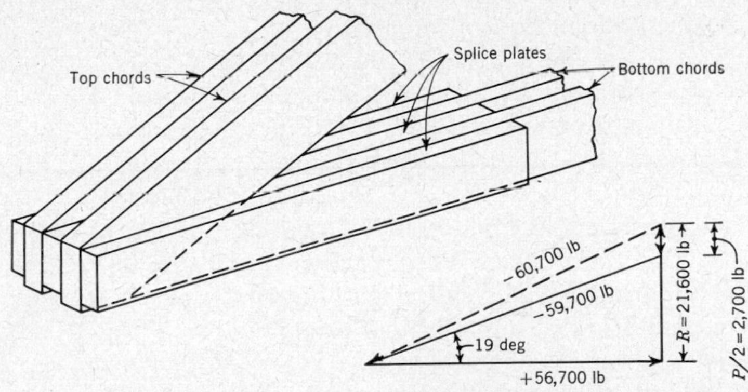

Fig. 5.31 Heel joint

With the top-chord member extended slightly below the splice plates to guarantee bearing, the vertical component (18,900 lb) of the top-chord stress is transferred directly to the support in bearing. In addition, the connections between the splice plates and the top chord need be adequate only for the horizontal component (56,700 lb), which equals the bottom-chord stress. If the bottom chords or the splice plates are in bearing, the connection must be adequate for the resultant (60,700 lb) of the top-chord stress and the end-panel load. Obviously the assumed conditions will permit simpler details.

Assuming 4-in. split rings in the top chord, two faces, 2⅝-in. lumber, 90 per cent seasoning factor, 115 per cent duration factor, and 19-deg angle of load, the allowable load per ring equals 5,600 lb. Thus 10.1 split rings (56,700 lb divided by 5,600 lb) are required. As there are four faces for installation of connectors, a multiple of 4 would be used, or 12 rings. Spacing, end, and edge distance must be adequate for 84 per cent of full value (10.1 divided by 12). Thus end distance on the top chord may be 4¾ in. and the minimum edge distance, 2¾ in.

The same rings in the splice plates carry the identical load (56,700 lb), but angle to grain is 0 deg, or parallel. The adjusted allowable load per ring, based on two faces in the center splice plates, is 5,800 lb, and thus 9.8 rings are required. Obviously 12 rings must be provided, as required in the top chord, and 81 per cent of connector value. End distance in the splice plates (tension) may be 5¼ in. and the minimum edge distance, 2¾ in. The basic connector value is slightly higher for the rings in one face of the outside splice plates, but the lower value for the center plate is used for all. The computation for the rings in the splice plate is the same as for the rings in the connection of the splice to the bottom-chord members.

With 3 x 10 top-chord members, rings could be placed on gauge lines 2 in. off the centerline and provide the required 2¾-in. edge distance. With 3 x 8 and 2 x 8 splice plates, the rings could be on 1-in. gauge lines. The available parallelogram area for the three ¾-in. bolts, each with four rings, is shown in Fig. 5.32a. Two alternative locations for the rings are shown in Fig. 5.32b. The greater spacing provides connector values of more than 100 per cent, whereas the smaller spacing along the centerline of the splice plates is just in excess of minimum requirements. The maximum values are preferable.

If there are three or more bolts in a joint, and if the lumber is assumed unseasoned or only partially seasoned, some designers install stitch bolts, usually ⅜- or ½-in. diameter, in the member that is loaded at an angle to the grain. The bolts prevent undue opening of checks or splits that may develop, and, to be most effective, should be tightened as the lumber seasons in place.

The required bearing area on the diagonal cut end of the chords must also be checked. If *c* parallel equals 1,200 psi and *c* perpendicular 390 psi, the allowable bearing at 71 deg (90 deg — 19 deg) to grain (using the Hankinson formula) is 420 psi. This figure may be increased 15 per cent for snow load. The required bearing area is thus 45 sq in. (21,600 reaction divided by 420×1.15), or a length of bearing of 8½ in. (45 divided by 5.25, the width of two 3-in. members). Use of a steel bearing plate will increase the allowable *c* parallel value and permit a slightly smaller bearing area (see Chap. 13, NDS Table 2). If bearing is on a wooden plate on top of the column, bearing area is based on compression on the plate at 90 deg to grain. A metal bearing

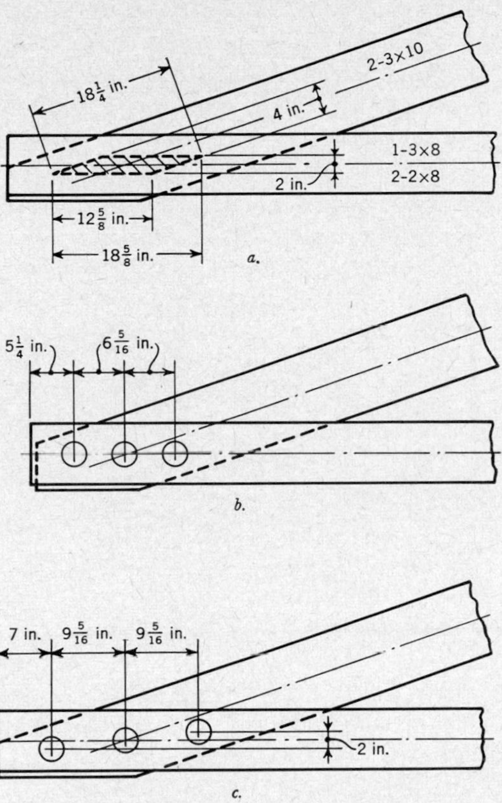

Fig. 5.32 Heel-joint details

a. Available parallelogram area for bolts
b. Minimum spacing and end distance
c. Maximum spacing and end distance

plate is preferable and can be made larger than the beam or truss end area if required.

5.57 Column connections As noted in Sec. 5.47, requirements for column-to-truss, column-to-knee-brace and column-to-foundation connections vary according to the design assumptions. Columns without base fixity require greater capacity in knee-brace and truss connections. For the unfixed column of Fig. 5.20, the requirements for truss connection were 6,800 lb and for knee-brace shear 10,575 lb, with 50 per cent of shear to each column. For a fixed column, the requirements would be 3,400 and 7,175 lb, respectively.

Bolts are generally used for truss-to-column connections if only two or three are needed, but shear plates may be used with metal shapes for heavy load requirements. Three common methods of truss-to-column framing are shown in Fig. 5.33. Two ¾-in. bolts are required

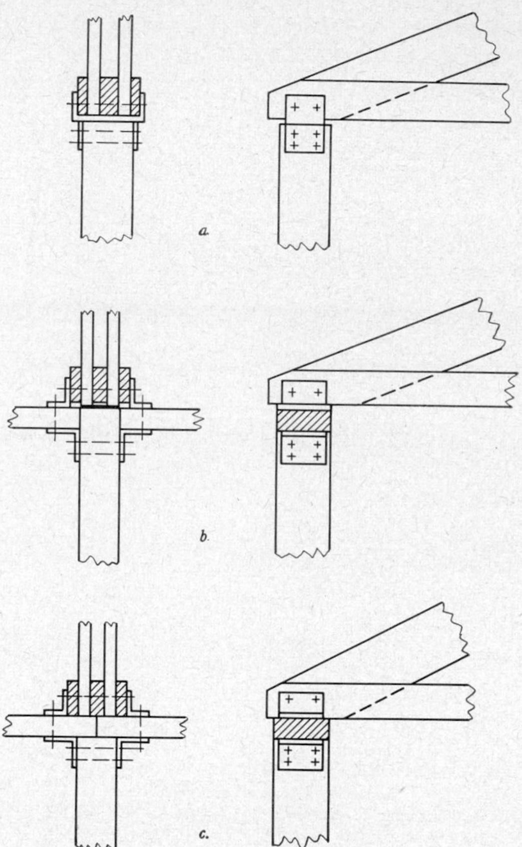

Fig. 5.33 Typical truss-to-column connections

a. Steel column cap
b. Steel angles and bearing plate
c. Steel angles and bearing on wood plate.

for 6,800 lb parallel to grain in the heel joint, and four bolts for 6,800 lb perpendicular to grain in the top of the column or in the plate.

If the knee brace is at a 40-deg angle with the column, the stress in the brace would be 16,400 lb for an unfixed column and 11,200 lb for a fixed-end column. Either four 4-in. split rings with two bolts or six ¾-in. bolts are required for the unfixed condition, whereas only two rings with one bolt or four ¾-in. bolts are required for the fixed-end condition; similar connections are needed for knee-brace-to-truss. The connections to the column must be analyzed as eccentric joints.

For the foundation connections of Fig. 5.20, shear requirements range from 3,020 to 4,530 lb. Two ¾-in. bolts are adequate for shear alone. Figure 5.21 illustrated possible column anchorage and methods of developing end fixity. Timber connectors, usually shear plates, may be desirable if more than several bolts are required. Metal bearing plates are also desirable.

5.58 Seven-member joints Multiple-member joints heretofore considered have been five members or less in thickness. In such joints, three members meet, two of which are two-piece members and one a single member. Design procedure for a seven-member joint such as that shown in Fig. 5.34 is similar, but the determination of angle of

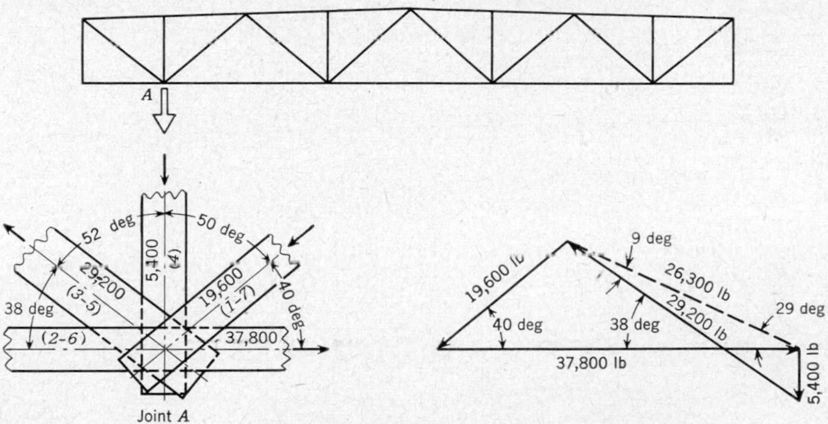

Fig. 5.34 Seven-member joint with stress diagram

load to grain is somewhat more complicated. Figure 5.34 corresponds to a bottom-chord panel-point joint in the flat Warren truss of Fig. 5.22. The member positions shown are the most efficient ones permitted by connection requirements. A joint stress diagram is also included.

As in previous examples, the analysis is most easily undertaken by working from the outside member toward the center of the joint thickness. Apart from the detailed calculations already covered, the following are the requirements for bolts or timber connectors in the various members:

1. Connection of outside diagonal web members (*1–7*) to bottom chords (*2–6*) must be adequate for the stress in diagonals (19,600 lb)

acting parallel to grain in diagonals and at 40 deg to grain in chords. It is necessary to check connections in both members, but normally the requirements for the chord will control because the chord is loaded at the greater angle of load to grain.

2. Connection of chords (*2–6*) to tension diagonals (*3–5*) must be adequate for the resultant (26,300 lb) of the stress in diagonals (19,600 lb) and the stress in bottom chords (37,800 lb). This resultant acts at 9 deg to grain in diagonals and 29 deg to grain in chords. The chord requirements will normally control.

3. Connection of tension diagonals (*3–5*) to vertical (*4*) must be adequate for the stress in vertical (5,400 lb) acting parallel to grain in vertical and at 52 deg to grain in diagonals. The requirements in the diagonal will normally control. The requirement for this connection can also be expressed as the resultant of two factors, the load on the connection between diagonal and chord (26,300 lb) and the stress in the diagonal (29,200 lb) that gives the same result (5,400 lb).

Assuming 4-in. split rings and 3-in. lumber partially seasoned, one possible solution to the preceding requirements is shown in Fig. 5.35.

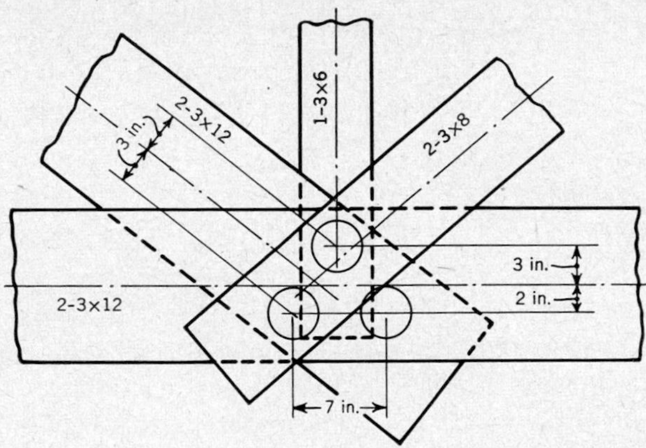

Fig. 5.35 Seven-member joint detail

For such lumber, $\frac{3}{8}$-in. or $\frac{1}{2}$-in. stitch bolts are recommended for the chords and the 3 x 12 diagonals as a precautionary measure against progressive splits during subsequent seasoning.

5.59 Gusset-plate joints Gusset-plate joints are used if members are arranged in the same plane, such as in a monochord truss. Gusset plates are usually steel but may be glued-laminated members, plywood, or even solid sawed lumber. A typical gusset-plate joint is the heel joint of a bowstring truss. The connection requirements between top and bottom chords of the bowstring are more than can be developed with heel splice plates, such as those used for the pitched truss of Fig. 5.31.

As gusset plates provide greater area for installation of fastenings than other connections, they are most often used for heavily stressed joints or as a means of eliminating short wood splice plates to minimize thickness of joints.

For the heel joint of the bowstring, the steel gusset is usually a "U" strap with the vertical sawed end of the top chord bearing on the end of the strap and the bottom sawed end of the top chord bearing on the support. If bearing values for this design exceed those allowable for the wood, the gusset may be fabricated as a seat for the square-cut top chord. Bearing on the support will then be provided through the gusset plate itself. Either way, the connection of the gusset to the bottom chord is similar, with the loads acting parallel to the grain of the bottom chord. Typical details are shown in Fig. 5.36.

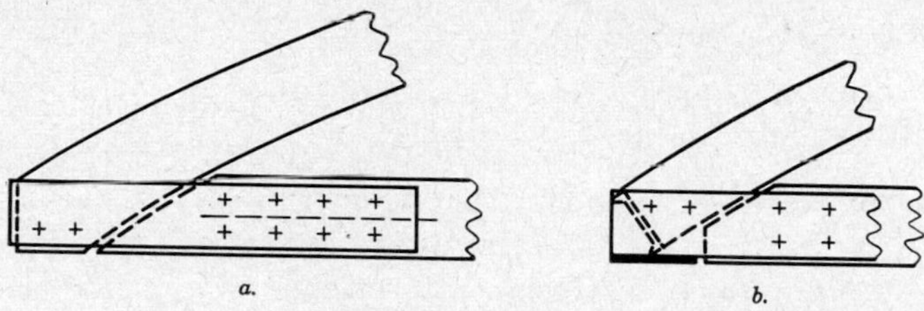

Fig. 5.36 Heel-joint details for bowstring truss

a. Top-chord bearing *b. Steel-strap bearing*

If rows of bolts with or without connectors (shear plates) are used in a single-width steel plate in a bottom chord, spacing between any two rows should not exceed 5 in. in unseasoned lumber unless care is taken to control or eliminate possible seasoning checks. This provision for bolt spacing should be applied to all chord splice plates to minimize secondary stresses.

Steel gusset plates are designed on the basis of accepted steel standards. Minimum thickness is usually determined by bolt bearings. A steel channel section or heavier plate may be necessary to compensate for bending moment on the end of the "U" strap. Steel gusset plates for web-member joints may be of solid plate steel or welded steel straps. Gussets should be standardized as much as possible to keep costs to a minimum. Standardization can be most easily accomplished for the bowstring web joints, as required capacity does not vary greatly from joint to joint within a given truss.

5.60 Rod-and-block joints Consider the web-member joint in the pitched truss of Fig. 5.27 as a rod-and-block joint. The joint may be designed for a split chord, single-compression web member, or a one-piece chord or web member.

The split-chord joint can be designed with connectors to the chord to carry the resultant of the diagonal and vertical (Fig. 5.37a) or, if

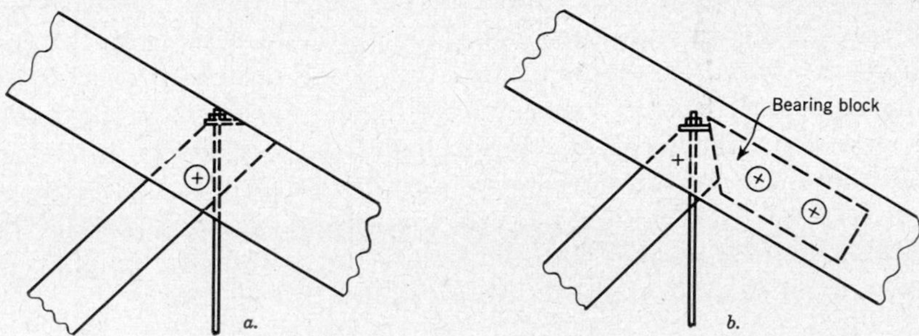

Fig. 5.37 Rod-and-block joint designed as split chord

larger capacity is required for the chord connection, with a bearing block having the required connectors (Fig. 5.37b). Required bearing area under the washer for the rod is determined by the allowable compression at the angle to grain, as is the required bearing on the bearing block. Maximum efficiency for wood-to-wood bearing is obtained if the bearing is at the same angle to the grain in each piece. Thus the bearing line should equally divide the angle between the two members. For the bearing-block design, an extra bolt through the chords or a pin into the bearing block is needed to hold the diagonal in position, particularly during erection.

For a single solid chord member, 6 x 10 or 6 x 12, details can be similar to those in Fig. 5.38. In Fig. 5.38b, the chord section is not reduced by the notching required for the diagonal bearing in Fig. 5.38a. The reduced chord section must be checked regardless. With glued-laminated top chords, the bearing block of Fig. 5.38b is laminated to the chord, thus eliminating the connectors indicated.

If tension-rod stresses require an unreasonably large bearing area on the top or bottom of the top chord, such as in a flat truss, the required area may be reduced by using a plate between the diagonal and the chord as shown in Fig. 5.38c. Either the plate must be welded to the rod or the rod threaded the depth of the chord, with a nut recessed into the bottom of the chord behind the plate. To determine required thickness, metal bearing plates are analyzed as short beams.

The separate wood-bearing plates may be fastened to the chords

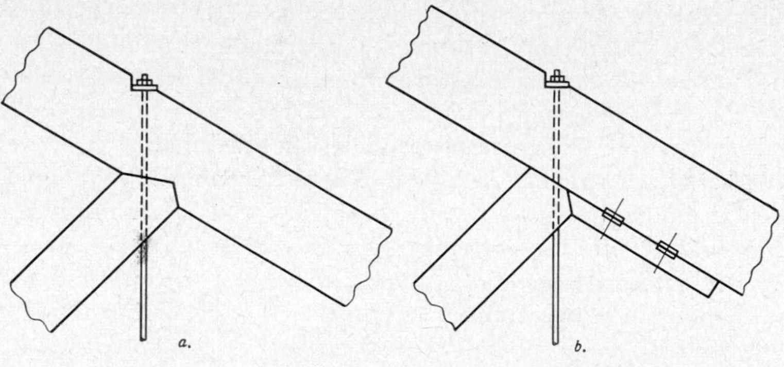

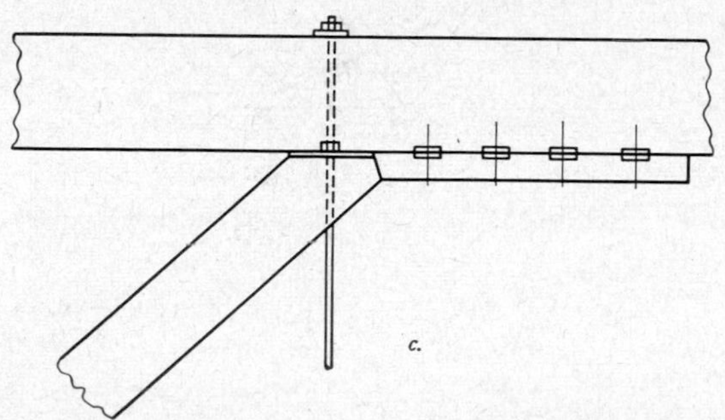

Fig. 5.38 Rod-and-block joint designed as monochord

with either lag screws or bolts, with or without connectors. All such short bearing blocks should be of well-seasoned, straight-grained lumber, selected for high quality and preferably of vertical- or edge-grain stock.

5.61 Nailed joints The design procedure for nailed joints is simpler than for bolts and timber connectors because the only variables are species of material, condition of the lumber, and embedment of the nails. A nail size is generally selected that will give the proper embedment for the thickness of material used. The species of lumber and seasoning condition of the lumber at fabrication are assumed.

It is important that the wood tolerate the required number of nails in the joint area without undue splitting. To increase the nailing area and to reduce splitting, plywood gusset or splice plates are frequently used. Spacing of nails to hold splitting to a minimum varies so much for different species that no precise design recommendations can be made. Some specifications arbitrarily recommend a minimum nail spacing and end distance of ½ the nail length and a minimum edge distance of ¼ the nail length. Spacing in terms of nail diameter—for example, a 10-diameter spacing and a 5-diameter edge distance—is also used on occasion. This method provides slightly larger distances than those based on nail length. These general recommendations may be taken as guides, but for a specific problem the designer must rely on his experience with the particular species.

Nailed joints are generally limited to more lightly stressed joints and to material of maximum 2-in. thickness so that preboring will not be necessary to avoid splitting. If it is necessary to prebore, then it will probably be more economical to use bolts or timber connectors.

Figure 5.39 illustrates a pitched trussed rafter of the type widely used

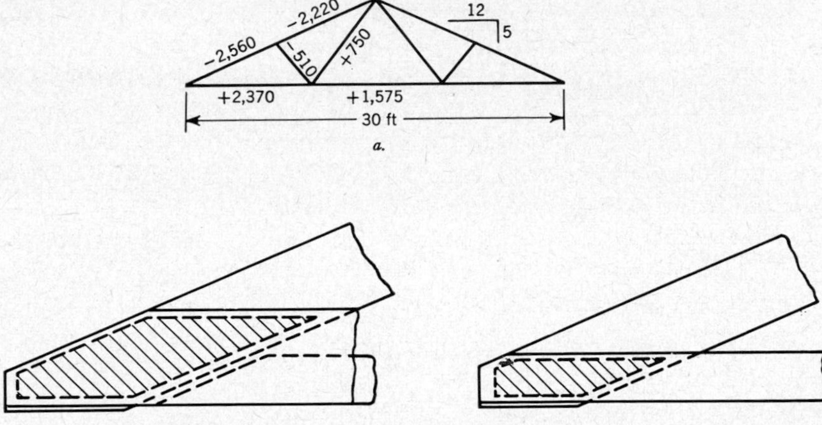

Fig. 5.39 Typical pitched-truss rafter

a. Stress diagram b. Nailed heel joint with gusset or splice plates c. Lapped-splice heel joint.

for homes and other small-span buildings (span usually not exceeding 50 ft). The stresses shown are for 35-lb roof and 10-lb ceiling load, 24-in. spacing, a 30-ft span, and 5:12 roof slope. For grades and species of material customarily used in housing, rafters would be 2 x 6, ceiling joists 2 x 4, and web members either 2 x 4 or 1-in. lumber. For partially seasoned lumber, a 90 per cent season factor may be applied to the basic nail values and a 115 per cent duration factor can be used for snow load. (See Sec. 3.17.)

Assume that the members are lapped at the joints so that the nails are in single shear and that the species of lumber is of the southern pine, Douglas fir, or larch variety. For two members of equal thickness, the required penetration for softwoods of ⅔ the nail length cannot be obtained (see Chap. 13, NDS). Thus the basic nail value must be reduced to the proportion of penetration or embedment furnished to penetration required. With a 16d nail, 3½-in. long, the penetration in two 2-in. members would be 1⅝ in., compared to the 2⅓ in. (⅔ of 3½ in.) required, or 70 per cent of basic nail values.

The heel joint is the most highly stressed connection, requiring a connection capacity of 2,370 lb if the bottom edge of the rafter is in bearing, or 2,560 lb if only the ceiling joist bears. To join two 2-in. members, nails should penetrate through the far member and preferably be clinched. In lieu of clinching, a special nail might be used to improve withdrawal resistance in the far member. A 16d nail would penetrate the 3¼ in. of material and still provide ¼ in. for clinching.

Adjusted allowable load per 16d nail is 77.5 lb (107 × 0.70 × 0.90 × 1.15). With the rafter bearing, the required number of nails in the lap is 31 (2,370 divided by 77.5). If the preceding general recommendations for nail spacing and edge distance are followed, it will be impossible to locate the required 31 nails in the small lapped area available. Apart from the empirical spacing rules, it is doubtful that 31 nails could be driven without undue splitting in most species.

Additional joint area can be provided by using larger members or by placing the ceiling joist and rafter in the same plane and using larger splice plates or gusset plates on each side. Both solutions, however, require extra labor and material for the extra pieces required. For comparison, this heel joint would be adequate for a lapped joint with one 2½-in. split ring and one ½-in. bolt, or with five ½-in. or four ⅝-in. bolts, but it would also be difficult to obtain proper spacing for the bolts in the lapped area.

If splice or gusset plates are used, nail size may be based on combined thickness of the plate and the rafter for single shear, and on the total thickness plus length for clinching for double shear. Although there are no standards, double shear values are frequently assumed to be twice those for single shear.

If the ceiling joist is spliced at the center of the span, the fastenings are designed for axial load plus the stresses acting perpendicular to the grain in order to resist the bending moment due to the ceiling load. A discussion of nailed plywood gusset-plate connections is included in Chap. 9.

5.62 Lag-screw joints The design of lag-screw joints is similar to that of bolt joints except that a minimum amount of penetration of the screw end is necessary to provide the withdrawal resistance furnished by the nut in a bolted joint. Lag screws are frequently used alone or with connectors if through bolts are impractical or undesirable because of appearance. There are many interrelated factors to be considered, as listed in Chap. 13. A simplified design procedure is outlined in Table 12.34 of Chap. 12.

6

Arches

LAMELLA ROOF CONSTRUCTION

6.1 Lamella roof construction Lamella roof construction, originating in Europe in 1908, was introduced to the United States in 1925. The lamella roof (Fig. 6.1) is made up of relatively short timbers of uniform length, called lamellas. Bevelled and bored at the ends and bolted together at an angle, the lamellas form a network of decorative structural timber. Standard lamella roofs employ the common or eccentric joint (Fig. 6.2a), whereas special roofs and very large spans use special joint connector plates (Fig. 6.2b).

The lamella roof and other arches afford an economical type of building with high center clearances, as for auditoriums; gymnasiums; field houses; indoor tennis, basketball, and badminton courts (in which the roof arch should follow the missile's trajectory curve); exhibition halls, and various other public buildings and hangars.

A network of lamellas forms an arch of mutually braced and stiffened timbers. As it is an arch rather than a truss, the roof exerts a horizontal thrust in addition to a vertical reaction. The resultant of these reactions is a roof thrust that is distributed to thrust supports—tie rods or buttresses, usually spaced from 12 to 20 ft apart—by timber, steel, or concrete sill beams between the supports. If continuous wall support for the sill beam is available, it need be designed for the horizontal thrust only (Fig. 6.3).

The four principal types of lamella roofs are the tied segmental arch, the buttress segmental arch, the parabolic arch, and the gothic arch (see Fig. 6.4).

6.2 Tied segmental arch The thrust of a tied segmental arch is resisted by tie rods or wood ties (see Fig. 6.4a). This method is commonly used if buildings occupy full lots or if the style of architecture

Courtesy Summerbell Roof Structures, Inc.

Fig. 6.1 Lamella roof (90-ft span)

prohibits the use of buttresses or cantilevered columns to resist the roof thrust.

The horizontal thrust, H, taken by the tie rod is determined by the formula:

$$H = \frac{(\text{dead} + \text{live load})(\text{square of the span} \times \text{tie-rod spacing})}{8 \times \text{roof rise}}$$

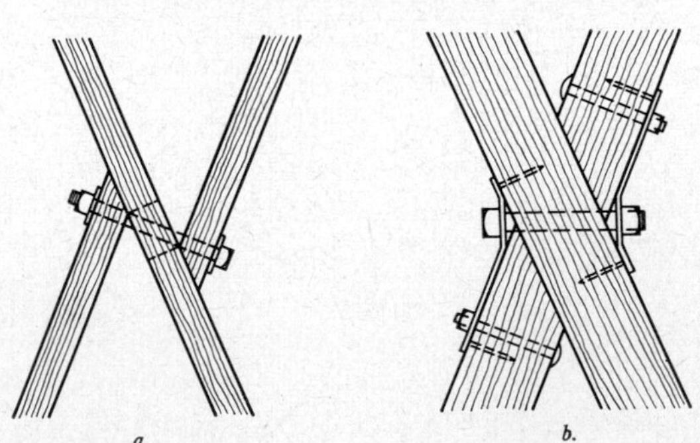

Fig. 6.2 Typical lamella joints

a. Common joint *b. Special joint*

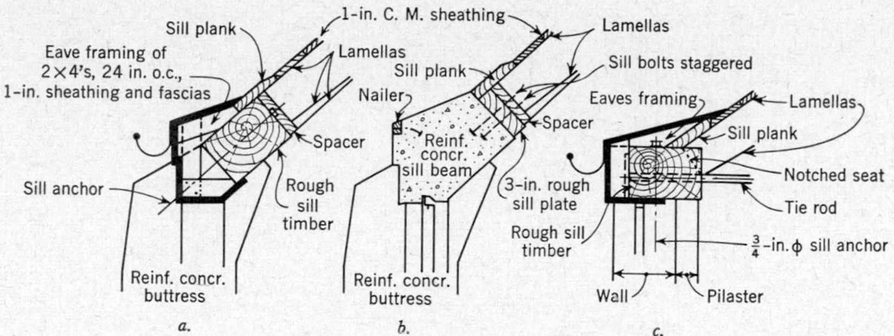

Fig. 6.3 Typical sill details

a. Tilted-timber sill
b. Reinforced-concrete sill
c. Flat-timber sill

The tie-rod area required at the root of the threads is obtained by dividing H by the allowable tensile stress for steel. The roof rise varies between 14 and 17 per cent of the roof span. If tied in this manner, a lamella roof is entirely self-supporting and exerts only vertical pressure. This pressure is equivalent to the live and dead load upon the wall or column supports. The roof must be properly anchored, of course, to resist wind action.

6.3 Buttress segmental arch In a buttress segmental arch (Fig. 6.4b), the thrust that is the resultant of horizontal and vertical reaction is resisted by buttresses, concrete or steel-beam columns, timber or steel bents, or rigid-frame bents (see Fig. 6.5). The roof rise varies between 14 and 25 per cent of the roof span, the usual rise being about 20 per cent. The buttresses permit the use of low and light sidewalls.

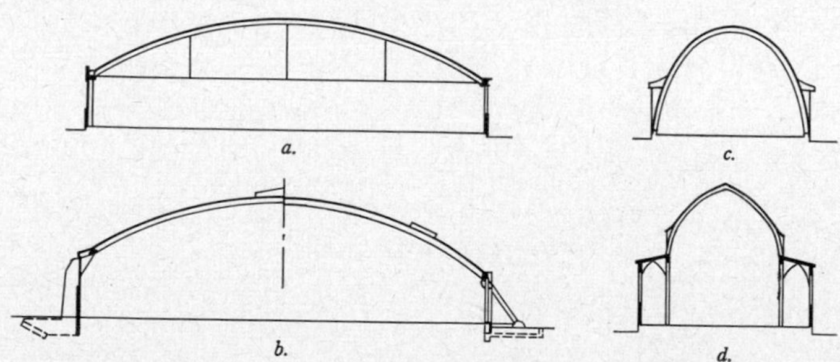

Fig. 6.4 Types of lamella roofs

a. Tied segmental arch
b. Buttress segmental arch
c. Parabolic arch
d. Gothic arch

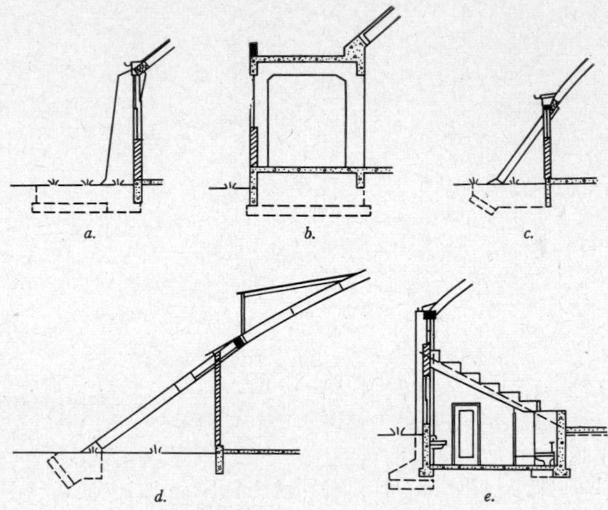

Fig. 6.5 Methods of absorbing roof thrust

a. Concrete buttress
b. Concrete rigid frame
c. Wood A-frame
d. Cantilevering timber strut
e. Tied concrete buttress

6.4 Parabolic arch A roof with a parabolic arch (Fig. 6.4c) usually rises from the floor line or from the top of a low foundation wall reinforced to resist the relatively low horizontal-thrust component. The floor construction acts as the tie membrane. The parabolic lamella roof combines wall and roof construction into one unit.

6.5 Gothic arch The gothic lamella roof is constructed as a three-hinged arch. It can be used with tie rods to cover buildings having a trapezoidal floor plan. For use in church design (Fig. 6.4d), it can rise from side-aisle height to span the nave. For use in storage sheds for grain, salt, or cottonseed, where provision must be made for overhead conveyors, it can rise from the top of low, buttressed foundation walls.

6.6 Roof plans Three main structural arrangements are possible with the lamella roof. Variations and combinations of these arrangements provide ample design leeway to meet most roof-contour requirements.

1. The continuous lamella roof (Fig. 6.6a) carries the network from gable wall to gable wall, acting as a horizontal wind-truss between gable walls.

2. The lamella roof with a sloped raftered end, or ends (Fig. 6.6b), stops its network 15 to 20 ft from one or both ends. The remaining space is covered by simple rafters supported by the end arch of the lamella roof and the end wall. These raftered ends give a warped surface of varying slope.

3. The lamella roof with broached ends (Fig. 6.7) is formed by intersection with other lamella roofs of the same radius springing from the end walls. The broached ends may be rectangular or multi-sided. Lamella roofs can also intersect, as needed, for "L," "T," "U," or cross-shaped floor plans.

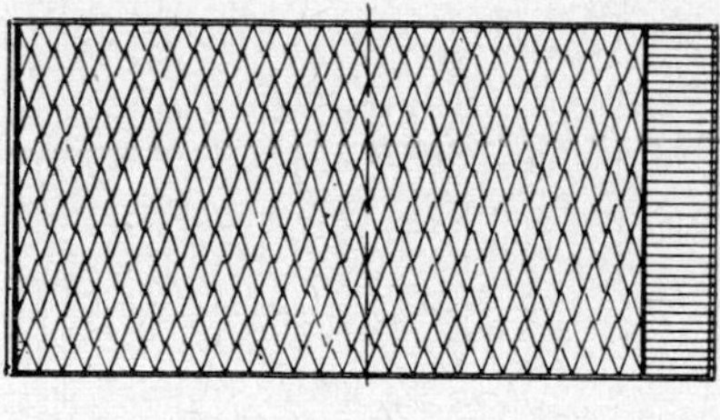

a. *b.*

Fig. 6.6 Lamella roof, continuous and raftered ends

a. Continuous
b. Raftered

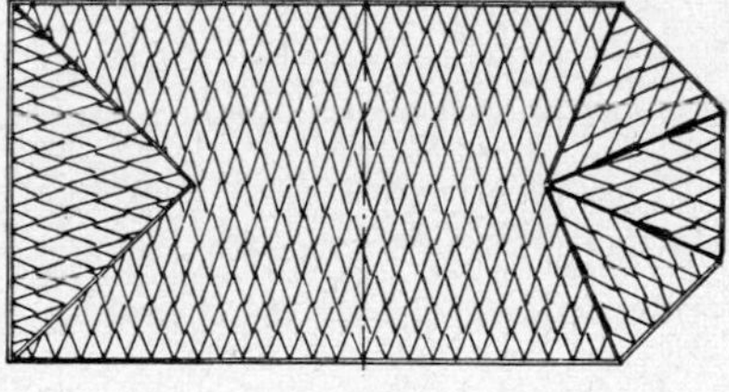

Fig. 6.7 Lamella roof, broached ends

6.7 Design Lamella roofs follow the arch principle and can be regarded as being either two-hinged, for segmental circular or parabolic types, or as three-hinged, for the Gothic type. In addition to dead loads and conventional live loads prescribed by local or state building codes, they are analyzed for strong winds in the South and for unbalanced loads in regions where snows occur. Special analysis is required for spot or traveling cranes for loads up to 5,000 lb, or for suspension of special mechanical or heating equipment. Short lamella roofs are checked for shell action if rigid gable support is available, and for wind action against gable ends. Spans are limited only by the availability of sawed lumber sections in sizes up to 4 x 20, or of laminated sections in even larger sizes.

6.8 Wind resistance The lamella network forms a curved wind truss spanning from gable wall to gable wall. The gable walls may thus be designed as structural members that are supported at top and bottom against wind pressure. (See Fig. 6.8.) In the direction of the arch, the curvature diverts rather than blocks the wind. The effective wind

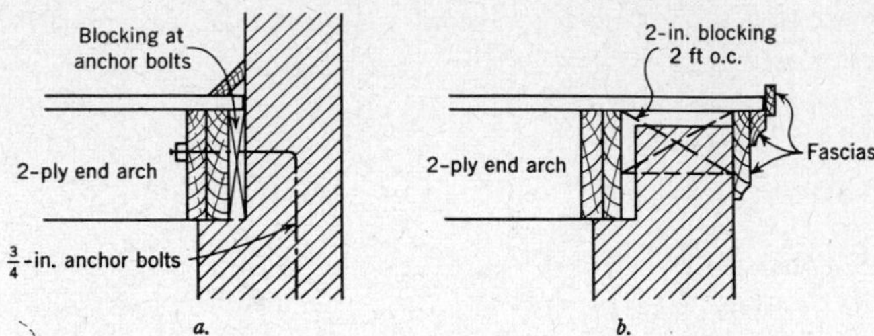

Fig. 6.8 Structural details for 12-in. gable walls

a. Gable with parapet *b. Gable with fascia*

pressure against cylindrical objects like chimneys, tanks, and curved roofs is generally accepted as ⅔ of the wind pressure against a plane equal to the vertical projection of the curved object.

The relatively closely spaced lamellas permit effective anchorage of the roof to the sidewalls. As all connections are bolted, a lamella roof offers a high resistance against interior pressure due to winds or other causes.

6.9 Erection Lamella roofs are usually erected from a movable scaffold having the width of the roof and the depth of one bay, i.e., the spacing between buttresses or tie rods. After placement of the timber sills—or spacers if steel or concrete beams are being used—the lamella network is woven from the sill up, from both sides, to meet and be connected in the center. Spacer boards over the lamella joints assure uniform spacing and prevent the network from spreading laterally both during fabrication and after the scaffold has been moved into the next bay for the weaving of another roof section (see Fig. 6.9).

Wood sheathing or stripping for other types of decking is applied after the network has been completed, fabrication again proceeding from the sill beams up.

6.10 Short-form computations Lamella roofs are basically a network of intersecting beam columns forming a two-hinged arch as deep as the individual beam columns and as wide as the length of the roof. An abridged design procedure for a segmental arch roof is given in the following paragraphs.

The desired span, L; desired rise, r; and radius, R, are all expressed in feet. The dead load, g; live load, p; drift or unbalanced load (snow load over one-half side of the span), s; and wind load, w, are all expressed in pounds per square foot. Reactions are expressed in pounds, and moments in foot-pounds per foot of length of roof. For the various loadings, the reactions and moments are:

1. For dead load g (see Fig. 6.10a):

$$\begin{aligned} V &= 0.5gL\sqrt{1 + 16/3(r/L)^2} \\ H &= VL/2r - gR \\ P' &= H(R - r)/R - VL/2R \\ \max M &= -0.068\, gr^2 \end{aligned}$$

2. For live load p over full span (see Fig. 6.10b):

$$\begin{aligned} V &= 0.5pL \\ H &= p(R - 0.57356r) \\ P' &= H(R - r)/R - VL/2R \\ M &= -0.09092pr^2 \end{aligned}$$

3. For snow load s on one side only (see Fig. 6.10c):

$$V_l = sL/8 \qquad V_r = 3sL/8$$
$$H = s/2(R - 0.57356r)$$
$$P'_l = H(R - r)/R + V_lL/2R \qquad P'_r = H(R - r)/R + V_rL/2R$$
$$M = V_l(L/2) - Hr - R(\sqrt{V_l^2 + H^2} - H)$$

Courtesy Roof Structures, Inc.

Fig. 6.9 Lamella erection (120-ft span)

4. For wind load w (see Fig. 6.10d):

$$V = wr^2/2L$$

$$H_l = 19wr/64 \qquad H_r = 45wr/64$$

$$P'_l = (19 - 3r/R)wr/64 \qquad P'_r = (45 - 29r/R)wr/64$$

$$M = 0.154wr^2$$

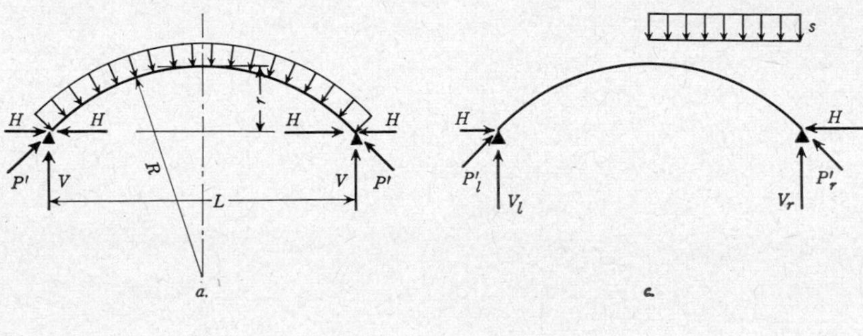

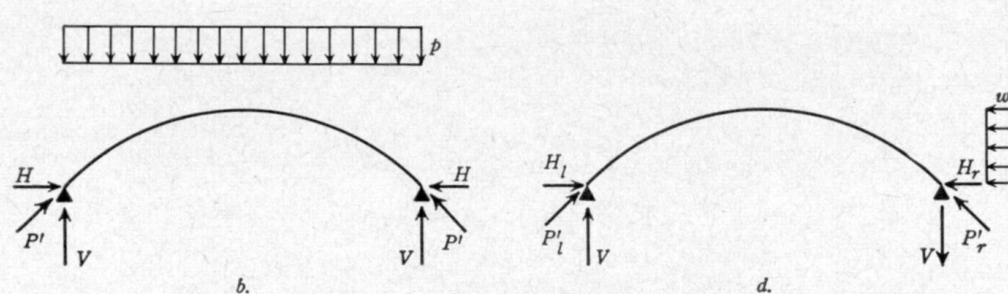

Fig. 6.10 Load-reaction diagrams

The spacing of lamellas is usually 4 ft or slightly less for lamellas 12 ft long, 4½ ft or slightly less for 14-ft lamellas, and 5 ft or slightly less for 16-ft lamellas. Spacing is measured parallel to the length of the roof, from center to center of the lamellas. It is equal to the short diagonal of the diamond shapes formed by their intersection. The enclosed angle between intersecting lamellas (twice the angle of inclination with respect to the axis of the arch) should not exceed 45 deg. Preferably it should be 38 to 40 deg.

At any intersection of lamellas, one lamella is continuous and therefore can take bending and compression, whereas the other lamellas are bolted to the continuous one, and therefore can take compression only. The sine of the angle of inclination equals the spacing of lamellas divided by the net length of a lamella. The net length of a lamella is the length, measured center to center, between its end connections and can be assumed to be about 6 to 8 in. less than the over-all length. This figure allows for beveled cuts on the end.

Thrusts (axial compression) and moments must be established for combinations of dead and live load, dead and drift load, and dead and wind load. The thrusts are then multiplied by ½ the lamella spacing divided by the cosine of the inclination. The moments are multiplied by the lamella spacing divided by the cosine of inclination. The resulting stresses for each combination are equal to the thrust divided by the sectional area (P'/A) plus the moment multiplied by 12 and divided by the section modulus ($12\ M/S$) of the chosen lamella. The maximum stress obtained for any combination shall be analyzed as for combined compression and bending with the permissible stresses for the stress grade as adjusted for the duration of loading.

The vertical shear introduced to the continuous lamella by the spliced lamellas is established for the maximum loading combination by multiplying the moment by 4 and dividing the result by the length of the lamella between end bolts. The resulting value is the required capacity of the fastenings perpendicular to grain in the lamella joint. Ordinarily, 2 x 8 and 2 x 10 lamellas receive one bolt and six or eight nails per joint.

The connection (bolts and nails) is designed to resist the vertical shear; it is also analyzed for load and as an eccentric joint. A tension is computed for the bolts that, neglecting friction, will balance the component of the thrust in the spliced lamella that is parallel to the through (unspliced) lamella.

The tension in the bolt (eccentric type) is equal to the thrust in the lamella divided by the tangent of twice the angle of inclination (the intersection angle). The washer area must be adequate for this load bearing perpendicular to the grain on the spliced lamella. The values for bolt tension and bearing perpendicular to grain are conservative, because any friction developed will lessen the theoretical bolt tension and thus lessen the stresses in bearing.

The bearing force perpendicular to the grain on the through lamella is equal to the thrust in the lamella divided by the sine of twice the angle of inclination. The unit bearing stress, based on the area of the diagonally cut end of the spliced lamella, must be within the allowable compression perpendicular to grain for the grade of lumber used.

The horizontal shear in the spliced lamella can be established by dividing ¾ of the vertical shear (determined above) by the net cross section of the end of the lamella.

More accurate and detailed calculations of the lamella stresses can be made by using the column analogy or the Van Karman method. The computation follows the theory of the two-hinged arch as outlined in Johnson, Bryan and Turneaure's book entitled *The Theory and*

Practice of Modern Framed Structures,[1] and as presented here in Sec. 6.18.

DETERMINATE AND INDETERMINATE ARCHES

6.11 Indeterminate frames Although most timber structures are statically determinate, there are advantages in the use of indeterminate frames because of the generally lower design stresses and consequent economy. The economic advantages of the structural frame may be offset to some degree, however, by the more complicated framing and possibly by the heavier foundation requirements of rigid frames. Except for unusually large spans or unusual shape or framing requirements, indeterminate frames are seldom used in timber.

Aside from two-hinged laminated arches and the lamella arch system, the most common indeterminate frames include rigid laminated frames, two-hinged and rigid trussed arches, segmental arches, and continuous trusses. Standard methods of engineering analysis are used for these frames, but deformation in the connections must be considered in addition to elastic deformation of the members.

6.12 Truss–column bents Trusses with column and knee braces or with integral trussed columns are not usually considered as rigid frames for vertical loads. Columns with knee braces and trussed columns are usually analyzed only for vertical truss reaction and for lateral loads.

6.13. Trussed and framed arches Trussed (Fig. 6.11) or framed (Fig. 6.12) arches are most usually designed as statically determinate, three-hinged arches because moment-resisting splices are difficult and expensive to frame. Sometimes, however, moment-resisting connections are made at the center hinge, and frequently the outer supports are not actually hinged but are flat end bearing. As a result, a certain amount of two-hinged action is obtained.

Trussed and framed arches may be less expensive to fabricate than glued-laminated arches even though larger member sizes may be required. Their design from a structural analysis standpoint is basically the same as that of glued-laminated arches. The elastic deflection of glued-laminated lumber may be greater than that of solid-sawed timber, because of the higher ratio of stresses to modulus of elasticity. However, the deflection due to joints or necessary connections may

[1] New York, John Wiley & Sons, 1917, Part II, Art. 128, p. 142.

Fig. 6.11 Three-hinged trussed arch

72-ft span; 10 ft on centers

result in a greater over-all deflection in a framed- or trussed-arch structure.

Framed arches of the gothic type utilize either a knee brace or steel gusset plates to develop the moment resistance required at the haunch section.

6.14 Segmental arches The commonly used segmental arch presents several indeterminate problems. In its simplest form, it consists of two relatively thin members side by side with staggered splices. Each member acts alternately as a splice plate for the other. These members usually have their outer edge sawed to the arc of a circle. As the ends of each member or splice plate are cut to butt, the direct stress is assumed to be carried in bearing. The moment-resisting couple is provided by timber connectors, bolts, or nailing. As sawing to curvature produces a variable cross section, the centerline of the piece does not run parallel to the straight edge. Bearing at the end of the piece may thus create an additional bending moment, which must also be considered.

6.15 Glued-laminated arches Glued-laminated members have opened up for timber the field of long-span arches that was formerly reserved almost entirely for steel and reinforced concrete (see Fig.

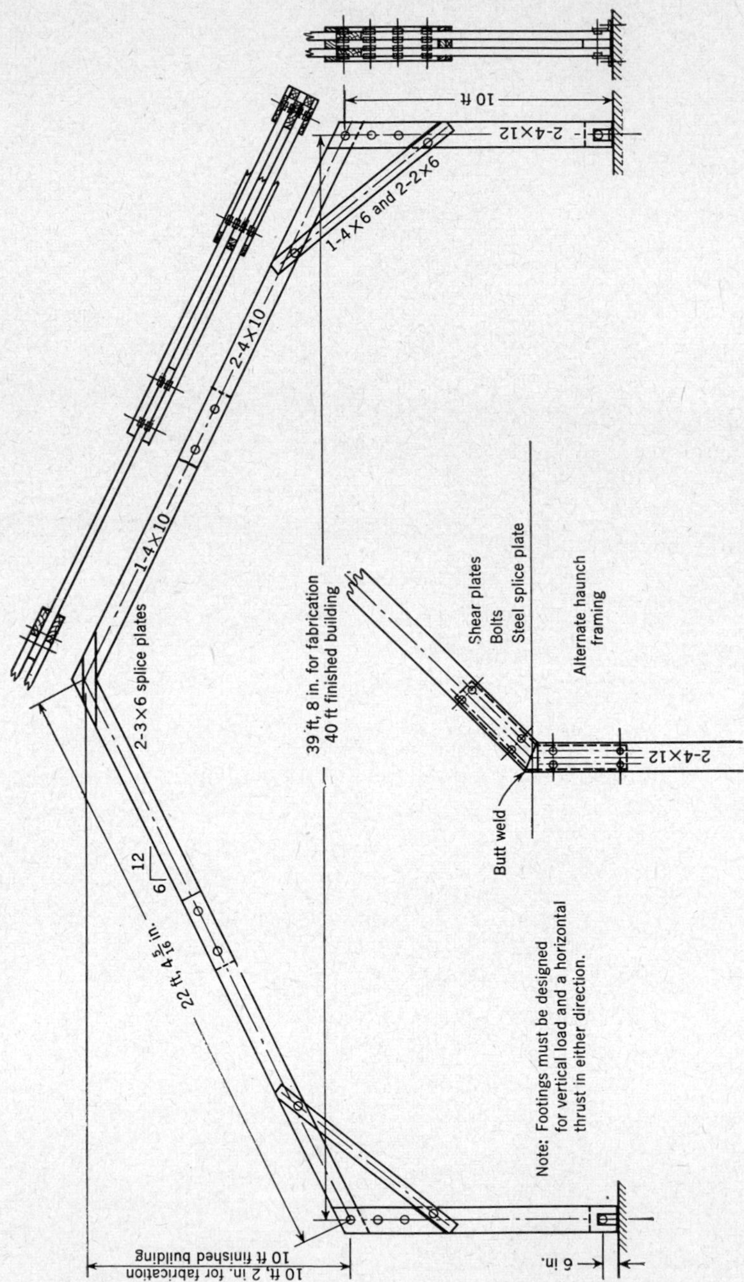

Fig. 6.12 Framed arch, details

Courtesy Unit Structures, Inc.

Fig. 6.13 Glued-laminated arches

Twelve 242-ft span, 11 x 46-in. interior arches; center rise, 74 ft.

6.13). They have also found application as smaller-span, decorative arches for churches, chapels, and all-purpose rooms. There are limitations in fabrication and shipping, however, which a designer should investigate before venturing to design with this relatively new structural medium.

There are three primary fabrication limitations: the capability of the laminator to make and handle large members, the open-and-closed assembly time required for the glue used, and the maximum size that transportation equipment and route clearance will permit.

A modern laminating plant has sufficient facilities to permit the assembly of any size member that can be shipped. Such facilities include a straight press long enough for beams and chord members of up to 130 ft in length (Fig. 6.14), and equipment for curved members up to 120 ft (Fig. 6.15). The rise of a single segment is somewhat dependent upon the length of the member, and also is restricted by shipping limitations to about 13 ft.

The open-and-closed assembly time is that period of time from the spreading of the glue on the first lamination until the application of

Courtesy Timber Structures, Inc.

Fig. 6.14 Lay-up for glue-laminating straight members

Courtesy Unit Structures, Inc.

Fig. 6.15 Finishing operations for glued-laminated curved members

the pressure. It varies according to the type of glue used and the temperature and relative humidity in the plant. Laminators should be consulted for large or unusual sections.

Shipping facilities have a great deal to do with the limitations of large assemblies. If marine transportation is available close to both plant and job site, such large assemblies as the U-shaped frames for use in wooden ships can be transported in one piece. If rail or truck facilities must be used, however, members more than 13 ft deep are usually considered too large. Occasionally the use of underslung freight cars permits greater depths, but careful checking is required (see Fig. 6.16).

Courtesy Timber Structures, Inc.

Fig. 6.16 Shipping arches by rail

The use of field moment splices permits the shipping of assemblies that would otherwise be out of the question. These splices should be designed to take care of not only the moment at the point of splice but also the axial compression and shear. A competent laminator employs engineers who are well grounded in the design of such splices and who know the methods by which they may be made as inconspicuous as possible. Moment splices have been developed that permit splicing at the junction of the wall and roof arms of two- and three-hinged arches. Such splices provide greater economy both in fabrication and shipment.

6.16 Three-hinged arches Three-hinged arches may take many shapes (see Figs. 6.13 and 6.17), from a constant-section and constant-curvature arch to one with a vertical wall arm and a nearly flat roof arm. Those with a very low rise are usually quite impractical because the horizontal thrust is very large, and consequently very large moments have to be developed in the haunch. Such shapes are often resolved into two-hinged arches with a substantially reduced thrust and

Courtesy McKeown Bros. Co.

Fig. 6.17 Three-hinged boomerang arch

haunch moment, or even into a simple span beam. Simple-span laminated beams have been built for spans up to 104 ft and should not be overlooked as an alternative to rigid-frame construction for spans up to 100 ft.

Three-hinged arches are often used as the basic frame for hammer-beam arches and those which have ornate falsework added to simulate old-style timber-arch framing. Such arches are usually designed as simple three-hinged arches; the additional built-up members are not considered as part of the structural frame. Often appearance rather than economy is primary; and heavier members are more in keeping with the style of the building.

6.17 Two-hinged arches Two-hinged arches (see Fig. 6.18) are indeterminate, and their analysis is complicated. Such arches have the advantage of reduced thrust and bending moment and can be broken down to more convenient transportation sizes by splices at or near points of contraflexure.

Constant-section, constant-curvature two-hinged arches present the most economical method of spanning any area by arches. Tie rods are usually the most economical means of resisting the horizontal thrust. The general shape requirements of a building will usually determine

Fig. 6.18 Two-hinged arch

Note moment splices under monitor windows.

the most desirable type of arch. The designer should remember that the farther an arch deviates from a circular arc, the greater the moment and consequently the greater the size and cost. Parabolic arches, the most economical for uniform balanced loads, are more difficult for shop lay-up and less economical for unbalanced loads.

DESIGN OF TWO-HINGED ARCHES

6.18 Precise method As previously mentioned, two-hinged arches are statically indeterminate structures. Because this text is not intended as a reference on structural analysis, all the ramifications of arch design will not be discussed. However, the average designer will find the following methods of analysis—based on an arch that is uniformly loaded, as with planks or joists equally spaced—helpful in preparing preliminary designs for estimating purposes. A more accurate analysis may be necessary either for special loading conditions, such as balcony or other concentrated loads, or for arches with supports on different elevations.

A precise method of design for two-hinged arches (see Fig. 6.19) is outlined below:

1. Lay out one-half of the arch into a convenient number of equal divisions. Usually ten such divisions will be sufficiently accurate; however, the more divisions, the more precise the results. Next compute the x and y distances, and enter them in a table similar to that shown in Fig. 6.20.
2. List the dead-load and live-load values for the points of division in the proper columns. It should be noted that vertical live loads, such as snow (computed in pounds per square foot), act vertically and uniformly along the horizontal projection of the arch. Dead loads are usually uniform per unit length of arch but vary along the horizontal projection. It is not possible, therefore, to combine vertical live loads and dead loads in one column.
3. Considering the entire arch as a simple span beam, compute the bending moments, MS, at the division points assumed in step 1, and enter in the proper columns.
4. Multiply the MS values by y values, and list.
5. Compute horizontal thrust, H, by the formula shown in Fig. 6.20. This formula neglects the effect of tie-rod elongation or spread in abutments, which is usually small.
6. Proceed with the design, once this H value has been determined, in the same way as for statically determinate problems.

Although suitable for all types and shapes of constant-section two-hinged arches, the above method is laborious and time-consuming. For many arches, the following coefficient method is more convenient.

6.19 Coefficient method The coefficient method of arch analysis is particularly adaptable to constant-radius, uniform-section, low-rise two-hinged arches with level supports and uniform loading. Special arches require analysis by more detailed methods.

The coefficients of Table 6.1 apply to unit loads and represent stress values per square foot of roof, per foot of span, and per foot length of building measured perpendicular to span of arches. Values are tabu-

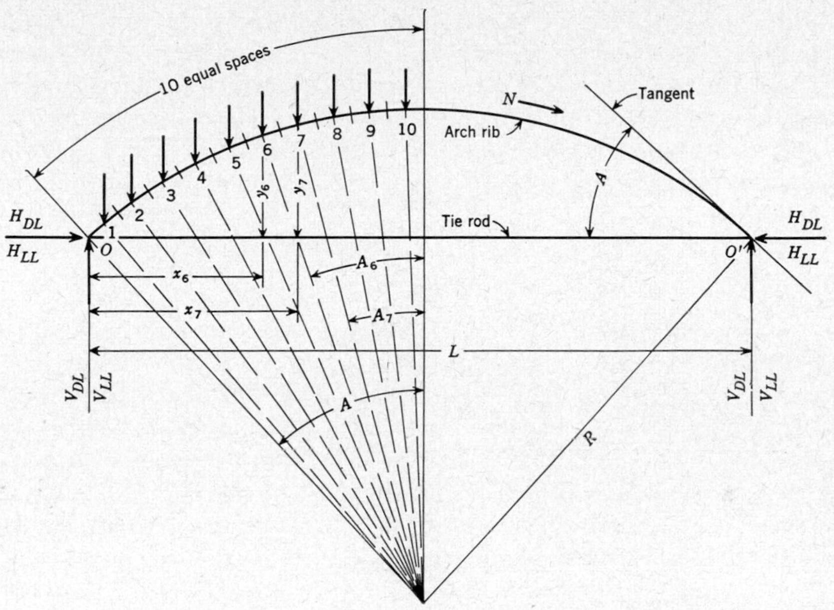

Fig. 6.19 Two-hinged arch diagram

A = *Tangent angle; also ½ center angle*
DL = *Dead load*
H = *Horizontal thrust*
L = *Span*
LL = *Live load*
M = *Bending moment on arch*
MS = *Bending moment of arch as simple beam*
N = *Normal thrust P along arch*
R = *Radius of curvature*
V = *Vertical reaction*
x = *Horizontal ordinate at division point*
y = *Vertical ordinate at division point*
Σ = *Summation of values*

lated for heel angles of 28 to 43 deg and for ratios of span to rise of from 5:1 to 8:1. Dead load is computed per unit per length of arch and live load per unit of length of the horizontal projection of arch. The coefficients reflect this variation.

Coefficients are given for bending moment, M, axial compression, P', and horizontal thrust at base, H. Coefficients permit solutions for conditions of balanced loads and any degree of half-span unbalanced loads. Horizontal thrust is maximum for balanced loads, and coefficients of H are given only for this condition.

6.20 Maximum moment (M) The maximum moment (in inch-pounds) of the arch is equal to the coefficient of M multiplied by the

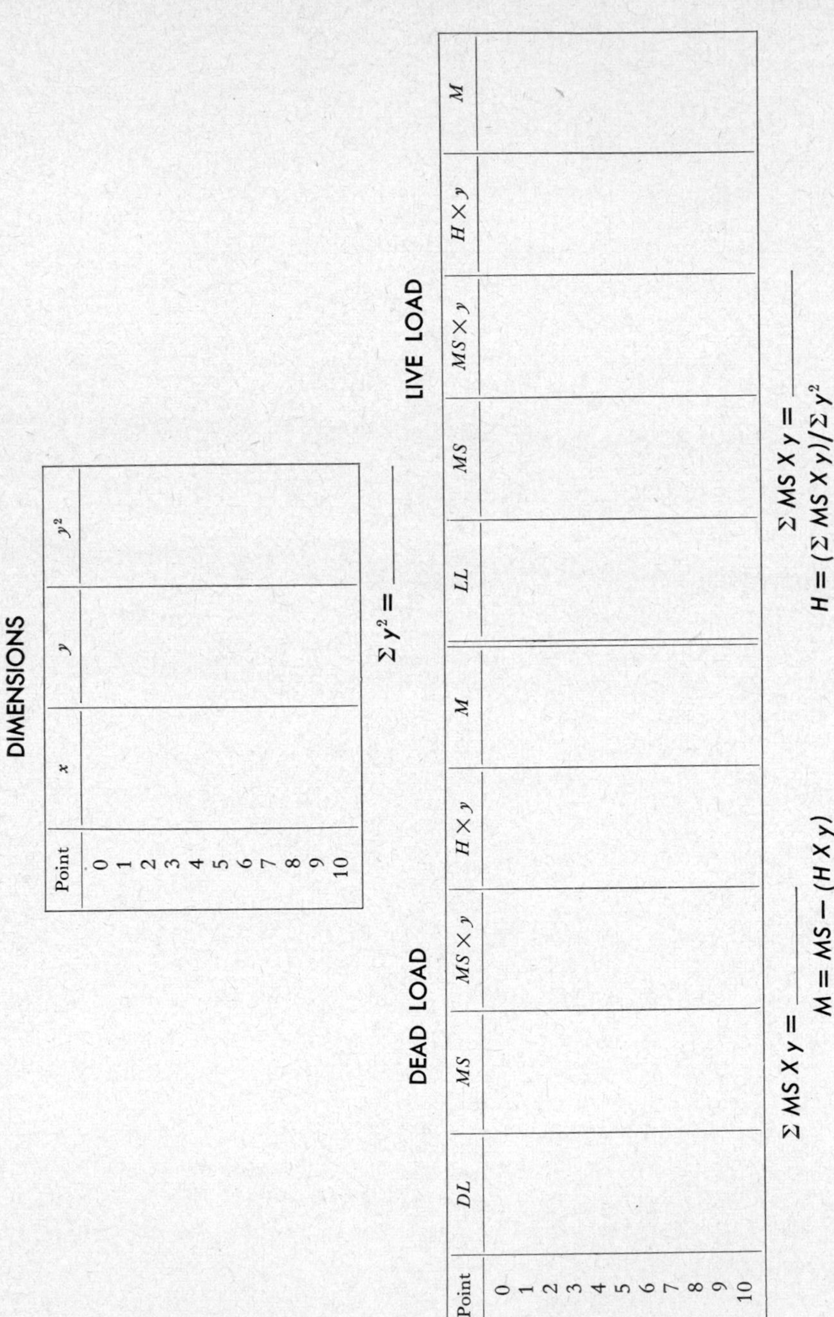

DIMENSIONS

Point	x	y	y^2
0			
1			
2			
3			
4			
5			
6			
7			
8			
9			
10			

$\Sigma y^2 =$ ______

	DEAD LOAD					LIVE LOAD				
Point	DL	MS	$MS \times y$	$H \times y$	M	LL	MS	$MS \times y$	$H \times y$	M
0										
1										
2										
3										
4										
5										
6										
7										
8										
9										
10										

$\Sigma MS \times y =$ ______ $\qquad \Sigma MS \times y =$ ______

$M = MS - (H \times y) \qquad H = (\Sigma MS \times y)/\Sigma y^2$

Fig. 6.20 Two-hinged arch calculation form

load (in pounds per square foot) by the bay length (in feet) by the square of the span (in square feet):

$$M = \text{coefficient } M \times w \times B \times L^2$$

Maximum moment usually occurs under unbalanced load conditions. For balanced live and dead loads, the maximum moments occur at approximately 15 per cent of the span from each hinge. For balanced dead load and unbalanced live load, maximum moment occurs at approximately 25 per cent of the span from the hinge on the least loaded side.

6.21 Axial compression (P') The maximum axial compression force in the arch (in pounds) is equal to the coefficient of P' multiplied by the load (in pounds per square foot) by the bay length (in feet) by the span (in feet):

$$P' = \text{coefficient } P' \times w \times B \times L$$

For balanced loading, use the sum of the thrusts obtained by application of dead- and live-load coefficients for balancing loading. For unbalanced loading, use the same procedure as for moments.

Axial compression values, like moment values, should always be for the same location so that they can be properly used together in the combined stress formula.

6.22 Horizontal thrust (H) As the maximum horizontal thrust at the hinges is reached under balanced loads, unbalanced-load conditions need not be considered, except possibly for foundation requirements. The maximum horizontal thrust is equal to the coefficient of H multiplied by the load (in pounds per square foot) by the bay length (in feet) by the span (in feet):

$$H = \text{coefficient } H \times w \times B \times L$$

6.23 Vertical reaction (V) Vertical reactions may be determined by analytical means using the following theorems: (1) summation of vertical forces equal zero, and (2) moments clockwise equal moments counter-clockwise. For balanced loading, each reaction is equal to ½ the total live and dead loads on the arch.

For balanced-load conditions, use the coefficients for M, P', and H itemized as 1, 2, and 3, respectively, in Table 6.1.

For full unbalanced-load conditions, use item 3 for H and items 4 and 5 for M and P' respectively.

For half or other partial ratio of unbalancing, use item 3 for H, items 4 and 5 for that portion of live load which is unbalanced, and items 6 and 7 for that portion of live load which is balanced.

TABLE 6.1 Two-hinged arch coefficients

Ratio–Span/rise		8.022	7.733	7.464	7.212	6.975	6.752	6.542	6.343
Tangent angle		28 deg	29 deg	30 deg	31 deg	32 deg	33 deg	34 deg	35 deg
Balanced 15 per cent									
M 1	Dead	.0120	.0130	.0144	.0155	.0168	.0180	.0192	.0204
	Live	.0180	.0192	.0203	.0218	.0230	.0244	.0258	.0273
P′ 2	Dead	1.074	1.046	1.019	.9920	.9680	.9420	.9200	.8970
	Live	1.060	1.030	1.004	.9750	.9500	.9240	.9000	.8760
H 3	Dead	.9870	.9600	.9315	.9040	.8790	.8540	.8285	.8040
	Live	.9630	.9340	.9060	.8800	.8530	.8280	.8030	.7800
Unbalanced 25 per cent									
M 4	Dead	.0028	.0033	.0039	.0044	.0049	.0055	.0060	.0066
	Live	.1901	.1902	.1904	.1905	.1907	.1908	.1909	.1910
P′ 5	Dead	1.0100	.9810	.9530	.9290	.9100	.8910	.8720	.8535
	Live	.4985	.4845	.4660	.4502	4406	.4300	.4196	.4050
M 6	Live	.0075	.0080	.0084	.0090	.0097	.0105	.0113	.0121
P′ 7	Live	1.0100	.9750	.9400	.9090	.8800	.8550	.8300	.8050

As an illustration, for a condition of 30-psf live and 12-psf dead load with half unbalancing, the coefficients are selected as follows:

For *H,* use item 3 with 30-psf live and 12-psf dead loads.

For *M,* use item 4 with 15-psf live and 12-psf dead loads plus item 6 with 15-psf live load.

For *P′,* use item 5 with 15-psf live and 12-psf dead loads plus item 7 with 15-psf live load.

6.24 Example of calculations

Arch data:

Span = 86 ft
Spacing = 17 ft
Loading = 20 psf live load,
10 psf dead load
Tangent angle = 42 deg
Radius = 64 ft

Allowable stresses:

$c = 2{,}180$ psi
$f = 2{,}280$ psi
$E = 1{,}800{,}000$ psi

TABLE 6.1 (Cont.)

Ratio–Span/rise		6.155	5.977	5.808	5.648	5.495	5.349	5.210	5.077
Tangent angle		36 deg	37 deg	38 deg	39 deg	40 deg	41 deg	42 deg	43 deg
Balanced 15 per cent									
M [1]	Dead	.0216	.0228	.0240	.0251	.0264	.0276	.0294	.0324
	Live	.0290	.0308	.0325	.0344	.0369	.0402	.0421	.0442
P' [2]	Dead	.8763	.8573	.8394	.8229	.8060	.7925	.7733	.7654
	Live	.8504	.8307	.8121	.7945	.7780	.7623	.7474	.7333
H [3]	Dead	.7791	.7570	.7360	.7159	.6969	.6788	.6611	.6446
	Live	.7577	.7351	.7136	.6932	.6737	.6551	.6373	.6202
Unbalanced 25 per cent									
M [4]	Dead	.0071	.0084	.0096	.0108	.0120	.0132	.0144	.0155
	Live	.1912	.1916	.1919	.1924	.1928	.1932	.1936	.1941
P' [5]	Dead	.8351	.8149	.7959	.7779	.7596	.7449	.7294	.7150
	Live	.3989	.3882	.3781	.3684	.3593	.3506	.3423	.3343
M [6]	Live	.0129	.0137	.0145	.0157	.0173	.0193	.0213	.0234
P' [7]	Live	.7840	.7630	.7450	.7240	.7080	.6910	.6750	.6600

Courtesy Timber Structures, Inc.

[1, 2, 3] For balanced loadings at critical section that is 15 per cent of span from hinge on either side.

[4, 5] For unba'anced loadings at critical s ction that is 25 per cent of span from hinge on least loaded side.

[6, 7] For balanced loadings at section that is 25 per cent of span from hinge on least loaded side.

Maximum moment for full unbalanced condition (in inch-pounds):

$$M_{DL} = 0.0144 \times 10 \times 17 \times 86^2 = 18{,}100$$
$$M_{LL} = 0.1936 \times 20 \times 17 \times 86^2 = 487{,}000$$
$$M = 505{,}100$$

Axial thrust (in pounds):

$$P'_{DL} = 0.7294 \times 10 \times 17 \times 86 = 10{,}660$$
$$P'_{LL} = 0.3423 \times 20 \times 17 \times 86 = 10{,}000$$
$$P' = 20{,}660$$

Maximum horizontal thrust–tension in tie rod (in pounds):

$$\begin{aligned} H_{DL} &= 0.6611 \times 10 \times 17 \times 86 = 9{,}660 \\ H_{LL} &= 0.6373 \times 20 \times 17 \times 86 = 18{,}620 \\ H &= 28{,}280 \end{aligned}$$

Maximum vertical reaction (in pounds):

$$\begin{aligned} V_{DL} &= 10 \times 17 \times 46 = 7{,}820 \\ V_{LL} &= 20 \times 17 \times 43 = 14{,}600 \\ V &= 22{,}420 \end{aligned}$$

Assuming lateral support for the arch in order to permit full compression parallel to grain stresses, the required arch section is:

$$\begin{aligned} A = P'/c &= 20{,}660/2{,}180 = 19.5 \text{ sq in.} \\ S = M/f &= 505{,}100/2{,}280 = 222 \text{ cu in.} \end{aligned}$$

Try a 5¼ x 19½ section, $S = 333$, $A = 102$. Then:

$$\begin{aligned} M/Sf + P'/Ac &= \frac{505{,}100}{333 \times 2{,}280} + \frac{20{,}660}{102 \times 2{,}180} \\ &= 0.67 + 0.09 = 0.76 \end{aligned}$$

The slenderness ratio (l/d) of the arch thus determined must be checked in the vertical direction normal to the roof plane. The length of arch acting as a column in a vertical plane is the length of arch between hinges and points of contraflexure, or between points of contraflexure. Frequently ½ the arch length is used. Points of contraflexure usually occur at about ¼ the arch length from the hinge for balanced loading, and a point of contraflexure usually occurs near the centerline of span for unbalanced loadings. The least dimension d used in the column formula is the depth of the arch.

One method of analysis that may be used is that for eccentric columns (see Chap. 13, NDS Appendix B):

$$l/d = 46 \times 12 \text{ (½ length of arch)} \div 19\tfrac{1}{2} \text{ (depth of arch)} = 28.3$$

The allowable compression parallel to grain, c, for an l/d ratio of $28.3 = 675 \times 1.15 = 775$. As the ratio is greater than 20, and the bending moment is known, the simplest of the eccentric column formulas may thus be used:

$$\frac{M/S}{f - P/A} + \frac{P/A}{c} \leq 1$$

$$\frac{505{,}100/333}{2{,}280 - 20{,}660/102} + \frac{20{,}660/102}{775} = 0.73 + 0.26 = 0.99$$

Though a smaller section might have satisfied the A and S requirements, it would not have been satisfactory for the eccentric column analysis.

The arch section is also checked for radial tension or compression as noted in Chap. 13. The maximum moment previously determined, being negative, produces radial compression. To save computing the lesser value of maximum positive moment, which produces radial tension, the section chosen may be evaluated for maximum negative-moment resistance for radial stresses. In this example, the selected section is adequate for radial tension for more than 6 times the negative moment in the arch.

DESIGN OF THREE-HINGED ARCHES

6.25 Design procedure Three-hinged arches are statically determinate and may be designed by the three equations of statics. The following typical example of a three-hinged arch (see Fig. 6.21) illustrates

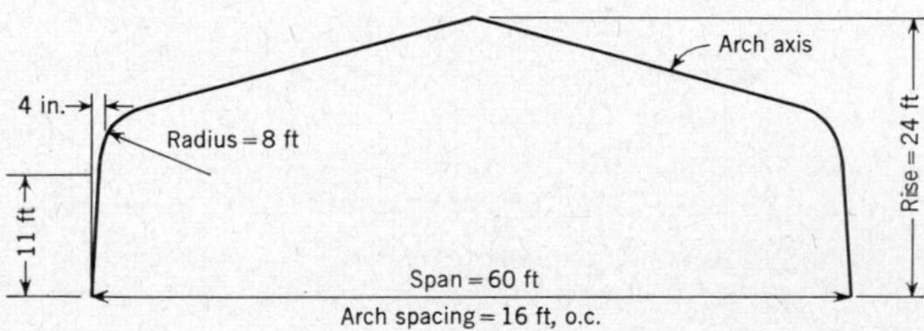

Fig. 6.21 Typical three-hinged arch design

a design procedure used by many designers. The 4-in. dimension at the haunch, indicating a slope from vertical of the leg section, is an estimate of the amount of taper in the leg. The 4-in. dimension will be adequate for a taper of 8 in. and will give conservative bending moments if the actual taper determined in design is more than 8 in. The outer face of the leg is usually vertical, and all of the taper occurs on the inner face. The assumed radius at the centerline of a haunch of 8 ft is almost the minimum radius that can be used. If possible, a larger radius should be used to permit thicker laminations or, conversely, in order to permit a larger adjusted f value for the same thickness.

Assume a live load (snow) of 30 psf, a dead load of 15 psf, and a wind load of 20 psf on projected area, or 320 lb per lin ft. Assume the following allowable stresses:

f = 2,000 increased 15 per cent for snow, or 2,300 psi
f_t = 2,200 increased 15 per cent for snow, or 2,530 psi
c = 1,900 increased 15 per cent for snow, or 2,190 psi
H = 165 increased 15 per cent for snow, or 190 psi
C = 390 increased 15 per cent for snow, or 450 psi

At the curved portion of the arch, the allowable f value must be modified for the curvature factor:

$$f = 2{,}300 \times [1 - 2{,}000(t/R)^2]$$

Assuming ⅝-in. laminations, then $t = 0.625$, $R = 96$, and the factor $= 0.915$. Thus:

$$f = 2{,}300 \times 0.915 = 2{,}110 \text{ psi}$$

6.26 Loading reactions The reactions for various conditions of loading (see Fig. 6.22) may be computed from the following equations, in which:

W = load, in pounds per linear foot
L = span, in feet
r = rise, in feet
V_l = vertical reaction, left, in pounds
V_r = vertical reaction, right, in pounds
H = horizontal reaction, in pounds

Uniform load on full span:

$$V_l = V_r = WL/2 \qquad H = WL^2/8r$$

Uniform load on one-half span:

$V_r = 3WL/8$ (on loaded side) $\qquad H = WL^2/16r$
$V_l = WL/8$ (on unloaded side)

Wind load on one side:

$V_l = V_r = Wr^2/2L$ (acting downward on windward side and upward on leeward side)
$H_l = 3Wr/4$ (on windward side)
$H_r = Wr/4$ (on leeward side)

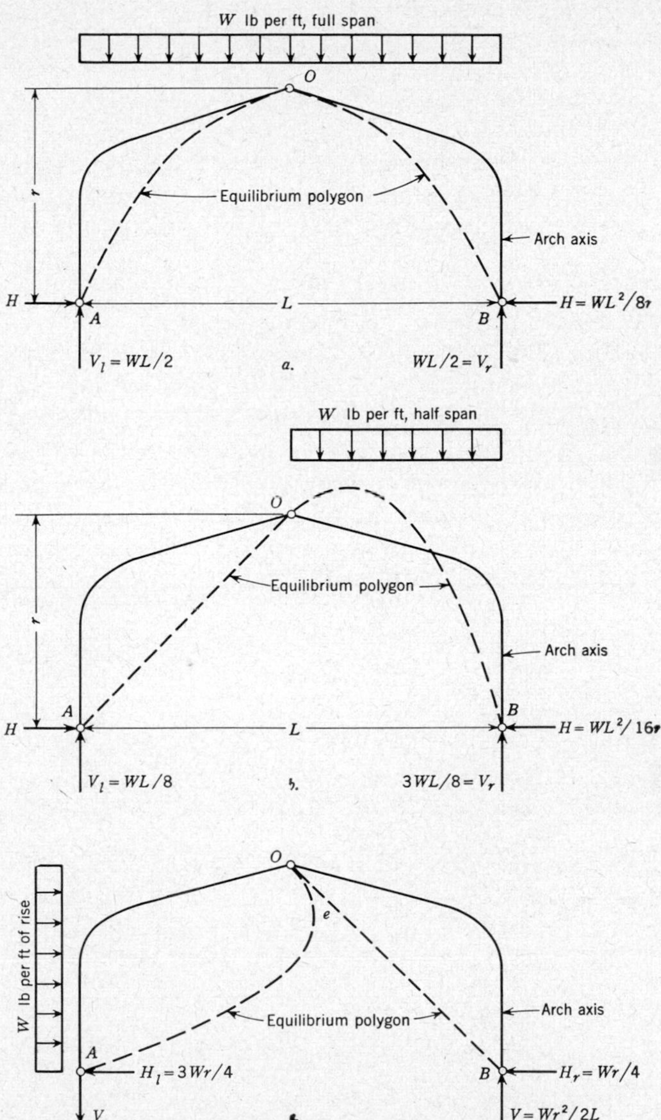

Fig. 6.22 Three-hinged-arch loading reactions

a. *Equilibrium polygon—parabola with vertex at crown hinge* O
b. *Equilibrium polygon—straight line* A *to* O, *parabola* O *to* B *with its vertex* L/*8 to the right and* r/*8 above* O
c. *Equilibrium polygon—parabola* A *to* O *with its vertex at* e, L/*16 to the right and* r/*4 below* O, *and straight line O* to *B*.

Tabulated below are the reactions (in pounds) for various combinations of loadings:

LOAD	V_l	V_r	H_l	H_r
Dead plus live	21,600	21,600	13,500	13,500
Dead	7,200	7,200	4,500	4,500
Live (right)	3,600	10,800	4,500	4,500
Live (left)	10,800	3,600	4,500	4,500
Wind (left)	1,536−	1,536+	5,760 (r)	1,920 (r)
Wind (right)	1,536+	1,536−	1,920 (l)	5,760 (l)

6.27 Equilibrium polygons Once the reactions have been determined, it is advisable, although not necessary, to draw an equilibrium polygon for each condition of load. The polygons may be drawn rapidly by following the method outlined in Fig. 6.22 and by remembering that the offset from a tangent to a parabola varies as the square of the distance. After the equilibrium polygons have been drawn (see Fig. 6.23) the moment at any point may be determined for vertical loads by multiplying the length of a vertical line between the arch axis and the equilibrium polygon by the reaction H. For horizontal forces,

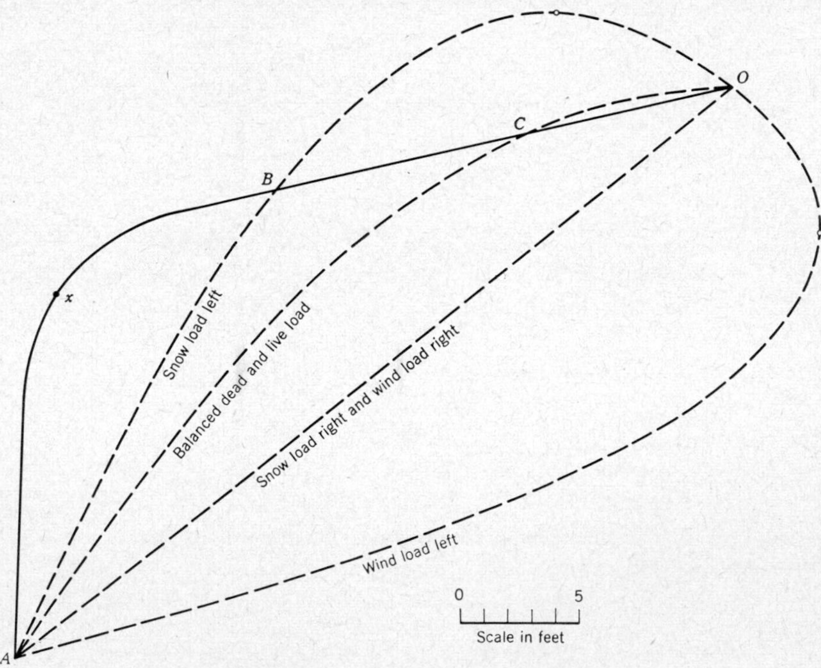

Fig. 6.23 Equilibrium polygon

the moment at any point is the vertical reaction multiplied by the length of a horizontal line between the arch axis and the equilibrium polygon. The advantage of these equilibrium polygons is that the points of maximum moment may be determined quickly by inspection, and the sign of the moment readily determined.

For vertical loads, axis moments are positive if the equilibrium polygon lies above the arch; if it lies below, they are negative. For horizontal loads, a moment at a point on the arch axis between the equilibrium polygon and the load is positive. If the equilibrium polygon and the load are to the same side of a point on the arch axis, the moment at that point is negative. Thus on the left side of the arch, the polygons indicate positive moment for wind on the left but negative moment for wind on the right (Fig. 6.23).

6.28 Maximum moment, thrust, and shear Table 6.2 indicates the maximum moments at point x for the curves of Fig. 6.23. Point x was determined by measurement of the moment arms to the polygons and is approximately at the center of the haunch arc.

TABLE 6.2 Maximum moments at point "x" for curves of Fig. 6.23

Load	Moment arm *in.*	Force *lb*	Moment *in.-lb*
Balanced dead and live	150	13,500 (H)	−2,030,000
Balanced dead only	150	4,500 (H)	−675,000
Wind left	376	1,536 (V)	+577,000
Wind right	223	1,536 (V)	−343,000
Snow left	138	4,500 (H)	−622,000
Snow right	174	4,500 (H)	−783,000

It is obvious that the maximum moment occurs under full balanced load even if the moment due to dead load is added to the other conditions.

Like moment, the direct axial stress or thrust will generally be maximum at the center of the haunch for this shape of arch. Maximum shear normal to the arch axis will generally occur either at the lower hinges or at either point of tangency of the curved haunch section. Both the thrust and the shear are generally maximum for full balanced loading. Wind-load combinations with dead load may be critical in areas of little or no snow or vertical live load.

6.29 Determination of thrust and shear Figure 6.24 illustrates a graphical method of determining the thrust and shear at any point. Half the arch axis is shown and also an equilibrium polygon for bal-

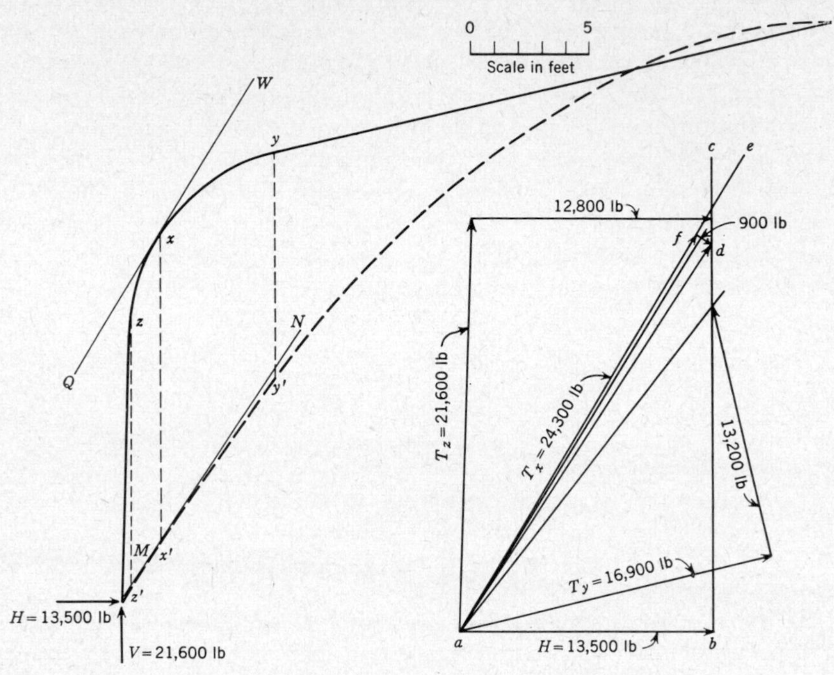

Fig. 6.24 Thrust and shear diagrams

anced dead load plus live load. In the force diagram, line *ab* represents *H* (13,500 lb) to scale, and *bc* is perpendicular to *ab*. A line through point *a* parallel to *MN*, which is tangent to the equilibrium polygon at *x′*, intersects *bc* at *d*. Line *ae* is parallel to the tangent *QW* to the arch axis at point *x*, and represents the direction of the arch axis at that point. If *df* is drawn perpendicular to *ae*, *af* then represents in amount and direction the thrust or axial stress in the arch axis to the right of point *x*, and *df* the shear acting normal to the arch axis to the right of point *x*. Values of the axial stress and shear are also shown for points *y* and *z*. The value of 900 lb for shear at point *x* indicates that that point is not exactly the point of maximum moment, as the shear would be 0 lb at point of maximum moment. However, the accuracy is close enough for practical purposes. More accuracy could have been obtained if the diagrams had been drawn to a larger scale.

6.30 Design of principal sections In most arches of this shape, the haunch or knee section is determined by the requirements for moment and axial stress as determined above. The straight arm and leg sections are generally proportioned for appearance and the need to meet purlin dimensions. The depth at the crown is always made at least equal to the width of the member and preferably 1¼ or more times the width. The arm and leg sections are generally overdesigned by such procedure. However, for special loading conditions or supports on different levels, it is desirable to select several points along the arch axis and set up tables of maximum moments, shears, and axial stresses for various conditions of load. The arch cross section selected should be then checked at these points.

In the selection of the arch cross section for this example, ⅝-in. laminations, a 9-in. dressed width of member, and lateral support of the legs will be assumed.

6.31 Design of knee or haunch Assume that $P = 24{,}300$ lb (see Fig. 6.24), $M = 2{,}030{,}000$ in.-lb, and shear normal to axis $= 900$ lb. Then:

$$P/Ac + M/Sf \leq 1$$
$$24{,}300/A(2{,}190) + 2{,}030{,}000/S(2{,}110) = 11.1/A + 963/S$$

Try a $9 \times 26\frac{7}{8}$ section, $A = 242$ and $S = 1{,}085$. This section is satisfactory for direct stress and bending. The f value of 2,110 is based on bending radius at the arch axis and should be recomputed for the radius of the inside lamination. For the present arch, this radius would be ½ the haunch depth (say 13½ in.) less than 8 ft. The recomputed f value is 2,040, and the section is still satisfactory. As t/R equals 0.625/82.5, or 1/132, which is less than 1/125, the ratio of lamination thickness to radius is not critical.

6.32 Check for column action Once the trial section at point x has been checked by the common combined-stress formula, the section should also be checked for column action in the vertical plane, with a column length equal to the length of arch between the hinge (point A) and the point of contraflexure for uniform loading (point C) of Fig. 6.23.

One method is to consider the arch segment AC as a column with side loads and eccentricity, and use the procedure of Chap. 13, NDS Appendix B.

If the l/d ratio in a vertical plane is 11 or less, no further check is necessary for the section at point x.

The l/d ratio of the arch section in the example equals the length of arch (27 ft × 12) divided by the depth of trial sections at x (26⅞ in.), or 16.5. Therefore the eccentric column analysis may be used. For an l/d ratio of 20 or more, the eccentric column formula is:

$$\frac{M/S}{f - P/A} + \frac{P/A}{c} \leq 1$$

Interpolation between l/d ratios of 11 and 20 may be accomplished by using a percentage of P/A in the denominator of the first term equal to:

$$\frac{l/d \text{ in vertical plane} - 11}{20 - 11} \times 100$$

or:

$$\frac{16.5 - 11}{20 - 11} \times 100 = 5.5/9 \times 100 = 61 \text{ per cent}$$

For an l/d ratio of 16.5, the allowable c value will be limited by the compression parallel value for the grade of lumber used, or 2,190 psi.

The trial section may thus be checked as follows:

$$\frac{2{,}030{,}000/1{,}085}{2{,}040 - 0.61(24{,}300/242)} + \frac{24{,}300/242}{2{,}190} \leq 1$$

$$0.943 + 0.046 = 0.989 < 1$$

The complete half arch AO can be checked in a similar manner for bending at section x and also for axial load at x due to snow, wind load right, or wind load left. It is often obvious that such conditions are less critical, but a check is necessary in case of doubt. Shear at section x is not critical.

The negative bending moment will cause a radial compressive stress. The allowable radial compressive stress equals the allowable compression perpendicular to grain. Thus:

$$S_R = \frac{3M}{2Rbh} = \frac{3 \times 2{,}030{,}000}{2 \times 109.4 \times 242} = 115 \text{ psi} < 450$$

6.33 Design of section at lower hinges The required depth of section at the lower hinges is dependent on the horizontal shear. As $H = 3V/2bh$, then:

$$h = 3V/2bH = \frac{3 \times 13{,}500}{2 \times 9 \times 190} = 7.9 \text{ in. required}$$

Therefore assume a depth of 10 in.

A check for bearing area shows a capacity of 196,000 lb (9 × 10 × 2,-190), which is greater than the required 21,600 lb. A depth of 10 in. provides a taper on the inside of the leg of 16⅜ in. and a slope in the leg axis of 8 3/16 in., which is greater than the 4 in. originally assumed.

6.34 Design of section at crown The section should be at least 9 in. deep at the crown. If the roof framing is to consist of purlins 8 ft on centers, 6 x 10's would suffice. Thus the depth at the crown should be at least 10 in. A check for horizontal shear in the arch at this point will show the 10-in. depth to be satisfactory.

With the knee section and the two end sections thus determined, the intermediate sections will taper from the knee down to the ends of the leg and arm. It may be necessary to check sections of the arch other than those at hinge and crown as eccentric columns, using the reduced section due to the taper from the haunch. The less the taper to crown and to hinge, the less chance that these other sections will be critical.

If section *BD* is checked, the *f* value need not be reduced for curvature. If the half arch *AD* is checked for wind combined with dead load, a larger increase in stresses (33⅓ per cent) is permissible for wind loading.

In computing *l/d* ratio for tapered sections, the depth at the section in question is frequently used, without consideration for the increase or reduction in depth to either side.

Typical crown and base details are shown in Fig. 6.25.

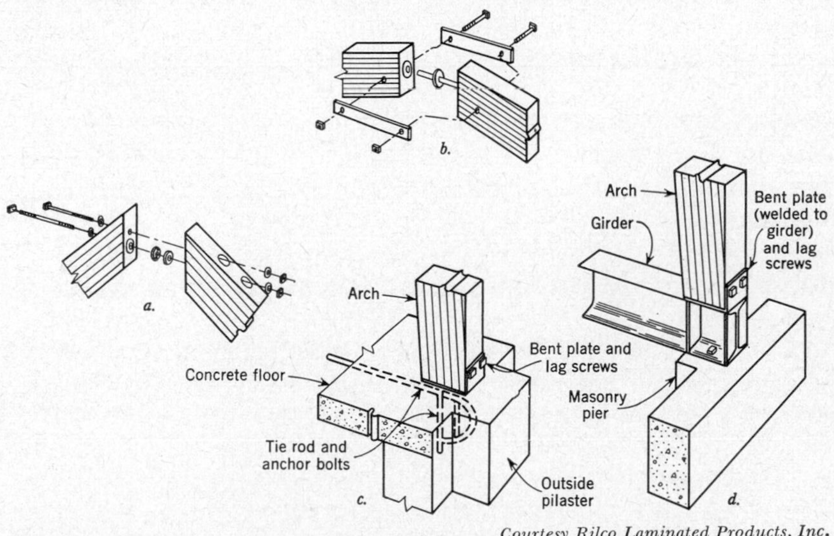

Courtesy Rilco Laminated Products, Inc.

Fig. 6.25 Three-hinged-arch crown and base details

a. Crown detail (one machine bolt, washers, threaded rod, two shear plates)
b. Crown detail (one rod, two shear plates, two steel plates, two machine bolts)
c. Base detail (horizontal thrust is absorbed by tie rod)
d. Base detail (horizontal thrust is absorbed by steel beam)

7

Special Framing

COMPOSITE TIMBER-CONCRETE CONSTRUCTION

7.1 Composite construction Composite construction is the combination of different structural materials in a manner that utilizes the preferred strength property of each material. Under axial stress or in flexure, moreover, each material functions as though the whole section were homogeneous. Specifically, the development of a composite timber-concrete section depends on an efficient means of providing adequate shear resistance or bond between the two different materials at their juncture plane.

Composite timber construction combines concrete and lumber in such a way that the concrete is in compression and the wood in tension when the structure is stressed in flexure. For continuous spans in which negative bending exists over the supports, stresses are reversed. The wood acts in compression, and tension reinforcing steel is necessary in the concrete portion of the section. Temperature reinforcing is also placed in both transverse and lateral directions of the concrete portion. Lumber for such construction is usually preservatively treated by pressure processes to guarantee long service life.

Longer service life and also greater economy have been the prime reasons for the development of this kind of structural system. The concrete provides a safe and enduring wearing surface for today's heavy and fast-moving loads, and wood and concrete effectively combined distribute concentrated loads over a wide area. A composite section also permits the use of small sizes of lumber for larger spans and heavier loadings.

Wood usually comprises the tension portion of the cross sections of the various types of composite constructions. It is used for several reasons. First, wood parts or members are easily fabricated prior to placement. Once in place, moreover, they are frequently sufficient to support the dead load of the structure while concrete is being placed. They may also be capable of supporting equipment used in construction, although the strength of self-supporting parts should be closely checked beforehand. Temporary supports may sometimes be desirable to limit deflection of the timber section during concrete pour, or to reduce the dead-load bending stress.

Two basic types of composite construction, "T" beams and slabs, have been developed, and also a variety of methods for achieving the desired results.

7.2 Composite "T" beams One basic type of deck consists of a concrete slab on timber stringers arranged as a series of "T" beams. The timber stringer forms the stem and the concrete slab the flange. Composite beams of this sort are usually of simple span. The concrete slab must be adequate to act as a slab spanning between stringers.

The horizontal shear stress existing between the slab and the stringers is resisted by a series of daps cut into the top of each stringer. Large spikes are also partially driven into prebored holes along the tops of the stringers (see Fig. 7.1) to prevent any vertical separation of the components.

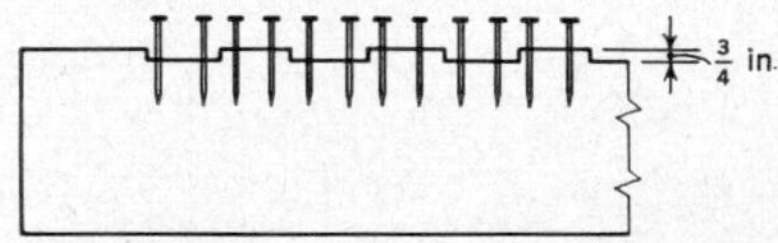

Fig. 7.1 Composite timber-concrete "T" beam deck

If spans are long and deep stringers are required, the use of glued-laminated stringers eliminates the problems of seasoning common to solid sawed timber of large dimensions.

Several methods of developing the horizontal shear at the juncture between the concrete flange and the timber stringer stem have been tested. As no great difference was found between the systems tried, daps in the upper edge of the stringers, plus uplift spikes, are commonly used for bridge construction for economy of materials and fabrication labor.

Flange width of 4 times the width of the stem has been tested, and current recommendations are that this limitation not be exceeded until further data are available. The slab or flange must be adequate as a reinforced slab in order to span between the timber stems. Depth of the concrete slab is usually 6 in. or more.

The tests made included loading to ultimate stress, repeated loading at less than ultimate stress, and the effect of temperature changes in producing secondary stresses.

7.3 Connections for temperature shear stress Analysis has shown that secondary temperature bending stresses are not large; they are thus usually ignored in design. Secondary temperature shearing stresses additive to those from normal bending, however, must be considered in the designing of the shear keys or daps in the top of the stringer. These stresses are induced by the thermal expansion or contraction of concrete, both of which are resisted by the wood. For all practical purposes, wood is normally unaffected by changes in temperature. Design of the shear connection for temperature requirements is as follows:

$$n = A_c f_c / s$$

in which:

n = number of shear connections required for temperature stress
A_c = area of concrete flange considered to be involved by the restraining timber stem
f_c = unit stress in concrete induced by temperature change within the range selected
s = the value of each shear connection

The shear connections for temperature change are uniformly distributed along the beam length. Such connections are required in addition to those required for horizontal shear.

The area of concrete flange, A_c, restrained by the timber is assumed as ⅓ the total, because the flange is only partially restrained by the timber.

The unit stress in the concrete, f_c, introduced by temperature change is the product of the coefficient of expansion for the concrete, the temperature change from the temperature at time of construction, and the modulus of elasticity. For a coefficient of expansion of concrete of 0.0000055 per deg F, modulus of elasticity of 3,000,000 psi, and temperature range of 70°F, f_c would be 1,155 psi. The 70° range of temperature would provide for a range from 0° to 140°F if the concrete is poured at 70°F, or from −20° to 120°F if poured at 50°F.

The value, or allowable load, for each shear connection, s, may be determined in one of three ways, according to the type of connection: (1) by test for special devices, (2) on the basis of allowable working stresses for common fastenings, and (3) on the basis of allowable shear and bearing values of concrete and wood for the daps or notches in the top of a stringer. With an allowable shear of 75 psi for the concrete and 120 psi for the wood, the dap length would be about 5/8 of the spacing of daps. For simplicity, length of daps is frequently made 1/2 the spacing, or about 3 to 4 in. for spacing from 6 to 8 in. A depth of dap of from 1/2 to 3/4 in. is suggested; greater depth will not increase shear resistance.

In order to combine temperature shear requirements with shear requirements for dead and live loads, it is sometimes more convenient to express the formula as pounds per inch of length, or:

$$ns/L = A_c f_c/L$$

7.4 Stress analysis Stress analysis involves two phases: (1) the determination of extreme fiber stress due to bending, and (2) the determination of shearing stresses at the junction point of two materials with proper connection details. If it is assumed that the junction connection is adequate, that it is without inelastic deformation and has elastic characteristics in keeping with the material of the beam, then the beam may be designed in the ordinary manner by transforming the composite section into an equivalent homogeneous section. The procedure is to multiply the flange width by the ratio of the modulus of elasticity of concrete to the modulus of elasticity for the species of timber used, E_c/E_w. Subsequent design with the transformed dimensions will be the same as for a homogeneous timber beam.

7.5 Design of a composite "T" beam To illustrate the general design properties of a composite timber-concrete "T" beam, assume a 6 x 16 timber stringer with a 6-in. concrete-slab deck serving as the flange. Assume that $E_c/E_w = 1$, and that the allowable normal load working stresses are $f = 1{,}900$, $c = 1{,}400$, $H = 120$. These values correspond approximately to grades of Douglas fir and southern pine frequently used in construction. Also assume that $c = 800$ psi for concrete.

The composite section, with the top of the timber dapped and set 3/4 in. into the bottom of the slab, is shown in Fig. 7.2. The effective flange width is considered to be 4 times the nominal width of the timber stem, or equal to the spacing of stringers, whichever is less. If the E_c/E_w ratio had been assumed at 1½ or 2, which might be proper for well cured concrete or wood of a lower modulus, the section of Fig. 7.2 would be transformed in the design to an equivalent flange width of 36 in. for the 1½ ratio, or to 48 in. for a ratio of 2. An E_c/E_w ratio of 1 is more accurate than 1½ or 2 for concrete that is only partially cured.

The neutral axis of the composite section of Fig. 7.2 is 6.74 in. from

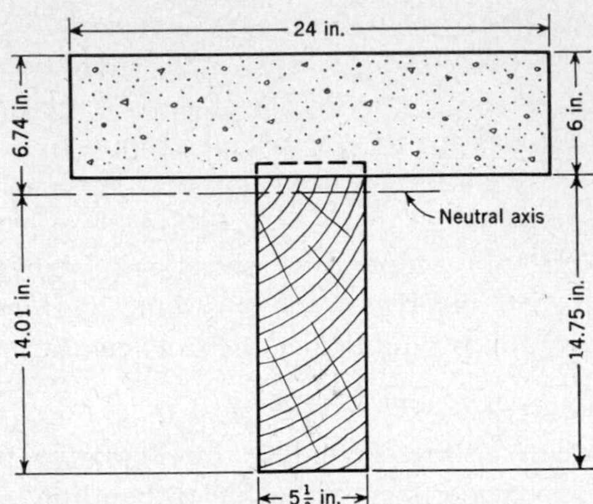

Fig. 7.2 Typical "T" beam section

the top surface. The moment of inertia of the section about the neutral axis is 7,460 in.[4]

The bending capacity of the section based on 800-psi concrete working stress is:

$$7{,}460 \times 800/6.74 = 885{,}000 \text{ in.-lb}$$

The bending capacity of the section based on 1,900-psi working stress in bending, f, of the wood is:

$$7{,}460 \times 1{,}900/14.01 = 1{,}010{,}000 \text{ in.-lb}$$

These capacities are for live loads only, because dead load is assumed to be carried by the timber stringer both while the concrete sets and thereafter. Thus the preceding live-load limit for the wood will be reduced by the dead-load bending moment in an actual problem.

The limit for the concrete is for normal live load, including impact of moving loads. The timber limit, less dead-load moment, is applicable for either normal load or moving loads excluding impact.

In practice, the analysis for stress in extreme fiber is the reverse of the above, because the live- and dead-load bending moments are known. The extreme fiber stress is calculated as a check against the allowable extreme fiber in bending stresses for the concrete (live-load moment with composite section) and for the timber (live-load moment with composite section, plus dead-load moment with net timber section).

Horizontal shear stress is maximum at the junction of the concrete and the timber. At this junction only the net area remaining after the top of the beam has been notched is effective in shear resistance.

The unit horizontal shear stress, H, may be determined by the formula:

$$H = VvA/Ib$$

in which:

V = vertical shear
I = moment of entire section about the neutral axis
b = width of the beam
A = area of transformed beam above or below section at which shear is to be determined
v = distance of center of gravity of area A from the neutral axis

If it is assumed that one-half the top surface is notched (length of notch equal to ½ the spacing of notches), the effective horizontal shear resistance is ½ that of a solid timber, and the permissible H value for the formula would be ½ the allowable stress for the grade of timber selected (½ of 120, or 60 psi for the original assumptions).

The horizontal shear formula may be rewritten:

$$V = HIb/vA, \qquad \text{or} \qquad Hb = VvA/I$$

Evaluating the composite section as shown in Fig. 7.2:

$$V = \frac{60 \times 7{,}462 \times 5.5}{3.74 \times 6 \times 24} = 4{,}570 \text{ lb allowable vertical shear}$$

This V does not consider the horizontal shear-connection requirement for secondary stresses due to temperature change, as previously discussed. The formula of Sec. 7.3 for shear connections for temperature stress, computed in pounds per inch of length, may be combined with the above equation for Hb. The resultant formula represents the combined stress per inch of length for a beam b wide:

$$Hb = VvA/I + A_c f_c/L$$

7.6 Composite timber-concrete slabs Many slab decks of composite timber-concrete construction have been built throughout North America. They are used for bridges, wharves, docks, and buildings. Initial development and full-scale tests were made in 1933 by the Service Bureau of the American Wood Preservers' Institute. Additional tests of actual structures were subsequently made by the State Roads Commission of Maryland, at the University of Illinois, and by the Forest Products Laboratory of Canada.

The two popular types of composite timber-concrete slabs use a laminated wood deck as the base or form for the concrete surface and for the tension portion of the composite section. General design procedure for fiber stress due to bending is the same for both. The design difference between them lies in the details used in developing shear and uplift resistance at the juncture of the timber and the concrete.

The laminated decks are made of 2-in. lumber (nominal) with the tops of alternate laminations 2 in. higher than the adjacent pieces. This design is accomplished in one of two ways. Either alternate laminations are fabricated 2 in. deeper than the adjacent pieces, or every alternate lamination is staggered 2 in. above its adjacent piece (see Fig. 7.3). Either way, each successive lamina is fastened to the adjacent

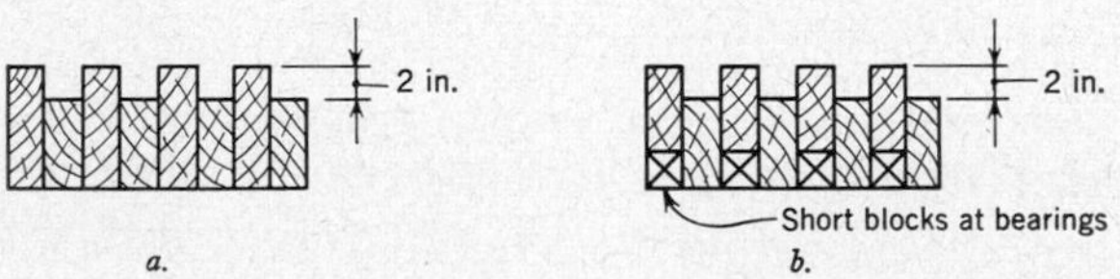

Fig. 7.3 Cross sections of laminated portions of composite decks

a. Alternate widths *b. Same width*

lamina by spiking, special metal dowels, or other positive means. Properly staggered 30d nails on about 24-in. spacing have been found satisfactory.

In order to reduce field labor, laminations are frequently shop-assembled into panels by conventional nailing, end joined in the field by "finger" joints about 12 in. long (Fig. 7.4), and appropriately spaced

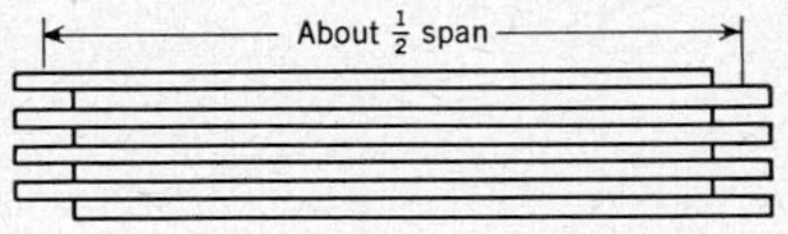

Fig. 7.4 Prefab deck section

Finger joints at ends of shop-assembled panels.

and staggered at points of least stress. The panels are then fastened to adjacent panels by long spiral dowels driven into prebored holes. A dowel spacing of up to 36 in. is practical.

7.7 Shear developers A patented metal "shear developer" was the first device used to develop shear resistance in the composite sections. Shear developers are triangular steel plates driven into precut slots at intervals along the channels between adjacent laminations (see Fig. 7.5). This method was selected from 13 methods tested. During the tests, the shear plates were tried at various angles to determine their resistance to the uplift of the concrete slab. Other types of standard fastenings were also investigated for uplift resistance, and 60d spikes on 24-in. centers, at an angle facing away from the center of the span, were ultimately adopted. The spikes are partially driven into the top edge of the higher lamination only. Spiral dowels, which are driven vertically, may be substituted for the uplift spikes.

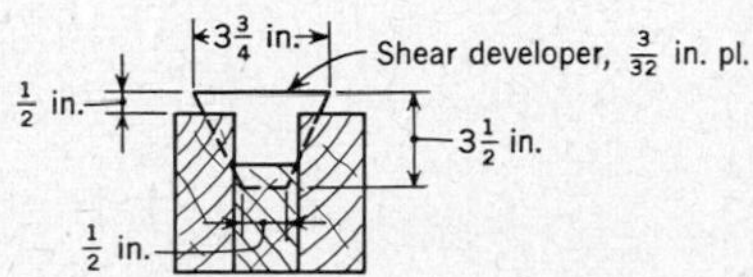

Fig. 7.5 Standard shear developer, installed

Installation recommended by the American Wood Preserver's Institute.

Tests have established the value of a shear developer (1,750 lb is recommended by the Service Bureau, AWPI) and the efficiency of the composite section as a beam (efficiencies approximating 100 per cent are obtainable).

It is interesting to note that at ultimate test loads, most of the beams failed for reasons not associated with the shear connection. Some failed because of compression in the concrete, and some because of tension in the laminations. Given the normal variability of materials, various types of failure are to be expected in a well proportioned section. Although there are two neutral axes in the composite section, subsequent tests have shown that the closeness of the two axes is such that departure from the theory of linear distribution of stress between extreme fibers in homogeneous members is not warranted.

7.8 Shear castellations The distinguishing difference between composite slabs using metal shear developers and spikes, and slabs depending on fabricated laminations, is the absence in the latter of hardware for resisting horizontal shear and uplift forces. Horizontal shear in this type of slab is resisted by castellations cut ½ in. deep into the tops of all laminations. Unit shear stress in the materials is low because each lamination is dapped, and shear resistance is developed over the total width of the slab. The bearing surfaces at the ends of the daps, which are calculated to transmit shear between the wood and concrete, are sloped at an angle of 30 deg from the vertical to reduce stress concentrations (see Fig. 7.6).

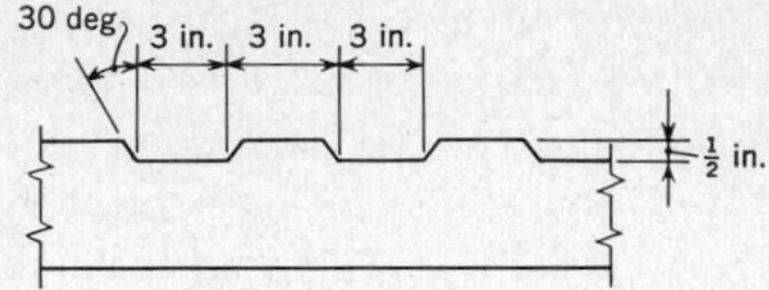

Fig. 7.6 Shear daps for composite slab

Castellated daps appear in all laminations of the modified composite deck slab of the West Coast Lumbermen's Association.

Vertical components of forces are adequately resisted by grooves milled the full length of each upstanding lamination to form a positive bond and resistance to uplift (see Fig. 7.7).

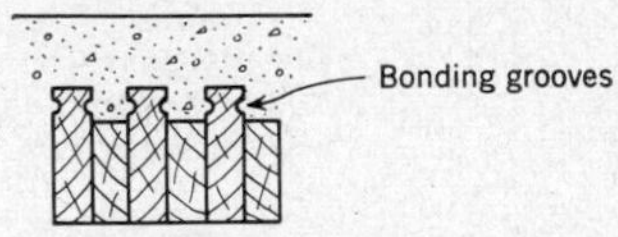

Fig. 7.7 Uplift grooves for composite slab

Typical cross section of West Coast Lumbermen's Association composite slab showing method of bonding to resist uplift.

7.9 Load distribution of composite slabs The earliest tests to determine transverse distribution of highway wheel loads were made in 1939 by the State Road Commission of Maryland on a bridge in which metal shear developers were used.

In these tests, bending moment for a single wheel load was distributed over 15.1 ft. By calculating the percentage of deflection caused by four wheels of passing vehicles at normal distances from a critical point and adding that percentage to a unit deflection assumed for one wheel at the critical point, a distribution of 5.1 ft was arrived at for a single wheel load. A 5-ft transverse distribution for bending moment is thus recommended.

It has been customary to assume a somewhat narrower transverse load distribution for shear than for moment calculations, because the critical position of the load for maximum shear will be closer to the support. Tests at the Bureau of Standards substantiate this assumption. Thus a transverse distribution of 4 ft for shear is recommended.

Test results of the Forest Products Laboratory of Canada confirm the fact that ample transverse distribution of loads does take place. These tests were conducted on an end span of a four-span bridge deck, designed for H-20 loading using castellated laminations.

For a continuous composite slab, the portions subject to negative moment will have a different stiffness factor, *EI,* from that in the section under positive moment. This difference will be reflected in the moment of inertia by the usual method of reducing the section to a transformed equivalent section of one material.

7.10 Point of inflection The point of inflection of a span can be determined from the factors in Table 7.1. These are based on the supposition that the portions of a span under negative and positive moments have different moments of inertia. As laminations are of necessity spliced at close intervals, the actual point of inflection for laminated pieces will be closer to the support than for unspliced pieces. Thus, to establish a table for positive and negative moments as percentages of simple-span moments, additional adjustment factors have to be applied.

TABLE 7.1 Maximum continuous-span bending moments

Span	Uniform dead-load moments				Live-load moments			
	Wood subdeck		Composite slab		Concentrated load		Uniform load	
	Pos.	Neg.	Pos.	Neg.	Pos.	Neg.	Pos.	Neg.
	per cent of simple span bending moments							
Interior	50	50	55	45	75	25	75	55
End	70	60	70	60	85	30	85	65
Two-span [1]	65	70	60	75	85	30	80	75

[1] Continuous beam of two equal spans.

Normally on continuous-span structures, one-third of the laminations, or panel sections, are spliced at each quarter-span point, and one-third over the interior supports. Laminations are not spliced in the center half of the span unless the reduced effective section caused by the splices is considered in the design. (The reduced section is considered in the design at interior supports.)

7.11 Distribution of bending moments in continuous spans Both positive and negative moments are to be distributed in accordance with Table 7.1. Impact should be considered in computing stresses for concrete and steel but neglected for wood.

7.12 Design The combination in a structural member of two elements having different mechanical properties requires the formulation of a design premise. The formulation that follows is based on the elastic properties of the materials:

$E_c/E_w = 1$ for slab in which the net concrete thickness above the wood is less than ½ the over-all depth of the composite section

$E_c/E_w = 2$ for slab in which the net concrete thickness above the wood is at least ½ the over-all depth of the composite section

$E_s/E_w = 18.75$ for Douglas fir and southern pine

The use of net concrete-slab thickness equal or greater than ½ the over-all depth of composite section has little, if any, advantage for most highway structures, because the allowable loads will more likely be controlled by the lumber stresses.

Design procedure for composite slabs is similar to that for composite "T" beams previously described, except that shear requirements for temperature change are neglected. Expansion joints, however, should be provided in a concrete slab on not more than 160-ft centers.

Design analysis is usually on the basis of a section 12 in. wide. Figure 7.8 shows representative transformed design sections for a typical

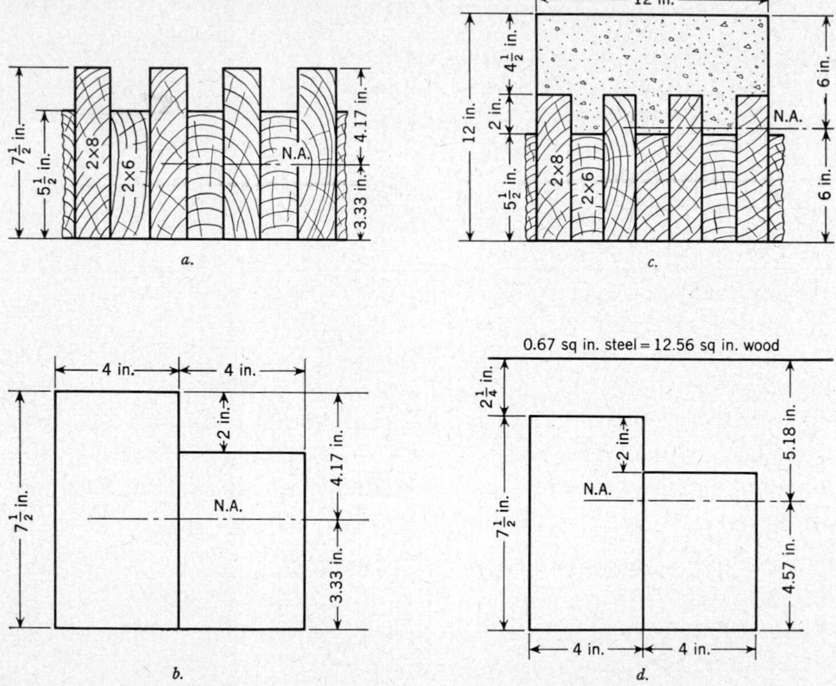

Fig. 7.8 Transformed design sections for typical 12-in. slab

a. Wood section at midspan *c. Composite section at midspan*
b. Wood section at support *d. Composite section at support*

12-in. deep slab, indicating wood section to carry dead load, composite section for positive bending moment, and steel-wood section at interior support for negative bending moment. For each of the sections shown, c equals the distance from the base to the center of gravity of the section. In Fig. 7.8a, each height of lamination has a width of 6 in. Calculations for c are as follows:

$$\begin{array}{rr} 6 \times 7\tfrac{1}{2} = 45 & 45 \times 3.75 = 168.75 \\ 6 \times 5\tfrac{1}{2} = \underline{33} & 33 \times 2.75 = \underline{90.75} \\ 78 & 259.50 \end{array}$$

$$c = 259.50/78 = 3.33 \text{ in.}$$

The moment of inertia of a wood section at midspan is thus:

$$\begin{aligned} 6(4.17)^3/3 &= 145.0 \\ 6(2.17)^3/3 &= 20.4 \\ 12(3.33)^3/3 &= \underline{147.6} \\ I &= 313.0 \text{ in.}^4 \end{aligned}$$

In Fig. 7.8b, only two-thirds of the plank strips are continuous over the support and the section may be sketched as shown to simplify calculation. The moment of inertia for a wood section at support is therefore ⅔ of that for the midspan section, or ⅔ of 313.0. Thus:

$$\begin{aligned} c &= 3.33 \text{ in.} \\ I &= 208.7 \text{ in.}^4 \end{aligned}$$

In Fig. 7.8c, the section is considered homogeneous if $E_c/E_w = 1$. Thus for a composite section at midspan:

$$\begin{aligned} c &= 6.00 \text{ in.} \\ I &= 12(12)^3/12 = 1{,}728 \text{ in.}^4 \end{aligned}$$

For a composite section at support (Fig. 7.8d), only two-thirds of the laminations are effective because of joints in the plank strips at support. Each height of lamination in a 12-in. width of slab has therefore a width of 4 in., instead of 6 in. as at midspan. Computations for c are as follows:

$$\begin{array}{rr} 30.00 \times 6.00 = & 180.00 \\ 22.00 \times 7.00 = & 154.00 \\ \underline{12.56} \times 0 = & \underline{0} \\ 64.56 & 334.00 \end{array}$$

$$\begin{aligned} c_s &= 334.00/64.56 = 5.18 \text{ in.} \\ c_w &= 4.57 \text{ in.} \end{aligned}$$

Computations for I are as follows:

Steel: $\frac{5}{8}$ in. ϕ at 9 in. and $\frac{1}{2}$ in. ϕ at 9 in. = 0.67 sq in. per ft width of slab
Wood: 0.67 × 18.75 = 12.56 sq in.

$$
\begin{aligned}
4(2.93)^3/3 &= 33.6 \\
4(0.93)^3/3 &= 1.0 \\
8(4.57)^3/3 &= 254.4 \\
12.56(5.18)^2 &= \underline{336.6} \\
I &= 625.6 \text{ in.}^4
\end{aligned}
$$

Figure 7.9 shows typical slab sections based on an E_c/E_w ratio of 1 and varying from 10 to 14½ in. in over-all depth. Table 7.2 lists properties of the typical slab sections of Fig. 7.9 and is helpful in estimating

TABLE 7.2 Properties of sections shown in Fig. 7.9

Section	Moment of inertia, I[1]	Resisting moment[1]			Distance to extreme fiber, c[1]		
		Concrete	Steel	Wood	Concrete	Steel	Wood
Midspan section—composite (no splices)							
1	1,000	160,000		290,000	5.00		5.00
2	1,396	202,000		314,000	5.54		6.46
3	1,396	202,600		314,000	5.54		6.46
4	1,728	230,400		418,000	6.00		6.00
5	2,541	299,000		478,000	6.80		7.70
Support section—composite (⅓ wood laminations spliced)							
1a	349		83,750	112,000		4.00	3.75
1b	455		126,500	127,000		3.45	4.30
2a	508		104,500	120,000		4.66	5.09
2b	654		153,100	139,000		4.10	5.65
3a	508		104,500	120,000		4.66	5.09
3b	654		153,100	139,000		4.10	5.65
4a	626		116,000	164,000		5.18	4.57
4b	809		168,000	188,000		4.62	5.13
5a	887		141,900	177,000		6.00	6.00
5b	1,436		254,100	262,000		5.42	6.58
Midspan section—wood only (no splices)							
1	117			71,800			2.36
2	232			89,600			3.75
3	232			89,600			3.75
4	313			136,000			3.33
5	512			157,000			4.75
Support section—wood only (⅓ wood laminations spliced)							
1	78			95,500			2.36
2	155			59,900			3.75
3	155			59,900			3.75
4	209			91,000			3.33
5	342			104,600			4.75

[1] $E_c/E_w = 1$; 800 psi concrete; 18,000 psi reinforcing steel; 1,450 psi wood in bending or tension; 1,200 psi wood in compression.

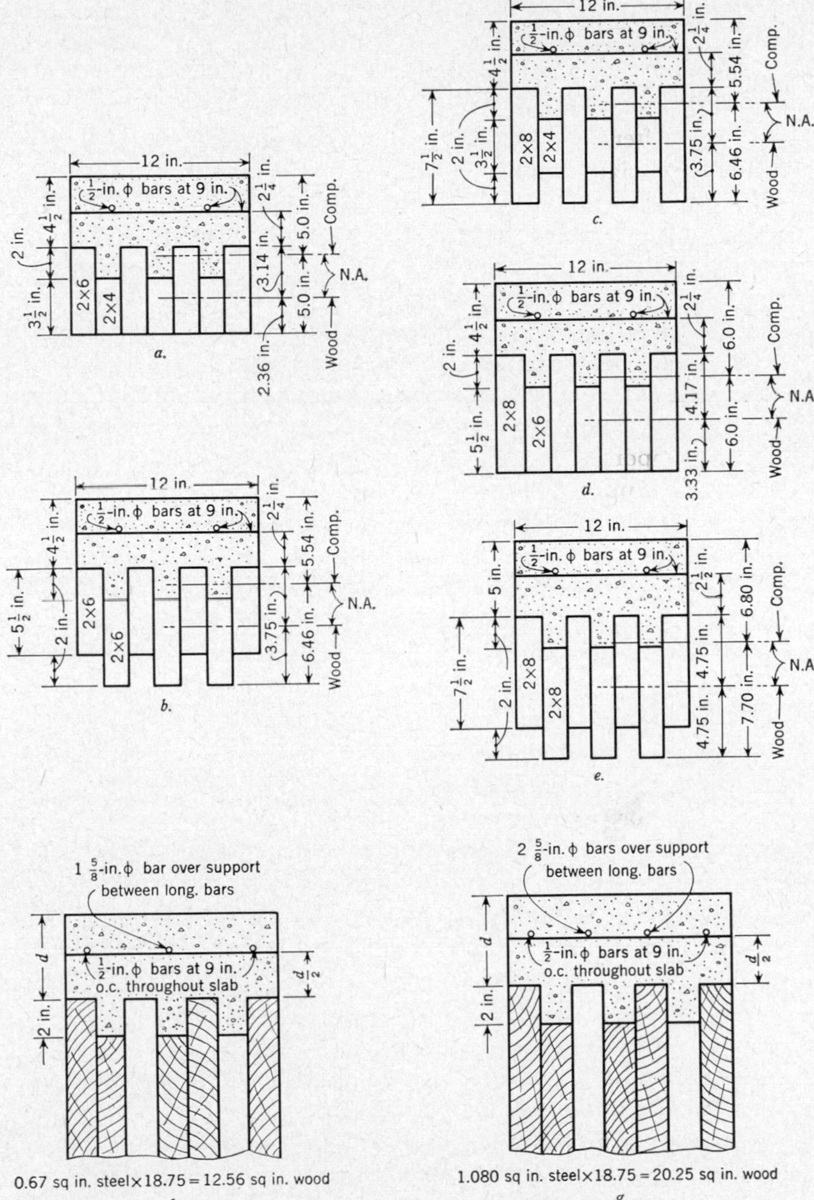

Fig. 7.9 Typical composite slab sections

Properties of these sections are shown in Table 7.2.

approximate slab size, which can then be checked by detailed computations. The step-by-step design procedure is as follows:

1. Compute dead load of estimated slab section and of necessary construction loads during pour and before curing.
2. Compute, as for a simple span, bending moments due to dead loads (Step 1), and apply constants for wood subdeck from Table 7.1.
3. Compute moment of inertia of wood subdeck at centerline (Fig. 7.8a) and at interior supports (Fig. 7.8b). Determine distance, c, from neutral axis to extreme fiber. Although the distance to the upper extreme fiber is sometimes greater, the distance to the lower fiber is critical because the live load adds substantially to the lower fiber stress.
4. Determine from Steps 2 and 3 the extreme fiber unit stress in wood due to dead loads, $Mc/I = fwd$, at centerline and at interior supports.
5. Compute, as for a single span, bending moments due to uniform dead loads after curing, and also concentrated or uniform live loads. Apply appropriate constants from Table 7.1. Concentrated wheel loads have an assumed distribution over 5 ft wide, which takes into consideration the effect of equal wheel loads in adjacent lanes.
6. Compute moments of inertia of composite sections at centerline of span (Fig. 7.8c) and at support (Fig. 7.8d). Determine distance, c, from neutral axis to extreme fiber of wood, concrete, and steel. Allowance for impact or dynamic loading must be added to the static moments if these are used to determine steel and concrete stresses.
7. Using the M, c, and I values of Steps 5 and 6, determine as in Step 4 the extreme fiber unit stress in the wood at centerline (tension), wood at support (compression), concrete at centerline (compression), and steel at support (tension). The concrete and steel unit stresses thus determined are for the equivalent section and are multiplied by E_c/E_w and E_s/E_w ratios, respectively, to determine the actual unit stresses in the concrete and steel.
8. The unit stress in the wood of Step 4 adds to the unit stress in the wood of Step 7 to give the total wood stress at centerline and at the support.
9. The total unit stresses of Steps 7 and 8 must not exceed the allowable stress for the respective materials.
10. Compute maximum vertical shear adjacent to supports, neglecting the shear due to dead load of the slab and wood. This shear is considered carried by the wood. Neglect uniform or fixed live loads and other dead loads within a distance 3 times the slab depth from the support. Concentrated moving wheel loads are assumed distributed over a 4-ft width of slab and placed 3 times the depth of slab or one-quarter the span, whichever is less, from the support.

11. Using the vertical shear of Step 10, compute the horizontal shear at the mid-depth of the top wood grooves. Use either the transformed concrete-wood section for areas of positive moment or the steel-wood section for areas of negative moment (see Fig. 7.8d).

12. Compute the required spacing of shear developers from Step 11, or check the adequacy of the castellations based on the allowable shear for the concrete or the wood. For dap length equal to ½ the dap spacing, the concrete shear will likely control, and thus it may be desirable to make the dap length about ⅓ the dap spacing to balance more nearly the allowable shear ($H_c = 75$, $H_w = 150$).

13. Spacing of shear developers required at the support is generally used as far as the quarter-span point and then increased uniformly to the spacing required (but not more than 24 in.) by possible vertical shear near the centerline of span.

BEARING POWER OF PILES

7.13 Types of piles Driven piles occasionally penetrate only a thin layer of soft earth before bearing up on an unyielding stratum, such as rock, that can support heavy concentrated loads. Under these conditions, the pile is a timber column and is designed as such. However, lateral support can be assumed for the portion of the pile in the ground in any but the very poorest soils.

Friction piles develop load-bearing capacity through friction with the surrounding soil mass that they penetrate. They probably constitute the great majority of piles in use. Loading tests are the best means of determining the load-carrying capacity of friction piles, and such tests are sometimes required as the basis for design. Often, though, tests may be too expensive and therefore impracticable on small- or medium-size jobs. Capacities are then estimated from a driving formula.

7.14 Bearing capacity formulas Numerous formulas have been proposed for estimating the bearing capacity of driven piles. The Wellington or *Engineering News* formulas are often used. They are simple, quickly solved, and as reliable as most empirical methods for estimating the capacities of timber piles, which are light in comparison with the hammer or ram used to drive them into place.

$$P = \frac{2WH}{S + 1.0} \quad \text{for gravity hammers}$$

$$P = \frac{2WH}{S + 0.1} \quad \text{for single-acting steam hammers}$$

$$P = \frac{2H(W + Ap)}{S + 0.1} \quad \text{for double-acting steam hammers}$$

in which:

P = safe bearing power, in pounds
W = weight, in pounds, of striking parts of hammer
H = height of fall, in feet
A = area of piston, in square inches
p = steam pressure, in pounds per square inch, at the hammer
S = the average penetration, in inches, per blow for the last 5 to 10 blows for gravity hammers and the last 10 to 20 blows for steam hammers

The efficiency of the hammer blow depends on the ratio of the weight of the hammer or driving ram to that of the pile, and decreases rapidly as the pile weight increases, as shown in Fig. 7.10. Efficiency may be

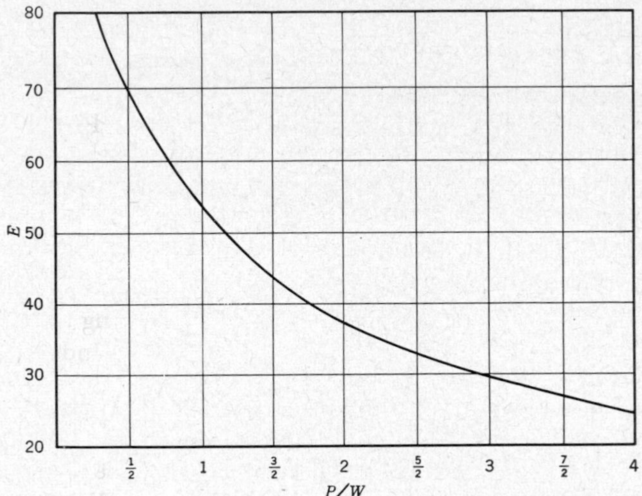

Fig. 7.10 Efficiency of hammer blow (per *cent*)

computed by the equation:

$$E = \frac{1}{1 + P/W} + \frac{\lambda^2}{1 + W/P}$$

in which:

P = weight of pile, in pounds
W = weight of hammer
λ = coefficient of restitution (0.25 for iron on hardwood)

For estimating capacities of long and heavy piles, the *Engineering News* formulas should be multiplied by the factor:

$$\frac{2W}{2W + w}$$

in which:

w = weight of the pile, in pounds
W = weight of striking parts of the hammer, in pounds

Closely grouped friction piles do not develop the same capacity as do an equal number of similar piles driven to the same bearing in the same soil but spaced far enough apart so that there is no contribution of load from neighboring piles. A friction pile creates pressure over considerable areas at depth, and with closely driven piles there is an overlapping of pressure bulbs.

7.15 Group load reduction The following formula, known as the Converse–LaBarre formula, is suggested by the American Association of State Highway Officials for estimating the reduction of single-pile loads if piles are driven in groups:

$$E = 1 - \phi\frac{(n - 1)m + (m - 1)n}{90mn}$$

in which:

E = the efficiency or percentage of the single pile value to be used for each pile in group
n = the number of piles in each row
m = the number of rows in each group
d = the average diameter of the pile
s = center-to-center spacing of piles
ϕ = the angle expressed in degrees
$\tan \phi = d/s$

7.16 Pile bents The design of pile bents is largely empirical. The proportioning of forces acting on the various members of a bent involves too many assumptions to be capable of exact analysis. Through the years, bent types have become somewhat standardized by the trial and error of experience. For the usual single-track railway trestle, bents usually contain six piles, and for those under highway bridges with deck widths up to 26 or 28 ft, four or more piles. Pile spacing may sometimes be controlled by shear or bending in the caps. If practical, spacing should be sufficient to prevent overlapping of pressure bulbs in the soil, which decreases the bearing value of the piles. If pile heads are from 2 to 3 ft apart at cut-off or cap level, the outer piles are frequently battered to provide a greater separation below ground.

Lateral loads from wind or from moving live loads are resisted by sway bracing and by batter piles, usually of 1:12 to 3:12 batter. If they have adequate penetration in firm soil, all piles in a bent act as cantilevers and have some resistance to lateral forces. Battering the outer piles on each side of a bent provides considerable resistance, and if the bent is sway-braced, it tends to act as a unit. Bracing should be fastened to the piles as securely as possible, for fastenings are frequently the weakest point in the bracing system. If large lateral forces and considerable vibration are likely, as in railroad trestles, spike-grid timber connectors and bolts should be used for fastening braces to the piles or posts. Bolts are generally adequate for attaching the sway bracing on highway bridges, unless considerable height is involved and large areas exposed to wind. Even for highway bridges, however, the stronger attachment secured by use of grids is desirable, because rigid connections contribute to unit action in the bent.

If horizontal forces act on the structure, piles on opposite sides of the group axis may receive quite different loads. Such pile groups are so designed that the piles on one side of the group will not be overloaded under any combinations of forces. Uplift resistance of 40 per cent of the friction bearing value is commonly permitted.

The load on each pile may be calculated by the following formula, which is derived from the equation for stress in a plane subjected simultaneously to a direct force and to bending moment:

$$W = (1/n \pm ey/\Sigma y^2) \times 100$$

in which:

W = the load to any pile at a distance y from the neutral axis of the group, in per cent of the total vertical load. The "plus" in the formula applies if the pile is on the side of the group toward which the lateral load acts, or on the same side of the group centroid as the load producing the bending moment

n = number of piles in the group

e = eccentricity or distance from the axis of group to the application of resultant

y = the distance of the pile in question from the center of gravity of the pile group

Σy^2 = the summation of the squares of all the y's $(y_1^2 + y_2^2 + y_3^2)$

The moment of inertia of the pile group equals $I + \Sigma ay^2$, in which I is the moment of inertia of each pile and a is the area of a pile head. As *a* can usually be taken as unity and the *I* of a single pile is small, the quantity Σy^2 represents with sufficient accuracy the moment of inertia of the pile group.

A general example of a pile group subject to a vertical load and a bending moment due to both horizontal load and eccentricity of vertical load is shown in Fig. 7.11. The variable spacing indicated is seldom used; it is included merely to illustrate the design procedure.

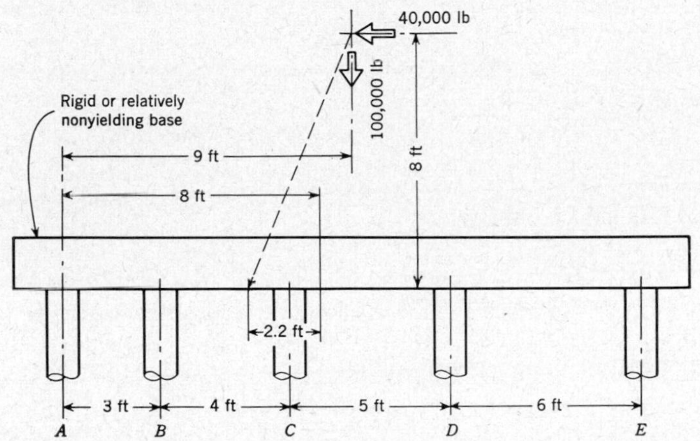

Fig. 7.11 Pile spacing and loading

The center of gravity of the five piles, the centroid of the group, would be as indicated, 1 ft to the right of pile *C*. In this example, the vertical load creates bending moment clockwise about the centroid, and the horizontal force creates counter-clockwise bending.

$$\begin{aligned} 100{,}000 \times 1 &= +100{,}000 \text{ ft-lb} \\ 40{,}000 \times 8 &= \underline{-320{,}000 \text{ ft-lb}} \\ & -220{,}000 \text{ ft-lb} \end{aligned}$$

$$e = 220{,}000/100{,}000 = 2.2\text{-ft eccentricity of resultant of forces with respect to centroid}$$

Using the preceding equation:

Pile *A*:	$y_1 = 8$	$y_1^2 = 64$
Pile *B*:	$y_2 = 5$	$y_2^2 = 25$
Pile *C*:	$y_3 = 1$	$y_3^2 = 1$
Pile *D*:	$y_4 = 4$	$y_4^2 = 16$
Pile *E*:	$y_5 = 10$	$y_5^2 = 100$
		$\Sigma y^2 = 206$

The portion of the 100,000-lb vertical load distributed to each pile is as follows:

$$
\begin{aligned}
W_A &= 1/5 + (2.2 \times 8)/206 &&= 0.20 + 0.085 = &&28.5 \text{ per cent}\\
W_B &= 1/5 + (2.2 \times 5)/206 &&= 0.20 + 0.053 = &&25.3 \text{ per cent}\\
W_C &= 1/5 + (2.2 \times 1)/206 &&= 0.20 + 0.011 = &&21.1 \text{ per cent}\\
W_D &= 1/5 - (2.2 \times 4)/206 &&= 0.20 - 0.043 = &&15.7 \text{ per cent}\\
W_E &= 1/5 - (2.2 \times 10)/206 &&= 0.20 - 0.106 = &&\underline{9.4} \text{ per cent}\\
& && &&100.0 \text{ per cent}
\end{aligned}
$$

In addition to the vertical load, each pile will resist $\frac{1}{5}$ of the horizontal load, or 8,000 lb.

POLE LINES

7.17 Pole lines Poles supporting power and telephone lines, except those guyed to resist lateral forces, are essentially cantilever beams. Column or axial loads usually are of small consequence and can be ignored unless the span lengths are long and there are many heavy conductors. Nor is it necessary to consider the slenderness ratio of the column except rarely, if axial loads are heavy. Ordinary span lengths even under the worst icing conditions impose only small vertical loads. Unbalanced horizontal pulls at angle points or at dead ends usually are balanced by guys that convert the pole into a strut carrying only vertical or axial load.

Unbalanced line tensions may occur on different sides of a pole if wire spans between poles are unequal. A wood pole, however, deflects sufficiently under moderate pulls to permit an increased sag of conductors on the side of greater tension. The sag helps to equalize the forces acting on the two sides of the pole.

If wires or lines break, deflection of the pole resulting from unbalanced tension lightens the pole load and thus usually prevents pole failure, or limits breakage to short sections.

Pole lines have frequently been designed for tensions in direction of the line equivalent to 50 per cent of the ultimate or breaking strength of the attached wires. If tensions exceed this percentage appreciably, they are above the proportional limit of the metal. The wires will then stretch considerably, thus relieving the poles of excessive loads. At dead ends, however, the supporting structures are usually required to be strong enough to resist full tension exerted by all wires. At angle points, too, poles are frequently guyed for all horizontal forces acting at these points, and the pole is simply a strut carrying the vertical component of the guy load.

Usually the severest forces acting on a pole line having equal spans, all conductors intact, and supports at the same elevation, are those induced by a wind normal to the line when the conductors are covered with thick radial coatings of ice. In this condition, the line presents a greater projected area to the wind and imposes heavier loads on the supported poles.

7.18 Formulas for wind and icing The most generally used formula for determining wind pressure on a conductor is that developed from experiments by H. W. Buck:

$$F = 0.0025V^2$$

in which:

F = pressure, in pounds per square foot, of projected area of cylindrical wire
V = corrected wind velocity, in miles per hour

The wind force P per lineal foot of conductor is then:

$$P = 0.0025V^2 \times d/12$$

in which d equals the diameter of the wire plus twice the thickness of the ice that encircles it. The weight of ice is taken at 57 lb per cu ft.

Bernard E. Lowe in "Rural Line Design Investigations" developed the following formulas for determining the weight of ice per foot length of conductor and the combined weight of conductor and ice per linear foot:

$$W_l = 1.254r(d + r)$$

in which:

W_l = weight of ice, in pounds per foot length of conductor
d = diameter of conductor, in inches
r = radial thickness of ice, in inches

$$\begin{aligned} W_t &= 1.254r(d + r) + 3.02d^2 \quad \text{(for solid copper)} \\ &= 1.254r(d + r) + 2.36d^2 \quad \text{(for stranded copper)} \end{aligned}$$

in which:

W_t = combined weight of conductor and ice, in pounds per linear foot of conductor

The combined horizontal wind pressure, *P*, and the weight of the conductor, W_t, may act simultaneously. The resultant force, W_r, acting on the conductor per foot then is:

$$W_r = \sqrt{W_t^2 + P^2}$$

The horizontal pull, *H*, on the pole exerted by the loaded cable is given by the formula:

$$H = wl^2/8S$$

in which:

w = load, in pounds per foot of cable
l = length of span, in feet
S = sag of cable, in feet

The minimum conductor loadings for various conditions are given in the *National Electrical Safety Code*.[1] In general, however, the radial thickness of ice varies from zero to ½ in., depending on locality, and the wind pressure from 4 to 9 psf, with the greater wind pressure in areas of no ice.

7.19 Permissible working stresses As noted in Chap. 13, ten classes of poles are available, of which seven classes are based on a specified breaking load applied horizontally 2 ft from the top of the pole. Thus poles may often be selected on the basis of this breaking standard. If a safety factor of 2 is desired for a horizontal pull of 1,500 lb applied near the top of a pole, a class-3 pole providing a breaking load of 3,000 lb will be sufficient.

If more exact or detailed analysis is required, permissible working stresses for pole design may be obtained by applying a factor of safety —generally 2 for new lines—to the established modulus of rupture given in Chap. 13. Pole dimensions are also given, from which moment of inertia and section modulus may be computed.

POLE FRAME STRUCTURES

7.20 Pole columns and beams Poles may often be used to advantage as beams and columns in structural applications as well as for foundation piles and transmission lines. They find frequent application as columns and vertical elements in trestles, warehouses, pavilions,

[1] NBS Handbook H30 available from U.S. Government Printing Office.

towers, and farm buildings. In such structures, pole columns provide increased lateral stability and, by eliminating concrete foundations, also cut the cost of construction. They are also suitable for use as beams, for example, as crossarms in H-pole transmission lines.

If a pole is to have siding or other exterior covering applied, it is frequently set with the taper to the inside of the building in order to provide a vertical exterior surface. If unusually long poles are used with the outer face vertical, the effect of eccentricity of vertical load should be considered. Preservative treatment should be considered for poles set in concrete or in the ground. (See Sec. 3.18–3.25.)

7.21 Ground fixity The amount of fixity provided by the embedment of a pole in the ground is an important consideration for lateral loads. Unfortunately, however, there are no specific recommendations for lateral bearing values. Fixity is related to the composition, moisture content, and type of soil and may be increased by embedding or encasing the pole in concrete. Experience with a particular type of structure is the best guide. The lateral pressure at ground line normally should not exceed, and possibly should be less than, allowable vertical soil-bearing values. Ground drainage should be provided to keep the area of embedment as dry as possible. Preferably the encasing concrete should be reinforced in some manner. Pole embedment of 4 to 4½ ft is common, and is regarded by some designers as satisfactory for average soils without specific fixity or bearing computations.

In addition to fixity, the vertical load-carrying capacity is limited by the bearing capacity of the soil. As poles used in this way are embedded a relatively short distance compared to their over-all length, friction between the pole and the soil is normally neglected. Recommended bearing capacities for various soils in tons per square foot are as follows:

SOIL	BEARING CAPACITY
	tons psf
Soft clay	½–1
Ordinary clay and sand	1½–2
Moderately dry clay	2–3
Hard dry sand and clay	4
Gravel or coarse sand well consolidated	6
Hard rock	15

If more capacity is required than the local conditions provide, cross pieces are sometimes bolted to the bottom of the pole in order to increase bearing area. The same method is used to provide better anchorage to resist overturning. Encasing concrete also increases the bearing area for vertical loads.

If poles are used in small buildings, such as farm structures, the poles are usually set in the holes and temporarily braced in the approximate position in which they are to remain. Other framing and bracing is installed before the holes are backfilled so that slight inaccuracies in framing or pole setting may be adjusted. For larger structures, there is usually a transit available; thus the poles may be set accurately and the hole backfilled or concreted before other framing begins.

7.22 Required cross-sectional area Round and square wood members of the same cross-sectional area and equal working stresses will carry the same loads in both bending and compression and will have approximately the same stiffness. To compute the required size of a round column or pole, a square column should be designed first and then a round column of a diameter that will give an equivalent area substituted. To allow for the taper of poles used as columns, the diameter d to be used for computing P/A in the Euler column formula should be taken at a distance from the point at which the smaller end of the pole is laterally supported equal to ⅓ of the unsupported length of the pole. This procedure will provide sufficient strength to prevent failure from buckling. The unit compressive stress at the smaller end of the column should also be computed, because it must not exceed the allowable stress for compression parallel to the grain.

7.23 Working stresses Required working stresses for poles that are used structurally in a manner and under conditions similar to those for sawed lumber are presently a matter of individual engineering judgment. Just as higher bending stresses are used for pole lines (see Sec. 7.19), so are they used for pole structures such as pole barns, signboards, and outdoor theater screens. Designers have employed these higher stresses for years satisfactorily, among them stresses for extreme fiber in bending that are up to 50 per cent higher than those of Table 7.3. In many structural pole uses, there is less hazard to life or property than is found in other constructions, and higher stresses may well be justified.

If the same safety level is desired for poles as that provided by structurally graded lumber, the unit working stresses of Table 7.3 are recommended in the absence of comprehensive test data. In general, these stresses are about the same as those for sawed lumber for compression perpendicular to grain and modulus of elasticity, and 60 per cent of those of basic clear wood for compression parallel to grain, extreme fiber in bending, and horizontal shear.

TABLE 7.3 Recommended allowable working stresses for poles [1]

Species of lumber	Extreme fiber in bending	Compression perpendicular to grain	Compression parallel to grain	Horizontal shear	Modulus of elasticity
Cedar (northern and southern white)	730	210	550	65	880,000
Cedar (western red)	860	240	690	80	1,100,000
Cypress (southern)	1,250	360	1,050	100	1,320,000
Douglas fir (West Coast)	1,450	390	1,050	85	1,760,000
Hemlock (West Coast)	1,250	360	870	75	1,540,000
Larch (western)	1,450	390	1,050	85	1,650,000
Oak (red and white)	1,350	600	980	120	1,650,000
Pine (southern)	1,450	390	1,050	105	1,760,000
Redwood	1,160	320	980	65	1,320,000

[1] These recommended stresses are for normal loading and dry use conditions. They may be adjusted for duration of loading and service conditions in a way similar to that for sawed lumber (see Chap. 13).

FORMWORK AND CENTERING

7.24 Formwork and centering Framing employing either glued or sawed timbers is often used in formwork and centering for large structures, such as concrete-arch or steel bridges and long-span concrete shells (see Fig. 7.12).

For the construction of concrete buildings, retaining walls, and small dams, the forms generally consist of sheathing, walls, and studs and braces of small sizes and on close spacing. Such formwork is usually a part of the contractor's engineering work rather than of the design of the structure.

There are many large projects, such as concrete bridges and thin-shell concrete roofs, that require sturdy and movable long-span centering structures. Although temporary and removable, these structures must be well designed and built because the stability of tons of materials and the lives of many workmen are at stake.

Timber falsework has been used many times for large culverts, dam tunnels, and railroad and highway tunnels. If tunnel work is exten-

Courtesy Timber Structures, Inc.

Fig. 7.12 Arch roof forming

Four spans for 155-ft arch

sive and centering forms are needed for the concrete linings, it is quite feasible to provide forms that can be lowered and folded back upon a carriage that is transportable along the tunnel.

Usually the centering structure must be suitable to support multiple pours, either duplicate lanes in width or duplicate spans in length. Large centering projects require considerable planning to provide an efficient and economical duplication of units, and proper timing and sequence of movements.

Centering and formwork should be designed for maximum re-use, suitability for erection operations, and easy handling. Demolition and salvage qualities should be kept in mind, because much of the material will often have resale value. The design of large centering structures requires close cooperation with the general contractor. A knowledge of his equipment and his plans for handling the work is an absolute necessity. Timing is of great importance.

Centering structures that are high and narrow may need guy cables to hold them safely against the wind when they are moved or even when in place to receive the pour.

Form structures are usually supported on blocks, jacks, or wedges while concrete is being poured and cured. They are then lowered upon wheels and moved along tracks into new locations for repeat operations. If moving equipment permits, forms should be moved as a whole; if this is not possible, they should be moved in large units. Sometimes, however, conditions require that forms be demountable into small pieces that can be moved by manpower.

If centering is over water, it may be necessary to use long spans. No underwater operations should be undertaken without a full knowledge of currents, tides, depths, and the character of stream or lake beds. It must be fully realized, moreover, that aquatic work may be quite costly. Sometimes by-passes or right-of-way must be maintained for traffic through framework.

As centering structures deflect, they change the shape of the concrete structure they are forming. Deflection consideration is thus required in both the main structure and in the sheathing and joists that transfer load to the form structure. Lack of proper deflection analysis may produce a sagged appearance in the finished surfaces and also increase the amount of concrete needed.

If deflection does not control, some designers use slightly higher working stresses for formwork and centering, because they are temporary structures and thus not subject to decay or future load increases. It seems reasonable to use a 20 per cent increase over normal loading values. For some minor members such as joists and sheathing, for which deflection may be the prime consideration, nonstructural grades of lumber may be used. Because of the temporary nature of the construction, moreover, hardware and ironwork does not need to be galvanized.

7.25 Hydraulic pressure When concrete is poured, a heavy hydraulic pressure develops that remains in force until the concrete has started to set. The hydraulic pressure of liquid concrete against vertical forms is 2½ times that of water. This heavy pressure must be considered as one of the live loads for the design of the forms. As a rule, form designers also allow 60- to 100-psf vertical live load for weight of workmen and tools. The lateral pressure of the concrete may be influenced by the following factors:

1. Method of placing concrete
2. Rate of filling the form
3. Temperature of the concrete
4. Consistency and proportion of the mix
5. Size and shape of form and amount and distribution of reinforcing steel.

The pressure on vertical forms should be computed on the basis that fresh concrete is a liquid weighing 150 lb per cu ft. The hydrostatic head from this load continues to build up as additional fresh concrete enters the form for approximately 30 minutes. After this time, there seems to be no increase in the maximum pressure because of increased depth or head. Thus the rate of pour may be restricted or specified as a certain number of feet per hour for very deep forms. Unlimited pour would otherwise require unusually heavy forming. The strength of the cleats, boards, ties, and other parts of the forms for walls and columns must be considered in relation to the depth of concrete to be poured in any 30-minute period. In cold weather, a longer period may be necessary.

After the concrete has obtained its initial set, the hydraulic actions are reduced to zero, and there is no longer any pressure against the lateral restraining forms. However, in some arrangments the weight of the concrete may rest on the forms, and the concrete will be too green for some time to permit form removal. Specifications often require a 14- to 21-day cure before form removal, but high-early-strength cements may need less cure time.

7.26 Structural components Forms and centering, like other large timber structures, are designed according to standard engineering procedures and composed of structural units such as columns, beams,

Courtesy Cartwright and Morrison

Fig. 7.13 Arch bridge forming (80-ft spans)

trusses, arches, and bracing. Centering structures may consist of a series of girders or trusses. Bowstring trusses or glued-laminated arches may best fit the curved shapes of a concrete arch or dome (see Fig. 7.13). The basic design of these components for forms and centering does not differ from that for other uses except that more attention is given to deflection.

Some forms are arranged to make extensive use of duplicate panels, which are rapidly fabricated on pattern jigs. Curved forms such as those required for tanks and standpipes may use curved panels made up of plywood sheets (see Sec. 9.11) fastened to curved glued-laminated wales. Because of its strength and smooth surface, plywood has found extensive use in structural and architectural formwork.

Additional helpful information about concrete weights and pressures and recommended sizes and spacings of sheathing, studs, wales, and girts is available from the Portland Cement Association and from manufacturers of concrete accessories.

FLOOR, ROOF, AND WALL DIAPHRAGMS

7.27 Design of wood diaphragms Wind, earthquakes, and bomb explosions create lateral forces for which resistance must be provided beyond that usually adequate for vertical live and dead loads. A convenient method of providing such resistance is to add sufficient strength or stiffness to ordinary functional floors, roofs, and walls so that each of them will act as a diaphragm, capable of safely transmitting the assumed lateral forces to or from the ground.

The design of wood diaphragms has received considerable attention during the past 20 years because of the severe damage caused by earthquakes on the Pacific Coast to buildings previously considered good construction. Buildings are perhaps the greatest hazard to life and property during earthquakes. The danger may be avoided if due attention is paid to the lateral resistance of floors, roofs, walls, and their connections, and to properly designed foundations.

A diaphragm is a relatively thin, usually rectangular element of a structure that is capable of withstanding shear in its plane. By its rigidity, its limits the deflection or deformation of other parts of the structure to tolerable magnitudes.

Wood diaphragms may be: (1) solid (vertical laminations nailed or glued); (2) braced (struts and ties); (3) sheathed (usually 1-in. boards, one or two layers, nailed to joists or studs); (4) plywood (panels nailed or glued to studs or joists); or (5) composite (any combination of the above, such as lamella roofs).

7.28 Distribution of forces Figure 7.14 represents an ordinary one-story building with a wood-sheathed roof, subjected to an earthquake. With ground motion in the direction *A–A,* a lateral force, *F,* is considered as being applied at the top of the side wall. This force is equal

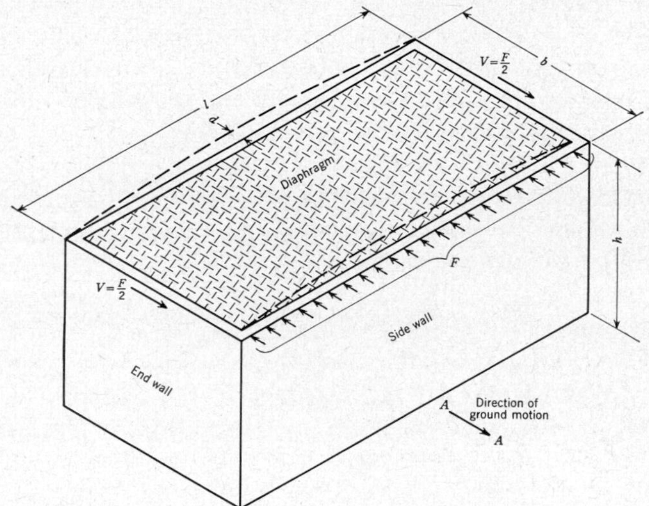

Fig. 7.14 Roof diaphragm action with lateral loads

to the mass of the roof diaphragm plus a portion of the mass of the side wall multiplied by the acceleration due to the earthquake.

$$F = Ma$$

One-half the mass of the side wall may be resisted by the roof diaphragm and ½ by the foundations. But both front and rear walls must be considered.

This lateral force must be resisted in some manner and carried down to the foundation if the side walls are not adequate by themselves—acting from the foundation as cantilevers or as horizontal beams—to resist the bending moment produced by *F*. An economical way to accomplish such resistance is to provide a roof that will transmit the load by diaphragm action from the side walls to the top of the end walls, and from there through the end walls (which must be adequate as shear walls or vertical diaphragms) to the foundation.

The roof diaphragm will deflect an amount, *d,* relative to the end walls. It is necessary to design the diaphragm so that this deflection is kept within the limits that can be tolerated by the side walls. Such deflections may be on the order of ¼ to 2 in. or more at the centerline of the side wall, depending on the height of side wall and the material of which it is constructed. Wood frame walls have the advantage over ordinary masonry walls of being more flexible or yielding before rupture, thus cushioning earthquake and other short-duration lateral forces. In addition, it is necessary to design all connections between boundaries of diaphragm and both side walls and end walls so that shears and direct stresses due to load F will be safely resisted. The effect of openings, such as doors, windows, and skylights in reducing the rigidity of diaphragms is an important matter that has had comparatively little study.

A wood diaphragm is commonly assumed to act in a manner similar to a plate girder, in which the flanges (boundary members at right angles to applied load) resist the bending moment, and the web (studs or joists to which some type of sheathing is attached) resists shear. As in a plate girder, the two flanges are assumed to act as a couple, the lever arm of which is the depth (dimension parallel to load) of the diaphragm. Thus the resultant compression in the loaded flange and tension in the unloaded flange may be calculated by dividing the bending moment due to F by the depth of the diaphragm.

7.29 Web shear resistance The shear resistance of the web is not readily determined. It depends on several factors, the most important of which is probably the method of attaching sheathing members to the boundary members and to the studs or joists comprising the framework of the diaphragm. As nails are commonly used for this purpose, the web cannot be considered as homogeneous. Empirical values for shear modulus, determined from tests, have been suggested for certain types of diaphragms, but no comprehensive design procedures are available for the many possible combinations of framing method, size, and other variables.

Such empirical values, for a given type of diaphragm, must take into consideration the deflection of the web, which will vary in accordance with the length-to-depth ratio of the diaphragm. Given a shear modulus for the web, and assuming the entire diaphragm acts as a plate girder (that is, that the web is fully shear-resistant), the deflection of the diaphragm can be calculated by the usual beam formulas.

7.30 Safe shear stresses The arbitrary yardstick by which wood diaphragms are frequently rated is the maximum shear stress produced by F divided by the depth, b, of the diaphragm. The safe load thus expressed will, for any given diaphragm, reflect its rigidity in proportion to the length-breadth ratio of the diaphragm.

Safe shear stresses will vary from 100 lb per lin ft of depth—for a single transverse layer of boards laid on joists that are perpendicular to the top of the side wall—to several hundred pounds—for two layers of boards laid diagonally and in perpendicular directions on the same face of the joists.

Some types of wood diaphragms, such as the double diagonally sheathed, may be analyzed by common engineering principles. The double-diagonal type can be designed as a multiple-web latticed girder, although the effect of the movement of the nailed connections is not capable of exact analysis. The deflection under a given load F can usually be kept within tolerable limits by specifying a minimum number and size of nails at joint details. Chords or flanges and connections must be provided to develop the stresses.

7.31 Maximum diaphragm deflection A formula for determining the maximum allowable deflection of the top of a building wall, and consequently of any diaphragm designed to restrain the wall to such deflection, has been developed in California for masonry or concrete walls or piers. This formula is:

$$d = 75H^2F_b/Et$$

in which:

d = maximum allowable deflection, in inches
H = wall or pier height between horizontal supports, in feet (but not less than 10)
F_b = allowable unit compressive stresses in flexure, increased $33\frac{1}{3}$ per cent, of material in the wall or piers
E = modulus of elasticity of the wall or pier material
t = wall thickness or effective pier depth, in inches

F_b and E values for typical wall types are as follows:

WALL TYPE	F_b	E
Reinforced grouted brick masonry	$4/3 \times 500$	1,500,000
Reinforced grouted concrete unit masonry	$4/3 \times 400$	1,500,000
Reinforced concrete	$4/3 \times 900$	2,000,000
Plain brick masonry	$4/3 \times 135$	1,500,000

The application of the formula to various types of walls is shown graphically in Fig. 7.15. Although by no means the last word on the subject, this empirical formula is considered to provide reasonable

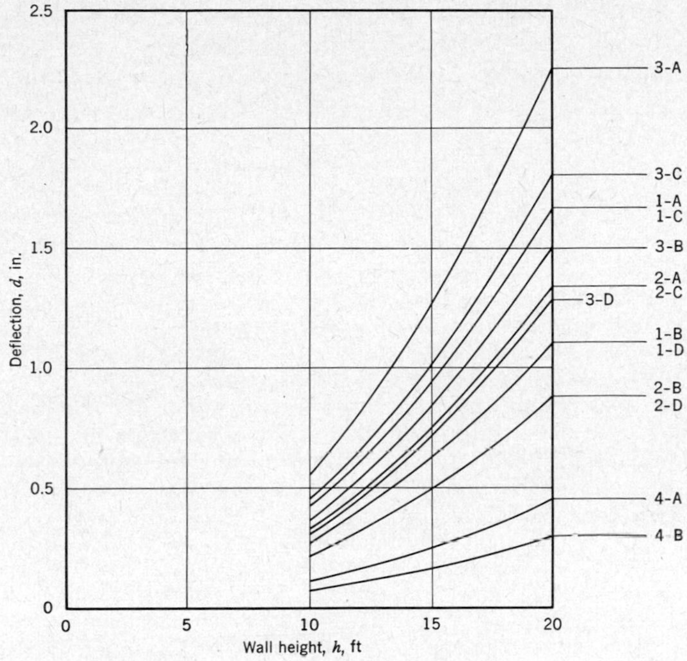

Fig. 7.15 Allowable deflection in masonry walls and piers

1-A *8-in. grouted reinforced brick masonry*
1-B *12-in. grouted reinforced brick masonry*
1-C *12-in. grouted reinforced brick pier* (t = *8 in.)*
1-D *16-in. grouted reinforced brick pier* (t = *12 in.)*

2-A *8-in. grouted concrete unit masonry, reinforced*
2-B *12-in. grouted concrete unit masonry, reinforced* (t = *12 in.)*
2-C *12-in. grouted concrete unit masonry, reinforced pier* (t = *8 in.)*
2-D *16-in. grouted concrete unit masonry, reinforced pier* (t = *12 in.)*

3-A *8-in. reinforced concrete wall*
3-B *12-in. reinforced concrete wall*
3-C *12-in. reinforced concrete pier* (t = *10 in.)*
3-D *16-in. reinforced concrete pier* (t = *14 in.)*

4-A *8-in. unreinforced plain brick wall*
4-B *12-in. unreinforced plain brick wall*

limitations upon the deflection of a bracing system. Principal vertical reinforcement of masonry piers should be not less than 0.008 times the area of the pier at ground line.

7.32 UBC provisions Present practice with some building code enforcement agencies is to limit the maximum span-depth ratios for specific types of diaphragms, and, in addition, to require that calculated shears not exceed certain arbitrary magnitudes.

The following provisions for wood diaphragms are excerpted from Sec. 2511 of the PCBOC Uniform Building Code.[1]

(a) GENERAL Wood and plywood diaphragms may be used to resist horizontal forces in horizontal and vertical distributing or resisting elements, provided the deflection in the plane of the diaphragm, as determined by calculations, tests, or analogies drawn therefrom, does not exceed the permissible deflection of attached distributing or resisting elements.

Permissible deflection shall be that deflection up to which the diaphragm and any attached distributing or resisting element will maintain its structural integrity under assumed load conditions, i.e., continue to support assumed loads without danger to occupants of the structure.

Connections and anchorages capable of resisting the design forces shall be provided between the diaphragms and the resisting elements. Openings in diaphragms which materially affect their strength shall be fully detailed on the plans, and shall have their edges adequately reinforced to transfer all shearing stresses.

Size and shape of diaphragms shall be limited as set forth in [Table 7.4].

In buildings of wood construction where rotation is provided for, transverse shear-resisting elements normal to the longitudinal element shall be provided at spacings not exceeding 1½ times the width for conventional diagonally sheathed diaphragms or 2 times the width for special diagonally sheathed or plywood diaphragms.

TABLE 7.4 Maximum diaphragm dimension ratios

Type of diaphragm	Horizontal diaphragms	Vertical diaphragms
	Max. span-to-width ratios	Max. height-to-width ratios
Diagonal sheathing, conventional	3:1	2:1
Diagonal sheathing, special	4:1	3½:1
Plywood, nailed all edges	4:1	3½:1
Plywood, blocking omitted at intermediate joints	4:1	2:1

In masonry or concrete buildings, wood and plywood diaphragms shall not be considered as transmitting lateral forces by rotation.

(b) DIAGONALLY SHEATHED DIAPHRAGMS *1. Conventional construction* Such wood diaphragms shall be made up of 1-in. nominal sheathing boards laid at an angle of approximately 45 deg to supports. Sheathing boards shall be directly nailed to each intermediate bearing member with not less than two 8d nails for 1-in. by 6-in. (1 x 6) boards and three 8d nails for boards 8 in. or wider, and in addition three 8d nails and four 8d nails shall be used for 6-in. and 8-in. boards, respectively, at the diaphragm boundaries. End

[1] Copyright 1955 Pacific Coast Building Officials Conference.

joints in adjacent boards shall be separated by at least two boards between joints on the same support. Boundary members at edges of diaphragms shall be designed to resist direct tensile or compressive chord stresses and shall be adequately tied together at corners.

Conventional wood diaphragms may be used to resist shears, due to wind or seismic forces, not exceeding 300 lb per lin ft of width.

2. *Special construction* Special diagonally sheathed diaphragms shall conform to conventional construction and, in addition, shall have all elements designed in conformance with the provisions of this Code.

Each chord or portion thereof may be considered as a beam, loaded with a uniform load per foot equal to 50 per cent of the unit shear due to diaphragm action. The load shall be assumed as acting normal to the chord, in the plane of the diaphragm and either toward or away from the diaphragm. The span of the chord, or portion thereof, shall be the distance between structural members of the diaphragm, such as the joists, studs, and blocking, which serve to transfer the assumed load to the sheathing.

Special diagonally sheathed diaphragms shall include conventional diaphragms sheathed with two layers of diagonal sheathing at 90 deg to each other and on the same face of the supporting members.

Special diagonally sheathed diaphragms may be used to resist shears due to wind or seismic loads, provided such shears do not stress the nails beyond their allowable safe lateral strength and do not exceed 600 lb per lin ft of width.

For allowable shears in plywood diaphragms, see Sec. 9.28–9.36 and Table 9.6 of Chap. 9. They are substantially the same as UBC provisions for plywood.

Although wood diaphragms are not presently subject to exact mathematical design formula, those constructed in accordance with ordinary good practice have proved effective in many earthquakes and tornados. With more test data available, it may be expected that they will provide still more useful and economical methods for providing structural stability, especially when freedom of architectural design is desired.

CRANE BEAMS

7.33 Crane beams Timber has a natural advantage over other materials for crane beams or girders because of its ability to absorb tremendous impact forces. Impact seldom need be considered because allowable stresses may be increased 100 per cent. A timber girder has great torsional strength and lateral stability if depth-to-breadth ratio is not more than 2 or 2½ to 1.

Lack of information regarding wheel loading seems to cause more inconvenience than the actual design of the crane beam. To assist the designer, figures for wheel loadings are given in Table 7.5. These are

TABLE 7.5 Loads and clearances for electric cranes

Capacity *tons*	Span c-to-c rails *ft*	Wheel base *b* [1] *ft*	Wheel base b_1 [1] *ft*	Max. load per wheel *lb*	Vertical clearance *c* [1] *ft*	Side clearance *d* [1] *in.*	ASCE rail *lb per yd*
	40	9		13,000	6	10	50
5	60	10		15,000	6	10	50
	80	11		18,000	6	10	50
	40	9		20,000	6	12	60
10	60	10		23,000	6½	12	60
	80	11		26,000	6½	12	60
	40	10		30,000	7	12	60
15	60	11		33,000	7	12	60
	80	12		36,000	7	12	60
	40	10½		35,000	7½	12	80
20	60	11½		39,000	7½	12	80
	80	12		43,000	7½	12	80
	40	11		50,000	8	13	80
30	60	12		54,000	8½	13	80
	80	13		59,000	8½	13	80
	40	12		66,000	8½	14	100
40	60	13		71,000	9	14	100
	80	14		77,000	9	14	100
	40	13		80,000	9½	15	100
50	60	13		85,000	10	15	100
	80	14		90,000	10	15	100
	60	12	5	65,000	12	16	100
75	80	14	5	70,000	12½	16	100

[1] See Fig. 7.16 for *b*, *c*, and *d* notation.

approximations only; wheel loads available from the manufacturer should be used if a specific crane has been selected because there is quite a variation between makes, rate of travel, and manner of operation (cab-, floor-, or hand-operated).

7.34 Design considerations The maximum moment for crane girders is found by placing one of the loads at the centerline, or at ¼ the wheel spacing beyond the centerline if such placement brings both wheels onto the same span. The arrangement that produces the greatest moment should be used. (See Fig. 7.16.)

Maximum shear for design purposes is obtained by placing one wheel at 3 times the depth of the beam from the support, or at the quarter point if that placement produces the greater reaction.

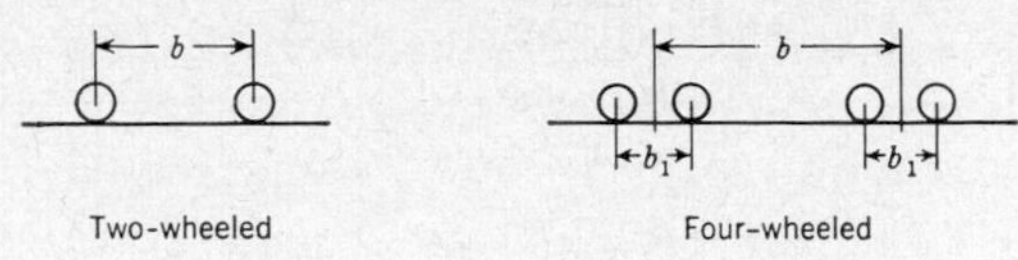

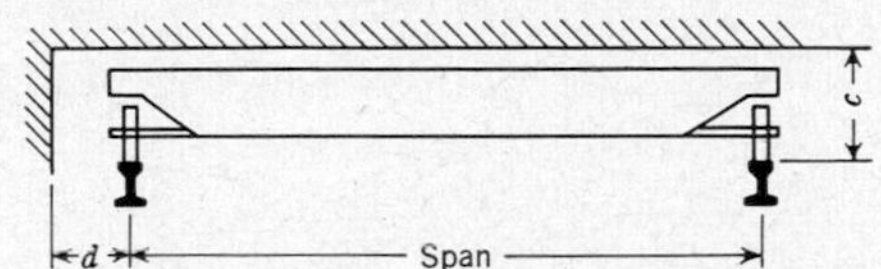

Fig. 7.16 Wheel spacings and clearance diagrams for electric cranes

The lateral force on crane runways that resists the effect of moving crane trolleys should be 20 per cent, if not otherwise specified, of the sum of the weights of the lifted load and of the crane trolley (but exclusive of other parts of the crane) applied at the top of the rail, ½ to each side of the runway. This force is to be considered as acting in either direction normal to the runway rail.

For longitudinal bracing, the design load should be 10 per cent, if not otherwise specified, of the maximum wheel loads of the crane applied at the top of the rail.

Some crane manufacturers specify wheel loads that include a certain percentage for impact. Designs should take this factor into account because it is not necessary to add impact loads to wheel loads for timber design unless there is a steel connection through which the load passes or unless impact exceeds 100 per cent of other normal loads. Impact must be considered for steel-to-steel connections but not for steel or metal timber fastenings.

On extremely long spans, the crane girders must be checked for lateral instability, but this factor will seldom enter into calculations even for spans of 40 to 50 ft. If necessary, the carrying capacity of beams unsupported laterally may be checked by formulas found in the *Wood Handbook*.[1]

Crane girders should be designed for limited deflection in order to avoid wracking of joints and undue movement. The deflection should preferably be limited to $1/240$ for hand-operated cranes and to $1/360$ for high-speed cranes, both percentages based on total dead and live load at the point of maximum moment.

[1] Forest Products Laboratory, U.S. Department of Agriculture.

7.35 Design materials Either solid sawed timber or glued-laminated members are satisfactory for crane girders. Large sizes of sawed timber should preferably be free of heart center (FOHC) to minimize seasoning checks, and allowance should be made in fastening and bearing details for probable shrinkage after erection. Glued-laminated members, for all practical purposes, eliminate problems of seasoning and shrinkage and are available in any required size or length.

Corbels or steel-column caps are preferable to bolsters as a means of obtaining sufficient bearing at beam ends, especially in sawed timber construction in which shrinkage may be a factor.

7.36 Design of a glued-laminated crane girder Calculations for a typical glued-laminated, hand-operated crane girder with a load distribution such as that shown in Fig. 7.17 are as follows:

Girder data:		Allowable stresses:
Span	= 24 ft	$f = 2{,}600$
Capacity	= 20 tons	$c = 415$
Maximum wheel load	= 25,600 lb	$E = 1{,}800{,}000$
Wheel spacing	= 8 ft, 4 in.	$H = 165$

$$\Sigma M_{R_1} = 0$$

$$= \left(\frac{100 \times 24 \times 24}{2}\right) + (25{,}600 \times 5.75) + (25{,}600 \times 14.08) - 24R_2$$

$$R_2 = \frac{28{,}800 + 147{,}200 + 360{,}448}{24} = 536{,}448/24 = 22{,}300 \text{ lb}$$

$$M_x = (22{,}300 \times 119) - \left(\frac{100 \times 9.92 \times 9.92}{2}\right)(12) = 2{,}594{,}000$$

$$S = M/f = 2{,}594{,}000/2{,}600 = 998$$

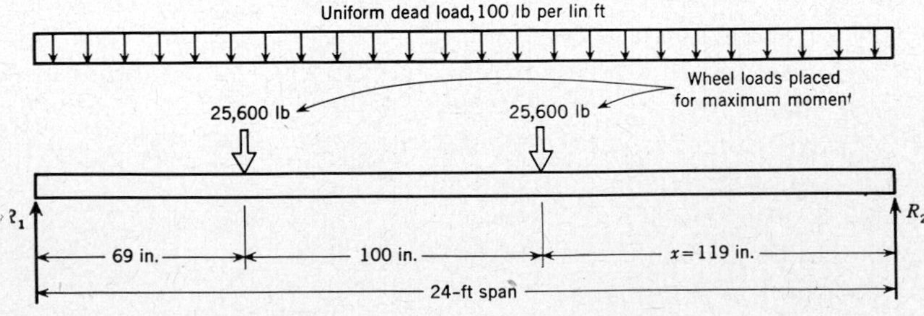

Fig. 7.17 Crane beam loading

Try an 11 x 26 section, $S = 1{,}239$, $A = 286$. Check for shear with one wheel 78 in. (3 x 26) from the support or at the quarter point. The quarter point will control the equation, $\Sigma M_{R_1} = 0$.

$$R_2 = \frac{\dfrac{100 \times (24)^2}{2} + 25{,}600(9.67 + 18.0)}{24} = 30{,}715 \text{ lb}$$

$$A = 3V/2H = \left(\frac{3}{2}\right)\left(\frac{30{,}715}{165}\right) = 279 \text{ sq in.}$$

Therefore an 11 x 26 section is satisfactory for bending and shear. Check for combined bending with 10 per cent of nominal crane capacity as horizontal load:

$$M_v = 2{,}594{,}000 \text{ in.-lb}$$

The reaction at R_2, neglecting dead load of the beam, and with wheels placed for maximum moment, is 21,100 lb. Assuming 1-lb wheel loads only, this reaction will be 21,100 divided by 25,600. Thus the moment for these 1-lb wheel loads will be $(21{,}100 \times 119)/25{,}600 = 98.3$ in.-lb, and the moment in the horizontal direction due to 10 per cent of nominal crane capacity (4,000 lb per side or 2,000 lb per wheel) will be $98.3 \times 2{,}000 = 196{,}600$ in.-lb. Then:

$$\frac{M_v}{S_v \times f_v} + \frac{M_h}{S_h \times f_h} \text{ should be} \leq 1$$

in which:

f_v = allowable unit stress in extreme fiber in bending for horizontally laminated beams (see Chap. 13, NDS Table 20a)

f_h = allowable unit stress in extreme fiber in bending for vertically laminated beams—equal to f for the grade of material used, or to weighted average of f value if more than one grade is used (assume combination No. 11 for Douglas fir)

$$S_h = \frac{11 \times 11 \times 26}{6} = 524$$

$$\frac{2{,}594{,}000}{1{,}239 \times 2{,}600(1.15)} + \frac{196{,}600}{524 \times 1{,}310(1.15)} = 0.700 + 0.249 = 0.949 \leq 1$$

It will be noted that the allowable stresses in extreme fiber in bending have been increased 15 per cent, as for two months' duration of load. If in the designer's opinion the combined vertical and horizontal loads will affect the structure for longer durations, it will be necessary to increase the width of the beam. To determine the size required for vertical load only, normal duration of load is used.

The area required for bearing with one wheel 1 ft from the support is calculated as follows:

$$R_1 = 25{,}600(14.67 + 23.00) \,/\, 24 = 40{,}107 \text{ lb}$$

Add 1,200 lb dead load to this reaction due to live load and the total reaction equals 41,307. Bearing area required = 41,307/415 = 100 sq in. Therefore a cap 20 in. long should be used to provide bearing for both adjoining beams.

In checking the beam for deflection, the loads are most conveniently considered one at a time (see Fig. 7.17):

$$\Delta x = \frac{Pa^2b^2}{3EIL} = \frac{25{,}600 \times (119)^2 \times (169)^2}{3 \times 1{,}800{,}000 \times 16{,}111 \times 288} = 0.413 \text{ in.}$$

$$\Delta x = \left[\frac{Pbx}{6EIL}\right][L^2 - b^2 - x^2]$$

$$= \left[\frac{25{,}600 \times 69 \times 119}{6 \times 1{,}800{,}000 \times 16{,}111 \times 288}\right][(288)^2 - (69)^2 - (119)^2]$$

$$= 0.268 \text{ in.}$$

$$\Delta x = \left[\frac{Wx}{24EI}\right][L^3 - 2Lx^2 + x^3]$$

$$= \left[\frac{100 \times 119}{24 \times 1{,}800{,}000 \times 16{,}111}\right][(288)^3 - 2(288)(119)^2 + (119)^3]$$

$$= 0.257 \text{ in.}$$

$$\text{Total } \Delta = 0.413 + 0.268 + 0.257 = 0.938 \text{ in.}$$

$$\text{Allowable } \Delta = \frac{24 \times 12}{240} = 1.2 \text{ in.}$$

COLLAR BEAMS

7.37 Collar beams Collar beams, often called collar ties, are horizontal members installed substantially below the ridge of a pitched-rafter roof, usually in the upper half of the rafter length. They are thought to reduce the effective length of rafters and thus provide either a stronger roof or permit the use of smaller rafter sizes. Usually collar beams are loaded in compression; reference to them as "ties" is therefore misleading. They frequently are not installed at each rafter but only on every third or fourth rafter.

The frame consisting of the collar beam, rafter, and ceiling joist is indeterminate. It is not factually known, moreover, how a collar beam on one rafter helps an adjacent rafter without one. However, collar beams and short members joining opposite rafters just below the ridge do act as ties for uplift forces such as winds may develop.

Most tables of rafter sizes and spans do not indicate any reduction in rafter span because collar beams are used. Consequently, if the beams are not installed on each rafter, their size and spacing are usually chosen rather arbitrarily, and no credit is taken for decreasing rafter sizes.

7.38 Analysis of collar-beam frames A roof frame with collar beams may be analyzed as an indeterminate frame. The analysis is based on assumed sizes of members. As true analysis takes elastic deformation into account, it could be somewhat complicated for a designer not well acquainted with the method of "least work" and similar theory. Such a designer can make an approximate analysis.

As the elastic deformation is relatively minor, approximate values for direct stress in the collar and direct stress and bending moments in the rafter can be determined for balanced loading by considering the rafter as a beam on three supports and continuous over the center (collar-beam) support. Vertical design loads must be converted to equivalent normal loads. This conversion will give values for the normal-to-rafter components of the stresses across the ridge, the collar beam, and the ceiling-joist tie; and the total stresses can then be determined.

For uniform balanced loading, this approximate method will indicate much less bending moment than if the analysis had been based on the bending of a simple rafter. However, if the frame is assumed to be rigid for determining the vertical reactions of a full unbalanced live load, a similar analysis sometimes yields a higher bending moment (negative) on the more lightly loaded side than that given by a simple rafter. Local requirements determine the amount of unbalanced load required, and thus affect the relative economy of collar beams and rafters alone.

Unless collar beams are placed at each rafter, an indeterminate analysis, whether exact or approximate, is probably not justified, and no allowance should be made for them. Even if the beams are installed on each rafter and properly designed, the savings obtained from the use of smaller rafter sizes may be almost nullified by the extra lumber needed for the collars, not to mention the extra labor of cutting and placing each beam.

7.39 Calculations Assume a 24-ft span with 13-ft rafters, 5:12 slope, 16-in. spacing of rafters, 30-psf live load, 10-psf dead load, and a collar beam $\frac{1}{3}$ down from the ridge. Fig. 7.18 illustrates stresses in the collar beam and the ceiling tie, and the maximum bending moments determined by an approximate solution for these particular conditions. The stresses indicated in parentheses are for full load on the right rafter and only dead load on the left. The other stresses are for balanced full load. The bending moments indicated on the right rafters are maximum for balanced load, those on the left, for unbalanced load.

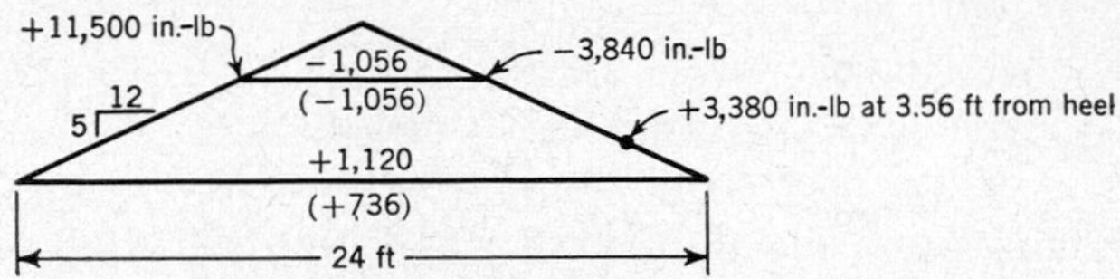

Fig. 7.18 Framing with collar beam

As determined by the approximate solution for these conditions, the maximum bending moment at the collar beam with full balanced load is only ⅓ that for a simple rafter. If full unbalanced live load has to be considered, however, the maximum bending moment at the collar beam on the unloaded side is the same as that for a simple rafter.

Assuming a grade of lumber with tabulated allowable bending stress, f, of 1,100 psi (1,265 psi for two months' duration), a 2 x 6 rafter is required with a 2 x 6 collar beam, neglecting the unbalanced load condition. For simple rafters or with full unbalanced live load, a 2 x 8 is required.

RAFTER SPANS

7.40 Rafter sizes To avoid introducing different recommendations for different slopes, most tables for rafter sizes are based on an analysis of rafters as simple beams. The sloped length of the rafter from wall to ridge is taken as the span length needed for the simple beam formula. This is a conservative approach as it provides for a larger bending moment than that obtained by true engineering analysis.

Vertical live load is usually specified as load per square foot of horizontal projection, and it is logical to assume that the same weight of snow would fall on a pitched roof as on a flat surface. The use of the sloped length in the simple-beam bending formula and of unit load based on horizontal projection actually gives a greater total load for a pitched roof than for a flat roof, a solution that is certainly conservative.

If rafter size is not selected from a standard table, an intermediate approximate solution may be obtained without a complete analysis. By this method, one value of l in the simple beam bending formula is used as the slope length and the other value of l as the horizontal projection of the span. The use of one value of l as the slope length is usually conservative enough to compensate for the direct stress neglected in the rafter. Direct stress varies with the slope in proportion to the component of the load parallel to the rafter.

7.41 Complete stress calculations If tabulated values or the preceding approximate calculations require sizes that seem unreasonable or are just in excess of the capacity of the next smaller size, it may be desirable to make complete calculations for the rafter. If size is limited by deflection, the vertical loading should be converted to equivalent normal loading, and the slope length used in computations.

A complete stress calculation requires the determination of the combined stress due to direct stress and bending moment. For uniform load, the direct stress in the rafter member increases from the peak to the outer wall. Bending moment is based on the actual design load on the rafter, the span being considered either as sloped or as a horizontal projection, depending on whether the loading is wind or vertical live load. Credit should be given for collar beams only if they are installed on each rafter and an analysis is made of the resulting indeterminate frame to determine the exact stresses in the beam, rafter, and ceiling tie member.

For the conditions indicated in Fig. 7.19, the tabulated sizes of 13-ft rafters based on allowable bending in extreme fiber of 1,265 psi indicate that a section modulus of 10.7 is required. If one value of l in the

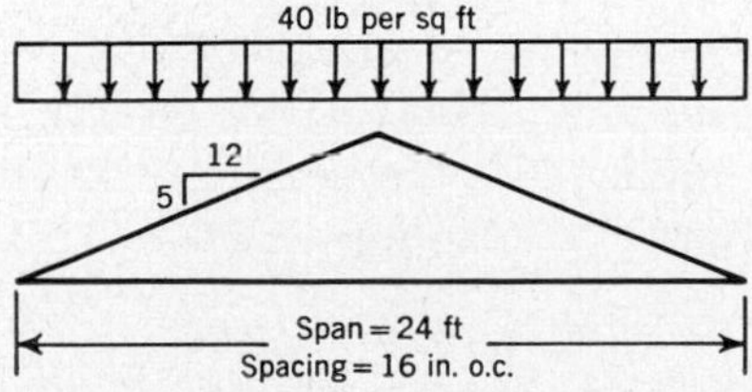

Fig. 7.19 Simple rafter framing

bending formula is taken as the horizontal span, or 12 ft, the required section modulus is 9.9. A 2 x 8 rafter will be required in both cases.

If the rafter is analyzed for combined bending due to vertical load and direct compression stress (assuming tabulated $c = 900$ and

$E = 1{,}600{,}000$), the required area is 0.8 sq in., and the required section modulus, 9.1. A 2 x 8 rafter is still required.

RAFTER AND CEILING–JOIST CONNECTIONS

7.42 Rafter connections Rafter connections in the light framing typical of housing have become more or less standardized by carpenters in terms of a certain number and size of nail. Such a practice disregards the design standards applied to other types of framing, such as trussed rafters, which are also widely used in housing and for small-span buildings. Although there is no intention to question the adequacy of arbitrary nailing practices, it is inconsistent to engineer a trussed-rafter roof and not to do likewise with a conventional rafter roof.

In the example of Sec. 7.41, the thrust of the rafter amounts to 768 lb. If four nails are used, which is an average number, there will be a load of 192 lb per nail. This is considerably more than twice the load per nail permitted on an engineering basis for 10d to 16d nails, the sizes normally used.

A combination of factors apparently assist the otherwise inadequate rafter connections in small structures. The engineering design load seldom, if ever, occurs. Most building codes require live roof loads in snow areas that are equivalent to from 30 to 40 in. of snow. Diaphragm action of the roof, and possibly of the ceiling, is probably effective in transferring the thrust along the wall until it may be resisted by the tie action of end walls and interior cross walls (see Sec. 7.27–7.32). Some stiffness and cantilever resistance is also provided by masonry and frame side walls.

Although arbitrary nailing practice may be satisfactory for small structures, the designer should consider the possible need for more than ordinary nailing if rafter spans are long, roof slope is low, cross walls are widely spaced, or if diaphragm action or rigidity of the roof is questionable.

7.43 Ceiling–joist connections Similar comments to those for rafters apply to ceiling–joist connections that act as tie members for the rafters. The tension in such ceiling joists resulting from the rafter thrust may need special consideration, particularly if a large number of joists are cut, as for a stairway. Diaphragm action of flooring or ceiling material apparently helps in average house framing to transfer the tension to adjacent joists that are continuous.

HIP RAFTERS

7.44 Hip rafters Hip rafters, like collar beams, are indeterminate, only to a greater extent. It is not well known how much of a hip-roof load is carried by arch action and how much by action of the hip rafter as a simple beam supported at the wall and at the peak. The distribution seems incapable of exact determination, although there is little doubt that both arch and beam action contribute to the strength.

If experience is consulted, it seems reasonably safe to assume that, for normal spans and slopes of 4:12 or higher, the hip rafter will carry only a small load acting as a simple beam, provided it is a single-length member. Most of the load is probably carried by arch action, providing there is proper tie in at least one direction, usually by ceiling joists, between the ends of the jack rafters.

If there were complete arch action, the hip rafter would serve merely as a framing point for the jack rafters and theoretically would be unnecessary after the roof sheathing is placed. A minimum, arbitrarily recommended size for hip rafters is at least one size larger in depth than the jack rafters and preferably two sizes, As a hip rafter is more likely to act as a simple beam on lower slopes and longer spans, larger or doubled hip rafters may be desirable for these conditions. The choice must be based on the designer's judgment and experience.

7.45 Peak loading If the hip rafter frames to an independent structural unit such as a truss or trussed rafter at the peak, a concentrated load should be considered as introduced into the analysis by the possible beam action of the hip rafter. For the small-span construction typical of housing, it is sometimes arbitrarily assumed that 50 per cent of the hip-roof load is carried by the hip rafter. The resultant reaction of the hip rafter at the peak is then used in the design of the structural element or truss at the peak. Figure 7.20 shows a 45-deg hip rafter calculated for use with 13-ft rafters and 40-lb load (50 per cent of load considered in bending, neglecting direct stress). A 2 x 12 hip rafter and 2 x 8 jack rafters will be required if it is assumed that 50 per cent of the load is carried by beam action.

7.46 Valley rafters Valley rafters have triangular loading conditions similar to those found in hip rafters, except that the loading increases toward the outer wall or support rather than toward the ridge. Unlike hip rafters, however, valley rafters receive no relief because of arch action and must therefore be designed as inclined beams.

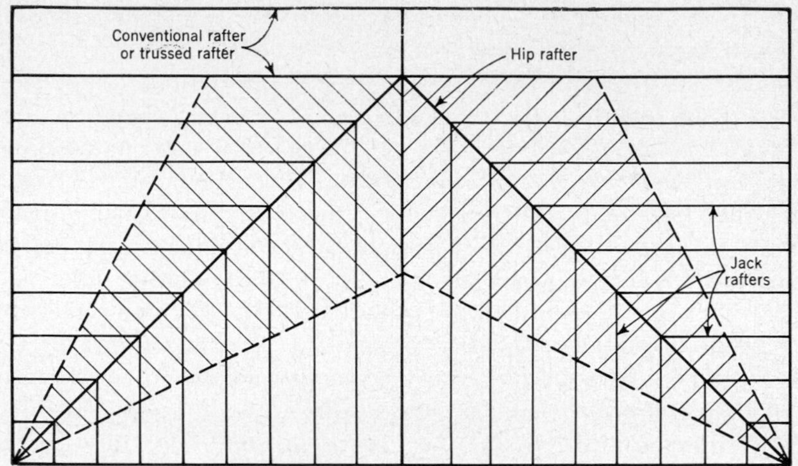

Fig. 7.20 Plan of hip roof

Shaded area shows roof area contributing load to hip rafters.

RAFTERS WITH RAISED TIE MEMBER

7.47 Raised tie members For architectural reasons, for savings in side-wall height, or for added central clearance, the cross-tie member (often a ceiling joist) is frequently not installed at the top of the side wall but fastened to the rafter 1 ft or so above the plate (see Fig. 7.21).

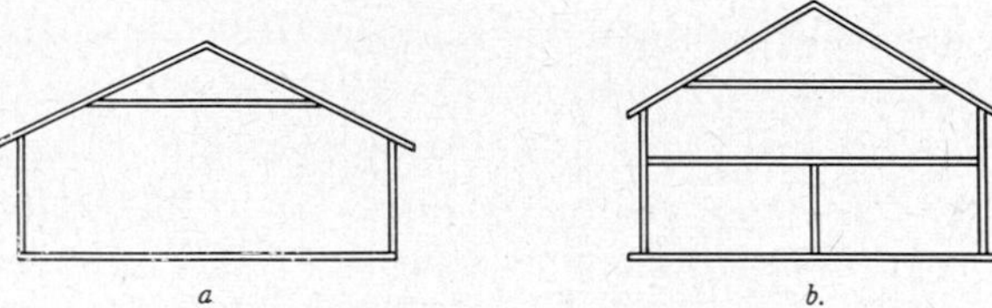

Fig 7.21 Cove ceilings

a. For extra head room *b. For reducing exterior wall height*

Such a tie member frequently requires a rafter of larger than usual size. This type of construction is referred to as a cove ceiling in some areas.

Unless resistance to lateral thrust is provided at the top of the wall, the rafter extension below the tie member should be designed as a cantilever. In residential frame walls, partial or full lateral-thrust resistance can be provided by using full-length rather than conventional studs with a short knee wall, or by using larger wall-plate members tied laterally at intervals by cross walls. For heavier construction, masonry walls and/or reinforced bond beams may be used.

If lateral-thrust resistance is not provided and the tie is more than about $1/8$ the rafter length from the wall, the bending moment will be larger than that allowable for a simple rafter, and a larger size rafter may be required. If the tie is about $3/10$ the rafter length from the wall, the bending moment will be about double that for a simple rafter. Rafter sizes should thus be closely checked, and consideration given to possible negative moment due to rafter overhang.

MOMENT-RESISTING SPLICES

7.48 Moment-resisting splices The simplest moment-resisting splice involves the splicing of two short beams to make a longer length. Such a splice with mechanical fastenings is technically never as good as a single solid length, although it may perform satisfactorily. If full-length material is available, even at increased cost, it will probably be more economical, considering the labor and material cost of the splice. For these reasons, moment-resisting splices should be avoided if possible.

If such splices cannot be avoided, special consideration should be given to the elimination of the deflection normally caused by the elastic and inelastic deformation in the fastening. If it is not provided for, this deflection may prove greater than that in a simple beam. More important, it could result in looseness in a frame that is subject to reversal bending-moment stresses, as are certain types of arches. Simple splices may be cambered in anticipation of initial deflection, and special splices of a kind frequently used in arches are often prestressed to remove the initial deformation.

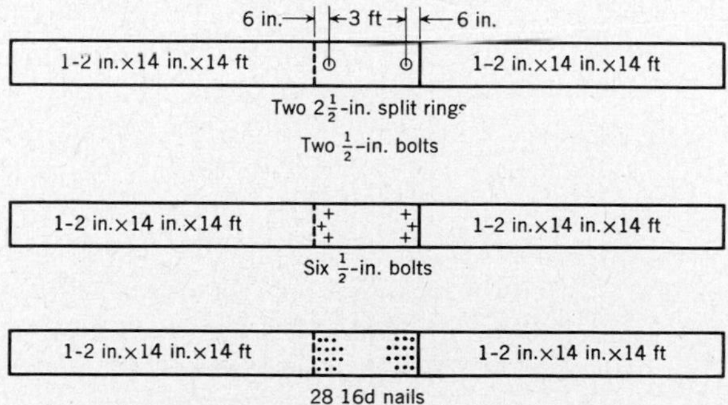

Fig. 7.22 Moment-resisting splices

All moment-resisting connections must be designed with care and analyzed as eccentric joints are for shear. As in eccentric joints, the allowable load is often limited by shear in the lumber rather than by the capacity of the fastening.

Figure 7.22 illustrates spliced joists showing number of nails, bolts, or connectors required for a span of 24 ft, joists 16 in. on centers, and 40-psf load.

8

Exterior Structures

PIERS AND WHARVES

8.1 Advantages of timber construction Wood pile and timber superstructure is the system of construction most commonly used for waterfront structures. Timber has a number of advantages over other materials for these structures, including (1) economy both in initial construction and in years of service, (2) an inherent ability to absorb impact matched by no other material, (3) a comparatively large bulk for ground bearing and relative stability, and (4) an ability to "give" and adjust and thus to absorb or cushion tremendous forces without damage. Timber structures are easily repaired, easily adapted to changing needs, and have high salvage and reuse value.

8.2 Wave action Although waterfront structures are designed by the usual engineering methods for vertical loads, methods of design based largely on experience are used for the less well defined horizontal forces acting on the structure. Consideration is given to wave action and to current pressure as well as to the shock pressures or impact caused by ship maneuvering.

Wave action on piers may be computed by the following formula:

$$P = 125h^2(\tan \theta)$$

in which the point of application is assumed to be at $\frac{3}{8}h$ and:

P = wave pressure, in pounds per linear foot of wave or per square foot of pier area at $\frac{3}{8}h$

h = height of wave, in feet

θ = maximum angle between centerline of pier and wave front (min θ = 15 deg)

Current pressures may be computed by the formula:

$$P = KWV^2/64.4$$

in which:

P = pressure, in pounds per square foot
V = velocity of current, in feet per second
W = weight of water, in pounds per cubic foot
K = a constant

$KW/64.4$ equals 1.5 for flat surfaces and 0.75 for round surfaces. A minimum pressure of 150 psf should be used in streams subject to floods.

8.3 Protection In wood waterfront structures, untreated piles and timber may be damaged by three deteriorating agencies—decay, insects (termites and wharf borers), and marine borers. Insects, which require air for survival, and decay both attack wood above the water level. Marine borers, active only in salt water or tidewater, attack below it. Wood below mud line is safe from both borers and decay. Waterfront structures should be preservatively treated by a standard pressure process unless they are temporary or unless local experience indicates little need for such treatment for the type of construction and life expectancy required.

The moisture conditions conducive to decay in wood are equally conducive to rust in steel and the corrosion of some metals. Salt-water air is particularly destructive to unprotected steel. Unless corrosion-resistant metals are used, protective coating methods, such as galvanizing, are recommended for all hardware involved in the construction.

Table 8.1 serves as a guide to preservatives, absorptions, and conditions of exposure in the treatment of timber for waterfront structures. The data are taken from Standard C18-54 of the AWPA. (Also see Tables 3.2, 3.3, and 3.4 of Chap. 3.)

8.4 Piling The proper selection of timber for waterfront structures is dependent not only upon the conditions of exposure but also upon a general study of the traffic expected. The amount and kind of traffic will affect the width of structure, the necessary freeboard, and the required depth of water. The last factor, of course, directly influences the length of piles.

The allowable bearing capacity of the piles of a pier or wharf normally determines the pile spacing and thus controls the general design. Information on the design of wood piles may be found in

Chap. 7. In general, however, the safe bearing value of wood piles is dependent upon:

1. The size, length, and physical characteristics of the pile itself
2. The soils on which the pile tip rests
3. The soils through which the pile is driven
4. The unsupported length of pile from a firm foundation

The spacing of piles and allowable load is frequently determined by local experience rather than by driving formulas (see Sec. 7.14). For almost 100 years, the design of numerous wood finger piers in New York Harbor has been predicated upon pure friction ("hung") piles. The piles have been spaced 5 ft on centers in the bents, with bent spacing at 10 ft, giving 50 sq ft of deck area per pile. In New York, such a design permits the use of decks capable of carrying live loads of 500 psf and dead loads of 100 psf, or 30,000 lb per pile.

Columns for covered superstructures are often spaced 20 ft on centers, and the cargo doors detailed to fit into 20-ft bays. It should be noted, however, that separate pilings are driven to support the columns for the superstructure. The column footings do not form a part of the substructure deck supports. Rather they consist of groups of four to six piles each, cut off at mean low water, with timber caps and deck planking that in turn carry the pedestals upon which the shed column rests.

If additional frictional resistance is required for the outboard piles, it has been common practice to lag the section of long piles below mud line. Lagging consists of bolting two or four 6 x 8 timbers parallel to the piles before driving the piles into place.

Other means of procuring greater bearing from bent-supporting piles consist of spacing piles on 2½-ft centers in the bent or driving double bents on 2½- to 3-ft centers. Local soil conditions and experience, however, sometimes preclude such close spacing. Double bents are capped and decked over with timber to carry the pedestals on which the deck rests.

8.5 Corner pile clusters An important design detail for piers extending out from the shoreline is the corner pile clusters at the outboard corners. At these points, the pier must have great stability and the ability to withstand the wear and abrasion caused by ships being warped into or out of the pier slip (see Fig. 8.1).

8.6 Fenders Fender systems are most commonly thought of in connection with ship docking facilities, but they are also used as protective devices for bridge piers and similar structures over navigable waters (see Fig. 8.2). The purpose of the fender is twofold. It must

TABLE 8.1 Standard minimum retention of preservative in pressure-treated piles and timbers for marine construction

(Pile cut-offs, field cuts, and bolt holes should be protected in accordance with AWPA Standard M4.)

Substructure—Members in water				
Type of member	Coastal waters		Fresh water or ground contact	
	Creosote	Creosote-coal tar solution	Creosote	Creosote-coal tar solution
	lb per cu ft			
Round piles				
Southern yellow pine	20	20	12	12
Norway pine			12	12
Douglas fir	14	14	12	12
Red oak			12	12
Bench caps, plumbposts, bracing, cribbing, sheet piles, fenders, chocks, etc.				
Southern yellow pine	16	16	12	12
Douglas fir [1]	12	12	10	10
Gum			10	10
Red oak			10	10

[1] Douglas fir timbers 3 in. or more thick should be incised.

absorb the shock of impinging vessels so that neither the pier, which it is designed to protect, nor the ship itself is damaged. Fender systems are almost always made of wood pile and timber elements. Fenders are attached to the ship-side faces and the ends of the pier or wharf. They are composed of a row of vertical piles driven on 5-ft centers to points a few feet deep into the harbor bottom. They are separated by sawed timbers called chocks, which are framed into the vertical fender piles at their tops and at points of high and low water. As the fender piles are usually larger in diameter than the chocks, they extend outward from the chocks and thereby absorb the heaviest mechanical wear. Fenders are expendable protective devices that should be replaced as soon as the wear they were designed to absorb becomes excessive.

The species used for fenders must be high in resistance to mechanical abrasion. As many species are satisfactory, choice is usually a matter of availability and relative cost to service life. As decay usually starts

TABLE 8.1 (Cont.)

Substructure—Members out of water				
Type of member	Creosote	50–50 Creosote-petroleum mixture	Chromated zinc chloride [2]	Tanalith (Wolman salts) [2]
	lb per cu ft			
Caps, stringers, subfloor decking, chocks, etc.				
Southern yellow pine	12	14	1.0	0.5
Douglas fir [1]	10	12	1.0	0.5
Gum	10	12	1.0	0.5

Superstructure				
Posts, trusses, rafters, purlins, sheathing, walkways backing, composite deck laminations:				
Southern yellow pine	8	10	0.75	0.35
Douglas fir [1]	8	10	0.75	0.35
Gum	8	10	0.75	0.35
Red oak	8	10	0.75	0.35

[2] Salt treatments listed for the prevention of decay. They are not recommended as equivalent to creosote but may be used for material to be painted.

Fig. 8.1 Corner pile cluster

Fig. 8.2 Fender piles

at the butt or top ends of fender piles, it is recommended that these ends be protected with wood preservative followed by a bitumastic sealing coat.

8.7 Deck systems The design of pier and wharf decks is naturally dependent upon the live loads that they must safely carry as well as the bent spacing provided by the substructure bents. Decking is usually applied in two layers. The subplanking of 3- to 4-in thickness is laid transversely to the stringers, which span between caps (see Fig. 8.3), and a top layer of 2-in. plank is laid at 90 deg to the subdeck. The

Fig. 8.3 Timber deck

top planking is thereby readily replaceable if abraded by heavy traffic. If it is desired to protect timber decking from mechanical wear, a bituminous or concrete wearing surface may be applied over the wood subplanking. Another form of deck is the composite timber-concrete deck discussed in detail in Chap. 7.

Fig. 8.4 Timber piling for concrete deck

8.8 Bulkheads Timber bulkheads are composed of sawed-timber sheet piles supported by a line of round vertical piles, to which are bolted two or more lines of horizontal timber walers. Bulkheads for waterfront structures are designed to resist the thrust of storm-driven waves and thus to protect the land at the shoreline from encroachment by the sea. They must also be able to act as retaining walls to restrain active and passive earth pressures as well as the surcharge of structures built on the land side of the bulkhead wall.

The stability of bulkhead retaining walls is dependent upon: (1) the thickness and lengths of the sheet piles, which in turn are dependent upon the soils into which the piles are driven and upon the height of fill on the land side of the structure; (2) the size, length, and spacing of the line piles supporting the sheet piles with the attached wales; and (3) the anchorage system. Typical anchorage systems for bulkhead walls are shown in Figs. 8.5 and 8.6. Tie rods should be of either corrosion-resistant alloy metals or steel rods carefully coated with an efficient protective coating. Tie rods may be attached to the wales at one or

Fig. 8.5 Bulkhead anchorage

Note horizontal piles to increase anchorage capacity.

Fig. 8.6 Bulkhead anchorage

Struts are for compression and rods for tension.

two points. If single rods are used, attachment is usually at a point ⅔ up the bulkhead height from the sea-side bottom. For high bulkheads, attachment is at points ⅓ and ⅔ up from the sea-side bottom.

8.9 Relieving-platform bulkheads Relieving-platform bulkheads (Fig. 8.7) may be considered as primarily marginal wharf structures. They consist of a land-side solid line of vertical sheet-pile bulkhead that is built as a part of a deep-water wharf carrying a sea wall at the water's edge.

Fig. 8.7 Relieving platform bulkhead

Note sheet piling on right, platform or wharf on left.

The platform consists of closely driven vertical pile bents, stay-lathed and capped with either timber caps and planking or with a concrete slab poured around and over the wood piles at cut-off. Batter or spur piles are placed to give stability to the sheet-pile bulkhead. On the water side of the platform, a gravity retaining wall is erected above the platform deck. Its purpose is to retain the earth fill placed on the deck up to the desired grade (see Fig. 8.8).

8.10 Jetties or groins Jetties or groins are installed primarily to stabilize sandy ocean beaches from the erosive actions of the sea caused by littoral drift (currents moving along the shore line). They have proved to be effective and long-lived structures. See Fig. 8.9 for the elemental type of construction of a typical groin.

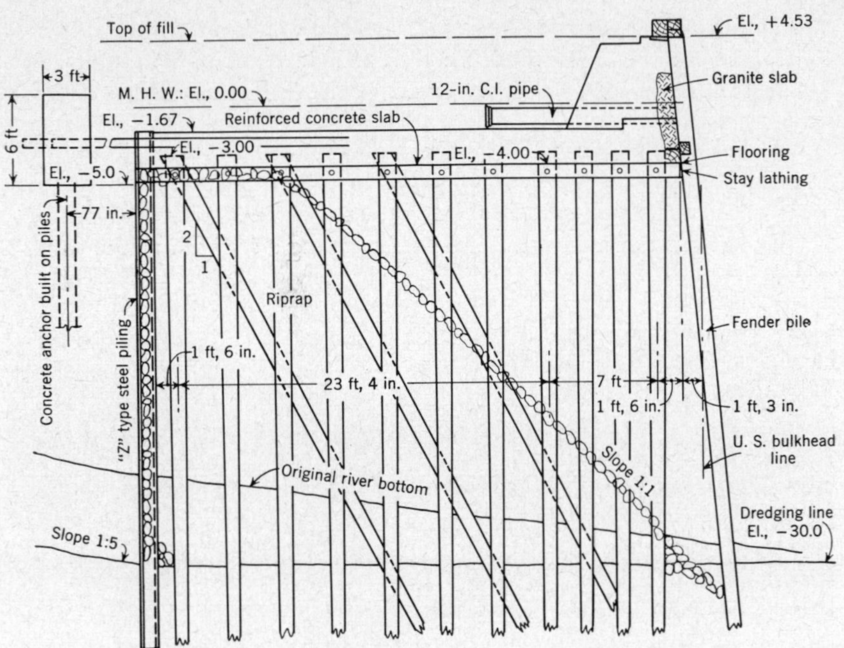

Fig. 8.8 Relieving platform bulkhead, typical section

8.11 Dolphin clusters Dolphin clusters are groups of piles driven as is shown in Fig. 8.10. Dolphins may also consist of a number of closely driven piles wrapped together at the top. Their primary purpose is to provide a stable marine element that will protect a pier or wharf from collision and assist in warping ships to their final mooring place.

The number of piles in a dolphin depends upon the depth of water and consistency of the harbor bottom, the strength of the pile species, and the impact stresses of heavy craft moving at a maximum assumed speed.

A design for a long-lived and stable dolphin consists of a core of pressure-treated vertical piles, separated in the tidal zone by 12 x 12 pressure-creosoted timbers set in two directions and securely wrapped by cable. Around this stable and permanent core, a single line of closely driven untreated fender piles is driven to take the wear of water craft. If the outer ring of piles becomes so abraded as to require replacement, it can be readily removed and replaced without damage to the permanent central core cluster.

Fig. 8.9 Timber groin

Fig. 8.10 Dolphin cluster

8.12 Ferry slips Timber ferry racks (see Figs. 8.11 and 8.12) are shaped to conform to the outlines of the gunwales of the boats they service. They consist usually of three lines of vertical piles called banks. Each bank is connected by two or three lines of 12 x 12 solid or laminated walers. The piles of the bank adjacent to the ferry slip are of full length. Those in the second bank are shorter, and the piles of the third shorter still. Each bank acts independently. The thrust of the boat is absorbed by the high bank, which transmits the force to the second, and so on to the third. The banks are not interconnected. For the final absorption of the thrust, groups of buttress piles are driven behind the inner lines of piles (see Fig. 8.12).

The slip wall consists of vertical or diagonal timbers approximately 4 x 10 in. in section that are bolted to the horizontal walers of the high bank of piles immediately adjacent. If abraded by wear, these planks are readily replaceable.

8.13 Rock cribs Rock cribs are usually not designed but rather proportioned on the basis of experience. They are used to support bridges (see Fig. 8.13) and docks or to protect shorelines against scour. They are most often used in places where rock supplies are plentiful

Fig. 8.11 Ferry slips

and space is ample. Cribs are composed of rock and of timber piers under vertical loads and act as gravity retaining walls to resist horizontal forces. As they are porous, no hydraulic pressure is built up within them.

Framework can consist of rough or dressed 10 x 10's or 12 x 12's laid horizontally—with log-cabin corners without mortises—and well driftbolted. Timber connectors can be effectively used at joints to

Fig. 8.12 Ferry slips

Fig. 8.13 Timber rock crib

increase the strength of structure. Fill material can be secured from the nearest stone or rock supply. Rock fill produces a lateral pressure on the timber frame. Arrangements should be such that the timber cells do not greatly exceed 10 or 12 ft on a side.

Bottom of cribs should be well embedded below surface wash or scour of wave and current. The height should not be much greater than the width unless the top is stabilized laterally by the adjoining framing of dock or bridge.

8.14 Fire safety Modern construction methods for pile and timber piers or wharf structures provide for the effective control of the spread of fire. Transverse underdeck fire-tight bulkheads, such as a double wall of 2- or 3-in. plank walls, can be attached back-to-back to the pile bent and cap, with planks at an angle of 45 or 90 deg to the opposite side. These bulkheads should extend from about 1 ft below mean-low-water up to the underside of the deck. Spacings should not be in excess of about 150 ft and preferably should be much less. Such bulkheads make it possible for an incipient fire to be compartmentalized or isolated and thus brought under control.

If timber deck stringers are used, solid bridging or blocking should be installed at each bent to act as fire stops and also at midbent points if bent spacings are large. Additional fire-safety devices are also recommended, such as automotive underdeck sprinkler systems and cellar nozzle holes built into the pier decks. See rules of the National Fire Protection Association on "Piers and Wharves" for details.[1]

FRAMED TOWERS

8.15 Framed towers Towers of wood are more frequently used than most people realize. Wood tanks on wood towers on top of buildings provide fire protection and stabilize water pressure; wood tanks on

Fig. 8.14 Tank tower

wood towers line the railroads and are scattered over deserts (Fig. 8.14); wood lookout towers for forest fire protection may be found on mountains throughout all forest areas; and wood towers for "drive-in" theater screens (Fig. 8.15) dot the entire national landscape.

[1] Bulletin 87, "Standards for Construction and Protection of Piers and Wharves."

Fig. 8.15 Outdoor screen tower

Towers are designed for vertical loads and for horizontal loads of wind, and in some areas, of earthquake. Usually the horizontal loads are critical. Customary tower framing consists of the legs needed to support the load, horizontal struts, and diagonal bracing members. Depending on economic considerations, foundation conditions, available ground area, or other factors, towers are designed to be either free-standing or guyed.

8.16 Horizontal-load problems A free-standing framed tower subject to horizontal forces (usually wind or earthquake) is designed as a cantilever truss. The legs and diagonal bracing members are subject to reversal of stresses. Double-crossed diagonal web members of either steel rods or wood are frequently used so that the diagonal members need be considered as acting only in tension. A horizontal earthquake (seismic) force on a free-standing tower is different from a wind load.

As the horizontal force used in earthquake design is a percentage of the weight of a structure and of the load that it supports, design stresses in a tank tower, for example, will be maximum when the tank is full. Because of the great weight supported at some distance above the base, the horizontal design loads for the weight of the water are likewise applied at the top of the tower. Anchorage to foundations is thus especially critical in tank towers subject to earthquake.

Transmission-line towers have special horizontal-load problems if a power line breaks. Such breaks are most apt to be caused by accumulated ice load on the lines. The line tension on the unbroken side of the tower, plus the line dead load and any ice load, may cause torsion in the tower. (See Sec. 7.18.)

In a guyed tower, there is no cantilever action below the guy line. Under either horizontal wind or earthquake forces, the compression stress in the tower legs is increased because of the vertical component of the tension stress in the guy system.

8.17 Leg design The number of legs needed by a tower will depend on the load it is to carry and the kind of service it is to perform. Some three-legged radio towers have been built, but three-legged towers are not as common as four-legged ones because of the problem of connecting struts and diagonal braces at an angle to square-sided lumber. Four-legged towers are used for all tower purposes except large tank towers. For those towers that must carry heavy loads, it is sometimes advantageous to use three pieces of lumber in an "L" arrangement at each of the four corners. Loading beams across the top of the legs should be able to distribute the load uniformly to each piece in each leg, and the outstanding piece forming the angle leg should provide the necessary area for strut and bracing connections and permit concentric joints at panel points. Another method used to simplify connection of struts and braces to a single leg is to offset panel-point joints on adjacent faces of each leg. The offset allows the bolts to pass through the leg one set above the other. Although this method requires that the usual horizontal struts be placed at a slight slope, each leg and each set of braces will be identical. Fabrication and assembly are therefore simplified.

8.18 Tank towers Tank towers, because of the great weight supported, present special problems. As the weight of water produces a vertical load in all the columns and as wind forces produce compression stresses in the leeward columns and tension in the windward columns, it is necessary to investigate the tower legs for both full and empty tank conditions in order to determine maximum compression and tension stresses. The diameters of wood tanks commonly vary by increments of 2 ft to as much as 30 ft, and sometimes more. Heights of tanks also vary in increments of 2 ft, with a maximum stave length of about 20 ft. A 20-ft tank of 30-ft diameter will have a capacity of 100,000 gallons, or a weight, when full of fresh water, of 834,500 lb. As wood tanks are generally not fastened to the tops of towers, it is important to keep the ratio of height to diameter such that an empty tank will not be overturned by wind. It is this possibility that usually dictates the 20-ft maximum stave length.

To support the bottom of a large wood tank and to distribute the load uniformly to the legs, a series of closely spaced chime joists are used. The chime joists are cut to lengths that fit within the inside diameter of the tank and are placed normal to the plane of the bottom planks. The chime joists also provide a horizontal shear connection between the tank and the tower because the bottom of the side-wall staves extends below the bottom of the tank in which the chime joists are fitted. A second series of joists or dunnage beams that bear directly on caps are uniformly spaced normal to the plane of the chime joists. In order to keep the caps from being overly large, legs or columns are usually spaced not more than 8 ft on centers. A tank of 150,000 gallon capacity and 37-ft diameter, 100 ft above ground, usually has 21 legs. Smaller-capacity tanks will have from 4 to 12 legs, depending on load and diameter of tank. Horizontal shear stresses higher than those normally allowable are permitted by some designers for the chime and dunnage joists and for the caps.

To increase resistance to overturning by widening the base, the legs of towers are customarily battered. Batter of 1½ in 12 in. is common. Some tank towers with multiple legs and a height of not over 20 ft, however, have all legs vertical. Although in theory there is no limit to the height of wood tank towers, heights seldom exceed 100 ft. This elevation gives sufficient head or water pressure for customary uses. Wood towers have been built for special purposes, however, that are over 300 ft tall.

8.19 Theater screen towers Next to tank towers, towers for drive-in theater screens present the most common tower problem. Critical design stresses are caused by wind pressure and are usually much greater than those for open-sided or skeleton towers. Although screen towers may be guyed, most are free-standing (see Fig. 8.16). Primary design is based on wind pressures (or seismic forces) normal to the screen, but it is important that proper resistance to forces parallel to the screen be provided by bracing or by making the screen face self-

Fig. 8.16 Free-standing screen tower

sheathing. As ground area is usually not restricted, a maximum base width that is consistent with reasonably sized horizontal struts should be used in order to improve stability, reduce deflection, and permit more economical foundations. If codes do not control, some designers permit higher-than-usual unit stresses for such structures on the assumption that maximum winds are infrequent and not hazardous to life because of the improbability of the theater's being in use under storm conditions.

8.20 Special design considerations It is particularly important that all fabrication be accurate so that parts will assemble easily, particularly those which are to be connected in the air. It is desirable to preassemble as many sections or pieces as can be hoisted and handled in the air. Shear-plate timber connectors make excellent high-strength joints that simplify connections in the air of the preassembled sections. It may sometimes be possible to preassemble the whole side of a low tower on the ground and then erect it by a tilt-up method. For these reasons, method of erection should be considered in the design.

For permanent structures, all wood members exposed to the weather should be pressure treated after fabrication with an appropriate wood preservative unless the heartwood of a recognized naturally durable species is used. For equal permanence in all parts, hardwood should be galvanized. In some localities, lightning rods should be installed.

TIMBER BRIDGES

8.21 Timber bridges The history of engineered timber construction began with the old covered bridge. Needless to say, the necessity of a cover to protect a bridge from decay by keeping moisture out of its joints has been almost wholly eliminated by modern preservative treatments or the use of the heartwood of durable species. Either method provides decay resistance without adding greatly to the dead load. Further protection is provided by designing joint and support details to minimize pockets that might trap moisture, by performing all feasible fabrication, cutting, and boring before treatment, and by field treating all wood exposed during site construction.

One of the primary structural considerations with bridges is the problem of stresses in horizontal shear. It has long been recognized that normal analysis for horizontal shear and the recommended unit stresses seem overly conservative with respect to highway bridge structures carrying large concentrated moving wheel loads. Few of the thousands of timber stringer bridges in use today would qualify by rigid engineering standards. Although data are not available to substantiate a more liberal distribution of load, some designers, on the basis of experience and considering the short duration of maximum load, use a larger distribution factor or allow considerable increase in recommended unit stress.

The demands made on today's highways for constant improvement in alignment and increased capacity are not conducive to the long-term survival of bridges. A useful life of more than 50 years would be unusual. Structures should thus be designed for ease of roadway widening and structure salvage wherever practical. Timber bridges easily meet the general requirements. In addition, they offer the advantage of being able to absorb impact stresses to the degree that impact may be neglected.

8.22 Timber trestles The simplest and most widely used type of timber bridge is the timber trestle. The trestle is particularly suited to widening and other alterations and has a high salvage value should its roadway be relocated. Although it is an essentially simple structure, the details are important because much of the design is based on long experience rather than engineering theory.

A timber trestle is usually supported on a substructure of pile bents (Fig. 8.17) or frame bents, sometimes called post bents (Fig. 8.18). For a roadway width of 24 ft, four or five piles or posts are used, with the outer piles battered 2 in 12. Frame bents may rest on concrete pedestals, a continuous concrete footing, or piling. Concrete footings are used if foundations are solid, and the choice between pedestals or a continuous footing depends on scour conditions.

Fig. 8.17 Timber trestle on pile bents

A composite post on a pile bent is used if pile penetration or height of bent is such that piles longer than those normally available are required. The piling is cut off close to the ground line and capped with a sill on which the posts bear. Composite post on pile framing is also used if pile bearing value is low, and more than the usual number of piles are driven in the line supporting the sill. Pile and frame bents are capped with 12 x 12 or larger timbers. Caps are driftbolted into the tops of piles or posts.

Pile bents 5 ft or more high and frame bents of all heights are sway-braced. Single-story sway bracing is used to heights of 30 ft, and multi-

Fig. 8.18 Timber trestle on frame bents

story sway bracing is used for higher bents, with each story limited to about 30 ft. Pairs of horizontal sash braces divide each story. Longitudinal tower bracing, fastened to outer piles only, follows the same pattern of heights and stories as that of the bent-bracing system. However, tower bracing is used only between every fourth span on low trestles up to 15 ft high, between every third span for heights of from 15 to 25 ft, and every second span for those over 25 ft. Bracing is usually of 3 x 8 lumber, bolted at each intersection with each pile or post. Sway bracing is extended and bolted to the ends of caps.

The spacing of bents is partially determined by the commercial lengths of stringers, which are fabricated in even-foot increments. Consequently, bents have odd-foot spacings, such as 15 or 19 ft for stringer lengths of 16 and 20 ft, respectively, the two lengths most commonly built. The ends of interior stringers are lapped and bolted side by side at the bearing on the caps. Exterior stringers are butted at ends and joined with a splice pad or plate. Usually one end of every other stringer is driftbolted to the bent caps. If there is danger of the stringers' floating off the deck because of high water, spiral dowels instead of driftbolts provide the stronger anchorage necessary. Spiral dowels may be used similarly in drifting caps to piles or posts.

Bending moment and possibly horizontal shear may be the critical factors in the design of stringers. Many highway departments neglect horizontal shear, however. Size of stringers ranges from 4 x 12 to 8 x 24, depending on span and loading, and spacing is about 18 in. or more. Stringers should have solid bridging at the ends to hold them in line and also to form a fire stop under the deck at each bent. Fire curtains should also be provided at intervals of about 100 ft. These curtains usually consist of 2- or 3-in. solid planking that is spiked to the bents and extends downward from the stringers or deck at least 5 ft and horizontally at least to the ends of the caps. Bridging, either of the solid or "X" type, should also be placed between stringers at midspan or, on long spans, at the third-points.

A crown for deck drainage may be obtained in three ways. If a wearing surface is not used, the simplest method is to slope the deck wholly to one side by sloping the cut-off of the piles or posts of each bent. Super-elevation on curved decks with or without a wearing surface is also achieved in this way. If a uniform thickness of wearing surface is desired, the roadway may be crowned each way from the centerline by the use of notches on the bottom at each end of the stringers. From the stringer at the roadway centerline, which is not notched, the notches get progressively deeper to the outer stringers. These notches should be adzed or jointed and never sawed for depth, because the sharp reentrant angle caused by sawing often becomes the focal point for splitting. The better method for crowning is to thicken the wearing surface toward the roadway centerline.

8.23 Bridge decks Selection of decks for trestles and other timber bridges depends largely on traffic density. The oldest type is the plank deck, suitable for light traffic, or for temporary structures such as detour bridges. If many high-speed, heavy loads are carried, there is a tendency for the spikes that hold the plank to the stringers to wear loose and withdraw. Spiral grooved spikes, highly resistant to withdrawal, are recommended for spiking planks to stringers in a permanent structure. Planks are occasionally 3 but more often 4 in. thick by 8 to 12 in. wide and are surfaced on four sides. A complete wearing surface is not usually placed on a plank deck, but metal-plate or plank driving strips are sometimes used.

Laminated decks of either 2 x 4 or 2 x 6 strips are more resistant to loosening and require less maintenance than plank decks because of the frequency and better efficiency of the nailing. Each lamination is toenailed with a spike to each stringer, and toenails strongly resist withdrawal. In addition, each lamination is nailed frequently to the preceding lamination with spikes long enough to penetrate the two pieces and part of the third. In the past, it was customary practice to specify that laminated floor strips be surfaced on one side and one edge (S1S1E). Such surfacing is no longer the general commercial practice in lumber manufacture, and as the net standard size is the same if four sides are surfaced (S4S), the S1S1E requirement is not recommended.

A sheet asphalt or asphaltic-macadam wearing surface is usually placed on laminated decks. The minimum thickness for asphaltic-macadam surfacing is about 3 in. at the curb and 4 in. at the centerline; sheet asphalt is 2 in. or more thick, depending on wear conditions. If the highway itself is paved with concrete, it is frequently desirable to provide the same concrete surfacing on the bridge deck. A composite timber-concrete "T"-beam design may prove economical, such as that described in more detail in Chap. 7. Also, a concrete slab may be formed on the stringers by first overlaying them with 1-in. boards, or by setting short lengths of boards between them that are flush with their tops (see Chap. 7). The boards rest on ledger strips nailed to the sides of the stringers. This method permits removal of forming after the concrete has set. If it is to be left in place, the lumber should be preservatively treated or the heartwood of a naturally durable species should be used. The slabs must be reinforced for temperature changes.

Composite timber-concrete slabs are used for the same range of span as are trestle decks. They provide a superior, economical deck structure that is practically exempt from structural maintenance. Deflection under load is quite small.

8.24 Girder bridges Girder bridges are satisfactory for (1) medium-length spans that exceed the practical limits of both the trestle and composite timber-concrete slabs, (2) spans of lengths less than those economical for truss construction, and (3) spans for which trusses are not desirable for reasons of appearance or clearance. Glued-laminated structural lumber has opened up a new field of timber engineering, including a new approach to the design of girder spans. Information on glued-laminated structural lumber can be found in Chaps. 6, 7, and 8. Details of girder bridges using this material are relatively simple.

Substructures can be quite similar to those used for trestle bridges, except that additional piles or posts may be necessary to accommodate the greater span reaction. As wood has a very low coefficient of thermal expansion, no expansion details are needed for the timber at girder bearings. Girder seats usually consist of a plate and a pair of short angles, one on each side of the girder. The angles and plate are bolted to the cap, and the angles in turn are bolted to the girders to hold them in alignment and transmit lateral forces to the substructure.

As glued-laminated members may be shop-formed to curvature, it is a simple matter to camber the girders. Width, depth, and length are limited by practical considerations only. As nominal 2-in. lumber is normally used for laminations, depths of girders are usually multiples of 1⅝ in., which is the net surfaced thickness of 2-in. lumber. The width-to-depth ratio is usually from 1:3 to 1:5. But the exact finished widths, which are less than commercial widths, should be those adhered to in commercial practice so that the entire member may be surfaced to width after gluing. (See Chap. 13, NDS, par. 901-A-1.)

Lateral bracing between girders is determined by the width-to-depth ratio of a girder, and by the lateral forces, which increase as the span increases. Considering width-to-depth ratio only, no lateral support is required if the ratio is 1:2 or less, but fire stopping at bents is recommended. If the ratio is not over 1:5, the ends of the girders should be braced, possibly in the form of solid fire stopping. Greater ratios should also be accompanied by midspan struts between girders and at the bottom flange. The top flange of bridge girders is restrained by the types of decks ordinarily used. If lateral forces are investigated, it will often be found that the large section modulus of a girder about a vertical axis will be sufficient to resist the lateral moment. However, if a single exterior girder is not strong enough, then all of the girders may be made to resist the force by introducing struts along the bottom flange between girders, with the deck strutting the top flange. Seldom will it be necessary to use horizontal lateral trussing at the bottom flange or vertical transverse "X" bridging for the usual lengths of timber-girder spans.

Girder spacing and the cantilever overhang of decks requires a heavier deck on girder spans than that needed on trestle spans. Laminated decks or composite timber-concrete slabs are suitable. For greater salvage potential, a nailing plank may be fastened to the girder tops with heavy lag bolts and the decking spiked to these planks. The deck may then be ripped off without seriously damaging the wood fibers of the girders. The nailing strip can be easily replaced if the girders are re-used, or if the deck is to be replaced.

8.25 Truss bridges Pioneer bridge builders spanned well over 200 ft with timber trusses. Modern timber connectors and glued-laminated chords, which either eliminate or reduce the number of chord splices, make possible timber bridge-truss spans of considerable length, even with modern heavy traffic demands.

Substructures for short bridge trusses may be of pile or framed bents that are almost as simple as those used for trestles. However, the vertical loads will be greater and will be concentrated at the ends of the trusses, with the result that a close spacing of piles or posts is necessary at these points. Long spans that carry greater dead and live loads will require substantial piers of timber, stone, or concrete. Frequently two spans will rest on one pier, an arrangement that doubles the load and necessitates doubling the bearing area for the ends of the trusses. As there is a minimum spacing for driving piling in a cluster, close spacing of pile tops may be achieved by driving a cluster of four piles on a four-way batter. If more than four piles are needed, they may be driven at the minimum spacing, cut off at ground line, and capped with a crib. Closely spaced posts are then framed on top. Similar post framing is used on concrete footings.

Lateral forces are much greater for trusses than for short stringer or girder spans and require a carefully designed system of sway bracing on the substructure bents or piers. Capping of bents for short truss spans is similar to that for trestle spans, but for long-span trusses, and especially multiple spans, a system of cribbing is used to cap the piles or posts. This system provides the large truss bearing area needed and distributes the load uniformly to each pile or post in a cluster. As with timber girders, no expansion detail is needed at the ends of timber trusses. Bearing plates, clip angles, and bolts secure and align trusses on bents or piers.

Deck-truss bridges, those with the truss beneath the roadway (Fig. 8.19), are more economical than through-truss bridges (Fig. 8.20), because their substructures and lateral bracing systems are narrower and the floorbeams smaller because of the shorter beam span. Trussed floorbeams, moreover, can be used. However, the use of deck trusses may be limited by the bridge site and the necessary under-clearance. Deck trusses may be of the bowstring or parallel-chord type. If a bowstring truss is used, the truss verticals are extended to a level line under the floorbeams. Through-truss bridges may also be of the bowstring or parallel-chord type, but the bowstring is usually the more economical because of the lower stresses in the web members.

Three factors determine the length of truss panels: (1) economical spacing of floorbeams, (2) minimal number of joints, and (3) avail-

Fig. 8.19 Deck-truss bridge

Fig. 8.20 Through-truss bridge

ability of lumber lengths. Floor systems require many members of the same length. As large quantities of lumber of the same size and length tend to increase cost, it is advisable to study the floor system carefully in determining truss-panel lengths. As a rule, lumber in lengths up to 20 ft is available in good quantity. A panel length of 19 ft is thus practical, which is also a good spacing for floorbeams.

Live loads on floors are constant to a span of 14 ft. They increase only by about 1.4 per cent for each additional foot of span to approximately 18 ft, and by about half that percentage for spans over 18 ft to spans nearly twice that length. Hence, the variation in live loads on floorbeams in relation to span is not great, and the effect of spacing floorbeams at less than 19 ft is to increase their number unnecessarily. A spacing over 19 ft might adversely affect the economy of the flooring because, by increasing the floor dead load, it would also increase floorbeam size, with a resultant decrease in lumber availability. If the required sizes and lengths for floor beams and stringers or deck are available, a panel length of about 19 ft is suggested. The designer should verify the availability of lumber sizes and lengths or consider using glued-laminated structural members.

The deformation of truss members and truss joints is an important consideration in truss design. If a multi-leaf tension chord is spliced, all leaves should be spliced at the same point. If one leaf is spliced and the other is not, the combined inelastic and elastic deformation in the one piece pitted against elastic deformation alone in the other will cause a stress distribution between the pieces that differs from the design assumption. Likewise, a joint that is framed for bearing but supplemented by bolts will not work as a unit because of the difference in deformation in bearing and the fastenings. Details such as these have been known to cause trouble.

Glued-laminated members are ideal for the top chords of bowstring trusses as they can be preformed to the radius of the chord (see Fig. 8.21). Such members are also excellent for the bottom chords of long-span trusses because the long lengths in which they can be fabricated eliminate splices. Truss joints should be detailed so as to minimize pockets that may retain moisture, even if the lumber is of a naturally durable species or has been preservatively treated.

8.26 Arch bridges If site conditions require a bridge of more than the usual height from foundation to roadway, arches provide a most economical type of span because of their minimal substructure framing (see Fig. 8.22). Timber arches are usually of two-hinged or three-hinged design (see Chap. 6). Some form of anchorage must be

Fig. 8.21 Trial assembly timber truss

Fig. 8.22 Framed arch bridge

provided at the spring line, and both design and erection may be simplified if these anchors are made to act as hinges. Two-hinged designs are more frequently used on shorter spans, and three-hinged designs on the longer.

Arches may be composed of built-up sections, such as latticed members of trussed arches, single or multiple heavy sawed timbers, or glued-laminated members formed to the desired shape. As built-up arches require considerable framing, the labor cost is high. Solid sawed timber arches are designed as short chords bridging from point to point on the arch curvature. These points are located where post bents are placed to support the deck. As the post and abutting arch members come together in a compression joint, the trio of pieces tends to complicate joint details. Simplification may be achieved by joining all members with steel gusset plates that are designed for erection loads and for any tension loads that may occur from stress reversal or lateral forces. The ends of the timber members must be closely fitted, or left with a few inches of separation and the cavity thus formed filled with a high-strength concrete. Arches joined in this fashion should have three hinges so that the joints between members need not be designed for bending moment. Glued-laminated arches are normally factory built to the shape desired. So long as their size is not limited by transport facilities, such arches eliminate the need for joints. Usually a crown hinge will divide long spans sufficiently to meet transportation limitations.

8.27 Culverts Wood culverts may be of round or rectangular section. Both forms are flexible so that the culvert is not damaged if nominal, unequal settlement occurs. Round, wire-bound pipe culverts are available with inside diameters of 6 to 18 in. Steel-banded culverts range from 12 to 72 in. in diameter. The larger the diameter, the closer the bands are spaced. Wood pipe culverts should be buried at least 2 diameters below the roadway. If the diameter is large, with a deep overburden, the culvert should be reinforced at intervals with side clamps consisting of pairs of vertical posts or horizontal tie rods, or with heavier wood staves and more closely spaced bands. Back-filling around pipe culverts should be placed uniformly on each side and well tamped in place. Rectangular culverts, usually called box culverts, are mostly of laminated 2 x 4, 2 x 6, 2 x 8, or wider pieces, spiked together. The size of the lamination is determined by the size of the culvert. Box culverts may be from about 18 in. to 10 ft high and from 2 to 10 ft in span. They may be composed of single or multiple boxes. The larger sizes are frequently used for cattle passes.

8.28 Railway bridges Timber railway bridges (see Figs. 8.17 and 8.18) are almost exclusively of a trestle type similar to that used for highways in design and construction. Because of the heavier loadings, spans are smaller and stringers are naturally grouped beneath the rail. As the large-sized stringers required are sometimes difficult to obtain in solid sawed lumber, some railroads have resorted in recent years to glued-laminated members. General construction recommendations are included in the standards of the American Railway Engineering Association.

Railway bridges are either open-deck, with the ties supported directly on the stringers, or ballasted-deck, with the ties embedded in the ballast and the ballast in turn supported on timber or concrete deck above the stringers. The advantages of greater stability and better load distribution of the ballasted-deck are offset somewhat by the added dead-load requirements. The ballasted-deck is higher in initial cost but generally requires less expensive maintenance, partially because of the cushioning effect of the ballast.

Because of their heavier live loads, more posts or piles are needed for railway trestle bents than for highway structures, and their greater vibration and lateral load forces require stronger bracing. Details are often based on experience rather than design analysis.

8.29 Pedestrian bridges Overpass bridges for pedestrians are becoming increasingly important with today's high-speed and limited-access expressways. The design problems are simple as load requirements are no more severe than those of normal roof or floor construction and the usual types of trusses, arches, or glued-laminated members can be adapted, the latter particularly if appearance is a factor.

MARINE GLUED-LAMINATED CONSTRUCTION

8.30 Marine laminating The development of marine laminating is one of the outstanding construction achievements of the past decade. Examples of its use by the Navy are in minesweepers of 165- and 138-ft lengths, as well as smaller minesweepers and other wooden boats, barges, and auxiliaries.

Laminating of structural members for marine service (see Fig. 8.23) was made possible by the development of improved and more practical waterproof adhesives during World War II. Early waterproof adhesives

Fig. 8.23 Glued-laminated ship ribs and stern section

required curing at temperatures of 300°F or higher, but newer types of adhesives—usually of a resorcinol or melamine type—made it possible to cure at temperatures of about 140°F for hardwoods and as low as 85°F for softwoods. This lowering of the curing temperature and developments in quality control have greatly broadened the economic market for marine laminating.

Marine laminating is important to the structural designer, because there are many exterior applications for glued-laminated construction that require waterproof glues of the same type used in naval work. The method of design for ship construction is the same as that for ordinary structural work except that tests and experience have led to the frequent use of higher working stresses than are justified by theory alone.

Waterproof laminating for ship construction is a specialized technical operation requiring a precise series of tolerances. All steps in the laminating procedure from surfacing to glue spreading, to curing, require more rigid control than those for average structural use. The need for added quality control is partly caused by the use conditions and partly by the characteristics of waterproof-type glues, which are not as foolproof as other glues and must be carefully employed for proper results. U.S. Navy requirements call for a quality control consisting of inspection of the facilities of the fabricator, and of block shear tests of the laminated pieces to determine the adequacy of the glue-line. Delamination or accelerated exposure tests are usually required for hardwood members. Naval use is the most severe test of waterproof glues.

For ordinary exposed structural use, most fabricators maintain quality production control in accordance with recommended practice. Delamination or block shear tests are not usually necessary because internal stresses due to normal variations in moisture content are not sufficiently large to cause delamination.

9

Plywood

CLASSIFICATION OF PLYWOOD

9.1 Definition of plywood Plywood may be defined as a cross-banded assembly made of layers of veneer or veneers—usually an odd number of them, with the grain direction of adjacent piles at right angles to one another—in combination with a lumber core or plys, and joined with an adhesive. Two types of plywood are recognized, veneer plywood and lumber core plywood. This chapter deals only with veneer plywood, as it is the type most commonly used in structural applications. Lumber core is common to furniture construction and millwork items such as doors.

Plywood is manufactured from many species of timber. Hardwood plywood is used chiefly for decorative paneling and for certain industrial applications, such as crating.

9.2 Properties of plywood The properties of plywood, aside from the characteristics of the veneer used in its assembly, stem chiefly from its cross-laminated construction. Plywood utilizes the strength and stability of wood along the grain by laying alternate veneer sheets at right angles, thus providing strength both parallel and perpendicular to the grain of the face ply. The important gain in perpendicular strength, however, involves some decrease in strength of the panel lengthwise. The cross-lamination similarly provides resistance to splitting, improved dimensional stability, and warp-resistance, and therefore the practicability of large panel width and length.

9.3 Types and grades of plywood Douglas fir plywood is produced chiefly under U.S. Commercial Standard USCS45. Most other softwood plywood is produced under the Western Softwood Plywood Standard, USCS122. Hardwood plywood generally follows requirements of USCS35 for the particular species involved.

The two basic types of plywood, exterior and interior, are dependent on the durability of adhesives used. Exterior (or waterproof) plywood is made only with hot-pressed phenolic-resin adhesives that are insoluble, irreversible, and moldproof. It is designed to be permanently waterproof in any service that will not destroy the wood itself.

Interior (or water-resistant) plywood is made by either cold- or hot-press processes using protein adhesives—such as soya bean, blood, or combinations of the two—or hot-press-extended phenolic resins. Interior plywood is designed to withstand casual wetting during construction, and to be permanently durable under service conditions if the long-term moisture content of wood does not exceed 18 to 20 per cent.

Exterior and interior plywood is manufactured in several grades, which are determined by the appearance and physical characteristics of the veneers not only in the faces (or backs) but also in the inner plies. Interior-type panels of the sheathing, concrete form, and underlayment grades are required by the 1955 Standard (USCS45-55) to have a specified mold resistance. For complete details concerning grades, the designer should refer to the U.S. Commercial Standard for the type of plywood being used.

9.4 Veneer requirements The general requirements for the veneers that establish the grade of the plywood are:

1. *A* veneer, formerly called "Sound," has a smooth surface suitable for painting, with no open defects, knots, or holes, but possibly containing neatly made repairs (such as patches or shims), most of which blend in with the grain of panel to permit stained or varnish finishes. Special "natural finish" (*N*) panels with rigidly limited repairs are also available from a number of mills.
2. *B* veneer is a solid-surface sheet except for specified minor defects permitting round plugs as well as other approved repairs. It is suitable for concrete forms, underlayment, and general utility uses in which appearance is a consideration.
3. *C* veneer permits 1-in. knotholes and pitch pockets, splits $3/16$ in. wide and tapering to a point, and certain other minor open defects. Used as "face" for sheathing, it is the lowest grade admitted in any exterior panel or in an interior concrete-form grade.
4. *D* veneer permits $2\frac{1}{2}$-in. knotholes, 2-in. pitch pockets, and splits limited in width ($\frac{1}{4}$ to $\frac{1}{2}$ in.), length, and tapering. It is not permitted in any exterior panel or in an interior concrete-form grade, but is commonly used for inner plies of other interior grades and as "backs" for *A–D*, *C–D*, and similar plywood combinations.

9.5 Common uses of types and grades Panels are designated according to the quality of veneers on their face and back; for example, *A–A* signifies a panel with an *A* veneer on each face, *A–C* one with an *A* face and a *C* back, *B–D* a *B* face and a *D* back.

A–A and *A–B* (interior or exterior) are mostly for cabinet work or industrial uses if appearance or paintability of both faces is important. As exterior grades, they are used for boat construction, highway signs, etc.

A–D (interior) is a one-sided paneling material of various uses.

C [repaired]–*D* (interior) is designed primarily as a floor underlayment or as a base for other materials.

C–D (interior) is used for roof and wall sheathing, subflooring, and interior utility purposes.

B–B (interior or exterior), when oiled and edge-sealed, is principally used for concrete forms.

A–C (exterior) is used for one-sided exposure, such as siding, soffits, store fronts, and signs.

C–C (exterior) is used as unsanded sheathing.

B–C (exterior) is a utility grade.

9.6 Sizes and thicknesses Some of the commonly available standard sizes and thicknesses are shown in Table 9.1. The width of these standard panels is 48 in. For a complete list of sizes produced, consult the applicable Commercial Standard.

STRENGTH PROPERTIES OF PLYWOOD

9.7 Tension, compression, and flexure If plywood is subjected to a tensile or compressive force lengthwise, only those plies having their grain running lengthwise are considered as resisting the load. The cross plies are stressed across the grain and are incapable of contributing any significant amount of strength under such conditions.

Similarly, in bending or flexure, only the plies running parallel to the span are usually considered in computing the moment of inertia and section modulus of the cross section. For example, in Fig. 9.1, the computation for the moment of inertia would be as follows:

$$I = 12/12[(5/8)^3 - (3 \times 0.14)^3 - (0.14)^3] = 0.173 \text{ in.}^4$$

If the grain of the face plies runs at right angles to the span, then only the crossbands, *c*, would be considered in computing the moment of inertia:

$$I = 12/12[(3 \times 0.14)^3 - (0.14)^3] = 0.071 \text{ in.}^4$$

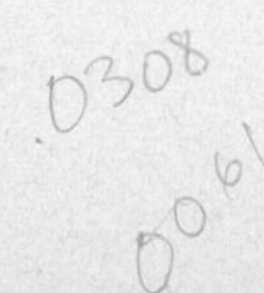

TABLE 9.1 Commonly available sizes and thicknesses of plywood

Grade	Length *in.*	Thicknesses (sanded, except for sheathing grades) *in.*	Min. No. of plies
Interior type			
A–A, A–B, A–D, B–D	84, 96, 108, 120	¼, ⅜ ½, ⅝, ¾	3 5
B–B	96	⅝, ¾	5
C (repaired)–*D*	96	¼, ⅜ ½, ⅝, ¾	3 5
C–D (unsanded)	96	5/16, ⅜ ½, ⅝, ¾	3 5
Exterior type			
A–A, A–B, A–C, B–C	84, 96, 108 120	¼, ⅜ ½, ⅝, ¾	3 5
C–C (unsanded)	96	5/16, ⅜ ½, ⅝	3 5
B–B	96	⅝, ¾	5

It should be noted, however, that for precise calculations—as in airplane design, in which absolute efficiency of material is vital—more exact methods of calculation are available in the "Design of Wood Aircraft Structures." [1]

9.8 Shear Shearing stresses in plywood are of two distinctly different types, either one of which may be the critical factor in design. One kind of shear is that which is perpendicular to the plane of the panel—for example, horizontal (or vertical) shear in a built-up beam with a plywood web. This shear is computed over the full cross-sectional area of the panel. If the direction of stress is parallel or perpendicular to the face grain, twice the basic horizontal shear stress for clear material ($2 \times 120 = 240$ psi for Douglas fir) is allowed, with suitable reduction for the plywood grades. If the direction of stress is at 45 deg to the face grain, 4 times the basic horizontal stress is allowed. A common example of this type of shear is found in plywood used as wall sheathing or as a diaphragm in designing for earthquakes.

The second type of shear is that which occurs in the plane of the

[1] Army-Navy-Civil (ANC) Committee Bulletin 18, available from U.S. Government Printing Office.

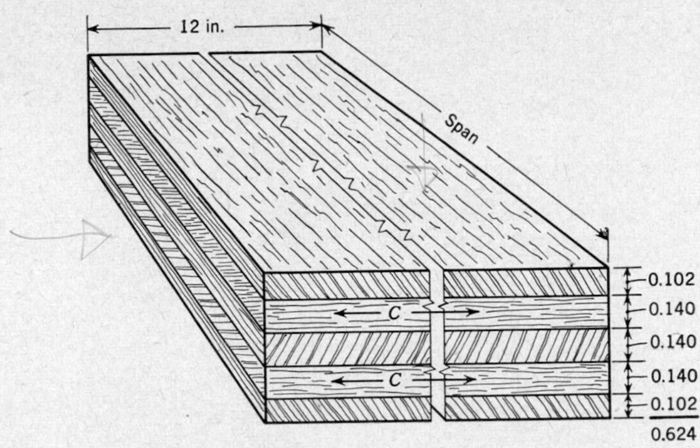

Fig. 9.1 Diagram for plywood "I" computations

panel. In plywood, the wood fibers in the ply at right angles to the shearing force tend to roll, and a so-called "rolling shear" is induced. Resistance of plywood against this type of shear is about ⅓ that offered by wood parallel to the grain. Because beam checking and other factors that considerably reduce the basic stress for lumber are not present in plywood, the Forest Products Laboratory suggests a unit shear in "plane of plies" of ¾ the basic horizontal shear stress ($3/4 \times 120 = 90$ psi for Douglas fir.)

9.9 Working stresses Working stresses for plywood are based on the strength properties and basic stresses for wood as determined by the Forest Products Laboratory. Recommended unit stresses are given in Table 12.33 of Chap. 12. Design methods and allowable stresses for plywood in structural use appear in Table 9.2.

Working stresses for the various structural grades of solid lumber are predicated on allowable knots, slope of grain, pitch pockets, and other similar natural-growth characteristics of the grade that reduce the effective cross section of the piece. In plywood, the same principles apply, but because of the nature of the plywood, such localized defects have a relatively smaller influence on the strength of the panel as a whole. For example, slope of grain in plywood generally need not be considered, and any effect it may have on strength is reflected in average test values, to which safety factors are applied for determining working stresses.

Checking is of an entirely different nature in plywood than in sawed lumber. It does not reduce the effective cross section and appears to have no significant effect on ordinary strength properties, except shear.

TABLE 9.2 Design methods and allowable stresses for plywood

Property	Direction of stress with respect to direction of face grain *deg*	Area to be considered [1]	Unit stress to be used [1]
Tension	0 or 90	Cross-sectional area of parallel plies [2] only	Unit stress for extreme fiber in bending
	±45	Full cross-sectional area	One-sixth unit stress for extreme fiber in bending
Compression	0 or 90	Cross-sectional area of parallel plies [2] only	Unit stress in compression parallel to grain
	±45	Full cross-sectional area	One-third unit stress in compression parallel to grain
Bearing at right angles to plane of plywood		Loaded area	Unit stress in compression perpendicular to grain
Load in bending	0 or 90	Bending moment $M = KSI/c$ in which S = unit stress for extreme fiber in bending; I = moment of inertia computed on basis of parallel plies only; c = distance from neutral axis to outer fiber of outermost ply having its grain in the direction of the span; $K = 1.50$ for three-ply plywood having the grain of the outer plies perpendicular to the span; $K = 0.85$ for all other plywood.	Unit stress for extreme fiber in bending
Deflection in bending	0 or 90	Deflection may be calculated by the usual formulas, taking the moment of inertia as that of the parallel plies plus 1/20 that of the perpendicular plies. (If face plies are parallel, the calculation may be simplified, with but little error, by taking the moment of inertia as that of the parallel plies only.)	Unit value for modulus of elasticity

[1] The suggested simplified methods of calculation apply reasonably well with usual plywood types under ordinary conditions of service. It is recognized, however, that they are not entirely valid for all types of plywood and plywood constructions, or for all spans and span-depth ratios. Also

TABLE 9.2 (Cont.)

Property	Direction of stress with respect to direction of face grain *deg*	Area to be considered [1]	Unit stress to be used [1]
Deformation in tension or compression	0 or 90	Cross-sectional area of parallel plies [2] only	Unit value for modulus of elasticity
Shear through thickness	0 or 90	Full cross-sectional area	Double unit stress in horizontal shear [3]
	±45	Full cross-sectional area	Four times unit stress in horizontal shear [3]
Shear in plane of plies	0 or 90	Full shear area when loaded normal to the plane of plies	Three-fourths unit stress in horizontal shear [3]

the methods given are not applicable to structures so proportioned that the plywood is in the buckling range, in which event the results will be too high.

[2] By "parallel plies" is meant those plies whose grain direction is parallel to the direction of principal stress.

[3] For unit shear stresses in webs of built-up beams and in panels with stressed covers, see *Technical Data Handbook*, DFPA, or Forest Products Laboratory Bulletin R1630, from which the preceding data were taken.

Certain plywood characteristics such as knots, knotholes, and pitch pockets, reduce the cross-sectional area. Consequently, the basic stresses for clear material are reduced a proper percentage for each of the several plywood grades in order to allow for the factors permitted in that grade under the current U.S. Commercial Standard.

9.10 Special treatment against decay and fire If protection of plywood against either decay or fire is desired, pressure treatment similar to that used for lumber should be employed. It appears to have no significant effect on strength properties. Only exterior-type plywood should be specified for this type of service, particularly if water-borne salts are to be used, because the integrity of the phenolic-resin adhesive is not affected by the treatment or by decay or fire.

9.11 Plywood bending radii Approximate minimum bending radii for Douglas fir plywood are listed in Table 9.3. These are average values applicable to areas of reasonably clear, straight grain and in a dry condition. Repairs and defects, including short grain, may cause rupture at a somewhat longer radius. Shorter radii may be obtained by wetting or steaming. These methods carry some risk of face check-

TABLE 9.3 Approximate bending radii for Douglas fir plywood

Thickness *in.*	Radius across grain *ft*	Radius along grain *ft*
¼	1¼	2
⅜	3	4½
½	6	8
⅝	8	10
¾	10	12

ing and grain raising, however, and possibly delamination unless an exterior type of plywood is used.

Although the tabulated radii are believed to be as short as can normally be used, tests on small, clear specimens indicate that actual breaking radii are frequently shorter. For example, test specimens of five-ply plywood have broken at radii approximately ½, and of three-ply at ⅔, of the tabulated values.

Table 9.3 may also be used as a guide for plywood of other species having a different modulus of elasticity or bending strength from Douglas fir plywood. Bending radius should be increased for species of higher modulus or lower bending strength and reduced for lower modulus or higher bending strength.

STRUCTURAL APPLICATIONS OF PLYWOOD

9.12 Structural applications Plywood has many structural applications. The recommendations of this section for the more common ones are based on the use of Douglas fir plywood. The designer should keep in mind that these recommendations are offered only as a guide. They sometimes may be at variance with local codes, but they will generally conform to most codes.

9.13 Subflooring The maximum spacings of supports for plywood subflooring appear in Table 9.4. Face grain must be perpendicular to the supports. It is recommended that spans be limited to values shown because of possible effect of concentrated loading. Actual safe uniform load is in excess of 150 psi ($E = 1{,}600{,}000$ psi).

Blocking should be installed at the edges of the plywood flooring unless 25⁄32-in. wood-strip finish floor is used. If the wood strips are perpendicular to the supports, ½-in. material can be used on a 2-ft span.

TABLE 9.4 Maximum center-to-center spacing of supports for plywood subflooring and roof sheathing

	Plywood thickness in.	Max. spacing of supports, c. to c. in.		
Subflooring	½	16		
	⅝	20		
	¾	24		
		Spacings for various loads in.		
		20 psf	30 psf	40 psf
Roof sheathing	5/16 (rough)	20 [1]	20	20
	⅜ (rough)	24 [1]	24	24
	½ (rough)	32 [1]	32	30
	⅝ (rough)	42 [1]	42	39
	¾ (sanded)	48 [1]	47	42

[1] It is recommended that these spans not be exceeded for any load condition because of possible effect of concentrated loading.

9.14 Roof sheathing Maximum spacings for plywood roof sheathing, with face grain perpendicular to the supports and the plywood continuous over two or more spans, appear in Table 9.4. Deflection is arbitrarily limited to $1/240$ of span. For other permissible deflections, spans may be adjusted accordingly, except that there can be no increase for spans limited by concentrated loading ($E = 1{,}600{,}000$ psi).

Two-span continuous beams can be increased 6½ per cent, except as noted in Table 9.4, and still be within the deflection limit. If spans exceed 28 in. for ½-in. thicknesses, 32 in. for ⅝-in., or 36 in. for ¾-in., blocking or other suitable edge support should be provided. Flat roofs intended to be walked on should be designed as floors.

9.15 Sidewall sheathing For plywood sidewall sheathing, 5/16-in. sheathing (*C–D*) should be used. It is applied either vertically or horizontally, with studs 16 in. on centers and 6d common nails not more than 6 in. on centers at perimeter of panel and 12 in. on other bearings. Plywood ⅜-in. thick is required perpendicular to the studs for a 24-in. spacing. No other bracing is ordinarily required.

If plywood is used as a base for siding and shingles, wood or asphalt shingles may be applied conventionally. Asbestos–cement shingles, however, should be applied with 1⅛-in., 12 gauge (0.104 in.) screw-type nails, 30 rings to the inch. Wood siding should be nailed to the studs.

9.16 Concrete forms For concrete forms, a concrete-form grade of plywood of either exterior or interior type should be used, depending on the number of re-uses intended. For special architectural finishes, resin-impregnated overlay panels are available.

BUILT-UP PLYWOOD BEAMS

9.17 Built-up plywood beams Plywood beams are built-up members consisting of one or more vertical plywood webs to which lumber flanges are attached along the top and bottom edges. They may be fabricated with nails, bolts, or glue, or with combinations of these fasteners. Plywood beams combine stiffness with light weight and are adaptable to both shop and site fabrication. Because of these properties, they are particularly adaptable to certain construction uses, such as movable catwalks and conveyor belt supports. For such relatively light loads as these, spans have ranged up to 100 ft. In buildings, they have been used as lintels, floor beams, roof girders, and ridge beams.

Douglas fir plywood is commonly used for built-up beams. It may be of any grade permitted in U.S. Commercial Standard CS45, either rough or sanded, provided the type is appropriate to the use conditions, and the proper working stresses are used. Plywood of other manufacture is also satisfactory if proper working stresses are determined according to the principles used for Douglas fir plywood. Flange lumber should be stress-graded. Available plywood and lumber sizes should be considered, and the design should be based on net lumber size, after resurfacing, if the plywood is shop-laminated.

If beams are shop-built, more refined methods of fabrication are possible than if site-built. Individual flange laminations can be scarf-jointed, and better control over gluing conditions, particularly pressure application, is possible.

Site-built beams are generally nailed or nail-glued. If nail-glued, one nail to each 8 to 10 sq in. of glue joint is considered satisfactory. It is permissible to butt-joint individual laminas within a laminated flange providing joints are well staggered, and considered in the design. Butt joints should not be considered as transmitting stress, although they do not detract from the stiffness of the beam if there are two or more laminations in the flange.

9.18 Simplified beam design method An accurate method of designing plywood beams based on recognized engineering principles can be found in "Technical Data on Plywood." [1] This method is recom-

[1] Douglas Fir Plywood Association, Tacoma, Washington.

mended if a close and economical design is involved. However, there is an approximate method that is easier to apply. It is recommended for designs for which exact results would be an unnecessary refinement.

This approximate method assumes that the lumber flanges resist the bending moment and the plywood webs resist the shear. Lumber is joined to full length, with glued scarf joints or butt joints used where the stress permits. Plywood panels are butted over a solid stiffener and require a plywood splice plate only on the inside of the beam (see Fig. 9.2). If butt joints are used, they must be well staggered, preferably both in flange and web, and the design must take into account the reduced cross section where it is critical.

The suitable beam depth may vary somewhat. Generally it ranges from $1/8$ to $1/12$ of the span, although ratios up to $1/22$ have been successfully used, and should ordinarily be chosen so that the beam may be cut with minimum waste from a standard width of plywood.

9.19 Required web thickness The total plywood web thickness required, t, can be found from the approximate formula:

$$t = 5V/4hv$$

in which:

V = the maximum shear, in pounds
h = the beam depth, in inches
v = the allowable shear stress, in pounds per square inch, through the thickness of the plywood for the grade used (see Chap. 12, Table 12.33)

As an example, v equals 192 psi for exterior A–C plywood. If a box-beam section with two webs is used, each web should be $t/2$ in. thick.

9.20 Flange size The required size of the top and bottom lumber flanges can be found by the formula:

$$A = M/ch_1$$

in which:

A = the net area, in square inches, of *each* lumber flange, after deducting any butt joints that occur in or near the critical cross sections
M = the bending moment, in inch-pounds
c = allowable lumber stress in compression parallel with the grain, in pounds per square inch
h_1 = the center-to-center distance between flanges, in inches

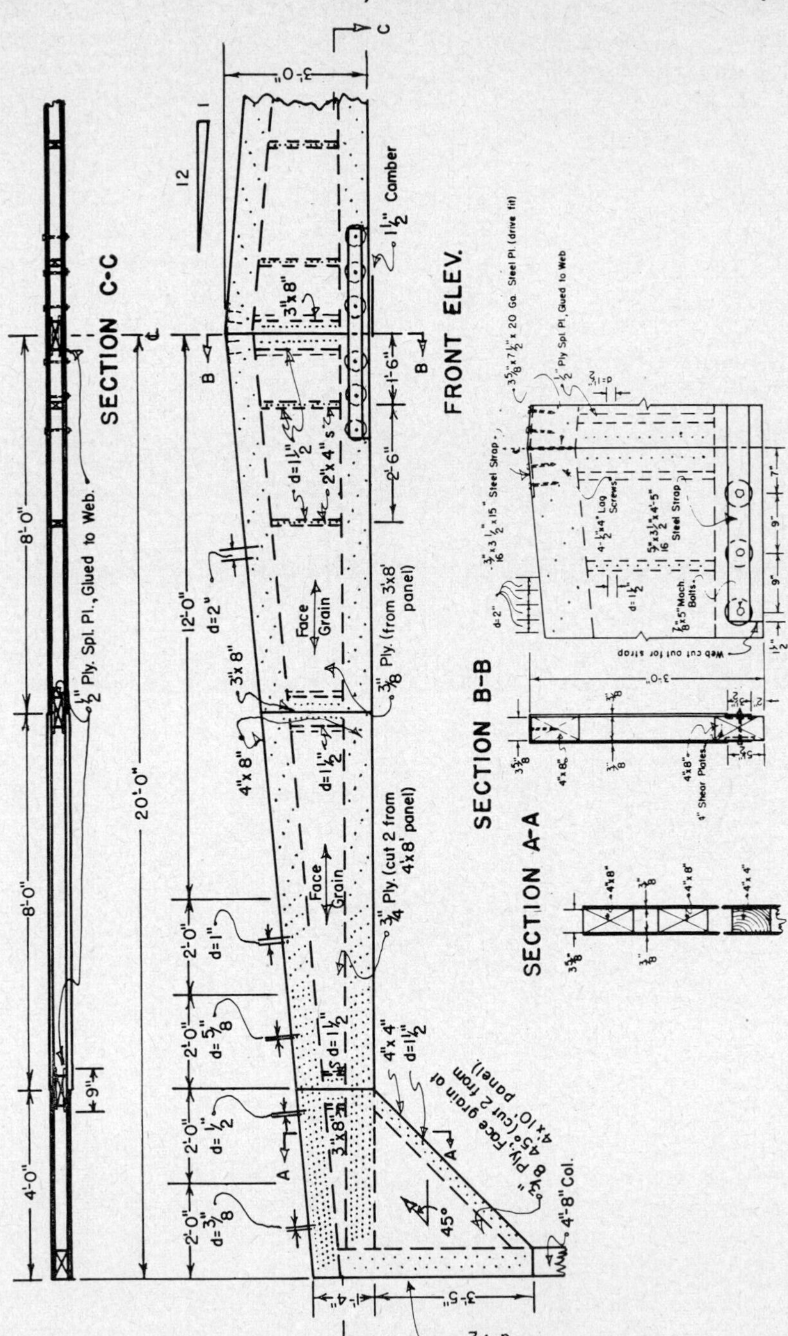

Fig. 9.2 Beam 1: 40-ft nailed plywood girder

Exterior A–C *plywood; design load, 375 lb per lin ft;* f, *1,700 psi.*

The area of tension flange may be found more accurately by using the allowable bending stress instead of compression stress in the above formula.

To have sufficient contact area between the flanges and web if the surfaces are glued, the flange depth should be at least 4 times the adjoining plywood web thickness. If only nailing is used, a greater depth may be required to avoid splitting. After the required flange area and depth is found, the width is determined, and the flange may be selected as either a single piece or a number of pieces of lumber.

9.21 Nail spacing For a box beam that is nailed only, the nail spacing on each side of the flange-web connection can be found from the formula:

$$p = 2rh_1/V$$

in which:

p = the nail spacing, in inches
r = the allowable lateral nail bearing load, in pounds
h_1 and V are the quantities previously defined

Note that the nail spacing is closest at the ends where the shear is highest and decreases towards midspan in proportion to the shear.

9.22 Shear transfer at splices If the web panels are spliced, enough nails or screws, or better yet, glue, should be provided to transfer the full shear at the section. A satisfactory arrangement in a box beam is to use a plywood splice plate at least 6 in. wide on the inner surface of each web, solidly backed with a lumber stiffener (see Fig. 9.2). A glued splice plate on both sides of each web provides a stronger joint, however, and permits the web to resist bending as well as shear (see Fig. 9.3). Bending resistance of the web is neglected in the approximate design method.

9.23 Stiffeners Vertical lumber stiffeners should be placed over the support and at points of concentrated load. Moreover, intermediate stiffeners should be placed near the ends of the beams where the shear stress is high in order to reinforce the webs against buckling. The webs should be glued or well nailed to all stiffeners, and the latter should fit snugly against both flanges. Intermediate stiffener spacing depends on the plywood thickness and the clear distance between flanges as well as the ratio of the actual stress in the plywood to its allowable value. This relation is shown in Fig. 9.4.

The upper flanges of beams—particularly deep, narrow beams—should be supported against lateral buckling. This support is often provided by roof joists set flush with the girder top on a ledger strip.

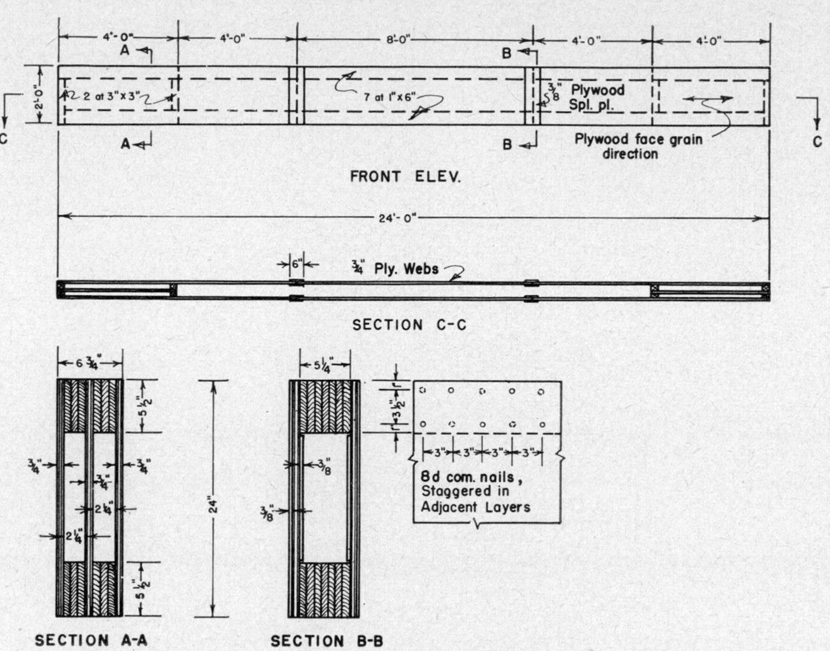

Fig. 9.3 Beam 2: 24-ft nail-glued plywood girder

Exterior A–C *plywood; design load, 660 lb per lin ft; dry lumber;* f, *1,700 psi; end joints in flange butted and staggered at least 24 in.; all side-grain contact surfaces glued and nailed.*

Unless beams are glued, it is desirable to place a few light cross bolts through their upper flanges to prevent lateral buckling of the individual pieces.

9.24 Deflection Deflection of beams of a depth at least $1/12$ of their span is usually considerably less than the customary allowable deflection of $1/360$ of span. Deflection may be computed approximately by the usual deflection formulas, with the computed value increased by 25 per cent for shear deformation. Deflection may be readily offset if the beam is fabricated with a suitable camber.

9.25 Design example As an example of the application of the approximate design method, let a box beam be designed to span 30 ft, with 10-ft spacing, 30-psf live load, and 10-psf dead load.

$$\begin{aligned} \text{Total load} &= 10(30 + 10) = 400 \text{ lb per lin ft} \\ W &= 400 \times 30 = 12{,}000 \text{ lb} \\ \text{Bending moment } M &= Wl/8 = 12{,}000(30 \times 12)/8 = 540{,}000 \text{ in.-lb} \\ \text{Maximum shear } V &= W/2 = 6{,}000 \text{ lb} \end{aligned}$$

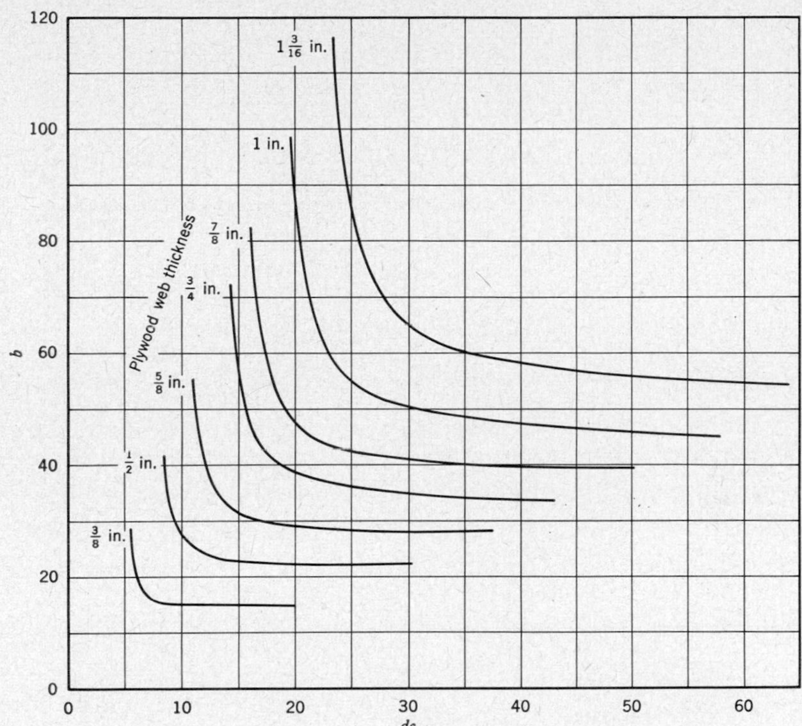

Fig. 9.4 Spacing of stiffeners for plywood beams

b = *clear distance between stiffeners, in inches*

d_c = *clear distance between flanges, in inches*

Basic stiffener spacing b *will prevent web buckling and develop full plywood shear strength when the shear stress in the web is the full allowable value. The spacing may be increased from* b *up to* 3b *as the shear stress decreases from full to* ½ *the allowable value.*

Assume a beam depth of 36 in. and v of 180 psi, a value which corresponds to a number of Douglas fir plywood grades. To find web thickness:

$$t = 5V/4hv = 5(6{,}000)/4(36)(180) = 1.16 \text{ in.}$$

The stock thickness most nearly meeting requirements is two webs of ⅝ in., giving a total thickness, t, of 1.25 in.

If other factors are equal, the most economical of the six grades of plywood that permit a v of 180—the value used above—should be chosen. The *B–C* and *B–B* face grades are more expensive than the *C–C* or *C–D* face grades and would be chosen only if appearance were a factor. Oiled grades would not be used for gluing. Interior grades are satisfactory for most indoor or protected uses. Thus the interior *C–D* grade will be used whether the flanges are to be glued or nailed to the beam.

For lumber with allowable compression parallel to grain of 1,200 psi, the flange area required is:

$$A = M/ch_1 = 540{,}000/(1{,}200)(32) = 14.0 \text{ sq in.}$$

Select for each flange two 2 x 4's with two 1 x 4's placed between them, giving a gross area of 17.2 sq in. The two 1 x 4's in place of another 2 x 4 provide better percentage distribution of flange splices in the center portion of the span. Place the 4-in. faces parallel with the plywood webs, and arrange butt joints in the 2 x 4's so they occur outside the quarter-points of the span. The 1 x 4's may be butt-jointed at any convenient place, but all joints, including those of the web, should be staggered at least 2 ft. Plywood webs will be spliced every 8 ft with a ⅝ x 6-in. splice plate glued to the inner side of each web.

This beam will be stiffer and probably stronger if nail-glued, but as many nails will be required to set the glue as would be if the beam were nailed only. Nail spacing on the flanges at the ends, where shear is a maximum, is determined as follows for 16d common nails having an allowable load of 160 lb each:

$$p = 2rh_1/V = 2(160)(32)/6{,}000 = 1.71 \text{ in.}$$

Nails will be spaced 1¾ in. along the length but staggered in two lines to lessen splitting, and driven into each side, both top and bottom. Spacing can increase uniformly toward midspan, but should not exceed about 6 in. Upper flange pieces will be restrained from buckling laterally if ⅜-in. bolts are placed every 24 in.

Stiffeners ripped from 2 x 6's will be set in over the supports and also at intermediate points as determined for ⅝-in. plywood with a clear distance between flanges of 29 in. (see Fig. 9.4). As the clear spacing is 28 in., the 2-in. intermediate stiffeners may be spaced 30 in. on centers at the ends, the spacing increasing uniformly to 3 times 28 in., or 84 in. at midspan.

As the beam is relatively deep and narrow, its upper flange will require good lateral bracing from the roof framing. Such bracing may be accomplished by setting joists on a ledger or otherwise hanging them so that their upper surface is nearly flush with the beam, with allowance made for their subsequent shrinkage. They should be well spiked to the beam and tied across, preferably with panel sheathing.

9.26 Box-beam tables To aid the selection of a suitable cross section for a preliminary design, Table 9.5 gives allowable bending moments and shears for selected box-beam sections. These sections offer a practical range of constructions as they represent stock sizes of lumber and plywood.

The table is based on the more accurate design method given in "Technical Data on Plywood." It assumes that glued construction is used, that workmanship is good, and that flanges and webs are spliced to develop their full bending moment at all critical sections. Beams designed by the simplified method will be slightly less efficient and require more material. The following conditions were also assumed in the table:

1. The lumber flanges used have a working stress of 1,700 psi in bending. If other grades are used, bending moments and shears may be adjusted proportionally.
2. Plywood webs may be either rough or sanded. Their grain is parallel with the span. The spacing of intermediate stiffeners is such as to develop the full web shear stress where required.

9.27 Typical beam designs Shown in Figs. 9.2, 9.3, and 9.5 are three examples of plywood beams. Allowable stresses are based on 1,700 psi for lumber and exterior *A–C* plywood. All three beams were designed by the precise rather than the approximate method. Details follow:

1. Beam 1 (Fig. 9.2) is a 40-ft beam that is nailed only (except at the web splices). It is suitable for site-built construction, and the design load is 375 lb per lin ft. The web is designed to resist shear only, not bending moment, and account is taken of the ability of the inclined upper flange to resist shear. The plywood gusset plate at the knee brace runs at 45 deg to the beam axis so as to take advantage of the doubled allowable shear stress at that angle. Consequently, thinner plywood may be used. The knee brace and gusset may be omitted, but their use adds lateral bracing and permits the beam and column to act integrally as a rigid frame bent. Column design should take this factor into account.
2. Beam 2 (Fig. 9.3) is a 24-ft nail-glued beam, suitable for site-built construction. Butt joints in the flange laminations are staggered. Design load is 660 lb per lin ft, which would occur with a 30-psf live load and 11-psf dead load if beams are spaced 16 ft.
3. Beam 3 (Fig. 9.5) is a 36-ft beam. It is an example of shop glued-laminated construction in which the flanges are horizontally laminated, then assembled between webs. Shear capacity at the shallow end is

TABLE 9.5 Allowable bending moments and shears on plywood box beams

(Moments, in 1,000 inch-pounds, are underlined. Shears are in pounds.)

18-in. Depth

Flange depth, in.		3/8-in. Webs				1/2-in. Webs				5/8-in. Webs			3/4-in. Webs		
Flange width: Nominal lumber sizes	Total width, in.	1 5/8	2 5/8	3 5/8	5 5/8	1 5/8	2 5/8	3 5/8	5 5/8	2 5/8	3 5/8	5 5/8	2 5/8	3 5/8	5 5/8
1 at 2 in.	1 5/8												149 3,990	172 3,900	204 3,700
3 at 1 in.	2 1/4			166 2,040	208 1,875			188 2,670	230 2,480		204 3,310	248 3,090	177 4,070	207 3,980	250 3,710
2 at 2 in.	3 1/4		180 2,150	220 2,050			200 2,800	242 2,700	304 2,500		257 3,350	322 3,110	220 4,000	263 4,020	325 3,740
1 at 4 in.	3 5/8	141 2,220	195 2,150			172 2,630	216 2,820	262 2,700		232 3,480	279 3,370	350 3,130	236 3,880	283 4,030	352 3,750
3 at 2 in.	4 7/8									285 3,530	348 3,400			352 4,070	445 3,760
1 at 6 in.	5 5/8	195 2,210				214 2,380								393 4,100	

TABLE 9.5 Allowable bending moments and shears on plywood box beams (Cont.)

(Moments, in 1,000 inch-pounds, are underlined. Shears are in pounds.)

Flange depth *in.*		3/8-in. Webs			1/2-in. Webs			5/8-in. Webs			3/4-in. Webs		
		1 5/8	2 5/8	3 5/8	2 5/8	3 5/8	5 5/8	2 5/8	3 5/8	5 5/8	2 5/8	3 5/8	5 5/8
Flange width													
Nominal lumber sizes	Total width *in.*	24-in. Depth											
2 at 2 in.	3 1/4		261 2,910	324 2,840	296 3,790	364 3,720	471 3,520	322 4,660	392 4,590	500 4,370	330 5,600	398 5,520	507 5,240
1 at 4 in.	3 5/8	203 2,970	286 2,925	354 2,850	318 3,810	393 3,740	512 3,530	344 4,700	421 4,640	542 4,390	354 5,640	429 5,570	550 5,280
3 at 2 in.	4 7/8		356 2,970	450 2,870	392 3,870	490 3,790		417 4,780	518 4,700	678 4,420	427 5,260	526 5,630	686 5,300
1 at 6 in.	5 5/8	278 3,030	401 2,970		436 3,895	550 3,805		461 4,820	576 4,700		473 5,100	583 5,660	770 5,320

TABLE 9.5 Allowable bending moments and shears on plywood box beams (Cont.)

(Moments, in 1,000 inch-pounds, are underlined. Shears are in pounds)

Flange depth, in.		½-in. Webs			⅝-in. Webs			¾-in. Webs				⅞-in. Webs			
Flange width: Nominal lumber sizes	Total width, in.	2⅝	3⅝	5⅝	2⅝	3⅝	5⅝	2⅝	3⅝	5⅝	7½	2⅝	3⅝	5⅝	7½
		30-in. Depth													
1 at 4 in.	3⅝	432	531	705	473	574	748	480	581	760	883	541	646	825	951
		4,790	4,750	4,580	5,880	5,860	5,670	7,080	7,020	6,810	6,515	8,070	8,040	8,500	7,540
3 at 2 in.	4⅞	526	655	879	566	698	925	572	708	937	1,108	634	771	1,000	1,178
		4,880	4,820	4,610	6,010	5,960	5,730	7,020	7,150	6,880	6,560	7,620	8,220	7,940	7,610
1 at 6 in.	5⅝	584	727		620	774	1,032	630	785	1,046	1,241	690	846	1,110	1,310
		4,910	4,850		6,050	6,000	5,760	6,760	7,200	6,930	6,590	7,300	8,270	7,980	7,650
4 at 2 in.	6½	650	816		686	862		697	871	1,173		757	933	1,240	1,464
		4,950	4,875		6,100	6,030		6,540	7,240	6,950		7,000	8,340	8,040	7,650

TABLE 9.5 Allowable bending moments and shears on plywood box beams (Cont.)

(Moments, in 1,000 inch-pounds, are underlined. Shears are in pounds.)

Flange depth, in.		⅝-in. Webs		¾-in.			⅞-in. Webs				1-in. Webs			
		3⅝	5⅝	3⅝	5⅝	7½	3⅝	5⅝	7½	9½	3⅝	5⅝	7½	9½
Flange width														
Nominal lumber sizes	Total width, in.	**36-in. Depth**												
1 at 4 in.	3⅝						<u>840</u> 9,700				<u>815</u> 11,180			
3 at 2 in.	4⅞	<u>892</u> 7,200	<u>1,188</u> 7,020	<u>905</u> 8,650	<u>1,213</u> 8,430	<u>1,443</u> 8,130	<u>990</u> 9,900	<u>1,293</u> 9,700	<u>1,537</u> 9,400	<u>1,750</u> 9,020	<u>970</u> 11,400	<u>1,280</u> 11,140	<u>1,510</u> 10,760	<u>1,715</u> 10,320
1 at 6 in.	5⅝	<u>985</u> 7,250	<u>1,322</u> 7,060	<u>1,000</u> 8,700	<u>1,346</u> 8,470	<u>1,612</u> 8,160	<u>1,090</u> 10,000	<u>1,437</u> 9,770	<u>1,705</u> 9,420	<u>1,950</u> 9,050	<u>1,065</u> 11,500	<u>1,415</u> 11,220	<u>1,680</u> 10,800	<u>1,920</u> 10,380
4 at 2 in.	6½	<u>1,090</u> 7,310	<u>1,477</u> 7,080	<u>1,110</u> 8,780	<u>1,503</u> 8,510	<u>1,803</u> 8,180	<u>1,190</u> 10,050	<u>1,595</u> 9,800	<u>1,900</u> 9,480		<u>1,170</u> 11,600	<u>1,574</u> 11,250	<u>1,880</u> 10,850	<u>2,160</u> 10,400

TABLE 9.5 Allowable bending moments and shears on plywood box beams (Cont.)

(Moments, in 1,000 inch-pounds, are underlined. Shears are in pounds.)

Flange depth, in.		¾-in. Webs				⅞-in. Webs				1-in. Webs				1⅛-in. Webs			
		3⅝	5⅝	7½	9½	3⅝	5⅝	7½	9½	3⅝	5⅝	7½	9½	3⅝	5⅝	7½	9½
Flange width																	
Nominal lumber sizes	Total width, in.	**48-in. Depth**															
1 at 6 in.	5⅝									1,570 15,400	2,080 15,250	2,510 14,950	2,890 14,530	1,724 16,950	2,240 16,920	2,660 16,600	3,060 16,200
4 at 2 in.	6½	1,610 11,750	2,190 11,650	2,660 11,320	3,114 11,000	1,760 13,480	2,350 13,400	2,830 13,100	3,280 12,750	1,720 15,530	2,310 15,400	2,790 15,000	3,230 14,600	1,865 16,750	2,470 17,100	2,940 16,750	3,410 16,300
1 at 8 in.	7½	1,780 11,850	2,440 11,700	2,980 11,390		1,930 13,600	2,590 13,460	3,140 13,120	3,660 12,800	1,890 15,100	2,560 15,500	3,110 15,100	3,630 14,660	2,040 16,100	2,720 17,200	3,270 16,800	3,790 16,380
1 at 10 in.	9½	2,120 12,000	2,940 11,850			2,270 13,750	3,100 13,600	3,760 13,220		2,230 14,300	3,070 15,700	3,750 15,150		2,370 15,100	3,230 17,450	3,900 16,920	4,550 16,450

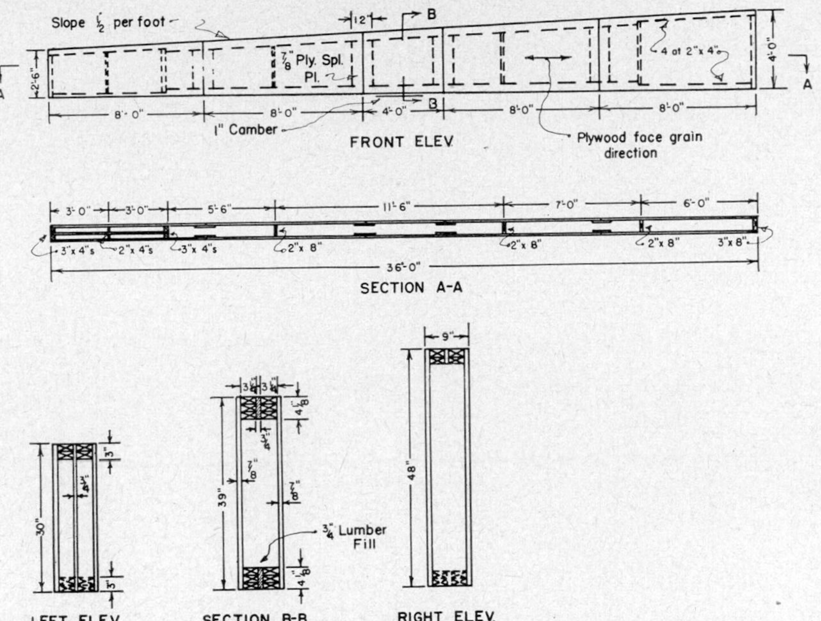

Fig. 9.5 Beam 3: 36-ft shop-laminated plywood girder

Exterior A–C *plywood; design load, 640 lb per lin ft; dry lumber;* f, *1,700 psi; end joints in flange scarfed at 1:12 slope and glued; all side-grain contact surfaces glued.*

increased by the addition of a short plywood panel. Because outer-web splice plates are omitted for appearance's sake, the web is figured to take only shear, and no flexure. Design load is 640 lb per lin ft. Thus this beam is suitable for use at a 20-ft spacing with a 20-psf live load and 12-psf dead load.

PLYWOOD DIAPHRAGMS

9.28 Plywood diaphragms Plywood diaphragms consist of framing members covered with plywood. The plywood is usually attached to one side with nails, although glue has also been used. The diaphragm's important function is to brace a building against horizontal wind or seismic forces and to transmit these forces into the foundations (see Chap. 7).

Diaphragms may be classified as horizontal or vertical. Horizontal diaphragms include floors and roofs, the latter normally pitched or curved, whereas vertical diaphragms include walls and partitions. Horizontal plywood diaphragms may be basically designed as plate girders acting as simple or continuous beams over supports—such as partitions or end walls—that are capable of transmitting shear to the foundation. A vertical diaphragm acts more nearly like a cantilever beam, with its base anchored to a foundation while load is being applied along its upper edge in the plane of the plywood.

The plywood sheathing acts as the fully shear-resistant web of a girder, and shear stresses can be calculated on this basis. Flexural stresses are carried by continuous members at the boundaries of the diaphragm. Intermediate framing members such as joists and studs stiffen the diaphragm against buckling and serve as splicing members at edges of plywood panels.

9.29 Length-width ratios To limit deflection, a maximum ratio of span length to diaphragm width of 4:1 is suggested for unblocked horizontal diaphragms (those without blocking or splices under the plywood panel joints that extend between joists or framing members). Possibly ratios should be more restrictive if plywood is used with masonry or concrete walls rather than with wood or steel frame walls. No such arbitrary ratio is recommended for blocked horizontal diaphragms; instead it is suggested that dimensions be limited by the allowable diaphragm shear and by the permissible deflection of the attached walls (see Sec. 7.31). An accurate method of calculating deflections is given in Sec. 9.36. Allowable shears are not affected by length-width ratio.

A maximum ratio of height to width of 3½:1 is suggested for a vertical blocked plywood diaphragm. Ratios for an unblocked member have not been set but should no doubt be lower, possibly 2:1.

9.30 Framing Joist or stud framing is normally designed primarily to resist vertical loads, with sizes and spacing governed accordingly. For diaphragm framing, however, there is an added consideration. Diaphragm stress values—being governed by the strength of the nails attaching the plywood to lumber—increase with the thickness of framing because of the additional nailing room provided if the plywood is butted at its centerline. Shear values for diaphragms on 1⅝-in. framing have been found in tests to be 11 per cent less than those on 2⅝-in. and thicker framing. Framing members thinner than 1⅝ are not desirable in a nailed diaphragm in which panels butt on the framing. Panels less than 12 in. wide should not be considered as carrying shear and may have to be compensated for by an increase in nailing in adjacent areas. Narrow panel pieces should thus be avoided if possible.

Shear strength is not directly affected by load direction in the framing members. The layout of these members, however, determines the direction of unblocked panel edges, which do affect strength, as do continuous panel joints (see Sec. 9.33).

Blocking between framing at the panel edges should be no thinner than the framing itself, but it need be no thicker than 2⅝ in. in order to develop full nail-bearing values. Blocking need be no deeper than necessary to receive and hold the nails if its only function is to splice the plywood. Generally, however, at least one line of blocking is made full depth. It may then do double duty as joist bridging by distributing into the diaphragm any loads applied perpendicular to the joists. Diagonal cross bridging is not recommended in blocked diaphragms if load is applied perpendicular to the joists because its resulting scissors-like action has been found capable of splitting the joists at high loads.

9.31 Boundary members Boundary members must be designed to resist direct stresses only (both tension and compression). The chord stress on a horizontal plywood diaphragm can be found by dividing the bending moment by the distance between chords times the cross-sectional area of that part of the chord which is continuous:

$$\text{Stress} = \frac{\text{Moment}}{\text{Chord area} \times \text{Diaphragm width}}$$

With wood framing, the continuous member on which the joists rest (such as the wall plate or upper chord of a truss) can be used to carry the bending stress, provided shear from the plywood is transferred into it. If the plywood cannot be nailed directly to the continuous member, it can be nailed to full-depth blocking placed between joists. The blocking in turn is nailed directly to the plate or truss chord, or to other blocking that is so nailed. Chords made with cut-in blocking have been found capable of developing full diaphragm shear strength, providing that all nailing between such members is designed to develop the shear (see Fig. 9.6).

Boundary members must provide an adequate nailing surface, because more nailing is usually required on these members than on interior joists or studs. If a concrete wall or bond-beam serves as the boundary, outer joists and headers must be effectively bolted or anchored to it. With steel framing, the joist ends can be bolted to welded clips, or set between blocking bolted to the beam, with the blocking serving as a nailing surface (see Fig. 9.7).

Corner connections of horizontal diaphragms with wood framing

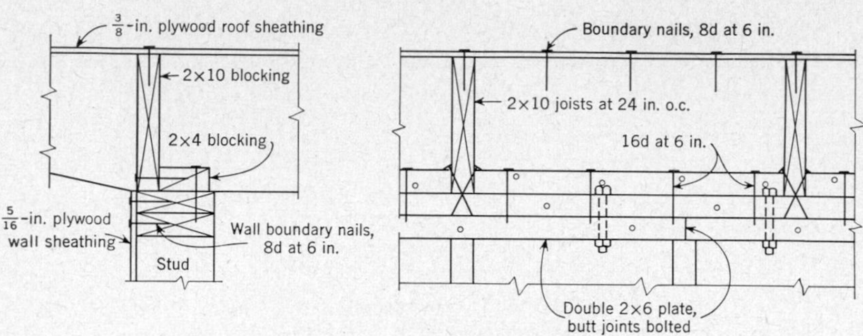

Fig. 9.6 Wood plate detail

may be simply lapped and nailed, because plywood sheathing develops no appreciable component tending to open the corner. Anchorage along the boundaries of horizontal diaphragms should be provided against the small vertical forces that develop from the twisting caused by application of the sheathing to only one side of the frame. Such anchorage is normally provided by the wall connections. Vertical diaphragms with large height-width ratios may require carefully designed anchors attached to the outer studs to resist overturning.

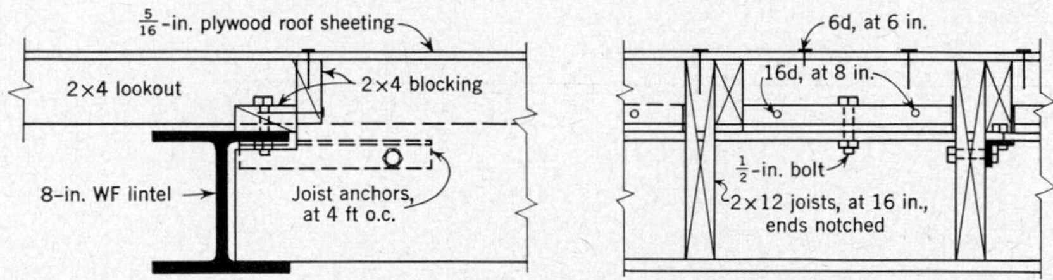

Fig. 9.7 Steel lintel detail

9.32 Plywood size The thickness of plywood required for a horizontal diaphragm will usually depend on vertical load and framing spacing (see Sec. 9.13 and 9.14). For vertical diaphragms, sheathing thickness should be not less than $\frac{1}{4}$ in. for studs spaced 16 in. and $\frac{3}{8}$ in. for 24-in. spacing. These span-thickness combinations are such that plywood buckling will not occur from shear stress within the shears listed in Table 9.6.

Diaphragm shear requirements may conceivably govern the thickness. The shears given in Table 9.6, however, are below the shear-stress limits in the plywood itself. If shears in excess of these tabular values are used (found by dividing the total shear by the plywood thickness and net diaphragm width—discounting any openings at the section

TABLE 9.6 Allowable shears for wind or seismic loadings on blocked Douglas fir plywood diaphragms using Douglas fir and southern pine framing [1]

Minimum plywood [2] thickness *in.*	Common nail size	Allowable shear *lb per ft* — Nail spacing on all plywood panel edges [3] — For framing member 2⅝ in. or more in width			For framing member less than 2⅝ in. but not less than 1⅝ in. in width		
		6 in.	4 in.	3 in.	6 in.	4 in.	3 in.
5⁄16 [4]	6d	280	420	475	250	375	420
⅜	8d	400	600	675	360	530	600
½	10d	480	720	820	425	640	730

[1] For other species, adjust values accordingly.
[2] For Douglas fir plywood grades having inner plies of species other than Douglas fir, use next greater thickness or reduce shears ¼.
[3] If the force acting along either boundary or any line of continuous panel joints exceeds ¾ of the tabulated value, nail spacing along such boundary or line shall be reduced by ⅓.
[4] These values may be used with ¼-in. plywood if perpendicular loads permit its use.

under consideration), the allowable shear stress in Table 12.33 of Chap. 12 should not be increased by more than ⅓ for short-time loading. Actual ultimate loads on full-scale test specimens range from 3 to 7 times the tabular values.

It should be noted also that for Douglas fir plywood grades having inner plies of other species than Douglas fir, the next greater thickness should be used, or else tabulated shears reduced 25 per cent.

9.33 Panel layout Shear strength is higher if the load is applied perpendicular to continuous, unstaggered panel edges than if applied parallel. The difference in strength occurs because panel rotation under load brings into bearing otherwise understressed nails in intermediate framing members in adjacent panel courses. Both loadings must be investigated in a design, as the load may be applied in either direction, whereas the panels can be staggered only in one. Thus the full values of table 9.6 apply if loads are perpendicular to continuous panel edges, whereas only 75 per cent of these values are permitted if loads are parallel.

In order to utilize full tabular values for loading parallel to continuous joints, nail spacing should be reduced by ⅓ along those joints. Normally this nailing increase applies only to those lines in the maximum shear area. It may be noted that as all four boundaries function like continuous joints, the same provision for increased nailing applies to them. However, the normal rectangular, horizontal diaphragm is fully stressed in only one rather than both directions, so that additional nailing is seldom required on more than the two short-length boundaries.

9.34 Omission of blocking So far as diaphragm action is concerned, the blocking at panel edges acts primarily as a shear splice and stiffener against edge buckling. It may sometimes be omitted if allowable shears are reduced.

If load is applied perpendicular to the unblocked panel edges and to the continuous joints, shears should not exceed ⅔ of the values given in Table 9.6 for 6-in. nail spacing. For other panel arrangements, shears should be limited to 50 per cent of the tabulated values for 6-in. nail spacing.

9.35 Nailing The load per nail on a panel nailed the same way on all four edges is determined by dividing the shear per foot by the number of nails per foot. Allowance should also be made in both the lumber and plywood for the edge distance of the nail. However, edge distance is a relatively small factor, because the load is applied essentially parallel with the framing member and the plywood edge. Theoretically it is only the edge nails that resist shear, but in practice the intermediate nails also contribute, as already mentioned, because of the rotation of adjacent staggered panels.

The intermediate nails also serve to prevent panel buckling, particularly that which is caused by compression from adjacent panels. Intermediate nails should be spaced not more than 12 in. A closer spacing will increase the strength, particularly as edge nailing is increased, but by an undetermined amount.

As not all areas of a diaphragm may be subjected to the same shear stress, it is possible to vary the nailing schedule to suit the need. Practical considerations suggest that such a schedule should not be so complicated as to cause confusion in the field. A nail spacing greater than 6 in. on panel edges is not recommended.

9.36 Deflection The deflection of a horizontal diaphragm may be limited by permissible deflections of attached walls and partitions, particularly if they are of masonry construction. The center deflection of a horizontal plywood diaphragm acting as a simple beam under uniform load is the sum of the bending, shear, and nail deflections, and can be determined from the following formula:

$$d = 5vL^3/8EAb + vL/4Gt + 0.094Ie_n$$

in which:

d = deflection, in inches
v = shear, in pounds per foot
L = span, in feet
E = elastic modulus of chords, in pounds per square inch
A = effective cross-sectional area of chords, in square inches
b = width of diaphragm, in feet
G = shear modulus, in pounds per square inch (110,000 psi for Douglas fir plywood at 12-per cent moisture content)
t = plywood thickness, in inches
e_n = nail slip, in inches, at load per nail

The nail slip, e_n, is found from Fig. 9.8 by reference to the proper plywood-nail combination (or interpolated values), using as the load per nail the shear per foot in the critical shear area divided by the

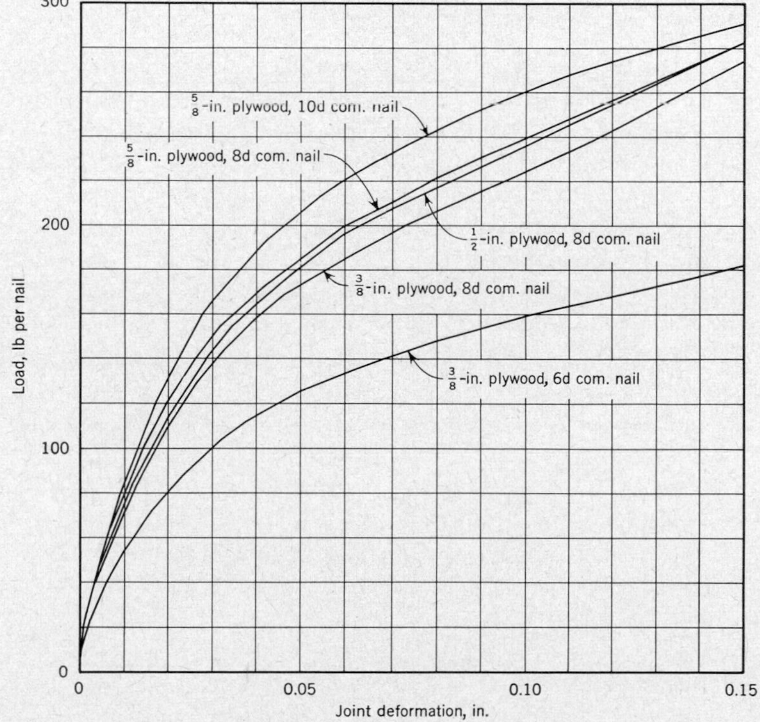

Fig. 9.8 Lateral bearing stiffness of plywood joints

Douglas fir lumber; green when nailed; tested after seasoning to 13 per cent moisture content; avg. sp. gr. = 0.48.

number of nails per foot on panel edges. (Increased nailing at boundary or continuous joints is not considered, because this is usually a local deviation.) The curves are drawn for the extreme case of joints made with green lumber that is allowed to season before loading. If seasoned lumber is used, deflection will be substantially reduced.

Tests have shown that nailed plywood diaphragms behave elastically. Repetitive loadings to the design value do not produce any significant set or increase in deflection rate.

9.37 Openings Openings such as skylights in horizontal diaphragms should be framed and nailed carefully. A reasonable practice is to double framing members around openings of considerable size and to nail them as for boundaries. The area of the opening should be discounted in calculating shear requirements and nailing schedules.

STRESSED-SKIN PANELS

9.38 Stressed-skin panels A stressed-skin panel is an assembly in which the covering acts integrally with the framing to resist flexure in a plane normal to the covering. Such a panel usually consists of several longitudinal framing members, separated by headers, with plywood panels glued to both sides. They are most commonly used as walls, floors, and roofs in prefabricated housing because they are light in weight and thin in cross section. However, the design method is applicable to longer spans, the limit on length being the availability of continuous framing members.

For a panel to qualify as a stressed-skin panel, the following conditions should be met:

1. Covers must be *glued* to both sides of the framing
2. Covers and framing must be continuous or adequately spliced longitudinally
3. Headers are required with thin, deep framing members
4. Clear distance between longitudinal framing members must not exceed twice the basic spacing, b

Gluing is most readily accomplished in a press or with some form of positive pressure, such as clamps. However, if these are not available, panels may be nail-glued satisfactorily if due precautions are observed. The design method is outlined below; for further details consult "Technical Data on Plywood."

9.39 Design method The most convenient design method for stressed-skin panels is to assume a section based on available sizes and check its properties. Ordinarily an "I" section consisting of one framing member and its contributing cover-panel areas may be used.

First the basic spacing, b, is determined for both the top and bottom covers by the following formulas (see Chap. 12, Table 12.32):

$$b = 31h\sqrt{h/t_{||}} \quad \text{for 3-ply material}$$
$$b = 36h\sqrt{h/t_{||}} \quad \text{for 5-ply or more}$$

in which:

h = plywood thickness
$t_{||}$ = thickness of plies parallel to the longitudinal framing

Find the neutral axis and moment of inertia of the "I" section (frequently unsymmetrical), considering the cover width either as extending only halfway to the adjacent framing members or as b plus the framing member thickness, whichever value is less. Consider only longitudinal plies.

The allowable resisting moment of the section is calculated both for tension and compression by using appropriate values of the section modulus and working stresses from Table 12.33 of Chap. 12 if the clear distance between framing members is $\frac{1}{2}b$ or less. If clear distance exceeds $\frac{1}{2}b$, these stresses are reduced proportionately from 100 to 67 per cent at a spacing of b, with no further decrease up to a value of $2b$. This reduction is to guard against buckling of the covers.

Deflection may be calculated by using the moment of inertia as determined above and the elastic modulus of plywood covers. Allowable shear may be governed either by rolling shear between the framing member and the cover, or by horizontal shear in the lumber framing member itself. Both values should be checked by the formula:

$$H = VQ/It$$

in which Q is the statical moment about the neutral axis of the longitudinal-grain material outside the critical shear plane under consideration, and t is the thickness of the longitudinal framing member.

The strength and stiffness of the cover between framing members should also be checked. End headers are ordinarily used if nominal framing-member depth exceeds twice the width. The headers should be continuous across the panel to provide some rigidity in this direction. Blocking is frequently cut in between longitudinals at the third-points of the span. If panel length exceeds available plywood length, the plywood is preferably scarf-jointed. As a less desirable alternative, the plywood may be glued to plywood backing plates cut between longitudinals, and backed in turn with blocking.

PLYWOOD FASTENINGS

9.40 Bolts Many plywood-lumber bolted joints have been tested and results are available from the Douglas Fir Plywood Association; however, actual design recommendations have not been crystallized, pending further tests. In general, tests have shown that grain direction makes less difference in strength than might be anticipated from unit bearing values. Plywood loaded at 45 deg to the face grain requires less end distance (towards the load) and more edge distance (perpendicular to the load) to develop full strength than if loaded at 0 or 90 deg to the grain.

A critical edge and end distance, important in fixing bolt placement and spacing in a joint, was found to exist for various bolt sizes, plywood thicknesses, and grain directions. For example, with ¾-in. plywood, a ¾-in. bolt requires an end distance of 6 in. at 0 or 90 deg and 3 in. at 45 deg, with corresponding edge distances of 1½ in. and 2¼ in. At lesser distances, load reduction may be taken as proportional to the reduction in end and edge distance, but such distances should not be less than ½ that required for full load.

Critical end distances parallel or perpendicular to grain may be taken as 3 in. in tension for a ½-in. bolt with ½- to ¾-in. plywood, and 4 in. for a ¾-in. bolt with ½- and ⅝-in. plywood, increasing to 6 in. for ¾-in. plywood (3 in. for all thicknesses at 45 deg). Critical edge distances range from 1 to 3 in.

It has been suggested that allowable loads be obtained by multiplying the projected bolt area by the allowable compression stress on each veneer, considering the angle of load with respect to grain. Stress values for the appropriate grade and exposure condition would be used; no correction for the slenderness ratio of the bolt would be employed. Bolt loads computed by this method may be logical but appear conservative. Accordingly, some designers suggest that they be doubled. Based on the tests of ½-in. and ¾-in. bolts, such doubled loads have safety factors exceeding 3.6 on the ultimate and 1.6 on the proportional limit, the values ordinarily used for wood construction if end and edge distances equal or exceed critical values given above.

For example, the allowable load in double shear for ¾-in. bolt with two ⅝-in. side members, in dry condition, and loaded parallel to plywood grain, would be determined as follows:

GRAIN DIRECTION	TOTAL VENEER AREA		ALLOWABLE STRESS		LOAD
	sq in.		*psi*		*lb*
Parallel	$\frac{3}{4} \times 2 \times \frac{3}{8} = 0.56$	$\times$	1,460	=	820
Perpendicular	$\frac{3}{4} \times 2 \times \frac{1}{4} = 0.38$	$\times$	408	=	152
			Total	=	972

If this value is doubled, as some suggest, the allowable load will be 1,944 lb.

Test loads on this construction yielded proportional limits averaging 5,080 lb and ultimates of 8,070 lb with a 2½-in. seasoned Douglas fir center member.

9.41 Timber connectors Heavily loaded gusset plates for major structural members may employ timber connectors. These are generally used in conjunction with specially ordered thick plywood, ranging from 1⅝ in. to 3⅝ in. It is suggested that allowable loads for timber connectors in plywood be based on values for sawed lumber with an assumed 60-deg angle of load to grain.

NAIL BEARING

9.42 Nails in shear In most nailed joints, plywood is the member under the nail head, whereas a piece of wood receives the nail shank. Thus the strength of the joint in lateral bearing is often governed by the allowable load of the nail in the wood. However, depending on the nail size and type, plywood thickness, and lumber species, the joint strength may be limited by the plywood. For example, with a Douglas fir nailing piece, and an 8d com. nail, ½-in. plywood develops failure in the wood piece, whereas ⅜-in. plywood fails in the plywood itself, although at loads almost as great as for ½-in. plywood.

In general, the thinnest plywood that will develop full or nearly full nail strength with wood of similar specific gravity is 5/16 in. for 6d com., ⅜ in. for 8d com., ½ in. for 10d com., and ⅝ in. for 16d. com. nails. Use of wood pieces more or less dense might respectively reduce or increase these thicknesses.

The full joint strength will be developed if the distance between the nail and the plywood edge in the direction of stress is a minimum of ½ to ¾ in., depending on plywood thickness and nail sizes. Moreover, the distance to the edge of the wood piece parallel with the load should equal 1 in. or more. Furthermore, regardless of the direction of load, an edge distance of at least ⅜ in. is recommended for the plywood.

In most joints in which the nails are highly stressed, such as in shear diaphragms, the load is actually directed essentially parallel with the wood member and with the plywood edge, so that edge distance is not a very critical factor. If gusset plates are used, however, the edge distances may be critical, and they will therefore influence the location of nails.

If the load is parallel with the wood piece, the nail spacing may limit the attainment of full joint strength because of the tendency for close nailing to split the wood. Nails may be spaced quite close in plywood without danger of splitting, but a spacing closer than 4 in. has been found to cause some reduction in strength in Douglas fir lumber. For example, a 3-in. spacing has been found to reduce lumber nail-bearing strength by 15 per cent with 8d and 10d com. nails. Moreover, if plywood is nailed to opposite edges of 2 x 4 lumber, with its edges butted at the centerline and 10d nails spaced 3 in. on each edge, the joint strength is reduced about $\frac{1}{4}$ if the stud is dry (no reduction if green). An 8d nail causes no load reduction in either case. Also 3 x 4 lumber nailed on both edges with 8d or 10d nails, spaced $1\frac{1}{2}$ in. on centers and staggered, suffers no loss in strength.

With the qualifications listed above, it is recommended that the allowable nail-bearing values in lumber be used for plywood also if the plywood is nailed to wood of a given species. Particular note should be paid to the fact that a thicker plywood may be required to develop the strength of the denser species. Increased values for short durations of load are recommended for wood.

The deformation of nailed joints under load is important for such computations as the deflection of plywood diaphragms. Deformation curves for common plywood thicknesses and nail sizes, with Douglas fir wood pieces, are given in Fig. 9.8. They are based on joints made while the wood was still green and tested after it was fully seasoned, in order to obtain conservative values.

Casing or finish nails are sometimes used structurally in exposed panels where appearance is a factor. Such nails are generally about half as effective in bearing as the same penny size of common nail because of their smaller head and thinner shank size. Special mechanically applied fasteners are also very suitable for such uses.

If common nails are used in double shear with plywood gusset plates, their normal allowable load may be doubled. Such nails are driven through the gusset plate on each side of a lumber piece (normally of 2-in. thickness). Nails must be long enough to allow at least $\frac{3}{8}$ in. of their point for clinching, and clinching should be accomplished perpendicular to the direction of stress. Deformation of such joints is less at double the normal nail value than it is for joints in single shear at the normal load.

9.43 Nails in withdrawal If plywood serves as a nailing base, such as for the attachment of shingles, the thicknesses commonly used for sheathing (usually 5/16 in. and 3/8 in.) exhibit adequate nail-holding properties. For example, the withdrawal load of an 11-gauge galvanized roofing nail averages approximately 51 lb for 5/16-in., 67 lb for 3/8-in., and 85 lb for 1/2-in. plywood.

Nails with deformed shanks hold much more. A 12-gauge aluminum nail with a screw-threaded shank (15 revolutions per inch of shank length, 16-deg helix angle) averaged 79 lb for 5/16-in. plywood when tested dry, or about 80 per cent more than a smooth shank nail of comparable gauge.

The degree of seasoning of the plywood has a marked effect on withdrawal resistance. Initial holding power is much better if the plywood's moisture content is high (18–20 per cent) rather than low (5–7 per cent). The holding power of nails generally decreases as wood dries and increases as its moisture content increases. The action is reversible and does not depend upon the original condition of the wood.

9.44 Gusset plates Plywood can be used for gusset plates because its strength in all directions is high and reasonably well balanced. Applications range from light residential roof-truss gusset plates to rigid-frame knees.

Gusset-plate design may involve computations for shear, flexure, tension or compression, or combinations of these properties. These stresses may be applied at various angles with respect to the face grain of the plywood, depending on the direction of the framing members. If secondary stresses due to eccentricity are present, they must also be considered.

As the strength properties of plywood vary with the grain direction and veneer construction, it is necessary either to assume the orientation that will produce the weakest condition at all planes under consideration, or else to specify the face-grain direction. If the latter alternative is chosen, available panel sizes should be considered and a practical cutting schedule established.

Allowable stresses at angles of 0, 45, and 90 deg with the face grain are given in Table 12.33 of Chap. 12. A straight-line interpolation is permissible for intermediate angles. For properties such as flexure or tension, which are affected by both the unit stress and the veneer construction, the interpolation should be based on the product of these two factors.

For example, the allowable tensile strength of $\frac{3}{4}$-in. exterior *A–C* plywood at 30 deg to the face grain is required. The tensile strength at 0 deg is 1,875 psi × 4.5 sq in., or 8,440 lb per ft of width; and at 45 deg, it is 320 psi × 9.0 sq in., or 2,880 lb. Then at 30 deg, the allowable tensile is $8{,}440 - \frac{30}{45}(8{,}440 - 2{,}880)$, or 4,734 lb per ft (see Tables 12.32 and 12.33).

Connections may be made with nails, bolts, connectors, or glue. Fastenings should be adequate to develop the full design loads imposed by the framing members, except for certain compression members in which the bearing of both pieces is primarily on end grain. The gusset plate for such members is used only to keep them in alignment.

Under certain conditions, glue may be used to transmit stress in gusset plates. With carefully controlled fabrication, plywood gusset plates have been successfully scarf-jointed and glued to lumber members of equal thickness to form a uniplanar rigid frame. Gusset plates may also be glued on both sides of intersecting lumber members in rigid frames or trusses. The glue for this purpose may be set under pressure from bolts or nails, depending somewhat on the size of the members joined, although a positive pressure arrangement, as with clamps, is preferred. If glue is used in conjunction with mechanical fasteners, the glue should be designed to carry the entire load, as glued joints are so much more rigid than mechanically connected ones that the joint will not deform enough to bring the fasteners into play.

The magnitude and direction of the resultant stress from the various framing members should be considered in the determination of the allowable rolling shear and grain direction of the plywood gusset plate. If the grain direction is not known, it may be conservatively assumed as parallel to or perpendicular to the face grain, because values are higher at 45 deg. Rolling shear stress values may be interpolated as a straight line variation between 0 (or 90) and 45 deg. Only the contact area between gusset plate and framing member should be considered as resisting stress, and the rolling shear stress value should be used (not the allowable shear parallel with the grain, even though the load may be applied parallel with the plywood grain).

The lumber and the plywood should be at approximately the moisture content they will reach in service, because a varying moisture content can occasion joint failure by changing joint dimensions.

9.45 Design example Figure 9.9a illustrates a pitched trussed rafter of the type widely used for homes and other small-span buildings. The span of such rafters usually does not exceed 50 ft. The stresses

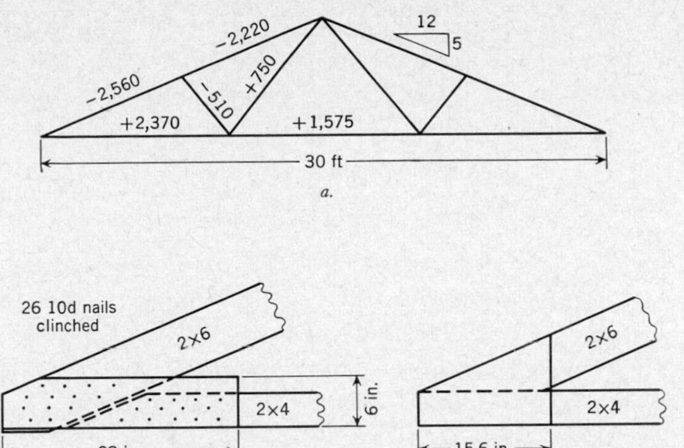

Fig. 9.9 Plywood gusset plates, details

shown are for a 35-lb roof and 10-lb ceiling load, 24-in. spacing, 30-ft span, and 5:12 roof slope. For grades of material and species customarily used in housing, rafters would be 2 x 6, ceiling joists 2 x 4, and web members, either 2 x 4 or 1-in. lumber. Assume that the design required is for the heel joint. One-half-inch plywood gussets will be used, with nails in double shear. Assume that the lumber is either Douglas fir or southern pine and is partially seasoned at the time of fabrication.

As the live load on the truss is probably based on snow loading, normal-load nail values may be increased 15 per cent; but as the lumber may be only partially seasoned at the time of fabrication, 90 per cent of the allowable nail value may be used. Therefore 10d nails, which will permit clinching and thus double shear values, will have a load capacity of 195 lb per nail (94 × 1.15 × 0.90 × 2). As the upper chord extends slightly below the lower chord (see Fig. 9.9b), the vertical component of the axial stress in the upper chord is carried by direct bearing on the wall plate. Therefore the joint is designed for the horizontal component of the axial stress in the upper chord, which is equal to the stress in the lower chord. The joint will then require 13 10d nails (2,370/195) in the upper chord and 13 in the lower chord, or a total of 26 10d nails for the joint.

With ½-in. plywood, the allowable stress in tension parallel to the face plies varies from 1,970 to 1,690 psi, depending on the grade chosen. The area of parallel-to-face-grain plies is 3.6 sq in. per 12 in. of width for ½-in. plywood, or 0.3 sq in. per inch of width (see Chap. 12,

Tables 12.32 and 12.33). The required combined width of the two plywood splice plates for 1,690 psi would be 4.67 in. (2,370 divided by 1,690 × 0.3), or say a 2⅜-in. width of splice plate on each side.

The width of plate is undoubtedly controlled by the nail spacing required to prevent splitting in the 2 x 6 rafter, and wider splice plates will probably be needed if the general criteria for edge distance, ¼ nail length, and for spacing, ½ nail length, are used.

If the rafter is not bearing on the support and is cut at the top edge of the 2 x 4 bottom chord, as shown in Fig. 9.9c, the connection to the top chord must be adequate for 2,560 lb. The shear in the plane of the plies in the gusset or splice plate will then be 2,370 lb. The allowable shear varies from 210 to 152 psi, depending on the grade chosen (see Table 12.33). Thus the required length of gusset plate in Fig. 9.9c is 15.6 in. (2,370 divided by 2 × ½ × 152).

There are no well-established principles for the design of glued structural joints at an angle of load to grain, or for general construction gluing conditions.

If the gusset plates are glued to the wood members, the allowable glue shear value between the face ply and the wood should probably not exceed the values for rolling shear in plywood. Even more conservative values may be desirable, depending on the quality of the gluing. If the principles of Sec. 5.2 are applied, the shear value for parallel-to-grain gluing should not exceed 60 per cent of the parallel-to-grain shear value, or about 80 psi. The values should be reduced, furthermore, as the angle between the grain of face ply and of the wood increases. Conservative design is recommended.

As secondary stresses caused by deflection of the members of the truss are difficult if not incapable of exact analysis, there is further reason for larger glue areas than might be determined from computations. Frequently such joints are designed essentially as nailed joints and the gluing added primarily for stiffness.

10

Fabrication, Assembly, Erection, and Maintenance

10.1 General practices Timber is the most easily worked of all structural materials. Simplicity of fabrication with commonly available tools is one of the prime reasons for its continuing economy and popularity through the years.

Although a designer may not be directly concerned with the fine points of timber fabrication, assembly, erection, and maintenance—unless engaged for supervision of such work—a knowledge of general practices will often prevent costly details.

FABRICATION

10.2 Timber fabricators Increased use of timber as an engineered structural material, particularly during and since World War II, has fostered the growth of a new group of specialists, the timber fabricators, to furnish prefabricated timber on the same basis that steel, concrete, and other building trade work may be subcontracted. These fabricators, employing efficient plant facilities and experienced personnel, are able to furnish prefabricated or glued-laminated lumber at reasonable cost everywhere, thus permitting the contractor to concentrate on the general contract work with which he is most familiar. Some fabricators are also able to furnish assembly and erection services. The general problems of timber fabrication are the same, however, whether the work is subcontracted to timber fabricators or handled by the contractor.

10.3 Equipment Either portable or fixed power tools are suitable for timber fabrication. As greater accuracy and higher production are usually achieved with fixed tools, however, they are preferred. Maximum labor economy is obtained from minimum handling and the concentration of a maximum number of operations at one position. Fabricating lines are thus recommended that make use of several power saws and drill presses that can be adjusted as needed along a roller-bed table. (See Fig. 10.1.)

Fig. 10.1 Fabricating production line

Note placement of multiple saws and drill presses to minimize handling.

Tools must be maintained in good working condition to provide clean and accurate cuts. Systematic tool sharpening, adjustment, and maintenance usually pays for itself in higher and better quality production and in savings in subsequent assembly.

Specialized facilities and control are needed for glued-laminated work, such as glue storage, mixing and spreading equipment, wood-moisture meters, gauges for checking lumber thickness, room temperature and humidity control, surface thermometers, surfacing machinery, torque wrenches and other devices to control clamping pressure, and high-temperature curing rooms for waterproof glue work. Apparatus for checking or testing quality-control specimens and complete recording of data as evidence of fabrication control are desirable.

10.4 Material The fabricator must purchase and stockpile the materials to be fabricated or furnished under the contract. Although this activity is largely one of purchase and supply, it also involves inspection of the lumber to insure that the specified sizes and grades are furnished, and particularly that miscellaneous hardware is of the correct size and manufacture to fit the fabricated lumber.

Some overage should normally be purchased to allow for waste, mismanufacture, damage, or loss. A small oversupply of lumber, bolts, timber connectors, washers, and simple steel fittings may save much time and expense later. Such overage naturally is included in cost estimates.

Bolt lengths should be such that extra thread is available for tightening to compensate for permissible variation in lumber sizes or for tightening after seasoning shrinkage has occurred. If bearing of shear plates or metal plates on bolt threads is not allowed, longer bolts should be available in which the threaded length is entirely beyond the joint and extra washers provide the tightening leeway.

Material must be properly handled and protected before, during, and after fabrication to prevent damage. Orderly marking and stacking and weather protection will pay dividends. Ends of members should be coated with end sealer soon after fabrication to retard rapid end seasoning and thus to minimize end checking. On large projects, the use of different colors in the end sealer will aid in identifying members.

10.5 Lumber selection Lumber is usually purchased according to standard commercial grades (based on American Lumber Standards) for joist and plank (J&P), beam and stringer (B&S), or post and timber (P&T). The latter is graded for use primarily in compression. Normally J&P or B&S grades are graded for the use of their entire length as a simple span beam in bending, and must be further graded or selected for high axial stresses or for use as continuous beams over two or more spans. (See Chaps. 2 and 11.)

Although some species of lumber may be purchased according to special grade provisions and although some standard grading rules make provision for axial-load grading, the contractor or fabricator usually selects lumber for highly stressed members on the basis of its freedom from large knots and other growth characteristics that might appear at critical points, such as joints. This method usually does not involve undue waste as the lower quality pieces or parts of pieces can usually be used for less highly stressed members.

Proper selection of lumber is most important for bottom-chord truss (tension) members and for tension splice plates. Lumber for these important members should normally be of high quality with small knot sizes, minimum slope of grain, high density, and low moisture content. Selection is based first on the quality of the entire piece, and further selection or adjustment may be made, if the full length is not needed, so as to position knots away from joints or other critical areas.

Strength need not normally be a factor in the choice of stress-graded lumber for glued-laminated members, but the appearance of the finished member may dictate that no knots or knotholes be visible. In preference to attempting to select lumber to avoid edge knots, some fabricators rout out exposed knots on the edge of pieces and insert clear "patches." Clear lumber is often used, however, for the top or bottom lamination if a clear finish is desired.

10.6 Prefabrication The term prefabrication is used to describe a fabricating procedure in which individual members of a truss or structural frame are cut to length, bored for bolts and timber connectors, and otherwise worked to finished form so that they will be ready for assembly in the structural unit without any but the most minor cutting or fitting that can be accomplished only at the time of assembly. Prefabrication is the process used by most timber fabricators if units are to be shipped knocked-down for assembly at the site. Contractors doing their own fabrication usually prefabricate if a considerable number of identical units are required.

Prefabrication requires that detailed shop drawings be prepared of the entire truss or frame with all members clearly identified by marking and with computed dimensions that are controlling shown for the frame. The drawings usually include assembly or erection diagrams. Shop drawings are also prepared for each member showing dimensions of all cuts, holes, timber connectors, daps, and other such details. It is important that shop dimensions be computed on the basis of the cambered-truss position, if camber is specified, so that the camber can be built in during fabrication. Usually both the top and bottom chords of trusses should be cambered so that their effective depth will be the same as that assumed in the stress analysis.

10.7 Templates Full-size templates, usually of plywood, are made for each member from the shop drawings. Templates for longer members frequently are made of two thin wood strips, as long as the member, with plywood plates at the ends and intermediate points to mark cut-offs and joint details. The longitudinal wood strips are spaced the width of the member apart to align the template automatically along the length of the member. Blunt pointed punches can be used through holes in the plywood portion of the templates to mark bolt-hole locations. Special "spring-back" punches mounted at each hole on the templates speed marking and pay for themselves quickly in labor savings. An oversize punch that makes a blunt centering mark and a concentric circle mark larger than the bolt-hole size provides for a subsequent check on the accuracy of bolt-hole boring (see Fig. 10.2). Template markings are usually circled with crayon or other easily seen marking, and identified by code to signify the size of hole, type of timber connector, or other work to be done.

Fig. 10.2 Punch-marking members from templates

For members requiring only a single hole with or without a connector at each end or at intermediate points, it is feasible to bore and groove without template markings. Stops that position the member under a fixed drill are used instead. This method of bench stops is most often used for simple fabrications such as trussed rafters, and for truss web members that have only a single bolt hole at each joint.

Templates are often assembled in order to check their accuracy and the dimensions of the truss itself (see Fig. 10.3). They obviously should be sturdily made to withstand repeated handling without losing shape and accuracy.

10.8 Preassembly fabrication The alternative to prefabrication is preassembly fabrication, in which all the members of a truss or frame are laid together in their final position and then marked and bored, grooved for connectors, dapped, and so on, so that a complete unit is fabricated at once. (See Fig. 10.4.) This method is often used, by contractors particularly, if only a few units are needed. It saves the work of preparing templates for each member, although templates can still be used to mark the individual joints. Templates for the prefabrication system can be prepared by this method.

Courtesy Weyerhaeuser Sales Co.

Fig. 10.3 Checking templates by lay-out

As the members for similar units prepared by preassembly are usually not interchangeable, each member must be marked so that it can be reassembled in the same order and position in which it was fabricated. For this reason, preassembly is most often used for job-site fabrications, although units may also be shipped wholly or partially assembled. The system is most often used with lapped or multiple-member joints in which bolt holes can be bored through the entire truss thickness, and the members disassembled if necessary to groove for connectors. As portable drills are most suitable, it is important that the drill be plumbed to bore straight through the assembly.

After the first truss or unit is laid in place, blocks are often placed by the sides of each member so that members for subsequent units can easily be positioned. In such a horizontal lay-up, the required camber is introduced by placing the chord members in cambered position before boring any holes.

Fig. 10.4 Preassembly of a segmental bowstring

10.9 Workmanship Quality of fabrication workmanship is an intangible that defies definition in terms of exact tolerances or accuracy. Acceptable accuracy ranges widely, depending upon the exact detail involved. The end-to-end length of a truss member not in end bearing may have a tolerance of ½ in. or even more, but a top-chord member in end bearing must be accurately cut to length or provision must be made, possibly by thin metal shims, to bring it to proper length and bearing. The over-all length of a supporting column does not usually require close tolerance. Some saw cuts can be quite rough and ragged, but those for end bearing should be smooth. Cabinet-maker tolerances may be needed in some details, such as scarf joints and the surfacing of laminates for glued-laminated members. In general, better than average carpenter accuracy is needed for framed structural units.

The smoothness necessary for saw cuts, bolt holes, and connector grooves requires sharp tools and a not too rapid feed. A reasonable accuracy for distance between holes in opposite ends, or for the overall length, of end-bearing truss members seems to be within $\frac{1}{16}$ to $\frac{1}{8}$ in. The shorter the member, the more important is close tolerance. A goal for accuracy between adjacent mating fastenings in the same joint might be $\frac{1}{2}$ the clearance between the fastening and the hole or groove, which would be in the order of $\frac{1}{32}$ in. Probably the best measure of accuracy is ease of assembly, provided bolt holes and connector grooves are of proper size and are not intentionally made oversize to provide easy fit. Obviously, oversize holes or grooves should not be permitted.

10.10 Glued-laminated members Proper fabrication of glued-laminated members requires high quality workmanship and strict quality control procedure. These requirements usually preclude field fabrication and call for technically supervised shop fabrication (see Chap. 6, Figs. 6.14 and 6.15). In brief, the lumber used must be of structural grade, of controlled moisture content, and of uniform thickness. Glue must be of a type approved for the use conditions involved, and standard specifications for gluing procedure must be followed, including proper glue storage, mixing and consistency, pot life, rate of spread, temperature of glue-line during lay-up, limited open and closed assembly time, specified clamping pressure, and controlled time-temperature curing.

Laminations are normally of nominal 1- or 2-in. lumber, seasoned, and dressed or surfaced just prior to gluing. The 2-in. lumber is used where bending radius permits and for flat or straight members. If laminations are to be bent to substantial curvature, it is necessary to pre-glue scarf splices in the curved area to obtain a continuous lamination within that area. Many fabricators pre-glue all scarf joints regardless of curvature.

Glues most commonly used are casein for interior work, and phenolics, resorcinols, and melamines for exterior or waterproof service. A detailed discussion of the many factors involved will be found in "Fabrication and Design of Glued-Laminated Wood Structural Members." [1]

[1] Technical Bulletin 1069, Forest Products Laboratory, U.S. Department of Agriculture, available from the U.S. Government Printing Office.

10.11 Shipment Except for local delivery, framed structures are usually shipped knocked-down, with similar members packed together and clearly marked for position and order of assembly as shown on shop or working plans. Hardware is packaged separately but usually shipped with the frame to avoid loss and insure that all material arrives at the same time. The method of shipment should be left to the judgment of the timber fabricator, if possible. Several small jobs may often be combined in a single shipment for freight savings. Shipments can also be combined with unfabricated lumber.

As preservative treatment for trusses and similar framed structures is usually applied after fabrication, it may often be accomplished during a stop-over in transit and thus may save on freight cost.

ASSEMBLY

10.12 Assembly If fabrication has been accurate, assembly is the simplest operation in the construction of a timber structure. The key to efficient assembly is a good organization of component parts and a planned order of work. Assembly normally should be as near the erection point as possible, usually on a flat surface inside or adjacent to the site. Like members should be stockpiled together, preferably in positions relative to their position in the assembly, with the heavy members situated for the shortest haul. An inventory should be taken at the time of stockpiling. If space is at a premium, units may be assembled flat and then tilted up for stacking side by side. Erection procedure should be planned before assembly so that assembled units will not be in the way and can be erected with a minimum of haul. Some timber fabricators are able to furnish assembly and erection services as part of their contract.

Trusses are normally assembled laid flat in stacks of three or four. The first truss is assembled on blocks high enough to permit bolt heads or nuts to be held underneath and to allow placement of lifting slings (see Fig. 10.5). Bolts are usually inserted upward through the bottom pieces to aid in aligning subsequent members. Shear plate timber connectors are fastened into their grooves with nails, and other connectors are placed as the build-up progresses. As connectors are not visible after assembly, due precaution must be taken to insure that they are installed during the assembly.

Undue force should not be necessary in assembly and should not be permitted. The "sledge hammer" fit is not a good one even though it

Fig. 10.5 Truss assembly

is tight; there is danger of damage to the members and the connections, although, unfortunately, it may not appear until later. Some few connections may require persuasion, but care should be exercised. Often a study of the stubborn joint will indicate a means of tilting or rotating a member, tilting a connector in a groove, or bending a bolt to simplify the fit. Occasionally another member can be substituted, and the original member will work more easily on another assembly. Grossly misfit joints can be rebored during assembly for a larger size bolt, or it may be possible to relocate the original bolt away from the misfit hole.

If fabricated members are to be stored for some time prior to erection, they should be at least subassembled and protected from the weather. Delayed assembly may cause difficulty because of change in dimension of members due to change in moisture content.

Clip angles for anchorage, bracing, or purlin seats can be installed on the ground, and often knee braces can also be installed and rotated and temporarily fastened out of the way parallel with the bottom chord.

Assembly procedure for multiple-span units may require consideration of erection problems, and even partial or sectional assembly may be necessary for unusually large spans, with sections supported by falsework and joined in the air. Assembly is usually most efficient when accomplished flat on the ground, but vertical assembly and assembly in place are sometimes necessary. Bridges and other outdoor structures often present unusual assembly and erection problems.

ERECTION

10.13 Field erection Erection equipment should be selected on the basis of the loads to be lifted and the height and working space for erection. Rental of a costlier but more suitable crane is usually preferable to "stretching" a piece of equipment and gambling with life and material. Framing presents the greatest hazard after erection has commenced and joist, sheathing, and other auxiliary construction is still not in place. Adequate bracing should be near at hand and installed immediately, particularly for compression members such as top chords. Temporary as well as permanent bracing is usually necessary until other framing, such as roof joists and sheathing, has been completed. Guy cables with turnbuckles provide easy adjustment and can be used to plumb and align units properly. (See Fig. 10.6.)

Fig. 10.6 Truss erection

Some units may require spreader beams or a heavy timber lashed or fastened to the arch or truss top chord to prevent buckling during erection.

If more than a single line is desirable, pick-up or sling points are usually established at panel points near the one-third span points in order to minimize erection stresses. When the assembly is raised to vertical position, the line should be kept as vertical as possible in order to minimize whipping action. A pick-up from the side away from an attached column is usually desirable. Members should be protected from injury at sling points by cushioning or blocking. All joints should be tight at time of erection. Care should be exercised in landing construction material as well as supporting construction equipment on a skeleton frame or completed portion so that the concentrated loads will not endanger the structure.

STRUCTURAL INSPECTION AND MAINTENANCE

10.14 Structural maintenance Little if any structural maintenance is normally required for properly designed and built timber structures. As discussed in other chapters, unit design recommendations are based on customary construction practices and conditions and contain a safety factor that normally precludes the need for such maintenance. To insure proper maintenance, however, it is important to distinguish between structural characteristics and normal appearance or seasoning characteristics.

10.15 Routine inspection A general inspection is recommended within the first year of service for heavy structures in which the timber becomes well seasoned after assembly. Because of shrinkage during seasoning, sufficient looseness may have developed in the bolts so that tightening will be necessary to keep the faces of the members in reasonably close relationship. Usually no maintenance other than tightening in the first year or so is necessary during the life of the structure.

Inspection not only for bolt tightness but for the general condition of the joints and the members is usually desirable from three to six months after erection. For buildings, the check should be made after the first heating season. It is important to remember that most so-called seasoning defects in unseasoned material are anticipated and taken care of by adjustments in the design values. The inspector should look primarily for the following defects:

1. General looseness of joints, such as more than $\frac{1}{16}$-in. average opening between members or any one opening approaching $\frac{1}{8}$ in.

2. Excessive deflection, elongation of bolt holes, or other signs of unusual joint movement (a proper joint will seldom move more than $\frac{1}{32}$ in.).

3. Splits or checks of unusual size or length, particularly those tending to run across the face or thickness of a member and out the side or edge, those which the forces in the joints may cause to increase in size or length, and those on bolt centers in short splice plates.

4. Twisting or bowing of members or misaligned sections.

10.16 Bolt tightening For normal dead and light live load, joints can be tightened by turning up the bolts without jacking the trusses to relieve the load (see Fig. 10.7). When washers begin to embed in the

Courtesy Timber Structures, Inc.

Fig. 10.7 Truss bolt-tightening operation

wood, the joint is usually as tight as possible, and as a rule there is no need to relieve the load or use oversize washers or separate clamping arrangements. Sometimes grooves that are too shallow prevent complete closure of connector joints, but small openings are not serious. Connector joints may be checked with a probe, such as a hacksaw blade, to be sure the connectors are installed. A probe check is particularly desirable if there is any sign of trouble. If connectors have been omitted, joint reinforcement will be necessary. Normally one bolt tightening is sufficient unless the framing was totally unseasoned when erected, or unless the assemblies are composed of large-size members, such as beam and stringer grades, for which complete seasoning may take a year or more. The approximate amount of shrinkage of unseasoned timber can be estimated at about $\frac{1}{32}$ in. per inch of thickness or width. A typical truss of about 12-in. thickness will thus shrink about $\frac{3}{8}$ in. Normally, bolts should be tightened during the humid season, so that the timber will not swell subsequently—because of seasonal increase in moisture content—and force the washer into the wood.

10.17 Splits and checks Splits and checks are probably the most common cause of concern to the layman. As there are no precise rules, the evaluation of these normal seasoning characteristics is a matter of engineering judgment. Probably 75 per cent of them are not serious and do not require maintenance. The two best criteria for such defects are a knowledge of their cause and of the potential seriousness of an increase in their size or length. A knowledge of the cause will usually indicate whether an increase in size or length can be expected. Checks are usually unimportant. Most splits are the result of seasoning shrinkage, aggravated by connections to other members that prevent a piece from shrinking normally. The internal cross-grain stresses thus set up between the connections cause the member to split. Tests indicate that the reduction in split-ring joint strength due to normal splitting is adequately covered by the 20-per cent reduction in design value recommended for unseasoned lumber.

A short split running parallel to the edges or at an angle corresponding to that permitted by the grade is usually not serious. A bolt hole bored at the end of a split will frequently arrest it. Stitch bolts or yokes around the member near the joint help prevent further opening of a split but should not be used for closure unless forces in the joint have increased the size of the split beyond that caused by shrinkage. Splits through connector joints are not particularly serious because the connector covers a wide area, whereas a split through a bolt hole may greatly reduce the strength of that bolt unless adjacent bolts prevent the wood from spreading under the wedge action of the bolt.

If the need for maintenance is debatable and subsequent inspection is planned, the size and length of a split may be marked on the member, with the date, and checked later. Obviously, if other maintenance of a similar nature is needed near the same area, the doubtful split may be included at little extra cost. A split that has not increased in size or length by the time of a second inspection is usually not serious.

Tension members, particularly chord members and their splice plates, are most vulnerable to the effect of splits and should be dealt with accordingly.

10.18 Member alignment Twisting and bowing of members may be a sign of improper design, bracing, joint trouble, or partial member failure due to use of an improper grade for the particular service. If none of these reasons appear to be responsible, the trouble may stem from seasoning that is in itself not serious, or it may have been present from the time of erection because of inaccurate fabrication. Bowing of single compression members should usually be corrected by stiffening plates or braces. Bowing of one piece of a two-piece member, on the other hand, requires study and analysis to determine whether the bow should be corrected or merely prevented from increasing. Straightening the bowed member may force it to carry a higher percentage of the load. Such redistribution may be undesirable, as the bow may have properly balanced the stresses.

10.19 Inspection responsibility Inspections are usually most efficient if decisions are made on the site by the inspector or the crew. It is nearly impossible, or at the least inefficient, to have to draw conclusions on the basis of notes and sketches alone, regardless of the completeness of observations. For average minor problems encountered in general inspections, the decisions are not difficult and the remedies neither complicated nor expensive.

Maintenance inspection of an old structure or one showing signs of trouble calls for ingenuity in locating the real cause of trouble, estimating whether it is progressive and whether the structure is safe, and determining the proper and most economical remedy.

Prior to inspection, the design should be studied to determine its adequacy, as poor design details may be the cause of trouble. Such a study will also provide a basis by which to judge whether the structure was built as designed and whether more load is being carried than had been contemplated.

10.20 Deflection Deflection is not itself a sign of trouble provided it is not caused by failure of members or connections. Too frequently laymen think a structure is failing because they find the truss is deflected below horizontal. Often such deflection should have been expected because of an initial neglect to provide camber, or to apply it properly. More than average deflection may be expected in structures built of unseasoned material, or with less truss depth than that normally recommended. A sudden and substantial increase in deflection without change in load, however, is usually a sign of trouble. Frictional forces in joints will sometimes delay normal joint deformation and permit a sudden increase in deflection as the wood shrinks and the forces are finally overcome. Excessive deflection is primarily a result rather than a cause of trouble. Deflection can affect secondary stresses adversely, but such stresses tend to be dissipated over a period of time, particularly in unseasoned lumber.

If the cause of deflection is determined and corrected, or if the deflection gives no sign of increasing or causing other trouble, it is usually not necessary to attempt to recamber the structure. Proper recambering is expensive because it requires that the structure be shored and the lengths of members adjusted. If the structure appears to be satisfactory except for deflection, it is often more economical to adjust roof and ceiling supports to eliminate the low spots than to recamber the trusses.

10.21 Methods of repair There is no aspect of timber construction requiring more careful planning and ingenuity than in-place repair. Repair problems may involve the reinforcement of joints weakened by inadequate fastenings or damaged or decayed wood in the joint area, and also the reinforcement or repair of members impaired by bad splitting or failures. As there are usually alternative methods of effective repair, cost is the primary consideration if appearance is not a factor. An outside piece can be removed and replaced with relative ease. An interior piece is expensive to remove, however, and normally is reinforced, although a new member can be added to the truss to compensate for the damage. If a member is added, it is important to check the transfer of stresses, because the new member may alter the original connection requirements.

For over-all economy in repair, as little fitting as possible should be accomplished in place. Reinforcement and repair should be designed for a maximum of shop work and a minimum of erection work. Thus a yoke clamp that can be bolted around a member to arrest splitting will probably be more economical than a stitch bolt, which requires boring a hole through the member in the air. The yoke clamp, moreover, does not reduce the net section area of the member. Should damage be extreme, threaded steel rods with steel shapes can be attached to the wood with a minimum of fitting. These rods are quite suitable for the repair of tension members.

Normally, lapped joints may be reinforced most easily by driving additional bolts, pins, or dowels with a tight fit in prebored holes. Damaged members may be reinforced in a similar manner with extra pieces scabbed to the sides.

10.22 Minimum maintenance through design The experienced designer knows how to guard against conditions that may lead to undue maintenance. If unseasoned lumber is to be used, details are designed where possible to permit shrinkage of adjacent pieces without setting up the internal stresses that increase the chances of splitting. Thus in chord splices, saw kerfs may be provided between rows of bolts, or split splice plates may be used. Additional end distances on bolts—up to 12 in. for splice plates—reduce the possibility that normal end checks will extend into the joint area. End coating or sealing of the members during fabrication reduces end checking.

For those joints in which seasoning will set up internal drying stresses between connections, some designers provide stitch bolts in the original design. These can be easily retightened at the time of general tightening. If seasoning is a factor, one firm specifies stitch bolts for members loaded at an angle to the grain on opposite faces in opposing directions provided two or more bolts with connectors are required. Stitch bolts are also specified for members loaded at a substantial angle to the grain if three or more bolts with connectors are required. With these safeguards, usually only bolt tightening is necessary for unseasoned or partially seasoned lumber.

10.23 Excessive maintenance Although every designer understandably wants to be on the safe side, experience has shown that some inspectors waste thousands of dollars on unnecessary maintenance. If there is room for doubt, a subsequent inspection is usually many times cheaper than an across-the-board recommendation to repair or replace every piece that shows splitting or checking. Except for possible bolt tightening, trusses that require maintenance are the exception and not the rule.

10.24 Glued-laminated members Usually no maintenance is required for glued-laminated members or assemblies fabricated in accordance with recommended practice. Problems of shrinkage are minimized because the lumber used in laminating is properly seasoned. Infrequently there is some question of checking, splitting, or delamination.

Checking and splitting are normally of minor importance, but their effect may be evaluated in relation to the shear requirements of the section at which they occur. If splitting or delamination increases, corrective measures—such as reinforcement with tightly fitted pins, bolts, or dowels—may be necessary. Many such defects are localized in character and are caused either by slight errors in quality control during laminating or improper handling or exposure to the weather during shipment or erection. Seldom are the defects progressive in nature.

Some seasoning shrinkage is found even in glued-laminated members, however, because they are usually laminated of lumber with a 12 to 15 per cent moisture content that may further season to 8 to 10 per cent if used in heated buildings. This additional seasoning often explains minor checking, and the increased shrinkage may require some bolt tightening, particularly in members of large widths or thicknesses. The shrinkage, however, will normally be only $\frac{1}{3}$ to $\frac{1}{4}$ that of equal-size solid sawed members.

Any general delamination requires extensive analysis for reinforcement because regluing in place is of doubtful value and mechanical fastenings will not develop the efficiency of the original glued-laminated member. The addition of cover-plates is frequently the best solution.

11

Specification Forms

11.1 Preparation of specifications Preparation of specifications has developed into a specialized, intricate operation, often involving a great amount of detail to eliminate or lessen the chance of misunderstanding between buyer and seller. The precise specification can also serve as a legal measuring stick in disputes over material furnished or services performed. Because of their complexity, no attempt shall be made here to suggest the detailed wording, form, or quality of specifications for a particular use.

An understanding of the basic provisions of specifications for engineered timber construction should enable a writer to tailor forms to any particular project. Complete textbooks are available on the subject and may be referred to for details.

For the sake of simplicity, specifications normally use established industry and manufacturing standards as reference for standard materials and sometimes for services and workmanship. These standards are periodically amended to simplify problems of purchase and supply.

The present chapter is confined to three aspects of specifications for engineered timber construction: (1) minimum provisions, (2) alternate or special provisions, and (3) unnecessary detail.

11.2 Lumber The grading rules for the various lumber species, based on American Lumber Standards, are used as the reference standards for quality of lumber. (See Chap. 13, NDS.) The minimum lumber specification usually includes:

1. End use (studs, joists, sheathing, trusses)
2. Species
3. Commercial grade
4. Commercial grading rules under which graded

Some specifications also include a summary of the allowable normal unit working stresses required by the design, but more frequently this listing of required strength properties is included only on the structural plans. Such a list normally includes values for:

1. Extreme fiber in bending, f
2. Compression parallel to grain, c
3. Compression perpendicular to grain, $c_{\perp}$
4. Horizontal shear, H
5. Modulus of elasticity, E

The list occasionally includes the allowable axial tension factor, t (often the same as f).

Alternative and special provisions may include:

1. Specific acceptable alternative species and grades
2. Requirements for grade marking or certification of quality
3. Specific grade provisions or size descriptions *if* the lumber does not conform to industry standards.
4. Provision for preservative treatment

It is desirable not only to provide for alternatives but to list them specifically rather than with the general recommendation, "or equal." The specification should define who is responsible for approving alternative material or services that are submitted as "equal" but not precisely identified in the specification.

Quality of lumber—particularly for uses in which strength properties are important, such as for engineered structures—is assured by the grade mark of, or certificate of inspection issued by, a recognized lumber grading or inspection bureau or agency on the basis of stress-grade specification requirements (see Chap. 2, Fig. 2.1). Grade marking is practical for lumber that is inspected and used or fabricated at the building site, but not usually so for lumber fabricated away from the site and inspected at the site. The grade marking may be removed in the cutting and working of the lumber. The fabricator may then be required to furnish a certificate of inspection to prove the proper grade was purchased, and to certify that only proper grades were used in the fabrication.

Special grade provisions, or nonstandard sizes, are to be avoided because they are expensive and often all but unattainable in small orders. The reworking or reselection of standard grades and sizes on the job is often the best solution to special requirements. Reselection for axial-tension members is quite common.

Many standard grades for construction lumber do not contain moisture-content limitations; although desirable, they are not a necessity for most situations. Such limitations in a specification may therefore constitute a special grade provision, depending upon the size and species of timber involved; if so, they should be avoided. If the moisture-content provision is part of the standard grade provision, it need not be repeated in the job or material specification.

Specifications sometimes include details on knot size, slope of grain, and standard sizes. As these merely duplicate the provisions of industry standards, they are unnecessary. The primary danger of such details is that they may be misinterpreted by inexperienced personnel as a means of grading lumber. Grading should be left to those personnel and agencies specialized and experienced in applying and interpreting the established rules.

11.3 Glued-laminated lumber The four reference standards for glued-laminated members are:

1. "Standard Specification for Design and Fabrication of Structural Glued-Laminated Lumber" [1]
2. "Standard Specification for Structural Glued-Laminated Southern Pine." [2]
3. "Standard Specification for the Design and Fabrication of Hardwood Glued-Laminated Lumber for Structural, Marine, and Vehicular Uses" [3]
4. "Inspection Manual for Structural Glued-Laminated Lumber" [4]

Of necessity, these standards (see Chap. 13, NDS) include details of design practice, gluing procedure, and technical data, and the reference details need not be repeated in a job specification. All four standards are based on principles set forth in "Fabrication and Design of Glued-Laminated Wood Structural Members." [5] The minimum specifications include:

1. Use conditions
2. Species and applicable reference specification
3. Stress requirements

The use conditions specify either dry or wet use and thus dictate the type of glue. Prolonged use with temperatures above 150°F—which require adjustment in working stresses—should be specified, if appropriate.

Stress requirements are listed for the various properties as indicated in Sec. 11.2, so that the fabricator may have the choice of an exact

[1] West Coast Lumbermen's Association.

[2] Southern Pine Inspection Bureau.

[3] Southern Hardwood Producers, Inc.; Appalachian Hardwood Manufacturers, Inc.; and Northern Hemlock & Hardwood Manufacturers Association.

[4] American Institute of Timber Construction.

[5] Technical Bulletin 1069, Forest Products Laboratory, U.S. Department of Agriculture.

glued-laminated grade combination to meet the needs. This part of the specification is omitted, however, if the design and details are to be prepared by the fabricator. The specification then need only state that members should be designed and fabricated, in accordance with the "reference standard," for the load requirements indicated on the plan.

Alternative and special provisions for glued-laminated lumber may include:

1. Acceptable alternative species and appropriate reference specification
2. Provision for inspection or certification of quality
3. Provisions for surface treatment or finishing
4. Provision for preservative treatment
5. Provision for protection in shipping
6. Provision for proper handling and storage at destination and at job site

As inspection by an independent agency during manufacture adds to the cost, certification by the laminator that the lamination is in accordance with the reference standards is usually acceptable.

Provisions for surface treatment or finishing for appearance should be well defined, but frequently it is desirable to leave the actual final finish—such as staining, painting, or varnishing—either to the laminator at the plant or the contractor on the site. The end result of the finished structure is what is important, not when or where the finish is applied. Laminated members require proper protection from weather during shipping and erection, but the particular means of protection are normally left to the laminator and the contractor.

Pressure preservative treatment may be applied to the lumber before laminating—the more expensive method—or to the laminated member after gluing. Treatment after lamination is usually regarded as satisfactory for all average service conditions. The sizes and shapes of members to be treated after lamination are restricted by the capacities of available pressure-treating cylinders. Timber fabricators and treating firms should be consulted for limitations and suggestions.

11.4 Poles and piling The usual reference standard for poles is "American Standard Specifications and Dimensions for Wood Poles"[1] (see Chap. 13). The minimum pole specification includes:

1. Species and alternatives, if desired
2. Class of pole (structural requirement)

[1] American Standards Association, adopted by reference in the National Electrical Safety Code.

3. Reference standard
4. Length
5. Type of preservative treatment, if any

The choice of species is largely a matter of size or length, availability, service life, and cost, because all poles of the same class furnish the same ultimate strength. Although naturally durable species and nonpressure treatments provide adequate service life under some service conditions, pressure preservative treatment is desirable for maximum service life.

The reference standards for piles include the ASTM "Specification for Round Timber Piles D25-55," and the timber pile specifications of the American Railway Engineering Association (AREA), and of the American Association of State Highway Officials (AASHO). The first is the most widely used, but there is no substantial difference between the three standards (see Chap. 13). The minimum pile specification includes:

1. Species and alternatives, if desired
2. Class of pile (A, B, C in ASTM)
3. Reference standard
4. Length
5. Type of preservative treatment, if any

In specifying standard poles and piling, there is no need to include details from the reference specifications, nor details of the preservative-treatment process unless it is nonstandard.

11.5 Preservative treatment The reference standards often used for pressure preservative treatments are Federal Specification TT-W-571C and the standard specifications of the American Wood Preservers' Association (see Chap. 13, NDS). A specification for preservative treatment may be added to the basic specifications for any wood product such as those previously outlined for lumber, glued-laminated lumber, poles, and piling. The pressure-treatment specification includes:

1. Wood product involved
2. Reference standard
3. Type of process and alternatives, if desired
4. Type of preservative and alternatives, if desired
5. Minimum retention of preservative

The specification should require that all feasible fabrication be accomplished prior to treatment and that field treatment of cuts be made after treatment. The retention required varies with use, species, type of preservative, process employed, and size of members or poles.

The specification need not include penetration nor deal with details of the actual treatment process, as these factors are covered by industry and standard requirements.

If nonpressure processes are considered acceptable, the specification should define the process or retention results required. Nonpressure processes should normally be judged adequate only on the basis of experience involving the same species, sizes, and use conditions.

11.6 Plywood The reference standards for plywood include U.S. Commercial Standards CS45-55 for Douglas fir plywood; CS122 for western softwood plywood; and CS35 for hardwood plywood, which is seldom used in construction (see Chap. 9 for details of commercial standards for Douglas fir plywood). Established specification procedure includes:

1. Species
2. Number of plies
3. Width of panel (measured across grain of face ply)
4. Length of panel (measured along grain of face ply)
5. Type of use (exterior, interior)
6. Grades of face plies (face appearance)
7. Finish of faces (sanded or unsanded)
8. Finished thickness
9. Reference standard
10. Provision for grade marking, if desired

Width is always specified before length. All standard grades, except sheathing, are sanded unless otherwise specified. Any grade may be specifically ordered unsanded, although usually only in quantity lots through the mills. The most common thickness for unsanded plywood is $\frac{1}{16}$ in. more than the regular standard dimensions; thus a $\frac{3}{8}$-in. sanded grade would be $\frac{7}{16}$ in. thick if unsanded. Sheathing, however, comes unsanded in standard thicknesses of $\frac{5}{16}$, $\frac{3}{8}$, $\frac{1}{2}$, $\frac{5}{8}$, and $\frac{3}{4}$. Any special requirements should usually be checked for availability through suppliers.

11.7 Fastenings Reference standards for commercial hardware items such as bolts, lag screws, nails, screws, and similar common fastenings are usually the appropriate ASTM or Federal specification. Specifications are usually general unless a special metal or form is desired that is not covered by the standards. The manufacturers' recommendations are then frequently used. Suggested specifications for timber connectors are given in Chap. 13 (NDS and DM).

12

Reference Data

CONTENTS OF CHAPTER 12

A WEIGHTS OF COMMERCIALLY IMPORTANT WOODS GROWN IN THE UNITED STATES

TABLE 12.1

American Standard lumber nomenclature	Weight per cu ft *lb*	
	Green	Air-dry (12-per cent moisture content)
Alder, red	46	28
Ash, black or brown	52	34
Ash, commercial white [1]	48	41
Ash, Oregon	46	38
Aspen	43	26
Basswood	42	26
Beech	54	45
Birch, commercial yellow [2]	57	44
Birch, paper	50	38
Butternut	46	27
Cedar, Alaska	36	31
Cedar, aromatic red	37	33
Cedar, incense	45	—
Cedar, Port Orford	36	29
Cedar, western red	27	23
Cedar, northern white	28	22
Cedar, southern white	26	23
Cherry, black	45	35
Chestnut	55	30
Cottonwood, eastern	49	28
Cottonwood, northern black	46	24
Cypress, southern	51	32
Douglas fir (coast region)	38	34
Douglas fir (Inland Empire region)	36	31
Douglas fir (Rocky Mountain region)	35	30
Elm, commercial soft [3]	55	36
Elm, rock	45	25
Fir, balsam	45	25
Fir, commercial white [4]	46	27
Gum, black	45	35
Gum, red	50	34
Hackberry	50	37
Hemlock, eastern	50	28
Hemlock, West Coast	41	29
Hickory, pecan [5]	62	45
Hickory, true [6]	63	51
Larch, western	48	36
Locust, black	58	48
Magnolia, cucumber	49	33
Magnolia, evergreen	59	35

A WEIGHTS OF COMMERCIALLY IMPORTANT WOODS GROWN IN THE UNITED STATES (Cont.)

TABLE 12.1 (Cont.)

American Standard lumber nomenclature	Weight per cu ft *lb* Green	Weight per cu ft *lb* Air-dry (12-per cent moisture content)
Maple, hard [7]	55	42
Maple, soft [8]	47	35
Oak, red [9]	64	44
Oak, white [10]	63	47
Pine, Idaho white	35	27
Pine, lodgepole	39	29
Pine, longleaf southern	55	41
Pine, northern white	36	25
Pine, Norway	42	34
Pine, ponderosa	45	28
Pine, shortleaf southern	52	36
Pine, sugar	52	25
Poplar, yellow	38	28
Redwood	50	28
Spruce, eastern [11]	34	28
Spruce, Engelmann	39	23
Spruce, Sitka	33	28
Sycamore	52	34
Tamarack	47	37
Walnut, black	58	38

[1] Average of biltmore white ash, blue ash, green ash, and white ash.
[2] Average of sweet birch and yellow birch.
[3] Average of American elm and slippery elm.
[4] Average of lowland white fir and white fir.
[5] Average of butternut hickory, nutmeg hickory, water hickory, and pecan.
[6] Average of bigleaf shagbark hickory, mockernut hickory, pignut hickory, and shagbark hickory.
[7] Average of black maple and sugar maple.
[8] Average of bigleaf maple, red maple, and silver maple.
[9] Average of black oak, laurel oak, pin oak, red oak, scarlet oak, southern red oak, swamp red oak, water oak, and willow oak.
[10] Average of burr oak, chestnut oak, post oak, swamp chestnut oak, swamp white oak, and white oak.
[11] Average of black spruce, red spruce, and white spruce.

B WEIGHTS OF STANDARD LUMBER SIZES PER LINEAR FOOT

TABLE 12.2

Nominal size *in.*	Weight of piece per lin ft *lb*						Board feet per linear foot of piece
	Weight of wood per cu ft						
	25 lb	30 lb	35 lb	40 lb	45 lb	50 lb	
1 × 4	0.5	0.6	0.7	0.8	0.9	1.0	⅓
1 × 6	0.8	0.9	1.1	1.2	1.4	1.5	½
1 × 8	1.0	1.2	1.4	1.6	1.8	2.0	⅔
1 × 10	1.3	1.5	1.8	2.1	2.3	2.6	5/6
1 × 12	1.6	1.9	2.2	2.5	2.8	3.1	1
2 × 2	0.5	0.6	0.6	0.7	0.8	0.9	⅓
2 × 4	1.0	1.2	1.4	1.6	1.8	2.0	⅔
2 × 6	1.6	1.9	2.2	2.5	2.9	3.2	1
2 × 8	2.1	2.5	3.0	3.4	3.8	4.2	1⅓
2 × 10	2.7	3.2	3.8	4.3	4.8	5.4	1⅔
2 × 12	3.2	3.9	4.5	5.2	5.8	6.5	2
2 × 14	3.8	4.6	5.3	6.1	6.9	7.6	2⅓
3 × 4	1.7	2.0	2.3	2.6	3.0	3.3	1
3 × 6	2.6	3.1	3.6	4.1	4.6	5.1	1½
3 × 8	3.4	4.1	4.8	5.5	6.2	6.8	2
3 × 10	4.3	5.2	6.1	6.9	7.8	8.7	2½
3 × 12	5.2	6.3	7.3	8.4	9.4	10.5	3
3 × 14	6.2	7.4	8.6	9.8	11.1	12.3	3½
3 × 16	7.1	8.5	9.9	11.3	12.7	14.1	4
4 × 4	2.3	2.7	3.2	3.7	4.1	4.6	1⅓
4 × 6	3.5	4.2	5.0	5.7	6.4	7.1	2
4 × 8	4.7	5.7	6.6	7.6	8.5	9.4	2⅔
4 × 10	6.0	7.2	8.4	9.6	10.8	12.0	3⅓
4 × 12	7.2	8.7	10.1	11.6	13.0	14.5	4
4 × 14	8.5	10.2	11.9	13.6	15.3	17.0	4⅔
4 × 16	9.8	11.7	13.7	15.6	17.6	19.5	5⅓
6 × 6	5.3	6.3	7.4	8.4	9.5	10.5	3
6 × 8	7.2	8.6	10.0	11.5	12.9	14.3	4
6 × 10	9.1	10.9	12.7	14.5	16.3	18.1	5
6 × 12	11.0	13.2	15.4	17.6	19.8	22.0	6
6 × 14	12.9	15.5	18.0	20.6	23.2	25.8	7
6 × 16	14.8	17.8	20.7	23.7	26.6	29.6	8
6 × 18	16.7	20.1	23.4	26.7	30.1	33.4	9
8 × 8	9.8	11.7	13.7	15.6	17.6	19.5	5⅓
8 × 10	12.4	14.8	17.3	19.8	22.3	24.7	6⅔
8 × 12	15.0	18.0	21.0	24.0	27.0	29.9	8
8 × 14	17.6	21.1	24.6	28.1	31.6	35.2	9⅓
8 × 16	20.2	24.2	28.3	32.3	36.3	40.4	10⅔
8 × 18	22.8	27.3	31.9	36.5	41.0	45.6	12
8 × 20	25.4	30.5	35.5	40.6	45.7	50.8	13⅓

B WEIGHTS OF STANDARD LUMBER SIZES PER LINEAR FOOT (Cont.)

TABLE 12.2 (Cont.)

Nominal size *in.*	Weight of piece per lin ft *lb* — Weight of wood per cu ft						Board feet per linear foot of piece
	25 lb	30 lb	35 lb	40 lb	45 lb	50 lb	
10 × 10	15.7	18.8	21.9	25.1	28.2	31.3	8⅓
10 × 12	19.0	22.8	26.6	30.3	34.1	37.9	10
10 × 14	22.3	26.7	31.2	35.6	40.1	44.5	11⅔
10 × 16	25.6	30.7	35.8	40.9	46.0	51.1	13⅓
10 × 18	28.9	34.6	40.4	46.2	52.0	57.7	15
10 × 20	32.2	38.6	45.0	51.5	57.9	64.3	16⅔
10 × 24	38.8	46.5	54.3	62.0	69.8	77.6	20
12 × 12	23.0	27.6	32.1	36.7	41.3	45.9	12
12 × 14	27.0	32.3	37.7	43.1	48.5	53.9	14
12 × 16	30.9	37.1	43.3	49.5	55.7	61.9	16
12 × 18	34.9	41.9	48.9	55.9	62.9	69.9	18
12 × 20	38.9	46.7	54.5	62.3	70.1	77.9	20
12 × 24	46.9	56.3	65.7	75.1	84.5	93.8	24
14 × 14	31.6	38.0	44.3	50.6	57.0	63.3	16⅓
14 × 16	36.3	43.6	50.9	58.1	65.4	72.7	18⅔
14 × 18	41.0	49.2	57.4	65.6	73.8	82.0	21
14 × 20	45.7	54.8	64.0	73.1	82.3	91.4	23⅓
14 × 24	55.1	66.1	77.1	88.1	99.1	110.2	28

C DIMENSIONAL PROPERTIES OF AMERICAN STANDARD LUMBER SIZES

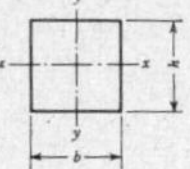

TABLE 12.3

Nominal size	American Standard dressed size (S4S)	Area of section	Moment of inertia		Section modulus	
in. $b \times h$	*in.* $b \times h$	*sq in.* $A = bh$	$I_{x-x} = bh^3/12$	$I_{y-y} = b^3h/12$	$S_{x-x} = bh^2/6$	$S_{y-y} = b^2h/6$
1 × 4	25/32 × 2⅝	2.83	3.10	0.14	1.71	0.37
1 × 6	25/32 × 5⅝	4.39	11.59	0.22	4.12	0.57
1 × 8	25/32 × 7½	5.86	27.47	0.30	7.32	0.76
1 × 10	25/32 × 9½	7.42	55.82	0.38	11.75	0.97
1 × 12	25/32 × 11½	8.98	99.02	0.46	17.22	1.17
2 × 2	1⅝ × 1⅝	2.64	0.58	0.58	0.72	0.72
2 × 4	1⅝ × 3⅝	5.89	6.45	1.30	3.56	1.60
2 × 6	1⅝ × 5⅝	9.14	24.10	2.01	8.57	2.48
2 × 8	1⅝ × 7½	12.19	57.13	2.68	15.23	3.30
2 × 10	1⅝ × 9½	15.44	116.10	3.40	24.44	4.18
2 × 12	1⅝ × 11½	18.69	205.95	4.11	35.82	5.06
2 × 14	1⅝ × 13½	21.94	333.18	4.83	49.36	5.94
3 × 4	2⅝ × 3⅝	9.52	10.42	5.46	5.75	4.16
3 × 6	2⅝ × 5⅝	14.77	38.93	8.48	13.84	6.46
3 × 8	2⅝ × 7½	19.69	92.29	11.30	24.61	8.61
3 × 10	2⅝ × 9½	24.94	187.55	14.32	39.48	10.91
3 × 12	2⅝ × 11½	30.19	332.69	17.33	57.86	13.21
3 × 14	2⅝ × 13½	35.44	538.21	20.35	79.73	15.50
3 × 16	2⅝ × 15½	40.69	814.60	23.36	105.11	17.80
4 × 4	3⅝ × 3⅝	13.14	14.39	14.39	7.94	7.94
4 × 6	3⅝ × 5⅝	20.39	53.76	22.33	19.12	12.32
4 × 8	3⅝ × 7½	27.19	127.44	29.77	33.98	16.43
4 × 10	3⅝ × 9½	34.44	259.00	37.71	54.53	20.81
4 × 12	3⅝ × 11½	41.69	459.43	45.65	79.90	25.19
4 × 14	3⅝ × 13½	48.94	743.24	53.59	110.11	29.57
4 × 16	3⅝ × 15½	56.19	1,124.92	61.53	145.15	33.95
6 × 6	5⅝ × 5⅝	30.25	76.26	76.24	27.73	27.73
6 × 8	5⅝ × 7½	41.25	193.36	103.98	51.56	37.81
6 × 10	5⅝ × 9½	52.25	392.96	131.71	82.73	47.90
6 × 12	5⅝ × 11½	63.25	697.07	159.44	121.23	57.98
6 × 14	5⅝ × 13½	74.25	1,127.67	187.17	167.06	68.06
6 × 16	5⅝ × 15½	85.25	1,706.78	214.90	220.23	78.15
6 × 18	5⅝ × 17½	96.25	2,456.38	242.63	280.73	88.23
8 × 8	7½ × 7½	56.25	263.67	263.67	70.31	70.31
8 × 10	7½ × 9½	71.25	535.86	333.98	112.81	89.06
8 × 12	7½ × 11½	86.25	950.55	404.30	165.31	107.81
8 × 14	7½ × 13½	101.25	1,537.73	474.61	227.81	126.56
8 × 16	7½ × 15½	116.25	2,327.42	544.92	300.31	145.31
8 × 18	7½ × 17½	131.25	3,349.61	615.23	382.81	164.06
8 × 20	7½ × 19½	146.25	4,634.30	685.55	475.31	182.81
10 × 10	9½ × 9½	90.25	678.76	678.76	142.90	142.90
10 × 12	9½ × 11½	109.25	1,204.03	821.56	209.40	172.98

C DIMENSIONAL PROPERTIES OF AMERICAN STANDARD LUMBER SIZES (Cont.)

TABLE 12.3 (Cont.)

Nominal size	American Standard dressed size (S4S)	Area of section	Moment of inertia		Section modulus	
in.	*in.*	*sq in.*	$I_{x\text{-}x} =$	$I_{y\text{-}y} =$	$S_{x\text{-}x} =$	$S_{y\text{-}y} =$
$b \times h$	$b \times h$	$A = bh$	$bh^3/12$	$b^3h/12$	$bh^2/6$	$b^2h/6$
10 × 14	9½ × 13½	128.25	1,947.80	964.55	288.56	203.06
10 × 16	9½ × 15½	147.25	2,948.07	1,107.44	380.40	233.15
10 × 18	9½ × 17½	166.25	4,242.84	1,250.34	484.90	263.23
10 × 20	9½ × 19½	185.25	5,870.11	1,393.23	602.06	293.31
10 × 24	9½ × 23½	223.25	10,274.15	1,679.03	874.40	353.48
12 × 12	11½ × 11½	132.25	1,457.51	1,457.51	253.48	253.48
12 × 14	11½ × 13½	155.25	2,357.86	1,710.98	349.31	297.56
12 × 16	11½ × 15½	178.25	3,568.71	1,964.46	460.48	341.65
12 × 18	11½ × 17½	201.25	5,136.07	2,217.94	586.98	385.73
12 × 20	11½ × 19½	224.25	7,105.92	2,471.42	728.81	429.81
12 × 22	11½ × 21½	247.25	9,524.28	2,724.90	885.98	473.90
12 × 24	11½ × 23½	270.25	12,437.13	2,978.38	1,058.48	517.98
14 × 14	13½ × 13½	182.25	2,767.92	2,767.92	410.06	410.06
14 × 16	13½ × 15½	209.25	4,189.36	3,177.98	540.56	470.81
14 × 18	13½ × 17½	236.25	6,029.30	3,588.05	689.06	531.56
14 × 20	13½ × 19½	263.25	8,341.73	3,998.11	855.56	592.31
14 × 24	13½ × 23½	317.25	14,600.11	4,818.23	1,242.56	713.81

D PROPERTIES OF SECTIONS, GLUED-LAMINATED STRUCTURAL LUMBER

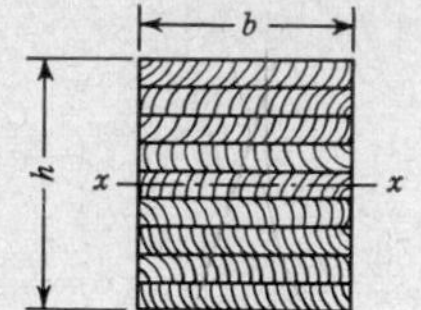

TABLE 12.4

(1⅝-in. laminations only; arranged in order of ascending section modulus)

Nom. width *in.*	No. of 1⅝-in. laminations[1]	Net finished size[1] *in.* $b \times h$	Area of section *sq in.*	Moment of inertia $I = \frac{bh^3}{12}$	Section modulus $S = \frac{bh^2}{6}$	Weight per lin ft at 12-per cent moisture content, *lb*
3	4	2¼ × 6½	14.6	51.5	15.8	3.45
4	4	3¼ × 6½	21.1	74.4	22.9	4.98
3	5	2¼ × 8⅛	18.3	101.	24.8	4.31
5	4	4¼ × 6½	27.6	97.3	29.9	6.52
6	4	5 × 6½	32.5	114.	35.2	7.67
3	6	2¼ × 9¾	21.9	174.	35.7	5.18
4	5	3¼ × 8⅛	26.4	145.	35.8	6.23
6	4	5¼ × 6½	34.1	120.	37.0	8.05
5	5	4¼ × 8⅛	34.5	190.	46.8	8.15
3	7	2¼ × 11⅜	25.6	276.	48.5	6.04
4	6	3¼ × 9¾	31.7	251.	51.5	7.48
6	5	5 × 8⅛	40.6	223.	55.0	9.59
6	5	5¼ × 8⅛	42.7	235.	57.8	10.1
5	6	4¼ × 9¾	41.4	328.	67.3	9.78
4	7	3¼ × 11⅜	37.0	399.	70.1	8.72
8	5	7 × 8⅛	56.9	313.	77.0	13.4
6	6	5 × 9¾	48.8	386.	79.2	11.5
6	6	5¼ × 9¾	51.2	406.	83.2	12.1
4	8	3¼ × 13	42.3	595.	91.6	9.97
5	7	4¼ × 11⅜	48.3	521.	91.7	11.4
6	7	5 × 11⅜	56.9	613.	108.	13.4
8	6	7 × 9¾	68.3	541.	111.	16.1
6	7	5¼ × 11⅜	59.7	644.	113.	14.1
4	9	3¼ × 14⅝	47.5	847.	116.	11.2
5	8	4¼ × 13	55.3	778.	120.	13.0
6	8	5 × 13	65.0	915.	141.	15.3
4	10	3¼ × 16¼	52.8	1,162.	143.	12.5
10	6	9 × 9¾	87.8	695.	143.	20.7
6	8	5¼ × 13	68.3	961.	148.	16.1
8	7	7 × 11⅜	79.6	859.	151.	18.8
5	9	4¼ × 14⅝	62.2	1,108.	152.	14.7
6	9	5 × 14⅝	73.1	1,303.	178.	17.3
5	10	4¼ × 16¼	69.1	1,520.	187.	16.3
6	9	5¼ × 14⅝	76.8	1,369.	187.	18.1
10	7	9 × 11⅜	102.	1,104.	194.	24.2
8	8	7 × 13	91.0	1,282.	197.	21.5

D PROPERTIES OF SECTIONS, GLUED-LAMINATED STRUCTURAL LUMBER (Cont.)

TABLE 12.4 (Cont.)

(1⅝-in. laminations only; arranged in order of ascending section modulus)

Nom. width *in.*	No. of 1⅝-in. laminations[1]	Net finished size[1] *in.* $b \times h$	Area of section *sq in.*	Moment of inertia $I = \frac{bh^3}{12}$	Section modulus $S = \frac{bh^2}{6}$	Weight per lin ft at 12-per cent moisture content, *lb*
6	10	5 × 16¼	81.3	1,788.	220.	19.2
5	11	4¼ × 17⅞	76.0	2,023.	226.	17.9
6	10	5¼ × 16¼	85.3	1,877.	231.	20.1
12	7	11 × 11⅜	125.	1,349.	237.	29.5
8	9	7 × 14⅝	102.	1,825.	250.	24.2
10	8	9 × 13	117.	1,648.	254.	27.6
6	11	5 × 17⅞	89.4	2,380.	266.	21.1
5	12	4¼ × 19½	82.9	2,626.	269.	19.6
6	11	5¼ × 17⅞	93.8	2,499.	280.	22.2
8	10	7 × 16¼	114.	2,503.	308.	26.8
12	8	11 × 13	143.	2,014.	310.	33.8
5	13	4¼ × 21⅛	89.8	3,339.	316.	21.2
6	12	5 × 19½	97.5	3,090.	317.	23.0
10	9	9 × 14⅝	132.	2,346.	321.	31.1
6	12	5¼ × 19½	102.	3,244.	333.	24.2
14	8	12½ × 13	163.	2,289.	352.	38.4
6	13	5 × 21⅛	106.	3,928.	372.	24.9
8	11	7 × 17⅞	125.	3,332.	373.	29.5
6	13	5¼ × 21⅛	111.	4,124.	390.	26.2
12	9	11 × 14⅝	161.	2,867.	392.	38.0
10	10	9 × 16¼	146.	3,218.	396.	34.5
6	14	5 × 22¾	114.	4,906.	431.	26.9
8	12	7 × 19½	137.	4,325.	444.	32.2
14	9	12½ × 14⅝	183.	3,258.	446.	43.1
6	14	5¼ × 22¾	119.	5,151.	453.	28.2
10	11	9 × 17⅞	161.	4,284.	479.	38.0
12	10	11 × 16¼	179.	3,933.	484.	42.2
6	15	5 × 24⅜	122.	6,034.	495.	28.8
16	9	14½ × 14⅝	212.	3,780.	517.	50.1
6	15	5¼ × 24⅜	128.	6,336.	520.	30.2
8	13	7 × 21⅛	148.	5,499.	521.	34.9
14	10	12½ × 16¼	203.	4,470.	550.	47.9
6	16	5 × 26	130.	7,323.	563.	30.7
10	12	9 × 19½	176.	5,561.	570.	41.4
12	11	11 × 17⅞	197.	5,235.	586.	46.4
6	16	5¼ × 26	137.	7,690.	592.	32.2

[1] With glued-laminated structural lumber, many additional sizes may be obtained. Greatest economy will result by using standard widths and depths that are multiples of standard board and dimension lumber thicknesses.

D PROPERTIES OF SECTIONS, GLUED-LAMINATED STRUCTURAL LUMBER (Cont.)

TABLE 12.4 (Cont.)

(1⅝-in. laminations only; arranged in order of ascending section modulus)

Nom. width *in.*	No. of 1⅝-in. laminations[1]	Net finished size[1] *in.* $b \times h$	Area of section *sq in.*	Moment of inertia $I = \frac{bh^3}{12}$	Section modulus $S = \frac{bh^2}{6}$	Weight per lin ft at 12-per cent moisture content, *lb*
8	14	7 × 22¾	159.	6,868.	604.	37.6
16	10	14½ × 16¼	236.	5,185.	638.	55.6
14	11	12½ × 17⅞	223.	5,949.	666.	52.7
10	13	9 × 21⅛	190.	7,071.	669.	44.9
8	15	7 × 24⅜	171.	8,448.	693.	40.3
12	12	11 × 19½	215.	6,797.	697.	50.6
16	11	14½ × 17⅞	259.	6,901.	772.	61.2
10	14	9 × 22¾	205.	8,831.	776.	48.3
8	16	7 × 26	182.	10,250.	789.	43.0
14	12	12½ × 19½	244.	7,724.	792.	57.5
12	13	11 × 21⅛	232.	8,642.	818.	54.8
8	17	7 × 27⅝	193.	12,300.	890.	45.6
10	15	9 × 24⅜	219.	10,860.	891.	51.8
16	12	14½ × 19½	283.	8,960.	919.	66.7
14	13	12½ × 21⅛	264.	9,820.	930.	62.3
12	14	11 × 22¾	250.	10,790.	949.	59.1
8	18	7 × 29¼	205.	14,600.	998.	48.3
10	16	9 × 26	234.	13,180.	1,014.	55.2
14	14	12½ × 22¾	284.	12,270.	1,078.	67.1
16	13	14½ × 21⅛	306.	11,390.	1,078.	72.3
12	15	11 × 24⅜	268.	13,280.	1,089.	63.3
8	19	7 × 30⅞	216.	17,170.	1,112.	51.0
10	17	9 × 27⅝	249.	15,810.	1,145.	58.7
8	20	7 × 32½	228.	20,030.	1,232.	53.7
14	15	12½ × 24⅜	305.	15,090.	1,238.	71.9
12	16	11 × 26	286.	16,110.	1,239.	67.5
16	14	14½ × 22¾	330.	14,230.	1,251.	77.9
10	18	9 × 29¼	263.	18,770.	1,283.	62.1
8	21	7 × 34⅛	239.	23,180.	1,359.	56.4
12	17	11 × 27⅝	304.	19,320.	1,399.	71.7
14	16	12½ × 26	325.	18,310.	1,408.	76.7
10	19	9 × 30⅞	278.	22,070.	1,430.	65.6
16	15	14½ × 24⅜	353.	17,500.	1,436.	83.4
8	22	7 × 35¾	250.	26,650.	1,491.	59.1
12	18	11 × 29¼	322.	22,940.	1,569.	75.9
10	20	9 × 32½	293.	25,750.	1,584.	69.0

D PROPERTIES OF SECTIONS, GLUED-LAMINATED STRUCTURAL LUMBER (Cont.)

TABLE 12.4 (Cont.)

(1⅝-in. laminations only; arranged in order of ascending section modulus)

Nom. width *in.*	No. of 1⅝-in. laminations[1]	Net finished size[1] *in.* $b \times h$	Area of section *sq in.*	Moment of inertia $I = \frac{bh^3}{12}$	Section modulus $S = \frac{bh^2}{6}$	Weight per lin ft at 12-per cent moisture content, *lb*
14	17	12½ × 27⅝	345.	21,960.	1,590.	81.5
16	16	14½ × 26	377.	21,240.	1,634.	89.0
10	21	9 × 34⅛	307.	29,800.	1,747.	72.5
12	19	11 × 30⅞	340.	26,980.	1,748.	80.2
14	18	12½ × 29¼	366.	26,070.	1,782.	86.3
16	17	14½ × 27⅝	401.	25,470.	1,844.	94.5
10	22	9 × 35¾	322.	34,270.	1,917.	75.9
12	20	11 × 32½	358.	31,470.	1,936.	84.4
14	19	12½ × 30⅞	386.	30,660.	1,986.	91.1
16	18	14½ × 29¼	424.	30,240.	2,068.	100.
10	23	9 × 37⅜	336.	39,160.	2,095.	79.4
12	21	11 × 34⅛	375.	36,430.	2,135.	88.6
14	20	12½ × 32½	406.	35,760.	2,201.	95.9
10	24	9 × 39	351.	44,490.	2,282.	82.8
16	19	14½ × 30⅞	448.	35,560.	2,304.	106.
12	22	11 × 35¾	393.	41,880.	2,343.	92.8
14	21	12½ × 34⅛	427.	41,390.	2,426.	101.
10	25	9 × 40⅝	366.	50,290.	2,476.	86.3
16	20	14½ × 32½	471.	41,480.	2,553.	111.
12	23	11 × 37⅜	411.	47,860.	2,561.	97.0
14	22	12½ × 35¾	447.	47,590.	2,663.	105.
10	26	9 × 42¼	380.	56,560.	2,678.	89.7
12	24	11 × 39	429.	54,380.	2,789.	101.
16	21	14½ × 34⅛	495.	48,020.	2,814.	117.
10	27	9 × 43⅞	395.	63,350.	2,888.	93.2
14	23	12½ × 37⅜	467.	54,380.	2,910.	110.
12	25	11 × 40⅝	447.	61,460.	3,026.	105.
16	22	14½ × 35¾	518.	55,210.	3,089.	122.
10	28	9 × 45½	410.	70,650.	3,105.	96.6
14	24	12½ × 39	488.	61,790.	3,169.	115.
12	26	11 × 42¼	465.	69,130.	3,273.	110.
16	23	14½ × 37⅜	542.	63,090.	3,376.	128.
14	25	12½ × 40⅝	508.	69,840.	3,438.	120.
12	27	11 × 43⅞	483.	77,420.	3,529.	114.
16	24	14½ × 39	566.	71,680.	3,676.	133.
14	26	12½ × 42¼	528.	78,560.	3,719.	125

[1] With glued-laminated structural lumber, many additional sizes may be obtained. Greatest economy will result by using standard widths and depths that are multiples of standard board and dimension lumber thicknesses.

D PROPERTIES OF SECTIONS, GLUED-LAMINATED STRUCTURAL LUMBER (Cont.)

TABLE 12.4 (Cont.)

(1⅝-in. laminations only; arranged in order of ascending section modulus)

Nom. width *in.*	No. of 1⅝-in. laminations[1]	Net finished size[1] *in.* $b \times h$	Area of section *sq in.*	Moment of inertia $I = \frac{bh^3}{12}$	Section modulus $S = \frac{bh^2}{6}$	Weight per lin ft at 12-per cent moisture content, *lb*
12	28	11 × 45½	501.	86,350.	3,795.	118.
16	25	14½ × 40⅝	589.	81,020.	3,988.	139.
14	27	12½ × 43⅞	548.	87,980.	4,010.	129.
12	29	11 × 47⅛	518.	95,930.	4,071.	122.
14	28	12½ × 45½	569.	98,120.	4,313.	134.
16	26	14½ × 42¼	613.	91,130.	4,314.	145.
12	30	11 × 48¾	536.	106,200.	4,357.	127.
14	29	12½ × 47⅛	589.	109,010.	4,627.	139.
12	31	11 × 50⅜	554.	117,180.	4,652.	131.
16	27	14½ × 43⅞	636.	102,060.	4,652.	150.
14	30	12½ × 48¾	609.	120,680.	4,951.	144.
16	28	14½ × 45½	660.	113,820.	5,003.	156.
14	31	12½ × 50⅜	630.	133,160.	5,287.	149.
16	29	14½ × 47⅛	683.	126,460.	5,367.	161.
16	30	14½ × 48¾	707.	139,990.	5,743.	167.
16	31	14½ × 50⅜	730.	154,470.	6,133.	172.

Courtesy West Coast Lumbermen's Association

[1] With glued-laminated structural lumber, many additional sizes may be obtained. Greatest economy will result by using standard widths and depths that are multiples of standard board and dimension lumber thicknesses.

E BENDING MOMENT FOR VARIOUS SPANS WHEN *W* EQUALS 10 LB PER LIN FT, OR *P* EQUALS 10 LB

TABLE 12.5

Span ft	Bending moment in.-lb			
	$M = Wl^2/8$	$M = Wl^2/10$	$M = Wl^2/12$	$M = PL/4$
1	15.	12.	10.	30
1 1/6	20.4	16.3	13.6	35
1⅓	26.7	21.3	17.8	40
1½	33.8	27.	22.5	45
1⅔	41.7	33.3	27.8	50
2	60.	48.	40.	60
2½	93.8	75.	62.5	75
3	135.	108.	90.	90
3½	183.8	147.	122.5	105
4	240.0	192.	160.	120
4½	303.8	243.	202.5	135
5	375.	300.	250.	150
5½	453.8	363.	302.5	165
6	540.0	432.	360.	180
6½	633.8	507.	422.5	195
7	735.	588.	490.	210
7½	843.8	675.	562.5	225
8	960.	768.	640.	240
8½	1,083.8	867.	722.5	255
9	1,215.	972.	810.	270
9½	1,353.8	1,083.	902.5	285
10	1,500.	1,200.	1,000.	300
10½	1,653.8	1,323.	1,102.5	315
11	1,815.	1,452.	1,210.	330
11½	1,983.8	1,587.	1,322.5	345
12	2,160.	1,728.	1,440.	360
12½	2,343.8	1,875.	1,562.5	375
13	2,535.	2,028.	1,690.	390
13½	2,733.8	2,187.	1,822.5	405
14	2,940.	2,352.	1,960.	420
14½	3,153.8	2,523.	2,102.5	435
15	3,375.	2,700.	2,250.	450
15½	3,603.8	2,883.	2,402.5	465
16	3,840.	3,072.	2,560.	480
16½	4,083.8	3,267.	2,722.5	495
17	4,335.	3,468.	2,890.	510
17½	4,593.8	3,675.	3,062.5	525
18	4,860.	3,888.	3,240.	540
18½	5,133.8	4,107.	3,422.5	555
19	5,415.	4,332.	3,610.	570
19½	5,703.8	4,563.	3,802.5	585
20	6,000.	4,800.	4,000.	600
20½	6,303.8	5,043.	4,202.5	615
21	6,615.	5,292.	4,410.	630
21½	6,933.8	5,547.	4,622.5	645
22	7,260.	5,808.	4,840.	660
22½	7,593.8	6,075.	5,062.5	675

E BENDING MOMENT FOR VARIOUS SPANS WHEN *W* EQUALS 10 LB PER LIN FT, OR *P* EQUALS 10 LB (Cont.)

TABLE 12.5 (Cont.)

Span *ft*	Bending moment *in.-lb*			
	$M = Wl^2/8$	$M = Wl^2/10$	$M = Wl^2/12$	$M = PL/4$
23	7,935.	6,348.	5,290.	690
23½	8,283.8	6,627.	5,522.5	705
24	8,640.	6,912.	5,760.	720
24½	9,003.8	7,203.	6,002.5	735
25	9,375.	7,500.	6,250.	750
25½	9,753.8	7,803.	6,502.5	765
26	10,140.	8,112.	6,760.	780
26½	10,533.8	8,427.	7,022.5	795
27	10,935.	8,748.	7,290.	810
27½	11,343.8	9,075.	7,562.5	825
28	11,760.	9,408.	7,840.	840
28½	12,183.8	9,747.	8,122.5	855
29	12,615.	10,092.	8,410.	870
29½	13,053.8	10,443.	8,702.5	885
30	13,500.	10,800.	9,000.	900

F MOMENT RESISTANCE OF STANDARD LUMBER SIZES FOR VARIOUS DURATIONS OF LOAD

Resi ting moments of Table 12.6 are based on tabulated a! owable extreme fiber stress in bending, f, of 1,000 psi for durations of load frequently used. For combinations of various durations, the shorter duration of the combination is used, providing other combinations of longer duration do not control.

This table may be used in combination with Table 12.5 for uniformly loaded or single concentrated load; the values of Table 12.5, converted to proper load, furnish the required bending moment due to normal, snow, or wind loading. Table 12.6 then gives the size required to resist the required bending moment based on an f of 1,000. The values of Table 12.5 can most conveniently be used with this table if they are multiplied by the ratio of 1,000 to the allowable f for the grade used (normal loading). The resulting moment can then be used directly to choose a member size from this table to satisfy the duration of load involved.

For example, for a 50-psf load due to snow and dead load and for an f of 1,500 psi, the bending moment M of Table 12.5 is multiplied by 5 (50 ÷ 10) and by 0.67 (1,000 ÷ 1,500), and a member size is selected from Table 12.6 from the snow-load column.

The data of this table may be adjusted for other f values in direct proportion to the ratio of those values to 1,000. Thus if f equals 1,500, the moment resistance of a member is 1.5 (1,500 ÷ 1,000) times the value found in this table for the duration of loading involved.

TABLE 12.6 Moment resistance in inch-kips for various durations of load

(f = 1,000 psi, normal load)

Nominal size *in.*	Moment resistance *inch-kips*									
	Normal load		Snow load		Wind load		Impact		Permanent	
	x-x	*y-y*	*x-x*	*y-y*	*x-x*	*y-y*	*x-x*	*y-y*	*x-x*	*y-y*
1 × 4	1.71	0.37	1.97	0.43	2.28	0.49	3.42	0.74	1.54	0.33
1 × 6	4.12	0.57	4.74	0.66	5.49	0.76	8.24	1.14	3.71	0.51
1 × 8	7.32	0.76	8.42	0.87	9.76	1.01	14.64	1.52	6.59	0.68
1 × 10	11.75	0.97	13.51	1.12	15.67	1.29	23.50	1.94	10.58	0.87
1 × 12	17.22	1.17	19.80	1.35	22.96	1.56	34.44	2.34	15.50	1.05
2 × 2	0.72	.72	0.83	0.83	0.96	0.96	1.44	1.44	0.65	0.65
2 × 4	3.56	1.60	4.09	1.84	4.75	2.13	7.12	3.20	3.20	1.44
2 × 6	8.57	2.48	9.86	2.85	11.43	3.31	17.14	4.96	7.71	2.23
2 × 8	15.23	3.30	17.51	3.80	20.31	4.40	30.46	6.60	13.71	2.97
2 × 10	24.44	4.18	28.11	4.81	32.58	5.57	48.88	8.36	22.00	3.76
2 × 12	35.82	5.06	41.19	5.82	47.76	6.75	71.64	10.12	32.24	4.55
2 × 14	49.36	5.94	56.76	6.83	65.81	7.92	98.72	11.88	44.42	5.35
3 × 4	5.75	4.16	6.61	4.78	7.67	5.55	11.50	8.32	5.18	3.74
3 × 6	13.84	6.46	15.92	7.43	18.45	8.61	27.68	12.92	12.46	5.81
3 × 8	24.61	8.61	28.30	9.90	32.81	11.48	49.22	17.22	22.15	7.75
3 × 10	39.48	10.91	45.40	12.55	52.64	14.55	78.96	21.82	35.53	9.82
3 × 12	57.86	13.21	66.54	15.19	77.14	17.61	115.72	26.42	52.07	11.89
3 × 14	79.73	15.50	91.69	17.82	106.30	20.67	159.46	31.00	71.76	13.95
3 × 16	105.11	17.80	120.88	20.47	140.14	23.73	210.22	35.60	94.60	16.02

TABLE 12.6 Moment resistance in inch-kips for various durations of load (Cont.)

(f = 1,000 psi, normal load)

Nominal size *in.*	Moment resistance *inch-kips*									
	Normal load		Snow load		Wind load		Impact		Permanent	
	x-x	*y-y*	*x-x*	*y-y*	*x-x*	*y-y*	*x-x*	*y-y*	*x-x*	*y-y*
4 × 4	7.94	7.94	9.13	9.13	10.59	10.59	15.88	15.88	7.15	7.15
4 × 6	19.12	12.32	21.99	14.17	25.49	16.43	38.24	24.64	17.21	11.09
4 × 8	33.98	16.43	39.08	18.89	45.30	21.91	67.96	32.86	30.58	14.79
4 × 10	54.53	20.81	62.71	23.93	72.70	27.75	109.06	41.62	49.08	18.73
4 × 12	79.90	25.19	91.88	28.97	106.53	33.59	159.80	50.38	71.91	22.67
4 × 14	110.11	29.57	126.63	34.01	146.81	39.43	220.22	59.14	99.10	26.61
4 × 16	145.15	33.95	166.92	39.04	193.53	45.27	290.30	67.90	130.64	30.56
6 × 6	27.73	27.73	31.89	31.89	36.97	36.97	55.46	55.46	24.96	24.96
6 × 8	51.56	37.81	59.29	43.48	68.74	50.41	103.12	75.62	46.40	34.03
6 × 10	82.73	47.90	95.14	55.08	110.30	63.86	165.46	95.80	74.46	43.11
6 × 12	121.23	57.98	139.41	66.68	161.64	77.30	242.46	115.96	109.11	52.18
6 × 14	167.06	68.06	192.12	78.27	222.74	90.74	334.12	136.12	150.35	61.25
6 × 16	220.23	78.15	253.26	89.87	293.63	104.20	440.46	156.30	198.21	70.34
6 × 18	280.73	88.23	322.84	101.46	374.30	117.64	561.46	176.46	252.66	79.41
8 × 8	70.31	70.31	80.86	80.86	93.74	93.74	140.62	140.62	63.28	63.28
8 × 10	112.81	89.06	129.73	102.42	150.38	118.74	225.62	178.12	101.53	80.15
8 × 12	165.31	107.81	190.11	123.98	220.41	143.74	330.62	215.62	148.78	97.03
8 × 14	227.81	126.56	261.98	145.54	303.74	168.74	455.62	253.12	205.03	113.90
8 × 16	300.31	145.31	345.36	167.11	400.40	193.74	600.62	290.62	270.28	130.78
8 × 18	382.81	164.06	440.23	188.67	510.40	218.74	765.62	328.12	344.53	147.65
8 × 20	475.31	182.81	546.61	210.23	633.73	243.74	950.62	365.62	427.78	164.53

TABLE 12.6 Moment resistance in inch-kips for various durations of load (Cont.)

(f = 1,000 psi, normal load)

Nominal size *in.*	Moment resistance *inch-kips*									
	Normal load		Snow load		Wind load		Impact		Permanent	
	x-x	*y-y*	*x-x*	*y-y*	*x-x*	*y-y*	*x-x*	*y-y*	*x-x*	*y-y*
10 × 10	142.90	142.90	164.34	164.34	190.53	190.53	285.80	285.80	128.61	128.61
10 × 12	209.40	172.98	240.81	198.93	279.19	230.63	418.80	345.96	188.46	155.68
10 × 14	288.56	203.06	331.84	233.52	384.74	270.74	577.12	406.12	259.70	182.75
10 × 16	380.40	233.15	437.46	268.12	507.19	310.86	760.80	466.30	342.36	209.84
10 × 18	484.90	263.23	557.64	302.71	646.51	350.96	969.80	526.46	436.41	236.91
10 × 20	602.06	293.31	692.37	337.31	802.73	391.07	1,204.12	586.62	541.85	263.98
10 × 24	874.40	353.48	1,005.56	406.50	1,163.21	471.29	1,748.80	706.96	786.96	318.13
12 × 12	253.48	253.48	291.50	291.50	337.96	337.96	506.96	506.96	228.13	228.13
12 × 14	349.31	297.56	401.71	342.19	465.74	396.74	698.62	595.12	314.38	267.80
12 × 16	460.48	341.65	529.55	392.90	613.96	455.52	920.96	683.30	414.43	307.49
12 × 18	586.98	385.73	675.03	443.59	782.62	514.29	1,173.96	771.46	528.28	347.16
12 × 20	728.81	429.81	838.13	494.28	971.72	573.07	1,457.62	859.62	655.93	386.83
12 × 24	1,058.48	517.98	1,217.25	595.68	1,411.27	690.62	2,116.96	1,035.96	952.63	466.18
14 × 14	410.06	410.06	471.57	471.57	546.73	546.73	820.12	820.12	369.05	369.05
14 × 16	540.56	470.81	621.64	541.43	720.73	627.73	1,081.12	941.62	486.50	423.73
14 × 18	689.06	531.56	792.42	611.29	918.72	708.73	1,378.12	1,063.12	620.15	478.40
14 × 20	855.56	592.31	983.89	681.16	1,140.72	789.73	1,711.12	1,184.62	770.00	533.08
14 × 24	1,242.56	713.81	1,428.94	820.88	1,656.70	951.72	2,485.12	1,427.62	1,118.30	642.43

G MOMENT RESISTANCE OF STANDARD LUMBER SIZES FOR VARIOUS *E* VALUES

The moment resistances of standard lumber sizes in Table 12.7 may *not* be used to determine span L limited by deflection. They may be used to determine whether a given span will carry a specified load and still be within certain deflection limitations, such as 1/360. The table may also be used to determine a size of beam limited by a given deflection if the load, span, and species of lumber are known.

The table is based on simple beams loaded uniformly with allowable deflections of 1/360. For other allowable deflections, the tabular data may be modified by the inverse ratio of 1/360 to the desired allowable deflection. Thus, if it is desired to use an allowable deflection of 1/180, the tabulated data would be multiplied by 2. Similarly the tabulated data may be modified in direct proportion for other values of E. For example, for an E of 1,600,000, the tabulated values for an E of 1,000,000 would be multiplied by 1.6.

To determine whether a given size, species (E), load, and span will be within $\Delta = 1/360$, divide the proper tabulated value by the moment developed in the piece. If the resultant is larger than the span being used, the piece is satisfactory from a deflection standpoint.

Example:

10-ft span, 2 x 6 section, $E = 1{,}600{,}000$ psi

$W = 50$ lb per lin ft

$M = Wl^2/8 = 7{,}500$ in.-lb and

$$\frac{53{,}556 \times 1.6}{7{,}500} = 11.4 \text{ ft}$$

The 2 x 6 is therefore satisfactory 'or a 10-ft pan.

To determ ne a size limited by a deflect'on of 1/360 when the load, span, and species (E) are known, divide the tabulated va ues by the span of the piece, in feet, and compare resulting moment values with the moment of the piece.

Example:

10-ft span, $E = 1{,}760{,}000$ psi

$W = 50$ lb per lin ft

$M = Wl^2/8 = 7{,}500$ in.-lb

2 x 4 = 25,226 25,226 ÷ 10 = 2,523

2,523 in.-lb < 7,500 in.-lb (unsatisfactory)

2 x 6 = 94,258 94,258 ÷ 10 = 9,426

9,426 in.-lb > 7,500 in.-lb (satisfactory)

An alternative method for selecting the size of member is to multiply the bending moment, in inch-pounds, by the span, in feet, and compare the resultant value with the values in the table.

TABLE 12.7 Moment resistance of standard lumber sizes for various *E* values

(1/360 deflection)

Nominal size in.	$ML = EI/450$ in.-lb-ft							
	E = 1,000,000		E = 1,210,000		E = 1,540,000		E = 1,760,000	
	x-x	*y-y*	*x-x*	*y-y*	*x-x*	*y-y*	*x-x*	*y-y*
1 × 4	68.89	3.11	83.36	3.76	106.09	4.79	121.25	5.47
1 × 6	277.56	4.89	335.85	5.92	427.44	7.53	488.50	8.61
1 × 8	610.44	6.67	738.63	8.07	940.08	10.27	1,074.37	11.74
1 × 10	1,240.44	8.44	1,500.93	10.21	1,910.28	13.00	2,183.17	14.85
1 × 12	2,200.44	10.22	2,662.53	12.37	3,388.68	15.74	3,872.77	17.99
2 × 2	12.89	12.89	15.60	15.60	19.85	19.85	22.69	22.69
2 × 4	143.33	28.89	173.43	34.96	220.73	44.49	252.26	50.85
2 × 6	535.56	44.67	648.03	54.05	824.76	68.79	942.58	78.62
2 × 8	1,269.56	59.56	1,536.17	72.07	1,955.12	91.72	2,234.42	104.82
2 × 10	2,580.00	75.56	3,121.80	91.43	3,973.20	116.36	4,540.80	132.98
2 × 12	4,576.67	91.33	5,537.77	110.51	7,048.07	140.65	8,054.94	160.70
2 × 14	7,404.00	107.33	8,958.84	129.87	11,402.16	165.29	13,031.04	188.90
3 × 4	231.56	121.33	280.19	146.81	356.60	186.85	407.54	213.54
3 × 6	865.11	188.44	1,046.78	228.01	1,332.27	290.20	1,522.59	331.65
3 × 8	2,050.89	251.11	2,481.58	303.84	3,158.37	386.71	3,609.57	441.95
3 × 10	4,167.78	318.22	5,043.01	385.05	6,418.38	490.06	7,335.29	560.07
3 × 12	7,393.11	385.11	8,945.66	465.98	11,385.39	593.07	13,011.87	677.79
3 × 14	11,960.22	452.22	14,471.87	547.19	18,418.74	696.42	21,049.99	795.91
3 × 16	18,102.22	519.11	21,903.69	628.12	27,877.42	799.43	31,859.91	913.63
4 × 4	319.78	319.78	386.93	386.93	492.46	492.46	562.81	562.81
4 × 6	1,194.67	496.22	1,445.55	600.43	1,839.79	764.18	2,102.62	843.57
4 × 8	2,832.00	661.56	3,426.72	800.49	4,361.28	1,018.80	4,984.32	1,164.34
4 × 10	5,755.56	838.00	6,964.20	1,013.98	8,863.55	1,290.52	10,129.78	1,474.88
4 × 12	10,209.56	1,014.44	12,353.57	1,227.47	15,722.72	1,562.24	17,968.82	1,785.41

TABLE 12.7 Moment resistance of standard lumber sizes for various *E* values (Cont.)

(1/360 deflection)

Nominal size *in.*	$ML = EI/450$ *in.-lb-ft*							
	E = 1,000,000		E = 1,210,000		E = 1,540,000		E = 1,760,000	
	x-x	*y-y*	*x-x*	*y-y*	*x-x*	*y-y*	*x-x*	*y-y*
4 × 14	16,516.44	1,190.89	19,984.89	1,440.90	25,435.32	1,833.97	29,068.93	2,095.97
4 × 16	24,998.22	1,367.33	30,247.84	1,654.47	38,497.26	2,105.69	43,996.87	2,406.50
6 × 6	1,694.67	1,694.67	2,050.55	2,050.55	2,609.79	2,609.79	2,982.62	2,982.62
6 × 8	4,296.89	2,310.67	5,199.24	2,795.91	6,617.21	3,558.43	7,562.53	4,066.78
6 × 10	8,732.44	2,926.89	10,566.25	3,541.54	13,447.96	4,507.41	15,369.09	5,151.32
6 × 12	15,490.44	3,543.11	18,743.43	4,287.16	23,855.28	5,456.39	27,263.17	6,235.87
6 × 14	25,059.37	4,159.33	30,321.84	5,032.79	38,591.43	6,405.37	44,104.49	7,320.42
6 × 16	37,928.44	4,775.56	45,893.41	5,778.43	58,409.80	7,354.36	66,754.05	8,404.98
6 × 18	54,586.22	5,391.78	66,049.33	6,524.05	84,062.79	8,303.34	96,071.75	9,489.53
8 × 8	5,859.33	5,859.33	7,089.79	7,089.79	9,023.37	9,023.37	10,312.42	10,312.42
8 × 10	11,908.00	7,421.78	14,408.68	8,980.35	18,338.32	11,429.54	20,958.08	13,062.33
8 × 12	21,123.33	8,984.44	25,559.23	10,871.17	32,529.93	13,836.04	37,177.06	15,812.61
8 × 14	34.171.78	10,546.89	41,347.85	12,761.74	52,624.54	16,242.21	60,142.33	18,562.53
8 × 16	51,720.44	12,109.33	62,581.73	14,652.30	79,649.48	18,648.37	91,027.97	21,312.42
8 × 18	74,435.78	13,671.78	90,066.99	16,542.80	114,631.02	21,054.52	131,006.93	24,062.32
8 × 20	102,984.44	15,234.44	124,611.17	18,433.67	158,596.04	23,461.04	181,252.61	26,812.61
10 × 10	15,083.56	15,083.54	18,251.11	18,251.04	23,228.68	23,228.66	26,547.06	26,547.05
10 × 12	26,756.22	18,258.89	32,375.03	22,093.26	41,204.59	28,118.69	47,090.95	32,135.64
10 × 14	43,284.44	21,434.44	52,374.17	25,935.67	66,658.04	33,009.04	76,180.61	37,724.61
10 × 16	65,512.67	24,609.78	79,270.33	29,777.83	100,889.51	37,899.06	115,302.30	43,313.21
10 × 18	94,285.33	27,785.33	114,085.25	33,620.25	145,199.41	42,789.41	165,942.18	48,902.18
10 × 20	130,446.88	30,960.67	157,840.72	37,462.41	200,888.20	47,679.43	229,586.51	54,490.78
10 × 24	228,314.44	37,311.78	276,260.47	45,147.25	351,604.24	57,460.14	401,833.41	65,668.73

TABLE 12.7 Moment resistance of standard lumber sizes for various *E* values (Cont.)

(1/360 deflection)

Nominal size *in.*	$ML = EI/450$ *in.-lb-ft*							
	E = 1,000,000		E = 1,210,000		E = 1,540,000		E = 1,760,000	
	x-x	*y-y*	*x-x*	*y-y*	*x-x*	*y-y*	*x-x*	*y-y*
12 × 12	32,389.11	32,389.11	39,190.82	39,190.82	49,879.23	49,879.23	57,004.83	57,004.83
12 × 14	52,396.89	38,021.78	63,400.24	46,006.35	80,691.21	58,553.54	92,218.53	66,918.33
12 × 16	79,304.66	43,654.67	95,958.64	52,822.15	122,129.18	67,228.19	139,576.20	76,832.22
12 × 18	114,134.89	49,287.56	138,103.22	59,637.95	175,767.73	75,902.84	200,877.41	86,746.11
12 × 20	157,909.33	54,920.44	191,070.29	66,453.73	243,180.37	84,577.48	277,920.42	96,659.97
12 × 24	276,380.66	66,186.22	334,420.60	80,085.33	425,626.22	101,926.78	486,429.96	116,487.75
14 × 14	61,509.33	61,509.33	74,426.29	74,426.29	94,724.39	94,724.39	108,256.42	108,256.42
14 × 16	93,096.89	70,621.78	112,647.24	85,452.35	143,369.21	108,757.54	163,850.53	124,294.33
14 × 18	133,984.44	79,734.44	162,121.17	96,478.67	206,336.04	122,791.04	235,812.61	140,332.61
14 × 20	185,371.78	88,846.89	224,299.85	107,504.74	285,472.54	136,824.21	326,254.33	156,370.53
14 × 24	324,446.88	107,071.78	392,580.72	129,556.85	499,648.20	164,890.54	571,026.51	188,446.33

H SHEAR RESISTANCE OF STANDARD LUMBER SIZES

Table 12.8 presents the maximum vertical shear permissible—for various durations of load—for standard lumber sizes that are limited by an allowable horizontal shear, *H*, of 100 psi. In computations for the actual vertical shear in a given beam for comparison with the allowable tabulated value, that portion of the load which lies at a distance equal to the depth of the beam from the ends should be neglected; also, special procedure should be used for wheel loadings, as noted in Chap. 13, NDS. Shear generally will not control except in relatively short, deep beams.

The tabular data may be adjusted in straight proportion for other values of *H*. Thus if an *H* value of 120 is used, the data are multiplied by 1.2.

TABLE 12.8 Maximum vertical shear for beams limited by resistance to horizontal shear

($H = 100$ psi)

Nominal size *in.*	Maximum vertical shear *lb*				
	Normal load	Snow load	Wind load	Impact load	Permanent load
2 × 2	176	202	235	352	158
2 × 4	393	452	524	786	354
2 × 6	609	700	812	1,218	548
2 × 8	813	935	1,084	1,626	732
2 × 10	1,030	1,184	1,373	2,060	927
2 × 12	1,246	1,433	1,661	2,492	1,121
2 × 14	1,463	1,682	1,951	2,926	1,317
3 × 4	635	730	847	1,270	572
3 × 6	985	1,133	1,313	1,970	887
3 × 8	1,313	1,510	1,751	2,626	1,182
3 × 10	1,663	1,912	2,217	3,326	1,497
3 × 12	2,013	2,315	2,684	4,026	1,812
3 × 14	2,363	2,717	3,151	4,726	2,127
3 × 16	2,731	3,141	3,641	5,462	2,458
4 × 4	876	1,007	1,168	1,752	788
4 × 6	1,359	1,563	1,812	2,718	1,223
4 × 8	1,813	2,085	2,417	3,626	1,632
4 × 10	2,296	2,640	3,061	4,592	2,066
4 × 12	2,779	3,196	3,705	5,558	2,501
4 × 14	3,263	3,752	4,351	6,526	2,937
4 × 16	3,746	4,308	4,995	7,492	3,371
6 × 6	2,017	2,320	2,689	4,034	1,815
6 × 8	2,750	3,162	3,666	5,500	2,475
6 × 10	3,483	4,005	4,644	6,966	3,135
6 × 12	4,217	4,850	5,623	8,434	3,795
6 × 14	4,950	5,692	6,600	9,900	4,455
6 × 16	5,683	6,535	7,577	11,366	5,115
6 × 18	6,417	7,380	8,556	12,834	5,775

TABLE 12.8 Maximum vertical shear for beams (Cont.)

Nominal size *in.*	Maximum vertical shear *lb*				
	Normal load	Snow load	Wind load	Impact load	Permanent load
8 × 8	3,750	4,313	5,000	7,500	3,375
8 × 10	4,750	5,462	6,333	9,500	4,275
8 × 12	5,750	6,612	7,667	11,500	5,175
8 × 14	6,750	7,762	9,000	13,500	6,075
8 × 16	7,750	8,912	10,333	15,500	6,975
8 × 18	8,750	10,062	11,667	17,500	7,875
8 × 20	9,750	11,212	13,000	19,500	8,775
10 × 10	6,017	6,920	8,022	12,034	5,415
10 × 12	7,283	8,375	9,710	14,566	6,555
10 × 14	8,550	9,832	11,400	17,100	7,695
10 × 16	9,817	11,290	13,089	19,634	8,835
10 × 18	11,083	12,745	14,777	22,166	9,975
10 × 20	12,350	14,202	16,466	24,700	11,115
10 × 24	14,883	17,115	19,844	29,766	13,395
12 × 12	8,817	10,140	11,756	17,634	7,935
12 × 14	10,350	11,903	13,800	20,700	9,315
12 × 16	11,883	13,665	15,844	23,766	10,695
12 × 18	13,417	15,430	17,889	26,834	12,075
12 × 20	14,950	17,193	19,933	29,900	13,455
12 × 24	18,017	20,720	24,022	36,034	16,215
14 × 14	12,150	13,973	16,200	24,300	10,935
14 × 16	13,950	16,043	18,600	27,900	12,555
14 × 18	15,750	18,113	21,000	31,500	14,175
14 × 20	17,550	20,182	23,400	35,100	15,795
14 × 24	21,150	24,322	28,200	42,300	19,035

I COMMON EQUATIONS FOR BEAMS, COLUMNS, AND MEMBERS SUBJECT TO AXIAL STRESS AND BENDING

TABLE 12.9

Property	Equation
Beams	
Flexure, extreme fiber	$f = Mc/I = M/S$
Flexure, any fiber[1]	$f = My/I$
Horizontal shear (for rectangular beams)[2]	$H = 3V/2bh$

I COMMON EQUATIONS FOR BEAMS, COLUMNS, AND MEMBERS SUBJECT TO AXIAL STRESS AND BENDING (Cont.)

TABLE 12.9 (Cont.)

Property	Equation
Continuous beams (supports on same level)[3]	
Moments of inertia, uniform load	$M_1L_1 + 2M_2(L_1 + L_2) + M_3L_2 = -\frac{1}{4} W_1L_1^3 - \frac{1}{4} W_2L_2^3$ $M_1 + 4M_2 + M_3 = -\frac{1}{2} W_1L_1^2$ [if $L_1 = L_2$; $W_1 = W_2$]
Moments of inertia, concentrated loads[4]	$M_1L_1 + 2M_2 (L_1 + L_2) + M_3L_2 = -P_1L_1^2 (K_1 - K_1^3) - P_2L_2^2 (2K_2 - 3K_2^2 + K_2^3)$ $M_1 + 4M_2 + M_3 = -P_1L_1 (3K_1 - 3K_1^2)$ [if $L_1 = L_2$; $P_1 = P_2$; $K_1 = K_2$]
Members subject to axial stress and bending	
Compression[5]	$\frac{P/A}{c} + \frac{M/S}{f} \leqq 1$
Tension[5]	$\frac{P/A}{f} + \frac{M/S}{f} \leqq 1$
Simultaneous bending, both axes	$\frac{M_{x-x}}{f\,S_{x-x}} + \frac{M_{y-y}}{f\,S_{y-y}} \leqq 1$
Simple columns concentrically loaded (normal load)	
Compression parallel to grain[6]	$P/A = \frac{0.30E}{(l/d)^2}$
Spaced columns concentrically loaded (normal load)	
Compression parallel to grain[7]	
For condition "a"	$2\frac{1}{2}$ times simple-column values
For condition "b"	3 times simple-column values

[1] y = distance from neutral axis to fiber.

[2] See Chap. 13, NDS, par. 400-D-2.

[3] These equations are for beams with moments of inertia constant for each span. By writing such equations for each successive pair of spans and introducing the known values (usually zero) of end moments, all other moments can be found.

[4] P_1 = a concentrated load in the first of the two spans at the distance K_1L_1 from the first support.
P_2 = a concentrated load in the second of the two spans at the distance K_2L_2 from the second support.

[5] As used here, c represents either the adjusted allowable basic stresses for compression parallel to grain, or P/A as used in the equations for concentric columns, whichever is less. P/A as used here represents the actual axial stress on the section, rather than the P/A for columns.

[6] P/A shall not exceed the values for compression parallel to grain, c, for the grade and species used.

[7] P/A is limited as for simple solid columns.

J ALLOWABLE UNIT STRESSES FOR COLUMNS

In lieu of the Euler formula, the column curves of Fig. 12.1 provide a graphical method for determining allowable unit stresses for square or rectangular columns, or the equivalent. For any l/d ratio, the curves show the normal P/A allowable unit compressive stress for simple or spaced columns, according to the E value of the species.

If the P/A value determined from the curves exceeds the c value for the grade used, then the c value controls.

Once the maximum normal unit stress (P/A or c) has been determined for a particular E value, it may be adjusted for durations of loading (see Chap. 13, NDS) other than normal. The adjustments are: 90 per cent for permanently applied load; 115 per cent for two-month loading, as for snow; 133⅓ per cent for wind or earthquake; 200 per cent for impact.

Allowable normal P/A for other E values may be obtained by direct proportion from any curve. Thus the P/A for a certain l/d on the curve for an E of 1,760,000 is converted to other E values by multiplying P/A for an E of 1,760,000 by the ratio of the other E to 1,760,000. The E value curves given are those most often used.

If the moisture content of the wood is at or above fiber-saturation point—as it is if the wood is continuously submerged—the E and c values are reduced, E to 10/11 and c to 9/10 of tabulated values. The P/A value thus is 10/11 of the l/d value given by the curves for the dry value of E.

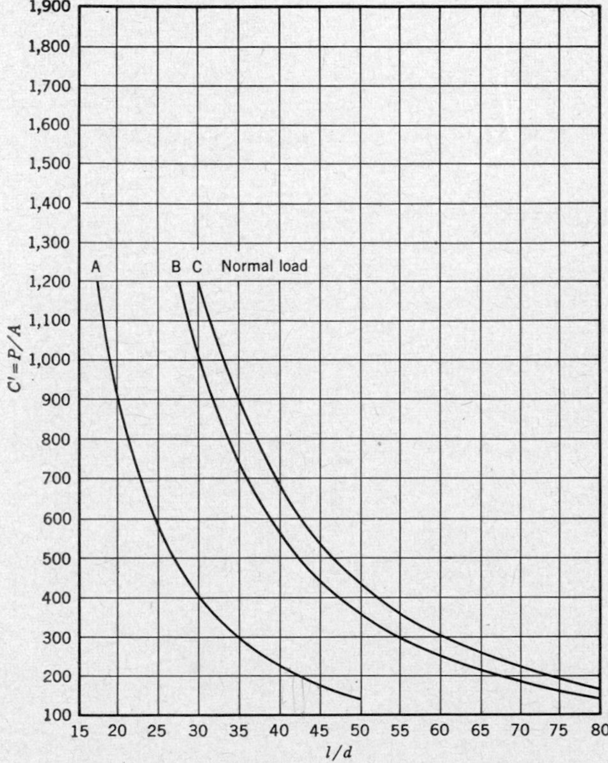

A—*Simple solid columns* $[C' = 0.3\ E \div (l/d)^2]$

B—*Spaced columns under Condition "a"; connectors located within 1/20 from the end* $[C' = 0.75\ E \div (l/d)^2]$

C—*Spaced columns under Condition "b"; connectors located within 1/20 to 1/10 from the end* $[C' = 0.9\ E \div (l/d)^2$; $P/A \leq$ *allowable c for grade specfied*]

Fig. 12.1 Column allowable unit stresses

E = *1,100,000 (1,000,000 increased 10 per cent for drying)*

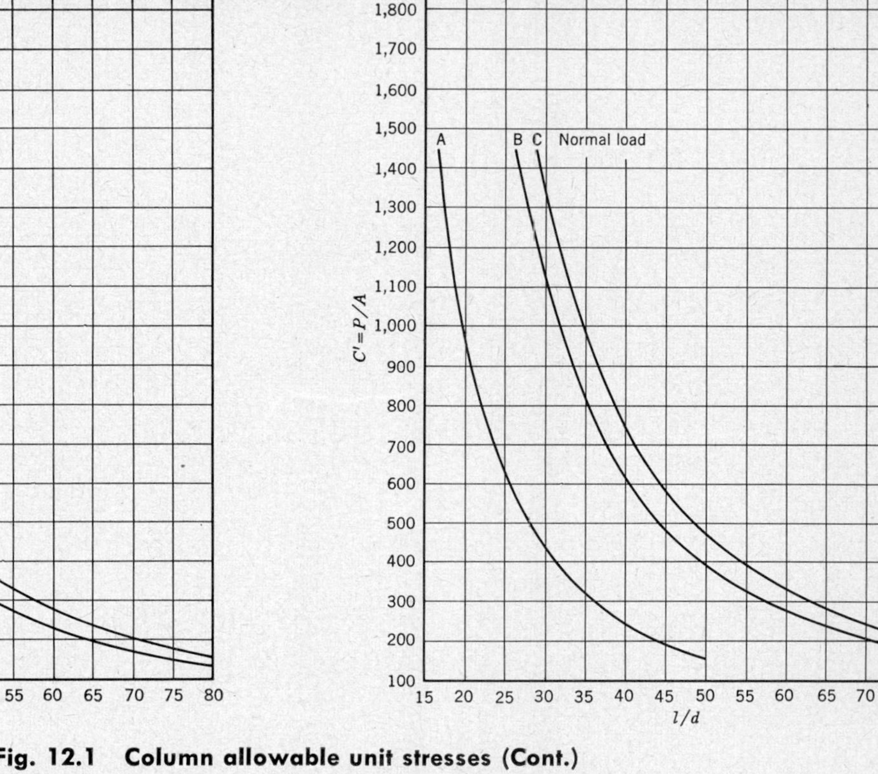

Fig. 12.1 Column allowable unit stresses (Cont.)

E = *1,210,000 psi (1,100,000 increased 10 per cent for drying)*

E = *1,320,000 psi (1,200,000 increased 10 per cent for drying)*

A—*Simple solid columns* [C′ = 0.3 E ÷ (l/d)²]
B—*Spaced columns under Condition "a"; connectors located within* 1/20 *from the end* [C′ = 0.75 E ÷ (l/d)²]
C—*Spaced columns under Condition "b"; connectors located within* 1/20 *to* 1/10 *from the end* [C′ = 0.9 E ÷ (l/d)²; P/A ≤ *allowable c for grade specified*]

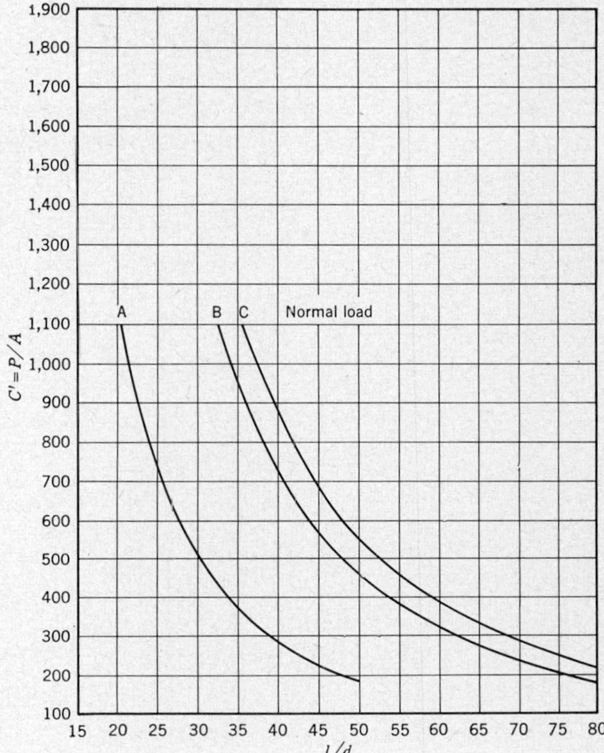

Fig. 12.1 Column allowable unit stresses (Cont.)

E = *1,430,000 psi (1,300,000 increased 10 per cent for drying)*

E = *1,540,000 psi (1,400,000 increased 10 per cent for drying)*

A—*Simple solid columns* [$C' = 0.3\ E \div (l/d)^2$]
B—*Spaced columns under Condition "a"; connectors located within* 1/20 *from the end* [$C' = 0.75\ E \div (l/d)^2$]
C—*Spaced columns under Condition "b"; connectors located within* 1/20 *to* 1/10 *from the end* [$C' = 0.9\ E \div (l/d)^2$; $P/A \leq$ *allowable c for grade specified*]

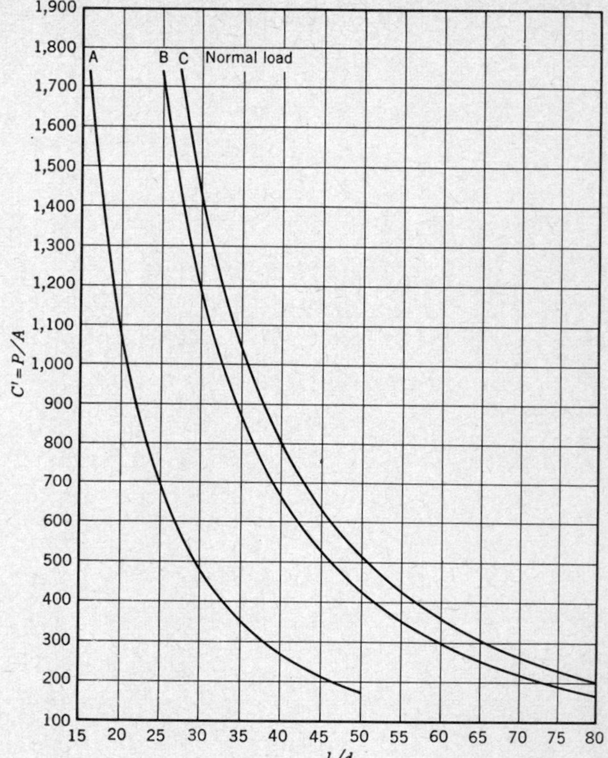

Fig. 12.1 Column allowable unit stresess (Cont.)

E = *1,650,000 psi (1,500,000 increased 10 per cent for drying)*

E = *1,760,000 psi (1,600,000 increased 10 per cent for drying)*

A—*Simple solid columns* [C′ = 0.3 E ÷ (l/d)²]

B—*Spaced columns under Condition "a"; connectors located within* l/20 *from the end* [C′ = 0.75 E ÷ (l/d)²]

C—*Spaced columns under Condition "b"; connectors located within* l/20 *to* l/10 *from the end* [C′ = 0.9 E ÷ (l/d)²; P/A ≤ *allowable c for grade specified*]

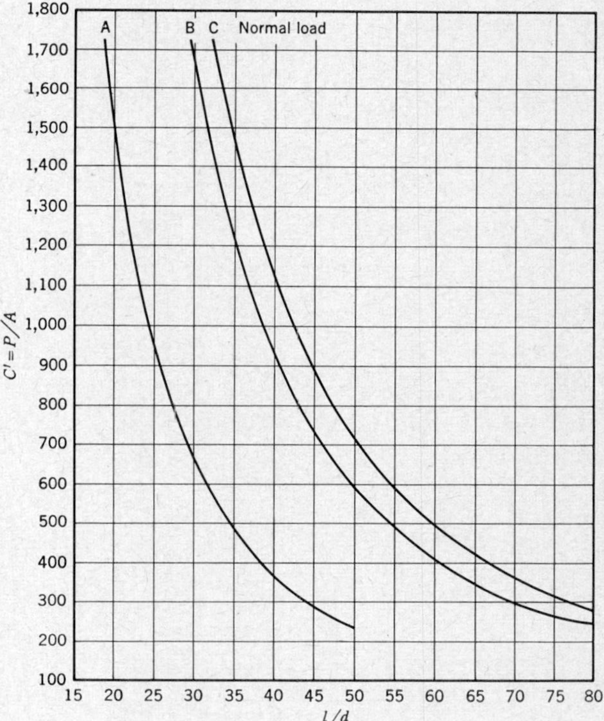

Fig. 12.1 Column allowable unit stresses (Cont.)

E = *1,800,000 psi (glued-laminated members)*

E = *1,980,000 psi (1,800,000 increased 10 per cent for drying)*

A—*Simple solid columns* [$C' = 0.3\,E \div (l/d)^2$]

B—*Spaced columns under Condition "a"; connectors located within* l/20 *from the end* [$C' = 0.75\,E \div (l/d)^2$]

C—*Spaced columns under Condition "b"; connectors located within* l/20 *to* l/10 *from the end* [$C' = 0.9\,E \div (l/d)^2$; $P/A \leq$ *allowable c for grade specified*]

K BEAM DIAGRAMS AND FORMULAS

1. SIMPLE BEAM—UNIFORMLY DISTRIBUTED LOAD

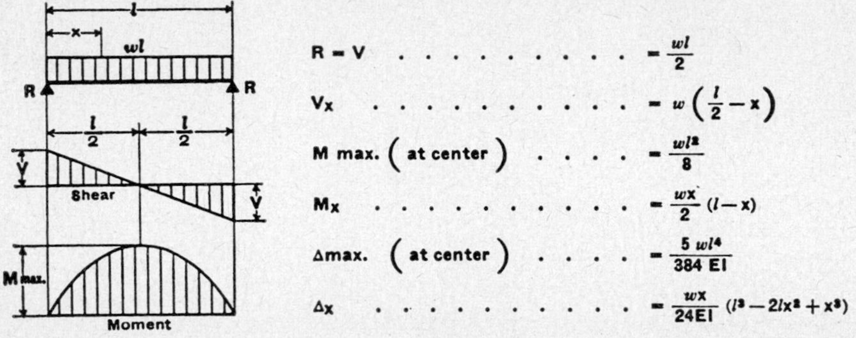

2. SIMPLE BEAM—LOAD INCREASING UNIFORMLY TO ONE END

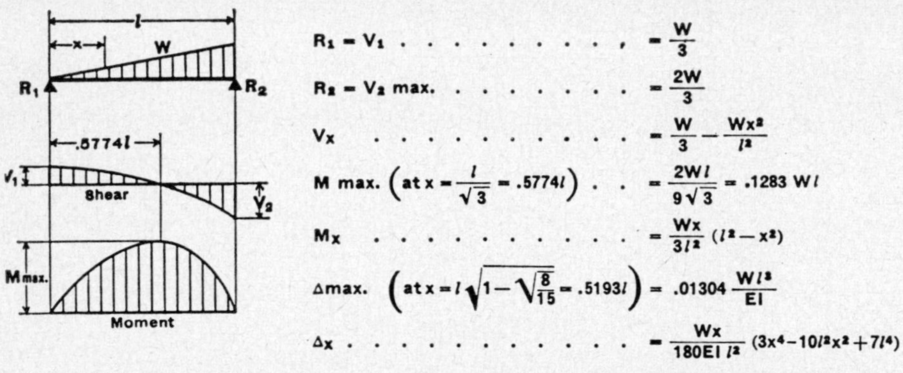

3. SIMPLE BEAM—LOAD INCREASING UNIFORMLY TO CENTER

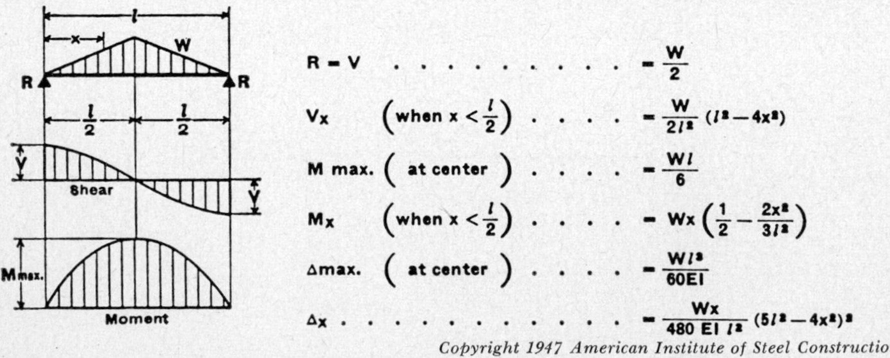

Fig. 12.2 Beam diagrams and formulas, static loading

4. SIMPLE BEAM—UNIFORM LOAD PARTIALLY DISTRIBUTED

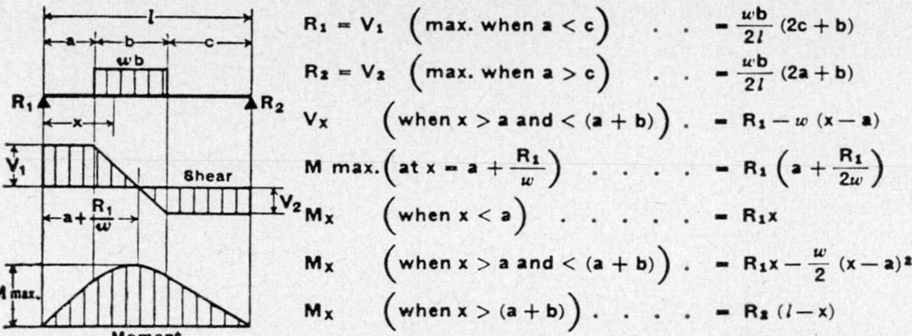

$$R_1 = V_1 \left(\text{max. when } a < c\right) \quad . \; . \quad = \frac{wb}{2l}(2c + b)$$

$$R_2 = V_2 \left(\text{max. when } a > c\right) \quad . \; . \quad = \frac{wb}{2l}(2a + b)$$

$$V_x \quad \left(\text{when } x > a \text{ and } < (a + b)\right) \quad . \quad = R_1 - w(x - a)$$

$$M \text{ max.} \left(\text{at } x = a + \frac{R_1}{w}\right) \quad . \; . \; . \; . \quad = R_1\left(a + \frac{R_1}{2w}\right)$$

$$M_x \quad \left(\text{when } x < a\right) \quad . \; . \; . \; . \; . \quad = R_1 x$$

$$M_x \quad \left(\text{when } x > a \text{ and } < (a + b)\right) \quad . \quad = R_1 x - \frac{w}{2}(x - a)^2$$

$$M_x \quad \left(\text{when } x > (a + b)\right) \quad . \; . \; . \; . \quad = R_2(l - x)$$

5. SIMPLE BEAM—UNIFORM LOAD PARTIALLY DISTRIBUTED AT ONE END

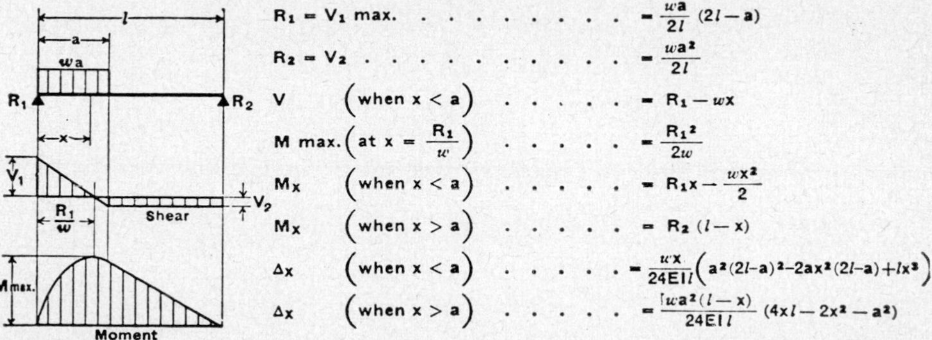

$$R_1 = V_1 \text{ max.} \quad . \; . \; . \; . \; . \; . \; . \; . \; . \quad = \frac{wa}{2l}(2l - a)$$

$$R_2 = V_2 \quad . \; . \; . \; . \; . \; . \; . \; . \; . \; . \quad = \frac{wa^2}{2l}$$

$$V \quad \left(\text{when } x < a\right) \quad . \; . \; . \; . \; . \quad = R_1 - wx$$

$$M \text{ max.} \left(\text{at } x = \frac{R_1}{w}\right) \quad . \; . \; . \; . \; . \quad = \frac{R_1^2}{2w}$$

$$M_x \quad \left(\text{when } x < a\right) \quad . \; . \; . \; . \; . \quad = R_1 x - \frac{wx^2}{2}$$

$$M_x \quad \left(\text{when } x > a\right) \quad . \; . \; . \; . \; . \quad = R_2(l - x)$$

$$\Delta x \quad \left(\text{when } x < a\right) \quad . \; . \; . \; . \; . \quad = \frac{wx}{24EIl}\left(a^2(2l-a)^2 - 2ax^2(2l-a) + lx^3\right)$$

$$\Delta x \quad \left(\text{when } x > a\right) \quad . \; . \; . \; . \; . \quad = \frac{wa^2(l - x)}{24EIl}(4xl - 2x^2 - a^2)$$

6. SIMPLE BEAM—UNIFORM LOAD PARTIALLY DISTRIBUTED AT EACH END

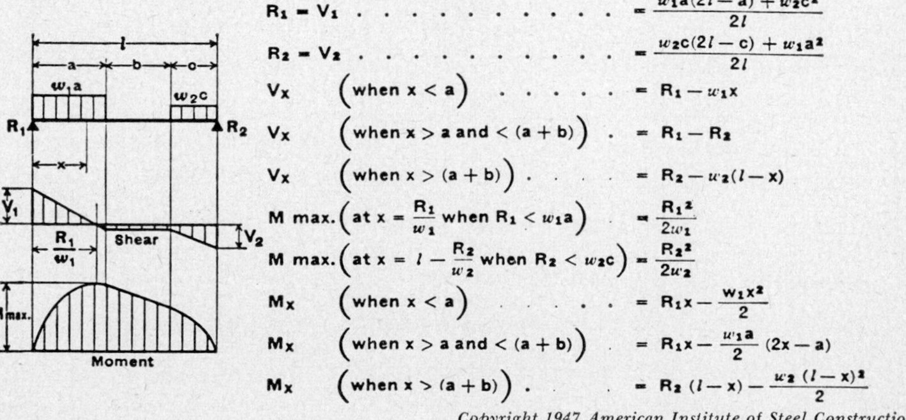

$$R_1 = V_1 \quad . \; . \; . \; . \; . \; . \; . \; . \; . \; . \quad = \frac{w_1 a(2l - a) + w_2 c^2}{2l}$$

$$R_2 = V_2 \quad . \; . \; . \; . \; . \; . \; . \; . \; . \; . \quad = \frac{w_2 c(2l - c) + w_1 a^2}{2l}$$

$$V_x \quad \left(\text{when } x < a\right) \quad . \; . \; . \; . \quad = R_1 - w_1 x$$

$$V_x \quad \left(\text{when } x > a \text{ and } < (a + b)\right) \quad . \quad = R_1 - R_2$$

$$V_x \quad \left(\text{when } x > (a + b)\right) \quad . \; . \; . \quad = R_2 - w_2(l - x)$$

$$M \text{ max.} \left(\text{at } x = \frac{R_1}{w_1} \text{ when } R_1 < w_1 a\right) \quad = \frac{R_1^2}{2w_1}$$

$$M \text{ max.} \left(\text{at } x = l - \frac{R_2}{w_2} \text{ when } R_2 < w_2 c\right) = \frac{R_2^2}{2w_2}$$

$$M_x \quad \left(\text{when } x < a\right) \quad . \; . \; . \; . \quad = R_1 x - \frac{w_1 x^2}{2}$$

$$M_x \quad \left(\text{when } x > a \text{ and } < (a + b)\right) \quad = R_1 x - \frac{w_1 a}{2}(2x - a)$$

$$M_x \quad \left(\text{when } x > (a + b)\right) \quad . \; . \quad = R_2(l - x) - \frac{w_2(l - x)^2}{2}$$

Fig. 12.2 Beam diagrams and formulas, static loading (Cont.)

7. BEAM OVERHANGING ONE SUPPORT—UNIFORMLY DISTRIBUTED LOAD

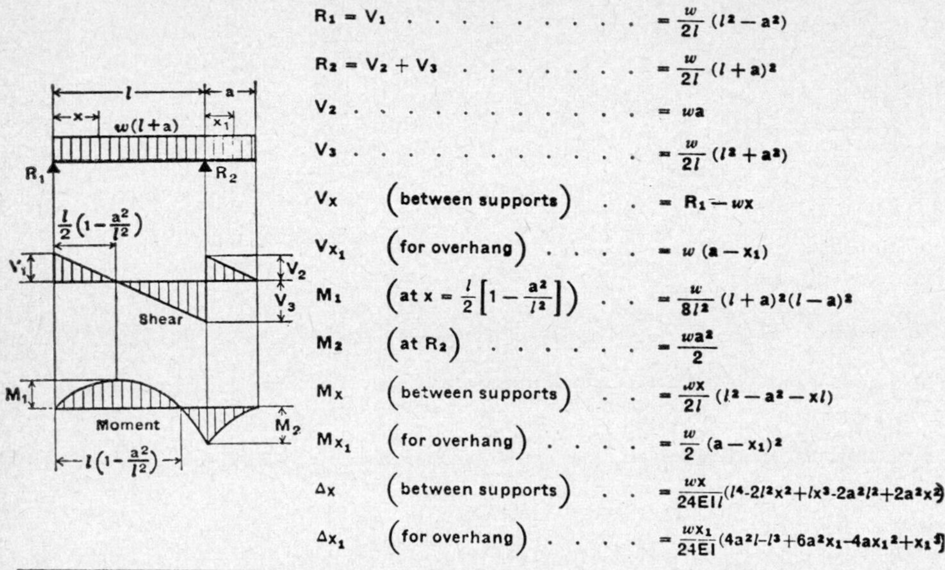

$R_1 = V_1 \ldots\ldots = \frac{w}{2l}(l^2 - a^2)$

$R_2 = V_2 + V_3 \ldots\ldots = \frac{w}{2l}(l + a)^2$

$V_2 \ldots\ldots = wa$

$V_3 \ldots\ldots = \frac{w}{2l}(l^2 + a^2)$

V_x (between supports) $\ldots = R_1 - wx$

V_{x_1} (for overhang) $\ldots = w(a - x_1)$

M_1 $\left(\text{at } x = \frac{l}{2}\left[1 - \frac{a^2}{l^2}\right]\right) \ldots = \frac{w}{8l^2}(l + a)^2(l - a)^2$

M_2 (at R_2) $\ldots = \frac{wa^2}{2}$

M_x (between supports) $\ldots = \frac{wx}{2l}(l^2 - a^2 - xl)$

M_{x_1} (for overhang) $\ldots = \frac{w}{2}(a - x_1)^2$

Δx (between supports) $\ldots = \frac{wx}{24EIl}(l^4 - 2l^2x^2 + lx^3 - 2a^2l^2 + 2a^2x^2)$

Δx_1 (for overhang) $\ldots = \frac{wx_1}{24EI}(4a^2l - l^3 + 6a^2x_1 - 4ax_1^2 + x_1^3)$

8. BEAM OVERHANGING ONE SUPPORT—UNIFORMLY DISTRIBUTED LOAD ON OVERHANG

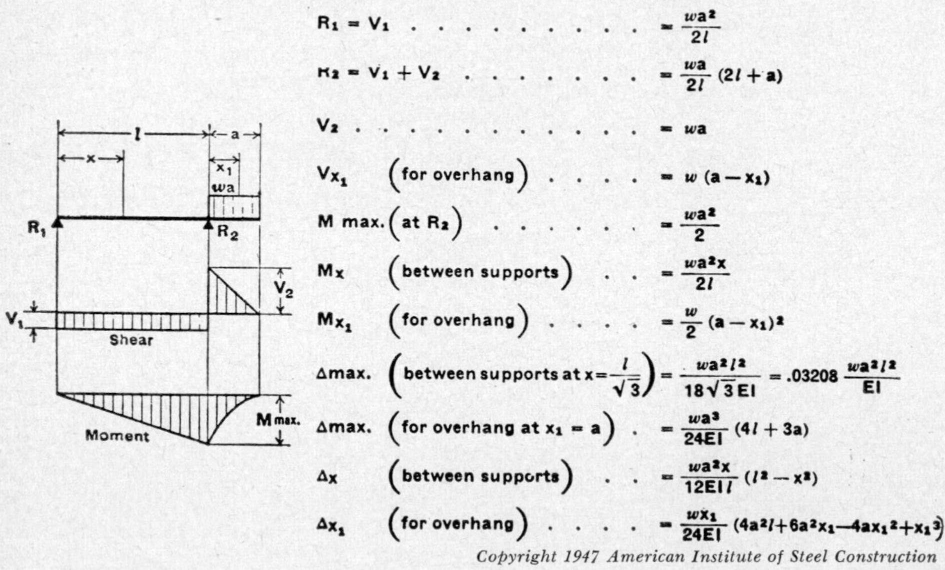

$R_1 = V_1 \ldots\ldots = \frac{wa^2}{2l}$

$R_2 = V_1 + V_2 \ldots\ldots = \frac{wa}{2l}(2l + a)$

$V_2 \ldots\ldots = wa$

V_{x_1} (for overhang) $\ldots = w(a - x_1)$

M max. (at R_2) $\ldots = \frac{wa^2}{2}$

M_x (between supports) $\ldots = \frac{wa^2x}{2l}$

M_{x_1} (for overhang) $\ldots = \frac{w}{2}(a - x_1)^2$

Δmax. $\left(\text{between supports at } x = \frac{l}{\sqrt{3}}\right) = \frac{wa^2l^2}{18\sqrt{3}EI} = .03208\,\frac{wa^2l^2}{EI}$

Δmax. (for overhang at $x_1 = a$) $\ldots = \frac{wa^3}{24EI}(4l + 3a)$

Δx (between supports) $\ldots = \frac{wa^2x}{12EIl}(l^2 - x^2)$

Δx_1 (for overhang) $\ldots = \frac{wx_1}{24EI}(4a^2l + 6a^2x_1 - 4ax_1^2 + x_1^3)$

Fig. 12.2 Beam diagrams and formulas, static loading (Cont.)

9. BEAM OVERHANGING ONE SUPPORT—UNIFORMLY DISTRIBUTED LOAD BETWEEN SUPPORTS

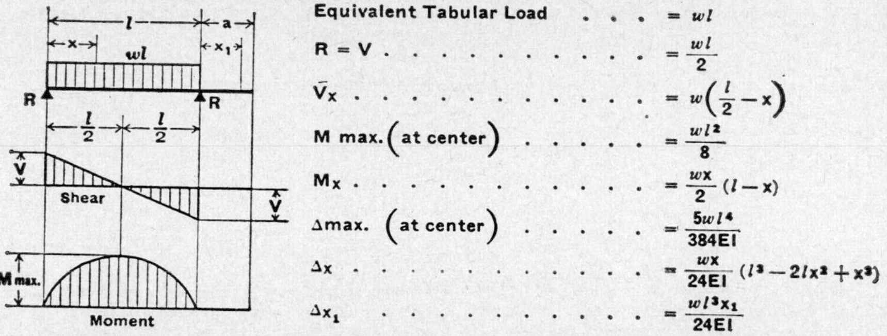

Equivalent Tabular Load	$= wl$
$R = V$	$= \frac{wl}{2}$
V_x	$= w\left(\frac{l}{2} - x\right)$
M max. (at center)	$= \frac{wl^2}{8}$
M_x	$= \frac{wx}{2}(l - x)$
Δmax. (at center)	$= \frac{5wl^4}{384EI}$
Δx	$= \frac{wx}{24EI}(l^3 - 2lx^2 + x^3)$
Δx_1	$= \frac{wl^3x_1}{24EI}$

10. BEAM OVERHANGING ONE SUPPORT—CONCENTRATED LOAD AT ANY POINT BETWEEN SUPPORTS

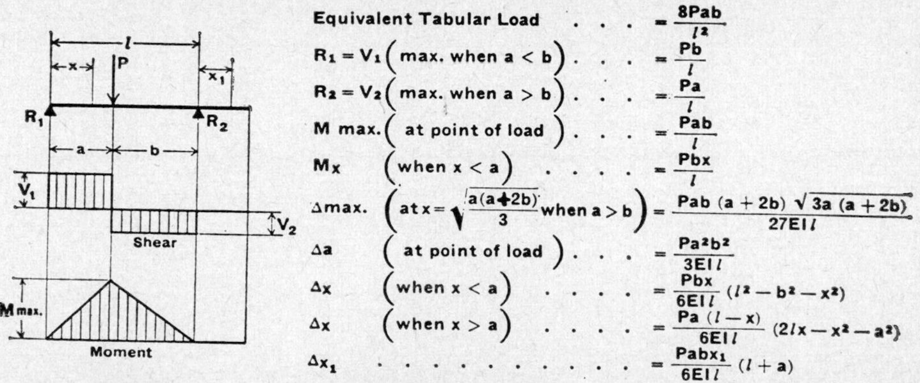

Equivalent Tabular Load	$= \frac{8Pab}{l^2}$
$R_1 = V_1$ (max. when $a < b$)	$= \frac{Pb}{l}$
$R_2 = V_2$ (max. when $a > b$)	$= \frac{Pa}{l}$
M max. (at point of load)	$= \frac{Pab}{l}$
M_x (when $x < a$)	$= \frac{Pbx}{l}$
Δmax. $\left(\text{at } x = \sqrt{\frac{a(a+2b)}{3}} \text{ when } a > b\right)$	$= \frac{Pab\,(a+2b)\sqrt{3a\,(a+2b)}}{27EIl}$
Δa (at point of load)	$= \frac{Pa^2b^2}{3EIl}$
Δx (when $x < a$)	$= \frac{Pbx}{6EIl}(l^2 - b^2 - x^2)$
Δx (when $x > a$)	$= \frac{Pa\,(l - x)}{6EIl}(2lx - x^2 - a^2)$
Δx_1	$= \frac{Pabx_1}{6EIl}(l + a)$

11. CONTINUOUS BEAM—TWO EQUAL SPANS—UNIFORM LOAD ON ONE SPAN

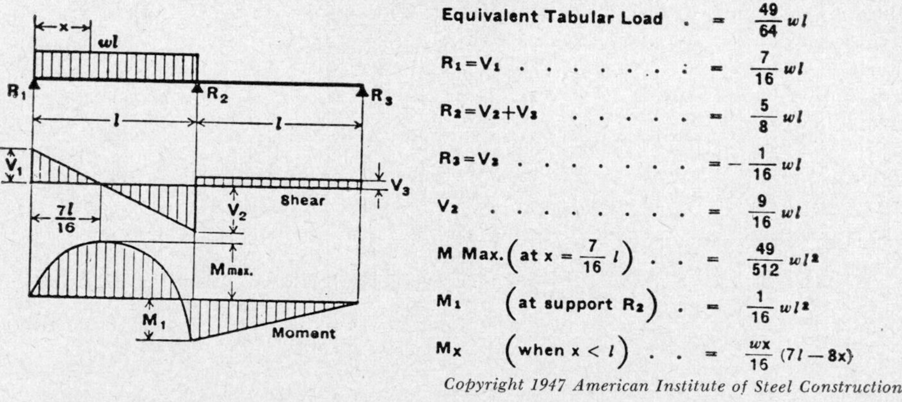

Equivalent Tabular Load	$= \frac{49}{64}wl$
$R_1 = V_1$	$= \frac{7}{16}wl$
$R_2 = V_2 + V_3$	$= \frac{5}{8}wl$
$R_3 = V_3$	$= -\frac{1}{16}wl$
V_2	$= \frac{9}{16}wl$
M Max. $\left(\text{at } x = \frac{7}{16}l\right)$	$= \frac{49}{512}wl^2$
M_1 (at support R_2)	$= \frac{1}{16}wl^2$
M_x (when $x < l$)	$= \frac{wx}{16}(7l - 8x)$

Fig. 12.2 Beam diagrams and formulas, static loading (Cont.)

12. CONTINUOUS BEAM DIAGRAMS

EQUAL SPANS, SIMILARLY LOADED, CONSTANT MOMENT OF INERTIA
SUPPORTS AT SAME LEVEL

UNIFORMLY DISTRIBUTED LOAD

Reaction and shear coefficients of wl

Moment coefficients of wl^2

w = Load per unit length

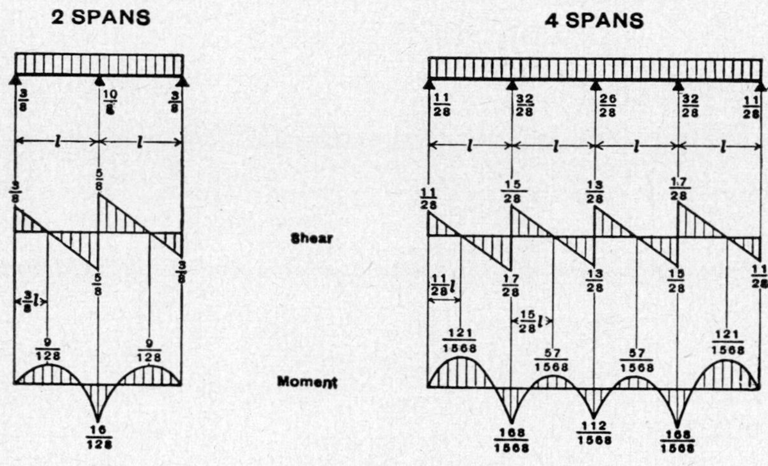

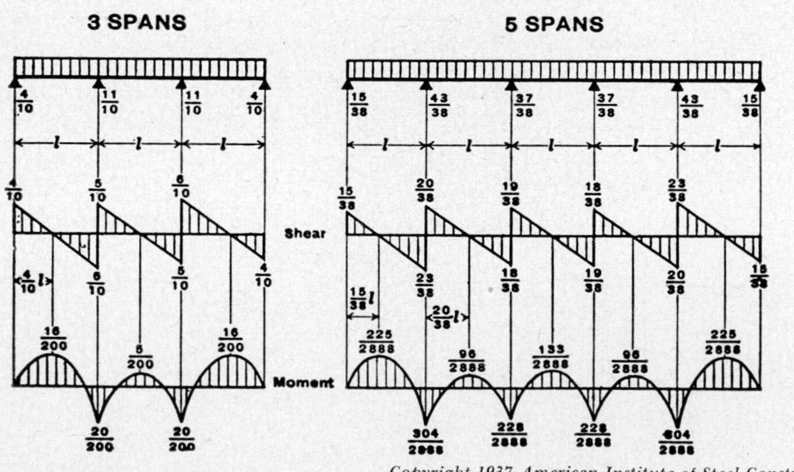

Fig. 12.2 Beam diagrams and formulas, static loading (Cont.)

13. SIMPLE BEAM—CONCENTRATED LOAD AT CENTER

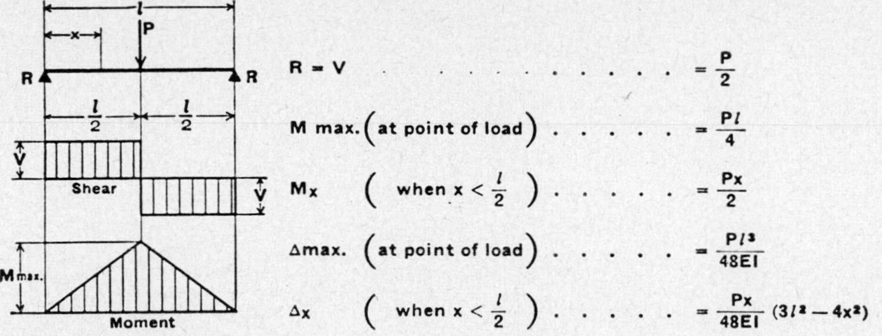

$R = V \ldots = \frac{P}{2}$

$M\ max. \left(\text{at point of load}\right) \ldots = \frac{Pl}{4}$

$M_x \left(\text{when } x < \frac{l}{2}\right) \ldots = \frac{Px}{2}$

$\Delta max. \left(\text{at point of load}\right) \ldots = \frac{Pl^3}{48EI}$

$\Delta x \left(\text{when } x < \frac{l}{2}\right) \ldots = \frac{Px}{48EI}(3l^2 - 4x^2)$

14. SIMPLE BEAM—CONCENTRATED LOAD AT ANY POINT

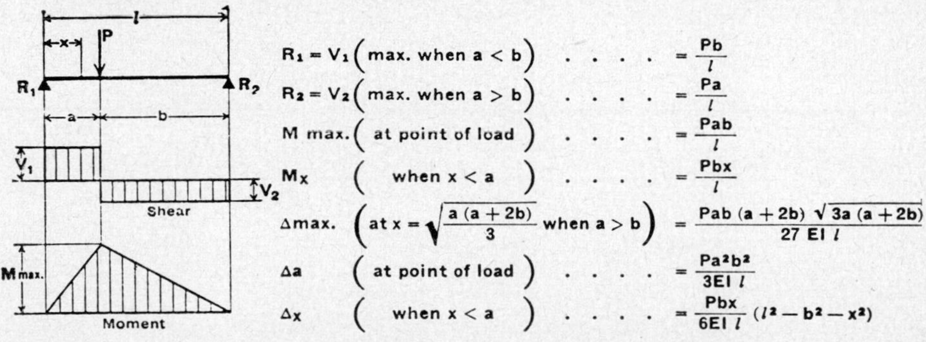

$R_1 = V_1 \left(\text{max. when } a < b\right) \ldots = \frac{Pb}{l}$

$R_2 = V_2 \left(\text{max. when } a > b\right) \ldots = \frac{Pa}{l}$

$M\ max. \left(\text{at point of load}\right) \ldots = \frac{Pab}{l}$

$M_x \left(\text{when } x < a\right) \ldots = \frac{Pbx}{l}$

$\Delta max. \left(\text{at } x = \sqrt{\frac{a(a+2b)}{3}} \text{ when } a > b\right) = \frac{Pab\,(a+2b)\sqrt{3a\,(a+2b)}}{27\,EI\,l}$

$\Delta a \left(\text{at point of load}\right) \ldots = \frac{Pa^2b^2}{3EI\,l}$

$\Delta x \left(\text{when } x < a\right) \ldots = \frac{Pbx}{6EI\,l}(l^2 - b^2 - x^2)$

15. SIMPLE BEAM—TWO EQUAL CONCENTRATED LOADS SYMMETRICALLY PLACED

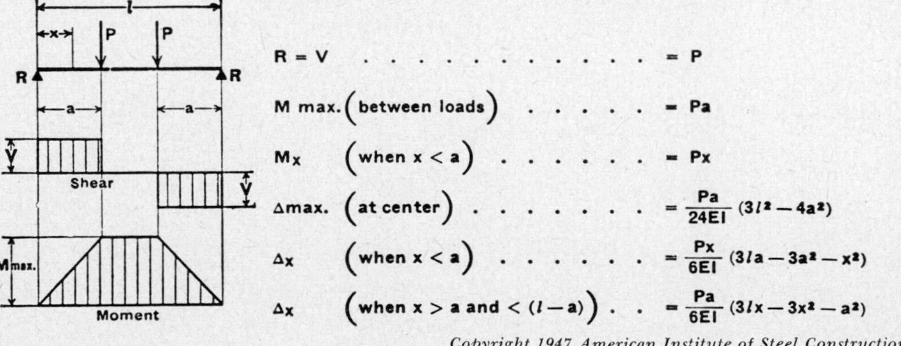

$R = V \ldots = P$

$M\ max. \left(\text{between loads}\right) \ldots = Pa$

$M_x \left(\text{when } x < a\right) \ldots = Px$

$\Delta max. \left(\text{at center}\right) \ldots = \frac{Pa}{24EI}(3l^2 - 4a^2)$

$\Delta x \left(\text{when } x < a\right) \ldots = \frac{Px}{6EI}(3la - 3a^2 - x^2)$

$\Delta x \left(\text{when } x > a \text{ and } < (l - a)\right) \ldots = \frac{Pa}{6EI}(3lx - 3x^2 - a^2)$

Fig. 12.2 Beam diagrams and formulas, static loading (Cont.)

16. SIMPLE BEAM—TWO EQUAL CONCENTRATED LOADS UNSYMMETRICALLY PLACED

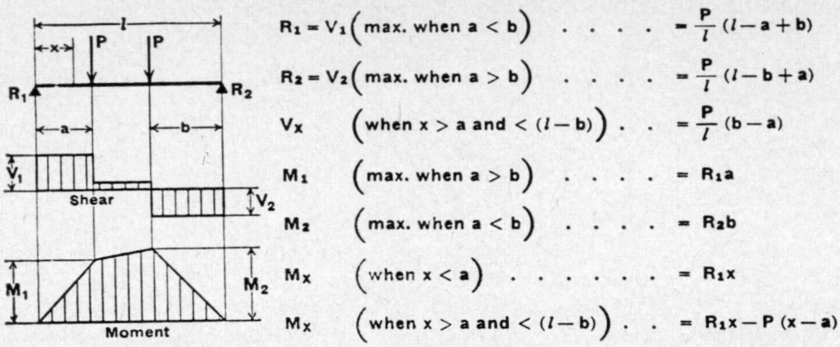

$R_1 = V_1$ (max. when $a < b$) . . . . $= \frac{P}{l}(l - a + b)$

$R_2 = V_2$ (max. when $a > b$) . . . . $= \frac{P}{l}(l - b + a)$

V_x (when $x > a$ and $< (l - b)$) . . $= \frac{P}{l}(b - a)$

M_1 (max. when $a > b$) . . . . $= R_1 a$

M_2 (max. when $a < b$) . . . . $= R_2 b$

M_x (when $x < a$) . . . . . . $= R_1 x$

M_x (when $x > a$ and $< (l - b)$) . . $= R_1 x - P(x - a)$

17. SIMPLE BEAM—TWO UNEQUAL CONCENTRATED LOADS UNSYMMETRICALLY PLACED

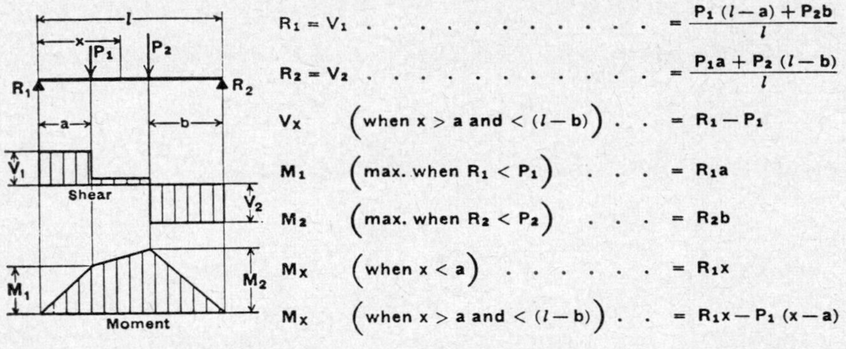

$R_1 = V_1$ . . . . $= \frac{P_1(l - a) + P_2 b}{l}$

$R_2 = V_2$ . . . . $= \frac{P_1 a + P_2(l - b)}{l}$

V_x (when $x > a$ and $< (l - b)$) . . $= R_1 - P_1$

M_1 (max. when $R_1 < P_1$) . . . $= R_1 a$

M_2 (max. when $R_2 < P_2$) . . . $= R_2 b$

M_x (when $x < a$) . . . . . . $= R_1 x$

M_x (when $x > a$ and $< (l - b)$) . . $= R_1 x - P_1(x - a)$

18. BEAM OVERHANGING ONE SUPPORT—CONCENTRATED LOAD AT END OF OVERHANG

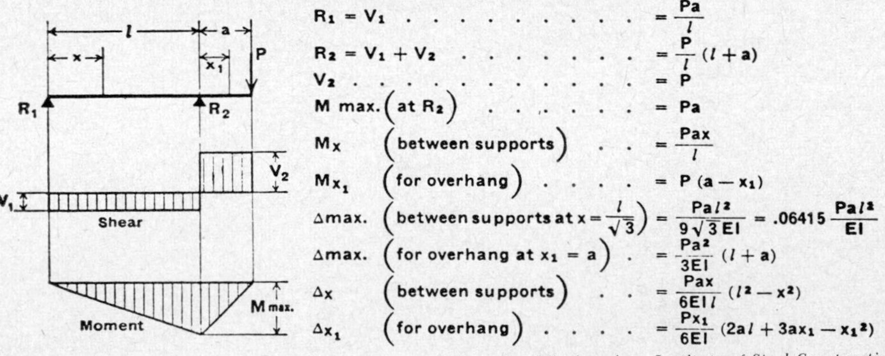

$R_1 = V_1$ . . . . $= \frac{Pa}{l}$

$R_2 = V_1 + V_2$ . . . . $= \frac{P}{l}(l + a)$

V_2 . . . . $= P$

M max. (at R_2) . . . . $= Pa$

M_x (between supports) . . $= \frac{Pax}{l}$

M_{x_1} (for overhang) . . . . $= P(a - x_1)$

Δmax. (between supports at $x = \frac{l}{\sqrt{3}}$) $= \frac{Pal^2}{9\sqrt{3}EI} = .06415\frac{Pal^2}{EI}$

Δmax. (for overhang at $x_1 = a$) . $= \frac{Pa^2}{3EI}(l + a)$

Δx (between supports) . . $= \frac{Pax}{6EIl}(l^2 - x^2)$

Δx_1 (for overhang) . . . . $= \frac{Px_1}{6EI}(2al + 3ax_1 - x_1^2)$

Fig. 12.2 Beam diagrams and formulas, static loading (Cont.)

19. CONTINUOUS BEAM DIAGRAMS

EQUAL SPANS, SIMILARLY LOADED, CONSTANT MOMENT OF INERTIA SUPPORTS AT SAME LEVEL

CONCENTRATED LOAD AT CENTERS

Reaction and shear coefficients of F **Moment coefficients of Fl**

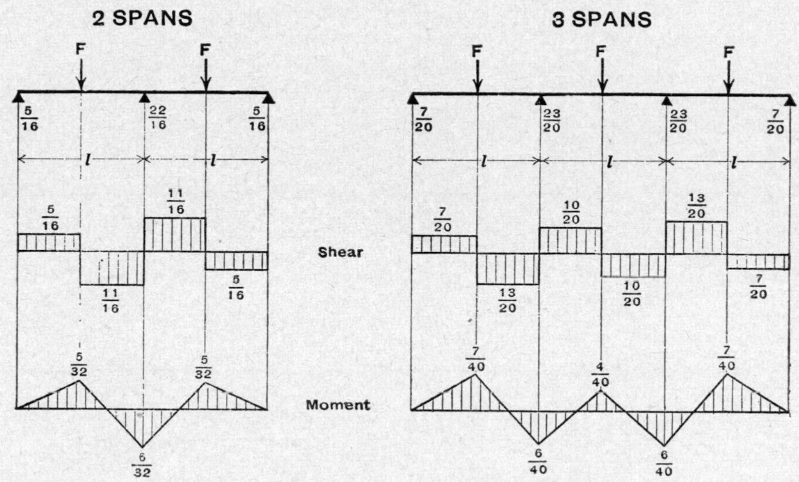

CONCENTRATED LOAD AT THIRD POINTS

Reaction and shear coefficients of F **Moment coefficients of Fl**

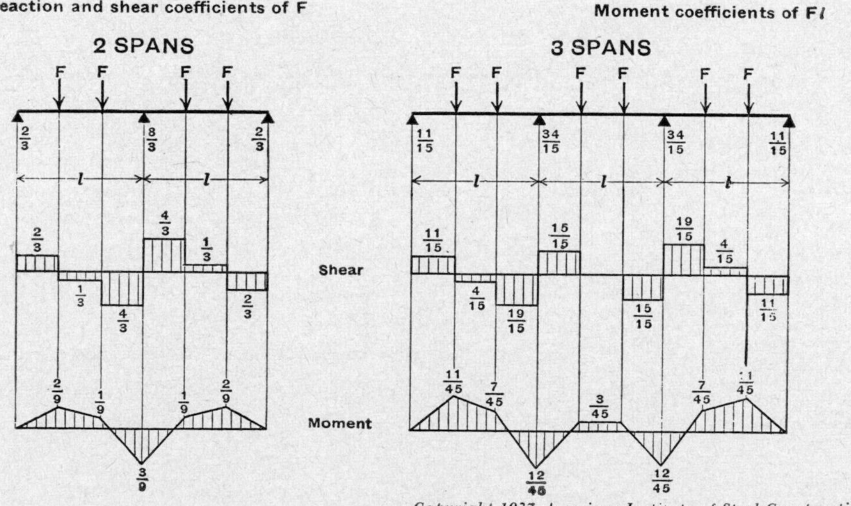

Fig. 12.2 Beam diagrams and formulas, static loading (Cont.)

20. CONTINUOUS BEAM—TWO EQUAL SPANS—CONCENTRATED LOAD AT CENTER OF ONE SPAN

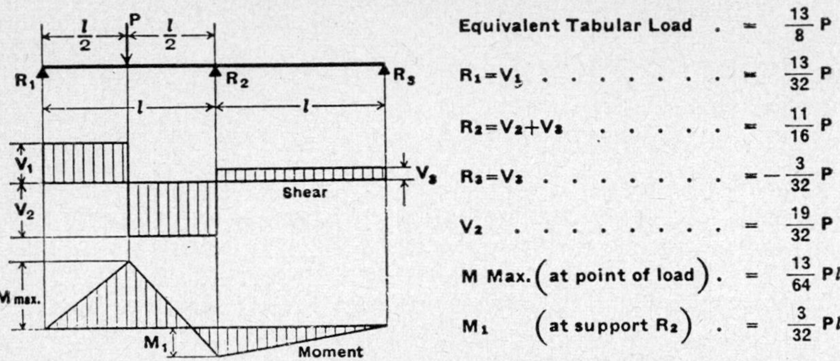

Equivalent Tabular Load . . . . $= \frac{13}{8} P$

$R_1 = V_1$ . . . . $= \frac{13}{32} P$

$R_2 = V_2 + V_3$ . . . . . . $= \frac{11}{16} P$

$R_3 = V_3$ . . . . $= -\frac{3}{32} P$

V_2 . . . . $= \frac{19}{32} P$

M Max. (at point of load) . $= \frac{13}{64} Pl$

M_1 (at support R_2) . $= \frac{3}{32} Pl$

21. CONTINUOUS BEAM—TWO EQUAL SPANS—CONCENTRATED LOAD AT ANY POINT

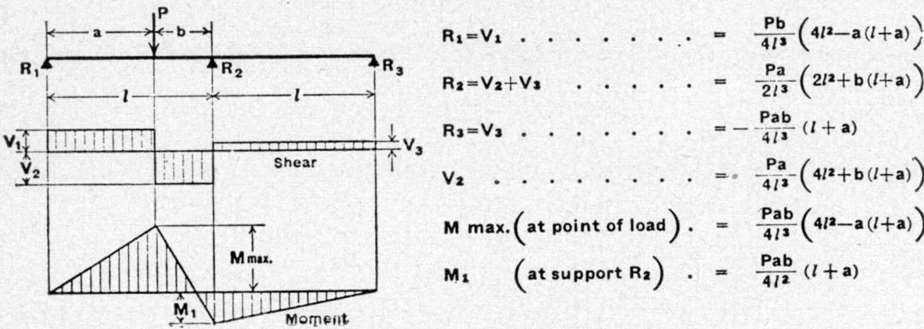

$R_1 = V_1$ . . . . $= \frac{Pb}{4l^3}\left(4l^2 - a(l+a)\right)$

$R_2 = V_2 + V_3$ . . . . . . $= \frac{Pa}{2l^3}\left(2l^2 + b(l+a)\right)$

$R_3 = V_3$ . . . . $= -\frac{Pab}{4l^3}(l+a)$

V_2 . . . . $= \frac{Pa}{4l^3}\left(4l^2 + b(l+a)\right)$

M max. (at point of load) . $= \frac{Pab}{4l^3}\left(4l^2 - a(l+a)\right)$

M_1 (at support R_2) . $= \frac{Pab}{4l^2}(l+a)$

22. BEAM FIXED AT ONE END, SUPPORTED AT OTHER—UNIFORMLY DISTRIBUTED LOAD

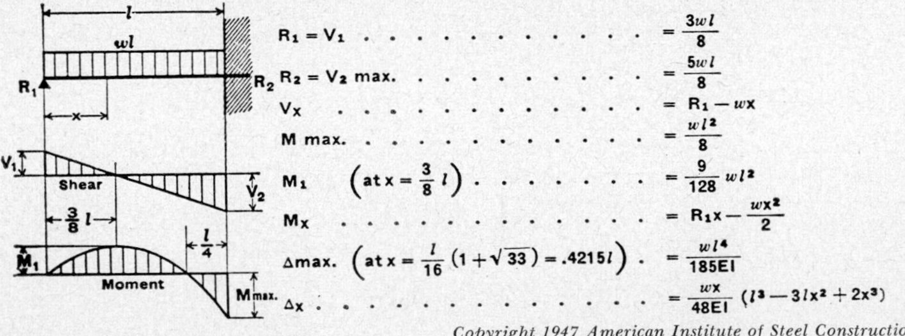

$R_1 = V_1$ . . . . $= \frac{3wl}{8}$

$R_2 = V_2$ max. . . . . $= \frac{5wl}{8}$

V_x . . . . $= R_1 - wx$

M max. . . . . $= \frac{wl^2}{8}$

M_1 $\left(\text{at } x = \frac{3}{8} l\right)$ . . . . $= \frac{9}{128} wl^2$

M_x . . . . $= R_1 x - \frac{wx^2}{2}$

Δmax. $\left(\text{at } x = \frac{l}{16}(1 + \sqrt{33}) = .4215l\right)$. $= \frac{wl^4}{185EI}$

Δx . . . . $= \frac{wx}{48EI}(l^3 - 3lx^2 + 2x^3)$

Fig. 12.2 Beam diagrams and formulas, static loading (Cont.)

23. CANTILEVER BEAM—LOAD INCREASING UNIFORMLY TO FIXED END

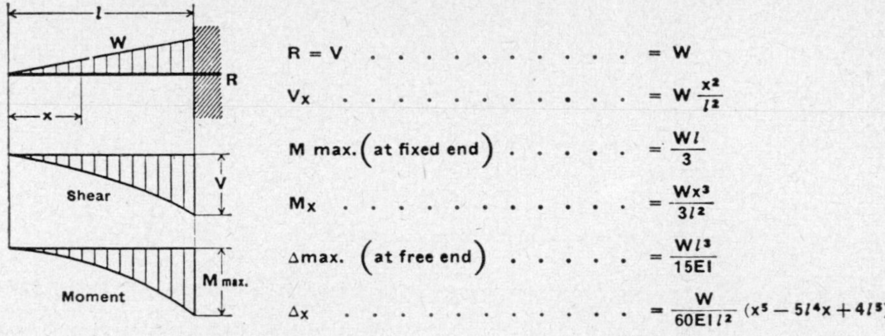

$$R = V \quad \dots\dots \quad = W$$

$$V_x \quad \dots\dots \quad = W\frac{x^2}{l^2}$$

$$M\ \text{max.}\left(\text{at fixed end}\right) \quad \dots\dots \quad = \frac{Wl}{3}$$

$$M_x \quad \dots\dots \quad = \frac{Wx^3}{3l^2}$$

$$\Delta\text{max.}\ \left(\text{at free end}\right) \quad \dots\dots \quad = \frac{Wl^3}{15EI}$$

$$\Delta x \quad \dots\dots \quad = \frac{W}{60EIl^2}(x^5 - 5l^4x + 4l^5)$$

24. CANTILEVER BEAM—UNIFORMLY DISTRIBUTED LOAD

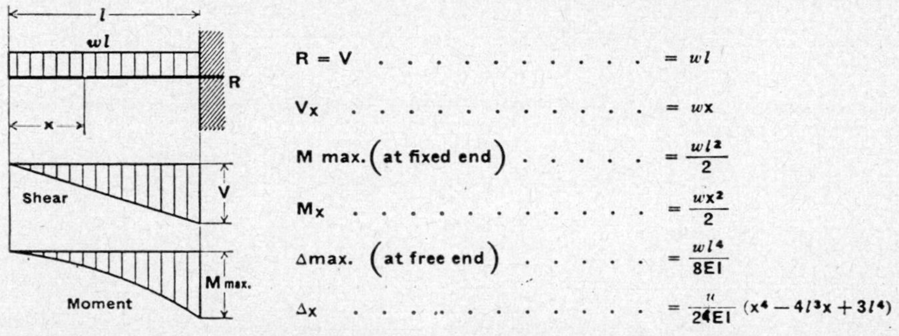

$$R = V \quad \dots\dots \quad = wl$$

$$V_x \quad \dots\dots \quad = wx$$

$$M\ \text{max.}\left(\text{at fixed end}\right) \quad \dots\dots \quad = \frac{wl^2}{2}$$

$$M_x \quad \dots\dots \quad = \frac{wx^2}{2}$$

$$\Delta\text{max.}\ \left(\text{at free end}\right) \quad \dots\dots \quad = \frac{wl^4}{8EI}$$

$$\Delta x \quad \dots\dots \quad = \frac{w}{24EI}(x^4 - 4l^3x + 3l^4)$$

25. BEAM FIXED AT ONE END, FREE BUT GUIDED AT OTHER—UNIFORMLY DISTRIBUTED LOAD

The deflection at the guided end is assumed to be in a vertical plane.

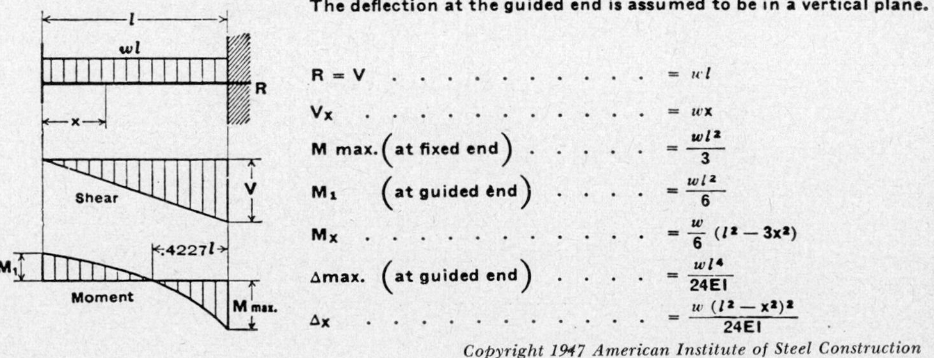

$$R = V \quad \dots\dots \quad = wl$$

$$V_x \quad \dots\dots \quad = wx$$

$$M\ \text{max.}\left(\text{at fixed end}\right) \quad \dots\dots \quad = \frac{wl^2}{3}$$

$$M_1\ \left(\text{at guided end}\right) \quad \dots\dots \quad = \frac{wl^2}{6}$$

$$M_x \quad \dots\dots \quad = \frac{w}{6}(l^2 - 3x^2)$$

$$\Delta\text{max.}\ \left(\text{at guided end}\right) \quad \dots\dots \quad = \frac{wl^4}{24EI}$$

$$\Delta x \quad \dots\dots \quad = \frac{w\,(l^2 - x^2)^2}{24EI}$$

Fig. 12.2 Beam diagrams and formulas, static loading (Cont.)

26. CANTILEVER BEAM—CONCENTRATED LOAD AT ANY POINT

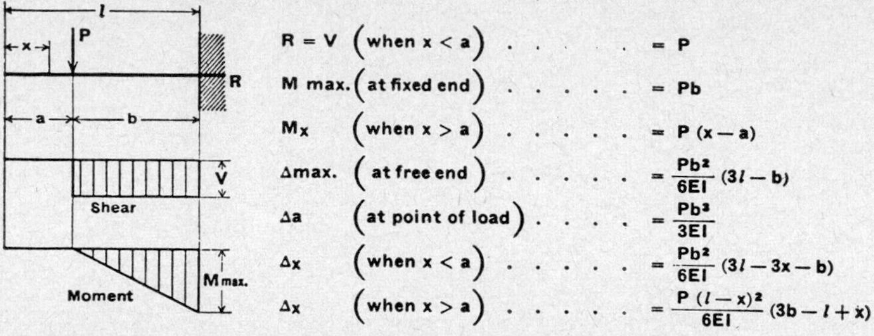

$R = V$ (when $x < a$) . . . . . . $= P$

M max. (at fixed end) . . . . . $= Pb$

M_x (when $x > a$) . . . . . $= P(x - a)$

Δmax. (at free end) . . . . . $= \dfrac{Pb^2}{6EI}(3l - b)$

Δa (at point of load) . . . . $= \dfrac{Pb^3}{3EI}$

Δx (when $x < a$) . . . . . $= \dfrac{Pb^2}{6EI}(3l - 3x - b)$

Δx (when $x > a$) . . . . . $= \dfrac{P(l - x)^2}{6EI}(3b - l + x)$

27. CANTILEVER BEAM—CONCENTRATED LOAD AT FREE END

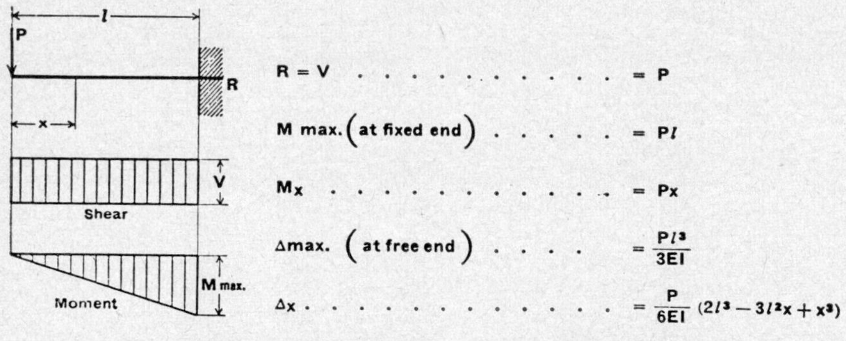

$R = V$ . . . . $= P$

M max. (at fixed end) . . . . . $= Pl$

M_x . . . . $= Px$

Δmax. (at free end) . . . . $= \dfrac{Pl^3}{3EI}$

Δx . . . . $= \dfrac{P}{6EI}(2l^3 - 3l^2x + x^3)$

28. BEAM FIXED AT ONE END, FREE BUT GUIDED AT OTHER—CONCENTRATED LOAD AT GUIDED END

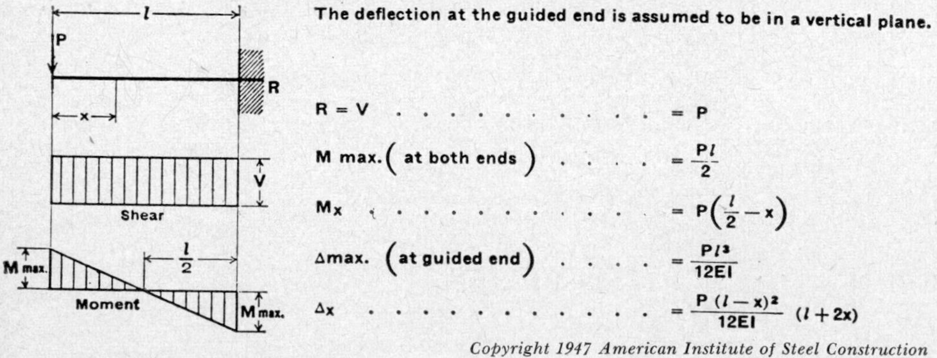

The deflection at the guided end is assumed to be in a vertical plane.

$R = V$ . . . . $= P$

M max. (at both ends) . . . . $= \dfrac{Pl}{2}$

M_x . . . . $= P\left(\dfrac{l}{2} - x\right)$

Δmax. (at guided end) . . . . $= \dfrac{Pl^3}{12EI}$

Δx . . . . $= \dfrac{P(l - x)^2}{12EI}(l + 2x)$

Fig. 12.2 Beam diagrams and formulas, static loading (Cont.)

29. BEAM FIXED AT ONE END, SUPPORTED AT OTHER— CONCENTRATED LOAD AT CENTER

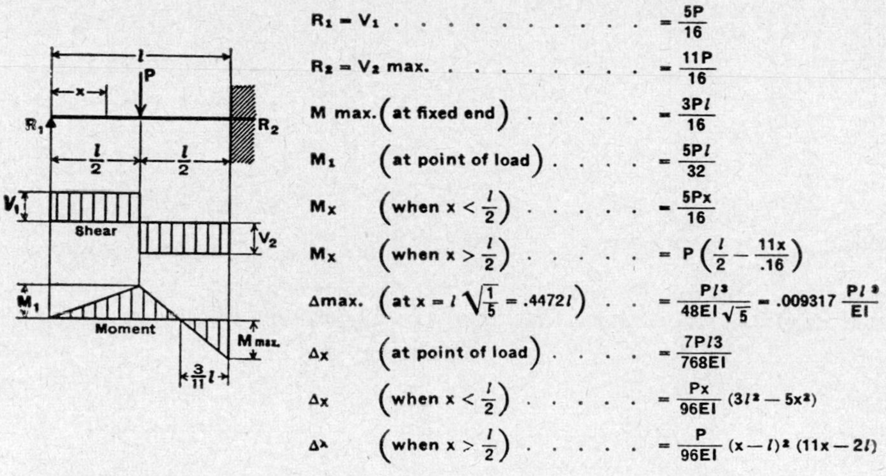

$R_1 = V_1 \ldots = \frac{5P}{16}$

$R_2 = V_2$ max. $\ldots = \frac{11P}{16}$

M max. (at fixed end) $\ldots = \frac{3Pl}{16}$

M_1 (at point of load) $\ldots = \frac{5Pl}{32}$

M_x $\left(\text{when } x < \frac{l}{2}\right) \ldots = \frac{5Px}{16}$

M_x $\left(\text{when } x > \frac{l}{2}\right) \ldots = P\left(\frac{l}{2} - \frac{11x}{16}\right)$

Δmax. $\left(\text{at } x = l\sqrt{\frac{1}{5}} = .4472l\right) \ldots = \frac{Pl^3}{48EI\sqrt{5}} = .009317\,\frac{Pl^3}{EI}$

Δx (at point of load) $\ldots = \frac{7Pl^3}{768EI}$

Δx $\left(\text{when } x < \frac{l}{2}\right) \ldots = \frac{Px}{96EI}(3l^2 - 5x^2)$

Δx $\left(\text{when } x > \frac{l}{2}\right) \ldots = \frac{P}{96EI}(x - l)^2(11x - 2l)$

30. BEAM FIXED AT ONE END, SUPPORTED AT OTHER— CONCENTRATED LOAD AT ANY POINT

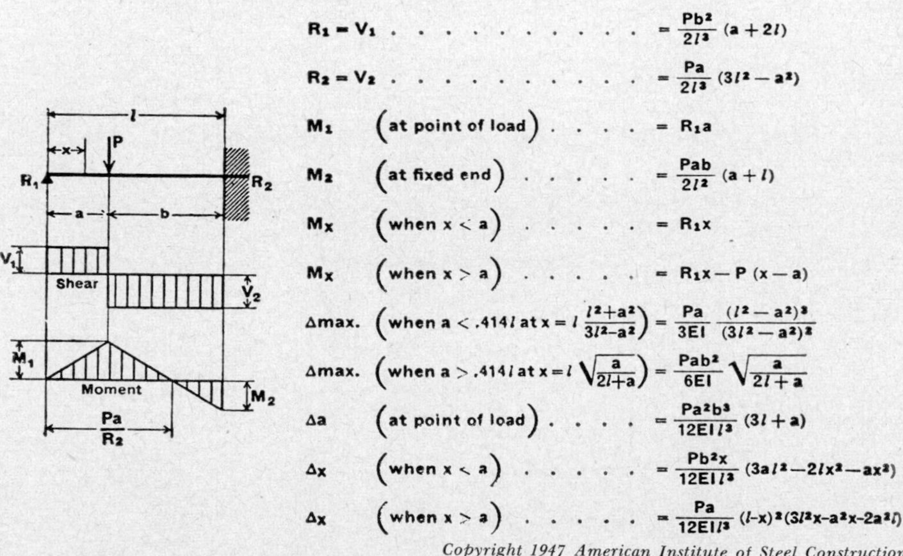

$R_1 = V_1 \ldots = \frac{Pb^2}{2l^3}(a + 2l)$

$R_2 = V_2 \ldots = \frac{Pa}{2l^3}(3l^2 - a^2)$

M_1 (at point of load) $\ldots = R_1 a$

M_2 (at fixed end) $\ldots = \frac{Pab}{2l^2}(a + l)$

M_x (when $x < a$) $\ldots = R_1 x$

M_x (when $x > a$) $\ldots = R_1 x - P(x - a)$

Δmax. $\left(\text{when } a < .414l \text{ at } x = l\,\frac{l^2 + a^2}{3l^2 - a^2}\right) = \frac{Pa}{3EI}\,\frac{(l^2 - a^2)^3}{(3l^2 - a^2)^2}$

Δmax. $\left(\text{when } a > .414l \text{ at } x = l\sqrt{\frac{a}{2l + a}}\right) = \frac{Pab^2}{6EI}\sqrt{\frac{a}{2l + a}}$

Δa (at point of load) $\ldots = \frac{Pa^2b^3}{12EIl^3}(3l + a)$

Δx (when $x < a$) $\ldots = \frac{Pb^2x}{12EIl^3}(3al^2 - 2lx^2 - ax^2)$

Δx (when $x > a$) $\ldots = \frac{Pa}{12EIl^3}(l - x)^2(3l^2x - a^2x - 2a^2l)$

Fig. 12.2 Beam diagrams and formulas, static loading (Cont.)

31. BEAM FIXED AT BOTH ENDS—UNIFORMLY DISTRIBUTED LOADS

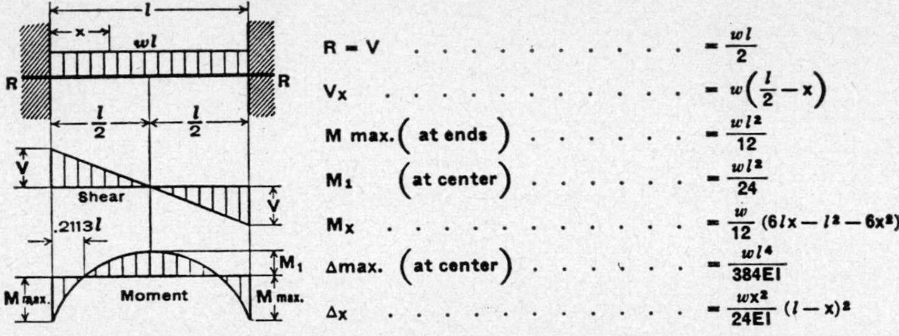

32. BEAM FIXED AT BOTH ENDS—CONCENTRATED LOAD AT CENTER

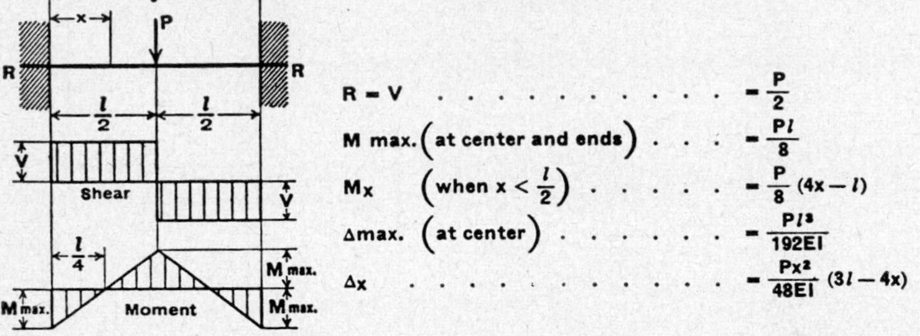

33. BEAM FIXED AT BOTH ENDS—CONCENTRATED LOAD AT ANY POINT

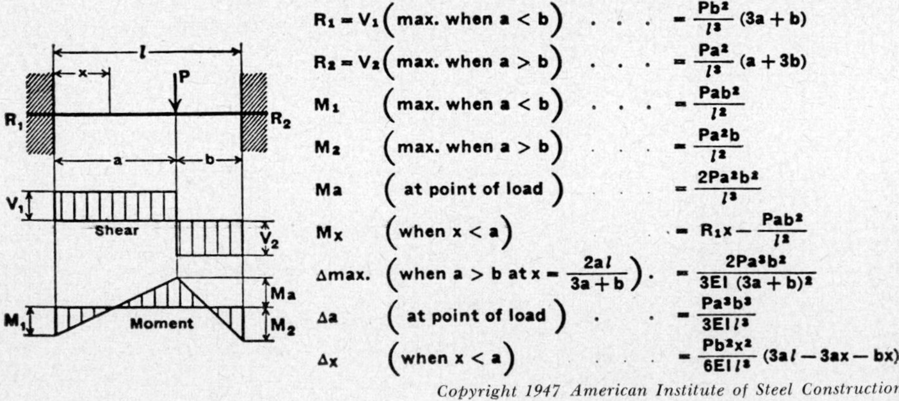

Fig. 12.2 Beam diagrams and formulas, static loading (Cont.)

1. SIMPLE BEAM—ONE CONCENTRATED MOVING LOAD

R_1 max. = V_1 max. (at x = o) . . . . $= P$

M max. $\left(\text{at point of load, when } x = \frac{l}{2}\right)$. $= \frac{Pl}{4}$

---

2. SIMPLE BEAM—TWO EQUAL CONCENTRATED MOVING LOADS

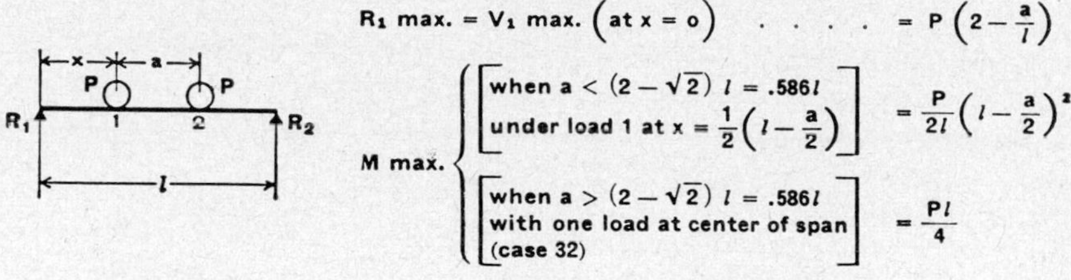

---

3. SIMPLE BEAM—TWO UNEQUAL CONCENTRATED MOVING LOADS

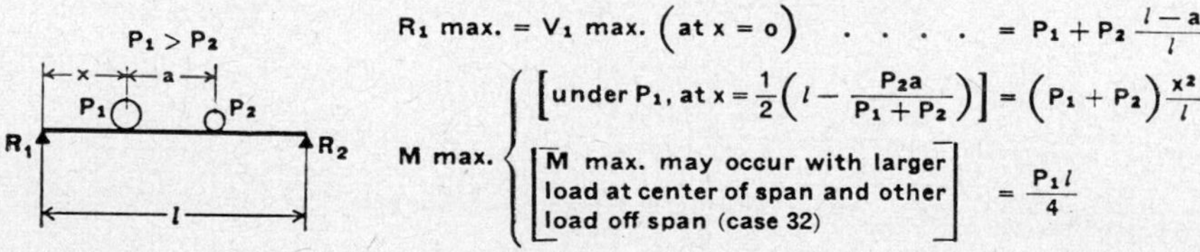

GENERAL RULES

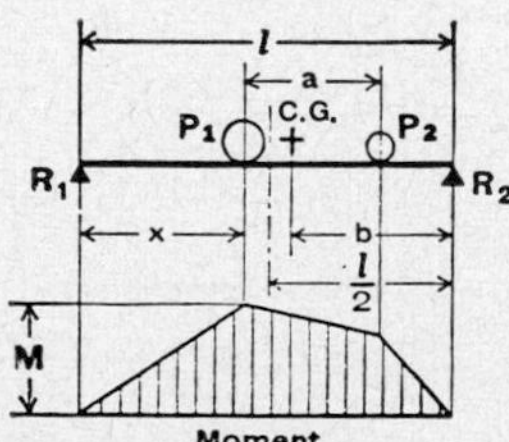

The maximum shear due to moving concentrated loads occurs at one support when one of the loads is at that support. With several moving loads, the location that will produce maximum shear must be determined by trial.

The maximum bending moment produced by moving concentrated loads occurs under one of the loads when that load is as far from one support as the center of gravity of all the moving loads on the beam is from the other support.

In the accompanying diagram, the maximum bending moment occurs under load P_1 when $x = b$. It should also be noted that this condition occurs when the center line of the span is midway between the center of gravity of loads and the nearest concentrated load.

Fig. 12.3 Beam diagrams and formulas, moving loads

L MAXIMUM SPANS FOR JOISTS AND RAFTERS

To determine the maximum safe span for a joist or rafter from Tables 12.10-12.26, first ascertain the allowable working stress for the species and grade of lumber being used by referring to the local building code or other proper authority. Then, in the table for the live load to be supported and opposite the required size of joist and spacing on centers, the maximum allowable span may be found under the column headed by the allowable working stress.

Spans may be governed by deflection, bending strength, or shear.

SPANS LIMITED BY DEFLECTION The span lengths under the column heading "Limited by deflection" were computed for a deflection caused by the assumed loads and not exceeding 1/360 of the span length. This is the limit usually chosen to prevent cracking, for example, in ceilings covered with some hard, inelastic material such as plaster. The weight of the plaster itself was ignored in the assumed loads for the deflection computations because the initial deflection from the dead load occurs before the plaster sets. If the ratio of live to dead loads is relatively high, the influence of the live loads, rather than the dead loads, is the principal factor to be considered. Also, with joisted floors, the flooring and the bridging be ween the joists serve to distribute moving or concentrated loads to adjoining members. The omission of the plaster weight in the load assumptions applies to deflection computations only; the full dead and live load is considered when computing for strength.

SPANS LIMITED BY BENDING The span lengths under the column heading "Determined by bending" may be used if ceilings are not plastered and deflection is not specifically l mited.

SPANS LIMITED BY HORIZONTAL SHEAR For the heavier loads for which horizontal shear may be a factor, the tables give the horizontal shear, *H*, induced by the load or each beam for the spans shown. If the horizontal shear shown in the tables is greater than that permitted for the material used another size joist or spacing should be selected within the proper shear limit. The latest recommendations of the Forest Products Laboratory were used in the horizontal shear computations.

DEAD LOAD ASSUMPTIONS The following average weights of various materials were used as the basis for the dead loads in computing the span lengths in the tables:

Finished floor	2.5 psf
Rough floor	2.5 psf
Roof sheathing	2.5 psf
Plaster and lath	10.0 psf
Roof coverings	
Group I (Assumed as 2.5 psf):	
Shingles	2.5 psf
Copper sheets	1.5 psf
Copper tile	1.75 psf
Three-ply ready roofing	1.00 psf
Group II (Assumed as 8 psf):	
Five-ply felt and gravel	7 psf
Slate, 3/16 in.	7¼ psf
Roman tile	8 psf
Spanish tile	8 psf
Ludowici tile	8 psf
Joists (Assumed as average weight of wood)	40 lb per cu ft

LIVE LOAD ASSUMPTIONS Live loads were assumed to be uniformly distributed.

PARTITIONS Spans shown in these tables were computed for the given live load plus the dead load and do not provide for additional loads such as partitions. If concentrated loads are imposed, the spans should be recomputed to provide for them.

TABLE 12.10 Maximum spans for ceil ng and attic-floor joists

Size of joists nominal *in.*	Spacing of joists center-to-center *in.*	Maximum allowable lengths, *L*, between supports				
		Span limited by deflection				
		E	1,000,000	1,210,000	1,540,000	1,760,000
CEILING JOISTS [1]						
			ft—in.			
2 × 4	12	*L*	9—4	10—0	10—10	11—4
	16	*L*	8—7	9—2	9—11	10—5
	24	*L*	7—7	8—1	8—10	9—2
2 × 6	12	*L*	14—2	15—1	16—5	17—2
	16	*L*	13—1	14—0	15—2	15—10
	24	*L*	11—8	12—5	13—6	14—1
2 × 8	12	*L*	18—6	19—8	21—4	22—4
	16	*L*	17—2	18—4	19—10	20—9
	24	*L*	15—4	16—4	17—9	18—6
2 × 10	12	*L*	22—11	24—5	26—6	27—8
	16	*L*	21—5	22—9	24—8	25—10
	24	*L*	19—2	20—6	22—2	23—2
2 × 12	12	*L*	27—2	28—11	31—5	32—10
	16	*L*	25—5	27—1	29—5	30—9
	24	*L*	23—0	24—6	26—6	27—9

[1] The span lengths are based on:
Maximum allowable deflection of 1/360 of the span length
Modulus of elasticity as noted for *E*
Dead load—Weight of joists plus plaster ceiling (10 psf)
Live load—None

TABLE 12.10 Maximum spans for ceiling and attic-floor joists (Cont.)

Size of joists nominal *in.*	Spacing of joists center-to-center *in.*	Maximum allowable lengths, *L*, between supports				
		Span limited by deflection				
		E	1,000,000	1,210,000	1,540,000	1,760,000
ATTIC—FLOOR JOISTS [2]						
			ft—in.			
2 × 4	12	*L*	6—6	7—0	7—7	7—11
	16	*L*	6—0	6—4	6—11	7—3
	24	*L*	5—3	5—7	6—0	6—4
2 × 6	12	*L*	10—1	10—9	11—8	12—2
	16	*L*	9—2	9—10	10—7	11—1
	24	*L*	8—1	8—7	9—4	9—9
2 × 8	12	*L*	13—4	14—2	15—4	16—1
	16	*L*	12—2	13—0	14—1	14—9
	24	*L*	10—9	11—5	12—5	13—0
2 × 10	12	*L*	16—9	17—10	19—4	20—2
	16	*L*	15—4	16—4	17—9	18—6
	24	*L*	13—6	14—5	15—8	16—4
2 × 12	12	*L*	20—1	21—5	23—2	24—3
	16	*L*	18—6	19—8	21—4	22—3
	24	*L*	16—4	17—5	18—10	19—8

[2] The span lengths are based on:
Maximum allowable deflection of 1/360 of the span length
Modulus of elasticity as noted for *E*
Dead load—Weight of joist
Weight of lath and plaster ceiling (10 psf)
Single thickness of flooring (2.5 psf)
Live load—20 psf of floor area

TABLE 12.11 Maximum spans for floor joists; live load 30 psf, uniformly distributed

Size of joists (nominal) in.	Spacing of joists center-to-center in.	Maximum allowable lengths, L, between supports											
		Span limited by deflection [1]					Span determined by bending [2]						
		E	1,000,000	1,210,000	1,540,000	1,760,000	f	1,000	1,100	1,450	1,700	1,900	2,150
			ft—in.					ft—in.					
2 × 6	12	L	9—10	10—5	11—4	11—11	L	11—0	11—6	13—2	14—4	15—1	16—1
	16	L	9—0	9—6	10—5	10—10	L	9—7	10—0	11—6	12—6	13—2	14—0
	24	L	7—11	8—5	9—1	9—6	L	7—10	8—3	9—6	10—3	10—10	11—6
2 × 8	12	L	13—0	13—10	15—0	15—9	L	14—6	15—2	17—5	18—11	20—0	21—3
	16	L	11—11	12—8	13—9	14—5	L	12—8	13—3	15—3	16—6	17—5	18—7
	24	L	10—6	11—2	12—1	12—8	L	10—5	10—11	12—7	13—7	14—4	15—3
2 × 10	12	L	16—4	17—5	18—11	19—9	L	18—2	19—1	21—11	23—8	25—1	26—8
	16	L	15—0	16—0	17—4	18—1	L	15—11	16—8	19—2	20—9	21—11	23—4
	24	L	13—3	14—1	15—3	16—0	L	13—2	13—9	15—10	17—2	18—1	19—3
2 × 12	12	L	19—8	20—11	22—8	23—9	L	21—10	22—11	26—3	28—5	30—1	32—0
	16	L	18—1	19—3	20—10	21—9	L	19—2	20—1	23—1	24—11	26—5	28—1
	24	L	15—11	17—0	18—5	19—3	L	15—10	16—7	19—1	20—8	21—10	23—3
2 × 14	12	L	22—11	24—5	26—5	27—8	L	25—5	26—7	30—7	33—1	35—0	37—3
	16	L	21—1	22—5	24—4	25—5	L	22—4	23—5	26—10	29—1	30—9	32—9
	24	L	18—8	19—10	21—6	22—6	L	18—6	19—5	22—4	24—2	25—6	27—2
3 × 6	12	L	11—5	12—2	13—2	13—9	L	13—9	14—5	16—6	17—10	18—11	20—1
	16	L	10—5	11—1	12—0	12—7	L	12—0	12—7	14—5	15—8	16—6	17—7
	24	L	9—2	9—10	10—7	11—1	L	9—11	10—4	11—11	12—11	13—8	14—6
3 × 8	12	L	15—0	16—0	17—4	18—1	L	18—0	18—11	21—9	23—6	24—10	26—5
	16	L	13—9	14—8	15—11	16—8	L	15—10	16—7	19—1	20—8	21—10	23—3
	24	L	12—2	13—0	14—1	14—9	L	13—1	13—9	15—9	17—1	18—1	19—3

TABLE 12.11 Maximum spans for floor joists; live load 30 psf, uniformly distributed (Cont.)

Size of joists (nominal)	Spacing of joists center-to-center	Maximum allowable lengths, L, between supports											
		Span limited by deflection [1]					Span determined by bending [2]						
		E	1,000,000	1,210,000	1,540,000	1,760,000	f	1,000	1,100	1,450	1,700	1,900	2,150
in.	*in.*		*ft—in.*					*ft—in.*					
3 × 10	12	L	18—9	20—0	21—8	22—8	L	22—6	23—7	27—2	29—4	31—1	33—0
	16	L	17—4	18—5	20—0	20—11	L	19—10	20—10	23—11	25—10	27—4	29—1
	24	L	15—4	16—4	17—9	18—6	L	16—6	17—3	19—10	21—6	22—9	24—2
3 × 12	12	L	22—6	23—11	25—11	27—2	L	26—11	28—2	32—5	35—1	37—1	39—5
	16	L	20—9	22—1	24—0	25—1	L	23—9	24—11	28—7	31—0	32—9	34—10
	24	L	18—6	19—8	21—4	22—3	L	19—10	20—9	23—10	25—10	27—4	29—0

[1] Maximum allowable deflection of 1/360 of the span length
Modulus of elasticity as noted for E
Dead load—Weight of joist
Double thickness of flooring (5 psf)
Weight of plaster ceiling ignored
Live load—30 psf with plastered ceiling

[2] Allowable stress in extreme fiber in bending as noted for f
Dead load—Weight of joist
Double thickness of flooring (5 psf)
Plastered ceiling (10 psf)
Live load—30 psf with plastered ceiling
40 psf with unplastered ceiling

TABLE 12.12 Maximum spans for floor joists; live load 40 psf

Size of joists (nominal)	Spacing of joists center-to-center	Maximum allowable lengths, L, between supports											
		Span limited by deflection [1]					Span determined by bending [2]						
		E	1,000,000	1,210,000	1,540,000	1,760,000	f	1,000	1,100	1,450	1,700	1,900	2,150
in.	*in.*		*ft—in.*					*ft—in.*					
2 × 6	12	*L*	9—1	9—8	10—6	11—0	*L*	10—0	10—5	12—0	13—0	13—9	14—7
	16	*L*	8—4	8—10	9—7	10—0	*L*	8—8	9—1	10—6	11—4	12—0	12—9
	24	*L*	7—3	7—9	8—5	8—9	*L*	7—2	7—6	8—7	9—3	9—10	10—6
2 × 8	12	*L*	12—1	12—10	13—11	14—7	*L*	13—2	13—10	15—7	17—2	18—2	19—4
	16	*L*	11—0	11—9	12—9	13—3	*L*	11—6	12—1	13—10	15—0	15—10	16—10
	24	*L*	9—8	10—4	11—2	11—8	*L*	9—6	9—11	11—5	12—4	13—1	13—11
2 × 10	12	*L*	15—2	16—2	17—6	18—4	*L*	16—7	17—5	20—0	21—7	22—10	24—4
	16	*L*	13—11	14—9	16—0	16—9	*L*	14—6	15—2	17—5	18—11	20—0	21—3
	24	*L*	12—3	13—0	14—1	14—9	*L*	11—11	12—6	14—4	15—7	16—5	17—6
2 × 12	12	*L*	18—4	19—5	21—1	22—0	*L*	19—11	20—11	24—0	26—0	27—6	29—3
	16	*L*	16—9	17—10	19—4	20—2	*L*	17—5	18—3	21—0	22—9	24—1	25—7
	24	*L*	14—9	15—9	17—0	17—10	*L*	14—5	15—1	17—4	18—9	19—10	21—1
2 × 14	12	*L*	21—4	22—8	24—7	25—9	*L*	23—3	24—4	28—0	30—3	32—0	34—1
	16	*L*	19—7	20—10	22—7	23—7	*L*	20—4	21—4	24—6	26—6	28—1	29—10
	24	*L*	17—3	18—5	19—11	20—10	*L*	16—10	17—8	20—3	21—11	23—3	24—8
3 × 6	12	*L*	10—7	11—3	12—2	12—9	*L*	12—6	13—1	15—1	16—3	17—3	18—4
	16	*L*	9—8	10—3	11—2	11—8	*L*	10—11	11—5	13—2	14—3	15—1	16—0
	24	*L*	8—6	9—1	9—10	10—3	*L*	9—0	9—5	10—10	11—9	12—5	13—2
3 × 8	12	*L*	13—11	14—10	16—1	16—10	*L*	16—6	17—3	19—10	21—6	22—9	24—2
	16	*L*	12—9	13—7	14—9	15—5	*L*	14—5	15—2	17—5	18—10	19—11	21—2
	24	*L*	11—3	12—0	13—0	13—7	*L*	11—11	12—6	14—4	15—6	16—5	17—6

TABLE 12.12 Maximim spans for floor joists; live load 40 psf (Cont.)

Size of joists (nominal) in.	Spacing of joists center-to-center in.	Maximum allowable lengths, L, between supports											
		Span limited by deflection [1]					Span determined by bending [2]						
		E	1,000,000	1,210,000	1,540,000	1,760,000	f	1,000	1,100	1,450	1,700	1,900	2,150
			ft—in.					*ft—in.*					
3 × 10	12	L	17—5	18—8	20—2	21—1	L	20—7	21—8	24—10	26—11	28—5	30—3
	16	L	16—1	17—1	18—7	19—5	L	18—1	19—0	21—10	23—7	25—0	26—7
	24	L	14—3	15—2	16—5	17—2	L	15—0	15—9	18—1	19—7	20—8	22—0
3 × 12	12	L	21—0	22—4	24—11	25—4	L	24—8	25—10	29—9	32—2	34—0	36—2
	16	L	19—4	20—7	22—4	23—4	L	21—9	22—9	26—2	28—4	30—0	31—11
	24	L	17—1	18—3	19—9	20—8	L	18—0	18—11	21—9	23—6	24—11	26—6

[1] Maximum allowable deflection of 1/360 of the span length
Modulus of elasticity as noted for E
Dead load—Weight of joist
Double thickness of flooring (5 lb)
Weight of plaster ceiling ignored
Live load—50 psf with plastered ceiling

[2] Allowable stress in extreme fiber in bending as noted for f
Dead load—Weight of joist
Double thickness of flooring (5 lb)
Plastered ceiling (10 lb)
Live load—50 psf with plastered ceiling
60 psf with unplastered ceiling

TABLE 12.13 Maximum spans for floor joists; live load 50 psf

Size of joists (nominal) in.	Spacing of joists center-to-center in.	Maximum allowable lengths, L, between supports											
		Span limited by deflection [1]					Span determined by bending [2]						
		E	1,000,000	1,210,000	1,540,000	1,760,000	f	1,000	1,100	1,450	1,700	1,900	2,150
			ft—in.					ft—in.					
2 × 6	12	L	8—6	9—1	9—10	10—4	L	9—2	9—8	11—1	12—0	12—8	13—6
	16	L	7—9	8—3	9—0	9—5	L	8—0	8—5	9—8	10—5	11—0	11—9
	24	L	6—10	7—3	7—11	8—3	L	6—7	6—11	7—11	8—7	9—1	9—8
2 × 8	12	L	11—4	12—1	13—1	13—8	L	12—2	12—9	14—8	15—11	16—10	17—10
	16	L	10—4	11—0	11—11	12—6	L	10—7	11—2	12—9	13—10	14—8	15—7
	24	L	9—1	9—8	10—6	10—11	L	8—9	9—2	10—6	11—4	12—0	12—9
2 × 10	12	L	14—3	15—2	16—6	17—3	L	15—4	16—1	18—6	20—0	21—2	22—6
	16	L	13—0	13—11	15—1	15—9	L	13—5	14—0	16—1	17—5	18—5	19—8
	24	L	11—6	12—3	13—3	13—10	L	11—0	11—7	13—3	14—4	15—2	16—2
2 × 12	12	L	17—2	18—4	19—10	20—9	L	18—5	19—4	22—3	24—1	25—5	27—1
	16	L	15—9	16—9	18—2	19—0	L	16—1	16—11	19—5	21—0	22—3	23—8
	24	L	13—10	14—9	16—0	16—9	L	13—3	13—11	16—0	17—4	18—4	19—6
2 × 14	12	L	20—1	21—5	23—2	24—3	L	21—6	22—7	25—11	28—1	29—8	31—7
	16	L	18—5	19—7	21—3	22—2	L	18—10	19—9	22—8	24—7	26—0	27—7
	24	L	16—2	17—3	18—9	19—7	L	15—7	16—4	18—9	20—3	21—5	22—10
3 × 6	12	L	9—11	10—7	11—6	12—0	L	11—7	12—1	13—11	15—1	15—11	17—0
	16	L	9—1	9—8	10—6	10—11	L	10—1	10—7	12—2	13—2	13—11	14—9
	24	L	8—0	8—6	9—2	9—7	L	8—3	8—8	10—0	10—10	11—5	12—2
3 × 8	12	L	13—1	14—0	15—2	15—10	L	15—3	16—0	18—5	19—11	21—0	22—5
	16	L	12—0	12—10	13—11	14—6	L	13—4	4—0	16—1	17—5	18—5	19—7
	24	L	10—7	11—3	12—3	12—9	L	11—0	11—6	13—3	14—4	15—2	16—2

TABLE 12.13 Maximum spans for floor joists; live load 50 psf (Cont.)

Size of joists (nominal) in.	Spacing of joists center-to-center in.	Maximum allowable lengths, L, between supports												
		Span limited by deflection [1]					Span determined by bending [2]							
		E	1,000,000	1,210,000	1,540,000	1,760,000	f	1,000	1,100	1,450	1,700	1,900	2,150
			ft—in.					ft—in.					
3 × 10	12	L	16—6	17—7	19—1	19—11	L	19—2	20—1	23—0	24—11	26—5	28—1
	16	L	15—2	16—1	17—6	18—3	L	16—9	17—7	20—2	21—10	23—2	24—7
	24	L	13—4	14—3	15—5	16—1	L	13—10	14—6	16—8	18—1	19—1	20—4
3 × 12	12	L	19—10	21—1	22—11	23—11	L	22—11	24—0	27—7	29—11	31—7	33—7
	16	L	18—2	19—5	21—0	22—0	L	20—2	21—1	24—3	26—3	27—9	29—6
	24	L	16—1	17—2	18—7	19—5	L	16—8	17—6	20—1	21—9	23—0	24—6

[1] Maximum allowable deflection of 1/360 of the span length
Modulus of elasticity as noted for E
Dead load—Weight of joist
Double thickness of flooring (5 lb)
Weight of plaster ceiling ignored
Live load—50 psf with plastered ceiling

[2] Allowable stress in extreme fiber in bending as noted for f
Dead load—Weight of joist
Double thickness of flooring (5 lb)
Plastered ceiling (10 lb)
Live load—50 psf with plastered ceiling
60 psf with unplastered ceiling

TABLE 12.14 Maximum spans for floor joists; live load 60 psf

Size of joists (nominal) in.	Spacing of joists center-to-center in.	Maximum allowable lengths, L, between supports: Span limited by deflection [1]					Span determined by bending [2]						
		E	1,000,000	1,210,000	1,540,000	1,760,000	f	1,000	1,100	1,450	1,700	1,900	2,150
			ft—in.					ft—in.					
2 × 6	12	L	8—1	8—7	9—4	9—9	L	8—7	9—0	10—4	11—2	11—10	12—7
		H	45	49	53	56	H	49	51	60	65	69	74
	16	L	7—4	7—10	8—6	8—11	L	7—6	7—10	9—0	9—9	10—4	11—0
		H	54	58	64	67	H	55	58	68	74	69	84
	24	L	6—6	6—11	7—6	7—10	L	6—1	6—5	7—4	8—0	8—5	9—0
		H	69	74	81	86	H	65	68	80	88	94	110
2 × 8	12	L	10—9	11—5	12—5	13—0	L	11—5	11—11	13—9	14—10	15—8	16—8
		H	46	49	54	57	H	49	52	60	66	70	75
	16	L	9—9	10—5	11—4	11—10	L	9—11	10—5	11—11	12—11	13—8	14—6
		H	54	58	64	67	H	55	58	68	74	79	85
	24	L	8—7	9—2	9—11	10—4	L	8—2	8—6	9—10	10—7	11—3	11—11
		H	69	74	82	86	H	65	69	81	88	94	101
2 × 10	12	L	13—6	14—5	15—8	16—4	L	14—4	15—0	17—3	18—8	19—9	21—0
		H	46	50	54	57	H	49	52	61	66	70	75
	16	L	12—4	13—2	14—3	14—11	L	12—6	13—1	15—1	16—4	17—3	18—4
		H	55	59	64	68	H	55	58	68	75	79	85
	24	L	10—10	11—7	12—6	13—1	L	10—3	10—9	12—4	13—5	14—2	15—1
		H	69	75	82	86	H	65	69	81	88	94	101
2 × 12	12	L	16—4	17—5	18—10	19—8	L	17—3	18—1	20—9	22—6	23—9	25—4
		H	47	50	55	57	H	50	52	61	66	71	75
	16	L	14—11	15—11	17—3	18—0	L	15—1	15—10	18—2	19—8	20—9	22—1
		H	55	59	65	68	H	56	59	69	75	80	85
	24	L	13—1	14—0	15—2	15—10	L	12—5	13—0	14—11	16—2	17—1	18—2
		H	70	75	82	87	H	65	69	81	89	94	101

TABLE 12.14 Maximum spans for floor joists; live load 60 psf (Cont.)

Size of joists (nominal) in.	Spacing of joists center-to-center in.	Maximum allowable lengths, L, between supports											
		Span limited by deflection [1]					Span determined by bending [2]						
		E	1,000,000	1,210,000	1,540,000	1,760,000	f	1,000	1,100	1,450	1,700	1,900	2,150
			ft—in.					*ft—in.*					
2 × 14	12	L	19—1	20—4	22—0	23—0	L	20—2	21—2	24—3	26—3	27—9	29—6
		H	47	50	55	58	H	50	53	61	67	71	76
	16	L	17—6	18—7	20—2	21—1	L	17—7	18—6	21—3	23—0	24—3	25—10
		H	55	60	65	68	H	56	59	69	75	80	86
	24	L	15—4	16—4	17—9	18—7	L	14—6	15—3	17—6	18—11	20—0	21—4
		H	70	75	83	87	H	65	69	81	89	95	102
3 × 6	12	L	9—5	10—0	10—11	11—4	L	10—10	11—4	13—0	14—1	14—11	15—10
		H	34	36	40	42	H	39	42	48	53	56	60
	16	L	8—7	9—2	9—11	10—5	L	9—5	9—10	11—4	12—3	13—0	13—10
		H	40	43	48	50	H	45	47	55	60	64	68
	24	L	7—7	8—1	8—9	9—1	L	7—9	8—1	9—4	10—1	10—8	11—4
		H	52	56	61	64	H	54	57	66	72	77	82
3 × 8	12	L	12—6	13—3	14—5	15—1	L	14—3	15—0	17—2	18—7	19—8	20—11
		H	34	37	40	42	H	40	42	49	53	56	60
	16	L	11—5	12—2	13—2	13—9	L	12—6	13—1	15—0	16—3	17—2	18—3
		H	41	44	48	50	H	45	48	55	60	64	69
	24	L	10—0	10—8	11—7	12—1	L	10—3	10—9	12—4	13—5	14—2	15—1
		H	52	56	62	65	H	54	57	66	72	77	82
3 × 10	12	L	15—8	16—9	18—1	18—11	L	17—11	18—10	21—7	23—4	24—9	26—4
		H	35	37	41	43	H	40	42	49	54	57	61
	16	L	14—4	15—4	16—7	17—4	L	15—8	16—6	18—11	20—6	21—8	23—0
		H	41	44	48	51	H	45	48	56	61	65	69
	24	L	12—8	13—6	14—7	15—3	L	12—11	13—7	15—7	16—11	17—10	19—0
		H	53	57	62	65	H	54	57	67	73	77	83

TABLE 12.14 Maximum spans for floor joists; live load 60 psf (Cont.)

3 × 12	12	*L*	18—10	20—1	21—9	22—9	*L*	21—6	22—7	25—11	28—0	29—8	31—7
		H	35	38	41	43	*H*	41	43	50	54	55	61
	16	*L*	17—4	18—5	20—0	20—11	*L*	18—10	19—9	22—9	24—7	26—0	27—8
		H	42	45	49	51	*H*	46	48	56	61	65	70
	24	*L*	15—3	16—3	17—8	18—5	*L*	15—7	16—4	18—10	20—4	21—6	22—11
		H	53	57	62	66	*H*	54	57	67	73	78	83
4 × 6	12	*L*	10—5	11—1	12—0	12—7	*L*	12—7	13—2	15—2	16—5	17—4	18—5
		H	28	30	33	34	*H*	34	36	42	46	48	52
	16	*L*	9—6	10—2	11—1	11—6	*L*	11—0	11—6	13—3	14—4	15—2	16—1
		H	33	35	39	41	*H*	39	41	47	52	55	59
	24	*L*	8—4	8—11	9—8	10—1	*L*	9—1	9—6	10—11	11—10	12—6	13—3
		H	43	46	50	53	*H*	47	49	57	63	66	71
4 × 8	12	*L*	13—9	14—8	15—11	16—7	*L*	16—7	17—4	19—11	21—7	22—10	24—3
		H	28	31	33	35	*H*	35	37	43	46	49	53
	16	*L*	12—7	13—5	14—7	15—3	*L*	14—6	15—3	17—6	18—11	21—3	21—3
		H	33	36	39	41	*H*	39	41	48	52	59	59
	24	*L*	11—1	11—10	12—10	13—5	*L*	12—0	12—7	14—5	15—8	16—6	17—7
		H	43	46	51	53	*H*	47	50	58	63	67	71
4 × 10	12	*L*	17—3	18—5	19—11	20—10	*L*	20—9	21—9	25—0	27—0	28—7	30—5
		H	29	31	34	35	*H*	35	37	43	47	50	53
	16	*L*	15—10	16—11	18—4	19—2	*L*	18—3	19—1	21—11	23—9	25—1	26—9
		H	34	36	40	42	*H*	39	42	48	53	56	60
	24	*L*	14—0	14—11	16—2	16—11	*L*	15—1	15—10	18—2	19—8	20—10	22—2
		H	44	47	51	54	*H*	47	50	58	63	67	72

[1] Maximum allowable deflection of 1/360 of the span length
Modulus of elasticity as noted for *E*
Dead load—Weight of joist
Double thickness of flooring (5 lb)
Weight of plaster ceiling ignored
Live load— 60 psf with plastered ceiling
Weight of plaster ceiling was included in computing horizontal shear *H* induced by load.

[2] Allowable stress in extreme fiber in bending as noted for *f*
Dead load—Weight of joist
Double thickness of flooring (5 lb)
Plastered ceiling (10 lb)
Live load— 60 psf with plastered ceiling
70 psf with unplastered ceiling
Total load was considered in computing the horizontal shear *H* induced by load.

TABLE 12.15 Maximum spans for floor joists; live load 70 ps`

Size of joists (nominal) in.	Spacing of joists center-to-center in.	Maximum allowable lengths, L, between supports											
		Span limited by deflection [1]					Span determined by bending [2]						
		E	1,000,000	1,210,000	1,540,000	1,760,000	f	1,000	1,100	1,450	1,700	1,900	2,150
			ft—in.					ft—in.					
2 × 6	12	L	7—9	8—3	8—11	9—4	L	8—1	8—6	9—9	10—6	11—2	11—10
		H	48	52	57	60	H	51	54	63	69	73	78
	16	L	7—0	7—6	8—8	8—6	L	7—0	7—4	8—6	9—2	9—8	10—4
		H	58	62	74	72	H	58	61	71	78	83	89
	24	L	6—2	6—7	7—2	7—5	L	5—9	6—0	6—11	7—6	7—11	8—5
		H	74	80	88	92	H	68	72	85	93	99	106
2 × 8	12	L	10—3	10—11	11—11	12—5	L	10—9	11—3	12—11	14—0	14—9	15—9
		H	49	52	58	60	H	51	54	63	69	73	79
	16	L	9—4	10—0	10—10	11—3	L	9—4	9—9	11—3	12—2	12—10	13—8
		H	58	63	69	72	H	58	61	72	78	83	89
	24	L	8—2	8—9	9—6	9—11	L	7—8	8—0	9—3	10—0	10—7	11—3
		H	75	80	88	93	H	69	73	85	93	100	107
2 × 10	12	L	12—11	13—9	15—0	15—7	L	13—6	14—2	16—3	17—7	18—8	19—10
		H	49	53	58	61	H	52	54	64	69	73	79
	16	L	11—10	12—7	13—8	14—3	L	11—9	12—4	14—2	15—4	16—3	17—3
		H	58	63	69	72	H	58	62	72	79	84	90
	24	L	10—4	11—1	12—0	12—6	L	9—8	10—2	11—8	12—7	13—4	14—2
		H	75	81	89	93	H	69	73	86	94	100	107
2 × 12	12	L	15—7	16—8	18—1	18—10	L	16—3	17—1	19—7	21—3	22—5	23—10
		H	50	53	58	61	H	52	55	64	70	74	79
	16	L	14—3	15—2	16—6	17—3	L	14—2	14—10	17—1	18—6	19—7	20—10
		H	59	63	70	73	H	59	62	72	79	84	90
	24	L	12—6	13—4	14—6	15—2	L	11—8	12—3	14—1	15—3	16—1	17—1
		H	75	81	89	93	H	69	73	86	94	100	107

TABLE 12.15 Maximum spans for floor joists; live load 70 psf (Cont.)

2 × 14	12	*L*	18—3	19—6	21—2	22—1	*L*	19—0	19—11	22—11	24—9	26—3	27—11
		H	50	54	59	62	*H*	52	55	64	70	75	80
	16	*L*	16—8	17—9	19—4	20—2	*L*	16—7	17—5	20—0	21—8	22—11	24—4
		H	59	64	70	73	*H*	59	62	73	79	84	90
	24	*L*	14—8	15—8	17—0	17—9	*L*	13—8	14—4	16—6	17—10	18—10	20—1
		H	75	81	89	94	*H*	69	73	86	94	100	108
3 × 6	12	*L*	9—0	9—7	10—5	10—10	*L*	10—2	10—8	12—3	13—3	14—0	14—11
		H	37	39	43	45	*H*	42	44	51	56	60	64
	16	*L*	8—3	8—9	9—6	9—11	*L*	8—10	9—4	10—8	11—7	12—3	13—0
		H	43	46	51	53	*H*	47	49	58	63	67	70
	24	*L*	7—3	7—8	10—4	8—9	*L*	7—3	7—8	8—9	9—6	10—0	10—8
		H	56	60	66	69	*H*	56	60	68	76	81	86
3 × 8	12	*L*	11—11	12—9	13—10	14—5	*L*	13—6	14—1	16—3	17—7	18—7	19—9
		H	37	40	44	46	*H*	42	45	52	57	60	64
	16	*L*	10—11	11—7	12—8	13—2	*L*	11—9	12—4	14—2	15—4	16—2	17—3
		H	43	47	51	54	*H*	47	50	58	63	67	72
	24	*L*	9—7	10—3	11—1	11—7	*L*	9—8	10—2	11—8	12—7	13—4	14—2
		H	56	60	66	69	*H*	57	60	70	76	81	87
3 × 10	12	*L*	15—0	16—0	17—5	18—2	*L*	16—11	17—9	20—5	22—1	23—4	24—10
		H	38	40	44	46	*H*	43	45	52	57	60	65
	16	*L*	13—9	14—8	15—11	16—7	*L*	14—10	15—6	17—10	19—3	20—5	21—9
		H	44	47	52	54	*H*	48	50	58	64	68	72
	24	*L*	12—1	12—11	14—0	14—7	*L*	12—2	12—9	14—8	15—11	16—10	17—11
		H	56	61	67	70	*H*	57	60	70	77	81	87
3 × 12	12	*L*	18—1	19—3	20—11	21—10	*L*	20—4	21—4	24—6	26—6	28—0	29—10
		H	38	41	45	47	*H*	43	45	53	57	61	65
	16	*L*	16—7	17—8	19—2	20—0	*L*	17—10	18—8	21—5	23—3	24—7	26—1
		H	44	47	52	55	*H*	48	50	59	64	68	73
	24	*L*	14—7	15—7	16—11	17—8	*L*	14—8	15—5	17—9	19—2	20—3	21—7
		H	57	61	67	70	*H*	57	60	70	77	82	88

TABLE 12.15 Maximum spans for floor joists; live load 70 psf (Cont.)

Size of joists (nominal) *in.*	Spacing of joists center-to-center *in.*	Maximum allowable lengths, *L*, between supports											
		Span limited by deflection [1]					Span determined by bending [2]						
		E	1,000,000	1,210,000	1,540,000	1,760,000	*f*	1,000	1,100	1,450	1,700	1,900	2,150
			ft—in.					*ft—in.*					
4 × 6	12	*L*	10—0	10—7	11—6	12—0	*L*	11—10	12—5	14—3	15—6	16—4	17—5
		H	30	32	35	37	*H*	37	38	45	49	52	55
	16	*L*	9—1	9—8	10—6	11—0	*L*	10—4	10—10	12—6	13—6	14—3	15—2
		H	36	38	42	44	*H*	41	43	51	55	58	62
	24	*L*	8—0	8—6	9—3	9—8	*L*	8—6	8—11	10—3	11—1	11—9	12—6
		H	46	49	54	57	*H*	49	52	61	66	70	75
4 × 8	12	*L*	13—2	14—0	15—3	15—11	*L*	15—8	16—5	18—10	20—5	21—7	22—11
		H	31	33	36	38	*H*	37	39	45	49	52	56
	16	*L*	12—1	12—10	14—0	14—7	*L*	13—8	14—4	16—6	17—10	18—11	20—1
		H	36	39	43	45	*H*	42	44	51	56	59	63
	24	*L*	10—7	11—4	12—4	12—10	*L*	11—3	11—10	13—7	14—9	15—7	16—7
		H	46	49	54	57	*H*	49	52	61	66	70	75
4 × 10	12	*L*	16—7	17—8	19—2	20—0	*L*	19—7	20—7	23—7	25—7	27—0	28—9
		H	31	33	36	38	*H*	37	39	46	50	53	56
	16	*L*	15—2	16—2	17—7	18—4	*L*	17—2	18—0	20—9	22—5	23—9	25—3
		H	37	39	43	45	*H*	42	44	51	56	59	64
	24	*L*	13—5	14—3	15—6	16—2	*L*	14—3	14—11	17—2	18—7	19—7	20—10
		H	46	50	55	60	*H*	50	52	61	67	71	76

[1] Maximum allowable deflection of 1/360 of the span length
Modulus of elasticity as noted for *E*
Dead load—Weight of joist
Double thickness of flooring (5 lb)
Weight of plaster ceiling ignored
Live load— 70 psf with plastered ceiling
Weight of plaster ceiling was included in computing horizontal shear *H* induced by load.

[2] Allowable stress in extreme fiber in bending as noted for *f*
Dead load—Weight of joist
Double thickness of flooring (5 lb)
Plastered ceiling (10 lb)
Live load— 70 psf with plastered ceiling
80 psf with unplastered ceiling
Total load was considered in computing the horizontal shear *H* induced by load.

TABLE 12.16 Maximum spans for floor joists; live load 80 psf

Size of joists (nominal)	Spacing of joists center-to-center	Maximum allowable lengths, *L*, between supports											
		Span limited by deflection [1]					Span determined by bending [2]						
		E	1,000,000	1,210,000	1,540,000	1,760,000	*f*	1,000	1,100	1,450	1,700	1,900	2,150
in.	*in.*		*ft—in.*					*ft—in.*					
2 × 6	12	*L*	7—5	7—11	8—7	9—0	*L*	7—8	8—0	9—3	10—0	10—7	11—3
		H	52	56	62	65	*H*	54	57	67	72	77	83
	16	*L*	6—9	7—2	7—10	8—2	*L*	6—8	7—0	8—0	8—8	9—2	9—9
		H	62	66	73	76	*H*	60	64	75	82	87	93
2 × 8	12	*L*	9—10	10—6	11—5	11—11	*L*	10—2	10—8	12—3	13—3	14—0	14—11
		H	52	56	61	64	*H*	54	57	66	72	77	82
	16	*L*	9—0	9—7	10—4	10—10	*L*	8—10	9—3	10—8	11—6	12—2	12—11
		H	62	67	73	77	*H*	61	64	75	82	88	94
	24	*L*	7—10	8—5	9—1	9—6	*L*	7—3	7—7	8—9	9—5	10—0	10—8
		H	79	85	93	98	*H*	71	75	89	97	104	112
2 × 10	12	*L*	12—5	13—3	14—4	15—0	*L*	12—10	13—5	15—5	16—8	17—8	18—9
		H	52	56	61	64	*H*	54	57	66	73	77	83
	16	*L*	11—4	12—1	13—1	13—8	*L*	11—2	11—8	13—5	14—6	15—5	16—4
		H	62	67	73	77	*H*	61	64	75	83	88	94
	24	*L*	10—0	10—7	11—6	12—0	*L*	9—2	9—7	11—1	11—11	12—8	13—5
		H	79	85	94	99	*H*	71	76	89	98	104	112
2 × 12	12	*L*	15—0	16—0	17—4	18—1	*L*	15—5	16—2	18—7	20—2	21—3	22—8
		H	52	56	62	65	*H*	54	57	67	73	78	83
	16	*L*	13—9	14—7	15—10	16—7	*L*	13—5	14—1	16—2	17—6	18—7	19—9
		H	63	67	74	78	*H*	61	65	76	83	88	94
	24	*L*	12—0	12—10	13—11	14—6	*L*	11—1	11—7	13—4	14—5	15—3	16—3
		H	79	85	94	99	*H*	72	76	89	98	104	112

TABLE 12.16 Maximum spans for floor joists; live load 80 psf (Cont.)

Size of joists (nominal) in.	Spacing of joists center-to-center in.	Maximum allowable lengths, L, between supports											
		Span limited by deflection [1]					Span determined by bending [2]						
		E	1,000,000	1,210,000	1,540,000	1,760,000	f	1,000	1,100	1,450	1,700	1,900	2,150
			ft—in.					ft—in.					
	12	L	17—7	18—9	20—3	21—2	L	18—0	18—11	21—9	23—6	24—11	26—6
		H	53	57	62	65	H	54	57	67	73	78	83
2 × 14	16	L	16—1	17—1	18—6	19—5	L	15—9	16—6	19—0	20—6	21—9	23—1
		H	63	68	74	78	H	61	65	76	83	89	95
	24	L	14—1	15—0	16—3	17—0	L	12—11	13—7	15—7	16—11	17—10	19—0
		H	80	86	94	99	H	72	76	90	98	105	112
	12	L	8—8	9—3	10—0	10—5	L	9—8	10—1	11—7	12—7	13—4	14—2
		H	39	41	45	48	H	44	46	53	58	62	66
3 × 6	16	L	7—11	8—5	9—1	9—6	L	8—5	8—10	10—1	10—11	11—7	12—4
		H	46	50	55	57	H	50	53	61	67	71	76
	24	L	6—11	7—4	8—0	8—4	L	6—11	7—3	8—4	9—0	9—6	10—1
		H	59	64	70	73	H	59	62	73	80	85	91
	12	L	11—6	12—3	13—3	13—10	L	12—9	13—5	15—5	16—8	17—7	18—9
		H	39	42	46	48	H	44	46	54	59	62	67
3 × 8	16	L	10—6	11—2	12—1	12—8	L	11—2	11—8	13—5	14—6	15—4	16—9
		H	47	50	55	58	H	50	53	62	67	71	76
	24	L	9—2	9—10	10—7	11—1	L	9—2	9—7	11—0	11—11	12—8	13—5
		H	60	64	70	74	H	59	63	73	80	85	91
	12	L	14—6	15—5	16—8	17—6	L	16—1	16—10	19—4	20—11	22—2	23—7
		H	39	42	46	49	H	44	47	54	59	63	67
3 × 10	16	L	13—3	14—1	15—3	16—0	L	14—0	14—9	16—11	18—4	19—4	20—7
		H	47	51	55	58	H	50	53	62	68	72	77
	24	L	11—7	12—5	13—5	14—0	L	11—7	12—2	13—11	15—1	15—11	17—0
		H	60	64	70	74	H	59	63	73	80	85	91

TABLE 12.16 Maximum spans for floor joists; live load 80 psf (Cont.)

	12	*L*	17—5	18—7	20—1	21—0	*L*	19—4	20—3	23—3	25—2	26—8	28—4
		H	40	43	47	49	*H*	45	47	55	60	63	68
3 × 12	16	*L*	15—11	17—0	18—5	19—3	*L*	16—11	17—9	20—4	22—0	23—4	24—9
		H	48	51	56	59	*H*	51	53	62	68	72	77
	24	*L*	14—0	14—11	16—2	16—11	*L*	13—11	14—7	16—9	18—2	19—3	20—5
		H	60	65	71	75	*H*	60	63	74	81	86	92
	12	*L*	9—7	10—3	11—1	11—7	*L*	11—3	11—10	13—7	14—8	15—6	16—6
		H	32	35	38	40	*H*	39	41	47	51	54	58
4 × 6	16	*L*	8—9	9—4	10—1	10—7	*L*	9—10	10—3	11—10	12—9	13—6	14—5
		H	38	40	44	46	*H*	43	45	53	57	61	65
	24	*L*	7—8	8—2	8—10	9—3	*L*	8—1	8—6	9—9	10—6	11—2	11—10
		H	48	52	57	60	*H*	51	54	63	69	73	78
	12	*L*	12—8	13—6	14—8	15—4	*L*	14—10	15—7	17—11	19—4	20—6	21—10
		H	32	34	37	39	*H*	39	41	47	51	54	58
4 × 8	16	*L*	11—7	12—4	13—5	14—1	*L*	13—0	13—7	15—8	16—11	17—11	19—1
		H	38	41	45	47	*H*	43	45	53	36	61	66
	24	*L*	10—3	10—11	11—9	12—4	*L*	10—9	11—3	12—11	14—0	14—9	15—9
		H	49	52	57	60	*H*	51	54	63	69	74	79
	12	*L*	15—11	17—0	18—5	19—3	*L*	18—8	19—7	22—5	24—4	25—8	27—4
		H	32	35	37	40	*H*	39	41	47	51	55	58
4 × 10	16	*L*	14—8	15—7	16—11	17—8	*L*	16—4	17—2	19—8	21—3	22—6	23—11
		H	38	41	45	47	*H*	43	46	53	58	62	66
	24	*L*	12—11	13—8	14—10	15—6	*L*	13—6	14—2	16—3	17—7	18—7	19—9
		H	49	52	57	60	*H*	52	55	64	70	74	79

[1] Maximum allowable deflection of 1/360 of the span length
Modulus of elasticity as noted for E
Dead load—Weight of joist
Double thickness of flooring (5 lb)
Weight of plaster ceiling ignored
Live load— 80 psf with plastered ceiling
Weight of plaster ceiling was included in computing horizontal shear H induced by load.

[2] Allowable stress in extreme fiber in bending as noted for f
Dead load—Weight of joist
Double thickness of flooring (5 lb)
Plaster ceiling (10 lb)
Live load— 80 psf with plastered ceiling
90 psf with unplastered ceiling
Total load was considered in computing the horizontal shear H induced by load.

TABLE 12.17 Maximum spans for floor joists; live load 90 psf

Size of joists (nominal) in.	Spacing of joists center-to-center in.	Maximum allowable lengths, L, between supports											
		Span limited by deflection [1]					Span determined by bending [2]						
		E	1,000,000	1,210,000	1,540,000	1,760,000	f	1,000	1,100	1,450	1,700	1,900	2,150
			ft—in.					ft—in.					
2 × 6	12	*L*	7—2	7—7	8—3	8—8	*L*	7—3	7—8	8—9	9—6	10—1	10—8
		H	55	59	65	68	*H*	56	59	69	76	81	86
	16	*L*	6—6	6—11	7—6	7—10	*L*	6—4	6—8	7—8	8—3	8—9	9—3
		H	65	70	76	81	*H*	63	67	78	86	91	98
2 × 8	12	*L*	9—6	10—2	11—0	11—6	*L*	9—8	10—2	11—8	12—7	13—4	14—2
		H	55	60	65	69	*H*	57	60	70	76	81	87
	16	*L*	8—8	9—3	10—0	10—6	*L*	8—5	8—10	10—2	11—0	11—7	12—4
		H	65	70	77	81	*H*	63	67	78	86	91	98
2 × 10	12	*L*	12—0	12—10	13—10	14—6	*L*	12—3	12—10	14—9	16—0	16—10	17—11
		H	56	60	66	69	*H*	57	60	70	77	81	87
	16	*L*	10—11	11—8	12—8	13—3	*L*	10—8	11—2	12—10	13—10	14—8	15—7
		H	66	71	78	82	*H*	63	67	79	86	92	98
	24	*L*	9—7	10—3	11—1	11—7	*L*	8—9	9—2	10—6	11—4	12—0	12—9
		H	84	90	99	105	*H*	74	79	93	102	109	117
2 × 12	12	*L*	14—6	15—5	16—9	17—6	*L*	14—9	15—5	17—9	19—2	20—4	21—7
		H	56	60	66	69	*H*	57	60	70	77	82	87
	16	*L*	13—3	14—1	15—3	16—0	*L*	12—10	13—5	15—5	16—9	17—8	18—10
		H	66	71	78	82	*H*	64	67	79	86	92	99
	24	*L*	11—7	12—4	13—5	14—0	*L*	10—6	11—1	12—8	13—9	14—6	15—6
		H	84	91	100	105	*H*	74	79	94	102	109	118

TABLE 12.17 Maximum spans for floor joists; live load 90 psf (Cont.)

Size	Spacing												
2 × 14	12	*L*	17—0	18—1	19—7	20—6	*L*	17—3	18—1	20—9	22—5	23—9	25—3
		H	56	61	66	70	*H*	57	61	71	77	82	88
	16	*L*	15—6	16—6	17—11	18—8	*L*	15—0	15—9	18—1	19—7	20—8	22—0
		H	66	71	78	82	*H*	64	68	79	87	92	99
	24	*L*	13—7	15—6	15—9	16—5	*L*	12—4	12—11	14—10	16—1	17—0	18—1
		H	84	91	100	105	*H*	74	79	94	102	110	118
3 × 6	12	*L*	8—4	8—11	9—8	10—1	*L*	9—2	9—8	11—1	12—0	12—8	13—6
		H	41	44	48	51	*H*	46	48	56	61	65	70
	16	*L*	7—7	8—1	8—9	9—2	*L*	8—0	8—5	9—8	10—5	11—0	11—9
		H	49	52	57	60	*H*	52	54	64	69	74	79
	24	*L*	6—8	7—1	7—8	8—1	*L*	6—7	6—11	7—11	8—7	9—1	9—7
		H	63	67	74	78	*H*	61	65	76	83	88	95
3 × 8	12	*L*	11—1	11—10	12—10	13—5	*L*	12—2	12—9	14—8	15—11	16—10	17—11
		H	42	45	49	51	*H*	46	49	57	62	66	70
	16	*L*	10—1	10—9	11—8	12—3	*L*	10—7	11—2	12—9	13—10	14—8	15—7
		H	49	53	58	61	*H*	52	55	64	70	74	79
	24	*L*	8—11	9—6	10—3	10—9	*L*	8—9	9—2	10—6	11—5	12—0	12—10
		H	63	68	74	78	*H*	62	65	76	83	89	95
3 × 10	12	*L*	14—0	14—11	16—2	16—10	*L*	15—4	16—1	18—6	20—0	21—2	22—6
		H	42	45	49	52	*H*	47	49	57	62	66	71
	16	*L*	12—9	13—7	14—9	15—5	*L*	13—5	14—0	16—1	17—5	18—6	19—8
		H	49	53	58	61	*H*	52	55	64	70	75	80
	24	*L*	11—3	12—0	13—0	13—7	*L*	11—0	11—7	13—3	14—4	15—2	16—2
		H	63	68	75	78	*H*	62	65	77	84	89	95
3 × 12	12	*L*	16—10	17—11	19—5	20—4	*L*	18—5	19—4	22—3	24—1	25—5	27—1
		H	42	46	50	52	*H*	47	49	58	63	67	71
	16	*L*	15—5	16—5	17—9	18—7	*L*	16—1	16—11	19—5	21—0	22—3	23—8
		H	50	53	59	62	*H*	52	55	65	70	75	80
	24	*L*	13—6	14—5	15—8	16—4	*L*	13—3	13—11	16—0	17—4	18—4	19—6
		H	63	68	75	79	*H*	62	66	77	84	89	96

TABLE 12.17 Maximum spans for floor joists; live load 90 psf (Cont.)

Size of joists (nominal) in.	Spacing of joists center-to-center in.	Maximum allowable lengths, L, between supports											
		Span limited by deflection [1]					Span determined by bending [2]						
		E	1,000,000	1,210,000	1,540,000	1,760,000	f	1,000	1,100	1,450	1,700	1,900	2,150
			ft—in.					*ft—in.*					
4 × 6	12	*L*	9—3	9—10	10—8	11—2	*L*	10—9	11—3	12—11	14—0	14—9	15—9
		H	34	36	39	41	*H*	40	42	49	53	56	60
	16	*L*	8—5	9—0	9—9	10—2	*L*	9—4	9—10	11—3	12—2	12—11	13—9
		H	40	43	47	50	*H*	45	48	55	60	64	69
	24	*L*	7—5	7—11	8—7	8—11	*L*	7—8	8—1	9—3	10—0	10—7	11—3
		H	52	56	61	64	*H*	54	57	66	72	77	82
4 × 8	12	*L*	12—3	13—1	14—2	14—9	*L*	14—2	14—11	17—1	18—6	19—7	20—10
		H	34	37	40	42	*H*	40	42	49	53	57	61
	16	*L*	11—2	11—11	12—11	13—6	*L*	12—5	13—0	14—11	16—2	17—1	18—2
		H	41	44	48	50	*H*	45	48	56	61	65	69
	24	*L*	9—10	10—6	11—4	11—11	*L*	10—2	10—8	12—3	13—4	14—1	15—0
		H	52	56	61	64	*H*	54	57	67	73	77	83
4 × 10	12	*L*	15—5	16—5	17—10	18—7	*L*	17—10	18—8	21—5	23—3	25—7	26—2
		H	34	37	40	42	*H*	40	43	50	54	57	61
	16	*L*	14—1	15—1	16—4	17—1	*L*	15—7	16—4	18—9	20—4	21—6	22—10
		H	41	44	48	51	*H*	46	48	56	61	65	70
	24	*L*	12—5	13—3	14—4	15—0	*L*	12—10	13—6	15—6	16—9	17—9	18—11
		H	52	56	62	65	*H*	54	57	67	73	78	83

[1] Maximum allowable deflection of 1/360 of the span length
Modulus of elasticity as noted for E
Dead load—Weight of joist
Double thickness of flooring (5 lb)
Weight of plaster ceiling ignored
Live load— 90 psf with plastered ceiling
Weight of plaster ceiling was included in computing horizontal shear H induced by load.

[2] Allowable stress in extreme fiber in bending as noted for f
Dead load—Weight of joist
Double thickness of flooring (5 lb)
Plastered ceiling (10 lb)
Live load— 90 psf with plastered ceiling
100 psf with unplastered ceiling
Total load was considered in computing the horizontal shear H induced by load.

TABLE 12.18 Maximum spans for floor joists; live load 100 psf

Size of joists (nominal) in.	Spacing of joists center-to-center in.	E	1,000,000	1,210,000	1,540,000	1,760,000	f	1,000	1,100	1,450	1,700	1,900	2,150
			Maximum allowable lengths, L, between supports										
			Span limited by deflection [1]					Span determined by bending [2]					
			ft—in.					ft—in.					
2 × 8	12	L	9—3	9—10	10—8	11—1	L	9—3	9—9	11—2	12—1	12—9	13—7
		H	58	62	69	72	H	58	62	72	79	84	90
	16	L	8—5	8—11	9—8	10—2	L	8—1	8—5	9—8	10—6	11—1	11—10
		H	69	74	81	86	H	66	69	82	89	95	102
2 × 10	12	L	11—8	12—5	13—5	14—0	L	11—8	12—3	14—1	15—3	16—2	17—2
		H	58	63	69	72	H	59	62	73	79	84	90
	16	L	10—7	11—4	12—3	12—10	L	10—2	10—8	12—3	13—3	14—0	14—11
		H	69	74	82	86	H	66	70	82	89	95	102
	24	L	9—3	9—11	10—9	11—3	L	8—4	8—9	10—1	10—10	11—6	12—3
		H	88	95	104	110	H	77	82	96	106	113	121
2 × 12	12	L	14—0	15—0	16—3	16—11	L	14—1	14—9	17—0	18—5	19—5	20—8
		H	59	63	69	73	H	59	62	73	80	85	91
	16	L	12—10	13—8	14—9	15—6	L	12—3	12—11	14—9	16—0	16—11	18—0
		H	69	75	82	86	H	66	70	82	90	96	102
	24	L	11—3	12—0	13—0	13—7	L	10—1	10—7	12—2	13—2	13—11	14—9
		H	88	95	104	110	H	77	82	97	106	113	122
2 × 14	12	L	16—5	17—6	19—0	19—10	L	16—6	17—3	19—10	21—6	22—9	24—2
		H	59	64	70	73	H	59	63	73	80	85	91
	16	L	15—0	16—0	17—4	18—1	L	14—4	15—1	17—4	18—9	19—10	21—1
		H	70	75	82	87	H	66	70	82	90	96	103
	24	L	13—2	14—0	15—3	15—11	L	11—10	12—5	14—3	15—5	16—3	17—4
		H	88	95	105	110	H	77	82	97	106	113	122

TABLE 12.18 Maximum spans for floor josts; live load 100 psf (Cont.)

Size of joists (nominal) *in.*	Spacing of joists center-to-center *in.*	Maximum allowable lengths, *L*, between supports											
		Span limited by deflection [1]					Span determined by bending [2]						
		E	1,000,000	1,210,000	1,540,000	1,760,000	*f*	1,000	1,100	1,450	1,700	1,900	2,150
			ft—in.					*ft—in.*					
3 × 6	12	*L*	8—1	8—7	9—4	9—9	*L*	8—10	9—3	10—7	11—6	12—2	12—11
		H	43	46	50	53	*H*	47	50	58	63	67	72
	16	*L*	7—4	7—10	8—6	8—11	*L*	7—8	8—0	9—3	10—0	10—7	11—3
		H	51	55	60	63	*H*	54	57	66	72	76	82
	24	*L*	6—6	6—11	7—6	7—10	*L*	6—3	6—7	7—7	8—2	8—8	9—3
		H	66	71	78	82	*H*	64	67	79	86	92	99
3 × 8	12	*L*	10—9	11—5	12—5	13—0	*L*	11—8	12—3	14—1	15—3	16—1	17—1
		H	43	47	51	54	*H*	48	50	59	64	68	73
	16	*L*	9—9	10—5	11—4	11—10	*L*	10—2	10—8	12—3	13—3	14—0	14—11
		H	51	55	60	63	*H*	54	57	66	72	77	82
	24	*L*	8—7	9—2	9—11	10—4	*L*	8—4	8—9	10—1	10—11	11—6	12—3
		H	66	71	78	82	*H*	64	68	79	87	92	99
3 × 10	12	*L*	13—6	14—5	15—8	16—4	*L*	14—8	15—5	17—8	19—2	20—3	21—7
		H	44	47	51	54	*H*	48	50	59	64	68	73
	16	*L*	12—4	13—2	14—3	14—11	*L*	12—10	13—5	15—5	16—9	17—8	18—10
		H	52	56	61	64	*H*	54	57	66	73	77	83
	24	*L*	10—10	11—7	12—6	13—1	*L*	10—6	11—1	12—8	13—9	14—6	15—6
		H	66	71	78	82	*H*	64	68	79	87	93	99
3 × 12	12	*L*	16—4	17—5	18—10	19—8	*L*	17—8	18—6	21—4	23—1	24—5	25—11
		H	44	47	52	54	*H*	48	51	59	65	69	73
	16	*L*	14—11	15—11	17—3	18—0	*L*	15—5	16—2	18—7	20—2	21—3	22—8
		H	52	56	61	64	*H*	54	57	67	73	78	83
	24	*L*	13—1	14—0	15—2	15—10	*L*	12—9	13—4	15—4	16—7	17—6	18—8
		H	67	72	79	83	*H*	64	68	80	87	93	100

TABLE 12.18 Maximum spans for floor josts; live load 100 psf (Cont.)

4 × 6	12	L	9—0	9—7	10—4	10—10	L	10—3	10—9	12—5	13—5	14—2	15—1
		H	36	38	42	44	H	42	44	51	55	59	63
	16	L	8—2	8—9	9—5	9—11	L	8—11	9—5	10—9	11—8	12—4	13—2
		H	42	45	49	52	H	47	50	57	63	66	71
	24	L	7—2	7—8	8—3	8—8	L	7—4	7—9	8—10	9—7	10—2	10—9
		H	54	58	64	67	H	56	59	69	75	80	85
4 × 8	12	L	11—11	12—8	13—9	14—4	L	13—7	14—3	16—4	17—9	18—9	19—11
		H	36	39	42	44	H	42	44	51	56	59	63
	16	L	10—10	11—7	12—6	13—1	L	11—10	12—5	14—4	15—6	16—4	17—5
		H	42	45	50	52	H	47	50	57	63	67	71
	24	L	9—6	10—2	11—0	11—6	L	9—9	10—3	11—9	12—9	13—6	14—4
		H	55	59	64	68	H	56	59	69	75	80	86
4 × 10	12	L	15—0	15—11	17—3	18—1	L	17—1	17—11	20—7	22—3	23—7	25—0
		H	37	39	43	45	H	42	45	52	56	60	64
	16	L	13—8	14—7	15—10	16—6	L	14—11	15—8	18—0	19—6	20—7	21—11
		H	43	46	50	53	H	47	50	58	63	68	72
	24	L	12—0	12—10	13—11	14—6	L	12—4	12—11	14—10	16—1	17—0	18—1
		H	55	59	65	68	H	56	59	69	76	81	86

[1] Maximum allowable deflection of 1/360 of the span length
Modulus of elasticity as noted for E
Dead load—Weight of joist
Double thickness of flooring (5 psf)
Weight of plaster ceiling ignored
Live load—100 psf with plastered ceiling
Weight of plaster ceiling was included in computing horizontal shear H induced by load

[2] Allowable stress in extreme fiber in bending as noted for f
Dead load—Weight of joist
Double thickness of flooring (5 psf)
Plastered ceiling (10 psf)
Live load—100 psf with plastered ceiling
110 psf with unplastered ceiling
Total load was considered in computing the horizontal shear H induced by load.

TABLE 12.19 Maximum spans for rafters and roof joists; 15-lb live load; group I covering

Size of joists (nominal)	Spacing of joists center-to-center	Maximum allowable lengths, L, between supports											
		Span limited by deflection [1]					Span determined by bending [2]						
		E	1,000,000	1,210,000	1,540,000	1,760,000	f	1,000	1,100	1,450	1,700	1,900	2,150
in.	*in.*		*ft—in.*					*ft—in.*					
2 × 4	12	L	7—7	8—1	8—10	9—2	L	10—6	11—0	12—7	13—8	14—5	15—4
	16	L	7—0	7—5	8—0	8—5	L	9—2	9—7	11—0	11—11	12—8	13—5
	24	L	6—1	6—6	7—1	7—5	L	7—7	7—11	9—1	9—10	10—5	11—1
2 × 6	12	L	11—8	12—5	13—6	14—1	L	15—11	16—9	19—2	20—9	22—0	23—5
	16	L	10—8	11—5	12—4	12—11	L	14—0	14—8	16—10	18—3	19—3	20—6
	24	L	9—5	10—1	10—11	11—5	L	11—7	12—2	14—0	15—1	16—0	17—0
2 × 8	12	L	15—4	16—4	17—9	18—6	L	20—10	21—10	25—1	27—2	28—9	30—7
	16	L	14—1	15—0	16—3	17—0	L	18—4	19—3	22—2	23—11	25—4	26—11
	24	L	12—6	13—4	14—5	15—1	L	15—4	16—0	18—5	19—11	21—1	22—5
2 × 10	12	L	19—2	20—6	22—2	23—2	L	25—11	27—2	31—2	33—9	35—8	38—0
	16	L	17—8	18—10	20—5	21—4	L	22—11	24—0	27—7	29—11	31—7	33—8
	24	L	15—9	16—9	18—2	19—0	L	19—2	20—1	23—1	25—0	26—5	28—2
2 × 12	12	L	23—0	24—6	21—6	27—9	L	30—9	32—3	37—1	40—2	42—5	45—2
	16	L	21—3	22—7	24—6	25—8	L	27—4	28—8	33—0	35—8	37—9	40—2
	24	L	18—11	20—2	21—10	22—10	L	23—0	24—1	27—8	30—0	31—8	33—9
2 × 14	12	L	26—8	28—5	30—9	32—2	L	35—6	37—3	40—7	43—11	46—6	49—5
	16	L	24—8	26—4	28—6	29—10	L	31—8	33—3	38—2	41—4	43—8	46—5
	24	L	22—0	23—6	15—5	26—7	L	26—9	28—0	32—2	42—0	36—10	39—2
3 × 6	12	L	13—5	14—3	15—5	16—2	L	19—7	20—6	23—7	25—6	27—0	28—9
	16	L	12—4	13—2	14—3	14—11	L	17—4	18—2	20—10	22—7	23—10	25—5
	24	L	10—11	11—8	12—8	13—3	L	14—6	15—2	17—5	18—10	19—11	21—3

TABLE 12.19 Maximum spans for rafters and roof joists; 15-lb live load; group I covering (Cont.)

Size of joists (nominal) in.	Spacing of joists center-to-center in.	Maximum allowable lengths, *L*, between supports											
		Span limited by deflection [1]					Span determined by bending [2]						
		E	1,000,000	1,210,000	1,540,000	1,760,000	*f*	1,000	1,100	1,450	1,700	1,900	2,150
			ft—in.					*ft—in.*					
3 × 8	12	*L*	17—6	18—8	20—3	21—2	*L*	25—4	26—7	30—7	33—1	35—0	37—2
	16	*L*	16—2	17—3	18—8	19—7	*L*	22—7	23—8	27—2	29—5	31—1	33—1
	24	*L*	14—5	15—5	16—8	17—5	*L*	19—0	19—11	22—11	24—9	26—2	27—10
3 × 10	12	*L*	21—9	23—2	25—2	26—3	*L*	31—3	32—10	37—8	40—10	43—2	45—11
	16	*L*	20—3	21—7	23—4	24—5	*L*	28—0	29—4	33—9	36—6	38—7	41—1
	24	*L*	18—1	19—3	20—11	21—10	*L*	23—8	24—10	28—6	30—11	32—8	34—9

[1] Maximum allowable deflection of 1/360 of the span length
Modulus of elasticity as noted for *E*

[2] Allowable stress in extreme fiber in bending as noted for *f*
Dead load—Weight of roof joist or rafter
Weight of roof sheathing (2.5 psf)
Weight of Group I roof coverings (2.5 psf)
Live load—Considered as acting normal to the surface in pounds per square foot of roof surface.

TABLE 12.20 Maximum spans for rafters and roof joists; 20-lb live load; group I covering

Size of joists (nominal) *in.*	Spacing of joists center-to-center *in.*	Maximum allowable lengths, *L*, between supports											
		Span limited by deflection [1]					Span determined by bending [2]						
		E	1,000,000	1,210,000	1,540,000	1,760,000	*f*	1,000	1,100	1,450	1,700	1,900	2,150
			ft—in.					*ft—in.*					
2 × 4	12	*L*	7—1	7—7	8—3	8—7	*L*	9—5	9—11	11—5	12—4	13—0	13—10
	16	*L*	6—6	6—11	7—6	7—10	*L*	8—3	8—8	9—11	10—9	11—5	12—1
	24	*L*	5—8	6—1	6—7	6—11	*L*	6—9	7—1	8—2	8—10	9—4	9—11
2 × 6	12	*L*	10—11	11—8	12—7	13—2	*L*	14—5	15—1	17—4	18—9	19—10	21—2
	16	*L*	10—0	10—8	11—6	12—1	*L*	12—8	13—3	15—3	16—6	17—5	18—6
	24	*L*	8—9	9—4	10—2	10—7	*L*	10—5	10—11	12—7	13—7	14—5	15—4
2 × 8	12	*L*	14—5	15—4	16—7	17—4	*L*	18—11	19—10	22—9	24—8	26—1	27—9
	16	*L*	13—3	14—1	15—3	15—11	*L*	16—8	17—5	20—0	21—8	22—11	24—5
	24	*L*	11—8	12—5	13—6	14—1	*L*	13—9	14—6	16—7	18—0	19—0	20—3
2 × 10	12	*L*	18—0	19—3	20—10	21—9	*L*	23—7	24—9	28—5	30—9	32—6	34—7
	16	*L*	16—7	17—8	19—2	20—0	*L*	20—10	21—10	25—1	27—2	28—8	30—6
	24	*L*	14—8	15—8	17—0	17—9	*L*	17—4	18—2	20—10	22—7	23—11	25—5
2 × 12	12	*L*	21—7	23—0	25—0	26—1	*L*	28—1	29—6	33—10	36—8	38—9	41—3
	16	*L*	19—11	21—3	23—0	24—1	*L*	24—11	26—1	30—0	32—6	34—4	36—6
	24	*L*	17—8	18—10	20—5	21—4	*L*	20—10	21—10	25—1	27—1	28—8	30—6
2 × 14	12	*L*	25—2	26—9	29—0	30—4	*L*	32—6	34—1	39—2	42—5	44—10	47—8
	16	*L*	23—3	24—9	26—10	28—0	*L*	28—11	30—4	34—10	37—8	39—10	42—5
	24	*L*	20—8	22—0	23—10	24—11	*L*	24—3	25—5	29—2	31—7	33—5	35—6
3 × 6	12	*L*	12—7	13—5	14—6	15—2	*L*	17—10	18—8	21—5	23—3	24—7	26—2
	16	*L*	11—7	12—4	13—4	13—11	*L*	15—9	16—6	18—11	20—6	21—8	23—0
	24	*L*	10—3	10—11	11—10	12—4	*L*	13—1	13—8	15—9	17—0	18—0	19—2

TABLE 12.20 Maximum spans for rafters and roof joists; 20-lb live load; group I covering (Cont.)

Size of joists (nominal)	Spacing of joists center-to-center	Maximum allowable lengths, L, between supports											
		Span limited by deflection [1]					Span determined by bending [2]						
		E	1,000,000	1,210,000	1,540,000	1,760,000	f	1,000	1,100	1,450	1,700	1,900	2,150
in.	*in.*		*ft—in.*					*ft—in.*					
3 × 8	12	*L*	16—6	17—7	19—0	19—11	*L*	23—2	24—4	27—11	30—3	32—0	34—0
	16	*L*	15—3	16—3	17—7	18—5	*L*	20—7	21—7	24—9	26—10	28—4	30—2
	24	*L*	13—6	14—5	15—7	16—4	*L*	17—2	18—0	20—9	22—5	23—9	25—3
3 × 10	12	*L*	20—7	21—11	23—9	24—10	*L*	28—9	30—2	34—7	37—6	39—7	42—2
	16	*L*	19—1	20—4	22—0	23—0	*L*	25—7	26—10	30—10	33—10	35—4	45—3
	24	*L*	17—0	18—1	19—7	20—6	*L*	21—6	22—7	25—11	28—0	29—8	31—0

[1] Maximum allowable deflection of 1/360 of the span length
Modulus of elasticity as noted for E

[2] Allowable stress in extreme fiber in bending as noted for f
Dead load—Weight of roof joist or rafter
Weight of roof sheathing (2.5 psf)
Weight of Group I roof coverings (2.5 psf)
Live load—Considered as acting normal to the surface in pounds per square foot of roof surface.

TABLE 12.21 Maximum spans for rafters and roof joists; 30-lb live load; group I covering

Size of joists (nominal) *in.*	Spacing of joists center-to-center *in.*	Maximum allowable lengths, *L*, between supports											
		Span limited by deflection[1]					Span determined by bending [2]						
		E	1,000,000	1,210,000	1,540,000	1,760,000	*f*	1,000	1,100	1,450	1,700	1,900	2,150
			ft—in.					*ft—in.*					
2 × 4	12	*L*	6—5	6—10	7—5	7—9	*L*	8—1	8—5	9—8	10—6	11—1	11—10
	16	*L*	5—10	6—3	6—9	7—0	*L*	7—0	7—4	8—5	9—2	9—8	10—3
	24	*L*	5—1	5—5	5—11	6—2	*L*	5—9	6—0	6—11	7—6	7—11	8—5
2 × 6	12	*L*	9—10	10—6	11—5	11—11	*L*	12—4	12—11	14—10	16—1	17—0	18—1
	16	*L*	9—0	9—7	10—5	10—10	*L*	10—9	11—4	13—0	14—1	14—10	15—10
	24	*L*	7—11	8—5	9—2	9—6	*L*	8—11	9—4	10—8	11—7	12—3	13—0
2 × 8	12	*L*	13—0	13—10	15—1	15—9	*L*	16—3	17—1	19—7	21—2	22—5	23—10
	16	*L*	11—11	12—8	13—10	14—5	*L*	14—3	14—11	17—2	18—7	19—8	20—11
	24	*L*	10—6	11—2	12—2	12—8	*L*	11—9	12—4	14—2	15—4	16—3	17—3
2 × 10	12	*L*	16—4	17—5	18—11	19—9	*L*	20—4	21—4	24—6	26—7	28—1	29—10
	16	*L*	15—0	16—0	17—5	18—1	*L*	17—10	18—9	21—6	23—4	24—8	26—1
	24	*L*	13—3	14—1	15—4	16—0	*L*	14—10	15—6	17—10	19—4	20—5	21—9
2 × 12	12	*L*	19—8	20—11	22—9	23—9	*L*	24—4	25—7	29—4	31—9	33—7	35—9
	16	*L*	18—1	19—3	20—11	21—9	*L*	21—5	22—6	25—10	28—0	29—7	31—6
	24	*L*	15—11	17—0	18—6	19—3	*L*	17—10	18—8	21—6	23—3	24—7	26—2
2 × 14	12	*L*	22—11	24—5	26—6	27—8	*L*	28—4	29—8	34—1	36—11	39—0	41—6
	16	*L*	21—1	22—5	24—5	25—5	*L*	25—0	26—2	30—1	32—7	34—5	36—7
	24	*L*	18—8	19—10	21—7	22—6	*L*	20—9	21—10	25—0	27—1	28—8	30—6
3 × 6	12	*L*	11—5	12—2	13—2	13—9	*L*	15—4	16—1	18—6	20—0	21—2	22—6
	16	*L*	10—5	11—1	12—1	12—7	*L*	13—6	14—2	16—3	17—7	18—7	19—9
	24	*L*	9—2	9—10	10—8	11—1	*L*	11—2	11—8	13—5	14—7	15—5	16—4

TABLE 12.21 Maximum spans for rafters and roof joists; 30-lb live load; group I covering (Cont.)

Size of joists (nominal)	Spacing of joists center-to-center	Maximum allowable lengths, L, between supports											
		Span limited by deflection [1]					Span determined by bending [2]						
		E	1,000,000	1,210,000	1,540,000	1,760,000	f	1,000	1,100	1,450	1,700	1,900	2,150
in.	*in.*		*ft—in.*					*ft—in.*					
3 × 8	12	L	15—0	16—0	17—5	18—1	L	20—2	21—1	24—3	26—3	27—9	29—6
	16	L	13—9	14—8	16—0	16—8	L	17—9	18—7	21—4	23—1	24—5	26—0
	24	L	12—2	13—0	14—1	14—9	L	14—9	15—6	17—9	19—3	20—4	21—7
3 × 10	12	L	18—9	20—0	21—9	22—8	L	25—1	26—3	30—2	32—8	34—7	36—9
	16	L	17—4	18—5	20—1	20—11	L	22—2	23—3	26—8	28—11	30—7	32—6
	24	L	15—4	16—4	17—9	18—6	L	18—6	19—5	22—3	24—1	25—6	27—2

[1] Maximum allowable deflection of 1/360 of the span length
Modulus of elasticity as noted for E

[2] Allowable stress in extreme fiber in bending as noted for f
Dead load—Weight of roof joist or rafter
Weight of roof sheathing (2.5 psf)
Weight of Group I roof coverings (2.5 psf)
Live load—Considered as acting normal to the surface in pounds per square foot of roof surface.

TABLE 12.22 Maximum spans for rafters and roof joists; 40-lb live load; group I covering

Size of joists (nominal) in.	Spacing of joists center-to-center in.	Maximum allowable lengths, L, between supports											
		Span limited by deflection [1]					Span determined by bending [2]						
		E	1,000,000	1,210,000	1,540,000	1,760,000	f	1,000	1,100	1,450	1,700	1,900	2,150
			ft—in.					ft—in.					
2 × 4	12	L	5—11	6—3	6—10	7—1	L	7—2	7—6	8—7	9—4	9—10	10—6
	16	L	5—4	5—9	6—2	6—6	L	6—3	6—6	7—6	8—1	8—7	9—1
	24	L	4—9	5—0	5—5	5—8	L	5—1	5—4	6—2	6—8	7—0	7—6
2 × 6	12	L	9—1	9—8	10—6	11—0	L	11—0	11—6	13—2	14—4	15—1	16—1
	16	L	8—4	8—10	9—7	10—0	L	9—7	10—0	11—6	12—6	13—2	14—0
	24	L	7—3	7—9	8—5	8—9	L	7—10	8—3	9—6	10—3	10—10	11—6
2 × 8	12	L	12—1	12—10	13—11	14—7	L	14—6	15—2	17—5	18—11	20—0	21—3
	16	L	11—0	11—9	12—9	13—3	L	12—8	13—3	15—3	16—6	17—5	18—7
	24	L	9—8	10—4	11—2	11—8	L	10—5	10—11	12—7	13—7	14—4	15—3
2 × 10	12	L	15—2	16—2	17—6	18—4	L	18—2	19—1	21—11	23—8	25—1	26—8
	16	L	13—11	14—9	16—0	16—9	L	15—11	16—8	19—2	20—9	21—11	23—4
	24	L	12—3	13—0	14—1	14—9	L	13—2	13—9	15—10	17—2	18—1	19—3
2 × 12	12	L	18—4	19—5	21—1	22—0	L	21—10	22—11	26—3	28—5	20—1	32—0
	16	L	16—9	17—10	19—4	20—2	L	19—2	20—1	23—1	24—11	26—5	28—1
	24	L	14—9	15—9	17—0	17—10	L	15—10	16—7	19—1	20—8	21—10	23—3
2 × 14	12	L	21—4	22—8	24—7	25—9	L	25—5	26—7	30—7	33—1	35—0	37—3
	16	L	19—7	20—10	22—7	23—7	L	22—4	23—5	26—10	29—1	30—9	32—9
	24	L	17—3	18—5	19—11	20—10	L	18—6	19—5	22—4	24—2	25—6	27—2
3 × 6	12	L	10—7	11—3	12—2	12—9	L	13—9	14—5	16—6	17—10	18—11	20—1
	16	L	9—8	10—3	11—2	11—8	L	12—0	12—7	14—5	15—8	16—6	17—7
	24	L	8—6	9—1	9—10	10—3	L	9—11	10—4	11—11	12—11	13—8	14—6

TABLE 12.22 Maximum spans for rafters and roof joists; 40-lb live load; group I covering (Cont.)

Size of joists (nominal)	Spacing of joists center-to-center	Maximum allowable lengths, L, between supports											
		Span limited by deflection [1]					Span determined by bending [2]						
		E	1,000,000	1,210,000	1,540,000	1,760,000	f	1,000	1,100	1,450	1,700	1,900	2,150
in.	*in.*		*ft—in.*					*ft—in.*					
3 × 8	12	L	13—11	14—10	16—1	16—10	L	18—0	18—11	21—9	23—6	24—10	26—5
	16	L	12—9	13—7	14—9	15—5	L	15—10	16—7	19—1	20—8	21—10	23—3
	24	L	11—3	12—0	13—0	13—7	L	13—1	13—9	15—9	17—1	18—1	19—3
3 × 10	12	L	17—5	18—8	20—2	21—1	L	22—6	23—7	27—2	29—4	31—1	33—0
	16	L	16—1	17—1	18—7	19—5	L	19—10	20—10	23—11	25—10	27—4	29—1
	24	L	14—3	15—2	16—5	17—2	L	16—6	17—3	19—10	21—6	22—9	24—2
3 × 12	12	L	21—0	22—4	24—11	25—4	L	26—11	28—2	32—5	35—1	37—1	39—5
	16	L	19—4	20—7	22—4	23—4	L	23—9	24—11	28—7	31—0	32—9	34—10
	24	L	17—1	18—3	19—9	20—8	L	19—10	20—9	23—10	25—10	27—4	29—0

[1] Maximum allowable deflection of 1/360 of the span length
Modulus of elasticity as noted for E

[2] Allowable stress in extreme fiber in bending as noted for f
Dead load—Weight of roof joist or rafter
Weight of roof sheathing (2.5 psf)
Weight of Group I roof coverings (2.5 psf)
Live load—Considered as acting normal to the surface in pounds per square foot of roof surface.

TABLE 12.23 Maximum spans for rafters and roof joists; 20-lb live load; group II covering

Size of joists (nominal)	Spacing of joists center-to-center	Maximum allowable lengths, L, between supports											
		Span limited by deflection [1]					Span determined by bending [2]						
		E	1,000,000	1,210,000	1,540,000	1,760,000	f	1,000	1,100	1,450	1,700	1,900	2,150
in.	in.		ft—in.					ft—in.					
2 × 4	12	L	6—8	7—1	7—9	8—1	L	8—7	9—0	10—4	11—3	11—10	12—7
	16	L	6—1	6—6	7—0	7—4	L	7—6	7—10	9—0	9—9	10—4	11—0
	24	L	5—4	5—8	6—2	6—5	L	6—2	6—6	7—5	8—0	8—6	9—0
2 × 6	12	L	10—3	10—11	11—10	12—5	L	13—2	13—10	15—10	17—2	18—2	19—4
	16	L	9—5	10—0	10—10	11—4	L	11—6	12—1	13—10	15—0	15—10	16—10
	24	L	8—3	8—9	9—6	10—0	L	9—6	9—11	11—5	12—4	13—1	13—11
2 × 8	12	L	13—7	14—6	15—8	16—5	L	17—4	18—2	20—10	22—7	23—10	25—5
	16	L	12—5	13—3	14—4	15—0	L	15—2	15—11	18—3	19—9	20—11	22—3
	24	L	10—11	11—8	12—8	13—3	L	12—7	13—2	15—2	16—4	17—4	18—5
2 × 10	12	L	17—0	18—2	19—8	20—7	L	21—8	22—8	26—1	28—3	29—10	31—9
	16	L	15—8	16—8	18—1	18—11	L	19—0	20—0	22—11	24—10	26—3	27—11
	24	L	13—10	14—9	15—11	16—8	L	15—10	16—7	19—0	20—7	21—9	23—2
2 × 12	12	L	20—5	21—9	23—7	24—8	L	25—10	27—2	31—2	33—9	35—8	37—11
	16	L	18—10	20—0	21—9	22—8	L	22—10	23—11	27—6	29—9	31—5	33—6
	24	L	16—8	17—9	19—3	20—1	L	19—0	19—11	22—11	24—9	26—2	27—10
2 × 14	12	L	23—10	25—4	27—6	28—9	L	30—0	31—6	36—1	39—1	41—4	44—0
	16	L	21—11	23—4	25—4	26—6	L	26—6	27—10	30—9	34—7	36—7	38—11
	24	L	19—5	20—9	22—6	23—6	L	22—2	23—3	26—8	28—10	30—6	32—6
3 × 6	12	L	11—10	12—8	13—8	14—4	L	16—4	17—2	19—8	21—3	22—6	23—11
	16	L	10—11	11—7	12—7	13—2	L	14—4	15—1	17—3	18—9	19—9	21—1
	24	L	9—7	10—3	11—1	11—7	L	11—11	12—6	14—4	15—6	16—5	17—6

TABLE 12.23 Maximum spans for rafters and roof joists; 20-lb live load; group II covering (Cont.)

Size of joists (nominal)	Spacing of joists center-to-center	Maximum allowable lengths, L, between supports											
		Span limited by deflection [1]					Span determined by bending [2]						
		E	1,000,000	1,210,000	1,540,000	1,760,000	*f*	1,000	1,100	1,450	1,700	1,900	2,150
in.	*in.*		*ft—in.*					*ft—in.*					
3 × 8	12	*L*	15—7	16—7	18—0	18—10	*L*	21—4	22—5	25—9	27—10	29—5	31—4
	16	*L*	14—4	15—4	16—7	17—4	*L*	18—10	19—9	22—8	24—7	26—0	27—8
	24	*L*	12—9	13—7	14—8	15—4	*L*	15—9	16—6	18—11	20—6	21—8	23—0
3 × 10	12	*L*	19—6	20—9	22—6	23—7	*L*	26—6	27—10	32—0	34—7	36—7	38—11
	16	*L*	18—0	19—2	20—10	21—9	*L*	23—6	24—8	28—4	30—8	32—5	34—6
	24	*L*	16—0	17—0	18—6	19—4	*L*	19—8	20—8	20—5	25—8	27—2	28—11
3 × 12	12	*L*	23—4	24—10	26—11	28—2	*L*	31—6	33—0	37—11	41—1	43—5	46—2
	16	*L*	21—7	23—0	24—11	26—0	*L*	28—0	29—5	33—9	36—7	38—8	41—1
	24	*L*	19—3	20—6	22—2	23—3	*L*	23—7	24—9	28—5	30—9	32—6	34—7

[1] Maximum allowable deflection of 1/360 of the span length
Modulus of elasticity as noted for *E*

[2] Allowable stress in extreme fiber in bending as noted for *f*
Dead load—Weight of roof joist or rafter
Weight of roof sheathing (2.5 psf)
Weight of Group II roof coverings (8 psf)
Live load—Considered as acting normal to the surface in pounds per square foot of roof surface.

TABLE 12.24 Maximum spans for rafters and roof joists; 30-lb live load; group II covering

Size of joists (nominal) in.	Spacing of joists center-to-center in.	Maximum allowable lengths, L, between supports											
		Span limited by deflection [1]					Span determined by bending [2]						
		E	1,000,000	1,210,000	1,540,000	1,760,000	f	1,000	1,100	1,450	1,700	1,900	2,150
			ft—in.					ft—in.					
2 × 4	12	L	6—1	6—6	7—0	7—4	L	7—6	7—10	9—1	9—9	10—4	11—0
	16	L	5—7	5—11	6—5	6—9	L	6—6	6—10	7—10	8—6	9—0	9—7
	24	L	4—10	5—2	5—7	5—11	L	5—4	5—7	6—6	7—0	7—5	7—10
2 × 6	12	L	9—5	10—0	10—10	11—4	L	11—6	12—1	13—11	15—0	15—11	16—11
	16	L	8—7	9—2	9—11	10—4	L	10—1	10—7	12—1	13—1	13—10	14—9
	24	L	7—6	8—0	8—8	9—1	L	8—3	8—8	10—0	10—9	11—5	12—2
2 × 8	12	L	12—5	13—3	14—5	15—0	L	15—3	15—11	18—4	19—10	21—0	22—4
	16	L	11—5	12—2	13—2	13—9	L	13—4	13—11	16—0	17—4	18—4	19—6
	24	L	10—0	10—8	11—7	12—1	L	11—0	11—6	13—2	14—4	15—1	16—1
2 × 10	12	L	15—8	16—8	18—1	18—11	L	19—1	20—0	23—0	24—10	26—4	28—0
	16	L	14—4	15—3	16—7	17—4	L	16—9	17—6	20—2	21—10	23—0	24—6
	24	L	12—8	13—6	14—7	15—3	L	13—10	14—6	16—8	18—0	19—1	20—3
2 × 12	12	L	18—10	20—1	21—9	22—9	L	22—10	24—0	27—6	29—10	31—6	33—6
	16	L	17—3	18—5	19—11	20—10	L	20—1	21—1	24—2	26—2	27—8	29—6
	24	L	15—3	16—3	17—7	18—5	L	16—8	17—6	20—0	21—8	22—11	24—5
2 × 14	12	L	22—0	23—5	25—4	26—6	L	26—7	27—10	32—0	34—8	36—8	39—0
	16	L	20—2	21—6	23—4	24—4	L	23—5	24—6	28—2	30—6	32—3	34—4
	24	L	17—10	19—0	20—7	21—6	L	19—5	20—5	23—5	25—4	26—10	28—6
3 × 6	12	L	10—11	11—7	12—7	13—2	L	14—5	15—1	17—4	18—9	19—10	21—1
	16	L	10—0	10—8	11—6	12—1	L	12—7	13—3	15—2	16—5	17—5	18—6
	24	L	8—9	9—4	10—2	10—7	L	10—5	10—11	12—6	13—7	14—4	15—3

TABLE 12.24 Maximum spans for rafters and roof joists; 30-lb live load; group II covering (Cont.)

Size of joists (nominal)	Spacing of joists center-to-center	Maximum allowable lengths, L, between supports												
		Span limited by deflection [1]					Span determined by bending [2]							
		E	1,000,000	1,210,000	1,540,000	1,760,000	*f*	1,000	1,100	1,450	1,700	1,900	2,150
in.	*in.*		*ft—in.*					*ft—in.*					
3 × 8	12	*L*	14—5	15—4	16—7	17—4	*L*	18—11	19—10	22—9	24—8	26—0	27—8
	16	*L*	13—2	14—1	15—3	15—11	*L*	16—7	17—5	20—0	21—8	22—11	24—4
	24	*L*	11—8	12—5	13—5	14—1	*L*	13—9	14—5	16—7	18—0	19—0	20—2
3 × 10	12	*L*	18—0	19—3	20—10	21—9	*L*	23—7	24—9	28—5	30—9	32—6	34—7
	16	*L*	16—7	17—8	19—2	20—0	*L*	20—9	21—10	25—0	27—1	28—8	30—6
	24	*L*	14—8	15—8	16—11	17—9	*L*	17—4	18—2	20—10	22—7	23—10	25—5
3 × 12	12	*L*	21—7	23—0	24—11	26—1	*L*	28—1	29—6	33—10	36—8	38—9	41—2
	16	*L*	19—11	21—3	23—0	24—0	*L*	24—10	26—1	29—11	32—1	34—3	36—6
	24	*L*	17—8	18—10	20—5	21—4	*L*	20—9	21—9	25—0	27—1	28—8	30—6

[1] Maximum allowable deflection of 1/360 of the span length
Modulus of elasticity as noted for *E*

[2] Allowable stress in extreme fiber in bending as noted for *f*
Dead load—Weight of roof joist or rafter
Weight of roof sheathing (2.5 psf)
Weight of Group II roof coverings (8 psf)
Live load—Considered as acting normal to the surface in pounds per square foot of roof surface.

TABLE 12.25 Maximum spans for rafters and roof joists; 40-lb live load; group II covering

Size of joists (nominal)	Spacing of joists center-to-center	Maximum allowable lengths, L, between supports											
		Span limited by deflection [1]					Span determined by bending [2]						
		E	1,000,000	1,210,000	1,540,000	1,760,000	f	1,000	1,100	1,450	1,700	1,900	2,150
in.	*in.*		*ft—in.*					*ft—in.*					
2 × 6	12	L	8—9	9—4	10—2	10—7	L	10—5	10—11	12—6	13—6	14—4	15—3
	16	L	8—0	8—6	9—3	9—8	L	9—1	9—6	10—11	11—9	12—6	13—3
	24	L	7—0	7—6	8—1	8—5	L	7—5	7—9	8—11	9—8	10—3	10—11
2 × 8	12	L	11—7	12—5	13—5	14—0	L	13—9	14—5	16—6	17—11	18—11	20—2
	16	L	10—7	11—4	12—3	12—9	L	12—0	12—7	14—5	15—7	16—6	17—7
	24	L	9—4	9—11	10—9	11—3	L	9—10	10—4	11—11	12—10	13—7	14—6
2 × 10	12	L	14—8	15—7	16—11	17—8	L	17—3	18—1	20—9	22—6	23—9	25—3
	16	L	13—5	14—3	15—6	16—2	L	15—1	15—10	18—2	19—8	20—10	22—1
	24	L	11—9	12—7	13—7	14—2	L	12—5	13—0	15—0	16—3	17—2	18—3
2 × 12	12	L	17—8	18—9	20—4	21—3	L	20—9	21—9	24—11	27—0	28—7	30—5
	16	L	16—2	17—3	18—8	19—6	L	18—2	19—0	21—10	23—8	25—0	26—7
	24	L	14—3	15—2	16—5	17—2	L	15—0	15—9	18—1	19—7	20—8	22—0
2 × 14	12	L	20—7	21—11	23—9	24—9	L	24—1	25—3	29—0	31—5	33—3	35—4
	16	L	18—10	20—1	21—9	22—9	L	21—2	22—3	25—6	27—7	29—2	31—1
	24	L	16—8	17—9	19—3	20—1	L	17—6	18—5	21—1	22—10	24—2	25—9
3 × 6	12	L	10—2	10—10	11—9	12—3	L	13—0	13—8	15—8	16—11	17—11	19—1
	16	L	9—4	9—11	10—9	11—3	L	11—4	11—11	13—8	14—10	15—8	16—8
	24	L	8—2	8—9	9—6	9—10	L	9—4	9—10	11—3	12—3	12—11	13—9
3 × 8	12	L	13—6	14—4	15—7	16—3	L	17—1	17—11	20—7	22—4	23—7	25—1
	16	L	12—4	13—2	14—3	14—10	L	15—0	15—9	18—1	19—7	20—8	22—0
	24	L	10—10	11—7	12—7	13—1	L	12—5	13—0	14—11	16—2	17—1	18—2

TABLE 12.25 Maximum spans for rafters and roof joists; 40-lb live load; group II covering (Cont.)

Size of joists (nominal) *in.*	Spacing of joists center-to-center *in.*	Maximum allowable lengths, *L*, between supports											
		Span limited by deflection [1]					Span determined by bending [2]						
		E	1,000,000	1,210,000	1,540,000	1,760,000	*f*	1,000	1,100	1,450	1,700	1,900	2,150
			ft—in.					*ft—in.*					
3 × 10	12	*L*	16—11	18—1	19—6	20—5	*L*	21—5	22—6	25—9	27—11	29—6	31—5
	16	*L*	15—6	16—6	17—11	18—9	*L*	18—10	19—9	22—8	24—7	26—0	27—8
	24	*L*	13—9	14—7	15—10	16—6	*L*	15—7	16—5	18—10	20—4	21—6	22—11
3 × 12	12	*L*	20—4	21—8	23—5	24—6	*L*	25—7	26—10	30—10	33—4	35—3	37—6
	16	*L*	18—8	19—11	21—7	22—6	*L*	22—7	23—8	27—2	29—5	31—1	33—1
	24	*L*	16—6	17—7	19—1	19—11	*L*	18—9	19—8	22—7	24—6	25—11	27—6

[1] Maximum allowable deflection of 1/360 of the span length
Modulus of elasticity as noted for *E*

[2] Allowable stress in extreme fiber in bending as noted for *f*
Dead load—Weight of roof joist or rafter
Weight of roof sheathing (2.5 psf)
Weight of Group II roof coverings (8 psf)
Live load—Considered as acting normal to the surface in pounds per square foot of roof surface.

TABLE 12.26 Maximum spans for rafters and roof joists; 50-lb live load; group II covering

Size of joists (nominal) in.	Spacing of joists center-to-center in.	Maximum allowable lengths, L, between supports											
		Span limited by deflection [1]					Span determined by bending [2]						
		E	1,000,000	1,210,000	1,540,000	1,760,000	f	1,000	1,100	1,450	1,700	1,900	2,150
			ft—in.					ft—in.					
2 × 6	12	L	8—3	8—10	9—7	10—0	L	9—6	10—0	11—6	12—5	13—2	14—0
	16	L	7—6	8—0	8—9	9—1	L	8—3	8—8	10—0	10—10	11—5	12—2
	24	L	6—7	7—0	7—8	8—0	L	6—10	7—2	8—2	8—10	9—5	10—0
2 × 8	12	L	11—0	11—8	12—8	13—3	L	12—7	13—3	15—2	16—5	17—5	18—6
	16	L	10—0	10—8	11—7	12—1	L	11—0	11—6	13—3	14—4	15—2	16—1
	24	L	8—10	9—4	10—2	10—7	L	9—0	9—6	10—11	11—9	12—5	13—3
2 × 10	12	L	13—10	14—9	16—0	16—9	L	15—10	16—8	19—1	20—8	21—10	23—3
	16	L	12—8	13—6	14—7	15—3	L	13—10	14—6	16—8	18—1	19—1	20—4
	24	L	11—1	11—10	12—10	13—5	L	11—5	12—0	13—9	14—10	15—9	16—9
2 × 12	12	L	16—8	17—9	19—3	20—2	L	19—1	20—0	23—0	24—10	26—3	28—0
	16	L	15—3	16—3	17—7	18—5	L	16—8	17—6	20—1	21—9	23—0	24—5
	24	L	13—5	14—4	15—6	16—2	L	13—9	14—5	16—7	17—11	19—0	20—2
2 × 14	12	L	19—6	20—9	22—6	23—6	L	22—3	23—4	26—9	29—0	30—8	32—7
	16	L	17—10	19—0	20—7	21—7	L	19—6	20—5	23—5	25—5	26—10	28—7
	24	L	15—9	16—9	18—2	19—0	L	16—1	16—11	19—5	21—0	22—2	23—7
3 × 6	12	L	9—8	10—3	11—1	11—8	L	11—11	12—6	14—5	15—7	16—6	17—6
	16	L	8—9	9—4	10—2	10—7	L	10—5	10—11	12—7	13—7	14—5	15—4
	24	L	7—9	8—3	9—0	9—4	L	8—7	9—0	10—4	11—2	11—10	12—7
3 × 8	12	L	12—9	13—7	14—9	15—5	L	15—9	16—6	19—2	20—7	21—9	23—2
	16	L	11—8	12—5	13—6	14—1	L	13—9	14—6	16—7	18—0	19—0	20—3
	24	L	10—3	10—11	11—10	12—5	L	11—5	11—11	13—9	14—10	15—9	16—9

TABLE 12.26 Maximum spans for rafters and roof joists; 50-lb live load; group II covering (Cont.)

Size of joists (nominal) in.	Spacing of joists center-to-center in.	Maximum allowable lengths, L, between supports												
		Span limited by deflection [1]					Span determined by bending [2]							
		E	1,000,000	1,210,000	1,540,000	1,760,000	f	1,000	1,100	1,450	1,700	1,900	2,150
			ft—in.					ft—in.						
3 × 10	12	L	16—0	17—1	18—6	19—4	L	19—9	20—9	23—10	25—9	27—3	29—0
	16	L	14—8	15—8	17—0	17—9	L	17—4	18—2	20—11	22—7	23—11	25—5
	24	L	12—11	13—10	14—11	15—8	L	14—4	15—0	17—3	18—8	19—9	21—1
3 × 12	12	L	19—3	20—6	22—3	23—3	L	23—8	24—10	28—6	30—10	32—8	34—9
	16	L	17—8	18—10	20—5	21—4	L	20—10	21—10	25—1	27—2	28—9	30—7
	24	L	15—7	16—8	18—0	18—10	L	17—3	18—1	20—10	22—6	23—10	25—4

[1] Maximum allowable deflection of 1/360 of the span length
Modulus of elasticity as noted for E

[2] Allowable stress in extreme fiber in bending as noted for f
Dead load—Weight of roof joist or rafter
Weight of roof sheathing (2.5 psf)
Weight of Group II roof coverings (8 psf)
Live load—Considered as acting normal to the surface in pounds per square foot of roof surface.

M SAFE UNIFORM LOADS FOR PLANK AND LAMINATED FLOORS

Table 12.27 gives the load per square foot for structural floors of varying thicknesses and working stresses.

The loads, limited by deflection, are based on a computed maximum deflection of 1/15 in. per ft, or 1/180 of the span, with the floor functioning as a simple beam over a single span. This deflection is twice that ordinarily considered the maximum for floor panels supporting a plastered ceiling but has been assumed as a reasonably permissible limit for ordinary purposes. If deflection is to be reduced, the percentage of decrease desired can be accomplished by decreasing the load in direct proportion. For example, one-half the loads shown in the table for a given thickness of flooring and a given modulus of elasticity will result in a computed deflection of 1/30 in. per ft (1/360), which is one-half the 1/180 ratio on which the table was computed. If load based on deflection is reduced, the bending stress reduces in the same proportion.

To find the safe loads for working stresses other than those given, multiply the load in the table by the ratio of the desired stress to some stress in the table. For example, the load on a floor of a given thickness with an extreme fiber stress in bending of 900 lb will be 9/10 of the load for a fiber stress of 1,000 lb, a value which may be found in the table. Likewise, a load for a fiber stress of 2,000 lb will be twice the safe load for a 1,000-lb stress.

No loads are given that are based on a bending strength of floor that would cause a sag of 2/15 in. per ft (1/90 of the span) or greater. Loads based on an E of 1,760,000 are also omitted.

If size is based on deflection, a grade of lumber must be selected to permit the proper bending stress.

TABLE 12.27 Safe uniform loads for plank and laminated floors

Span ft	American Standard thickness in. Nominal	Dressed	Load determined by bending psf f = 1,000	f = 1,100	f = 1,450	f = 1,700	f = 1,900	f = 2,150	Load determined by deflection of 1/180 of span psf E = 1,000,000 W	E = 1,000,000 f	E = 1,210,000 W	E = 1,210,000 f	E = 1,540,000 W	E = 1,540,000 f	E = 1,760,000 W	E = 1,760,000 f
4	2	1⅝	220	242	319	374	418	473	199	903	241	1,093	306	1,391	350	1,589
	3	2⅝	574	631	832	976	1,091	1,234	837	1,459	1,013	1,765	—	—	—	—
5	2	1⅝	141	155	204	240	268	303	102	722	123	874	157	1,112	180	1,271
	3	2⅝	367	404	532	624	697	789	429	1,167	519	1,412	661	1,797	755	2,054
	4	3⅝	701	771	1,016	1,192	1,332	1,507	1,129	1,611	1,366	1,949	—	—	—	—
6	2	1⅝	98	108	142	167	186	211	59	602	71	728	91	927	104	1,060
	3	2⅝	255	280	370	434	484	548	248	972	300	1,176	382	1,497	436	1,711
	4	3⅝	487	536	706	828	925	1,047	653	1,342	790	1,624	1,006	2,067	—	—
7	2	1⅝	72	79	104	122	137	—	37	516	48	624	57	795	65	908
	3	2⅝	187	206	271	318	355	402	166	833	201	1,008	256	1,283	292	1,466
	4	3⅝	358	394	519	609	680	770	411	1,151	497	1,393	633	1,772	723	2,026
8	2	1⅝	55	60	80	—	—	—	25	451	30	546	38	694	44	794
	3	2⅝	143	157	207	243	272	307	105	729	127	882	162	1,123	185	1,283
	4	3⅝	274	301	397	466	521	589	276	1,007	334	1,218	425	1,551	486	1,772
	6	5⅝	659	725	956	1,120	1,252	1,417	1,030	1,562	1,246	1,890	—	—	—	—
9	2	1⅝	43	47	62	—	—	—	17	401	20	485	26	618	30	706
	3	2⅝	113	124	164	192	215	243	73	648	88	784	112	998	128	1,140
	4	3⅝	216	238	313	367	410	464	194	895	235	1,083	299	1,378	341	1,575
	6	5⅝	521	573	755	886	990	1,120	723	1,389	875	1,681	1,113	2,139	—	—

TABLE 12.27 Safe uniform loads for plank and laminated floors (Cont.)

Span ft	American Standard thickness in.		Load determined by bending psf						Load determined by deflection of 1/180 of span psf							
	Nominal	Dressed	$f =$ 1,000	$f =$ 1,100	$f =$ 1,450	$f =$ 1,700	$f =$ 1,900	$f =$ 2,150	$E = 1{,}000{,}000$		$E = 1{,}210{,}000$		$E = 1{,}540{,}000$		$E = 1{,}760{,}000$	
									W	f	W	f	W	f	W	f
10	2	1⅝	35	38	—	—	—	—	13	361	16	437	20	556	23	635
	3	2⅝	92	101	133	156	175	—	54	583	65	705	83	898	95	1,026
	4	3⅝	175	192	254	298	332	376	141	805	171	974	217	1,240	248	1,417
	6	5⅝	422	464	612	717	802	907	527	1,250	638	1,512	812	1,925	—	—
	8	7½	750	825	1,088	1,275	1,425	1,612	1,250	1,667	1,512	2,017	—	—	—	—
11	2	1⅝	29	32	—	—	—	—	10	328	12	397	15	505	18	577
	3	2⅝	76	84	110	129	144	—	40	530	48	641	62	816	70	933
	4	3⅝	145	160	210	246	276	312	106	732	128	886	163	1,127	186	1,288
	6	5⅝	349	384	506	593	663	750	396	1,136	479	1,374	610	1,749	697	1,999
	8	7½	620	682	899	1,054	1,178	1,330	939	1,515	1,136	1,833	—	—	—	—
12	3	2⅝	64	70	93	109	—	—	31	486	38	588	48	748	54	855
	4	3⅝	122	134	177	207	232	262	82	671	99	812	126	1,033	144	1,181
	6	5⅝	293	322	425	498	557	630	306	1,042	370	1,261	471	1,605	538	1,834
	8	7½	521	573	755	886	990	1,120	723	1,389	875	1,681	1,113	2,139	—	—
13	3	2⅝	54	59	78	—	—	—	24	449	29	543	37	691	42	790
	4	3⅝	104	114	151	177	198	224	64	620	77	750	99	954	113	1,091
	6	5⅝	250	275	362	425	475	538	240	962	290	1,164	370	1,481	422	1,693
	8	7½	444	488	644	755	844	955	569	1,282	688	1,551	876	1,974	—	—
	10	9½	712	783	1,032	1,210	1,353	1,531	1,156	1,624	1,399	1,965	—	—	—	—
14	3	2⅝	47	52	68	—	—	—	19	417	23	504	29	642	33	734
	4	3⅝	89	98	129	151	169	—	51	575	62	696	78	886	90	1,012
	6	5⅝	215	236	312	366	408	462	192	893	232	1,080	296	1,375	338	1,572
	8	7½	383	421	555	651	728	823	455	1,190	550	1,440	701	1,833	801	2,094
	10	9½	614	675	890	1,044	1,167	1,320	926	1,506	1,120	1,822	—	—	—	—

TABLE 12.27 Safe uniform loads for plank and laminated floors (Cont.)

Span	American Standard thickness		Load determined by bending						Load determined by deflection of 1/180 of span							
	in.		psf						psf							
									E = 1,000,000		E = 1,210,000		E = 1,540,000		E = 1,760,000	
ft	Nominal	Dressed	f = 1,000	f = 1,100	f = 1,450	f = 1,700	f = 1,900	f = 2,150	W	f	W	f	W	f	W	f
15	4	3⅝	78	86	113	133	148	—	42	537	51	650	65	827	74	945
	6	5⅝	187	206	271	318	355	402	156	833	189	1,008	240	1,283	274	1,466
	8	7½	333	366	483	566	633	716	370	1,111	448	1,344	570	1,711	651	1,955
	10	9½	535	588	776	910	1,016	1,150	753	1,407	911	1,702	—	—	—	—
16	4	3⅝	68	75	99	116	—	—	34	503	41	609	52	775	60	885
	6	5⅝	165	182	239	280	314	355	129	781	156	945	199	1,023	227	1,374
	8	7½	293	322	425	498	557	630	129	781	156	945	199	1,203	227	1,374
	10	9½	470	517	682	799	893	1,010	620	1,319	750	1,596	955	2,031	—	—
	12	11½	689	758	999	1,171	1,309	1,481	1,100	1,597	1,331	1,932	—	—	—	—
17	4	3⅝	61	67	88	104	—	—	29	474	35	574	45	730	51	834
	6	5⅝	146	161	212	248	277	314	107	735	129	889	165	1,132	188	1,294
	8	7½	259	285	376	440	492	557	254	960	307	1,162	391	1,478	447	1,690
	10	9½	416	458	603	707	790	894	517	1,242	626	1,503	796	1,913	—	—
	12	11½	610	671	884	1,037	1,159	1,312	917	1,503	1,110	1,819	—	—	—	—
18	4	3⅝	54	59	78	—	—	—	24	447	29	541	37	688	42	787
	6	5⅝	130	143	188	221	247	280	90	694	109	840	139	1,069	158	1,221
	8	7½	231	254	335	393	439	497	214	926	259	1,120	330	1,426	377	1,630
	10	9½	371	408	538	631	705	798	436	1,173	528	1,419	671	1,806	767	2,064
	12	11½	544	598	789	925	1,034	1,170	773	1,420	935	1,718	—	—	—	—
19	4	3⅝	48	53	70	—	—	—	21	424	25	513	32	653	37	746
	6	5⅝	117	129	170	199	222	252	77	658	93	796	118	1,013	136	1,158
	8	7½	208	229	302	354	395	447	182	877	220	1,061	280	1,350	320	1,544
	10	9½	333	366	483	566	633	716	370	1,111	448	1,344	570	1,711	651	1,955
	12	11½	488	537	708	830	927	1,049	657	1,345	795	1,627	1,012	2,071	—	—

TABLE 12.27 Safe uniform loads for plank and laminated floors (Cont.)

Span ft	American Standard thickness in. Nominal	Dressed	Load determined by bending psf $f =$ 1,000	$f =$ 1,100	$f =$ 1,450	$f =$ 1,700	$f =$ 1,900	$f =$ 2,150	Load determined by deflection of 1/180 of span psf E = 1,000,000 W	E = 1,000,000 f	E = 1,210,000 W	E = 1,210,000 f	E = 1,540,000 W	E = 1,540,000 f	E = 1,760,000 W	E = 1,760,000 f
	4	3⅝	44	48	64	—	—	—	18	403	22	488	28	621	32	709
	6	5⅝	106	117	154	180	201	228	66	625	80	756	102	962	116	1,100
20	8	7½	187	206	271	318	355	402	156	833	189	1,008	240	1,283	274	1,466
	10	9½	301	331	436	512	572	647	318	1,056	385	1,278	490	1,626	560	1,859
	12	11½	441	485	640	750	838	948	563	1,278	681	1,546	867	1,968	—	—
	6	5⅝	96	106	139	163	182	—	57	595	69	720	88	916	100	1,047
21	8	7½	170	187	246	289	323	366	135	794	163	961	208	1,223	238	1,397
	10	9½	273	300	396	464	519	587	274	1,005	332	1,216	422	1,548	482	1,769
	12	11½	400	440	580	680	760	860	487	1,217	589	1,472	750	1,874	857	2,142
	6	5⅝	87	96	126	148	165	—	49	568	59	687	75	875	86	1,000
22	8	7½	155	170	225	264	294	333	117	758	142	917	180	1,167	206	1,334
	10	9½	249	274	361	423	473	535	239	960	289	1,162	368	1,478	421	1,690
	12	11½	364	400	528	619	692	783	423	1,162	512	1,406	651	1,789	744	2,045
	6	5⅝	80	88	116	136	152	—	43	543	52	657	66	836	76	956
23	8	7½	142	156	206	241	270	305	103	725	125	877	159	1,116	181	1,276
	10	9½	227	250	329	386	431	488	209	918	253	1,111	322	1,414	368	1,616
	12	11½	333	366	483	566	633	716	370	1,111	448	1,344	570	1,711	651	1,955
	6	5⅝	73	80	106	124	—	—	38	521	46	630	58	802	67	917
24	8	7½	130	143	189	221	247	280	90	694	109	840	139	1,069	158	1,221
	10	9½	209	230	303	355	397	449	184	880	223	1,065	283	1,355	324	1,549
	12	11½	306	337	444	520	581	658	326	1,065	394	1,289	502	1,640	574	1,874

N STUD WALLS—SAFE AXIAL LOADS AND ESTIMATED WEIGHT OF WALL COVERINGS

Table 12.28 gives the safe normal-duration loads per linear foot of stud wall for common S4S stud lengths of 7 to 12 ft, the studs spaced 16 in. on centers with their wider dimension at right angles to the plane of the wall. The strength of the stud column depends on the wider of the two cross-sectional dimensions of the stud if it has sufficient lateral bracing parallel to the wall.

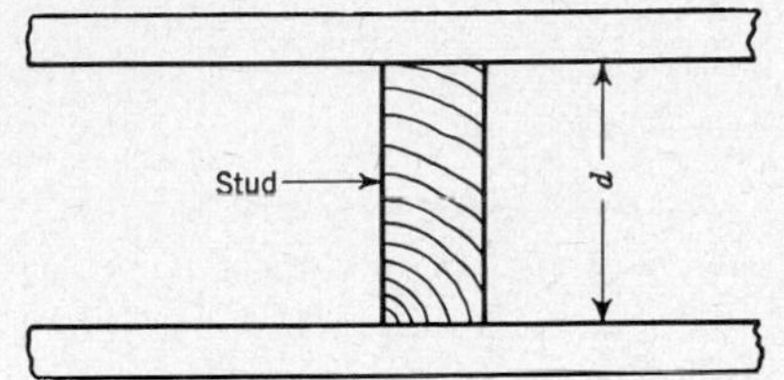

If it is desired to obtain the net load that may be superimposed on the stud wall, subtract the weight of the wall and its covering (Table 12.29) from the values in Table 12.28. As the weight of a stud is generally only a small percentage of the total load capacity of the wall, it is frequently neglected in computing the safe total load.

LATERAL SUPPORTS OF STUDS The loads in Table 12.28 are based on the assumption that the studs are laterally supported in a direction parallel to the stud wall either by a covering of sheathing or similar stiff materials well attached to the studs, by properly spaced rows of bridging inserted between the studs, or by comparable lateral support.

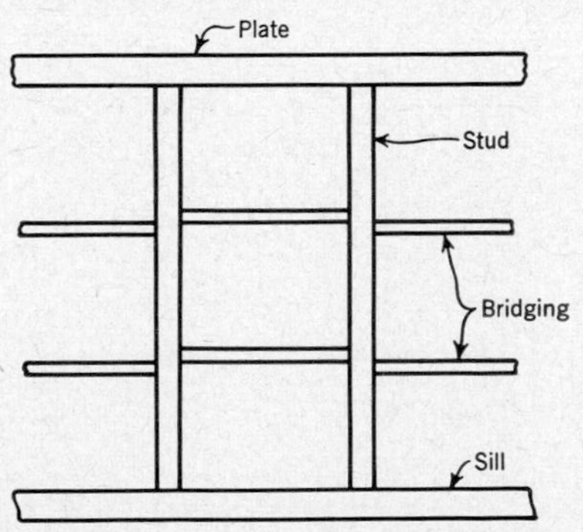

If lateral support for the studs is *not* provided by sheathing but rather by bridging alone, the spacing between rows of bridging or between the top or bottom plate and the adjacent row of bridging, should not exceed the following:

$$\frac{\text{Tabulated stud length (in.)} \times \text{actual stud thickness (in.)}}{\text{Actual stud width (in.)}}$$

For example, in a one-story stud wall without sheathing, 9 ft in height from plate to sill, and consisting of 2 x 6 S4S studs spaced 16 in. on centers, the row spacing of the bridging should not exceed:

$$\frac{(9\text{x}12) \times 1\tfrac{5}{8}}{5\tfrac{5}{8}} = 31 \text{ in.}$$

The maximum spacing between rows of stud bridging may also be obtained by multiplying the length of stud, in inches, by the appropriate spacing factor below.

SAFE LOADS FOR CONVENTIONAL STUD WALLS In using Table 12.28 to determine the safe load per linear foot of a stud wall having studs spaced 16 in. on centers, the following procedure should be observed:

1. Obtain the allowable unit stresses *c* and *E* for the species and grade of lumber to be used. They may be determined from building codes, the "National Design Specification for Stress-Grade Lumber and Its Fastenings" (see Chap. 13), or other proper references. They should be adjusted, as

SIZE S4S, IN.	2 x 3	2 x 4	3 x 4	4 x 4	2 x 6	3 x 6	2 x 8
Spacing factor for bridging	0.70	0.45	0.72	1.00	0.29	0.47	0.22

specified, for load durations other than normal, such as those for columns.

2. The safe load per linear foot of wall is found under the W for the length and size of stud involved and opposite the E for the species used. This value, however, must be checked as directed in step 3.

3. Under P/A and opposite the value of E for the species will be found the load per square inch of cross-sectional area that is imposed on the stud by the load, w, per linear foot on the wall. This unit load, P/A, is not permitted to exceed the allowable unit stress in compression parallel to the grain, c, for the grade of lumber used. If P/A in the table is found to be greater than c, then the maximum total load permitted on a stud of that size, length, and grade is c times the cross-sectional area of the stud in square inches. The load per linear foot of wall is 75 per cent of the resulting P for studs 16 in. on centers.

If the P/A shown in the table is less than the c permitted for the grade, then P/A is the maximum allowable unit load and the w in the table is the safe load per linear foot on the wall.

Safe loads for values of E between those shown in the table may be determined by interpolation or by multiplying the loads for an E of 1,000,000 by the ratio of the other E to 1,000,000.

SAFE LOADS FOR OTHER STUD SPACINGS To obtain the safe load per linear foot of wall having studs at other than 16 in. spacing on centers, multiply the values in Table 12.28 by the appropriate load factor below.

SAFE LOADS FOR STUD SIZES OTHER THAN THOSE LISTED To obtain the safe load per linear foot of wall for 3 x 8 studs, multiply 2 x 8 loads in Table 12.28 by 1.62; for 4 x 8 studs, multiply 2 x 8 loads by 2.23.

STUD SPACING, IN.	12	20	24	32	36	42	48
Load factor	1.33	0.80	0.67	0.50	0.44	0.38	0.33

TABLE 12.28 Safe axial loads per linear foot of stud walls

(P/A = safe axial loads of normal duration in pounds per square inch[1]; W = safe axial total load of normal duration in pounds per linear foot of wall.)

Stud length	Nominal size, *in.*	2 × 3		2 × 4		3 × 4		4 × 4		2 × 6		3 × 6		2 × 8	
ft	*E*	*P/A*	*W*	*P/A*	*W*	*P/A*	*W*	*P/A*	*W*	*P/A*	*W*	*P/A*	*W*	*P/A*	*W*
7	1,000,000	293	938	557	2,461	557	3,978	557	5,491	1,351	9,263	1,351	14,969	2,392	21,874
	1,210,000	355	1,135	674	2,978	674	4,813	674	6,644	1,635	11,208	1,635	18,112	2,894	26,468
	1,540,000	451	1,445	858	3,790	858	6,126	858	8,456	2,081	14,265	2,081	23,052	3,684	33,686
	1,760,000	516	1,651	980	4,331	980	7,001	980	9,664	2,378	16,303	2,378	26,345	4,210	38,498
8	1,000,000	224	717	427	1,887	427	3,050	427	4,209	1,026	7,035	1,026	11,368	1,832	16,753
	1,210,000	271	868	517	2,283	517	3,690	517	5,093	1,241	8,512	1,241	13,755	2,217	20,271
	1,540,000	345	1,104	658	2,906	658	4,697	658	6,482	1,580	10,834	1,580	17,507	2,821	25,800
	1,760,000	394	1,262	752	3,321	752	5,368	752	7,408	1,806	12,382	1,806	20,008	3,224	29,485
9	1,000,000	178	570	338	1,494	338	2,414	338	3,332	814	5,581	814	9,020	1,446	13,223
	1,210,000	215	690	409	1,808	409	2,921	409	4,032	985	6,753	985	10,914	1,750	16,000
	1,540,000	274	878	521	2,301	521	3,718	521	5,131	1,254	8,595	1,254	13,891	2,227	20,363
	1,760,000	313	1,003	595	2,629	595	4,249	595	5,864	1,433	9,823	1,433	15,875	2,545	23,272
10	1,000,000	144	461	274	1,211	274	1,957	274	2,701	661	4,532	661	7,324	1,172	10,718
	1,210,000	174	558	332	1,465	332	2,368	332	3,268	800	5,484	800	8,862	1,418	12,969
	1,540,000	222	710	422	1,865	422	3,014	422	4,160	1,018	6,979	1,018	11,279	1,805	16,506
	1,760,000	253	811	482	2,131	482	3,444	482	4,754	1,163	7,976	1,163	12,890	2,063	18,864
11	1,000,000	119	381	226	999	226	1,614	226	2,228	543	3,723	543	6,017	968	8,852
	1,210,000	144	461	273	1,209	273	1,953	273	2,696	657	4,505	657	7,281	1,171	10,711
	1,540,000	183	587	348	1,538	348	2,486	348	3,431	836	5,733	836	9,266	1,491	13,632
	1,760,000	209	671	398	1,758	398	2,841	398	3,921	956	6,552	956	10,590	1,704	15,580
12	1,000,000	100	320	190	840	190	1,357	190	1,873	458	3,140	458	5,075	814	7,525
	1,210,000	121	387	230	1,016	230	1,642	230	2,266	554	3,799	554	6,141	985	9,008
	1,540,000	154	493	293	1,294	293	2,090	293	2,884	705	4,836	705	7,816	1,254	11,469
	1,760,000	176	563	334	1,478	334	2,388	334	3,296	806	5,526	806	8,932	1,433	13,104

[1] P/A is not to exceed c, the allowable unit stress in compression parallel to grain, for species and grade of lumber used.

TABLE 12.29 Estimated weights of wall coverings per linear foot of stud wall

(This table gives the estimated weights of various stud-wall coverings. The total weight of wall covering is obtained by adding the weights of the appropriate individual items.)

Wall covering[1]	Weight per sq ft of wall surface *lb*	Weight of covering *lb per lin ft* Height of wall					
		7 ft	8 ft	9 ft	10 ft	11 ft	12 ft
Exterior:							
Wood siding							
8 in. beveled	1.5	10.5	12.0	13.5	15.0	16.5	18.0
6 in. drop	2.5	17.5	20.0	22.5	25.0	27.5	30.0
Wood shingles							
6½ in. to weather	1.1	7.7	8.8	9.9	11.0	12.1	13.2
Stucco on wood lath	8.0	56.0	64.0	72.0	80.0	88.0	96.0
Stucco on metal lath	9.0	63.0	72.0	81.0	90.0	99.0	108.0
Sheathing:							
Wood, 1 in.	2.5	17.5	20.0	22.5	25.0	27.5	30.0
Plywood, ⅜ in.	1.1	7.7	8.8	9.9	11.0	12.1	13.2
Fiber board, 1 in.	1.5	10.5	12.0	13.5	15.0	16.5	18.0
Fiber board, ½ in.	0.8	5.6	6.4	7.2	8.0	8.8	9.6
Paper, 50	0.1	0.7	0.8	0.9	1.0	1.1	1.2
Interior:							
Wood paneling, 1 in.	2.5	17.5	20.0	22.5	25.0	27.5	30.0
Plywood, 5/16 in.	1.0	7.0	8.0	9.0	10.0	11.0	12.0
Plaster on wood lath, ¾ in.	5.0	35.0	40.0	45.0	50.0	55.0	60.0
Plaster on metal lath, ¾ in.	6.0	42.0	48.0	54.0	60.0	66.0	72.0
Plaster, ½ in. on ⅜-in. gypsum board	6.0	42.0	48.0	54.0	60.0	66.0	72.0
Plaster, ½ in. on ½-in. insulating board	5.0	35.0	40.0	45.0	50.0	55.0	60.0

Courtesy National Lumber Manufacturers Association

[1] Weights of special products may be obtained from the catalogue of the manufacturer.

O TYPICAL ARCH SECTIONS FOR ESTIMATING

The typical sections for the arches of Tables 12.30 and 12.31 are based on conservative design criteria. The sections have been determined for vertical live and dead loads, which generally control for roof slopes up to 10 in 12 for Tudor arches and for low-rise (radius-equal-to-span), two-hinged arches. However, for some combinations of loading, horizontal or wind loads may control at lesser rise-to-span ratios, and all arches should be checked before final dimensions are determined. Normal lateral support is assumed for the two-hinged arches. The tables are useful for preliminary estimates of sizes required but are subject to revision for different structural grade combinations or other considerations of a local nature.

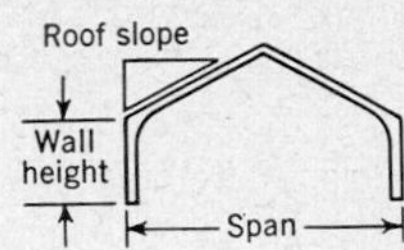

TABLE 12.30 Typical haunch sections of Tudor arches (three-hinged)

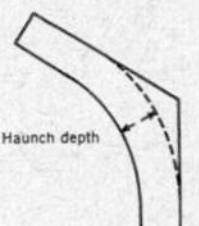

(Depth increments based on ¾-in. laminations)

Roof Slope	Wall height *ft*	Vertical loading, *lb per lin ft of span* 400	600	800	1,000	1,200
SPAN 30 FT						
3:12	8	3¼ × 9¾	5¼ × 9	5¼ × 12	5¼ × 15	5¼ × 17½
	10	3¼ × 10½	3¼ × 12	5¼ × 10½	5¼ × 12	5¼ × 15
	12	3¼ × 12	5¼ × 11¼	5¼ × 12¾	5¼ × 14¼	5¼ × 15¾
	14	5¼ × 10½	5¼ × 12¾	5¼ × 14¼	5¼ × 15¾	5¼ × 17¼
	16	5¼ × 11¼	5¼ × 13½	5¼ × 15	5¼ × 17¼	5¼ × 18¾
4:12	8	3¼ × 9	5¼ × 9	5¼ × 11¼	5¼ × 13¾	5¼ × 15¾
	10	3¼ × 10½	3¼ × 12	5¼ × 11¼	5¼ × 12¾	5¼ × 14¼
	12	3¼ × 12	5¼ × 11¼	5¼ × 12¾	5¼ × 14¼	5¼ × 15¾
	14	5¼ × 10½	5¼ × 12¾	5¼ × 14¼	5¼ × 15¾	5¼ × 16½
	16	5¼ × 11¼	5¼ × 13½	5¼ × 15¾	5¼ × 17¼	5¼ × 17¼
6:12	8	3¼ × 9	3¼ × 10½	5¼ × 9	5¼ × 9¾	5¼ × 11¼
	10	3¼ × 10½	5¼ × 9¾	5¼ × 12	5¼ × 12¾	5¼ × 14¼
	12	5¼ × 9¾	5¼ × 12	5¼ × 13½	5¼ × 15	5¼ × 16½
	14	5¼ × 10½	5¼ × 12¾	5¼ × 14¼	5¼ × 16½	5¼ × 18
	16	5¼ × 11¼	5¼ × 13½	5¼ × 15¾	5¼ × 17¼	5¼ × 18¾
8:12	8	3¼ × 10½	3¼ × 12	5¼ × 11¼	5¼ × 12¾	5¼ × 13½
	10	3¼ × 12	5¼ × 11¼	5¼ × 12¾	5¼ × 14¼	5¼ × 15¾
	12	5¼ × 10½	5¼ × 12¾	5¼ × 14¼	5¼ × 15¾	5¼ × 17¼
	14	5¼ × 11¼	5¼ × 13½	5¼ × 15	5¼ × 17¼	5¼ × 18¾
	16	5¼ × 12	5¼ × 14¼	5¼ × 15¾	5¼ × 18	5¼ × 19½
12:12	8	3¼ × 10½	3¼ × 12	5¼ × 11¼	5¼ × 12	5¼ × 13½
	10	3¼ × 12	5¼ × 11¼	5¼ × 12¾	5¼ × 14¼	5¼ × 15¾
	12	5¼ × 10½	5¼ × 12¾	5¼ × 14¼	5¼ × 15¾	5¼ × 17¼
	14	5¼ × 11¼	5¼ × 13½	5¼ × 15	5¼ × 17¼	5¼ × 18¾
	16	5¼ × 12	5¼ × 14¼	5¼ × 16½	5¼ × 18	5¼ × 19½
16:12	8	3¼ × 10½	5¼ × 10½	5¼ × 12	5¼ × 13½	5¼ × 14¼
	10	3¼ × 12	5¼ × 11¼	5¼ × 13½	5¼ × 15	5¼ × 15¾
	12	5¼ × 10½	5¼ × 12	5¼ × 14¼	5¼ × 15¾	5¼ × 17¼
	14	5¼ × 11¼	5¼ × 12¾	5¼ × 15	5¼ × 16½	5¼ × 21
	16	5¼ × 11¼	5¼ × 13½	5¼ × 16½	5¼ × 18	7 × 17¼
SPAN 40 FT						
3:12	10	5¼ × 9¾	5¼ × 13½	5¼ × 16½	5¼ × 20¼	7 × 18
	12	5¼ × 12	5¼ × 14¼	5¼ × 16½	5¼ × 20¼	7 × 17¼
	14	5¼ × 13½	5¼ × 16½	5¼ × 18¾	5¼ × 21	7 × 20¼
	16	5¼ × 14¼	5¼ × 17¼	5¼ × 20¼	7 × 18¾	7 × 21¾
	18	5¼ × 15	5¼ × 18¾	7 × 18	7 × 21	7 × 22½
4:12	10	5¼ × 9¾	5¼ × 12	5¼ × 16½	5¼ × 19½	7 × 17¼
	12	5¼ × 12	5¼ × 15	5¼ × 16½	5¼ × 19½	7 × 17¼
	14	5¼ × 13½	5¼ × 16½	5¼ × 18¾	5¼ × 21	7 × 20¼
	16	5¼ × 14¼	5¼ × 17¼	5¼ × 20¼	7 × 19½	7 × 21¾
	18	5¼ × 15	5¼ × 18¾	7 × 18	7 × 21	7 × 22½

TABLE 12.30 Typical haunch sections of Tudor arches (Cont.)

(Depth increments based on ¾-in. laminations)

Roof Slope	Wall height *ft*	Vertical loading, *lb per lin ft of span* 400	600	800	1,000	1,200
SPAN 40 FT						
6:12	10	5¼ × 10½	5¼ × 12¾	5¼ × 15	5¼ × 16½	5¼ × 18
	12	5¼ × 12	5¼ × 15	5¼ × 17¼	5¼ × 18¾	5¼ × 20¼
	14	5¼ × 13½	5¼ × 16½	5¼ × 18¾	5¼ × 21	7 × 19½
	16	5¼ × 14¼	5¼ × 17¼	5¼ × 20¼	7 × 19½	7 × 21
	18	5¼ × 15	5¼ × 18¾	5¼ × 21	7 × 21	7 × 21¾
8:12	10	5¼ × 11¼	5¼ × 14¼	5¼ × 16½	5¼ × 18	5¼ × 19¼
	12	5¼ × 12¾	5¼ × 15¾	5¼ × 18	5¼ × 20¼	7 × 18¾
	14	5¼ × 14¼	5¼ × 16½	5¼ × 19½	5¼ × 21	7 × 20¼
	16	5¼ × 15	5¼ × 18	5¼ × 20¼	7 × 19½	7 × 21¾
	18	5¼ × 15¾	5¼ × 18¾	5¼ × 21	7 × 21	7 × 22½
12:12	10	5¼ × 11¼	5¼ × 14¼	5¼ × 15¾	5¼ × 18	5¼ × 19½
	12	5¼ × 12¾	5¼ × 15	5¼ × 17¼	5¼ × 19½	5¼ × 21
	14	5¼ × 13½	5¼ × 16½	5¼ × 18¾	5¼ × 21	7 × 20¼
	16	5¼ × 14¼	5¼ × 17¼	5¼ × 20¼	7 × 19½	7 × 21
	18	5¼ × 15	5¼ × 18	5¼ × 21	7 × 20¼	7 × 22½
SPAN 50 FT						
3:12	10	5¼ × 12	5¼ × 18	7 × 18	7 × 22½	7 × 26¼
	12	5¼ × 14¼	5¼ × 17¼	7 × 16½	7 × 19½	7 × 23¼
	14	5¼ × 15¾	5¼ × 19½	7 × 18¾	7 × 21	7 × 23¼
	16	5¼ × 17¼	5¼ × 21	7 × 20¼	7 × 23¼	7 × 25½
	18	5¼ × 18¾	7 × 19½	7 × 22½	7 × 25½	7 × 27¾
4:12	10	5¼ × 11¼	5¼ × 15¾	7 × 15¾	7 × 20¼	7 × 24
	12	5¼ × 13½	5¼ × 16½	7 × 16½	7 × 18¾	7 × 21¾
	14	5¼ × 15¾	5¼ × 18¾	7 × 18¾	7 × 21	7 × 22½
	16	5¼ × 17¼	5¼ × 20¼	7 × 20¼	7 × 22½	7 × 24¾
	18	5¼ × 18	7 × 18¾	7 × 21¾	7 × 24	7 × 26¼
6:12	10	5¼ × 12	5¼ × 15	5¼ × 17¼	7 × 16½	7 × 20¼
	12	5¼ × 14¼	5¼ × 17¼	5¼ × 19½	7 × 18¾	7 × 20¼
	14	5¼ × 15¾	5¼ × 18¾	7 × 18¾	7 × 21	7 × 22½
	16	5¼ × 16½	5¼ × 20¼	7 × 20¼	7 × 22½	7 × 24
	18	5¼ × 18	7 × 18¾	7 × 21	7 × 24	7 × 25½
8:12	10	5¼ × 12¾	5¼ × 15¾	5¼ × 18	7 × 18	7 × 18¾
	12	5¼ × 14¼	5¼ × 18	5¼ × 20¼	7 × 19½	7 × 21¾
	14	5¼ × 15¾	5¼ × 19½	7 × 18¾	7 × 21	7 × 23¼
	16	5¼ × 16½	5¼ × 20¼	7 × 20¼	7 × 22½	7 × 24¾
	18	5¼ × 17¼	5¼ × 21	7 × 21	7 × 24	7 × 26¼
12:12	10	5¼ × 12¾	5¼ × 15¾	5¼ × 18	7 × 17¼	7 × 18¾
	12	5¼ × 14¼	5¼ × 17¼	5¼ × 19½	7 × 18¾	7 × 21
	14	5¼ × 15	5¼ × 18¾	5¼ × 21	7 × 20¼	7 × 22½
	16	5¼ × 16½	5¼ × 19½	7 × 19½	7 × 21¾	7 × 24
	18	5¼ × 17¼	5¼ × 21	7 × 20¼	7 × 23¼	7 × 25½

TABLE 12.30 Typical haunch sections of Tudor arches (Cont.)

(Depth increments based on ¾-in. laminations)

Roof Slope	Wall height *ft*	Vertical loading, *lb per lin ft of span* 400	600	800	1,000	1,200
SPAN 60 FT						
3:12	12	5¼ × 16½	7 × 17¼	7 × 21	7 × 26¼	9 × 24¾
	14	5¼ × 18¾	7 × 19½	7 × 21¾	7 × 24¾	9 × 24
	16	5¼ × 20¼	7 × 21	7 × 24	7 × 27	9 × 26¼
	18	7 × 18¾	7 × 22½	7 × 25½	9 × 25½	9 × 27¾
4:12	12	5¼ × 16½	5¼ × 20¼	7 × 19½	7 × 24	9 × 23¼
	14	5¼ × 18¾	7 × 19½	7 × 21¾	7 × 24¾	9 × 24
	16	5¼ × 20¼	7 × 21	7 × 24	7 × 26½	9 × 25½
	18	5¼ × 21	7 × 21¾	7 × 25½	9 × 24¾	9 × 27¾
6:12	12	5¼ × 16½	5¼ × 20¼	7 × 19½	7 × 21¾	7 × 24
	14	5¼ × 18	7 × 18¾	7 × 21	7 × 24	7 × 26¼
	16	5¼ × 19½	7 × 20¼	7 × 23¼	7 × 26¼	9 × 24¾
	18	5¼ × 21	7 × 21¾	7 × 24¾	7 × 27¾	9 × 26¼
8:12	12	5¼ × 17¼	5¼ × 20¼	7 × 20¼	7 × 21¾	7 × 24
	14	5¼ × 18¾	7 × 19½	7 × 21¾	7 × 24¾	7 × 27
	16	5¼ × 19½	7 × 20¼	7 × 23¼	7 × 26¼	9 × 25½
	18	5¼ × 20¼	7 × 21¾	7 × 24¾	7 × 27¾	9 × 27
11.2:12	12	5¼ × 16½	5¼ × 19½	7 × 19½	7 × 21¾	7 × 23¼
	14	5¼ × 17¼	5¼ × 21	7 × 21	7 × 23¼	7 × 25½
	16	5¼ × 18¾	7 × 19½	7 × 22½	7 × 24¾	7 × 27
	18	5¼ × 19½	7 × 20¼	7 × 26¼	7 × 26¼	9 × 25½
SPAN 70 FT						
3:12	14	5¼ × 21	7 × 22½	7 × 26¼	9 × 27	9 × 30
	16	7 × 20¼	7 × 24¾	7 × 27¾	9 × 28½	9 × 30
	18	7 × 21¾	7 × 26¼	9 × 26¼	9 × 30	9 × 32¼
	20	7 × 22½	7 × 27¾	9 × 27¾	9 × 30¾	9 × 33¾
4:12	14	5¼ × 21	7 × 22½	7 × 25½	7 × 27¾	9 × 27
	16	7 × 19½	7 × 24	7 × 27¾	9 × 27	9 × 30
	18	7 × 21	7 × 25½	9 × 25½	9 × 29¼	9 × 31½
	20	7 × 21¾	7 × 27	9 × 26¼	9 × 30¾	9 × 33
6:12	14	5¼ × 20¼	7 × 21¾	7 × 24¾	7 × 27¾	9 × 27
	16	7 × 19½	7 × 23¼	7 × 27	9 × 26¼	9 × 29¼
	18	7 × 20¼	7 × 24¾	9 × 25½	9 × 27¾	9 × 30¾
	20	7 × 21	7 × 25½	9 × 26¼	9 × 29¼	9 × 32¼
8:12	14	5¼ × 21	7 × 21¾	7 × 24¾	7 × 27¾	9 × 27
	16	7 × 19½	7 × 23¼	7 × 27	9 × 26¼	9 × 29¼
	18	7 × 20¼	7 × 24¾	9 × 24¾	9 × 27¾	9 × 30¾
	20	7 × 21	7 × 25½	9 × 26¼	9 × 29¼	9 × 31½
10.6:12	14	5¼ × 20¼	7 × 21	7 × 24	7 × 27	9 × 25½
	16	5¼ × 21	7 × 22½	7 × 25½	9 × 25½	9 × 27¾
	18	7 × 19½	7 × 23¼	7 × 27	9 × 27	9 × 29¼
	20	7 × 20¼	7 × 24¾	9 × 24¾	9 × 27¾	9 × 30¾

TABLE 12.30 Typical haunch sections of Tudor arches (Cont.)

(Depth increments based on ¾-in. laminations)

Roof Slope	Wall height *ft*	Vertical loading, *lb per lin ft of span* 400	600	800	1,000	1,200
		SPAN 80 FT				
3:12	14	7 × 20¼	7 × 24	9 × 25½	9 × 30	9 × 35¼
	16	7 × 22½	7 × 27	9 × 27¾	9 × 30¾	9 × 34½
	18	7 × 24	9 × 25½	9 × 29¼	9 × 32¼	9 × 36
	20	7 × 24¾	9 × 26¼	9 × 30¾	9 × 33¾	11 × 33¾
	22	7 × 25½	9 × 27	9 × 31½	9 × 35¼	11 × 35¼
4:12	14	7 × 19½	7 × 24¾	7 × 27¾	9 × 27¾	9 × 32¼
	16	7 × 21¾	7 × 27	9 × 27	9 × 29¼	9 × 33
	18	7 × 23¼	9 × 24¾	9 × 28½	9 × 31½	9 × 34½
	20	7 × 24¾	9 × 26¼	9 × 30	9 × 33¾	9 × 36
	22	7 × 26¼	9 × 27	9 × 30¾	9 × 35¼	11 × 33¾
6:12	14	7 × 18¾	7 × 23¼	7 × 27	9 × 26¼	9 × 28½
	16	7 × 20¼	7 × 24¾	9 × 25½	9 × 28½	9 × 30¾
	18	7 × 21¾	7 × 26¼	9 × 27	9 × 30	9 × 32¼
	20	7 × 23¼	9 × 24¾	9 × 27¾	9 × 31½	9 × 34½
	22	7 × 24¾	9 × 25½	9 × 29¼	9 × 33	9 × 36
8:12	14	7 × 19½	7 × 23¼	7 × 27	9 × 26¼	9 × 28½
	16	7 × 20¼	7 × 24¾	9 × 25½	9 × 28½	9 × 30¾
	18	7 × 21¾	7 × 26¼	9 × 27	9 × 30	9 × 32¼
	20	7 × 22½	7 × 27¾	9 × 28½	9 × 31½	9 × 33¾
	22	7 × 23¼	9 × 25½	9 × 29¼	9 × 32¼	9 × 35¼
10.2:12	14	5¼ × 21	7 × 22½	7 × 26¼	9 × 25½	9 × 27¾
	16	7 × 20¼	7 × 24	7 × 27¾	9 × 27	9 × 30
	18	7 × 21	7 × 25½	9 × 25½	9 × 29¼	9 × 31½
	20	7 × 21¾	7 × 27	9 × 27	9 × 30	9 × 33
	22	7 × 23¼	9 × 24¾	9 × 27¾	9 × 31½	9 × 34½

Courtesy Timber Structures, Inc.

TABLE 12.31 Constant radius—constant section two-hinged arches[1]

High rise (one-third of span)

Span	Rise	Radius	Section sizes required, *in.*					Max. horizontal thrust per 100 lb of design load
			Design load on horizontal projection, *lb per lin ft of arch*					
ft	*ft–in.*	*ft–in.*	400	600	800	1,000	1,200	*lb*
Depth increments based on 1 3/16-in. laminations								
50	16–8	27–1	5¼ x 9½	5¼ x 11⅞	5¼ x 13–1/16	5¼ x 14¼	5¼ x 15–7/16	1,830
60	20–0	32–6	5¼ x 11⅞	5¼ x 14¼	5¼ x 15–7/16	7 x 15–7/16	7 x 16⅝	2,200
70	23–4	37–11	5¼ x 13–1/16	5¼ x 16⅝	7 x 16⅝	7 x 17–13/16	7 x 19	2,560
Depth increments based on 1⅝-in. laminations								
80	26–8	43–3	5¼ x 16¼	7 x 16¼	7 x 17⅞	7 x 21⅛	7 x 22¾	2,930
90	30–0	48–9	7 x 16¼	7 x 17⅞	7 x 21⅛	9 x 21⅛	9 x 22¾	3,290
100	33–4	54–2	7 x 17⅞	7 x 19½	9 x 21⅛	9 x 22¾	9 x 24⅜	3,660
110	36–8	59–7	7 x 19½	9 x 19½	9 x 22¾	9 x 24⅜	9 x 26	4,030
120	40–0	65–0	7 x 21⅛	9 x 21⅛	9 x 24⅜	9 x 26	9 x 29¼	4,390

Table 12.31 is based upon conservative design criteria for construction with suitable structural grade combinations, but is subject to local considerations. Normal lateral support is assumed.

TABLE 12.31 Constant radius—constant section two-hinged arches [1] (Cont.)

Low rise (radius equals span)

(Depth increments based on 1⅝-in. laminations)

Span *ft*	Rise *ft–in.*	Section sizes required, *in.* Design load on horizontal projection, *lb per lin ft of arch*					Max. horizontal thrust per 100 lb of design load *lb*
		400	600	800	1,000	1,200	
50	6–8⅜	3¼ x 11⅜	5¼ x 11⅜	5¼ x 13	5¼ x 13	5¼ x 14⅝	4,700
60	8–0 7/16	5¼ x 11⅜	5¼ x 13	5¼ x 14⅝	5¼ x 16¼	7 x 16¼	5,640
70	9–4 9/16	5¼ x 13	5¼ x 14⅝	7 x 14⅝	7 x 16¼	7 x 17⅞	6,580
80	10–8⅝	5¼ x 14⅝	7 x 16¼	7 x 17⅞	7 x 19½	7 x 21⅛	7,520
90	12–1 7/16	5¼ x 16¼	7 x 17⅞	7 x 19½	7 x 21⅛	9 x 21⅛	8,860
100	13–4¾	7 x 16¼	7 x 19½	7 x 21⅛	9 x 21⅛	9 x 22¾	9,400
110	14–8⅞	7 x 17⅞	7 x 21⅛	9 x 21⅛	9 x 22¾	9 x 24⅜	10,340
120	16–0 15/16	7 x 19½	9 x 21⅛	9 x 22¾	9 x 24⅜	9 x 27⅝	11,280

Table 12.31 is based upon conservative design criteria for construction with suitable structural grade combinations, but is subject to local considerations. Normal lateral support is assumed.

TABLE 12.32 Moments of inertia, section moduli, and veneer areas for selected plywood constructions (12-in. widths)

Net plywood thickness *in.*	No. of plies	Nominal veneer thickness, *in.*			Parallel[3] plies only			Perpendicular[3] plies only			Weight, *lb per 1,000 sq ft* (approx., as shipped from mill)
		Faces[4]	Centers	Crossband	Area *sq in.*	Moment of inertia I *in.*[4]	Section modulus S *in.*[3]	Area *sq in.*	Moment of inertia I *in.*[4]	Section modulus S *in.*[3]	
1/4–S[1]	3	1/9	1/9		1.67	.0143	.114	1.33	.0014	.0247	790
5/16–R[2]	3	1/10+	1/10+		2.50	.0294	.188	1.25	.0011	.0215	950
5/16–S	3	1/8	1/8		2.25	.0286	.183	1.50	.0020	.0312	950
3/8–R	3	1/8	1/8		3.00	.0509	.271	1.50	.0020	.0312	1,125
3/8–S	3	1/8	3/16		2.25	.0461	.246	2.25	.0066	.0704	1,125
3/8–S	5	1/10	1/12	2–1/12	2.50	.0377	.201	2.00	.0150	.120	1,125
1/2–R	5	1/10	1/10	2–1/10	3.60	.0990	.396	2.40	.0260	.1735	1,525
1/2–S	5	1/8	1/8	2–1/10	3.60	.0926	.370	2.40	.0324	.1995	1,525
5/8–R	5	1/8	1/8	2–1/8	4.50	.1934	.619	3.00	.0507	.271	1,825
5/8–S	5	1/8	3/16	2–1/8	4.50	.1670	.534	3.00	.0771	.352	1,825
3/4–R	5	1/8	1/8	2–3/16	4.50	.299	.798	4.50	.123	.492	2,225
3/4–S	5	1/8	3/16	2–3/16	4.50	.251	.670	4.50	.171	.608	2,225
3/4–S	7	1/8	2–1/12	3–1/8	4.50	.286	.763	4.50	.136	.503	2,225

Courtesy Douglas Fir Plywood Association

[1] Sanded; [2] Rough; [3] Refers to direction of face grain; [4] For sanded panels, thickness is before sanding.

TABLE 12.33 Recommended working stresses[1] for plywood (Douglas fir) permanent loading, dry location[2]

(In bending, tension, and compression—except bearing and 45-deg stresses—consider only those plies with their grain direction parallel to the principal stress)

Type of stress	Exterior: DFPA, A-A	Exterior: DFPA, A-B; DFPA, A-C	Exterior: DFPA, B-C; DFPA, C-C; DFPA, B-B. Interior: B-B; C-D; C (Repaired)-D	Interior:[3] A-A; A-B; A-D; B-D; N-D
	psi			*percentage of exterior grade*
Extreme fiber in bending				
Face grain parallel to span	2,188	2,000	1,875	100
Face grain perpendicular to span	1,875	1,875	1,875	80
Tension				
Parallel to face grain (3-ply only[4])	2,188	2,000	1,875	100[6]
Perpendicular to face grain	1,875	1,875	1,875	80
± 45 deg to face grain	337	320	310	85
Compression				
Parallel to face grain (3-ply only[4])	1,605	1,460	1,375	100[6]
Perpendicular to face grain	1,375	1,375	1,375	70
± 45 deg to face grain	496	472	460	80
Bearing (on face)	405	405	405	100
Shear, rolling, in plane of plies[5]				
Parallel or perpendicular to face grain	79	72	68	75
± 45 deg	105	96	90	75

TABLE 12.33 Recommended working stresses[1] for plywood (Cont.)

Type of stress	Exterior: DFPA, A-A	Exterior: DFPA, A-B; DFPA, A-C	Exterior: DFPA, B-C; DFPA, C-C; DFPA, B-B; Interior: B-B; C-D; C (Repaired)-D	Interior:[3] A-A; A-B; A-D; B-D; N-D
	psi			*percentage of exterior grade*
Shear, in plane perpendicular to plies[5]				
Parallel or perpendicular to face grain	210	192	180	85
± 45 deg	420	384	360	85
Modulus of elasticity in bending				
Face grain parallel to span	1,600,000	1,600,000	1,600,000	100
Face grain perpendicular to span	1,600,000	1,600,000	1,600,000	70

Courtesy Douglas Fir Plywood Association

[1] For grades and thicknesses listed in USCS4554.

[2] For wet or damp locations where moisture content will exceed 16 per cent, decrease values shown for dry location for the following properties by 20 per cent: extreme fiber in bending; tension and compression both parallel and perpendicular to the grain and at 45 deg; bearing. There is no change in value for shear or modulus of elasticity.

[3] Apply the percentages of this column to the stresses for the corresponding exterior grade. Reductions are caused by the fact that various western softwoods, other than Douglas fir, may be used in the inner plies—for these interior grades only.

[4] For tension or compression parallel to grain in 5-ply or thicker, use values of 3-ply, but in next lower grade.

[5] For certain conditions where stress concentrations exist, these working stresses for rolling shear should be reduced by 50 per cent. See Table I, FPL Bulletin, "Approximate Methods of Calculating the Strength of Plywood."

[6] For 5 or more plies, use 90 per cent.

Q SIMPLIFIED DESIGN DATA FOR LAG SCREWS

The data of Table 12.34 provide a simplified design procedure for lag screws as an alternative to the more complicated methods of the National Design Specification in Chap. 13. Species of wood have been grouped for the table as follows:

Group 1:

Cedar: northern and southern white
Fir: balsam and commercial white
Hemlock, eastern
Pine: ponderosa, sugar, northern white, and western white
Spruce: Engelmann, red, Sitka, and white

Group 2:

Aspen and largetooth aspen
Basswood
Cedar: Alaska, Port Orford, western red
Chestnut
Cottonwood: black and eastern
Cypress, southern
Douglas fir (Rocky Mountain type)
Hemlock, West Coast
Pine, Norway
Redwood
Tamarack
Yellow poplar

Group 3:

Ash, black
Birch, paper
Douglas fir (coast region)
Elm (soft): American and (gray) slippery
Gum: black, red, and tupelo
Larch, western
Maple (soft): red and silver
Pine, southern
Sycamore

Group 4:

Ash: commercial white
Beech
Birch: sweet and yellow
Elm, rock
Hickory, true
Maple (hard): black and sugar
Oak: commercial red and white
Pecan

The design procedure is as follows:

SIDE-MEMBER THICKNESS KNOWN, PENETRATION UNLIMITED

1. Select the largest diameter to give either minimum value (62 per cent) or full value (100 per cent) for the side member.
2. Calculate length to give a percentage of penetration the same as the percentage value of the side member, i.e., 100 or 62 per cent.
3. Add to this length a length equal to the diameter to allow for washer and point.

SIDE-MEMBER THICKNESS KNOWN, TOTAL PENETRATION LIMITED

1. Find the largest diameter as limited by minimum penetration, subtracting a length equal to the diameter from total penetration.
2. Find the largest diameter as limited by the minimum side member.
3. Use the smaller of the two diameters. If the side member determines diameter, penetration may be reduced accordingly by interpolation.

LAG DIAMETER KNOWN OR SELECTED

Side member and penetration to be chosen

1. Select a side-member thickness and penetration to give 100 per cent values.
2. Add a length equal to the diameter.

Side-member thickness known and equal or greater than 100 per cent value

1. Select penetration to give 100 per cent value.
2. Add a length equal to the diameter.

Side-member thickness known and less than 100 per cent value

1. Interpolate to determine a percentage based on the side member.
2. Select a penetration to give the same percentage.
3. Add a length equal to the diameter.

TABLE 12.34 Lateral resistance of lag screws for wood side plates and normal load[1]

Diameter in.	Allowable load, full value[2] lb.		Penetration[3] in.		Thickness of side members[4] in.	
	Angle of load to grain deg		Full per cent	Min. per cent	Full per cent	Min. per cent
Group 1	0°	90°	100%	45%	100%	62%
3/16	65	65	2.09	.95	.67	.42
¼	113	110	2.75	1.25	.88	.55
5/16	176	150	3.44	1.56	1.09	.68
⅜	253	192	4.13	1.88	1.31	.81
7/16	406	288	4.81	2.19	1.53	.95
½	450	293	5.50	2.50	1.75	1.09
⅝	703	422	6.88	3.13	2.19	1.36
¾	1,013	557	8.25	3.75	2.63	1.63
⅞	1,378	717	9.63	4.38	3.06	1.90
1	1,800	900	11.00	5.00	3.50	2.17
Group 2	0°	90°	100%	52%	100%	62%
3/16	74	74	1.84	.95	.67	.42
¼	128	124	2.42	1.25	.88	.55
5/16	199	169	3.02	1.56	1.09	.68
⅜	287	218	3.63	1.88	1.31	.81
7/16	460	327	4.23	2.19	1.53	.95
½	510	332	4.84	2.50	1.75	1.09
⅝	797	478	6.04	3.13	2.19	1.36
¾	1,148	631	7.25	3.75	2.63	1.63
⅞	1,562	812	8.46	4.38	3.06	1.90
1	2,040	1,020	9.67	5.00	3.50	2.17
Group 3	0°	90°	100%	60%	100%	62%
3/16	82	82	1.58	.95	.67	.42
¼	143	139	2.08	1.25	.88	.55
5/16	222	189	2.60	1.56	1.09	.68
⅜	321	244	3.12	1.88	1.31	.81
7/16	514	365	3.64	2.19	1.53	.95
½	570	371	4.17	2.50	1.75	1.09
⅝	891	535	5.21	3.13	2.19	1.36
¾	1,283	706	6.25	3.75	2.63	1.63
⅞	1,746	908	7.29	4.38	3.06	1.90
1	2,280	1,140	8.33	5.00	3.50	2.17
Group 4	0°	90°	100%	71%	100%	62%
3/16	95	95	1.33	.95	.67	.42
¼	165	160	1.75	1.25	.88	.55
5/16	257	219	2.19	1.56	1.09	.68
⅜	371	282	2.63	1.88	1.31	.81
7/16	596	423	3.06	2.19	1.53	.95
½	660	429	3.50	2.50	1.75	1.09
⅝	1,031	619	4.38	3.13	2.19	1.36
¾	1,485	817	5.25	3.75	2.63	1.63
⅞	2,021	1,051	6.13	4.38	3.06	1.90
1	2,640	1,320	7.00	5.00	3.50	2.17

[1] For simplicity, increases in allowable load for thicker side members and for penetration of shank into the

R PROPERTIES OF BOLTS

TABLE 12.35 Screw threads

SCREW THREADS

American National Form

American Standard, B 1.1—1935.

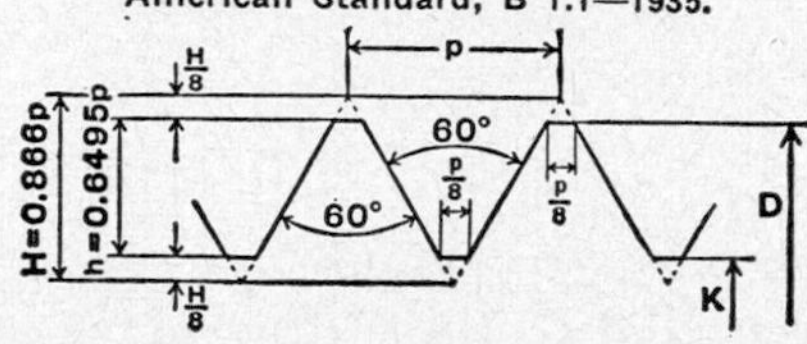

DIAMETER		AREA		Number of Threads per Inch
Total D In.	Net K In.	Total Dia., D Sq. In.	Net Dia., K Sq. In.	
¼	.185	.049	.027	20
⅜	.294	.110	.068	16
½	.400	.196	.126	13
⅝	.507	.307	.202	11
¾	.620	.442	.302	10
⅞	.731	.601	.419	9
1	.838	.785	.551	8
1⅛	.939	.994	.693	7
1¼	1.064	1.227	.890	7
1⅜	1.158	1.485	1.054	6
1½	1.283	1.767	1.294	6
1¾	1.490	2.405	1.744	5
2	1.711	3.142	2.300	4½
2¼	1.961	3.976	3.021	4½
2½	2.175	4.909	3.716	4
2¾	2.425	5.940	4.619	4

DIAMETER		AREA		Number of Threads per Inch
Total D In.	Net K In.	Total Dia., D Sq. In.	Net Dia., K Sq. In.	
3	2.675	7.069	5.621	4
3¼	2.925	8.296	6.720	4
3½	3.175	9.621	7.918	4
3¾	3.425	11.045	9.214	4
4	3.675	12.566	10.608	4
4¼	3.798	14.186	11.330	2⅞
4½	4.028	15.904	12.741	2¾
4¾	4.255	17.721	14.221	2⅝
5	4.480	19.635	15.766	2½
5¼	4.730	21.648	17.574	2½
5½	4.953	23.758	19.268	2⅜
5¾	5.203	25.967	21.262	2⅜
6	5.423	28.274	23.095	2¼

Sizes over 4″ are old U. S. Standard; there is no American Standard.
Dimensions are maximum; specify "Free Fit—Class 2." For Bolts from 2½″ to 6″ diameter it is always necessary to bill the number of threads per inch.

main member have not been introduced; also, the possible reduction, to a maximum of 80 per cent value, for bearing of threads on the side member has not been introduced. Thread bearing need be considered only if side-member thickness and penetration both exceed 80 per cent values. The data for wood side plates may be used for penetration for steel side plates. A considerable increase in allowable loads, up to 39 per cent, can be obtained by the more exact but complicated analysis of Chap. 13 (NDS, par. 700-702).

[2] See NDS for adjustments in allowable loads for duration of load (90 to 200 per cent), condition of lumber (40 to 100 per cent), service conditions (67 to 100 per cent), and other details. Allowable loads parallel to grain only (not perpendicular) may be increased 25 per cent for steel side plates. Use Hankinson formula for angles of load to grain between 0 and 90 deg.

[3] Interpolate in direct proportion for values between 100 per cent and minimum. Minimum value is for 5 diameters and is the same for all groups but gives a higher percentage for the harder woods. Full value varies from 11 diameters for Group 1 to 7 diameters for Group 4.

[4] Interpolate in direct proportion for intermediate values (see note 1). Values are the same for all groups. Full value equals 3.5 diameters and minimum value, 2 diameters.

TABLE 12.36 Length of bolt threads

LENGTH OF BOLT THREADS

American Standard, B 18.2—1941.

Length of Bolt Inches	Diameter of Bolt, Inches														
	1/4	3/8	1/2	5/8	3/4	7/8	1	1 1/8 1 1/4	1 3/8 1 1/2	1 5/8 1 3/4	1 7/8 2	2 1/4	2 1/2	2 3/4	3
	Minimum Thread Length														
1	3/4	3/4	3/4	3/4											
1 1/4	3/4	3/4	1	1	1										
1 1/2	3/4	7/8	1	1 1/8	1 1/8	1 1/8									
1 3/4	3/4	7/8	1	1 3/16	1 3/8	1 3/8	1 3/8								
2	3/4	1	1 1/4	1 1/4	1 3/8	1 9/16	1 5/8	1 5/8							
2 1/2	3/4	1	1 1/4	1 1/2	1 1/2	1 9/16	1 3/4	2	2						
3	7/8	1	1 1/4	1 1/2	1 3/4	1 3/4	1 3/4	2 1/8	2 1/2	2 1/2					
4	7/8	1	1 1/4	1 1/2	1 3/4	2	2 1/4	2 1/4	2 1/2	2 7/8	3 1/4	3 1/4	3 1/4		
5	7/8	1 3/16	1 1/4	1 1/2	1 3/4	2	2 1/4	2 3/4	2 3/4	2 7/8	3 1/4	3 5/8	4	4 1/8	4 1/4
6	7/8	1 3/16	1 1/2	1 1/2	1 3/4	2	2 1/4	2 3/4	3 1/4	3 1/4	3 1/4	3 5/8	4	4 1/8	4 3/4
8	7/8	1 3/16	1 1/2	1 13/16	2	2	2 1/4	2 3/4	3 1/4	3 3/4	4	4	4	4 1/8	4 3/4
10	7/8	1 3/16	1 1/2	1 13/16	2 1/8	2 7/16	2 1/2	2 3/4	3 1/4	3 3/4	4 1/4	4 3/4	4 3/4	4 3/4	4 3/4
12	7/8	1 3/16	1 1/2	1 13/16	2 1/8	2 7/16	2 3/4	2 3/4	3 1/4	3 3/4	4 1/4	4 3/4	5 1/4	5 3/4	6 1/4
16	1	1 3/16	1 1/2	1 13/16	2 1/8	2 7/16	2 3/4	3 1/4	3 1/4	3 3/4	4 1/4	4 3/4	5 1/4	5 3/4	6 1/4
20	1	1 3/8	1 1/2	1 13/16	2 1/8	2 7/16	2 3/4	3 3/8	4	4 5/8	4 3/4	4 3/4	5 1/4	5 3/4	6 1/4
30			1 3/4	1 13/16	2 1/8	2 7/16	2 3/4	3 3/8	4	4 5/8	5 1/4	5 7/8	6 1/2	6 1/2	6 1/2

For intermediate bolt lengths, same minimum thread length as for next shorter tabulated length.

TABLE 12.37 Bolt heads and nuts

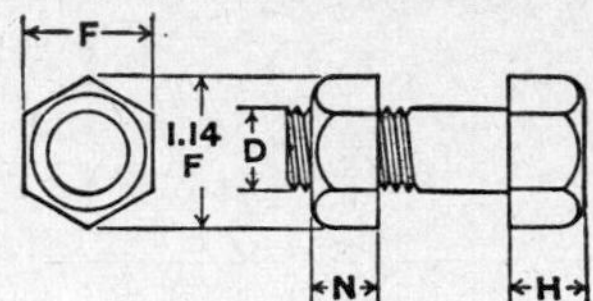

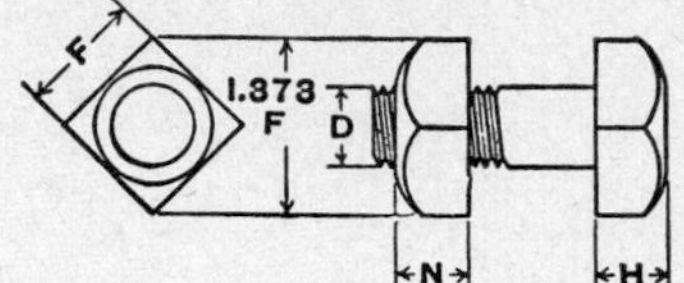

HEADS AND NUTS		American Standard Regular	American Standard Heavy
HEAD	Height, H	2/3 D	3/4 D + 1/16"
	Short Dia., F	1 1/2 D	1 1/2 D + 1/8"
NUT	Height, N	7/8 D	D
	Short Dia., F	1 1/2 D + 1/16" (D = 5/8" or less) 1 1/2 D (D greater than 5/8")	1 1/2 D + 1/8"

American Standard Bolt and Nut dimensions rounded to the nearest 1/16 inch, are those adopted by American Institute of Bolt, Nut and Rivet Manufacturers, American Standard B 18.2—1941. "American Standard Regular" formerly called Manufacturers Standard, American Standard, etc. "American Standard Heavy" formerly called United States Standard. Some fabricators have standard heads and nuts differing only slightly from the table. For bolts with countersunk heads the included angle is 78 degrees, the same as for rivets. See page 160 for dimensions.

STANDARD DIMENSIONS

HEAD

Dia. of Bolt In.	Series	Hexagon Diameter, In. Long	Hexagon Diameter, In. Short	Height In.	Square Diameter, In. Long	Square Diameter, In. Short
1/4	American Standard Regular	7/16	3/8	3/16	1/2	3/8
3/8		5/8	9/16	1/4	3/4	9/16
1/2		7/8	3/4	5/16	1	3/4
5/8		1 1/16	15/16	7/16	1 5/16	15/16
3/4		1 5/16	1 1/8	1/2	1 9/16	1 1/8
7/8		1 1/2	1 5/16	9/16	1 13/16	1 5/16
1		1 11/16	1 1/2	5/8	2 1/16	1 1/2
1 1/8		1 15/16	1 11/16	3/4	2 5/16	1 11/16
1 1/4		2 1/8	1 7/8	13/16	2 9/16	1 7/8
1 3/8		2 3/8	2 1/16	15/16	2 13/16	2 1/16
1 1/2		2 9/16	2 1/4	1	3 1/16	2 1/4
1 5/8		2 3/4	2 7/16	1 1/16	3 3/8	2 7/16
1 3/4		3	2 5/8	1 3/16	3 5/8	2 5/8
1 7/8		3 3/16	2 13/16	1 1/4	3 7/8	2 13/16
2		3 7/16	3	1 5/16	4 1/8	3
2 1/4		3 7/8	3 3/8	1 1/2	4 5/8	3 3/8
2 1/2		4 1/4	3 3/4	1 11/16	5 1/8	3 3/4
2 3/4		4 11/16	4 1/8	1 13/16	5 11/16	4 1/8
3		5 1/8	4 1/2	2	6 3/16	4 1/2
3 1/4	Former Manufacturers Std.	5 9/16	4 7/8	2 3/16	6 11/16	4 7/8
3 1/2		6	5 1/4	2 5/16	7 3/16	5 1/4
3 3/4		6 7/16	5 5/8	2 1/2	7 3/4	5 5/8
4		6 7/8	6	2 11/16	8 1/4	6
4 1/4		7 1/4	6 3/8	2 13/16	8 3/4	6 3/8
4 1/2		7 11/16	6 3/4	3	9 1/4	6 3/4
4 3/4		8 1/8	7 1/8	3 3/16	9 13/16	7 1/8
5		8 9/16	7 1/2	3 5/16	10 5/16	7 1/2
5 1/4		9	7 7/8	3 1/2	10 13/16	7 7/8
5 1/2		9 3/8	8 1/4	3 11/16	11 5/16	8 1/4
5 3/4		9 13/16	8 5/8	3 13/16	11 13/16	8 5/8
6		10 1/4	9	4	12 3/8	9

NUT

Dia. of Bolt In.	Series	Hexagon Diameter, In. Long	Hexagon Diameter, In. Short	Height In.	Square Diameter, In. Long	Square Diameter, In. Short
1/4	American Standard Regular	1/2	7/16	1/4	5/8	7/16
3/8		11/16	5/8	5/16	7/8	5/8
1/2		15/16	13/16	7/16	1 1/8	13/16
5/8		1 1/8	1	9/16	1 3/8	1
3/4		1 5/16	1 1/8	11/16	1 9/16	1 1/8
7/8		1 1/2	1 5/16	3/4	1 13/16	1 5/16
1		1 11/16	1 1/2	7/8	2 1/16	1 1/2
1 1/8		1 15/16	1 11/16	1	2 5/16	1 11/16
1 1/4		2 1/8	1 7/8	1 1/8	2 9/16	1 7/8
1 3/8		2 3/8	2 1/16	1 1/4	2 13/16	2 1/16
1 1/2		2 9/16	2 1/4	1 5/16	3 1/8	2 1/4
1 3/8	American Standard Heavy	2 1/2	2 3/16	1 3/8	3	2 3/16
1 1/2		2 11/16	2 3/8	1 1/2	3 1/4	2 3/8
1 5/8		2 15/16	2 9/16	1 5/8	3 1/2	2 9/16
1 3/4		3 1/8	2 3/4	1 3/4	3 3/4	2 3/4
1 7/8		3 3/8	2 15/16	1 7/8	4 1/16	2 15/16
2		3 9/16	3 1/8	2	4 5/16	3 1/8
2 1/4		4	3 1/2	2 1/4	4 13/16	3 1/2
2 1/2		4 7/16	3 7/8	2 1/2	5 5/16	3 7/8
2 3/4		4 7/8	4 1/4	2 3/4	5 13/16	4 1/4
3		5 1/4	4 5/8	3	6 3/8	4 5/8
3 1/4		5 11/16	5	3 1/4	6 7/8	5
3 1/2		6 1/8	5 3/8	3 1/2	7 3/8	5 3/8
3 3/4		6 9/16	5 3/4	3 3/4	7 7/8	5 3/4
4		7	6 1/8	4	8 7/16	6 1/8
4 1/4	Former U. S. Std.	7 7/16	6 1/2	4 1/4	8 15/16	6 1/2
4 1/2		7 13/16	6 7/8	4 1/2	9 7/16	6 7/8
4 3/4		8 1/4	7 1/4	4 3/4	9 15/16	7 1/4
5		8 11/16	7 5/8	5	10 1/2	7 5/8
5 1/4		9 1/8	8	5 1/4	11	8
5 1/2		9 9/16	8 3/8	5 1/2	11 1/2	8 3/8
5 3/4		10	8 3/4	5 3/4	12	8 3/4
6		10 3/8	9 1/8	6	12 1/2	9 1/8

S PROPERTIES OF WASHERS

Five types of washers are used in timber construction (see Table 12.38): (1) cast-iron ogee (Fig. a), (2) cast-iron ribbed (Fig. d), (3) malleable iron (Fig. g), (4) circular pressed steel (Fig. b), and (5) square plate washers (Fig. c). Washers of standard sizes and shapes may be bought from the manufacturers. For bolts over 2 in. in diameter, special cast-iron washers (Fig. d) are often used, although this type is very expensive unless a large number of one size is required.

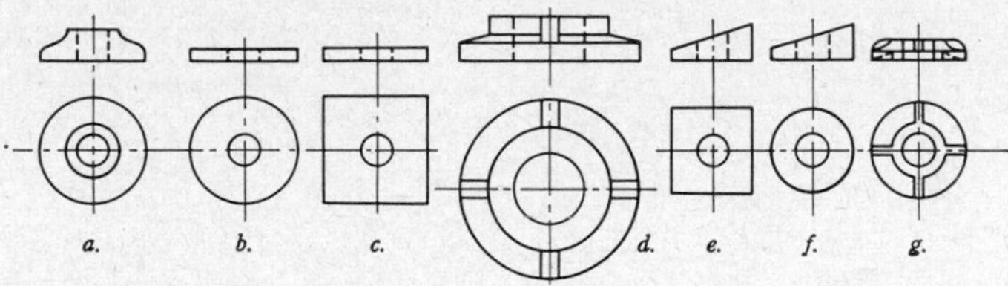

Beveled cast-iron washers (Figs. e and f), useful if the axis of the bolt makes an angle with the bearing surface, may also be purchased from the manufacturers. If the bolt makes an angle with the bearing surface, the timber may be notched instead and the beveled washer dispensed with, provided the notch does not reduce the timber section beyond a safe limit. Such bearing would be inclined to the direction of the fiber, and greater unit stresses can be taken advantage of. If notching is impracticable, especially if large washers are required, a combination of a large flat washer and a small beveled washer may be economical.

To determine the size of washer required, divide the tension in the bolt by the safe unit compression of the wood and add the area of the hole of the washer, which gives the gross area required. From this figure, the outside dimensions are computed. Washer thickness, if of wrought iron or steel, should be at least ⅛ its width or diameter. If of cast iron (Fig. a), the thickness should be not less than about ¼ its diameter. The square-plate washer should have a thickness of ½ the diameter of the bolt plus 1/16 in. If of the type shown in Fig. d, it may be designed similar to cast-iron shoes, the unit pressure upon the bottom of the washer being the allowable compression upon the wood. If the tension in the bolt is small, use standard washers.

TABLE 12.38 Washer dimensions

Diameter *in.*	Size of hole *in.*	Approximate number in a pound	Area of washer *sq in.*
Wrought-iron or steel-plate round washers[1]			
1⅜	9/16	27.0	1.3
1½	⅝	22.0	1.5
1¾	11/16	13.0	2.0
2	13/16	10.0	2.6
2¼	15/16	8.6	3.3
2½	1 1/16	6.2	4.0
2¾	1¼	5.2	4.5
3	1⅜	4.0	5.6
3¼	1½	2.8	6.5
3½	1⅝	2.5	7.6
3¾	1¾	2.4	8.6
4	1⅞	2.2	9.8
4¼	2	1.9	11.0
4½	2⅛	1.7	12.4
4¾	2⅜	1.0	13.3
5	2⅝	1.0	14.2
Wrought-iron or steel-plate square washers[2]			
2	9/16	5.0	3.8
2¼	¾	3.2	4.6
2½	⅞	2.5	5.7
3	1	1.7	8.2
3½	1⅛	.9	11.3
4	1⅛	.7	15.0
4½	1¼	.5	19.0
5	1½	.4	23.2
6	1⅝	.3	34.0
Cast-iron washers[3]			
2¼	⅝	3.3	3.8
2¾	¾	2.5	5.5
3¼	⅞	1.4	7.9
3¾	1	1.0	10.1
4	1⅛	.5	11.6
4½	1¼	.4	14.7
5	1⅜	.3	18.2
6	1¾	.2	25.9

[1] The size of hole in washer is 1/16 in. larger than the diameter of the bolt up to and including bolts 1 in. in diameter. For larger bolts, the hole is ⅛ in. larger.
[2] For size of bolts, see round-plate washers.
[3] The size of hole in washer is ⅛ in. larger than the diameter of the bolt up to and including bolts 1¼ in. in diameter. For larger bolts, the hole is ¼ in. larger.

T ALLOWABLE WORKING STRESSES FOR STEEL AND MASONRY BEARING

TABLE 12.39

Stress	Allowable unit stress [1] psi
Structural steel, rivets, bolts	
Tension	
Structural steel (net section)	20,000
Rivets (on area based on nom. dia.)	20,000
Bolts and other threaded parts (on nom. area at root of thread)	20,000
Compression	
Columns, axially loaded (gross section) [2]	
All members, $l/r \leq 120$	$17{,}000 - 0.485\,(l/r)^2$
Bracing and other secondary members, $l/r > 120$	$\dfrac{18{,}000}{1 - \dfrac{l^2}{18{,}000\,r^2}}$
Bending	
Rolled sections, plate girders, built-up members [3]	
Tension (on extreme fibers)	20,000
Compression (on extreme fibers)	
$ld/bt \leq 600$	20,000
$ld/bt > 600$	$\dfrac{12{,}000{,}000}{ld/bt}$
Pins (on extreme fibers)	30,000
Shearing	
Rivets	15,000
Pins and turned bolts in reamed or drilled holes	15,000
Unfinished bolts	10,000
Webs of beams and plate girders (gross section)	13,000
Bearing	
Rivets	
Double shear	40,000
Single shear	32,000
Pins and turned bolts in reamed or drilled holes	
Double shear	40,000
Single shear	32,000
Unfinished bolts	
Double shear	25,000
Single shear	20,000
Pins	32,000
Milled stiffeners (on contact area)	30,000
Fitted stiffeners (on contact area)	27,000
Expansion rollers and rockers (on contact area) [4]	$600d$

TABLE 12.39 Allowable stresses (Cont.)

Stress	Allowable unit stress [1] *psi*
Cast steel	
Compression	as for structural steel
Bearing	as for structural steel
Tension	¾ value for structural steel
Bending	¾ value for structural steel
Shearing	¾ value for structural steel
Wind loading	as for structural steel
Wind and other forces	as for structural steel

Masonry bearing

Material	Allowable compression *psi*
Granite	800
Sandstone and limestone	400
Portland Cement concrete (unless otherwise specified)	600
Hard brick in cement mortar	250

[1] Members subject to stresses *produced only by wind forces* may be proportioned for unit stresses 33⅓ per cent greater than those specified for dead and live-load stresses. A corresponding increase may be applied to the allowable unit stresses in their connecting rivets, bolts, or welds. Members subject to stresses *produced by a combination of wind and other loads* may be proportioned for unit stresses 33⅓ per cent greater than those specified for dead and live-load stresses, provided the section thus required is not less than that required for the combination of dead load, live load, and impact (if any). A corresponding increase may be applied to the allowable unit stresses in their connecting rivets, bolts, or welds.

[2] l = unbraced length of the column; and r = corresponding radius of gyration of section, both in inches.

[3] l = unsupported length; d = depth of members; b = width; t = thickness of compression flange, all in inches—except that l shall be taken as twice the length of the compression flange of a cantilever beam not fully stayed at its outer end against translation or rotation.

[4] Stress in lb per lin in.; d = diameter of rocker or roller, in inches.

U TYPICAL LIVE-LOAD REQUIREMENTS

Local and state building codes usually define exact live-load requirements for buildings within their jurisdiction. If no such code controls or if the code allows some judgment on the part of the designer, the discussion and suggestions of this section will be of assistance. Local codes are helpful as guides even though they may not legally control.

ROOF LOADS Roof live loads may include basic (no-snow) loads, snow load, water, ice, sleet, wind, and earthquake loads, and floor type loads for roof decks. Local weather bureaus are excellent sources of information for snow, ice, and wind loads.

Basic live loads in the range of 12 to 20 psf are used in areas of no snow, or where snowfalls are light, infrequent, and of short duration. This load provides an additional safety factor for unforeseen loads and for the weight of workmen and material during construction. If snow and other known live loads are not a factor, basic live load is frequently assumed to vary according to the shape of roof and according to the tributary roof area, as indicated in Table 12.40.

Snow live load may be estimated on the basis of maximum snow depths on the ground at any one time. Actual snow load on the ground may vary from 0 to 60 psf or more, depending upon locality. Snow is usually estimated at from 0.5 to 0.7 psf per inch of depth. Table 12.41 lists snow and basic live-load requirements for roofs in various city building codes, in pounds per square foot.

It is reasonable to assume that some shapes of roof retain less snow than others. For these roofs, snow live loads may be reduced, assuming that construction features such as parapet walls, monitors, valleys, and snow guards do not improve retention of the snow. Such features frequently bear close study. Table 12.42 shows reductions in snow and basic live loads for differing shapes of roof.

FLOOR LIVE LOADS Suggested values for uniformly distributed floor live loads are given in Table 12.43. Permissible live loads should be posted in warehouses, stores, and manufacturing plants.

Reduction of floor live loads for tributary areas on members and for successive floor loads on columns is permitted by many codes. A suggested reduction pattern for all members supporting 150 sq ft or more of floor is a 15 per cent reduction in unit live loads, and for columns, a further reduction of 5 per cent per floor up to 40 per cent. All concentrated live loads occurring singly or in combination with uniform live loads are considered in the design.

WIND LOADS For average structures, wind pressure should be considered as acting on the gross area of the vertical projection of the structure at not less than 15 psf for those portions of the building less than 60 ft above the ground, and at not less than 20 psf for those portions more than 60 ft above the ground. Greenhouses, lath houses, and farm structures, in which there is less hazard to life, are often designed for a pressure as low as 10 psf.

The wind pressure upon roof tanks, roof signs, or other exposed roof structures and their supports should be considered as acting on the gross area in any direction at not less than 30 psf. Pressure on circular tanks, towers, or stacks is assumed to act on 3/5 of the projected area. The relationship of wind velocity to pressure is given in Table 12.44.

On open framed structures, such as bridges or towers, with two sets of supporting frames, the pressure area should be 1½ times the net area of the framing members in the side exposed to the wind, and ½ again as much for each added set of frames.

There are few well-defined recommendations for wind-suction forces on structures, as model tests show considerable variation in pressure and suction distribution and magnitude for slight changes in shape or proportions. It has been suggested that all roofs be adequate for a minimum of 5 to 10 psf net suction. The designer may care to consult other references for a more detailed treatment of wind pressure and suction forces.

COMBINED SNOW AND WIND For average conditions, maximum snow and wind loads on roofs are not usually assumed to occur at the same time. Wind load is sometimes assumed as occurring on the windward slope with snow load on the leeward slope of pitched or arch roofs but even such a combination is unlikely. The effect of wind forces in distributing snow loads is usually recognized by the requirement that roofs be adequate for unbalanced snow load—varying from full unbalanced (full snow load on only one-half of roof) to half unbalanced (with full snow load on one-half of roof and one-half snow load on the other half). The roof structure must of course be adequate for full uniform snow load, and the unbalanced loading conditions are usually not critical, except possibly for web-member stress reversals in trusses and for bending moment in arch type roofs. Half-unbalanced snow load is considered more realistic than full unbalanced.

IMPACT AND VIBRATION FORCES The effect of very short duration loads, such as impact and vibration, can usually be neglected in timber structures, except for those portions made of materials for which these forces may be critical. Thus impact would normally not be considered for a wood beam but might be considered for the beam connections if the loads were transferred by metal shear. Similarly, a wood truss with metal splice plates would require consideration of impact for the metal splice plates.

For all practical purposes there is no fatigue limit in wood, and thus vibration is usually considered only as it might loosen threaded connections.

HIGHWAY LOADS Live and dead-load requirements for timber highway structures are given in great detail in standard specifications, such as the AASHO "Standard Specification for Highway Bridges."[1] Except for the infrequent project in which exact live loads can be determined and controlled, such as privately owned bridges, the AASHO specifications are the accepted standards for public structures and are used by most state and local highway departments and by Federal government agencies.

RAILROAD LOADS Like highway loads, railroad design loads are too specialized to warrant detailed discussion in this handbook. The designer should consult "Specifications for Design of Wood Bridges and Trestles for Railway Loading."[2] These specifications recommend the Cooper system of equivalent wheel loads.

EARTHQUAKE LOADS The following partial excerpt from the PCBOC "Uniform Building Code,"[3] represents the design load recommendation widely used in those western states where earthquake design is common practice:

> Structures in earthquake hazard zones shall be designed to resist earthquake forces. Where wind loads produce higher stresses, the wind loads shall be used in lieu of earthquake loads. For stresses induced by earthquake in timber structures, the proper short-time stress increase may be used. (*See the earthquake zone map of the United States in Fig. 12.4.*)
>
> (A) GENERAL Building or structure and every portion thereof shall be designed and constructed to resist stresses produced by lateral forces as provided below. Stresses shall be calculated as the effect of a force applied horizontally at each floor or roof level above the foundation. The force shall be assumed to come from any horizontal direction.
>
> All bracing systems both horizontal and vertical shall transmit all forces to the resisting members and shall be of sufficient extent and detail to resist the horizontal forces and shall be located symmetrically about the center of mass of the building or the building shall be designed for the resulting rotational forces about the vertical axis.
>
> Junctures between distinct parts of buildings, such as wings which extend

[1] American Association of State Highway Officials.

[2] American Railway Engineering Association Manual.

[3] Copyright 1955 Pacific Coast Building Officials Conference.

more than 20 ft from the main portion of the building, shall be designed at the juncture with other parts of the building for rotational forces, or the juncture may be made by means of sliding fragile joints having a minimum width of not less than 8 in.

(B) HORIZONTAL FORCE FORMULA In determining the horizontal force to be resisted, the following formula shall be used:

$$F = CW$$

in which:

F = the horizontal force, in pounds

W = the total dead load, tributary to the point under consideration, except for warehouses and tanks. For tanks, W shall equal the total dead load plus the total vertical design live-load tributary to the point under consideration, and for warehouses, W shall equal dead load plus one-half the live load. Machinery or other fixed concentrated loads shall be considered as part of the dead load

C = a numerical constant (*as shown in Table 12.45*)

TABLE 12.40 Basic roof live load (no snow)

Roof type	Basic load *psf* — Tributary loaded area for any structural element *sq ft*		
	0 to 200	201 to 600	over 600
Low rise [1]	20	16	12
Medium rise [2]	16	14	12
High rise [3]	12	12	12

[1] Low rise refers to roofs that are (1) flat; (2) pitched with rise less than 4 in. per foot, as occurs with parallel chord or slightly sloping top-chord trusses; (3) curved arches or domes with rise less than ⅛ of span.
[2] Medium rise refers to roofs that are (1) pitched with rise 4 in. per foot; (2) curved arches or domes with rise ⅛ of span to less than ⅜ of span or with radius ¾ or greater of the span, as occurs with most bowstring trusses and with many two-hinged arches.
[3] High rise refers to roofs that are (1) pitched with rise 12 in. per foot or greater, as occurs in most scissor and with most high-rise church trusses; (2) curved arches or domes with rise ⅜ or greater of the span or with radius less than ¾ of the span, such as Gothic barns.

TABLE 12.41 Snow and basic live load requirements of various city building codes

City	Load *psf*	City	Load *psf*
Chicago, Ill.	25	New Orleans, La.	20
Dallas, Tex.	20	New York, N. Y.	40
Denver, Col.	40	Portland, Ore.	25
Kansas City, Mo.	40	San Francisco, Calif.	15
Los Angeles, Calif.	15	Seattle, Wash.	25
Madison, Wis.	40	Spokane, Wash.	40
Minneapolis, Minn.	40	St. Louis, Mo.	40

TABLE 12.42 Suggested live loads (including snow) for various types of roof

Snow and basic live load psf	Suggested load psf — Type of roof: Low-rise	Medium-rise	High-rise
40	40	30	15
30	30	25	12
25	25	20	12
20	20	15	10
15	15	12	10
12	12	10	10

TABLE 12.43 Floor live loads

Occupancy	Load psf	Occupancy	Load psf
Apartments	40	Libraries, reading	60
Armories	150	Lofts	100
Auditoriums		Manufacturing, light	75
Fixed seats	50	Manufacturing, heavy	125
Movable seats	100	Marquees	40 to 60
Balconies		Offices	50
Fixed seats	50	Printing rooms	150
Movable seats	100	Public rooms	100
Bleachers	100	Rest rooms	50 to 100
Cornices	60	Roofs	12 to 40
Corridors, public	100	Schools	
Dance halls	100	Classrooms	40
Drill rooms	100	Corridors	100
Dwellings	40	Sidewalks	250
Fire escapes	100	Skating rinks	100
Garages	100	Stairways	100
Gymnasiums	100	Storage, light	125
Hospitals	40	Storage, heavy	250 (min.)
Hotels	40	Stores, light	75
Libraries, stock	125	Stores, heavy	100

TABLE 12.44 Relationship of wind velocity to pressure

Type of wind	Velocity *mph*	Pressure on vertical surface *psf*
Gentle breeze	10	0.5
Fresh breeze	20	1.5
Strong breeze	30	3.5
Gale	40	6.5
Strong gale	50	10.0
Whole gale	60	15.0
Hurricane	75 to 100 or more	25.0-40.0

TABLE 12.45 Horizontal force factors for seismic loading

Portion of structure	Direction of force	Numerical constant[1] *C*
Floors, roof, columns, and bracing in any story of a building or the structure as a whole[2]	Any direction horizontally	$\frac{.15}{N+4\frac{1}{2}}$
Bearing walls, non-bearing walls, partitions, and free-standing masonry walls over 6 ft in height[3]	Normal to surface of wall	0.05
Cantilever parapet and other cantilever walls, except retaining walls	Normal to surface of wall	0.25
Exterior and interior ornamentations and appendages	Any direction horizontally	0.25
Towers, tanks, towers and tanks plus contents, chimneys, smokestacks, and penthouses, if connected to or a part of a building	Any direction horizontally	0.05
Tanks, elevated tanks, smokestacks, standpipes, and similar structures not supported by a building	Any direction horizontally	0.025

[1] Coefficients are for minimum hazard in zone 1 areas; For zone 2, use 2 times the above *C* values; for zone 3, use 4 times the above *C* values. (See Fig. 12.4.)

[2] N equals number of stories above the story under consideration, provided that N for floors or horizontal bracing shall be only the number of stories contributing load.

[3] A minimum *F* value of 5 psf should be used.

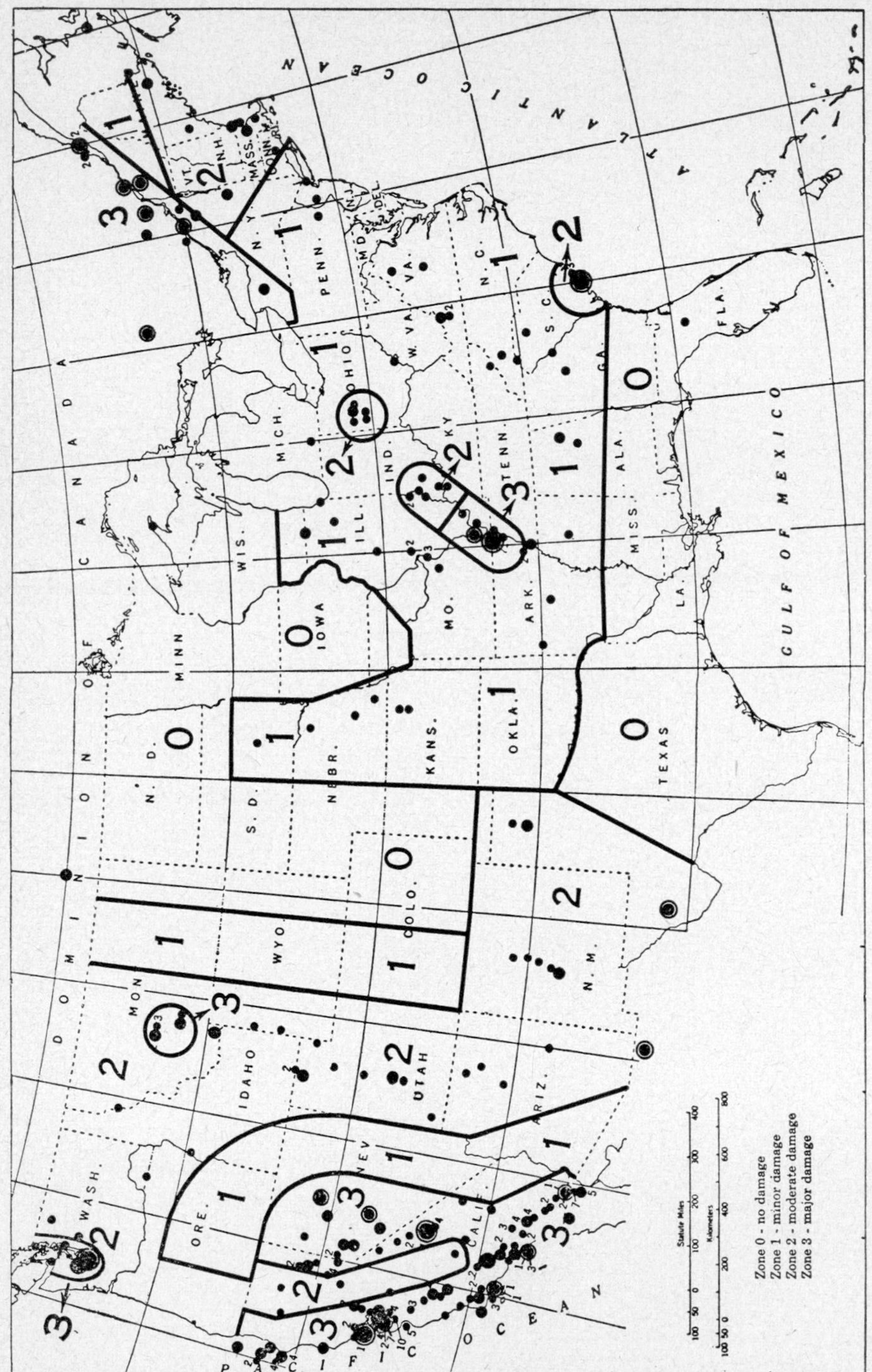

Fig. 12.4 Earthquake probability map of the United States

13

Design Standards

Reproduced in this chapter are those design standards—current at time of printing—which represent the practices recommended by the lumber industry and which are the most generally accepted standards for timber design and construction.

All standards are subject to change, and the users of this handbook several years after a printing may care to obtain separate copies of these standards to ascertain whether any change has been made that might substantially affect a design process or its results.

These design standards, presented in four sections, are as follows:

1. "National Design Specification for Stress-Grade Lumber and Its Fastenings" (herein referred to as "NDS"), established 1944, revised 1955, recommended by National Lumber Manufacturers Association, Washington, D. C.

2. "Design Manual for Timber Connector Construction" (herein referred to as "DM"), by Timber Engineering Company, Washington, D. C.

3. Portions of "American Standard Specifications and Dimensions for Wood Poles" (herein referred to as "ASA"), established by the American Standards Association.

4. Portions of "Specification For Round Timber Piles D25–55" (herein referred to as "ASTM"), established by the American Society for Testing Materials.

NATIONAL DESIGN SPECIFICATION FOR STRESS-GRADE LUMBER AND ITS FASTENINGS

Established 1944
Revised 1955

This specification is based on and recognizes the value of competent engineering design, accurate fabrication, and adequate supervision of construction where stress-grade lumber is used. With the lumber preparation, its installation and joining, and its fastenings conforming to good engineering practice, the application of the Specification affords a means of realizing more efficient and economical lumber structures.

Material which is qualified for the working stresses assigned to the grade is assured by the use of stress-grades of lumber identified by the grade mark of, or certificate of inspection issued by, a lumber grading or inspection bureau or agency recognized as being competent.

CONTENTS

NDS Part I. General—Stress-Grade Lumber

100—SCOPE

100–A. This specification defines the practice to be followed in design with, and in fabrication and erection of, stress-grade lumber (see par. 102-B), and structural glued-laminated lumber (see NDS Part IX) and also in design with, and installation of, the fastenings defined herein when used to connect stress-grade lumber or structural glued-laminated lumber.

In this Specification the word "shall" is mandatory and the word "should" is advisory.

100–B. The allowable unit stresses given in NDS Tables 1, 20, and 21 and the requirements in NDS Parts II and IX are for designs made and carried out under competent supervision and for lumber of assured grade.

100–C. Allowable unit stresses for species and grades of lumber not given in the following tables shall be established in accordance with the principles set forth in "American Lumber Standards, Simplified Practice Recommendation R16–53," and "Guide to the Grading of Structural Timber and Determination of Working Stresses," Miscellaneous Publication No. 185, United States Department of Agriculture, dated February, 1934, and the 1940 and 1948 supplements thereto, using 110 per cent of the values in columns 2, 3, 4 and 5 of Table 1 of the 1948 supplement for normal loading conditions. (For structural glued-laminated lumber, see NDS Part IX.)

101—GENERAL REQUIREMENTS

101–A. The quality of the wood and the design for load-supporting members when stress-grades are used shall conform to the standards hereinafter specified.

101–B. All members shall be so framed, anchored, tied, and braced that they have the necessary strength and rigidity.

101–C. In the engineering design, care should be taken that the connections, both at joints and splices, are such that each individual piece carries its proportional stress and consideration is given to stresses resulting from moment in joints.

102—STRESS-GRADE LUMBER

102–A. Lumber grades shall be specified by commercial grade names.

102–B. Stress-grade lumber consists of lumber classifications known as "Beams and Stringers," "Joists and Planks," and "Posts and Timbers," to each grade of which is assigned proper allowable unit stresses.

102–B–1. **Beams and stringers.** Lumber of rectangular cross-section, 5 or more in. thick and 8 or more in. wide, graded with respect to its strength in bending when loaded on the narrow face.

102–B–2. **Joists and planks.** Lumber of rectangular cross-section, 2 in. to, but not including, 5 in. thick and 4 or more in. wide, graded with respect to its strength in bending when loaded either on the narrow face as a joist or on the wide face as a plank.

102–B–3. **Posts and timbers.** Lumber of square or approximately square cross section 5 by 5 in. and larger, graded primarily for use as posts or columns carrying longitudinal load but adapted for miscellaneous uses in which strength in bending is not especially important.

NDS Part II. Allowable Unit Stresses for Stress-Grade Lumber

200—GENERAL STRESS PROVISIONS

200–A. Each wood structural member shall be of sufficient size to carry the dead and required live loads[1] without exceeding the allowable unit stress hereinafter specified. Adequate bracing and bridging to resist wind and other lateral forces shall be provided.

200–B. When stress-grade lumber is resawed, it shall be regraded and allowable unit stresses for the regraded material shall apply.

200–C. Minimum sizes of lumber members required by this specification refer to nominal sizes. American Lumber Standard dressed sizes (ref. 1, NDS Appendix R) shall be accepted as the minimum net sizes conforming to nominal sizes. Computations to determine the required sizes of members shall be based on the net dimensions (actual size) and not the nominal sizes. If rough sizes or finished sizes greater or smaller than American Lumber Standard dressed sizes are to be used, computations shall be predicated upon such actual sizes, provided they are specified on the plans or in a statement appended thereto. For convenience, nominal sizes may be shown on the plans.

200–D. Induced stresses, in pounds per square inch, computed on the basis of actual dimensions, shall not exceed the allowable unit stresses except as hereinafter modified for the respective species and grades in NDS Table 1. When the allowable unit stresses in this table are used, the lumber shall be identified by the grade mark of, or certificate of inspection issued by, a lumber grading or inspection bureau or agency recognized as being competent.

[1] Live loads as used herein include wind, snow, impact, earthquake, and other applied loads.

200–E. The allowable unit stresses in NDS Table 1 and adjustments thereof apply to lumber in any condition of seasoning unless otherwise provided herein.

201—ALLOWABLE STRESSES FOR NORMAL LOADING CONDITIONS

201–A. The allowable unit stresses in NDS Table 1 are applicable in all conditions other than those for which specific exceptions are made.

202—ALLOWABLE UNIT STRESSES FOR SERVICE CONDITIONS

202–A. The allowable unit stresses in NDS Table 1 and adjustments thereof apply to sawed lumber used under conditions continuously dry, such as in most covered structures. The allowable unit stresses for glued-laminated lumber for this condition of use are given in NDS Tables 20 and 21.

202–B. The allowable unit stresses in NDS Table 1 and adjustments thereof apply to lumber used under conditions where the moisture content of the wood is at or above the fiber-saturation point, as when continuously submerged, except that under such conditions of use the allowable unit stresses in compression parallel to grain shall be reduced 10 per cent, in compression perpendicular to the grain shall be reduced $\frac{1}{3}$ and the values for modulus of elasticity shall be reduced 1/11. The allowable unit stresses for glued-laminated lumber for this condition of use are given in NDS Tables 20 and 21.

202–C. The allowable unit stresses in NDS Tables 1, 20, and 21 and adjustments thereof apply to lumber pressure-impregnated by an approved process and preservative and to the heartwood of a durable species under dry or other conditions of use except as provided in par. 202-B.

203—ALLOWABLE UNIT STRESSES FOR SNOW, WIND, EARTHQUAKE, SHORT-TIME, OR IMPACT LOADING

203–A. When the duration of the full maximum load does not exceed the period indicated, increase the allowable unit stresses in NDS Tables 1, 20, and 21 as follows:

15 per cent for 2 months' duration, as for snow
25 per cent for 7 days' duration
33⅓ per cent for wind or earthquake
100 per cent for impact

Allowable unit stresses given in NDS Tables 1, 20, and 21 for normal loading conditions may be used without regard to impact if the stress induced by impact does not exceed the allowable unit stress for normal loading. The above increases are not cumulative. The resulting structural members shall not be smaller than required for a longer duration of loading. The provisions of this paragraph apply to the modulus of elasticity when used to determine allowable unit loads for columns, otherwise they do not apply thereto. These increases apply to mechanical fastenings except as otherwise noted. (See NDS Appendix H for explanation of application.)

204—ALLOWABLE UNIT STRESSES FOR FULL LOAD PERMANENTLY APPLIED

204–A. Where a member is fully stressed to the maximum allowable stress for many years, either continuously or cumulatively under the condition of maximum design load, use working stresses 90 per cent of those in NDS Tables 1, 20, and 21. The provisions of this paragraph apply to modulus of elasticity when used to determine allowable unit loads for columns, otherwise they do not apply thereto. The provisions of this paragraph apply to mechanical fastenings except as otherwise noted. (See NDS Appendix H for explanation of application.)

205—ALLOWABLE UNIT STRESSES FOR FLEXURE

205–A. Allowable unit stresses in flexure for Joist and Plank grades apply to material with the load applied to either the narrow or wide face.

205–B. Allowable unit stresses in flexure for Beam and Stringer grades apply only to material with the load applied to the narrow face.

205–C. Beam grades ordinarily are graded for use on simple spans. When used as a continuous beam, the grading provisions customarily applied to the middle third of the length of simple spans shall be applied to the middle two-thirds of the length of pieces to be used over double spans and to the entire length of pieces to be used over three or more spans.

205–D. For design formulas, see par. 400.

206—ALLOWABLE UNIT STRESSES FOR COMPRESSION PARALLEL TO GRAIN

206–A. The allowable unit stresses for compression parallel to grain in NDS Tables 1, 20, and 21, subject to the adjustments provided in par. 201, 202, 203, and 204, shall not be exceeded in any column nor in the individual members of a spaced column.

Within this limitation, the allowable unit stresses for various l/d ratios shall be determined by the column formulas given in par. 401.

207—ALLOWABLE UNIT STRESSES FOR COMBINED COMPRESSION AND FLEXURE

207–A. When members are subjected to loading which induces combined flexure and axial compressive stresses, a grade qualifying for a bending stress shall be used. (See NDS Tables 1, 20, and 21.)

207–B. For design formulas, see par. 403-B.

208—ALLOWABLE UNIT STRESSES FOR TENSION AND COMBINED TENSION AND FLEXURE

208–A. For design formulas, see par. 403-A and 404-A.

209—ALLOWABLE UNIT STRESSES FOR SHEAR

209–A. Induced stresses in horizontal shear shall be computed in accordance with par. 400-D.

209–B. Allowable unit stresses for shear in joint details may be 50 per cent greater than the horizontal shear values otherwise permitted.

210—ALLOWABLE UNIT STRESSES FOR BEARING PERPENDICULAR TO GRAIN

210–A. The allowable unit stresses for compression perpendicular to the grain in NDS Table 1 assume the material will be surface seasoned when installed.

210–B. In joists supported on a ribbon or ledger board and spiked to the studs, the allowable unit stresses in NDS Tables 1, 20, and 21 for compression perpendicular to grain may be increased by 50 per cent.

210–C. Allowable unit stresses in compression perpendicular to grain may be increased for bearings less than 6 in. in length and located 3 in. or more from the end of a timber in accordance with par. 400-E.

211—ALLOWABLE UNIT STRESSES FOR END BEARING OF COMPRESSION MEMBERS ON METAL PLATES OR STRAPS

211–A. If a wood compression member that bears on a metal plate or strap, e. g., as at the heel joint of a truss, contains no knot at the bearing greater in diameter than 1½ in. or ¼ the minimum cross-sectional dimension of the bearing area, whichever is the lesser, the allowable unit stress for bearing is the value for the species given in NDS Table 2, or, if the loading is at an angle to grain, shall be determined by the Hankinson formula (par. 405, NDS Appendix C), using the allowable unit stress parallel to grain from NDS Table 2 and allowable unit stress

NDS TABLE 2 Allowable unit stresses in bearing parallel to grain on metal plates, in pounds per square inch

(The allowable unit stresses below are for normal loading conditions. See other provisions of NDS Part II for adjustments of these tabulated allowable unit stresses.)

Species	Stress
Ash, white	1,600
Beech	1,750
Birch	1,750
Chestnut	1,150
Cypress, southern	1,600
Cypress, tidewater	1,600
Douglas fir, all regions, dense	1,875
Douglas fir, coast region, close grained	1,700
Douglas fir, coast region	1,600
Douglas fir, inland region, close grained	1,600
Douglas fir, inland region	1,500
Elm, rock	1,750
Elm, soft	1,150
Fir, white	1,050
Gum, black and red	1,150
Hemlock, eastern	1,050
Hemlock, West Coast	1,325
Hickory	2,200
Larch, dense	1,875
Larch, close grained	1,700
Larch	1,600
Maple, hard	1,750
Oak, red and white	1,475
Pecan	2,200
Pine, Norway	1,150
Pine, southern longleaf	1,875
Pine, southern dense	1,875
Pine, southern	1,600
Poplar, yellow	1,050
Redwood, close grained	1,600
Redwood	1,475
Spruce, eastern	1,150
Tupelo	1,150

perpendicular to grain from NDS Tables 1, 20, and 21 in accordance with the provision of par. 210.

212—ALLOWABLE UNIT STRESSES FOR COMPRESSION AT ANGLE TO GRAIN

212–A. The allowable unit stresses in compression on surfaces inclined to the grain shall be determined by the Hankinson formula. (See par. 211-A and 405 and NDS Appendix C.)

212–B. For end to end bearing on metal plate, see par. 401-D.

213—MODULUS OF ELASTICITY [1]

213–A. The values for modulus of elasticity in NDS Table 1 assume the lumber will be surface seasoned before it is fully loaded to the maximum allowable load. With sawed members thicker than 4 in., which season slowly, care should be exercised to avoid their being overloaded before an appreciable seasoning of the outer fibers has taken place, otherwise the values for modulus of elasticity in NDS Table 1 should be reduced 1/11.

214—SPECIFICATIONS AND PLANS

214–A. Lumber shall be specified by species and commercial grade names.

214–B. The allowable unit stresses used in the design should be indicated on the plans and working drawings. Whether the design is based on standard dressed, standard rough or special sizes should also be indicated.

NDS Part III. Design Loads

300—LOADS AND FORCES

300–A. Wood structures shall be designed to sustain the actual loads and forces applied, including:

300–A–1. Dead load.

300–A–2. Live load.[2]

- **(a)** Impact
- **(b)** Wind and other lateral, longitudinal, and uplift forces
- **(c)** Erection loads
- **(d)** Other forces

301—DEAD LOADS

301–A. The dead load consists of the weight of the appropriate portion of the wood structure and all material fastened thereto or permanently supported thereby.

302—LIVE LOADS

302–A. The live loads[2] depend on the code under which the structure is designed,

[1] The values for the modulus of elasticity in NDS Table 1 are applicable to the condition generally encountered in buildings. They have been revised from those in previous issues of this Specification to conform to the provisions of par. 213-A. These values and the associated provisions afford a more systematic recognition of the effect of seasoning on stiffness as indicated by the Forest Products Laboratory than has generally been past practice.

Most lumber literature extant as of the date of issue of this revision of the National Design Specification shows the values for modulus of elasticity corresponding to those in previous issues. However, new or revised editions of technical information from lumber industry sources will generally be amended to incorporate these corrected values of *E*.

[2] Live loads as used herein include wind, snow, impact, earthquake, and other applied loads.

NDS TABLE 1 Allowable unit stresses for stress-grade lumber

The allowable unit stresses below are for normal loading conditions. See other provisions of NDS Part II for adjustments of these tabulated allowable unit stresses. KEY TO GRADES: *C*, construction; *CS*, common structural; *DC*, dense construction; *DS*, dense structural; *DSS*, dense select structural; *IND*, industrial; *PS*, prime structural; *S*, structural; *SS*, select structural; *STD*, standard; *US*, utility structural. KEY TO GRADE RULES: *CRA*, California Redwood Association; *NHHMA*, Northern Hemlock and Hardwood Manufacturers Association; *NHLA*, National Hardwood Lumber Association; *NLMA*, Northeastern Lumber Manufacturers Association; *SCMA*, Southern Cypress Manufacturers Association; *SPIB*, Southern Pine Inspection Bureau; *WCLIB*, West Coast Lumber Inspection Bureau; *WPA*, Western Pine Association.

			Allowable unit stresses, *psi*				
1		*2*	*3*	*4*	*5*	*6*	*7*
Species and commercial grade[1]		Graded by	f, t[3]	H	$c\perp$	c	E
Ash, white							
2150 f	J&P	NHLA	2,150	145	600	1,700	1,650,000
1900 f	J&P–B&S		1,900	145	600	1,500	1,650,000
1700 f	J&P–B&S		1,700	145	600	1,325	1,650,000
1450 f	J&P–B&S		1,450	120	600	1,150	1,650,000
1300 f	B&S		1,300	120	600	1,050	1,650,000
1450 c	P&T				600	1,450	1,650,000
1200 c	P&T				600	1,200	1,650,000
1075 c	P&T				600	1,075	1,650,000
Beech							
Birch							
2150 f	J&P	NHLA	2,150	145	600	1,750	1,760,000
1900 f	J&P–B&S		1,900	145	600	1,525	1,760,000
1700 f	J&P–B&S		1,700	145	600	1,350	1,760,000
1450 f	J&P–B&S		1,450	120	600	1,150	1,760,000
1550 c	P&T				600	1,550	1,760,000
1450 c	P&T				600	1,450	1,760,000
1200 c	P&T				600	1,200	1,760,000
Chestnut							
1450 f	J&P	NHLA	1,450	120	360	1,200	1,100,000
1200 f	J&P–B&S		1,200	120	360	950	1,100,000
1075 c	P&T				360	1,075	1,100,000
Cypress, southern, coast type (tidewater red)							
1700 f	J&P–B&S	SCMA	1,700	145	360	1,425	1,320,000
1300 f	J&P–B&S		1,300	120	360	1,125	1,320,000
1450 c	P&T				360	1,450	1,320,000
1200 c	P&T				360	1,200	1,320,000
Cypress, southern, inland type							
1700 f	J&P–B&S	NHLA	1,700	145	360	1,425	1,320,000
1300 f	J&P–B&S		1,300	120	360	1,125	1,320,000
1450 c	P&T				360	1,450	1,320,000
1200 c	P&T				360	1,200	1,320,000

See footnotes at end of table.

NDS TABLE 1 Allowable unit stresses for stress-grade lumber (Cont.)

1		2	Allowable unit stresses, *psi*				
			3	4	5	6	7
Species and commercial grade [1]		Graded by	*f*, *t* [3]	*H*	$c\perp$	*c*	*E*
Douglas fir, coast region							
DSS[2]	LF	WCLIB	2,050	[5-6-8]120	455	1,500	1,760,000
SS	LF		1,900	[5-6-8]120	415	1,400	1,760,000
1500 f IND	LF		1,500	120	390	1,200	1,760,000
1200 f	LF		1,200	95	390	1,000	1,760,000
DSS[2]	J&P		2,050	[5-6-8]120	455	1,650	1,760,000
SS	J&P		1,900	[5-6-8]120	415	1,500	1,760,000
DC[2]	J&P		1,750	[5-7-8]120	455	1,400	1,760,000
C	J&P		1,500	[5-7-8]120	390	1,200	1,760,000
S	J&P		1,200	[5-7-8] 95	390	1,000	[10]1,760,000
DSS[2]	B&S		2,050	[9]120	455	1,500	1,760,000
SS	B&S		1,900	[9]120	415	1,400	1,760,000
DC[2]	B&S		1,750	[9]120	455	1,200	1,760,000
C	B&S		1,500	[9]120	390	1,000	1,760,000
DSS[2]	P&T		1,900	[9]120	455	1,650	1,760,000
SS	P&T		1,750	[9]120	415	1,500	1,760,000
DC[2]	P&T		1,500	[9]120	455	1,400	1,760,000
C	P&T		1,200	[9]120	390	1,200	1,760,000
Douglas fir, inland region							
SS[2]	J&P[4]	WPA	2,150	145	455	1,750	1,760,000
S	J&P[4]		1,900	100	400	1,400	1,650,000
CS	J&P[4]		1,450	95	380	1,250	1,650,000
SS[2]	P&T				455	1,750	1,760,000
S	P&T				400	1,400	1,650,000
CS	P&T				380	1,250	1,650,000
Elm, rock							
2150 f	J&P	NHLA	2,150	145	600	1,750	1,430,000
1900 f	J&P–B&S		1,900	145	600	1,525	1,430,000
1700 f	J&P–B&S		1,700	145	600	1,350	1,430,000
1450 f	J&P–B&S		1,450	120	600	1,150	1,430,000
1550 c	P&T				600	1,550	1,430,000
1450 c	P&T				600	1,450	1,430,000
1200 c	P&T				600	1,200	1,430,000
Elm, soft **Gum, black and red** **Tupelo**							
1700 f	J&P	NHLA	1,700	120	300	1,225	1,320,000
1450 f	J&P–B&S		1,450	120	300	1,050	1,320,000
1200 f	J&P–B&S		1,200	120	300	875	1,320,000
1075 c	P&T				300	1,075	1,320,000

See footnotes at end of table.

NDS TABLE 1 Allowable unit stresses for stress-grade lumber (Cont.)

			Allowable unit stresses, *psi*				
1		*2*	*3*	*4*	*5*	*6*	*7*
Species and commercial grade [1]		Graded by	*f, t* [3]	*H*	*c*⊥	*c*	*E*
Hemlock, eastern							
SS	J&P[4]–B&S[4]	NHHMA	1,300	85	360	850	1,210,000
PS	J&P[14–4]		1,200	60	360	775	1,210,000
CS	J&P[14–4]		1,100	60	360	650	1,210,000
US	J&P[14–4]		950	60	360	600	1,210,000
SS	P&T				360	850	1,210,000
Hemlock, West Coast							
SS	LF	WCLIB	1,600	[5–6–12] 100	365	1,100	1,540,000
1500 f IND	LF		1,500	100	365	1,000	1,540,000
1200 f IND	LF		1,200	80	365	900	1,540,000
SS	J&P		1,600	[5–6–12] 100	365	1,200	1,540,000
C	J&P		1,500	[5–11–12] 100	365	1,100	1,540,000
S	J&P		1,200	[5–11–12] 80	365	1,000	1,540,000
C	B&S		1,500	[13] 100	365	1,000	1,540,000
C	P&T		1,200	[13] 100	365	1,100	1,540,000
Hickory							
Pecan							
2150 f	J&P–B&S	NHLA	2,150	145	720	1,725	1,980,000
1900 f	J&P–B&S		1,900	145	720	1,550	1,980,000
1700 f	J&P–B&S		1,700	145	720	1,350	1,980,000
1550 c	P&T				720	1,550	1,980,000
1450 c	P&T				720	1,450	1,980,000
1325 c	P&T				720	1,325	1,980,000
Larch							
SS[2]	J&P[4]	WPA	2,150	145	455	1,750	1,650,000
S	J&P[4]		1,900	120	415	1,450	1,650,000
CS	J&P[4]		1,450	120	390	1,325	1,650,000
SS[2]	P&T				455	1,750	1,650,000
S	P&T				415	1,450	1,650,000
CS	P&T				390	1,325	1,650,000
Maple, hard							
2150 f	J&P	NHLA	2,150	145	600	1,750	1,760,000
1900 f	J&P–B&S		1,900	145	600	1,525	1,760,000
1700 f	J&P–B&S		1,700	145	600	1,350	1,760,000
1450 f	J&P–B&S		1,450	120	600	1,150	1,760,000
1550 c	P&T				600	1,550	1,760,000
1450 c	P&T				600	1,450	1,760,000
1200 c	P&T				600	1,200	1,760,000

See footnotes at end of table.

NDS TABLE 1 Allowable unit stresses for stress-grade lumber (Cont.)

1		2	Allowable unit stresses, *psi*				7
			3	4	5	6	
Species and commercial grade[1]		Graded by	*f, t*[3]	*H*	*c*⊥	*c*	*E*
Pine, southern[15]							
DS 86 KD[2-17-18]	2 in. thick only	SPIB	3,000	165	455	2,250	1,760,000
DS 72 KD[2-17-18]	"		2,500	150	455	1,950	1,760,000
DS 65 KD[2-17-18]	"		2,250	135	455	1,800	1,760,000
DS 58 KD[2-17-18]	"		2,050	120	455	1,650	1,760,000
No. 1 Dense KD[2-17-18]	"		2,050	135	455	1,750	1,760,000
No. 1 KD[17]	"		1,750	135	390	1,500	1,760,000
No. 2 Dense KD[2-17-18]	"		1,750	120	455	1,300	1,760,000
No. 2 KD[17]	"		1,500	120	390	1,100	1,760,000
DS 86[2 18]	2 in. thick only		2,900	150	455	2,200	1,760,000
DS 72[2-18]	"		2,350	135	455	1,800	1,760,000
DS 65[2-18]	"		2,050	120	455	1,600	1,760,000
DS 58[2-18]	"		1,750	105	455	1,450	1,760,000
No. 1 Dense[2-18]	"		1,750	120	455	1,550	1,760,000
No. 1	"		1,500	120	390	1,350	1,760,000
No. 2 Dense[2-18]	"		1,400	105	455	1,050	1,760,000
No. 2	"		1,200	105	390	900	1,760,000
DS 86[2-18]	3 in. & 4 in.	SPIB	2,900	150	455	2,200	1,760,000
DS 72[2-18]	" thick		2,350	135	455	1,800	1,760,000
DS 65[2-18]	"		2,050	120	455	1,600	1,760,000
DS 58[2-18]	"		1,750	105	455	1,450	1,760,000
No. 1 Dense SR[2-18]	"		1,750	120	455	1,750	1,760,000
No. 1 SR	"		1,500	120	390	1,500	1,760,000
No. 2 Dense SR[2-18]	"		1,400	105	455	1,050	1,760,000
No. 2 SR	"		1,200	105	390	900	1,760,000
DS 86[2-18]	5 or more in.		[16]2,400	150	455	1,800	1,760,000
DS 72[2-18]	" thick		[16]2,000	135	455	1,550	1,760,000
DS 65[2-18]	"		[16]1,800	120	455	1,400	1,760,000
DS 58[2-18]	"		[16]1,600	105	455	1,300	1,760,000
No. 1 Dense SR[2-18]	"		[16]1,600	120	455	1,500	1,760,000
No. 1 SR	"		[16]1,400	120	390	1,300	1,760,000
No. 2 Dense SR[2-18]	"		[16]1,400	105	455	1,050	1,760,000
No. 2 SR	"		[16]1,200	105	390	900	1,760,000
IND 86 KD[17]	1 in., 1¼ in.	SPIB	2,600	165	390	1,950	1,760,000
IND 72 KD[17]	and 1½ in. thick		2,200	150	390	1,650	1,760,000
IND 65 KD[17]	"		2,000	135	390	1,550	1,760,000
IND 58 KD[17]	"		1,750	120	390	1,400	1,760,000
IND 50 KD[17]	"		1,500	120	390	1,100	1,760,000
IND 86	"		2,500	150	390	1,900	1,760,000
IND 72	"		2,000	135	390	1,550	1,760,000
IND 65	"		1,750	120	390	1,350	1,760,000
IND 58	"		1,500	105	390	1,250	1,760,000
IND 50	"		1,200	105	390	900	1,760,000

See footnotes at end of table.

NDS TABLE 1 Allowable unit stresses for stress-grade lumber (Cont.)

			Allowable unit stresses, *psi*				
1		*2*	*3*	*4*	*5*	*6*	
Species and commercial grade [1]		Graded by	f, t [3]	H	$c\perp$	c	E
Oak, red and white							
2150 f	J&P	NHLA	2,150	145	600	1,550	1,650,000
1900 f	J&P–B&S		1,900	145	600	1,375	1,650,000
1700 f	J&P–B&S		1,700	145	600	1,200	1,650,000
1450 f	J&P–B&S		1,450	120	600	1,050	1,650,000
1300 f	B&S		1,300	120	600	950	1,650,000
1325 c	P&T				600	1,325	1,650,000
1200 c	P&T				600	1,200	1,650,000
1075 c	P&T				600	1,075	1,650,000
Pine, Norway							
PS	J&P[14–4]	NHHMA	1,200	75	360	900	1,320,000
CS	J&P[14–4]		1,100	75	360	775	1,320,000
US	J&P[14–4]		950	75	360	650	1,320,000
Poplar, yellow							
1500 f	J&P	NHLA	1,500	110	300	1,200	1,210,000
1250 f	J&P–B&S		1,250	110	300	950	1,210,000
1075 c	P&T				300	1,075	1,210,000
Redwood							
DS[2]	J&P[4]–B&S[4]	CRA	1,700	110	320	1,450	1,320,000
HS	J&P[4]–B&S[4]		1,300	95	320	1,100	1,320,000
DS[2]	P&T				320	1,450	1,320,000
HS	P&T				320	1,100	1,320,000
Spruce, Eastern							
1450 f S	J&P[4]	NLMA	1,450	110	300	1,050	1,320,000
1300 f S	J&P[4]		1,300	95	300	975	1,320,000
1200 f S	J&P[4]		1,200	95	300	900	1,320,000

[1] Abbreviations: (For description of classification of material, see par. 102-B) J&P=Joists and Planks; B&S=Beams and Stringers; P&T=Posts and Timbers; LF=Light Framing; KD=See Note 17; SR=Stress Rated.

[2] These grades meet the requirements for density.

[3] In tension members, the slope of grain limitations applicable to the middle portion of the length of the joist and plank and beam and stringer grades used shall apply throughout the length of the piece.

[4] The allowable unit stresses for tension parallel to grain, t, and for compression parallel to grain, c, given for these Joist and Plank and Beam and Stringer grades are applicable when the following additional provisions are applied to the grades:

The sum of the sizes of all knots in any 6 in. of the length of the piece shall not exceed twice the maximum permissible size of knot. Two knots of maximum permissible size shall not be within the same 6 in. of length of any face.

[5] Value applies to pieces used as planks.

[6] Value applies to 2-in. thick pieces of Select Structural grade used as joists.

[7] For 2-in. thick pieces of Construction and Standard Grades used as joists:

H = 120 when length of split is approximately equal to ½ the width of piece
H = 100 when length of split is approximately equal to the width of piece
H = 70 when length of split is approximately equal to 1½ times width of piece

or if no code governs, the designer's estimates of the particular service requirements for the structure, local weather conditions, and seismic disturbances, but this specification is predicated on the condition that the actual maximum loading is the loading assumed in the design.

303—RECORDING OF LIVE LOADS

303–A. The live loads used in the design of structures covered by this specification should be clearly marked on the design plans and working drawings.

304—POSTING OF LIVE LOADS

304–A. Posting of commercial and industrial structures indicating the design live loads is recommended (as additional assurance against overloading).

305—IMPACT

305–A. For wood structures carrying live loads which induce impact or vibration, the stresses should be computed as indicated in par. 203.

---

[8] For 3-in. thick pieces of Select Structural, Construction and Standard grades used as joists:
H = 120 when length of split is approximately 2¼-in.,
H = 80 when length of split is approximately 4½-in., and
For 4-in. thick pieces of Select Structural, Construction and Standard grade used as joists:
H = 120 when length of split is approximately 3-in.
H = 80 when length of split is approximately 6-in.

[9] For Beams and Stringers and for Posts and Timbers:
H = 120 when length of split is equal to ½ the nominal narrow face dimension
H = 100 when length of split is equal to the nominal narrow face dimension
H = 80 when length of split is equal to 1½ times the nominal narrow face dimensions

Note: Values for lengths of split other than those given in Notes 7, 8, and 9 are proportionate.

[10] Pieces of less than medium grain, when included in the grade of "STANDARD" may be considered as having a modulus of elasticity E of 1,320,000.

[11] For 2-in. thick pieces of Construction and Standard Grades used as joists:
H = 100 when length of split is approximately equal to ½ the width of piece
H = 80 when length of split is approximately equal to the width of piece
H = 60 when length of split is approximately equal to 1½ times width of piece

[12] For 3-in. thick pieces of Select Structural, Construction and Standard grades used as joists:
H = 100 when length of split is approximately 2¼-in.
H = 70 when length of split is approximately 4½-in., and
For 4-in. thick pieces of Select Structural, Construction and Standard grade used as joists:
H = 100 when length of split is approximately 3-in.
H = 70 when length of split is approximately 6-in.

[13] For Beams and Stringers and for Posts and Timbers:
H = 100 when length of split is equal to ¾ the nominal narrow face dimension
H = 90 when length of split is equal to the nominal narrow face dimension
H = 70 when length of split is equal to 1½ times the nominal narrow face dimension

Note: Values for lengths of splits other than those given in Notes 11, 12, and 13 are proportionate.

[14] These grades applicable to 2-in. thickness only.

[15] All stress-grades under the 1956 Grading Rules are all-purpose grades and apply to all sizes. Pieces so graded may be cut to shorter lengths without impairment of the stress rating of the shorter pieces.
Grade restrictions provided by the 1956 Grading Rules apply to the entire length of the piece, and each piece is suitable for use in continuous spans, over double spans or under concentrated loads without regrading for special shear or other special stress requirements.
The following variations apply to the provisions of par. 202-B for lumber in service under wet conditions or where the moisture content is at or above fiber-saturation point, as when continuously submerged, (a) the allowable unit stresses in bending, tension parallel to grain and horizontal shear shall be limited in all thicknesses to the stresses indicated for thicknesses of 5-in. and up; (b) the allowable unit stresses for compression parallel to grain shall be limited to the stresses indicated for thicknesses of 5-in. and up reduced by 10 per cent; (c) the allowable unit stresses for compression perpendicular to grain shall be reduced ⅓; and (d) the values for modulus of elasticity shall be reduced 1/11.

[16] These stresses apply for loading either on narrow face or on wide face, which is an exception to par. 102-B-1 and 205-B.

[17] KD = Kiln-dried in accordance with the provisions of par. 219 and 220 of the 1956 Grading Rules.

[18] Longleaf may be specified by substituting "Longleaf" for "Dense" in the grade name, and when so specified the same allowable stresses shall apply.

306—WIND

306–A. Adequate provision shall be made for all stresses caused by wind both during erection and after completion of the structure. The allowable unit stresses are specified in par. 203.

306–B. All roofs, as well as other affected portions of the structure, shall be designed for anchorage to resist uplift from wind. The actual dead weight of the portions of the structure affected may be deducted to determine net uplift. Roof decks shall be anchored to beams and beams anchored to columns, bearing partitions, or well down on the walls. Vertical anchorage from column to column shall be provided to give a dead load sufficient to resist the uplift. Columns and walls shall be anchored to footings if necessary. For uplift, the design values for the withdrawal and lateral resistance of metal fastenings in wood and allowable unit stresses for lumber may be increased 33⅓ per cent above those for normal loading. The design procedure for uplift should be in accordance with ref. 6 and 7, NDS Appendix R, except that the design values for lumber and fastenings given in this specification shall apply.

307—EARTHQUAKES AND OTHER FORCES

307–A. Structures in localities subject to earthquakes, hurricanes, and other extraordinary conditions shall be designed with due regard for such conditions and the relation of duration of loading to allowable unit stresses. (See NDS Part II.)

307–B. Structures designed to resist earthquake shock shall be designed and constructed to resist forces applied horizontally from any direction.

308—ERECTION

308–A. Proper provision shall be made to resist the short time stresses induced during erection increasing allowable unit stresses for the short time loading. (See NDS Part II.)

NDS Part IV. Design Formulas and Provisions

400—WOOD BEAMS

400–A. NOTATION (except where otherwise noted): Symbols used in the following formulas are:

b = breadth of section, in inches
$\triangle$ = deflection, in inches
E = modulus of elasticity
f = unit stress in extreme fiber in bending
h = depth of section, in inches
H = unit stress in horizontal shear
I = moment of inertia of the section
M = bending or resisting moment, maximum
n = distance from neutral axis to extreme fiber, in inches
P = total concentrated load, in pounds
L = span, in feet
l = span, in inches
S = section modulus
V = total vertical end shear or end reaction, in pounds
W = total uniformly distributed load, in pounds

400–B. BEAM SPAN. For simple beams the span shall be taken as the distance from face to face of supports plus one-half the required length of bearing at each end, and for continuous beams the span is the distance between centers of bearings on supports over which the beam is continuous.

400–C. FLEXURE

400–C–1. The extreme fiber stress in bending for a wood beam is:

$$f = \frac{Mn}{I} = \frac{M}{S}$$

400–C–2. For a rectangular beam b wide and h deep, this becomes:

$$f = \frac{M}{S} = \frac{6M}{bh^2}$$

400–C–3. For solid rectangular and square beams with the neutral axis perpendicular to depth at center:

$$I = \frac{bh^3}{12} = \text{moment of inertia}$$

$$S = \frac{I}{n} = \frac{bh^2}{6} = \text{section modulus}$$

400–C–4. A beam of circular cross section is assumed to have the same strength in flexure as a square beam having the same cross-sectional area. If a circular beam is tapered, it shall be considered a beam of variable cross section.

400–C–5. For cross sections of unusual shape such as extremely deep, narrow beams, "I" beams, and box beams, see NDS Appendix D.

400–C–6. Insofar as possible, notching of beams shall be avoided. For a beam notched at or near the middle of the span, the net depth shall be taken when determining the flexural strength. Notches at the ends do not affect flexural strength directly. For effect of notch on shear strength, see par. 400-D. The stiffness of a beam as determined from its cross section is practically unaffected by notches of reasonable depth and length, i.e., a notch depth equal to one-sixth the beam depth and a notch length equal to one-third the beam depth at any point along the beam.

400–C–7. Lateral moment distribution of a concentrated load from a critically loaded beam to adjacent parallel beams should be calculated. (See NDS Appendix A.)

400–C–8. Design procedure for panels with stressed covering shall conform to ref. 17 and 26, NDS Appendix R. (For additional data, see ref. 28.)

400–D. SHEAR

400–D–1. Vertical shear. Ordinarily it is unnecessary to compute or check the strength of beams in cross-grain (vertical) shear.

400–D–2. Horizontal shear. The maximum horizontal shearing stress in a wood beam shall be calculated by means of the formula:

$$H = \frac{VQ}{It}$$

in which:

Q = the statical moment of the area above or below the neutral axis.
t = the width of the beam at the neutral axis.

For a rectangular beam b inches wide and h inches deep, this becomes:

$$H = \frac{3V}{2bh}$$

This formula indicates shearing stresses greater than the actual stress. When calculating shear in a beam:[1]

(a) Take b as the full thickness of the beam.

(b) Select the allowable unit shearing stress for the species and grade. (Allowance for checks, end splits and shakes has been made in the allowable unit stresses.)

(c) When calculating the reactions:

(1) Take into account any relief to the beam resulting from load being distributed to adjacent parallel beams by flooring or other members of the construction. (See NDS Appendix A.)

[1] For a graphical representation of the total, single-beam, and two-beam reaction incorporated in these provisions, see NDS Appendix E.

(2) Neglect all loads within a distance from either support equal to the depth of the beam.

(3) If there are moving loads, place the largest one (keeping others in their normal relation) at 3 times the depth of the beam from the support or at the quarter point, whichever is the closer to the support.

(4) Consider all other loads in the usual manner. If a timber does not qualify for shear resistance under the foregoing procedure, the reactions shall be determined by the formulas:

For concentrated load

$$R = \frac{10P\,(l - x)\,(x/h)^2}{9l[2 + (x/h)^2]}$$

For uniformly distributed load

$$R = \frac{W}{2}\left(1 - \frac{2h}{l}\right)$$

in which:

h = depth of beam, in inches
l = span, in inches
P = concentrated load, in pounds
R = total modified end reaction or end shear, in pounds
W = total uniform load, in pounds
x = distance, in inches, from reaction to load.

For allowable unit stresses in shear, see NDS Part II.

400–D–3. Horizontal shear in notched beams. For notched beams, the shearing strength of a short, relatively deep beam notched on the lower face at the end is decreased by an amount depending on the relation of the depth of the notch to the depth of the beam. When designing a beam having a notch at its end, the desired bending load shall be checked against the load obtained by the formula

$$V = \left(\frac{2Hbd}{3}\right)\left(\frac{d}{h}\right)$$

in which d is the actual end depth above the notch. A gradual change in cross section compared with a square notch increases the shearing strength nearly to that computed for the actual depth above the notch.

For allowable unit stresses in shear for joint details, see par. 209-B.

400–D–4. Design of eccentric joints and of beams supported by fastenings. Eccentric connector and bolted joints and beams supported by connectors or bolts shall be designed so that H in the following formula does not exceed the allowable unit stresses in horizontal shear

$$H = \frac{3V}{2bh_e}$$

in which:

h_e(with connectors) = the depth of the member less the distance from the unloaded edge of the member to the nearest edge of the nearest connector.

h_e (with bolts only) = the depth of the member less the distance from the unloaded edge of the member to the center of the nearest bolt.

For allowable unit stresses in shear for joint details, see par. 209-B.

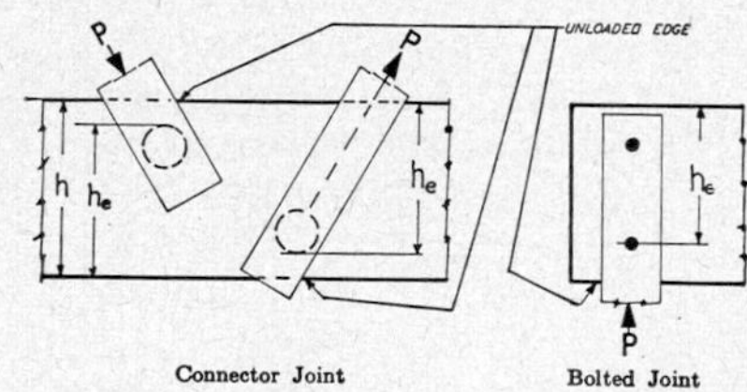

NDS Fig. 1 Showing h_e for member with various fastenings.

400–E. COMPRESSION PERPENDICULAR TO GRAIN

400–E–1. Also see par. 210. The allowable unit stresses for compression perpendicular to the grain, in NDS Tables 1, 20, and 21, apply to bearings of any length at the ends of the beam, and to all bearings 6 in. or more in length at any other location. When calculating the bearing area at the ends of beams, no allowance shall be made for the fact that, as the beam bends, the pressure upon the inner edge of the bearing is greater than at the end of the beam.

For bearings of less than 6 in. in length and not nearer than 3 in. to the end of a member, the maximum allowable load per square inch is obtained by multiplying the allowable unit stresses in compression perpendicular to grain by the following factor:

$$\frac{l + 3/8}{l}$$

in which l is the length of bearing in inches measured along the grain of the wood.

The multiplying factors for indicated lengths of bearing on such small areas as plates and washers become:

Length of bearing, in inches	½	1	1½	2	3	4	6 or more
Factor	1.75	1.38	1.25	1.19	1.13	1.10	1.00

In using the preceding formula and table for round washers or bearing areas, use a length equal to the diameter.

400–E–2. Primary members acting as beams should be supported at or near the bottom or unloaded edge. (See par. 400-D-4.)

400–F. DEFLECTION

400–F–1. Vertical deflection. If deflection is a factor in design, it shall be calculated by standard methods of engineering mechanics. Under design loading permanently applied, timber acquires a permanent set about equal to the original deflection, but the strength is not reduced.

400–F–2. Lateral deflection—floor joists. (The dimensions in the following provisions are nominal—not actual.) Joists should be bridged at intervals not exceeding 8 ft or 6 times their depth, whichever is the greater, between bridging or between bridging and bearing.

400–F–3. Lateral deflection—beams and roof joists. (The dimensions in the following provisions are nominal—not actual.)

The designer should apply the following approximate rules in providing lateral restraint for rectangular beams and roof joists.

(a) If the ratio of depth to breadth is 2 to 1, no lateral support is needed.

(b) If the ratio is 3 to 1, the ends shall be held in position.

(c) If the ratio is 4 to 1, the piece shall be held in line as in a well-bolted chord member in a truss.

(d) If the ratio is 5 to 1, one edge shall be held in line.

(e) If the ratio is 6 to 1, the provisions of par. 400-F-2 may be applied.

(f) If the ratio is 7 to 1, both edges shall be held in line.

(g) If a beam is subject to both flexure and compression parallel to grain, the ratio may be as much as 5 to 1, if one edge is held firmly in line, e.g., by rafters (or by roof joists) and diagonal sheathing. If the dead load is sufficient to induce tension on the under side of the rafters, the ratio for the beam may be 6 to 1.

(h) If the above conditions for lateral support are not provided, see ref. No. 2, NDS Appendix R, for guidance when determining strength.

400–F–4. Lateral deflection—arches and top chords of trusses.

(a) Where roof joists, not purlins, are used between arches or the top chords of trusses, the depth rather than the breadth of the arch or top-chord member (compression member) may be taken as its least dimension in determining the l/d ratio. The roof joists should be placed so that their upper edges are at least ½ in. above the tops of the arch or chord, but also placed low enough to provide adequate lateral support.

(b) When the roof joists are on top of an arch or top chord of a truss and are well spiked or otherwise securely fastened to the arch or top chord and to blocking placed in the spaces between the joists at the arch or chord and spiked or otherwise securely fastened to the arch or truss, the depth of the individual chord member may be used as the least dimension d in determining l/d. When not so fastened or blocked the breadth of the individual chord member shall be used as the least dimension d in determining l/d.

401—WOOD COLUMNS

Wood columns shall be designed in accordance with the following formulas and requirements (for allowable unit stresses, see NDS Part II and NDS Part IX):

401–A. NOTATION

A = area of column cross section, in square inches

c = allowable unit stress in compression parallel to grain adjusted in accordance with par. 201, 202, 203, and 204

d = dimension of least side of simple solid column and of least side of individual members of spaced columns, in inches

E = modulus of elasticity, adjusted in accordance with the provisions of par. 201, 202, 203, and 204

l = unsupported over-all length, in inches, between points of lateral support of simple columns or from center to center of lateral supports of continuous or spaced columns

l_2 = distance in spaced columns from center of connector in end blocks to center of spacer block, in inches

P = total load, in pounds

P/A = maximum load per unit of cross-sectional area

r = least radius of gyration of section

401–B. COLUMN CLASSIFICATIONS

401–B–1. Simple solid wood columns. Simple columns consist of a single piece or of pieces properly glued together to form a single member.

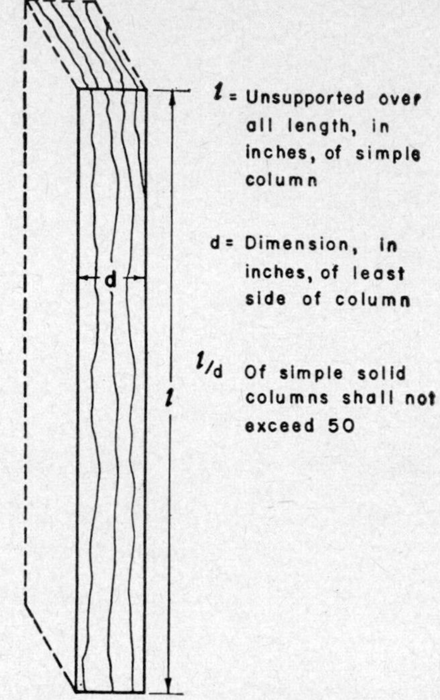

NDS Fig. 2 Simple solid column

401–B–2. Spaced columns, connector-joined. Spaced columns are formed of two or more individual members with their longitudinal axes parallel, separated at the ends and middle points of their length by blocking and joined at the ends by timber connectors capable of developing the required shear resistance. To obtain spaced-column action, end blocks with connectors and spacer blocks are required when the individual members of a spaced-column assembly have an l/d ratio greater than $\sqrt{\frac{0.30E}{c}}$; c and E being adjusted as provided in par. 201, 202, 203, and 204. For an assembly of members having a lesser l/d ratio, the individual members are designed as simple solid columns. Spaced columns are classified as to fixity, i.e., condition "a" or condition "b," which introduces a multiplying factor applicable in the design of its individual members as provided in par. 401-F-4. (See NDS Fig. 3.)

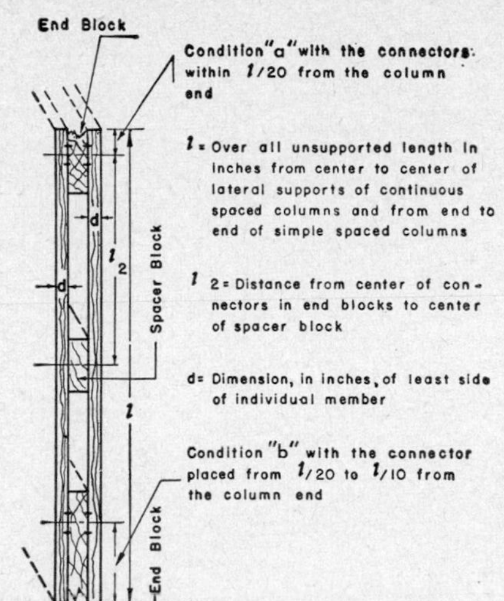

NDS Fig. 3 Spaced column, connector joined

401–B–3. **Built-up columns** (other than connector-joined spaced columns and glued-laminated columns) shall not be designed as solid columns but shall be designed in accordance with ref. 2, 23, NDS Appendix R, except that the allowable unit stresses herein apply.

401–C. *L/d* LIMITATIONS

401–C–1. For simple solid columns, l/d shall not exceed 50.

401–C–2. For individual members of a spaced column, l/d shall not exceed 80, nor shall l_2/d exceed 40.

401–D. COMPRESSION MEMBERS BEARING END TO END PARALLEL TO GRAIN

401–D–1. For end-to-end bearing of wood in compression members, the full allowable compressive stress parallel to grain, c, may be used provided that there is adequate lateral restraint, end cuts are accurately squared and parallel and, when the stress exceeds 75 per cent of the values in NDS Table 2, a metal plate of not less than 20 gauge is inserted with a snug fit between abutting ends.

401–D–2. The bearing stress parallel to grain, P/A, shall not exceed the allowable unit stress in compression parallel to grain, c, where P is the applied load and A is the end area in bearing.

401–E. SIMPLE SOLID COLUMNS

401–E–1. **End conditions.** These formulas for simple solid columns are based on pin-end conditions but shall be applied also to square-end conditions.

401–E–2. **Allowable unit loads for simple solid columns.** Allowable unit loads in pounds per square inch of cross-sectional area of simple solid columns shall be determined by the following formula, but the maximum unit load shall not exceed the values for compression parallel to grain, c, in NDS Tables 1, 20, and 21 adjusted in accordance with the provisions of par. 201, 202, 203, and 204. In applying the formula adjust the E value in NDS Tables 1, 20, and 21 in accordance with the provisions in par. 201, 202, 203, and 204.

$$P/A = \frac{\pi^2 E}{2.727(l/r)^2} = \frac{3.619\ E}{(l/r)^2}$$

For columns of square or rectangular cross section, this formula becomes:

$$P/A = \frac{0.30\ E}{(l/d)^2}$$

401–F. SPACED-COLUMN DESIGN

401–F–1. **Location of spacer and end blocks.** A single spacer block shall be located within the middle tenth of the column length, l, and, if so located, connectors are not required for this block. If there are two or more spacer blocks, the distance between any two blocks shall not exceed one-half the distance between centers of connectors in the end blocks. The requirements for connectors in spacer blocks when two or more blocks are used are the same as for end blocks.

End blocks shall be so placed that sufficient end and edge distances and spacings (see Part V) for the required minimum size and number of connectors are maintained in both end blocks and individual members, and connectors so placed that they comply with conditions "a" or "b," (NDS Fig. 3), depending on fixity factor assumed.

For spaced columns used as members of a truss, e.g., compression chords, a panel point which is stayed laterally shall be considered as the end of the spaced column and the portion of the web members between the individual pieces making up a spaced column may be considered as the end blocks. For spaced-column web members, joints at the tension chord may be considered stayed laterally by the tautness of the tension chord and by customary lateral braces between trusses.

If there are two or more connectors in a contact face, the position of the center of gravity of the group of connectors shall be used in measuring the distance from connectors in the end block to the end of the column for determining fixity condition "a" or "b" (NDS Fig. 3).

401–F–2. Dimensions of spacer and end blocks. The thickness of spacer and end blocks shall not be less than that of the individual members of the spaced column nor shall the thickness, width, and length of spacer and end blocks be less than that required for installation of connectors of a size and number (NDS Part V) capable of carrying a load equal to that computed from NDS Table 3. Spacer and end blocks of a thickness between that required above and one-half that thickness may be used, provided that the length of the blocks is made inversely proportional to the thickness in relation to required length of a full thickness block. Blocks thicker than a side member do not appreciably increase the load capacity. The load shall be considered to be applied in either direction parallel to the longitudinal axis of the individual member.

401–F–3. Load capacity of connectors in end-spacer blocks. To obtain spaced-column action the connectors in each pair of mutually contacting surfaces of end blocks and individual members at each end of a spaced column shall be of a size and number to provide a connector load capacity in pounds equal to the required cross-sectional area for compression in square inches of one of the individual members times the appropriate end-spacer block constant in NDS Table 3.

If connector-joined spaced columns are used in locations other than dry, the connector loads should be adjusted for such conditions in accordance with the provisions of NDS Part V.

If spaced columns are a part of a truss system or other similar framing, the connectors required by joint design may be sufficient for end-block connectors but should be checked against NDS Table 3.

NDS TABLE 3. End spacer-block constants for connector-joined spaced columns

l/d ratio of individual member in the spaced column[1]	End spacer-block constant[2]			
	Group A connector loads	Group B connector loads	Group C connector loads	Group D connector loads
0 to 11	0	0	0	0
15	38	33	27	21
20	86	73	61	48
25	134	114	94	75
30	181	155	128	101
35	229	195	162	128
40	277	236	195	154
45	325	277	229	181
50	372	318	263	208
55	420	358	296	234
60 to 80	468	399	330	261

[1] Constants for intermediate l/d ratios may be obtained by straight-line interpolation.

[2] For data on connector-load groups, see NDS Part V.

401–F–4. Allowable loads for spaced columns. The total allowable load for a spaced column is the sum of the allowable loads for each of its individual members determined as follows, except that the unit load for the individual members shall not exceed the values for compression parallel to grain, *c*, given in NDS Tables 1, 20, and 21 adjusted as provided in par. 201, 202, 203, and 204, nor shall such load exceed that permitted by the provisions of par. 502:

For condition "*a*": The allowable load for the individual members of a spaced column in which the connectors in end blocks are placed at the ends of the columns or not exceeding a distance of $l/20$ from the ends is 2½ times the load for a simple column determined in accordance with par. 401-E-2, or as determined by the formula:

$$P/A = \frac{0.75\,E}{(l/d)^2}$$

For condition "b": The allowable load for the individual members of a spaced column in which the connectors in end blocks are placed a distance of $l/20$ to $l/10$ from the ends and the blocks extend to the ends of the column is 3 times the load for a simple column determined in accordance with par. 401-E-2, or as determined by the formula:

$$P/A = \frac{0.90\,E}{(l/d)^2}$$

Check of load capacity: The total load capacity determined by the above procedure should be checked against the sum of the load capacities of the individual members taken as simple solid columns without regard to fixity factor using their greater *d* and the *l* between the lateral supports that provide restraint in a direction parallel to the greater *d*.

401–G. ROUND COLUMNS. The allowable load for a column of round cross section shall not exceed that for a square column of the same cross-sectional area, or as determined by the formula:

$$P/A = \frac{3.619\,E}{(l/r)^2}$$

provided, however, that P/A shall not exceed *c* adjusted as provided in this Specification.

401–H. TAPERED COLUMNS. In determining the *d* for column design, the diameter of a column tapered at one or both ends shall be taken as the sum of the minimum diameter and ⅓ the difference between the minimum and maximum diameters, but in no case shall it be assumed as more than 1½ times the minimum diameter. The induced unit compressive stress at the small end of a tapered column shall not exceed the allowable unit stress for a short column.

402—WOOD COLUMN BRACING

402–A. Column bracing shall be installed where necessary to resist wind or other lateral forces. (See NDS Appendix F.)

403—FLEXURAL AND AXIAL LOADING COMBINED

403–A. FLEXURE AND AXIAL TENSION COMBINED (NDS Fig. 4)

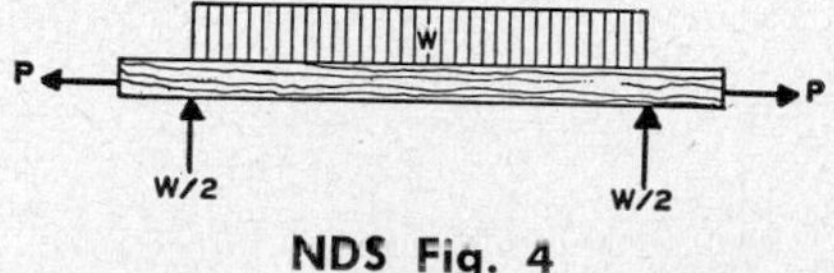

NDS Fig. 4

403–A–1. Unit stresses induced by loads.

Unit flexural stress = M/S
Unit axial tensile stress = P/A

403–A–2. Allowable unit stresses. Members subjected to both FLEXURE AND AXIAL TENSION shall be so proportioned that:

$$\frac{P/A}{t} + \frac{M/S}{f} \text{ shall not exceed 1}$$

403–B. FLEXURE AND AXIAL COMPRESSION COMBINED (NDS Fig. 5)

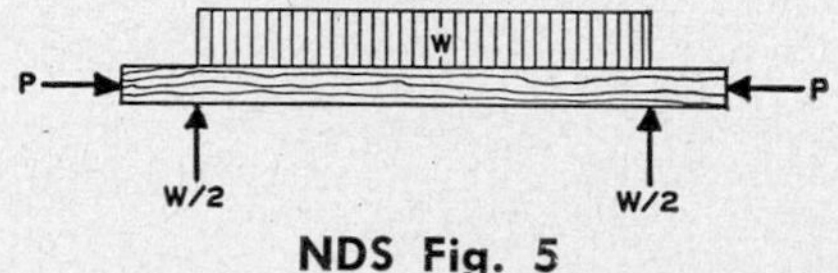

NDS Fig. 5

403–B–1. Unit stresses induced by loads.

Unit flexural stress = M/S
Unit axial compressive stress = P/A

403–B–2. Allowable unit stresses. Members subjected to both FLEXURE AND AXIAL COMPRESSION shall be so proportioned that:

$$\frac{P/A}{c} + \frac{M/S}{f} \text{ shall not exceed } 1$$

in which:

P = total axial load, in pounds
A = area of cross-section of member, in square inches
P/A = compressive stress induced by axial load, in pounds per square inch
M = total bending moment, in inch-pounds
S = section modulus of member
M/S = flexural stress induced by bending load, in pounds per square inch
f = allowable unit stress in pounds per square inch that would be permitted if flexure only existed
c = allowable unit stress in compression parallel to grain in pounds per square inch that would be permitted for column if only axial compression existed, i.e., for the l/d ratio of the column under consideration
t = allowable unit stress in tension parallel to grain in pounds per square inch, if only tension existed

403–C. In the case of spaced columns this combined-stress formula may be applied only if the bending is in a direction parallel to the greater d of the individual member.

403–D. Formulas for more accurate calculation of combined stresses are given in NDS Appendix B.

404—TENSION

404–A. TENSION PARALLEL TO GRAIN. The induced unit stress in axial tension parallel to grain of wood, P/A, shall not exceed t.

For allowable unit stress in tension, t, see NDS Tables 1, 20, and 21 and provisions of NDS Part II.

405—COMPRESSION AT ANGLE TO GRAIN (NDS Fig. 7)

405–A. The allowable unit stress in compression at an angle of load to grain between 0 deg and 90 deg shall be computed from the Hankinson formula:

$$N = \frac{PQ}{P \sin^2 \theta + Q \cos^2 \theta}$$

in which:

N = allowable unit stress acting perpendicular to the inclined surface
P = allowable unit stress in compression parallel to the grain
Q = allowable unit stress in compression perpendicular to the grain
θ = angle between the direction of the load and the direction of the grain

For tabulated values of $\sin^2 \theta$ and $\cos^2 \theta$ and graphical solution of Hankinson formula, see NDS Appendix C.

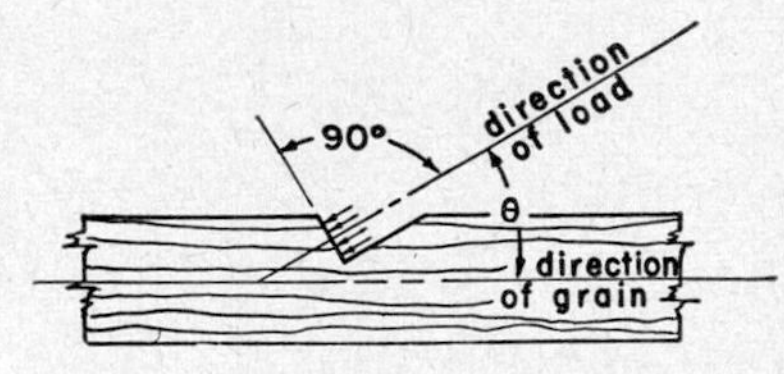

NDS Fig. 7

406—TIMBER-CONCRETE COMPOSITE CONSTRUCTION

406–A. For design procedure on timber-concrete composite construction, see ref. Nos. 15 and 16, NDS Appendix R, but use the allowable unit stresses and design values for lumber and fastenings given in this specification.

407—METAL PLATES

407–A. When used, metal plates (side or gusset) shall be designed in accordance with the applicable metal specification.

408—TRUSS BRACING

408–A. Bracing or diaphragms adequate to brace trusses to resist lateral forces shall be installed where necessary. (See NDS Appendix F.)

NDS Part V. Timber-Connector Joints

For timber-connector joints using stress-grade lumber and the timber-connector devices defined herein, the provisions of NDS Part V and the tabulated allowable connector loads herein apply:

500—BASIC DESIGN CONSIDERATIONS AND LIMITATIONS

500–A. CONNECTOR UNIT

500–A–1. For purposes of specifying allowable connector loads herein, a connector unit shall consist of one of the following:

(a) One split ring with its bolt in single shear; or

(b) One toothed-ring with its bolt in single shear; or

(c) Two shear plates used back to back in the contact faces of a timber-to-timber joint with their bolt in single shear; or one shear plate with its bolt in single shear used in conjunction with a steel strap or shape in a timber-to-metal joint.

500–A–2. In installation of connectors and bolts, a nut shall be placed on each bolt, and washers not smaller than the size specified in NDS Tables 8, 9, and 10 shall be placed between the outside wood member and the bolt head and between the outside wood member and nut. When an outside member is a steel strap or shape, the washer may be omitted except when needed to extend bolt length to prevent metal plate or shape from bearing on threaded portion of bolt when used in conjunction with shear plates.

500–B. NUMBER OF CONNECTORS

500–B–1. Tabulated loads are for *one* connector unit with bolt in shear in any joint of any number of members.

500–B–2. For a joint assembly in which two or more connector units of the same size are used in the contact faces with the connectors concentric with the same bolt axis or in which two or more bolts are used with connectors on separate bolts, the total allowable connector load shall be the sum of the allowable connector loads given for each connector unit used. This provision applies to all conditions except that connectors shall not be placed concentrically on the same bolt in the same timber surface except as provided in par. 500-B-3 and 500-B-4.

500–B–3. If grooves for two sizes of split rings are cut, concentric in the same timber surface, rings shall be installed in both grooves and the total allowable load shall be the tabulated load for the larger ring only.

500–B–4. Two toothed rings in combination of the sizes 2 and 3⅜ in., 2 and 4 in., or 2⅝ and 4 in. may be concentric to the same bolt between the same timber surfaces. For these combinations the total allowable connector load shall be the tabulated allowable load for the larger ring plus 25 per cent of the tabulated load for the smaller ring.

500–C. ALLOWABLE CONNECTOR LOADS

500–C–1. Allowable connector loads for normal loading conditions. The allowable connector loads given in NDS Tables 8, 9, and 10 are applicable for the connectors described in par. 500-D for all conditions other than those for which specific exceptions are made.

500–C–2. Other conditions of loading.

(a) Where a connector joint is fully loaded to the maximum allowable load for many years, either continuously or cumulatively under the conditions of maximum design load, use working stresses 90 per cent of those in NDS Tables 8, 9, and 10.

(b) When the duration of full maximum load does not exceed the period indicated, increase the allowable unit stresses in NDS Tables 8 and 10 as follows:

15 per cent for two months' duration, as for snow
25 per cent for seven days' duration
33⅓ per cent for wind or earthquake
100 per cent for impact

These increases are applicable to the tabulated loads for split rings and shear plates (except that the limitations in notes in NDS Table 10 apply for shear plates). These increases are not applicable to the tabulated loads for toothed rings. An increase of 20 per cent is permitted for wind, earthquake, or impact on toothed rings. Otherwise the same conditions of load duration apply to connectors as apply to lumber. (See par. 203-A.)

500–C–3. Condition of lumber.

(a) For connectors used in lumber which is seasoned to approximately 15 per cent moisture content to a depth of ¾ in. from the surface before fabrication and which will remain dry in service, the tabulated allowable connector loads as adjusted by par. 500-C-1 and 500-C-2 apply for all connectors.

(b) For connectors used in lumber which is fabricated before it is seasoned to a depth of ¾ in. from the surface and which later is seasoned either before erection or while in the structure, 80 per cent of the tabulated allowable connector loads as adjusted by par. 500-C-1 and 500-C-2 shall apply for all connectors.

(c) For lumber partially seasoned when fabricated, proportional intermediate connector values may be used.

(d) For connectors used in lumber which is fabricated in a seasoned or unseasoned condition and will remain wet in service, 67 per cent of the tabulated allowable connector loads as adjusted by par. 500-C-1 and 500-C-2 shall apply for all connectors.

500–D. QUALITY OF CONNECTORS

500–D–1. Specifications for timber connectors and tabulated loads and modifications thereof given herein are for connectors of a quality as follows:

(a) Split ring timber connectors manufactured from hot-rolled carbon steel meeting "Society of Automotive Engineers Specification SAE-1010" (1943). Each ring shall form a closed true circle with the principal axis of the cross-section of the ring metal parallel to the geometric axis of the ring. The ring shall fit snugly in the precut groove. This may be accomplished with a ring the metal section of which is beveled from the central portion toward the edges to a thickness less than at midsection or by any other method which will accomplish equivalent performance. It shall be cut through in one place in its circumference to form a tongue and slot. (See NDS Fig. 8.)

(b) Toothed ring timber connectors stamped cold from U. S. Standard 16 gauge hot-rolled sheet steel conforming to "American Society for Testing Materials Standard Specifications for Carbon Steel A 17-29, Type A, Grade 1," and bent cold to form a

SPLIT-RING

NDS Fig. 8

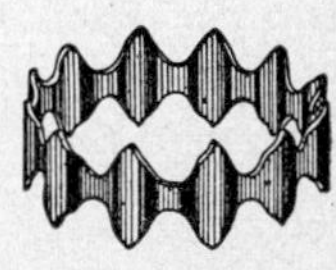

TOOTHED-RING

NDS Fig. 9

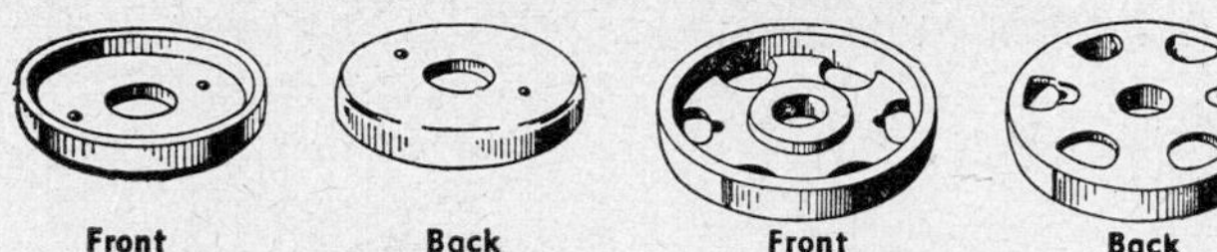

SHEAR PLATES

NDS Fig. 10 **NDS Fig. 11**

circular, corrugated, sharptoothed band and welded into a solid ring. The teeth on each ring shall be on a true circle and shall be parallel to the axis of the ring. The central band shall be welded to fully develop the strength of the band. (See NDS Fig. 9.)

(c) Shear plate timber connectors:

(1) Pressed-steel type—Pressed-steel shear plates manufactured from hot-rolled carbon steel meeting "Society of Automotive Engineers Specification SAE-1010" (1943). Each plate shall be a true circle with a flange around the edge, extending at right angles to the face of the plate and extending from one face only, the plate portion having a central bolt hole and two small perforations on opposite sides of the hole and midway from the center and circumference. (See NDS Fig. 10.)

(2) Malleable iron type—Malleable iron shear plates manufactured according to "American Society for Testing Materials Standard Specifications A 47-33, Grade 35018," for malleable iron castings. Each casting shall consist of a perforated round plate with a flange around the edge extending at right angles to the face of the plate and projecting from one face only, the plate portion having a central bolt hole reamed to size with an integral hub concentric to the bolt hole and extending from the same face as the flange. (See NDS Fig. 11.)

500–D–2. The tolerances in dimensions of the connector shall not be greater than those conforming to standard practices for the machine operations involved in manufacturing the connector.

500–E. SPECIES OF LUMBER

500–E–1. The tabulated loads for Groups A, B, C, and D in NDS Tables 8, 9, and 10 apply to stress-grades (NDS Tables 1, 20, and 21) of species as listed in NDS Table 7.

500–F. GRADE OF LUMBER

500–F–1. Tabulated connector loads shall apply to all stress-grades of a given species except where modifications for density are made as indicated in NDS Table 7.

500–G. GROOVES, DAPS, AND BOLT HOLES

500–G–1. Grooves, daps, and bolt holes of dimensions and shape given in NDS Tables 8, 9, and 10 as appropriate for the type and size of connector used shall be accurately cut or bored and oriented in contacting faces.

500–H. TIGHTNESS OF JOINTS

500–H–1. The allowable loads for connectors are based on the assumption that the faces of the members are brought into contact when the connectors are installed.

500–H–2. Tabulated connector loads and modifications thereof assume and allow for seasonal variations after the lumber has reached the moisture content normal to the conditions of service.

500–H–3. When lumber is not seasoned to the moisture content normal to the conditions of service, the joints should be drawn up by turning down the nuts on the bolts periodically until moisture equilibrium is reached so as to keep the adjacent faces of the members in contact.

500–I. SIDE MEMBERS—MATERIALS

500–I–1. Tabulated connector loads are for side members of wood.

500–I–2. If metal plates instead of wood side plates are used, the tabulated allowable connector loads for parallel-to-grain loading shall be modified in accordance with the notes on NDS Table 10.

500–J. THICKNESS OF LUMBER

500–J–1. Tabulated loads shall not be used for connectors installed in umber of a net thickness less than specified in NDS Tables 8, 9, and 10.

500–K. EDGE DISTANCE, CONNECTOR

(See NDS Tables 8, 9, and 10.)

500–K–1. Edge distance is the distance from edge of member to center of connector closest to the edge of the member measured perpendicular to the edge. (See NDS Figs. 12 and 13.)

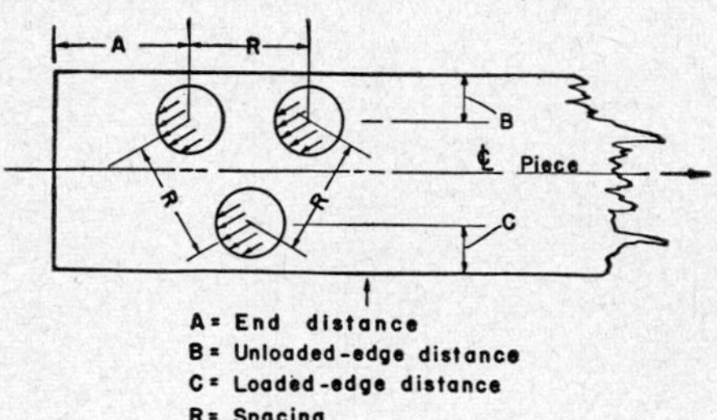

NDS Fig. 12

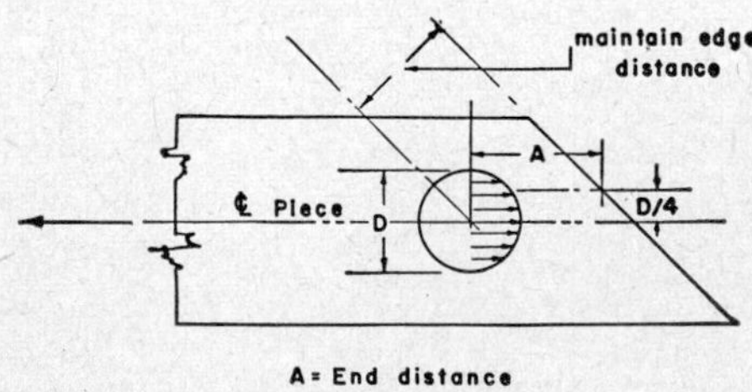

NDS Fig. 13

500–K–2. Member loaded parallel to grain (0 deg).

(a) The tabulated edge distances for parallel-to-grain loading for each connector are for maximum allowable loads and also are the minimum edge distances to be used.

500–K–3. Member loaded perpendicular to grain (90 deg).

(a) Unloaded-edge distance (at edge opposite loaded edge):

(1) Tabulated unloaded-edge distances for perpendicular-to-grain loading for each connector are those for maximum allowable loads, and are also the minimum unloaded-edge distances to be used, and are the same for all angles of load to grain.

(b) Loaded-edge distance (for edge toward which connector load acts):

The loaded-edge distance for perpendicular-to-grain loading is the distance from the center of the connector to the edge toward which the load acts.

(1) The first loaded-edge distance tabulated for each thickness for each connector is the minimum loaded-edge distance which may be used.

(2) The second loaded-edge distance tabulated for each thickness is the least loaded-edge distance which gives the maximum allowable load, i.e., any additional edge distance will not increase the load capacity.

(3) For loaded-edge distances intermediate of (1) and (2), the appropriate allowable connector loads are obtained by straight line interpolation between allowable loads given for maximum and minimum tabulated loaded-edge distances.

(4) For angles of load to grain of 45 deg to 90 deg, the tabulated loaded-edge distance for 90 deg shall be applied. For angles of load to grain of 0 deg to 45 deg, interpolate on a straight line between the tabulated loaded-edge distance for 0 deg and the tabulated loaded-edge distance for 90 deg.

500–L. END DISTANCES, CONNECTOR

(See NDS Tables 8, 9, and 10.)

500–L–1. End distance is the distance measured parallel to the grain from center of connector to the square cut end of the member. (See NDS Fig. 12.)

500–L–2. If the end of the member is not cut at right angles to its length, the end distance measured parallel to the centerline of the piece from any point on the center half of the connector diameter which is perpendicular to the centerline of the piece shall not be less than the end distance required for a square cut member. In no case shall the perpendicular distance from center of connector to sloping end cut of a member be less than the required edge distance. (See NDS Fig. 13.)

500–L–3. End distances for members loaded parallel to grain (0 deg).

(a) Tension member:

(1) For a tension member, the first tabulated tension-end distance for each connector is the minimum tension-end distance which may be used. With minimum tension-end distances, the loads permitted are 62½ per cent of tabulated loads for split rings and shear plates and 67 per cent for toothed rings.

(2) The second tabulated tension-end distance is the least tension-end distance which gives the maximum allowable load.

(3) For tension-end distances intermediate of (1) and (2), the appropriate allowable connector loads are obtained by straight-line interpolation between allowable loads given for maximum and minimum tabulated tension-end distances.

(4) If cross bolts are inserted near end of tension member, the maximum compression-end distance given for compression member at 0 deg angle of load to grain shall apply for maximum allowable load in tension.

(b) Compression member:

(1) For a compression member, the first tabulated compression-end distance for each connector is the minimum end distance which may be used. With minimum compression-end distances, the loads permitted are 62½ per cent of the tabulated loads for split rings and shear plates and 100 per cent for toothed rings.

(2) The second tabulated compression end distance is the least end distance which gives the maximum allowable load.

(3) For compression-end distances intermediate of (1) and (2), the appropriate allowable loads are obtained by straight-line interpolation between allowable loads given for minimum and maximum tabulated end distances.

500–L–4. End distances for members loaded perpendicular to grain (90 deg).

(a) Tension member:

(1) Tabulated end distances are the same as for members loaded parallel to grain (0 deg).

(b) Compression member:

(1) The first tabulated loaded-perpendicular-to-grain end distance is the minimum end distance which may be used. With minimum end distances, the loads permitted are 62½ per cent of tabulated allowable loads for split rings and shear plates and 67 per cent for toothed rings.

(2) The second tabulated loaded-perpendicular-to-grain end distance is the least end distance which gives the maximum allowable load.

(3) For end distances intermediate of (1) and (2), the loads are obtained by straight-line interpolation between allowable loads given for minimum and maximum tabulated end distances.

500–L–5. End distances for members loaded at angles to grain other than 0 deg and 90 deg.

(a) Tension member:

(1) End distances are the same for all angles of load to grain.

(b) Compression member:

(1) For loading at angles intermediate of 0 deg and 90 deg, the end distances shall be determined by straight-line interpolation.

500–M. SPACINGS, CONNECTOR

500–M–1. Spacing is the distance between centers of connectors measured along a line joining their centers. (See NDS Fig. 12.)

500–M–2. Spacings for members loaded parallel to grain (0 deg).

(See NDS Tables 8, 9, and 10.)

(a) Tension and compression members:

(1) Spacing parallel to grain, loaded parallel to grain:

a. For tension and compression members, the first tabulated spacings for each connector are the minimum spacings which may be used for loading parallel to grain. With minimum spacings, the loads permitted are 75 per cent of the tabulated allowable connector loads.

b. The second tabulated spacing is the least spacing which gives the maximum tabulated load.

c. For spacings intermediate between "a" and "b" above, the appropriate allowable loads are obtained by straight-line interpolation between allowable loads given for minimum and maximum tabulated spacings.

(2) Spacing perpendicular to grain, loaded parallel to grain:

a. The tabulated perpendicular-to-grain spacings are for tabulated loads and are also minimum spacings.

500–M–3. Spacings for members loaded perpendicular to grain (90 deg).

(See NDS Tables 8, 9, and 10.)

(a) Tension and compression members:

(1) Spacing parallel to grain, loaded perpendicular to grain:

a. For tension and compression members, spacings given are minimum and are 100 per cent of the tabulated load except as modified in par. 500-M-4.

(2) Spacing perpendicular to grain, loaded perpendicular to grain:

a. For compression and tension members, the first tabulated spacing for each connector provides for the allowable load corresponding to that tabulated for the minimum loaded-edge distance.

b. The second tabulated spacing provides for the allowable load corresponding to that tabulated for the loaded-edge distance for the maximum allowable load.

c. For spacings intermediate between "a" and "b" above, the appropriate allowable loads are obtained by straight line interpolation between allowable loads given for minimum and maximum tabulated spacings.

500–M–4. Spacings for members loaded at an angle of grain other than 0 deg and 90 deg and with connector axis at various angles with grain.

(See NDS Table 4.)

(a) Tension and compression members:

(1) The connector axis is a line joining the centers of two adjacent connectors located in the same contact face of a member in a joint.

(2) For tension and compression members loaded at an angle of load to grain (θ) other than 0 deg and 90 deg or with connector axis at any angle (ϕ) to grain other than 0 deg and 90 deg and for both angle of load (θ) and angle of connector axis (ϕ) at other than 0 deg and 90 deg to the grain, the least spacings for allowable connector loads obtained as provided by par. 500-N and 500-O shall be determined from the following formula and values for A and B given in NDS Table 4.

$$R = \frac{AB}{\sqrt{A^2 \sin^2 \phi + B^2 \cos^2 \phi}}$$

in which:

R = least spacing of connectors, measured in inches along connector axis, required for the angle of load to grain (θ) and angle of connector axis to grain (ϕ) used.

A = value in column (3), NDS Table 4, opposite the connector in column (1) and angle of load to grain in column (2) which are used.

B = value in column (4), NDS Table 4, opposite the connector in column (1) and angle of load to grain in column (2) which are used.

ϕ = angle of connector axis to grain.

(3) The values under C, column (5), NDS Table 4, are minimum allowable

NDS TABLE 4 Values for use with par. 500–M–4

1	2	3	4	5
Type and size of connector	Angle of load to grain, θ *deg*	*A* *in.*	*B* *in.*	*C* (75 per cent value) *in.*
2½ -in. split ring or 2⅝-in. shear plate	0	6¾	3½	3½
	15	6	3¾	3½
	30	5⅛	3⅞	3½
	45	4¼	4⅛	3½
	60–90	3½	4¼	3½
4-in. split ring or 4-in. shear plate	0	9	5	5
	15	8	5¼	5
	30	7	5½	5
	45	6	5¾	5
	60–90	5	6	5
2-in. toothed ring	0	4	2½	2½
	15	3⅝	2⅝	2½
	30	3¼	2¾	2½
	45	2⅞	2⅞	2½
	60–90	2½	3	2½
2⅝-in. toothed ring	0	5¼	3⅛	3⅛
	15	4¾	3⅜	3⅛
	30	4¼	3½	3⅛
	45	3¾	3⅝	3⅛
	60–90	3⅛	3¾	3⅛
3⅜-in. toothed ring	0	6¾	3⅞	3⅞
	15	6	4¼	3⅞
	30	5¼	4½	3⅞
	45	4½	4¾	3⅞
	60–90	3⅞	5	3⅞
4-in. toothed ring	0	8	4½	4½
	15	7⅛	4¾	4½
	30	6¼	5⅛	4½
	45	5⅜	5⅜	4½
	60–90	4½	5¾	4½

spacings for any angle of load to grain (θ) other than 0 deg and 90 deg. They are also the minimum allowable spacings for any angle of connector axis to grain (ϕ) other than 0 deg and 90 deg.

(4) For spacings intermediate between *R* and the minimum *C* from column 5, NDS Table 4, the allowable load shall be determined by straight-line interpolation between the load for *R* spacing and 75 per cent of the load for *R* spacing, respectively.

500–N. LOAD AT ANGLE TO GRAIN

500–N–1. The angle of load to grain is the angle between the direction of the resultant load acting on the member and the longitudinal axis of the member.

500–N–2. For angles of load to grain intermediate of parallel and perpendicular to grain, the allowable connector load shall be determined by application of the Hankinson formula (see par. 405 and Appendix C) between the allowable connector loads for parallel and perpendicular-to-grain loading given in NDS Tables 8, 9, and 10, except that:

(a) For *toothed rings*, allowable loads shall be determined as follows:

(1) The allowable connector loads for angles of load to grain of 45 deg to 90 deg shall be the same as the tabulated allowable connector load for an angle of load to grain of 90 deg.

(2) For angles of load to grain intermediate of 0 deg and 45 deg, the allowable connector loads shall be determined by application of the Hankinson formula between the allowable loads at angles of load to grain of 0 deg and 45 deg.

(b) For *shear plates* when the tabulated allowable loads are equal to the limits imposed in the notes in NDS Table 10, allowable loads at angles of load to grain other than parallel and perpendicular to grain shall be determined by the application of the Hankinson formula between the following units. The parallel-to-grain load for use in the formula shall be taken as 143 per cent of the perpendicular-to-grain load for the second loaded-edge distance tabulated for the thickness used. The tabulated perpendicular-to-grain load for the appropriate loaded-edge distance and thickness shall be used therewith in the formula. In no case, however, shall the allowable angle-to-grain load so determined be permitted to exceed the limits imposed by the notes in NDS Table 10.

500–O. INTER-RELATIONSHIP OF THICKNESS, DISTANCES, AND SPACING

500–O–1. Loads reduced because of thickness (see tabulated loads) do not permit any reduction of edge distance, end distance, or spacing and conversely loads reduced for edge distance, end distance, or spacing do not permit reduction of thickness.

500–O–2. When allowable load is reduced due to reduced edge distance, end distance, or spacing, the reduced allowable load for each shall be determined separately and the lowest allowable load so determined for any one connector shall apply. Such load reductions are not cumulative. Conversely, if the allowable load is reduced because of a reduced distance or spacing, the other distances or spacings may be reduced to those resulting in the same reduced allowable load.

501—USE OF LAG SCREWS INSTEAD OF BOLTS WITH TIMBER CONNECTORS

501–A. TYPE OF SCREW

501–A–1. The lag screw shall have a cut thread, not a rolled thread.

501–B. DIAMETER OF LAG SCREW

501–B–1. The shank of the lag screw shall have the same diameter as the bolt specified for the connector.

501–C. HOLE FOR SHANK AND THREADED PORTION

501–C–1. The hole for the shank shall be the same diameter as the shank.

501–C–2. The hole for the threaded portion of lag screw shall have a diameter equal to approximately 75 per cent of that of the shank. (See par. 700-H.)

501–D. ALLOWABLE LOADS

501–D–1. When lag screws instead of bolts are used with connectors, the allowable loads on connectors shall vary uniformly from full allowable load (allowable load for connector unit with common bolt) with an anchorage of threaded portion of lag screw equal to 9 times the diameter of the shank to 90 per cent of full allowable load with an anchorage of 5 times the shank diameter. With anchorage of less than 5 times the shank diameter, 75 per cent of full allowable connector load shall apply but the anchorage shall not be less than 3½ times the shank diameter.

502—NET SECTION

502–A. The net section shall be determined by subtracting from the full cross-sectional area of the timber the projected area of that portion of the connectors within the member and that portion of the bolt hole not within the connector projected area, located at the critical plane. (See NDS Fig. 14.)

NDS Fig. 14. Shaded area shows net cross section of timber

502–B. For sawed lumber the following provisions apply:

502–B–1. The stresses in the net section shall not exceed ⅞ of the allowable unit stress in bending for the grade of lumber used unless the provisions of par. 502-B-2 and 502-B-3 are observed.

502–B–2. If knots occur at the critical section, the cross-sectional area of the knots outside the area deducted for connectors and bolts should also be deducted in determining the net section.

502–B–3. In tension and compression members, the critical or net section of a timber in square inches shall not be less than that determined by dividing the total load in pounds which is transferred through the critical section of the member, by the appropriate constant in NDS Table 6.

502–C. For glued-laminated lumber the following provisions apply:

502–C–1. Knots at or near the critical section shall be disregarded in determining the net section.

502–C–2. The required net section in tension and compression shall be determined by dividing the total load in pounds which is transferred through the critical section of the member by the appropriate allowable unit compressive stress permitted for the glued-laminated material in NDS Part IX.

NDS TABLE 6 Constants for use in determining required net section in square inches

Duration of loading	Thickness of wood member *in.*	Constants for each connector-load group			
		Group A[1]	Group B[1]	Group C[1]	Group D
Normal	4 in. or less	2350	2000	1650	1300
	Over 4 in.	1850	1600	1300	1050
Permanent	4 in. or less	2100	1800	1500	1200
	Over 4 in.	1700	1450	1200	950
Snow	4 in. or less	2700	2300	1900	1500
	Over 4 in.	2150	1850	1500	1200
Wind or earthquake	4 in. or less	3100	2650	2200	1750
	Over 4 in.	2500	2150	1750	1400

[1] For woods in this group, see NDS Table 7.

NDS TABLE 7 Connector-load grouping of species when stress-graded

Connector-load grouping	Species
Group A	Ash, white Beech Birch Douglas fir (dense)[1] Elm, rock Hickory Pecan Maple, hard Oak, red and white Pine, southern (dense)[1]
Group B	Douglas fir (coast region) Elm, soft Larch, western Maple, soft Pine, southern Gum, black or red
Group C	Cypress, southern and tidewater red Hemlock, West Coast Pine, Norway Redwood Poplar, yellow Spruce, eastern Spruce, Sitka
Group D	Cedar, western red Fir, white Hemlock, eastern Pine, ponderosa Pine, sugar Pine, eastern white Pine, western white Spruce, Engelmann

[1] For grades qualifying as dense, see NDS Table 1.

503—DESIGN OF ECCENTRIC JOINTS AND BEAM SUPPORTS

503–A. For design of eccentric joint and connector supported beams, see par. 400-D-4.

NDS TABLE 8 Allowable loads for one split ring and bolt in single shear

(For normal loading conditions. See other provisions of NDS Part V for adjustments.)

Split-ring diam.	Bolt diam.	Number of faces of a piece containing connectors on same bolt	Thickness (net) of lumber	Loaded parallel to grain (0°)					Loaded perpendicular to grain (90°)					
				Edge distance	Allowable load per connector unit and bolt for—				Edge distance		Allowable load per connector unit and bolt for—			
					Group A woods*	Group B woods*	Group C woods*	Group D woods*	Unloaded-edge distance (edge opposite loaded edge)	Loaded-edge distance (edge toward which connector load acts)	Group A woods*	Group B woods*	Group C woods*	Group D woods*
Inches	*Inches*		*Inches*	*Inches*	*Pounds*	*Pounds*	*Pounds*	*Pounds*	*Inches*	*Inches*	*Pounds*	*Pounds*	*Pounds*	*Pounds*
2½	½	1	1 min.	1¾ min. or more	2,870	2,480	2,080	1,790	1¾ min. or more	1¾ min.	1,720	1,480	1,230	1,060
										2¾ or more	2,050	1,750	1,460	1,250
			1⅝ and thicker	1¾ min. or more	3,450	2,980	2,500	2,140	1¾ min. or more	1¾ min.	2,070	1,770	1,480	1,270
										2¾ or more	2,450	2,110	1,750	1,500
		2	1⅝ min.	1¾ min. or more	2,870	2,480	2,080	1,790	1¾ min. or more	1¾ min.	1,720	1,480	1,230	1,060
										2¾ or more	2,050	1,750	1,460	1,250
			2 and thicker	1¾ min. or more	3,450	2,980	2,500	2,140	1¾ min. or more	1¾ min.	2,070	1,770	1,480	1,270
										2¾ or more	2,450	2,110	1,750	1,500
4	¾	1	1 min.	2¾ min. or more	4,460	3,830	3,190	2,750	2¾ min. or more	2¾ min.	2,590	2,220	1,850	1,600
										3¾ or more	3,110	2,660	2,220	1,910
			1⅝ and thicker	2¾ min. or more	6,700	5,740	4,780	4,130	2¾ min. or more	2¾ min.	3,880	3,330	2,770	2,390
										3¾ or more	4,660	4,000	3,330	2,870
		2	1⅝ min.	2¾ min. or more	4,700	4,030	3,350	2,900	2¾ min. or more	2¾ min.	2,720	2,330	1,940	1,680
										3¾ or more	3,270	2,800	2,330	2,020
			2	2¾ min. or more	5,400	4,630	3,860	3,330	2¾ min. or more	2¾ min.	3,130	2,690	2,240	1,930
										3¾ or more	3,760	3,220	2,690	2,320
			2⅝	2¾ min. or more	6,580	5,630	4,700	4,060	2¾ min. or more	2¾ min.	3,810	3,270	2,720	2,350
										3¾ or more	4,570	3,920	3,270	2,820
			3 and thicker	2¾ min. or more	6,700	5,740	4,780	4,130	2¾ min. or more	2¾ min.	3,880	3,330	2,770	2,390
										3¾ or more	4,660	4,000	3,330	2,870

* For woods in this group, see NDS Table 7.

NDS TABLE 8 (Cont.) End distances and spacings for split rings and percentages of tabulated loads to use

Split-ring diam. (inches)	End distance						Spacing—center to center of connectors							
	Loaded parallel to grain (0°)				Loaded perpendicular to grain (90°)		Loaded parallel to grain (0°)				Loaded perpendicular to grain (90°)			
	Tension member (end toward which connector load acts)		Compression member (unloaded end)				Spacing parallel to grain		Spacing perpendicular to grain		Spacing parallel to grain		Spacing perpendicular to grain	
	Tension end distance (inches)	Percentage of tabulated loads	Compression end distance (inches)	Percentage of tabulated loads	End distance (inches)	Percentage of tabulated loads	Spacing (inches)	Percentage of tabulated loads	Spacing (inches)	Percentage of tabulated loads	Spacing (inches)	Percentage of tabulated loads	For spacing in inches of—	Use 100 percent of load given for loaded-edge-distance of—
2½	2¾ min 5½ or more	62.5 100	2½ min 4 or more	62.5 100	2¾ min 5½ or more	62.5 100	3⅜ min 6¾ or more	75 100	3½ min. or more.	100	3½ min. or more.	See par. 500–M–4.	3¼ min 4¼ or more	1¾ min. 2¾ or more.
4	3½ min 7 or more	62.5 100	3¼ min 5½ or more	62.5 100	3½ min 7 or more	62.5 100	4⅞ min 9 or more	75 100	5 min. or more.	100	5 min. or more.	See par. 500–M–4.	5 min 6 or more	2¾ min. 3¾ or more.

DIMENSIONS IN INCHES

	2½″	4″
Split ring:		
Inside diameter at center when closed	2½	4
Thickness of metal at center	.163	.193
Depth of metal (width of ring)	.750	1.000
Groove:		
Inside diameter	2.56	4.08
Width	.18	.21
Depth	.375	.50
Bolt hole:		
Diameter	9/16	13/16

	2½″	4″
Washers, standard:		
Round, cast iron or malleable iron, diameter	2⅛	3
Round, wrought iron (minimum):		
Diameter	1⅜	2
Thickness	3/32	5/32
Square plate:		
Length of side	2	3
Thickness	⅛	3/16
Projected area:		
Portion of one ring within member, sq. in.	1.10	2.25

NDS TABLE 9 Allowable loads for one toothed ring and bolt in single shear

(For normal loading conditions. See other provisions of NDS Part V for adjustments.)

Toothed ring diam.	Bolt diam.	Number of faces of a piece containing connectors on same bolt	Thickness (net) of lumber	Loaded parallel to grain (0°): Edge distance	Loaded parallel to grain (0°): Allowable load per connector unit and bolt for— Group A woods*	Group B woods*	Group C woods*	Group D woods*	Loaded perpendicular to grain (90°): Edge distance: Unloaded-edge distance (edge opposite loaded edge)	Loaded-edge distance (edge toward which connector load acts)	Loaded perpendicular to grain (90°): Allowable load per connector unit and bolt for— Group A woods*	Group B woods*	Group C woods*	Group D woods*
Inches	*Inches*		*Inches*	*Inches*	*Pounds*	*Pounds*	*Pounds*	*Pounds*	*Inches*	*Inches*	*Pounds*	*Pounds*	*Pounds*	*Pounds*
2	½	1	1 min.	1¼ min. or more	1,320	1,200	1,080	940	1¼ min. or more	1¼ min.	800	800	720	620
										2 or more	1,000	910	820	710
			1⅝ and thicker	1¼ min. or more	1,450	1,320	1,190	1,030	1¼ min. or more	1¼ min.	970	880	790	690
										2 or more	1,100	1,000	900	780
		2	1⅝ min.	1¼ min. or more	1,320	1,200	1,080	940	1¼ min. or more	1¼ min.	880	800	720	620
										2 or more	1,000	910	820	710
			2 and thicker	1¼ min. or more	1,450	1,320	1,190	1,030	1¼ min. or more	1¼ min.	970	880	790	690
										2 or more	1,100	1,000	900	780
2⅝	⅝	1	1 min.	1¾ min. or more	1,980	1,800	1,620	1,400	1¾ min. or more	1¾ min.	1,320	1,200	1,080	940
										2½ or more	1,500	1,370	1,230	1,070
			1⅝ and thicker	1¾ min. or more	2,480	2,250	2,020	1,760	1¾ min. or more	1¾ min.	1,650	1,500	1,350	1,170
										2½ or more	1,870	1,700	1,530	1,330
		2	1⅝ min.	1¾ min. or more	1,980	1,800	1,620	1,400	1¾ min. or more	1¾ min.	1,320	1,200	1,080	940
										2½ or more	1,500	1,370	1,230	1,070
			2	1¾ min. or more	2,190	1,990	1,790	1,550	1¾ min. or more	1¾ min.	1,460	1,330	1,190	1,030
										2½ or more	1,660	1,510	1,360	1,180
			2⅝ and thicker	1¾ min. or more	2,480	2,250	2,020	1,760	1¾ min. or more	1¾ min.	1,650	1,500	1,350	1,170
										2½ or more	1,870	1,700	1,530	1,330
3⅜	¾	1	1 min.	2¼ min. or more	2,570	2,340	2,110	1,830	2¼ min. or more	2¼ min.	1,720	1,560	1,400	1,220
										3¼ or more	2,040	1,850	1,670	1,450
			1⅝ and thicker	2¼ min. or more	3,470	3,160	2,840	2,460	2¼ min. or more	2¼ min.	2,320	2,110	1,900	1,640
										3¼ or more	2,750	2,500	2,250	1,950
		2	1⅝ min.	2¼ min. or more	2,570	2,340	2,110	1,830	2¼ min. or more	2¼ min.	1,720	1,560	1,400	1,220
										3¼ or more	2,040	1,850	1,670	1,450
			2	2¼ min. or more	2,820	2,560	2,310	2,000	2¼ min. or more	2¼ min.	1,880	1,710	1,540	1,330
										3¼ or more	2,230	2,030	1,820	1,580
			2⅝	2¼ min. or more	3,230	2,930	2,640	2,290	2¼ min. or more	2¼ min.	2,150	1,960	1,760	1,530
										3¼ or more	2,550	2,320	2,090	1,810
			3 and thicker	2¼ min. or more	3,470	3,160	2,840	2,460	2¼ min. or more	2¼ min.	2,320	2,110	1,900	1,640
										3¼ or more	2,750	2,500	2,250	1,950
4	¾	1	1 min.	2¾ min. or more	3,100	2,820	2,540	2,200	2¾ min. or more	2¾ min.	2,070	1,880	1,690	1,460
										3¾ or more	2,480	2,260	2,030	1,760
			1⅝ and thicker	2¾ min. or more	4,030	3,670	3,300	2,860	2¾ min. or more	2¾ min.	2,690	2,440	2,200	1,900
										3¾ or more	3,230	2,930	2,640	2,290
		2	1⅝ min.	2¾ min. or more	3,100	2,820	2,540	2,200	2¾ min. or more	2¾ min.	2,070	1,880	1,690	1,460
										3¾ or more	2,480	2,260	2,030	1,760
			2	2¾ min. or more	3,350	3,050	2,740	2,380	2¾ min. or more	2¾ min.	2,240	2,030	1,830	1,590
										3¾ or more	2,690	2,440	2,200	1,900
			2⅝	2¾ min. or more	3,780	3,440	3,090	2,680	2¾ min. or more	2¾ min.	2,520	2,290	2,060	1,790
										3¾ or more	3,020	2,750	2,470	2,140
			3 and thicker	2¾ min. or more	4,030	3,670	3,300	2,860	2¾ min. or more	2¾ min.	2,690	2,440	2,200	1,900
										3¾ or more	3,230	2,930	2,640	2,290

NDS TABLE 9 (Cont.) End distances and spacings for toothed rings and percentages of tabulated loads to use

Toothed ring diam. (inches)	End distance						Spacing—center to center of connectors							
	Loaded parallel to grain (0°)				Loaded perpendicular to grain (90°)		Loaded parallel to grain (0°)				Loaded perpendicular to grain (90°)			
	Tension member (end toward which connector load acts)		Compression member (unloaded end)				Spacing parallel to grain		Spacing perpendicular to grain		Spacing parallel to grain		Spacing perpendicular to grain	
	Tension end distance (inches)	Percentage of tabulated loads	Compression end distance (inches)	Percentage of tabulated loads	End distance (inches)	Percentage of tabulated loads	Spacing (inches)	Percentage of tabulated loads	Spacing (inches)	Percentage of tabulated loads	Spacing (inches)	Percentage of tabulated loads	For spacing in inches of—	Use 100 percent of load given for loaded-edge distance of—
2	2 min. 3½ or more	66.7 100	2 min. or more.	100	2 min. 3½ or more	66.7 100	2 min. 4 or more	75 100	2½ min. or more.	100	2½ min. or more	See par. 500–M–4.	2¼ min. 3 or more	1¼ min. 2 or more.
2⅝	2⅝ min. 4⅝ or more	66.7 100	2⅝ min. or more.	100	2⅝ min. 4⅝ or more	66.7 100	2⅝ min. 5¼ or more	75 100	3⅛ min. or more.	100	3⅜ min. or more.	See par. 500–M–4.	3 min. 3¾ or more	1¾ min. 2½ or more.
3⅜	3⅜ min. 5⅞ or more	66.7 100	3⅜ min. or more.	100	3⅜ min. 5⅞ or more	66.7 100	3⅜ min. 6¾ or more	75 100	3⅞ min or. more.	100	3⅞ min. or more.	See par. 500–M–4.	4 min. 5 or more	2¼ min. 3¼ or more.
4	4 min. 7 or more	66.7 100	4 min. or more.	100	4 min. 7 or more	66.7 100	4 min. 8 or more	75 100	4½ min. or more.	100	4½ min. or more.	See par. 500–M–4.	4¾ min. 5¾ or more	2¾ min. 3¾ or more.

DIMENSIONS IN INCHES

	2	2⅝″	3⅜″	4″
Toothed ring:				
Diameter	2	2⅝	3⅜	4
Thickness of metal	.061	.061	.061	.061
Depth	.94	.94	.94	.94
Depth of filet (minimum)	.25	.25	.25	.25
Bolt hole:				
Diameter	9/16	11/16	13/16	13/16

	2″	2⅝″	3⅜″	4″
Washers, minimum:				
Round, cast or malleable iron (diameter)	2	2⅝	3	3½
Square plate:				
Length of side	2	2½	3	3½
Thickness	3/16	¼	¼	⅜
Projected area:				
Portion of one ring within member (sq. in.)	.94	1.23	1.59	1.89

* For woods in this group, see NDS Table 7.

NDS TABLE 10 Allowable loads for one shear-plate unit and bolt in single shear

(For normal loading conditions. See other provisions of NDS Part V for adjustments. Loads tabulated below are for wood side plates. Also see notes following.)

Shear-plate diam.	Bolt diam.	Number of faces of a piece containing connectors on same bolt	Thickness (net) of lumber	Loaded parallel to grain (0°): Edge distance	Loaded parallel to grain (0°): Allowable load per connector unit and bolt for— Group A woods*	Group B woods*	Group C woods*	Group D woods*	Loaded perpendicular to grain (90°): Edge distance: Unloaded-edge-distance (edge opposite loaded edge)	Loaded-edge-distance (edge toward which connector load acts)	Loaded perpendicular to grain (90°): Allowable load per connector unit and bolt for— Group A woods*	Group B woods*	Group C woods*	Group D woods*
Inches	Inches		Inches	Inches	Pounds	Pounds	Pounds	Pounds	Inches	Inches	Pounds	Pounds	Pounds	Pounds
2 5/8	3/4	1	1 5/8 min. and thicker	1 3/4 min. or more	[1] 3,680	[1] 3,150	2,630	2,270	1 3/4 min. or more	1 3/4 min.	2,140	1,830	1,520	1,320
										2 3/4 or more	2,580	2,210	1,840	1,590
		2	1 5/8 min.	1 3/4 min. or more	2,860	2,450	2,040	1,760	1 3/4 min. or more	1 3/4 min.	1,660	1,420	1,190	1,020
										2 3/4 or more	2,000	1,720	1,430	1,230
			2	1 3/4 min. or more	[1] 3,480	[1] 2,980	2,480	2,140	1 3/4 min. or more	1 3/4 min.	2,020	1,730	1,440	1,240
										2 3/4 or more	2,430	2,090	1,740	1,500
			2 5/8 and thicker	1 3/4 min. or more	[1] 3,680	3,150	2,630	2,270	1 3/4 min. or more	1 3/4 min.	2,140	1,830	1,520	1,320
										2 3/4 or more	2,580	2,210	1,840	1,590
4	3/4	1	1 5/8 min.	2 3/4 min. or more	5,180	4,440	3,700	3,190	2 3/4 min. or more	2 3/4 min.	3,010	2,580	2,150	1,850
										3 3/4 or more	3,630	3,110	2,590	2,240
			1 3/4 and thicker	2 3/4 min. or more	[1] 5,550	[1] 4,760	3,970	3,420	2 3/4 min. or more	2 3/4 min.	3,220	2,760	2,300	1,980
										3 3/4 or more	3,890	3,330	2,780	2,400
		2	1 3/4 min.	2 3/4 min. or more	3,700	3,170	2,640	2,280	2 3/4 min. or more	2 3/4 min.	2,150	1,840	1,530	1,320
										3 3/4 or more	2,590	2,220	1,850	1,600
			2	2 3/4 min. or more	4,130	3,540	2,950	2,540	2 3/4 min. or more	2 3/4 min.	2,400	2,050	1,710	1,480
										3 3/4 or more	2,890	2,480	2,060	1,780
			2 5/8	2 3/4 min. or more	4,840	4,150	3,460	2,980	2 3/4 min. or more	2 3/4 min.	2,810	2,410	2,010	1,730
										3 3/4 or more	3,390	2,910	2,420	2,090
			3	2 3/4 min. or more	5,270	4,520	3,760	3,250	2 3/4 min. or more	2 3/4 min.	3,060	2,620	2,180	1,880
										3 3/4 or more	3,690	3,160	2,640	2,270
			3 5/8 and thicker	2 3/4 min. or more	[1] 5,550	4,760	3,970	3,420	2 3/4 min. or more	2 3/4 min.	3,220	2,760	2,300	1,980
										3 3/4 or more	3,890	3,330	2,780	2,400
4	7/8	1	1 5/8 min.	2 3/4 min. or more	5,180	4,440	3,700	3,190	2 3/4 min. or more	2 3/4 min.	3,010	2,580	2,150	1,850
										3 3/4 or more	3,630	3,110	2,590	2,240
			1 3/4 and thicker	2 3/4 min. or more	5,550	4,760	3,970	3,420	2 3/4 min. or more	2 3/4 min.	3,220	2,760	2,300	1,980
										3 3/4 or more	3,890	3,330	2,780	2,400
		2	1 3/4 min.	2 3/4 min. or more	3,700	3,170	2,640	2,280	2 3/4 min. or more	2 3/4 min.	2,150	1,840	1,530	1,330
										3 3/4 or more	2,590	2,220	1,850	1,600
			2	2 3/4 min. or more	4,130	3,640	2,950	2,540	2 3/4 min. or more	2 3/4 min.	2,400	2,050	1,710	1,480
										3 3/4 or more	2,890	2,480	2,060	1,780
			2 5/8	2 3/4 min. or more	4,840	4,150	3,460	2,980	2 3/4 min. or more	2 3/4 min.	2,810	2,410	2,010	1,730
										3 3/4 or more	3,390	2,910	2,420	2,090
			3	2 3/4 min. or more	5,270	4,520	3,760	3,250	2 3/4 min. or more	2 3/4 min.	3,060	2,620	2,180	1,880
										3 3/4 or more	3,690	3,160	2,640	2,270
			3 5/8 and thicker	2 3/4 min. or more	5,550	4,760	3,970	3,420	2 3/4 min. or more	2 3/4 min.	3,220	2,760	2,300	1,980
										3 3/4 or more	3,890	3,330	2,780	2,400

* For woods in this group, see NDS Table 7.

NDS TABLE 10 (Cont.) End distance and spacings for shear plates and percentages of tabulated loads to use

Shear-plate diam. (inches)	End distance: Loaded parallel to grain (0°): Tension member (end toward which connector load acts): Tension end distance (inches)	Percentage of tabulated loads	Compression member (unloaded end): Compression end distance (inches)	Percentage of tabulated loads	Loaded perpendicular to grain (90°): End distance (inches)	Percentage of tabulated loads	Spacing—center to center of connectors: Loaded parallel to grain (0°): Spacing parallel to grain: Spacing (inches)	Percentage of tabulated loads	Spacing perpendicular to grain: Spacing (inches)	Percentage of tabulated loads	Loaded perpendicular to grain (90°): Spacing parallel to grain: Spacing (inches)	Percentage of tabulated loads	Spacing perpendicular to grain: For spacing in inches of—	Use 100 percent of load given for loaded-edge distance of—
2⅝	2¾ min. 5½ or more	62.5 100	2½ min. 4 or more	62.5 100	2¾ min. 5½ or more	62.5 100	3⅜ min. 6¾ or more	75 100	3½ min. or more.	100	3½ min. or more.	See par. 500–M–4.	3¼ min. 4¼ or more	1¾ min. 2¾ or more.
4	3½ min. 7 or more	62.5 100	3¼ min. 5½ or more	62.5 100	3½ min. 7 or more	62.5 100	4⅞ min. 9 or more	75 100	5 min. or more.	100	5 min. or more.	See par. 500–M–4.	5 min. 6 or more	2¾ min. 3¾ or more.

DIMENSIONS IN INCHES

	2⅝″	4″	4″
Shear-plates:			
Material	Pressed steel.	Malleable iron.	Malleable iron.
Diameter of plate	2.62	4.02	4.02
Diameter of bolt hole	.81	.81	.94
Thickness of plate	.172	.20	.20
Depth of flange	.42	.62	.62
Circular Dap—Dimensions:			
A	2.63	4.03	4.03
B		1.55	1.55
C	1³⁄₁₆	1³⁄₁₆	1⁵⁄₁₆
D		0.97	.97
E	.19	.27	.27
F	.45	.64	.64
G	.25	.22	.22
H		.50	.50
I	2.25	3.49	3.49

bolt hole

	2⅝″	4″	4″
Steel strap or shapes for use with shear plates.			
Size of steel straps or shapes for use with shear plates shall be determined in accordance with Note 4.			
Hole diameter in straps or shapes for bolts	13/16	13/16	15/16
Bolt hole—Diameter in timber	1³⁄₁₆	1³⁄₁₆	1⁵⁄₁₆
Washers, standard:			
Round, cast or malleable iron, diameter	3	3	3½
Round, wrought iron, minimum:			
Diameter	2	2	2¼
Thickness	⁵⁄₃₂	⁵⁄₃₂	¹¹⁄₆₄
Square plate:			
Length of side	3	3	3
Thickness	¼	¼	¼
Projected area:			
Portion of one shear plate within member, square inches	0.98	2.48	2.48

Notes:

1. Loads preceded by "1" in the above table exceed those permitted by note 3 but are needed for proper determination of loads for other angles of load to grain. Note 3 limitations apply in all cases.

2. For metal side plates, tabulated loads apply except that for 4-in. shear plates the parallel-to-grain (not perpendicular) loads for wood side plates shall be increased 18, 11, 5 and zero per cent for groups A, B, C and D woods respectively, but loads shall not exceed those permitted by note 3.

3. The allowable loads for all loadings except wind shall not exceed 2,900 lb for 2 5/8-in. shear plates; 4,970 lb, and 6,760 lb, for 4 in. shear plates with 3/4-in. and 7/8-in. bolts respectively; or, for wind loading shall not exceed 3,870 lb, 6,630 lb, and 9,020 lb, respectively.

4. Metal side plates, when used, shall be designed in accordance with accepted metal practices. For steel, the following unit stresses in pounds per square inch are suggested for all loadings except wind; net section in tension 20,000; shear 10,000; double shear bearing 25,000; single shear bearing 20,000; for wind, these values may be increased one-third; if washers are provided and there is no bearing on bolt threads, bearing and shear values may be increased one-eighth.

NDS Part VI. Bolted Joints

For bolted joints using stress-grade lumber and the bolts defined herein, the provisions of Part VI and the tabulated allowable bolt loads herein apply.

600—BASIC DESIGN CONSIDERATIONS AND LIMITATIONS

600–A. TYPE OF LOAD

600–A–1. Tabulated allowable bolt loads are the maximum for normal loading. Pertinent adjustments of stresses and provisions of par. 200, 201, 202, 203, and 204 for lumber except as otherwise provided in NDS Part VI apply likewise to the tabulated bolt loads given in NDS Part VI.

600–B. NUMBER OF BOLTS

600–B–1. Tabulated loads are for *one* common bolt in double shear in a three-member joint.

600–B–2. Loads for more than one bolt, each of the same or miscellaneous sizes, are the sum of the loads permitted for each bolt. Spacings, end distances and edge distances shall be sufficient to develop the full strength of each bolt.

600–C. QUALITY OF BOLTS

600–C–1. Tabulated loads are for common bolts.

600–C–2. Where high-strength bolts are used, higher allowable loads are permissible in some cases as noted in ref. 9, NDS Appendix R. For high-strength bolts, allowable bolt loads given herein shall be modified proportionately, using basic provisions of the reference for guidance.

600–D. SPECIES OF LUMBER

600–D–1. Tabulated loads apply to species as given in NDS Table 12.

600–D–2. For proportionate loads for other species, see ref. 9, NDS Appendix R.

600–E. GRADE OF LUMBER

600–E–1. Tabulated loads apply to species irrespective of grade of lumber used.

600–F. CONDITION OF LUMBER

600–F–1. Tabulated loads are for bolts in lumber seasoned to a moisture content approximately equal to that to which it will eventually come in service.

600–F–2. For lumber installed at or above fiber saturation point and which becomes seasoned in place, allowable bolt loads shall be 40 per cent of the tabulated loads.

600–F–3. For lumber partially seasoned when fabricated, adjusted intermediate values may be used.

600–G. SERVICE CONDITIONS

600–G–1. Tabulated loads as adjusted for condition of lumber apply to bolted joints used under conditions continuously dry as in most covered structures.

600–G–2. When joints are to be exposed to weather, 75 per cent, and where always wet, 67 per cent of the tabulated loads apply.

600–H. BOLT HOLES

600–H–1. Bolt holes of a diameter permitting bolts to be driven easily and careful centering of holes in main members and splice plates are assumed.

600–H–2. Bolt holes shall be 1/32 in. to 1/16 in. larger than the bolt, depending on the size of the bolt.

600–H–3. Tight fit requiring forcible driving of bolts is not recommended.

600–I. NUTS AND WASHERS

600–I–1. Loosening of nuts, resulting from any shrinkage, is assumed and allowed for in the tabulated bolt loads.

600–I–2. Tabulated bolt loads shall apply for tight nuts also.

600–I–3. A washer not less than a standard cut washer, or in lieu thereof a metal plate or strap, shall be between the wood and the bolt head and between the wood and the nut.

600–J. SIDE MEMBERS—MATERIALS

600–J–1. Tabulated bolt loads are for side members of wood. Bearing thrust on side plates is assumed to be parallel to fibers.

600–J–2. When wood splice plates are used, the allowable load perpendicular-to-grain shall not exceed the load parallel-to-grain for any given size and quality of timbers.

600–J–3. When steel plates are used for side members, the tabulated loads for parallel-to-grain loading shall be increased by 25 per cent but no increase shall be made for perpendicular-to-grain loads. Steel plates shall be of ample strength.

600–K. SIDE MEMBERS—DIMENSIONS

600–K–1. Tabulated loads apply when side members of wood are each one-half the thickness of main member (see NDS Fig. 15).

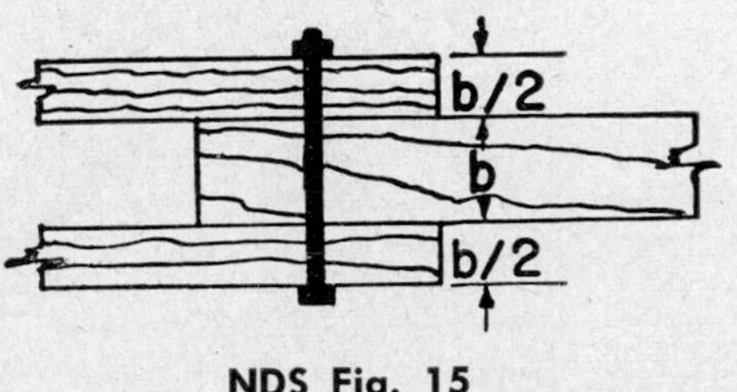

NDS Fig. 15

600–K–2. If side members are thicker than one-half the thickness of the main member, no increase in tabulated loads is permissible (see NDS Fig. 16).

NDS Fig. 16

600–K–3. When the side members are less than one-half the thickness of the main member, the tabulated loads indicated for a main member which is twice the thickness of thinnest side members used shall apply. For example, with 2-in. side members and a 10-in. center member, the tabulated loads for a 4-in. center member shall be used (see NDS Fig. 17).

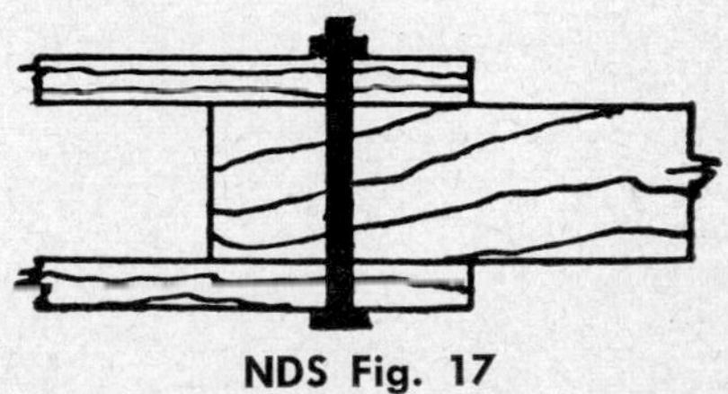

NDS Fig. 17

600–L. NUMBER OF MEMBERS IN JOINT

600–L–1. Tabulated loads are for a joint consisting of three members (double shear). Length of bolt, l, is measured in the main member (i.e., thickness of the piece). (See NDS Fig. 18.)

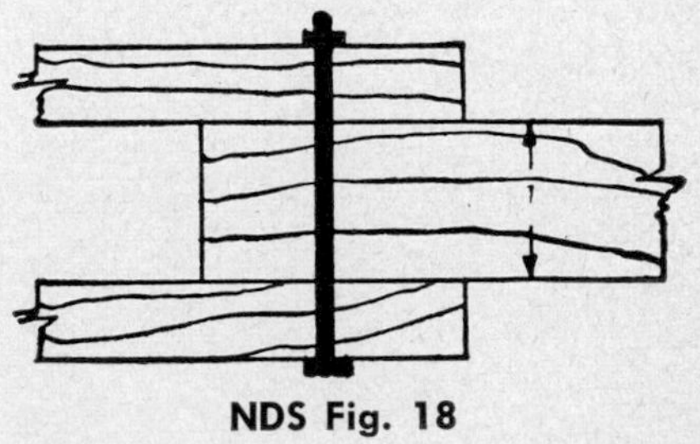

NDS Fig. 18

600–L–2. When a joint consists of two members (single shear) of equal thickness, one-half the tabulated load for a piece twice the thickness of one of the members shall apply (see NDS Fig. 19).

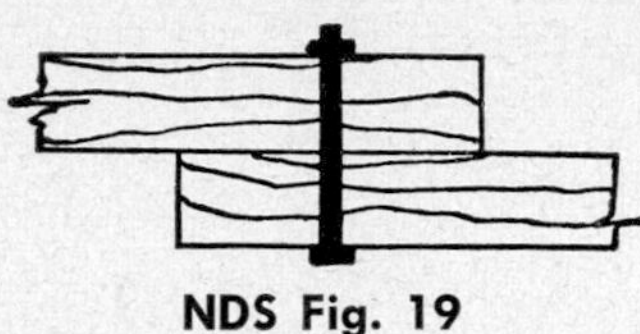

NDS Fig. 19

600–L–3. When members of a two-member joint are of unequal thickness, one-half the tabulated load for a piece twice the thickness of the thinner member shall apply (see NDS Fig. 20).

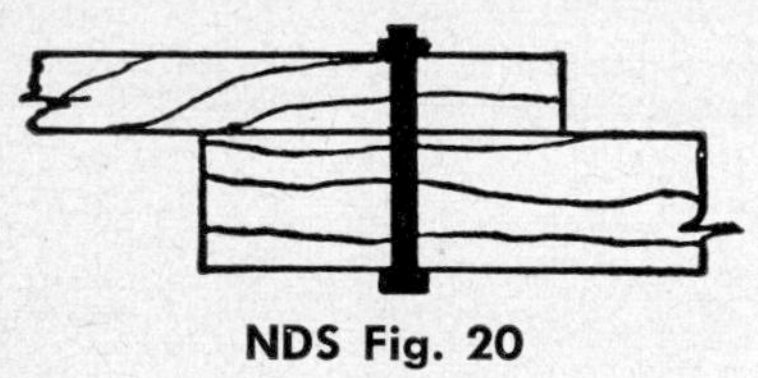

NDS Fig. 20

600–L–4. For multiple-member joints other than two or three members, of which the pieces are of equal thickness, the allowable load shall vary as the number of shear planes involved; the allowable load for each shear plane shall be equal to one-half the tabulated load for a piece the thickness of the member involved. Thus, when a joint consists of four members of equal thickness, 1½ times the tabulated load for a piece the thickness of one of the members shall apply (see NDS Fig. 21).

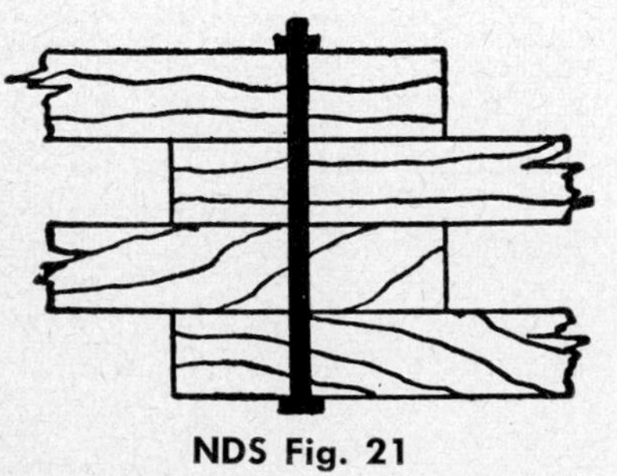

NDS Fig. 21

600—M. LOAD AT AN ANGLE WITH AXIS OF BOLT (NDS Fig. 22)

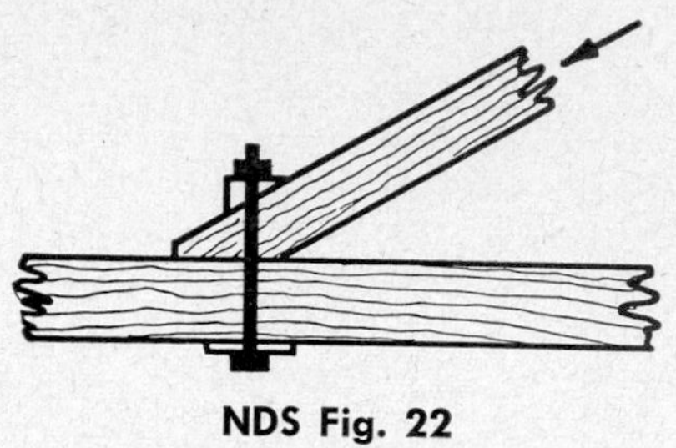

NDS Fig. 22

600–M–1. Tabulated loads are for loading acting perpendicular-to-axis of bolt.

600–M–2. If the load in a two-member joint acts at an angle with the axis of a bolt, the allowable load component acting at 90 deg with the bolt axis shall be equal to ½ the tabulated load for a bolt twice the length of the bolt length in the thinner piece. Ample bearing area under washers or plates shall be provided to resist the load component acting parallel to the axis of the bolt.

600–N. LOADS NEITHER PARALLEL NOR PERPENDICULAR TO GRAIN (NDS Fig. 23)

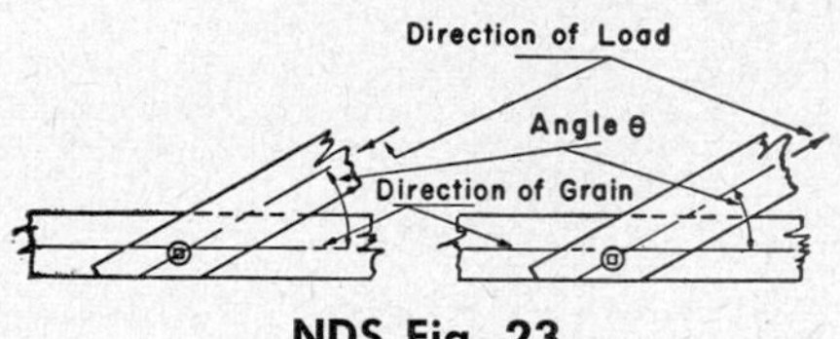

NDS Fig. 23

600–N–1. Allowable bolt loads acting in a direction inclined to grain shall be determined from the Hankinson formula which for total bolt loads, may be stated as follows:

$$N = \frac{PQ}{P \sin^2 \theta + Q \cos^2 \theta}$$

in which:

N = allowable load per bolt in a direction at inclination θ with the direction of the grain

P = allowable load per bolt in compression parallel to grain

Q = allowable load per bolt in compression perpendicular to grain

θ = angle between the direction of the load and the direction of the grain

For tabulated values of $\sin^2 \theta$ and $\cos^2 \theta$, and graphical solution of Hankinson formula, see Appendix C.

601—PLACEMENT OF BOLTS IN JOINT (NDS Fig. 24)

601–A. *l/d* OF BOLT

601–A–1. l/d of bolt is the ratio of its length, l, in main member, to its diameter, d.

601–B. CRITICAL SECTION

601–B–1. The critical section is that section of the member, taken at right angles to the direction of the load, which gives the maximum stress in the member based on the net area remaining after reducing it for bolt holes at that section.

601–B–2. For parallel to grain loading, net tension area remaining at critical section must equal at least 80 per cent of total area in bearing under all bolts at the joint in the particular timber in question for softwoods, and 100 per cent for hardwoods, for designs under par. 600-F-1, and 33 per cent and 42 per cent, respectively, for those under par. 600-F-2. For partial seasoning, proportional intermediate areas may be used.

601–C. ROW OF BOLTS

601–C–1. "Row of bolts" means a number of bolts placed in a line parallel to the direction of the load when parallel or perpendicular to grain.

601—D. SPACING

601–D–1. All spacings and distances given are measured from center of bolt.

601–E. SPACING OF BOLTS IN A ROW

601–E–1. For parallel-to-grain loading, the minimum spacing is 4 times bolt diameter d.

601–E–2. For perpendicular-to-grain loading:

(a) If design load approaches bolt-bearing capacity of side members, space same as parallel-to-grain.

(b) If design load is less than bolt-bearing capacity of side members, spacing may be reduced.

601–F. SPACING BETWEEN ROWS OF BOLTS

601–F–1. For parallel-to-grain loading, the spacing across the grain between rows of bolts is controlled by net section as provided in par. 601-B-2.

601–F–2. For perpendicular-to-grain loading, the spacing shall be at least 2½ times bolt diameter for l/d ratio of 2, and 5 times bolt diameter for l/d ratios of 6 or

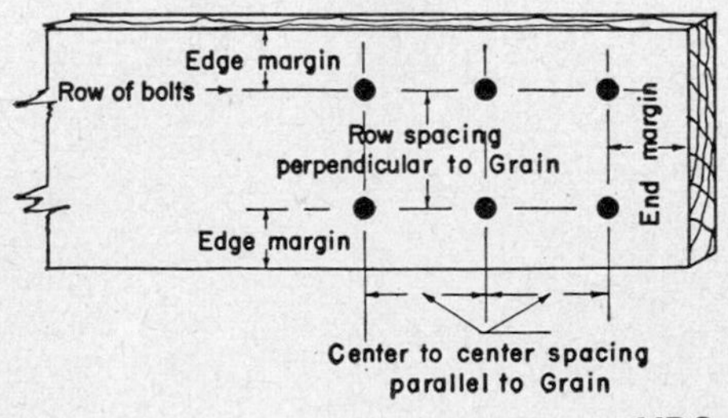

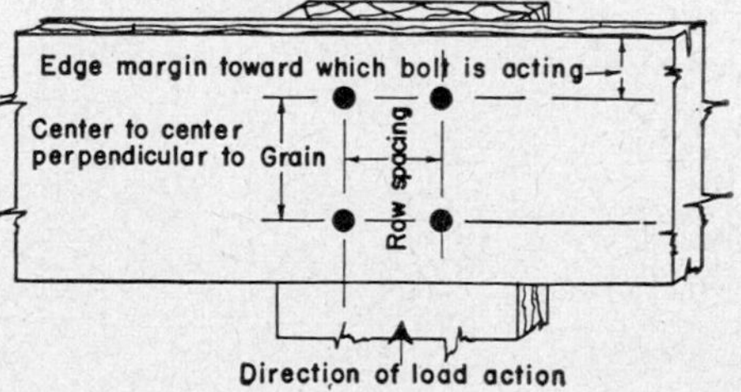

NDS Fig. 24

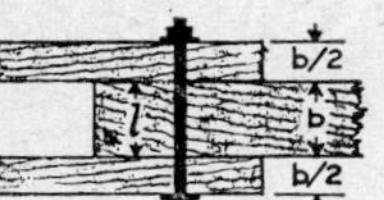

NDS TABLE 12 Allowable loads on one bolt loaded at both ends (double shear)[1]

(The allowable bolt loads below, in pounds, are for normal loading conditions. See other provisions of NDS Part VI for adjustments of these tabulated allowable bolt loads. Key: l = length of bolt in main member; d = bolt diameter; A = projected area of bolt; P = parallel to grain; Q = perpendicular to grain.)

				ASH, BLACK		ASH, WHITE		ASPEN		BEECH AND BIRCH		CEDAR, ALASKA		CEDAR, NORTHERN AND SOUTHERN WHITE		CEDAR, PORT ORFORD	
l	d	l/d	$A=l\,d$	P	Q	P	Q	P	Q	P	Q	P	Q	P	Q	P	Q
Inches	*Inches*		*Sq. in.*														
	½	3.3	.8125	610	450	1,010	750	580	225	1,120	750	750	380	540	270	850	380
	⅝	2.6	1.0156	760	510	1,290	850	710	250	1,430	850	930	420	670	310	1,070	420
1⅝	¾	2.2	1.2188	910	570	1,550	950	850	280	1,720	950	1,120	470	800	340	1,280	470
	⅞	1.9	1.4219	1,060	620	1,820	1,040	1,000	310	2,000	1,040	1,310	520	940	370	1,500	520
	1	1.6	1.625	1,220	680	2,070	1,140	1,140	340	2,290	1,140	1,500	570	1,070	410	1,720	570
	½	4.0	1.00	740	550	1,180	920	700	280	1,300	920	900	460	660	330	1,030	460
	⅝	3.2	1.25	940	630	1,560	1,050	890	310	1,730	1,050	1,160	520	830	380	1,320	520
2	¾	2.7	1.50	1,120	700	1,910	1,160	1,060	350	2,110	1,160	1,390	580	990	420	1,580	580
	⅞	2.3	1.75	1,310	770	2,230	1,280	1,240	380	2,460	1,280	1,620	640	1,160	460	1,850	640
	1	2.0	2.00	1,500	840	2,550	1,400	1,410	420	2,820	1,400	1,850	700	1,320	500	2,110	700
	½	5.3	1.3125	910	730	1,270	1,210	850	360	1,400	1,210	1,030	610	800	440	1,180	610
	⅝	4.2	1.6406	1,210	820	1,890	1,370	1,140	410	2,090	1,370	1,460	690	1,070	490	1,670	690
2⅝	¾	3.5	1.9688	1,470	920	2,420	1,530	1,390	460	2,670	1,530	1,810	760	1,300	550	2,060	760
	⅞	3.0	2.2969	1,720	1,010	2,900	1,680	1,620	500	3,200	1,680	2,120	840	1,520	600	2,420	840
	1	2.6	2.625	1,960	1,100	3,340	1,830	1,850	550	3,690	1,830	2,430	920	1,730	660	2,770	920
	½	6.0	1.50	960	830	1,290	1,330	900	420	1,420	1,330	1,050	690	850	500	1,200	690
	⅝	4.8	1.875	1,350	940	1,990	1,570	1,270	470	2,190	1,570	1,560	780	1,190	560	1,790	780
3	¾	4.0	2.25	1,670	1,050	2,650	1,740	1,580	520	2,930	1,740	2,030	870	1,480	630	2,320	870
	⅞	3.4	2.625	1,960	1,150	3,250	1,920	1,850	580	3,590	1,920	2,420	960	1,730	690	2,760	960
	1	3.0	3.00	2,240	1,260	3,790	2,100	2,110	630	4,180	2,100	2,770	1,050	1,980	750	3,170	1,050
	½	7.3	1.8125	960	950	1,290	1,390	900	500	1,420	1,390	1,050	830	850	600	1,200	830
	⅝	5.8	2.2656	1,490	1,140	2,000	1,850	1,400	570	2,220	1,850	1,640	950	1,310	680	1,870	950
3⅝	¾	4.8	2.7188	1,960	1,270	2,880	2,110	1,850	630	3,190	2,110	2,280	1,050	1,730	760	2,600	1,050
	⅞	4.1	3.1719	2,360	1,390	3,700	2,320	2,220	700	4,090	2,320	2,840	1,160	2,080	840	3,240	1,160
	1	3.6	3.625	2,710	1,520	4,430	2,530	2,550	760	4,880	2,530	3,320	1,270	2,390	910	3,790	1,270
	½	8.0	2.00	960	980	1,290	1,390	900	550	1,420	1,390	1,050	890	850	670	1,200	890
	⅝	6.4	2.50	1,500	1,250	2,010	1,950	1,420	630	2,220	1,750	1,640	1,050	1,330	750	1,870	1,050
4	¾	5.3	3.00	2,080	1,400	2,890	2,310	1,960	700	3,190	2,310	2,340	1,160	1,840	840	2,680	1,160
	⅞	4.6	3.50	2,550	1,540	3,830	2,560	2,400	770	4,230	2,560	3,000	1,280	2,250	920	3,430	1,280
	1	4.0	4.00	2,980	1,680	4,720	2,790	2,800	840	5,210	2,790	3,600	1,400	2,630	1,010	4,120	1,400
	½	9.0	2.25	960	960	1,290	1,340	900	590	1,420	1,340	1,050	900	850	710	1,200	900
	⅝	7.2	2.8125	1,500	1,350	2,010	1,980	1,420	710	2,220	1,980	1,640	1,170	1,330	850	1,870	1,170
4½	¾	6.0	3.375	2,160	1,570	2,890	2,520	2,040	790	3,190	2,520	2,360	1,310	1,910	940	2,700	1,310
	⅞	5.1	3.9375	2,780	1,730	3,940	2,880	2,620	860	4,350	2,880	3,160	1,440	2,460	1,040	3,610	1,440
	1	4.5	4.50	3,290	1,890	5,000	3,140	3,090	940	5,520	3,140	3,900	1,570	2,900	1,130	4,450	1,570
	1⅛	4.0	5.0625	3,770	2,050	5,970	3,420	3,540	1,030	6,590	3,420	4,560	1,710	3,320	1,230	5,210	1,710
	½	10.0	2.50	960	930	1,290	1,280	900	590	1,420	1,280	1,050	800	850	710	1,200	800
	⅝	8.0	3.125	1,500	1,380	2,010	1,960	1,420	780	2,220	1,960	1,640	1,260	1,330	940	1,870	1,260
5	¾	6.7	3.75	2,170	1,720	2,890	2,620	2,040	870	3,190	2,620	2,360	1,450	1,910	1,050	2,700	1,450
	⅞	5.7	4.375	2,910	1,920	3,940	3,140	2,740	960	4,350	3,140	3,210	1,600	2,570	1,150	3,670	1,600
	1	5.0	5.00	3,570	2,100	5,100	3,490	3,360	1,050	5,630	3,490	4,080	1,750	3,150	1,260	4,670	1,750
	1⅛	4.4	5.625	4,120	2,280	6,350	3,810	3,880	1,140	7,000	3,810	4,910	1,900	3,640	1,370	5,620	1,900

l	d	l/d	A=l d	ASH, BLACK		ASH, WHITE		ASPEN		BEECH AND BIRCH		CEDAR, ALASKA		CEDAR, NORTHERN AND SOUTHERN WHITE		CEDAR, PORT ORFORD	
				P	Q	P	Q	P	Q	P	Q	P	Q	P	Q	P	Q
Inches	*Inches*		*Sq. in.*														
	⅝	8.8	3.4375	1,500	1,360	2,010	1,910	1,420	830	2,220	1,910	1,640	1,270	1,330	990	1,870	1,270
	¾	7.3	4.125	2,170	1,820	2,910	2,660	2,040	960	3,190	2,660	2,380	1,590	1,920	1,150	2,700	1,590
5½	⅞	6.3	4.8125	2,960	2,100	3,940	3,310	2,780	1,060	4,350	3,310	3,230	1,760	2,610	1,270	3,670	1,760
	1	5.5	5.50	3,740	2,300	5,120	3,800	3,520	1,150	5,650	3,800	4,170	1,920	3,300	1,380	4,670	1,920
	1⅛	4.9	6.1875	4,440	2,510	6,440	4,190	4,180	1,260	7,110	4,190	5,110	2,090	3,920	1,510	5,840	2,090
	⅝	9.6	3.75	1,500	1,340	2,010	1,840	1,420	840	2,220	1,840	1,650	1,250	1,330	1,010	1,870	1,250
	¾	8.0	4.50	2,170	1,840	2,910	2,620	2,040	1,050	3,190	2,620	2,380	1,680	1,920	1,260	2,700	1,680
6	⅞	6.9	5.25	2,960	2,250	3,940	3,380	2,780	1,150	4,350	3,380	3,230	1,920	2,610	1,380	3,670	1,920
	1	6.0	6.00	3,840	2,510	5,140	4,040	3,620	1,260	5,680	4,040	4,210	2,100	3,390	1,510	4,810	2,100
	1⅛	5.3	6.75	4,690	2,740	6,500	4,540	4,420	1,370	7,200	4,540	5,270	2,280	4,140	1,640	6,020	2,280
	⅝	10.4	4.0625	1,500	1,300	2,010	1,800	1,420	830	2,220	1,800	1,650	1,230	1,330	990	1,870	1,230
	¾	8.7	4.875	2,170	1,820	2,910	2,560	2,040	1,100	3,190	2,560	2,380	1,700	1,920	1,320	2,700	1,700
6½	⅞	7.4	5.6875	2,960	2,350	3,940	3,410	2,780	1,250	4,350	3,410	3,230	2,070	2,610	1,500	3,670	2,070
	1	6.5	6.50	3,840	2,700	5,150	4,180	3,620	1,360	5,680	4,180	4,210	2,270	3,420	1,630	4,810	2,270
	1⅛	5.8	7.3125	4,810	2,970	6,500	4,820	4,520	1,480	7,200	4,820	5,290	2,470	4,240	1,780	6,050	2,470
	⅝	11.2	4.375	1,500	1,270	2,010	1,720	1,420	820	2,220	1,720	1,650	1,210	1,330	980	1,870	1,210
	¾	9.3	5.25	2,170	1,800	2,910	2,510	2,040	1,120	3,190	2,510	2,380	1,690	1,920	1,350	2,700	1,690
7	⅞	8.0	6.125	2,960	2,370	3,940	3,360	2,780	1,340	4,350	3,360	3,230	2,150	2,610	1,610	3,670	2,150
	1	7.0	7.00	3,840	2,850	5,150	4,250	3,620	1,470	5,680	4,250	4,210	2,440	3,420	1,760	4,810	2,440
	1⅛	6.2	7.875	4,920	3,190	6,500	5,050	4,630	1,600	7,200	5,050	5,340	2,660	4,340	1,920	6,110	2,660
	⅝	12.0	4.6875	1,500	1,220	2,010	1,670	1,420	810	2,220	1,670	1,650	1,200	1,330	970	1,870	1,200
	¾	10.0	5.625	2,170	1,760	2,910	2,420	2,040	1,110	3,190	2,420	2,380	1,660	1,920	1,330	2,700	1,660
7½	⅞	8.6	6.5625	2,960	2,340	3,940	3,300	2,780	1,400	4,350	3,300	3,230	2,180	2,610	1,680	3,670	2,180
	1	7.5	7.50	3,840	2,940	5,150	4,230	3,620	1,570	5,680	4,230	4,210	2,590	3,420	1,890	4,810	2,590
	1⅛	6.7	8.4375	4,920	3,370	6,500	5,140	4,630	1,710	7,200	5,140	5,340	2,850	4,340	2,050	6,110	2,850
	⅝	12.8	5.00	1,500	1,180	2,010	1,600	1,420	800	2,200	1,600	1,650	1,180	1,330	950	1,870	1,180
	¾	10.7	6.00	2,170	1,720	2,910	2,360	2,040	1,100	3,190	2,360	2,380	1,630	1,920	1,310	2,700	1,630
8	⅞	9.1	7.00	2,960	2,320	3,940	3,260	2,780	1,440	4,350	3,260	3,230	2,180	2,610	1,730	3,670	2,180
	1	8.0	8.00	3,840	2,950	5,150	4,190	3,620	1,680	5,680	4,190	4,210	2,680	3,420	2,010	4,810	2,680
	1⅛	7.1	9.00	4,920	3,530	6,500	5,210	4,630	1,830	7,200	5,210	5,340	3,040	4,340	2,190	6,110	3,040
	1¼	6.4	10.00	6,060	3,900	8,040	6,090	5,710	1,960	8,870	6,090	6,570	3,270	5,350	2,360	7,510	3,270
	¾	12.7	7.125	2,170	1,580	2,910	2,150	2,040	1,060	3,190	2,150	2,380	1,570	1,920	1,270	2,700	1,570
	⅞	10.9	8.3125	2,960	2,190	3,940	2,980	2,780	1,400	4,350	2,980	3,230	2,080	2,610	1,680	3,670	2,080
9½	1	9.5	9.50	3,840	2,860	5,150	3,960	3,620	1,790	5,680	3,960	4,210	2,680	3,420	2,150	4,810	2,680
	1⅛	8.4	10.6875	4,920	3,630	6,500	5,120	4,630	2,140	7,200	5,120	5,340	3,350	4,340	2,560	6,110	3,350
	1¼	7.6	11.875	6,060	4,310	8,040	6,190	5,710	2,330	8,870	6,190	6,570	3,820	5,350	2,800	7,510	3,820
	⅞	11.4	8.75	2,960	2,160	3,940	2,940	2,780	1,400	4,350	2,940	3,230	2,080	2,610	1,680	3,670	2,080
10	1	10.0	10.00	3,840	2,820	5,150	3,870	3,620	1,780	5,680	3,870	4,210	2,660	3,420	2,140	4,810	2,660
	1⅛	8.9	11.25	4,920	3,560	6,500	4,990	4,630	2,180	7,200	4,990	5,340	3,330	4,340	2,610	6,110	3,330
	1¼	8.0	12.50	6,060	4,320	8,040	6,140	5,710	2,450	8,870	6,140	6,570	3,930	5,350	2,950	7,510	3,930
	1	11.5	11.50	3,840	2,680	5,150	3,640	3,620	1,740	5,680	3,640	4,210	2,580	3,420	2,090	4,810	2,580
11½	1⅛	10.2	12.9375	4,920	3,440	6,500	4,710	4,630	2,180	7,200	4,710	5,340	3,260	4,340	2,620	6,100	3,260
	1¼	9.2	14.375	6,060	4,210	8,040	5,890	5,710	2,620	8,870	5,890	6,570	3,950	5,350	3,150	7,510	3,950
	1	12.0	12.00	3,840	2,610	5,150	3,560	3,620	1,730	5,680	3,560	4,210	2,560	3,420	2,070	4,810	2,560
12	1⅛	10.7	13.50	4,920	3,370	6,500	4,640	4,630	2,150	7,200	4,640	5,340	3,200	4,340	2,580	6,100	3,200
	1¼	9.6	15.00	6,060	4,180	8,040	5,770	5,710	2,630	8,870	5,770	6,570	3,920	5,350	3,150	7,510	3,920

[1] Three (3) member joint.

NDS TABLE 12 (Cont.) Allowable loads on one bolt loaded at both ends (double shear)[1]

l	d	l/d	$A=l\,d$	CEDAR, WESTERN RED		COTTON-WOOD, EASTERN		CYPRESS, SOUTHERN		DOUGLAS FIR, COAST REGION		DOUGLAS FIR, ROCKY MOUNTAIN TYPE		ELM, ROCK		ELM, SOFT	
				P	Q	P	Q	P	Q	P	Q	P	Q	P	Q	P	Q
Inches	*Inches*		*Sq. in.*														
	½	3.3	.8125	680	300	580	225	1,010	450	1,010	480	750	420	1,120	750	750	380
	⅝	2.6	1.0156	850	340	710	250	1,290	510	1,290	540	930	480	1,430	850	930	420
1⅝	¾	2.2	1.2188	1,010	380	850	280	1,550	570	1,550	600	1,120	530	1,720	950	1,120	470
	⅞	1.9	1.4219	1,190	420	1,000	310	1,820	620	1,820	670	1,310	580	2,000	1,040	1,310	520
	1	1.6	1.625	1,360	450	1,140	340	2,070	680	2,070	730	1,500	640	2,290	1,140	1,500	570
	½	4.0	1.00	840	370	700	280	1,180	550	1,180	590	900	520	1,300	920	900	460
	⅝	3.2	1.25	1,050	420	890	310	1,560	630	1,560	670	1,160	590	1,730	1,050	1,160	520
2	¾	2.7	1.50	1,250	470	1,060	350	1,910	700	1,910	750	1,390	650	2,110	1,160	1,390	580
	⅞	2.3	1.75	1,470	510	1,240	380	2,230	770	2,230	820	1,620	720	2,460	1,280	1,620	640
	1	2.0	2.00	1,670	560	1,410	420	2,550	840	2,550	890	1,850	780	2,820	1,400	1,850	700
	½	5.3	1.3125	1,010	490	850	360	1,270	730	1,270	780	1,030	680	1,400	1,210	1,030	610
	⅝	4.2	1.6406	1,360	550	1,140	410	1,890	820	1,890	880	1,460	770	2,090	1,370	1,460	690
2⅝	¾	3.5	1.9688	1,650	610	1,390	460	2,420	920	2,420	980	1,810	860	2,670	1,530	1,810	760
	⅞	3.0	2.2969	1,920	670	1,620	500	2,900	1,010	2,900	1,080	2,120	940	3,200	1,680	2,120	840
	1	2.6	2.625	2,190	730	1,850	550	3,340	1,100	3,340	1,170	2,430	1,030	3,690	1,830	2,430	920
	½	6.0	1.50	1,070	550	900	420	1,290	830	1,290	890	1,050	780	1,420	1,330	1,050	690
	⅝	4.8	1.875	1,510	630	1,270	470	1,990	940	1,990	1,000	1,560	880	2,190	1,570	1,560	780
3	¾	4.0	2.25	1,870	700	1,580	520	2,650	1,050	2,650	1,120	2,030	980	2,930	1,740	2,030	870
	⅞	3.4	2.625	2,190	770	1,850	580	3,250	1,150	3,250	1,230	2,420	1,080	3,590	1,920	2,420	960
	1	3.0	3.00	2,510	840	2,110	630	3,790	1,260	3,790	1,340	2,770	1,170	4,180	2,100	2,770	1,050
	½	7.3	1.8125	1,070	670	900	500	1,290	950	1,290	1,020	1,050	930	1,420	1,390	1,050	830
	⅝	5.8	2.2656	1,660	760	1,400	570	2,000	1,140	2,000	1,210	1,640	1,060	2,220	1,850	1,640	950
3⅝	¾	4.8	2.7188	2,190	840	1,850	630	2,880	1,270	2,880	1,350	2,280	1,180	3,190	2,110	2,280	1,050
	⅞	4.1	3.1719	2,630	930	2,220	700	3,700	1,390	3,700	1,490	2,840	1,300	4,090	2,320	2,840	1,160
	1	3.6	3.625	3,030	1,010	2,550	760	4,430	1,520	4,430	1,620	3,320	1,420	4,880	2,530	3,320	1,270
	½	8.0	2.00	1,070	710	900	550	1,290	980	1,290	1,040	1,050	990	1,420	1,390	1,050	890
	⅝	6.4	2.50	1,670	840	1,420	630	2,010	1,250	2,010	1,330	1,640	1,170	2,220	1,950	1,640	1,050
4	¾	5.3	3.00	2,330	930	1,960	700	2,890	1,400	2,890	1,490	2,340	1,300	3,190	2,310	2,340	1,160
	⅞	4.6	3.50	2,850	1,020	2,400	770	3,830	1,540	3,830	1,640	3,000	1,430	4,230	2,560	3,000	1,280
	1	4.0	4.00	3,330	1,120	2,800	840	4,720	1,680	4,720	1,790	3,600	1,560	5,210	2,790	3,600	1,400
	½	9.0	2.25	1,070	720	900	590	1,290	960	1,290	1,020	1,050	1,000	1,420	1,340	1,050	900
	⅝	7.2	2.8125	1,670	940	1,420	710	2,010	1,350	2,010	1,440	1,640	1,310	2,220	1,980	1,640	1,170
4½	¾	6.0	3.375	2,420	1,050	2,040	790	2,890	1,570	2,890	1,680	2,360	1,470	3,190	2,520	2,360	1,310
	⅞	5.1	3.9375	3,110	1,150	2,620	860	3,940	1,730	3,940	1,840	3,160	1,610	4,350	2,880	3,160	1,440
	1	4.5	4.50	3,670	1,260	3,090	940	5,000	1,890	5,000	2,010	3,900	1,760	5,520	3,140	3,900	1,570
	1⅛	4.0	5.0625	4,210	1,370	3,540	1,030	5,970	2,050	5,970	2,190	4,560	1,920	6,590	3,420	4,560	1,710
	½	10.0	2.50	1,070	700	900	590	1,290	930	1,290	990	1,050	990	1,420	1,280	1,050	800
	⅝	8.0	3.125	1,670	1,000	1,420	780	2,010	1,380	2,010	1,470	1,640	1,410	2,220	1,960	1,640	1,260
5	¾	6.7	3.75	2,420	1,160	2,040	870	2,890	1,720	2,890	1,830	2,360	1,630	3,190	2,620	2,360	1,450
	⅞	5.7	4.375	3,260	1,280	2,740	960	3,940	1,920	3,940	2,050	3,210	1,790	4,350	3,140	3,210	1,600
	1	5.0	5.00	3,990	1,400	3,360	1,050	5,100	2,100	5,100	2,240	4,080	1,960	5,630	3,490	4,080	1,750
	1⅛	4.4	5.625	4,610	1,520	3,880	1,140	6,350	2,280	6,350	2,440	4,910	2,130	7,000	3,810	4,910	1,900

l	d	l/d	A = l d	Cedar, Western Red P	Cedar, Western Red Q	Cottonwood, Eastern P	Cottonwood, Eastern Q	Cypress, Southern P	Cypress, Southern Q	Douglas Fir, Coast Region P	Douglas Fir, Coast Region Q	Douglas Fir, Rocky Mountain Type P	Douglas Fir, Rocky Mountain Type Q	Elm, Rock P	Elm, Rock Q	Elm, Soft P	Elm, Soft Q
Inches	*Inches*		*Sq. in.*														
	⅝	8.8	3.4375	1,670	1,020	1,420	830	2,010	1,360	2,010	1,450	1,640	1,430	2,220	1,910	1,640	1,270
	¾	7.3	4.125	2,420	1,270	2,040	960	2,910	1,820	2,910	1,940	2,380	1,780	3,190	2,660	2,380	1,590
5½	⅞	6.3	4.8125	3,310	1,410	2,780	1,060	3,940	2,100	3,940	2,240	3,230	1,970	4,350	3,310	3,230	1,760
	1	5.5	5.50	4,180	1,540	3,520	1,150	5,120	2,300	5,120	2,460	4,170	2,150	5,650	2,800	4,170	1,920
	1⅛	4.9	6.1875	4,960	1,670	4,180	1,260	6,440	2,510	6,440	2,680	5,110	2,340	7,110	4,190	5,110	2,090
	⅝	9.6	3.75	1,670	1,000	1,420	840	2,010	1,340	2,010	1,420	1,650	1,400	2,220	1,840	1,650	1,250
	¾	8.0	4.50	2,420	1,340	2,040	1,050	2,910	1,840	2,910	1,970	2,380	1,880	3,190	2,620	2,380	1,680
6	⅞	6.9	5.25	3,310	1,540	2,780	1,150	3,940	2,250	3,940	2,400	3,230	2,150	4,350	3,380	3,230	1,920
	1	6.0	6.00	4,290	1,680	3,620	1,260	5,140	2,510	5,140	2,680	4,210	2,350	5,680	4,040	4,210	2,100
	1⅛	5.3	6.75	5,240	1,830	4,420	1,370	6,500	2,740	6,500	2,920	5,270	2,560	7,200	4,540	5,270	2,280
	⅝	10.4	4.0625	1,670	990	1,420	830	2,010	1,300	2,010	1,390	1,650	1,380	2,220	1,800	1,650	1,230
	¾	8.7	4.875	2,420	1,360	2,040	1,100	2,910	1,820	2,910	1,940	2,380	1,900	3,190	2,560	2,380	1,700
6½	⅞	7.4	5.6875	3,310	1,650	2,780	1,250	3,940	2,350	3,940	2,510	3,230	2,310	4,350	3,410	3,230	2,070
	1	6.5	6.50	4,290	1,820	3,620	1,360	5,150	2,700	5,150	2,880	4,210	2,540	5,680	4,180	4,210	2,270
	1⅛	5.8	7.3125	5,370	1,980	4,520	1,480	6,500	2,970	6,500	3,170	5,290	2,770	7,200	4,820	5,290	2,470
	⅝	11.2	4.375	1,670	970	1,420	820	2,010	1,270	2,010	1,350	1,650	1,360	2,220	1,720	1,650	1,210
	¾	9.3	5.25	2,420	1,350	2,040	1,120	2,910	1,800	2,910	1,920	2,380	1,890	3,190	2,510	2,380	1,690
7	⅞	8.0	6.125	3,310	1,720	2,780	1,340	3,940	2,370	3,940	2,510	3,230	2,410	4,350	3,360	3,230	2,150
	1	7.0	7.00	4,290	1,960	3,620	1,470	5,150	2,850	5,150	3,040	4,210	2,740	5,680	4,250	4,210	2,440
	1⅛	6.2	7.875	5,450	2,130	4,630	1,600	6,500	3,190	6,500	3,400	5,340	2,980	7,200	5,050	5,340	2,660
	⅝	12.0	4.6875	1,670	960	1,420	810	2,010	1,220	2,010	1,300	1,650	1,340	2,220	1,670	1,650	1,200
	¾	10.0	5.625	2,420	1,330	2,040	1,110	2,910	1,760	2,910	1,880	2,380	1,860	3,190	2,420	2,380	1,660
7½	⅞	8.6	6.5625	3,310	1,740	2,780	1,400	3,940	2,340	3,940	2,500	3,230	2,440	4,350	3,300	3,230	2,180
	1	7.5	7.50	4,290	2,070	3,620	1,570	5,150	2,940	5,150	3,130	4,210	2,900	5,680	4,230	4,210	2,590
	1⅛	6.7	8.4375	5,450	2,280	4,630	1,710	6,500	3,370	6,500	3,590	5,340	3,200	7,200	5,140	5,340	2,850
	⅝	12.8	5.00	1,670	940	1,420	800	2,010	1,180	2,010	1,260	1,650	1,320	2,200	1,600	1,650	1,180
	¾	10.7	6.00	2,420	1,300	2,040	1,100	2,910	1,720	2,910	1,830	2,380	1,820	3,190	2,360	2,380	1,630
8	⅞	9.1	7.00	3,310	1,740	2,780	1,440	3,940	2,320	3,940	2,480	3,230	2,440	4,350	3,260	3,230	2,180
	1	8.0	8.00	4,290	2,150	3,620	1,680	5,150	2,950	5,150	3,150	4,210	3,010	5,680	4,190	4,210	2,680
	1⅛	7.1	9.00	5,450	2,440	4,630	1,830	6,500	3,530	6,500	3,760	5,340	3,410	7,200	5,210	5,340	3,040
	1¼	6.4	10.00	6,780	2,620	5,710	1,960	8,040	3,900	8,040	4,160	6,570	3,670	8,870	6,090	6,570	3,270
	¾	12.7	7.125	2,420	1,260	2,040	1,060	2,910	1,580	2,910	1,680	2,380	1,760	3,190	2,150	2,380	1,570
	⅞	10.9	8.3125	3,310	1,670	2,780	1,400	3,940	2,190	3,940	2,330	3,230	2,330	4,350	2,980	3,230	2,080
9½	1	9.5	9.50	4,290	2,140	3,620	1,790	5,150	2,860	5,150	3,050	4,210	3,000	5,680	3,960	4,210	2,680
	1⅛	8.4	10.6875	5,450	2,680	4,630	2,140	6,500	3,630	6,500	3,870	5,340	3,750	7,200	5,120	5,340	3,350
	1¼	7.6	11.875	6,780	3,060	5,710	2,330	8,040	4,310	8,040	4,600	6,570	4,280	8,870	6,190	6,570	3,820
	⅞	11.4	8.75	3,310	1,660	2,780	1,400	3,940	2,160	3,940	2,300	3,230	2,330	4,350	2,940	3,230	2,080
10	1	10.0	10.00	4,290	2,130	3,620	1,780	5,150	2,820	5,150	3,000	4,210	2,980	5,680	3,870	4,210	2,660
	1⅛	8.9	11.25	5,450	2,660	4,630	2,180	6,500	3,560	6,500	3,790	5,340	3,730	7,200	4,990	5,340	3,330
	1¼	8.0	12.50	6,780	3,140	5,710	2,450	8,040	4,320	8,040	4,600	6,570	4,400	8,870	6,140	6,570	3,930
	1	11.5	11.50	4,290	2,060	3,620	1,740	5,150	2,680	5,150	2,850	4,210	2,890	5,680	3,640	4,210	2,580
11½	1⅛	10.2	12.9375	5,450	2,600	4,630	2,180	6,500	3,440	6,500	3,670	5,340	3,650	7,200	4,710	5,340	3,260
	1¼	9.2	14.375	6,780	3,160	5,710	2,620	8,040	4,210	8,040	4,490	6,570	4,430	8,870	5,890	6,570	3,950
	1	12.0	12.00	4,290	2,040	3,620	1,730	5,150	2,610	5,150	2,790	4,210	2,860	5,680	3,560	4,210	2,560
12	1⅛	10.7	13.50	5,450	2,560	4,630	2,150	6,500	3,370	6,500	3,590	5,340	3,580	7,200	4,640	5,340	3,200
	1¼	9.6	15.00	6,780	3,140	5,710	2,630	8,040	4,180	8,040	4,460	6,570	4,390	8,870	5,770	6,570	3,920

[1] Three (3) member joint.

NDS TABLE 12 (Cont.) Allowable loads on one bolt loaded at both ends (double shear)[1]

	d	l/d	A=l d	FIR, BALSAM		FIR, WHITE		GUM		HEMLOCK, EASTERN		HEMLOCK, WEST COAST		HICKORY AND PECAN		LARCH, WESTERN	
				P	Q	P	Q	P	Q	P	Q	P	Q	P	Q	P	Q
Inches	*Inches*		*Sq. in.*														
1⅝	½	3.3	.8125	680	225	680	450	750	450	680	450	850	450	1,400	900	1,010	480
	⅝	2.6	1.0156	850	250	850	510	930	510	850	510	1,070	510	1,780	1,020	1,290	540
	¾	2.2	1.2188	1,010	280	1,010	570	1,120	570	1,010	570	1,280	570	2,150	1,130	1,550	600
	⅞	1.9	1.4219	1,190	310	1,190	620	1,310	620	1,190	620	1,500	620	2,500	1,250	1,820	670
	1	1.6	1.625	1,360	340	1,360	680	1,500	680	1,360	680	1,720	680	2,860	1,360	2,070	730
2	½	4.0	1.00	840	280	840	550	900	550	840	550	1,030	550	1,630	1,110	1,180	590
	⅝	3.2	1.25	1,050	310	1,050	630	1,160	630	1,050	630	1,320	630	2,160	1,250	1,560	670
	¾	2.7	1.50	1,250	350	1,250	700	1,390	700	1,250	700	1,580	700	2,630	1,400	1,910	750
	⅞	2.3	1.75	1,470	380	1,470	770	1,620	770	1,470	770	1,850	770	3,080	1,540	2,230	820
	1	2.0	2.00	1,670	420	1,670	840	1,850	840	1,670	840	2,110	840	3,520	1,680	2,550	890
2⅝	½	5.3	1.3125	1,010	360	1,010	730	1,030	730	1,010	730	1,180	730	1,740	1,450	1,270	780
	⅝	4.2	1.6406	1,360	410	1,360	820	1,460	820	1,360	820	1,670	820	2,610	1,650	1,890	880
	¾	3.5	1.9688	1,650	460	1,650	920	1,810	920	1,650	920	2,060	920	3,340	1,830	2,420	980
	⅞	3.0	2.2969	1,920	500	1,920	1,010	2,120	1,010	1,920	1,010	2,420	1,010	4,000	2,020	2,900	1,080
	1	2.6	2.625	2,190	550	2,190	1,100	2,430	1,100	2,190	1,100	2,770	1,100	4,610	2,200	3,340	1,170
3	½	6.0	1.50	1,070	420	1,070	830	1,050	830	1,070	830	1,200	830	1,770	1,600	1,290	890
	⅝	4.8	1.875	1,510	470	1,510	940	1,560	940	1,510	940	1,790	940	2,740	1,880	1,990	1,000
	¾	4.0	2.25	1,870	520	1,870	1,050	2,030	1,050	1,870	1,050	2,320	1,050	3,660	2,090	2,650	1,120
	⅞	3.4	2.625	2,190	580	2,190	1,150	2,420	1,150	2,190	1,150	2,760	1,150	4,480	2,300	3,250	1,230
	1	3.0	3.00	2,510	630	2,510	1,260	2,770	1,260	2,510	1,260	3,170	1,260	5,230	2,510	3,790	1,340
3⅝	½	7.3	1.8125	1,070	500	1,070	950	1,050	950	1,070	950	1,200	950	1,770	1,670	1,290	1,020
	⅝	5.8	2.2656	1,660	570	1,660	1,140	1,640	1,140	1,660	1,140	1,870	1,140	2,760	2,220	2,000	1,210
	¾	4.8	2.7188	2,190	630	2,190	1,270	2,280	1,270	2,190	1,270	2,600	1,270	3,980	2,530	2,880	1,350
	⅞	4.1	3.1719	2,630	700	2,630	1,390	2,840	1,390	2,630	1,390	3,240	1,390	5,110	2,780	3,700	1,490
	1	3.6	3.625	3,030	760	3,030	1,520	3,320	1,520	3,030	1,520	3,790	1,520	6,110	3,040	4,430	1,620
4	½	8.0	2.00	1,070	550	1,070	980	1,050	980	1,070	980	1,200	980	1,770	1,660	1,290	1,040
	⅝	6.4	2.50	1,670	630	1,670	1,250	1,640	1,250	1,670	1,250	1,870	1,250	2,770	2,340	2,010	1,330
	¾	5.3	3.00	2,330	700	2,330	1,400	2,340	1,400	2,330	1,400	2,680	1,400	3,990	2,780	2,890	1,490
	⅞	4.6	3.50	2,850	770	2,850	1,540	3,000	1,540	2,850	1,540	3,430	1,540	5,290	3,070	3,830	1,640
	1	4.0	4.00	3,330	840	3,330	1,680	3,600	1,680	3,330	1,680	4,120	1,680	6,510	3,350	4,720	1,790
4½	½	9.0	2.25	1,070	590	1,070	960	1,050	960	1,070	960	1,200	960	1,770	1,610	1,290	1,020
	⅝	7.2	2.8125	1,670	710	1,670	1,350	1,640	1,350	1,670	1,350	1,870	1,350	2,770	2,380	2,010	1,440
	¾	6.0	3.375	2,420	790	2,420	1,570	2,360	1,570	2,420	1,570	2,700	1,570	3,990	3,020	2,890	1,680
	⅞	5.1	3.9375	3,110	860	3,110	1,730	3,160	1,730	3,110	1,730	3,610	1,730	5,440	3,450	3,940	1,840
	1	4.5	4.50	3,670	940	3,670	1,890	3,900	1,890	3,670	1,890	4,450	1,890	6,900	3,770	5,000	2,010
	1⅛	4.0	5.0625	4,210	1,030	4,210	2,050	4,560	2,050	4,210	2,050	5,210	2,050	8,240	4,110	5,970	2,190
5	½	10.0	2.50	1,070	590	1,070	930	1,050	930	1,070	930	1,200	930	1,770	1,540	1,290	990
	⅝	8.0	3.125	1,670	780	1,670	1,380	1,640	1,380	1,670	1,380	1,870	1,380	2,770	2,350	2,010	1,470
	¾	6.7	3.75	2,420	870	2,420	1,720	2,360	1,720	2,420	1,720	2,700	1,720	3,990	3,140	2,890	1,830
	⅞	5.7	4.375	3,260	960	3,260	1,920	3,210	1,920	3,260	1,920	3,670	1,920	5,440	3,760	3,940	2,050
	1	5.0	5.00	3,990	1,050	3,990	2,100	4,080	2,100	3,990	2,100	4,670	2,100	7,040	4,190	5,100	2,240
	1⅛	4.4	5.625	4,610	1,140	4,610	2,280	4,910	2,280	4,610	2,280	5,620	2,280	8,750	4,570	6,350	2,440

l	d	l/d	A = l d	Fir, Balsam P	Fir, Balsam Q	Fir, White P	Fir, White Q	Gum P	Gum Q	Hemlock, Eastern P	Hemlock, Eastern Q	Hemlock, West Coast P	Hemlock, West Coast Q	Hickory and Pecan P	Hickory and Pecan Q	Larch, Western P	Larch, Western Q
Inches	Inches		Sq. in.														
	5/8	8.8	3.4375	1,670	830	1,670	1,360	1,640	1,360	1,670	1,360	1,870	1,360	2,770	2,300	2,010	1,450
	3/4	7.3	4.125	2,420	960	2,420	1,820	2,380	1,820	2,420	1,820	2,700	1,820	3,990	3,190	2,910	1,940
5½	7/8	6.3	4.8125	3,310	1,060	3,310	2,100	3,230	2,100	3,310	2,100	3,670	2,100	5,440	3,970	3,940	2,240
	1	5.5	5.50	4,180	1,150	4,180	2,300	4,170	2,300	4,180	2,300	4,670	2,300	7,070	4,560	5,120	2,460
	1⅛	4.9	6.1875	4,960	1,260	4,960	2,510	5,110	2,510	4,960	2,510	5,840	2,510	8,890	5,020	6,440	2,680
	5/8	9.6	3.75	1,670	840	1,670	1,340	1,650	1,340	1,670	1,340	1,870	1,340	2,770	2,210	2,010	1,420
	3/4	8.0	4.50	2,420	1,050	2,420	1,840	2,380	1,840	2,420	1,840	2,700	1,840	3,990	3,140	2,910	1,970
6	7/8	6.9	5.25	3,310	1,150	3,310	2,250	3,230	2,250	3,310	2,250	3,670	2,250	5,440	4,060	3,940	2,400
	1	6.0	6.00	4,290	1,260	4,290	2,510	4,210	2,510	4,290	2,510	4,810	2,510	7,100	4,840	5,140	2,680
	1⅛	5.3	6.75	5,240	1,370	5,240	2,740	5,270	2,740	5,240	2,740	6,020	2,740	8,970	5,450	6,500	2,920
	5/8	10.4	4.0625	1,670	830	1,670	1,300	1,650	1,300	1,670	1,300	1,870	1,300	2,770	2,160	2,010	1,390
	3/4	8.7	4.875	2,420	1,100	2,420	1,820	2,380	1,820	2,420	1,820	2,700	1,820	3,990	3,070	2,910	1,940
6½	7/8	7.4	5.6875	3,310	1,250	3,310	2,350	3,230	2,350	3,310	2,350	3,670	2,350	5,440	4,090	3,940	2,510
	1	6.5	6.50	4,290	1,360	4,290	2,700	4,210	2,700	4,290	2,700	4,810	2,700	7,100	5,020	5,150	2,880
	1⅛	5.8	7.3125	5,370	1,480	5,370	2,970	5,290	2,970	5,370	2,970	6,050	2,970	8,970	5,790	6,500	3,170
	5/8	11.2	4.375	1,670	820	1,670	1,270	1,650	1,270	1,670	1,270	1,870	1,270	2,770	2,070	2,010	1,350
	3/4	9.3	5.25	2,420	1,120	2,420	1,800	2,380	1,800	2,420	1,800	2,700	1,800	3,990	3,010	2,910	1,920
7	7/8	8.0	6.125	3,310	1,340	3,310	2,370	3,230	2,370	3,310	2,370	3,670	2,370	5,440	4,030	3,940	2,510
	1	7.0	7.00	4,290	1,470	4,290	2,850	4,210	2,850	4,290	2,850	4,810	2,850	7,100	6,000	5,150	3,040
	1⅛	6.2	7.875	5,450	1,600	5,450	3,190	5,340	3,190	5,450	3,190	6,110	3,190	8,970	6,050	6,500	3,400
	5/8	12.0	4.6875	1,670	810	1,670	1,220	1,650	1,220	1,670	1,220	1,870	1,220	2,770	2,000	2,010	1,300
	3/4	10.0	5.625	2,420	1,110	2,420	1,760	2,380	1,760	2,420	1,760	2,700	1,760	3,990	2,900	2,910	1,880
7½	7/8	8.6	6.5625	3,310	1,400	3,310	2,340	3,230	2,340	3,310	2,340	3,670	2,340	5,440	3,960	3,940	2,500
	1	7.5	7.50	4,290	1,570	4,290	2,940	4,210	2,940	4,290	2,940	4,810	2,940	7,100	5,070	5,150	3,130
	1⅛	6.7	8.4375	5,450	1,710	5,450	3,370	5,340	3,370	5,450	3,370	6,110	3,370	8,970	6,160	6,500	3,590
	5/8	12.8	5.00	1,670	800	1,670	1,180	1,650	1,180	1,670	1,180	1,870	1,180	2,770	1,930	2,010	1,260
	3/4	10.7	6.00	2,420	1,100	2,420	1,720	2,380	1,720	2,420	1,720	2,700	1,720	3,990	2,840	2,910	1,830
8	7/8	9.1	7.00	3,310	1,440	3,310	2,320	3,230	2,320	3,310	2,320	3,670	2,320	5,440	3,910	3,940	2,480
	1	8.0	8.00	4,290	1,680	4,290	2,950	4,210	2,950	4,290	2,950	4,810	2,950	7,100	5,030	5,150	3,150
	1⅛	7.1	9.00	5,450	1,830	5,450	3,530	5,340	3,530	5,450	3,530	6,110	3,530	8,970	6,250	6,500	3,760
	1¼	6.4	10.00	6,780	1,960	6,780	3,900	6,570	3,900	6,780	3,900	7,510	3,900	11,090	7,310	8,040	4,160
	3/4	12.7	7.125	2,420	1,060	2,420	1,580	2,380	1,580	2,420	1,580	2,700	1,580	3,990	2,580	2,910	1,680
	7/8	10.9	8.3125	3,310	1,400	3,310	2,190	3,230	2,190	3,310	2,190	3,670	2,190	5,440	3,580	3,940	2,330
9½	1	9.5	9.50	4,290	1,790	4,290	2,860	4,210	2,860	4,290	2,860	4,810	2,860	7,100	4,750	5,150	3,050
	1⅛	8.4	10.6875	5,450	2,140	5,450	3,630	5,340	3,630	5,450	3,630	6,110	3,630	8,970	6,140	6,500	3,870
	1¼	7.6	11.875	6,780	2,330	6,780	4,310	6,570	4,310	6,780	4,310	7,510	4,310	11,090	7,420	8,040	4,600
	7/8	11.4	8.75	3,310	1,400	3,310	2,160	3,230	2,160	3,310	2,160	3,670	2,160	5,440	3,530	3,940	2,300
10	1	10.0	10.00	4,290	1,780	4,290	2,820	4,210	2,820	4,290	2,820	4,810	2,820	7,100	4,640	5,150	3,000
	1⅛	8.9	11.25	5,450	2,180	5,450	3,560	5,340	3,560	5,450	3,560	6,110	3,560	8,970	5,990	6,500	3,790
	1¼	8.0	12.50	6,780	2,450	6,780	4,320	6,570	4,320	6,780	4,320	7,510	4,320	11,090	7,230	8,040	4,600
	1	11.5	11.50	4,290	1,740	4,290	2,680	4,210	2,680	4,290	2,680	4,810	2,680	7,100	4,370	5,150	2,850
11½	1⅛	10.2	12.9375	5,450	2,180	5,450	3,440	5,340	3,440	5,450	3,440	6,100	3,440	8,970	5,650	6,500	3,670
	1¼	9.2	14.375	6,780	2,620	6,780	4,210	6,570	4,210	6,780	4,210	7,510	4,210	11,090	7,070	8,040	4,490
	1	12.0	12.00	4,290	1,730	4,290	2,610	4,210	2,610	4,290	2,610	4,810	2,610	7,100	4,280	5,150	2,790
12	1⅛	10.7	13.50	5,450	2,150	5,450	3,370	5,340	3,370	5,450	3,370	6,100	3,370	8,970	5,570	6,500	3,590
	1¼	9.6	15.00	6,780	2,630	6,780	4,180	6,570	4,180	6,780	4,180	7,510	4,180	11,090	6,930	8,040	4,460

[1] Three (3) member joint.

NDS TABLE 12 (Cont.) Allowable loads on one bolt loaded at both ends (double shear)[1]

l	d	l/d	A=l d	MAPLE, HARD P	MAPLE, HARD Q	OAK, RED AND WHITE P	OAK, RED AND WHITE Q	PINE, NORTHERN (Eastern White), PONDEROSA, SUGAR, AND IDAHO WHITE P	PINE, NORTHERN (Eastern White), PONDEROSA, SUGAR, AND IDAHO WHITE Q	PINE, LODGEPOLE P	PINE, LODGEPOLE Q	PINE, NORWAY P	PINE, NORWAY Q	PINE, SOUTHERN P	PINE, SOUTHERN Q	POPLAR, YELLOW P	POPLAR, YELLOW Q
Inches	*Inches*		*Sq. in.*														
1⅝	½	3.3	.8125	1,120	750	940	750	710	380	680	330	750	330	1,010	480	680	330
	⅝	2.6	1.0156	1,430	850	1,200	850	890	420	850	370	930	370	1,290	540	850	370
	¾	2.2	1.2188	1,720	950	1,450	950	1,070	470	1,010	420	1,120	420	1,550	600	1,010	420
	⅞	1.9	1.4219	2,000	1,040	1,690	1,040	1,250	520	1,190	460	1,310	460	1,820	670	1,190	460
	1	1.6	1.625	2,290	1,140	1,930	1,140	1,430	570	1,360	500	1,500	500	2,070	730	1,360	500
2	½	4.0	1.00	1,300	920	1,100	920	860	460	840	410	900	410	1,180	590	840	410
	⅝	3.2	1.25	1,730	1,050	1,460	1,050	1,100	520	1,050	460	1,160	460	1,560	670	1,050	460
	¾	2.7	1.50	2,110	1,160	1,780	1,160	1,320	580	1,250	510	1,390	510	1,910	750	1,250	510
	⅞	2.3	1.75	2,460	1,280	2,080	1,280	1,540	640	1,470	560	1,620	560	2,230	820	1,470	560
	1	2.0	2.00	2,820	1,400	2,380	1,400	1,760	700	1,670	610	1,850	610	2,550	890	1,670	610
2⅝	½	5.3	1.3125	1,400	1,210	1,180	1,210	980	610	1,010	530	1,030	530	1,270	780	1,010	530
	⅝	4.2	1.6406	2,090	1,370	1,760	1,370	1,390	690	1,360	600	1,460	600	1,890	880	1,360	600
	¾	3.5	1.9688	2,670	1,530	2,250	1,530	1,720	760	1,650	670	1,810	670	2,420	980	1,650	670
	⅞	3.0	2.2969	3,200	1,680	2,700	1,680	2,020	840	1,920	740	2,120	740	2,900	1,080	1,920	740
	1	2.6	2.625	3,690	1,830	3,110	1,830	2,310	920	2,190	810	2,430	810	3,340	1,170	2,190	810
3	½	6.0	1.50	1,420	1,330	1,200	1,330	1,000	690	1,070	610	1,050	610	1,290	890	1,070	610
	⅝	4.8	1.875	2,190	1,570	1,850	1,570	1,490	780	1,510	690	1,560	690	1,990	1,000	1,510	690
	¾	4.0	2.25	2,930	1,740	2,470	1,740	1,930	870	1,870	770	2,030	770	2,650	1,120	1,870	770
	⅞	3.4	2.625	3,590	1,920	3,020	1,920	2,300	960	2,190	840	2,420	840	3,250	1,230	2,190	840
	1	3.0	3.00	4,180	2,100	3,530	2,100	2,640	1,050	2,510	920	2,770	920	3,790	1,340	2,510	920
3⅝	½	7.3	1.8125	1,420	1,390	1,200	1,390	1,000	830	1,070	730	1,050	730	1,290	1,020	1,070	730
	⅝	5.8	2.2656	2,220	1,850	1,860	1,850	1,560	950	1,660	830	1,640	830	2,000	1,210	1,660	830
	¾	4.8	2.7188	3,190	2,110	2,680	2,110	2,170	1,050	2,190	930	2,280	930	2,880	1,350	2,190	930
	⅞	4.1	3.1719	4,090	2,320	3,450	2,320	2,700	1,160	2,630	1,020	2,840	1,020	3,700	1,490	2,630	1,020
	1	3.6	3.625	4,880	2,530	4,120	2,530	3,160	1,270	3,030	1,110	3,320	1,110	4,430	1,620	3,030	1,110
4	½	8.0	2.00	1,420	1,390	1,200	1,390	1,000	890	1,070	780	1,050	780	1,290	1,040	1,070	780
	⅝	6.4	2.50	2,220	1,950	1,870	1,950	1,560	1,050	1,670	920	1,640	920	2,010	1,330	1,670	920
	¾	5.3	3.00	3,190	2,310	2,690	2,310	2,230	1,160	2,330	1,020	2,340	1,020	2,890	1,490	2,330	1,020
	⅞	4.6	3.50	4,230	2,560	3,570	2,560	2,860	1,280	2,850	1,130	3,000	1,130	3,830	1,640	2,850	1,130
	1	4.0	4.00	5,210	2,790	4,400	2,790	3,430	1,400	3,330	1,230	3,600	1,230	4,720	1,790	3,330	1,230
4½	½	9.0	2.25	1,420	1,340	1,200	1,340	1,000	900	1,070	790	1,050	790	1,290	1,020	1,070	790
	⅝	7.2	2.8125	2,220	1,980	1,870	1,980	1,560	1,170	1,670	1,030	1,640	1,030	2,010	1,440	1,670	1,030
	¾	6.0	3.375	3,190	2,520	2,690	2,520	2,250	1,310	2,420	1,150	2,360	1,150	2,890	1,680	2,420	1,150
	⅞	5.1	3.9375	4,350	2,880	3,670	2,880	3,010	1,440	3,110	1,270	3,160	1,270	3,940	1,840	3,110	1,270
	1	4.5	4.50	5,520	3,140	4,660	3,140	3,710	1,570	3,670	1,380	3,900	1,380	5,000	2,010	3,670	1,380
	1⅛	4.0	5.0625	6,590	3,420	5,560	3,420	4,340	1,710	4,210	1,510	4,560	1,510	5,970	2,190	4,210	1,510
5	½	10.0	2.50	1,420	1,280	1,200	1,280	1,000	800	1,070	770	1,050	770	1,290	990	1,070	770
	⅝	8.0	3.125	2,220	1,960	1,870	1,960	1,560	1,260	1,670	1,100	1,640	1,100	2,010	1,470	1,670	1,100
	¾	6.7	3.75	3,190	2,620	2,690	2,620	2,250	1,450	2,420	1,280	2,360	1,280	2,890	1,830	2,420	1,280
	⅞	5.7	4.375	4,350	3,140	3,670	3,140	3,060	1,600	3,260	1,410	3,210	1,410	3,940	2,050	3,260	1,410
	1	5.0	5.00	5,630	3,490	4,750	3,490	3,890	1,750	3,990	1,540	4,080	1,540	5,100	2,240	3,990	1,540
	1⅛	4.4	5.625	7,000	3,810	5,910	3,810	4,680	1,900	4,610	1,670	4,910	1,670	6,350	2,440	4,610	1,670

l	d	l/d	A=l d	MAPLE, HARD		OAK, RED AND WHITE		PINE, NORTHERN (Eastern White), PONDEROSA, SUGAR, AND IDAHO WHITE		PINE, LODGEPOLE		PINE, NORWAY		PINE, SOUTHERN		POPLAR, YELLOW	
				P	Q	P	Q	P	Q	P	Q	P	Q	P	Q	P	Q
Inches	*Inches*		*Sq. in.*														
	⅝	8.8	3.4375	2,220	1,910	1,870	1,910	1,560	1,270	1,670	1,120	1,640	1,120	2,010	1,450	1,670	1,120
	¾	7.3	4.125	3,190	2,660	2,690	2,660	2,250	1,590	2,420	1,400	2,380	1,400	2,910	1,940	2,420	1,400
5½	⅞	6.3	4.8125	4,350	3,310	3,670	3,310	3,060	1,760	3,310	1,550	3,230	1,550	3,940	2,240	3,310	1,550
	1	5.5	5.50	5,650	3,800	4,770	2,800	3,970	1,920	4,180	1,690	4.170	1,690	5,120	2,460	4,180	1,690
	1⅛	4.9	6.1875	7,110	4,190	6,000	4,190	4,870	2,090	4,960	1,840	5,110	1,840	6,440	2,680	4,960	1,840
	⅝	9.6	3.75	2,220	1,840	1,870	1,840	1,570	1,250	1,670	1,100	1,650	1,100	2,010	1,420	1,670	1,100
	¾	8.0	4.50	3,190	2,620	2,690	2,620	2,250	1,680	2,420	1,480	2,380	1,480	2,910	1,970	2,420	1,480
6	⅞	6.9	5.25	4,350	3,380	3,670	3,380	3,060	1,920	3,310	1,690	3,230	1,690	3,940	2,400	3,310	1,690
	1	6.0	6.00	5,680	4,040	4,790	4,040	4,000	2,100	4,290	1,840	4,210	1,840	5,140	2,680	4,290	1,840
	1⅛	5.3	6.75	7,200	4,540	6,050	4,540	5,020	2,280	5,240	2,010	5,270	2,010	6,500	2,920	5,240	2,010
	⅝	10.4	4.0625	2,220	1,800	1,870	1,800	1,570	1,230	1,670	1,090	1,650	1,090	2,010	1,390	1,670	1,090
	¾	8.7	4.875	3,190	2,560	2,690	2,560	2,250	1,700	2,420	1,490	2,380	1,490	2,910	1,940	2,420	1,490
6½	⅞	7.4	5.6875	4,350	3,410	3,670	3,410	3,060	2,070	3,310	1,820	3,230	1,820	3,940	2,510	3,310	1,820
	1	6.5	6.50	5,680	4,180	4,790	4,180	4,000	2,270	4,290	2,000	4,210	2,000	5,150	2,880	4,290	2,000
	1⅛	5.8	7.3125	7,200	4,820	6,050	4,820	5,040	2,470	5,370	2,180	5,290	2,180	6,500	3,170	5,370	2,180
	⅝	11.2	4.375	2,220	1,720	1,870	1,720	1,570	1,210	1,670	1,070	1,650	1,070	2,010	1,350	1,670	1,070
	¾	9.3	5.25	3,190	2,510	2,690	2,510	2,250	1,690	2,420	1,490	2,380	1,490	2,910	1,920	2,420	1,490
7	⅞	8.0	6.125	4,350	3,360	3,670	3,360	3,060	2,150	3,310	1,890	3,230	1,890	3,940	2,510	3,310	1,890
	1	7.0	7.00	5,680	4,250	4,790	4,250	4,000	2,440	4,290	2,150	4,210	2,150	5,150	3,040	4,290	2,150
	1⅛	6.2	7.875	7,200	5,050	6,050	5,050	5,090	2,660	5,450	2,340	5,340	2,340	6,500	3,400	5,450	2,340
	⅝	12.0	4.6875	2,200	1,670	1,870	1,670	1,570	1,200	1,670	1,050	1,650	1,050	2,010	1,300	1,670	1,050
	¾	10.0	5.625	3,190	2,420	2,690	2,420	2,250	1,660	2,420	1,460	2,380	1,460	2,910	1,880	2,420	1,460
7½	⅞	8.6	6.5625	4,350	3,300	3,670	3,300	3,060	2,180	3,310	1,920	3,230	1,920	3,940	2,500	3,310	1,920
	1	7.5	7.50	5,680	4,230	4,790	4,230	4,000	2,590	4,290	2,280	4,210	2,280	5,150	3,130	4,290	2,280
	1⅛	6.7	8.4375	7,200	5,140	6,050	5,140	5,090	2,850	5,450	2,510	5,340	2,510	6,500	3,590	5,450	2,510
	⅝	12.8	5.00	2,200	1,600	1,870	1,600	1,570	1,180	1,670	1,040	1,650	1,040	2,010	1,260	1,670	1,040
	¾	10.7	6.00	3,190	2,360	2,690	2,360	2,250	1,630	2,420	1,430	2,380	1,430	2,910	1,830	2,420	1,430
8	⅞	9.1	7.00	4,350	3,260	3,670	3,260	3,060	2,180	3,310	1,920	3,230	1,920	3,940	2,480	3,310	1,920
	1	8.0	8.00	5,680	4,190	4,790	4,190	4,000	2,680	4,290	2,360	4,210	2,360	5,150	3,150	4,290	2,360
	1⅛	7.1	9.00	7,200	5,210	6,050	5,210	5,090	3,040	5,450	2,680	5,340	2,680	6,500	3,760	5,450	2,680
	1¼	6.4	10.00	8,870	6,090	7,480	6,090	6,260	3,270	6,780	2,880	6,570	2,880	8,040	4,160	6,780	2,880
	¾	12.7	7.125	3,190	2,150	2,690	2,150	2,250	1,570	2,420	1,380	2,380	1,380	2,910	1,680	2,420	1,380
	⅞	10.9	8.3125	4,350	2,980	3,670	2,980	3,060	2,080	3,310	1,830	3,230	1,830	3,940	2,330	3,310	1,830
9½	1	9.5	9.50	5,680	3,960	4,790	3,960	4,000	2,680	4,290	2,360	4,210	2,360	5,150	3,050	4,290	2,360
	1⅛	8.4	10.6875	7,200	5,120	6,050	5,120	5,090	3,350	5,450	2,950	5,340	2,950	6,500	3,870	5,450	2,950
	1¼	7.6	11.875	8,870	6,190	7,480	6,190	6,260	3,820	6,780	3,360	6,570	3,360	8,040	4,600	6,780	3,360
	⅞	11.4	8.75	4,350	2,940	3,670	2,940	3,060	2,080	3,310	1,830	3,230	1,830	3,940	2,300	3,310	1,830
10	1	10.0	10.00	5,680	3,870	4,790	3,870	4,000	2,660	4,290	2,340	4,210	2,340	5,150	3,000	4,290	2,340
	1⅛	8.9	11.25	7,200	4,990	6,050	4,990	5,090	3,330	5,450	2,930	5,340	2,930	6,500	3,790	5,450	2,930
	1¼	8.0	12.50	8,870	6,140	7,480	6,140	6,260	3,930	6,780	3,460	6,570	3,460	8,040	4,600	6,780	3,460
	1	11.5	11.50	5,680	3,640	4,790	3,640	4,000	2,580	4,290	2,270	4,210	2,270	5,150	2,850	4,290	2,270
11½	1⅛	10.2	12.9375	7,200	4,710	6,050	4,710	5,090	3,260	5,450	2,860	5,340	2,860	6,500	3,670	5,450	2,860
	1¼	9.2	14.375	8,870	5,890	7,480	5,890	6,260	3,950	6,780	3,480	6,570	3,480	8,040	4,490	6,780	3,480
	1	12.0	12.00	5,680	3,560	4,790	3,560	4,000	2,560	4,290	2,250	4,210	2,250	5,150	2,790	4,290	2,250
12	1⅛	10.7	13.50	7,200	4,640	6,050	4,640	5,090	3,200	5,450	2,810	5,340	2,810	6,500	3,590	5,450	2,810
	1¼	9.6	15.00	8,870	5,770	7,480	5,770	6,260	3,920	6,780	3,450	6,570	3,450	8,040	4,460	6,780	3,450

[1] Three (3) member joint.

NDS TABLE 12 (Cont.) Allowable loads on one bolt loaded at both ends (double shear)[1]

				REDWOOD		SPRUCE, ENGELMANN		SPRUCE, EASTERN AND SITKA		TUPELO	
l	*d*	*l/d*	*A = l d*	*P*	*Q*	*P*	*Q*	*P*	*Q*	*P*	*Q*
Inches	*Inches*		*Sq. in.*								
	½	3.3	.8125	940	380	580	270	750	380	750	450
	⅝	2.6	1.0156	1,200	420	710	310	930	420	930	510
1⅝	¾	2.2	1.2188	1,450	470	850	340	1,120	470	1,120	570
	⅞	1.9	1.4219	1,690	520	1,000	370	1,310	520	1,310	620
	1	1.6	1.625	1,930	570	1,140	410	1,500	570	1,500	680
	½	4.0	1.00	1,100	460	700	330	900	460	900	550
	⅝	3.2	1.25	1,460	520	890	380	1,160	520	1,160	630
2	¾	2.7	1.50	1,780	580	1,060	420	1,390	580	1,390	700
	⅞	2.3	1.75	2,080	640	1,240	460	1,620	640	1,620	770
	1	2.0	2.00	2,380	700	1,410	500	1,850	700	1,850	840
	½	5.3	1.3125	1,180	610	850	440	1,030	610	1,030	730
	⅝	4.2	1.6406	1,760	690	1,140	490	1,460	690	1,460	820
2⅝	¾	3.5	1.9688	2,250	760	1,390	550	1,810	760	1,810	920
	⅞	3.0	2.2969	2,700	840	1,620	600	2,120	840	2,120	1,010
	1	2.6	2.625	3,110	920	1,850	660	2,430	920	2,430	1,100
	½	6.0	1.50	1,200	690	900	500	1,050	690	1,050	830
	⅝	4.8	1.875	1,850	780	1,270	560	1,560	780	1,560	940
3	¾	4.0	2.25	2,470	870	1,580	630	2,030	870	2,030	1,050
	⅞	3.4	2.625	3,020	960	1,850	690	2,420	960	2,420	1,150
	1	3.0	3.00	3,530	1,050	2,110	750	2,770	1,050	2,770	1,260
	½	7.3	1.8125	1,200	830	900	600	1,050	830	1,050	950
	⅝	5.8	2.2656	1,860	950	1,400	680	1,640	950	1,640	1,140
3⅝	¾	4.8	2.7188	2,680	1,050	1,850	760	2,280	1,050	2,280	1,270
	⅞	4.1	3.1719	3,450	1,160	2,220	840	2,840	1,160	2,840	1,390
	1	3.6	3.625	4,120	1,270	2,550	910	3,320	1,270	3,320	1,520
	½	8.0	2.00	1,200	890	900	670	1,050	890	1,050	980
	⅝	6.4	2.50	1,870	1,050	1,420	750	1,640	1,050	1,640	1,250
4	¾	5.3	3.00	2,690	1,160	1,960	840	2,340	1,160	2,340	1,400
	⅞	4.6	3.50	3,570	1,280	2,400	920	3,000	1,280	3,000	1,540
	1	4.0	4.00	4,400	1,400	2,800	1,010	3,600	1,400	3,600	1,680
	½	9.0	2.25	1,200	900	900	710	1,050	900	1,050	960
	⅝	7.2	2.8125	1,870	1,170	1,420	850	1,640	1,170	1,640	1,350
4½	¾	6.0	3.375	2,690	1,310	2,040	940	2,360	1,310	2,360	1,570
	⅞	5.1	3.9375	3,670	1,440	2,620	1,040	3,160	1,440	3,160	1,730
	1	4.5	4.50	4,660	1,570	3,090	1,130	3,900	1,570	3,900	1,890
	1⅛	4.0	5.0625	5,560	1,710	3,540	1,230	4,560	1,710	4,560	2,050
	½	10.0	2.50	1,200	800	900	710	1,050	800	1,050	930
	⅝	8.0	3.125	1,870	1,260	1,420	940	1,640	1,260	1,640	1,380
5	¾	6.7	3.75	2,690	1,450	2,040	1,050	2,360	1,450	2,360	1,720
	⅞	5.7	4.375	3,670	1,600	2,740	1,150	3,210	1,600	3,210	1,920
	1	5.0	5.00	4,750	1,750	3,360	1,260	4,080	1,750	4,080	2,100
	1⅛	4.4	5.625	5,910	1,900	3,880	1,370	4,910	1,900	4,910	2,280

more. For ratios between 2 and 5, the spacing shall be obtained by straight-line interpolation.

601–G. END DISTANCE

601–G–1. "End distance" is the distance from the end of a bolted timber to the center of the bolt hole nearest the end.

601–G–2. For parallel-to-grain loading, the end distance shall be:

(a) In tension, 7 times the bolt diameter for softwoods and 5 times for hardwoods.

(b) In compression, 4 times the bolt diameter.

601–G–3. For perpendicular-to-grain loading, when members abut at a joint, the strength of the joint shall be evaluated not only for the bolt load but also as a beam supported by fastenings as provided in par. 400-D-4.

601–H. EDGE DISTANCE

601–H–1. "Edge distance" is the distance from the edge of the timber to the center of the nearest bolt hole.

601–H–2. For parallel-to-grain loading, in tension or compression, the edge distance shall be at least 1½ times the bolt

NDS TABLE 12 (Cont.) Allowable loads on one bolt loaded at both ends (double shear)[1]

l	*d*	*l/d*	*A=l d*	REDWOOD		SPRUCE, ENGELMANN		SPRUCE, EASTERN AND SITKA		TUPELO	
				P	*Q*	*P*	*Q*	*P*	*Q*	*P*	*Q*
Inches	*Inches*		*Sq. in.*								
	5/8	8.8	3.4375	1,870	1,270	1,420	990	1,640	1,270	1,640	1,360
	3/4	7.3	4.125	2,690	1,590	2,040	1,150	2,380	1,590	2,380	1,820
5½	7/8	6.3	4.8125	3,670	1,760	2,780	1,270	3,230	1,760	3,230	2,100
	1	5.5	5.50	4,770	1,920	3,520	1,380	4,170	1,920	4,170	2,300
	1⅛	4.9	6.1875	6,000	2,090	4,180	1,510	5,110	2,090	5,110	2,510
	5/8	9.6	3.75	1,870	1,250	1,420	1,010	1,650	1,250	1,650	1,340
	3/4	8.0	4.50	2,690	1,680	2,040	1,260	2,380	1,680	2,380	1,840
6	7/8	6.9	5.25	3,670	1,920	2,780	1,380	3,230	1,920	3,230	2,250
	1	6.0	6.00	4,790	2,100	3,620	1,510	4,210	2,100	4,210	2,510
	1⅛	5.3	6.75	6,050	2,280	4,420	1,640	5,270	2,280	5,270	2,740
	5/8	10.4	4.0625	1,870	1,230	1,420	990	1,650	1,230	1,650	1,300
	3/4	8.7	4.875	2,690	1,700	2,040	1,320	2,380	1,700	2,380	1,820
6½	7/8	7.4	5.6875	3,670	2,070	2,780	1,500	3,230	2,070	3,230	2,350
	1	6.5	6.50	4,790	2,270	3,620	1,630	4,210	2,270	4,210	2,700
	1⅛	5.8	7.3125	6,050	2,470	4,520	1,780	5,290	2,470	5,290	2,970
	5/8	11.2	4.375	1,870	1,210	1,420	980	1,650	1,210	1,650	1,270
	3/4	9.3	5.25	2,690	1,690	2,040	1,350	2,380	1,690	2,380	1,800
7	7/8	8.0	6.125	3,670	2,150	2,780	1,610	3,230	2,150	3,230	2,370
	1	7.0	7.00	4,790	2,440	3,620	1,760	4,210	2,440	4,210	2,850
	1⅛	6.2	7.875	6,050	2,660	4,630	1,920	5,340	2,660	5,340	3,190
	5/8	12.0	4.6875	1,870	1,200	1,420	970	1,650	1,200	1,650	1,220
	3/4	10.0	5.625	2,690	1,660	2,040	1,330	2,380	1,660	2,380	1,760
7½	7/8	8.6	6.5625	3,670	2,180	2,780	1,680	3,230	2,180	3,230	2,340
	1	7.5	7.50	4,790	2,590	3,620	1,890	4,210	2,590	4,210	2,940
	1⅛	6.7	8.4375	6,050	2,850	4,630	2,050	5,340	2,850	5,340	3,370
	5/8	12.8	5.00	1,870	1,180	1,420	950	1,650	1,180	1,650	1,180
	3/4	10.7	6.00	2,690	1,630	2,040	1,310	2,380	1,630	2,380	1,720
8	7/8	9.1	7.00	3,670	2,180	2,780	1,730	3,230	2,180	3,230	2,320
	1	8.0	8.00	4,790	2,680	3,620	2,010	4,210	2,680	4,210	2,950
	1⅛	7.1	9.00	6,050	3,040	4,630	2,190	5,340	3,040	5,340	3,530
	1¼	6.4	10.00	7,480	3,270	5,710	2,360	6,570	3,270	6,570	3,900
	3/4	12.7	7.125	2,690	1,570	2,040	1,270	2,380	1,570	2,380	1,580
	7/8	10.9	8.3125	3,670	2,080	2,780	1,680	3,230	2,080	3,230	2,190
9½	1	9.5	9.50	4,790	2,680	3,620	2,150	4,210	2,680	4,210	2,860
	1⅛	8.4	10.6875	6,050	3,350	4,630	2,560	5,340	3,350	5,340	3,630
	1¼	7.6	11.875	7,480	3,820	5,710	2,800	6,570	3,820	6,570	4,310
	7/8	11.4	8.75	3,670	2,080	2,780	1,680	3,230	2,080	3,230	2,160
10	1	10.0	10.00	4,790	2,660	3,620	2,140	4,210	2,660	4,210	2,820
	1⅛	8.9	11.25	6,050	3,330	4,630	2,610	5,340	3,330	5,340	3,560
	1¼	8.0	12.50	7,480	3,930	5,710	2,950	6,570	3,930	6,570	4,320
	1	11.5	11.50	4,790	2,580	3,620	2,090	4,210	2,580	4,210	2,680
11½	1⅛	10.2	12.9375	6,050	3,260	4,630	2,620	5,340	3,260	5,340	3,440
	1¼	9.2	14.375	7,480	3,950	5,710	3,150	6,570	3,950	6,570	4,210
	1	12.0	12.00	4,790	2,560	3,620	2,070	4,210	2,560	4,210	2,610
12	1⅛	10.7	13.50	6,050	3,200	4,630	2,580	5,340	3,200	5,340	3,370
	1¼	9.6	15.00	7,480	3,920	5,710	3,150	6,570	3,920	6,570	4,180

[1] Three (3) member joint.

diameter, except that for *l/d* ratios more than 6, use ½ the distance between rows of bolts.

601–H–3. For perpendicular-to-grain loading, the edge distance nearest the edge toward which load is acting shall be at least 4 times the bolt diameter.

601–I. STAGGERED BOLTS

601–I–1. For parallel-to-grain loading with staggered bolts, special precaution shall be taken to provide sufficient area at the critical section. Adjacent staggered bolts shall be considered as being placed at the critical section.

601–I–2. For perpendicular-to-grain loading, if design load for main member is less than bolt bearing capacity of side timbers, staggering may be employed.

601–J. BOLTING FOR LOADS AT ANGLE TO GRAIN

601–J–1. It is virtually impossible to set up general rules regarding the alignment, spacing, and distances of bolts to cover all possible directions of applied load. Uniform stress in main members and a uniform distribution of load to all bolts, however, require that the gravity axis of the members shall pass through the center of resistance of the bolt groups.

602—DESIGN OF ECCENTRIC JOINTS AND BEAM SUPPORTS

602–A. For design of eccentric bolted joints and bolt supported beams, see par. 400-D-4.

NDS Part VII. Lag-Screw Joints

For machine (cut) thread lag-screw (lag-bolt) joints using stress-grade lumber and the lag screws defined herein, the provisions of NDS Part VII and the tabulated values herein apply.

700—PROVISIONS APPLICABLE TO BOTH WITHDRAWAL AND LATERAL RESISTANCE

700–A. TYPE OF LOAD

700–A–1. Allowable loads for lag screws in NDS Part VII are the maximum for normal loading. Pertinent adjustment of stresses and provisions of par. 200, 201, 202, 203, and 204 for lumber except as otherwise provided in NDS Part VII apply likewise to loads for lag screws given in NDS Part VII.

700–B. NUMBER OF LAG SCREWS

700–B–1. Loads given are for one lag screw either in withdrawal or in lateral resistance in single shear in a *two*-member joint.

700–B–2. Loads for more than one lag screw, each of the same or miscellaneous sizes, are the sum of the loads permitted for each lag screw provided that spacings, end distances, and edge distances are sufficient to develop the full strength of each lag screw.

700–C. QUALITY OF LAG SCREW

700–C–1. The following allowable loads are based on lag screws of metal having a yield point of 45,000 psi and a tensile strength of 77,000 psi.

700–C–2. For other metal, the values herein may be adjusted in proportion to the tensile strength of the metal for maximum allowable loads in withdrawal (par. 701-A) and in proportion to square roots of the yield point stresses of the metal for allowable loads in lateral resistance.

700–D. SPECIES OF LUMBER

700–D–1. The method of determining allowable loads for lag screws in the various species is indicated by formulas and provisions and tabulated values herein.

700–E. GRADE OF LUMBER

700–E–1. The allowable loads for lag screws in a given species apply to all grades of that species.

700–F. CONDITION OF LUMBER

700–F–1. The allowable loads given are for lag screws in lumber seasoned to a moisture content approximately equal to that to which it will eventually come in service.

700–F–2. For lumber installed unseasoned and which becomes seasoned in place, the allowable lag-screw loads shall be 40 per cent of those given.

700–F–3. For lumber partially seasoned when fabricated, proportional intermediate loads may be used.

700–G. SERVICE CONDITIONS

700–G–1. Allowable loads given herein as adjusted for condition of lumber apply to lag screw joints used under conditions continuously dry as in most covered structures.

700–G–2. Where joints are to be exposed to weather, 75 per cent, and where always wet, 67 per cent of the otherwise allowable loads apply.

700–H. LEAD HOLES

700–H–1. Lead holes shall be prebored as follows:

(a) The lead hole for the shank shall have the same diameter as the shank and the same depth as the length of unthreaded shank.

(b) The lead hole for the threaded portion shall have a diameter equal to 65 per cent to 85 per cent of the shank diameter in oak, 60 per cent to 75 per cent in Douglas fir and southern pine, and 40 per cent to 70 per cent in redwood and northern white pine and a length equal to at least the length of the threaded portion. The larger figure in each range shall apply to screws of the greater diameters. For other species the diameter shall be determined from the foregoing percentages by proportions based on the relative specific gravities of the species.

(c) Lead holes slightly larger than those specified in par. 700-H-1 (a) and (b) shall be used with lag screws of excessive length.

700–I. INSERTION

700–I–1. The threaded portion of the screw shall be inserted in its lead hole by turning with a wrench, not by driving with a hammer.

700–I–2. Soap or other lubricant shall be used on the screws, particularly with the denser species, to facilitate insertion and prevent damage to screw.

700–J. PENETRATION OF THREADED PORTION OF LAG SCREW

700–J–1. In determining the penetration of threaded portion of lag screw into a member, the reduced portion (threaded or gimlet point) shall not be considered as part of the threaded portion. (For dimensions of standard lag screws, see NDS Appendix I.)

701—WITHDRAWAL RESISTANCE

701–A. TENSILE STRENGTH OF LAG SCREW

701–A–1. In determining withdrawal resistance, the allowable tensile strength of lag bolt at net (root) section shall not be exceeded. Penetration of threaded portion of about 7 times the shank diameter in the denser species and 10 to 12 times the shank diameter in the softer species will develop approximately the ultimate tensile strength of the screw in axial withdrawal. (See par. 701-B.)

701–B. ALLOWABLE WITHDRAWAL LOAD IN SIDE GRAIN

701–B–1. The allowable load for lag screws in withdrawal from side grain with axis of the lag screw perpendicular to the fibers shall be determined from the formula:

$$p = 1800D^{3/4}G^{3/2}$$

in which:

p = allowable load per inch of penetration of threaded portion of lag screw into member receiving the point

D = shank diameter of lag screw, in inches (see NDS Appendix I)

G = specific gravity of oven-dry wood (see NDS Appendix G)

701–C. ALLOWABLE WITHDRAWAL LOAD IN END GRAIN

701–C–1. If possible, the design shall be such that lag screws are not loaded in withdrawal from end grain of wood. When this condition cannot be avoided, the allowable load in withdrawal from end grain shall not be taken as more than three-fourths of that for withdrawal from side grain.

702—LATERAL RESISTANCE

702–A. THICKNESS OF WOOD SIDE PIECE

702–A–1. The allowable loads for lateral resistance of lag screws given in par. 702-E are for wood side members having a thickness equal to 3.5 times the shank diameter.

702–A–2. For other ratios of thickness of side piece to shank diameter, the percentages given in NDS Table 13 shall be applied to the allowable loads for lateral resistance obtained from the formulas in NDS Table 15.

NDS TABLE 13 Percentages of allowable loads for ratio of thickness of side member to shank diameter

Ratio of thickness of side member to shank diameter of lag screw	Percentage of the allowable load for a ratio of 3.5	Ratio of thickness of side member to shank diameter of lag screw	Percentage of the allowable load for a ratio of 3.5
2.0	62.0	4.5	113.0
2.5	77.5	5.0	118.0
3.0	93.0	5.5	121.0
3.5	100.0	6.0	122.0
4.0	107.0	6.5	122.5

702–B STEEL SIDE PIECE

702–B–1. Where steel plates rather than wood side pieces are used, the allowable loads given by the formulas for parallel-to-grain loading (par. 702-E) may be increased by 25 per cent but no increase shall be made in the allowable loads for perpendicular-to-grain loading.

702–B–2. The stresses induced in the steel plate and at bearing of lag bolt on plate shall not exceed the allowable stresses for the metal used.

702–C. PENETRATION OF SHANK IN SIDE AND MAIN MEMBERS

702–C–1. The allowable loads given in par. 702-E are for the condition where the junction of the unthreaded shank and threaded portion of lag screw is at the plane of contact of the side and main member.

702–C–2. When the shank penetrates into the main member, the following percentage loads apply:

NDS TABLE 14 Percentages of allowable loads for ratio of penetration of shank into main member to shank diameter

Ratio of penetration of shank into main member to shank diameter	Percentage of allowable load for zero penetration	Ratio of penetration of shank into main member to shank diameter	Percentage of allowable load for zero penetration
0.0	100.0	4.5	135.0
0.5	104.0	5.0	136.0
1.0	108.0	5.5	137.0
1.5	112.5	6.0	138.0
2.0	117.0	6.5	138.5
2.5	122.0	7.0	139.0
3.0	126.5	7.5	139.0
3.5	130.5	8.0	139.0
4.0	133.0	8.5	139.0

702–C–3. When the portion of the shank and threaded portion of the lag screw is within the side member, the allowable load shall be determined from the actual penetration of shank by interpolation between the allowable load given in par. 702-C-1 for complete penetration of side member and 80 per cent of that load for no penetration (thread extended to head of screw).

702-D. DEPTH OF PENETRATION OF THREADED PORTION IN THE MAIN MEMBER

702-D-1. The formulas in par. 702-E for determining allowable loads for lateral resistance are based on a minimum penetration of the threaded portion of the lag screw into the main member of 11 times the shank diameter for Group 1 woods (the softer woods) to 7 times for Group 4 woods (the harder woods), when the ratio of thickness of side member to shank diameter is 3.5 and the length of the shank is equal to the thickness of the side member.

702-D-2. Higher ratios of thickness of side member to shank diameter (up to about 7 to 1 and in excess of 3.5, par. 702-A-2) and greater ratios of penetration of shank into main member to shank diameter (up to a ratio of about 7 to 1, par. 702-C-2) require greater depths of penetration into main member to develop the percentage loads given in NDS Table 13, par. 702-A-2 and NDS Table 14, par. 702-C-2. The required penetration of threaded portion into main member shall be obtained through multiplication of the standard penetration by a fraction having the square root of the product of the two percentage loads as the numerator and 100 per cent as the denominator. If the product of the two percentages is less than 100 per cent, due to the use of thin side members, or of side members thicker than the length of shank, or of both, the required depth of penetration of threaded portion into main member shall be obtained by direct proportion of the percentage product to 100 per cent for standard penetration, but shall not be less than 5 times the shank diameter.

If the above required penetration of threaded portion into main member cannot be obtained, the allowable loads given in par. 702-E shall be reduced in direct proportion of the actual penetration to the required penetration, but, if greater penetration than required is used, the allowable loads shall not be increased.

NDS TABLE 15 Equations for computing allowable lateral loads parallel-to-grain for lag screws screwed into side grain

Group	Species of wood	Equation
1	Cedar, northern and southern white Fir, balsam and commercial white Hemlock, eastern Pine, ponderosa, sugar, northern white and western white Spruce, Engelmann, red, Sitka and white	$P = 1{,}800D^2$
2	Aspen and largetooth aspen Basswood Cedar, Alaska, Port Orford and western red Chestnut Cottonwood, black and eastern Cypress, southern Douglas fir (Rocky Mountain type) Hemlock, West Coast Pine, Norway Redwood Tamarack Yellow poplar	$P = 2{,}040D^2$
3	Ash, black Birch, paper Douglas fir (coast region) Elm (soft), American and (gray) slippery Gum, black, red, and tupelo Larch, western Maple, (soft) red and silver Pine, southern Sycamore	$P = 2{,}280D^2$
4	Ash, commercial white Beech Birch, sweet and yellow Elm, rock Hickory, true Maple (hard), black and sugar Oak, commercial red and white Pecan	$P = 2{,}640D^2$

P = allowable load per lag screw, in pounds.
D = shank diameter of lag screw, in inches.

702–E. ALLOWABLE LOADS FOR LATERAL RESISTANCE WHEN THE LOADS ACT PARALLEL TO GRAIN AND LAG SCREW IS INSERTED IN SIDE GRAIN

702–E–1. Allowable loads for lateral resistance when the loads act parallel to grain, lag screw is inserted perpendicular to the fiber (i.e., in side grain of main member), and a wood side piece is used, shall be determined from the formulas in NDS Table 15 for the species under consideration.

702–E–2. For adjustment of loads for metal instead of wood side pieces, see par. 702-B.

702–F. ALLOWABLE LOADS FOR LATERAL RESISTANCE WHEN THE LOADS ACT PERPENDICULAR TO GRAIN AND LAG SCREW IS INSERTED IN SIDE GRAIN

702–F–1. Allowable loads for lateral resistance when the loads act perpendicular to grain, lag screw is inserted perpendicular to the fibers (i.e., in side grain of main member), and *wood* side piece is used, shall be determined by multiplying the allowable loads for lateral resistance parallel to grain for wood side plates by the factors from NDS Table 16.

NDS TABLE 16 Factors for computing allowable lateral loads for perpendicular-to-grain loading of lag screws screwed into side grain (see par. 702F)

Lag-screw diameter	Factor
3/16	1.00
¼	0.97
5/16	0.85
⅜	0.76
7/16	0.71
½	0.65
⅝	0.60
¾	0.55
⅞	0.52
1	0.50

702–F–2. The allowable loads for lateral resistance when the loads act perpendicular to grain are the same for both *metal* and *wood* side pieces.

702–G. ALLOWABLE LOADS FOR LATERAL RESISTANCE WHEN THE LOADS ACT AT ANGLES OTHER THAN 0 DEG AND 90 DEG WITH THE GRAIN AND THE LAG SCREW IS INSERTED IN SIDE GRAIN

702–G–1. When the load acts at an angle other than 0 deg and 90 deg with the grain, the lag screw is inserted perpendicular to the fiber (i.e., in side grain of main member), and either wood or metal side piece is used, the allowable loads for lag screws under lateral loading shall be determined from the Hankinson formula.

702–G–2. For Hankinson formula, see par. 600-N and NDS Appendix C.

702–H. ALLOWABLE LOADS FOR LATERAL RESISTANCE WHEN THE LOADS ACT PERPENDICULAR TO THE GRAIN AND THE LAG SCREW IS INSERTED IN END GRAIN

702–H–1. Allowable loads for lateral resistance when the loads act perpendicular to grain and the lag screw is inserted parallel to the fibers (i.e., in the end grain of the main member) shall be 2/3 of those for lateral resistance when the loads act perpendicular to the grain, the lag screw is inserted perpendicular to the grain (i.e., in the side grain of the main member) and a wood side piece is used.

703—PLACEMENT OF LAG SCREWS IN JOINT

703–A. The spacings, end distances, edge distances, and net section for lag-screw joints shall be the same as for joints with bolts of a diameter equal to the shank diameter of the lag screw used. (See par. 601.)

NDS Part VIII. Nail, Spike, Drift-Bolt, and Wood-Screw Joints

800—NAILED JOINTS

For nailed joints using stress-grade lumber and the nails defined herein, the provisions of par. 800 and the tabulated allowable nail loads herein apply.

800–A. GENERAL PROVISIONS

800–A–1. The following provisions (except par. 800-A-2) apply to common wire nails.

800–A–2. For nails other than common wire nails, allowable loads herein for common wire nails may be adjusted by proportion in accordance with the provisions of ref. 2, NDS Appendix R.

800–A–3. When more than one nail is used in a nailed joint, the total allowable load in withdrawal or lateral resistance is the sum of the allowable loads for the individual nails.

800–A–4. When a prebored hole having a diameter not exceeding approximately ¾ of that of the nail is used, the allowable load for the nail without a prebored hole applies in withdrawal and in lateral resistance.

800–B. TYPE OF LOAD

800–B–1. The allowable loads for nails given in par. 800 are maximum for normal loading. Pertinent adjustments of stresses and provisions of par. 200, 201, 202, 203, and 204 for lumber except as otherwise provided in par. 800 apply likewise to the allowable nail loads in par. 800.

800–C. WITHDRAWAL FROM SIDE GRAIN

800–C–1. If possible, the structural design shall be such that nails are not loaded in withdrawal. When this condition cannot be avoided, the following provisions shall apply:

(a) For common wire nails, the allowable withdrawal load per inch of penetration of a nail driven in side grain (perpendicular to fibers) of main member of seasoned wood or unseasoned wood which will remain wet shall be:

(1) Determined from the following formula:

$$p = 1{,}380\ G^{5/2}D$$

in which:

p = allowable load *per inch* of penetration into member receiving point
G = specific gravity of species of wood, oven-dry weight and volume (see NDS Appendix G)
D = diameter of nail, in inches

(For calculated loads, see NDS Appendix J.)

(b) When driven in unseasoned wood which will season subsequently under load, the allowable load from side grain shall be one-fourth of that given in par. 800-C-1 (a).

800–D. WITHDRAWAL FROM END GRAIN

800–D–1. The structural design shall be such that nails are not loaded in withdrawal from end grain of wood.

800–E. LATERAL RESISTANCE OF NAILS DRIVEN IN SIDE GRAIN OF WOOD

800–E–1. The allowable *load per common wire nail* in lateral resistance when driven in side grain (perpendicular to fibers) of seasoned wood with the load applied in any lateral direction shall be determined from the formulas in NDS Table 17. These loads apply only for conditions where the side piece and main member have approximately the same density and where the nail penetrates in the main member a minimum distance equal to $^2/_3$ of its length in softwoods and ½ in hardwoods. (For calculated loads, see NDS Appendix J.) Where side piece and main member have different densities, the lighter density controls. When the nail penetrates in the main member a lesser distance, the allowable load shall be determined by straight-line interpolation between zero load at zero penetration and full load at standard penetration, but the minimum penetration in the main member shall be ½ of the nail length in softwoods and $^2/_5$ of the nail length in hardwoods.

800–E–2. For nails driven into side grain of unseasoned wood which will remain wet or will be loaded before seasoning, the allowable load per nail in lateral resistance shall be ¾ of that given in par. 800-E-1.

800–E–3. Where metal side plates are used, the allowable load per nail given in par. 800-E-1 may be increased by 25 per cent.

800–F. LATERAL RESISTANCE OF NAILS DRIVEN IN END GRAIN OF WOOD

800–F–1. The allowable *load per nail* in lateral resistance for a common wire nail driven in the end grain (parallel to fibers) shall be $^2/_3$ of that given for nails in par. 800-E.

800–G. SPACING OF NAILS

800–G–1. The end distance, edge distances, and spacings of nails shall be such as to avoid unusual splitting of the wood.

800–H. TOENAILS

800–H–1. Withdrawal of toenails. The allowable withdrawal load per nail in toenailed joints, for all conditions of seasoning, is equivalent to two-thirds of that calculated according to par. 800-C-1 (a).

NDS TABLE 17 Allowable loads for common wire nails in lateral resistance when driven in side grain

(Equations for computing allowable lateral load for common wire nails driven perpendicular to the grain of wood in seasoned lumber, expressed in pounds per nail.)

Species	Equation
Aspen and largetooth aspen Basswood Butternut Cedar, northern and southern white, and western red Chestnut Cottonwood, black and eastern Fir, balsam and white Hemlock, eastern Pine, lodgepole, ponderosa, sugar, northern white, and western white Poplar, yellow Spruce, Engelmann, red, Sitka, and white	$P = 1{,}080\,D^{3/2}$
Cedar, Alaska, incense, Port Orford Cedar, eastern red Cypress, southern Douglas fir (Rocky Mountain region) Hemlock, West Coast Pine, Norway Redwood Tamarack	$P = 1{,}350\,D^{3/2}$
Alder, red Ash, black Birch, paper Elm, American and slippery Gum, black, red, and tupelo Hackberry Magnolia, cucumber Magnolia, evergreen Maple, bigleaf Maple (soft), red and silver Sugarberry Sycamore	$P = 1{,}500\,D^{3/2}$
Douglas fir (coast region) Larch, western Pine, southern	$P = 1{,}650\,D^{3/2}$
Ash, commercial white Ash, Oregon Beech Birch, sweet and yellow Cherry, black Elm, rock Hickory, true and pecan Locust, honey and black Maple (hard), black and sugar Oak, commercial red and white Walnut, black	$P = 2{,}040\,D^{3/2}$

P = allowable load per nail, in pounds
D = diameter of nail, in inches

800–H–2. Lateral resistance of toenails. The allowable lateral load per nail in a toenailed joint is equivalent to $^5/_6$ of that (for the same nail penetration) calculated according to par. 800-E-1 and 800-E-2.

Note: It is recommended that toenails be driven at an angle of approximately 30 deg with the piece and started approximately one-third the length of the nail from the end of the piece.

801—SPIKED JOINTS

For spiked joints using stress-grade lumber and the spikes defined herein, the provisions of par. 801 and the tabulated allowable spike loads herein apply.

801–A. GENERAL PROVISIONS

801–A–1. The following provisions (except par. 801-A-2) apply to common wire spikes with diamond or chisel points.

801–A–2. For boat spikes which are square in cross section, allowable loads given in ref. 2, Appendix R, shall be adjusted in proportion to values given herein for common wire spikes.

801–A–3. When more than one spike is used in a spiked joint, the total allowable load in withdrawal or lateral resistance is the sum of the allowable loads for the individual spikes.

801–B. TYPE OF LOAD

801–B–1. The allowable loads for spikes given in par. 801 are the maximum for normal loading. Pertinent adjustments of stresses and provisions of par. 200, 201, 202, 203, and 204 for lumber except as otherwise provided in par. 801 apply likewise to the allowable spike loads in par. 801.

801–C. WITHDRAWAL FROM SIDE GRAIN

801–C–1. If possible, the structural design shall be such that spikes are not loaded in withdrawal. When this condition cannot be avoided, the following provisions shall apply:

(a) For common wire spikes, the allowable withdrawal load per inch of penetration of spike driven in side grain (perpendicular to fibers) of seasoned wood or unseasoned wood which will remain wet shall be:

(1) Determined from formula in par. 800-C-1-(a). (For calculated loads, see NDS Appendix J.)

(b) When driven in unseasoned wood which will season subsequently under load, the allowable withdrawal load shall be one-fourth of that given in par. 801-C-1-(a).

801–D. WITHDRAWAL FROM END GRAIN

801–D–1. The structural design shall be such that spikes are not loaded in withdrawal from end grain of wood.

801–E. LATERAL RESISTANCE OF SPIKES DRIVEN IN SIDE GRAIN

801–E–1. The allowable *load per common wire spike* in lateral resistance when driven in side grain (perpendicular to fibers) of seasoned wood with the load applied in any direction shall be determined from the formulas in NDS Table 17. The loads apply only for conditions where the side piece and main member have approximately the same density and where the spike penetrates in the main member a minimum distance equal to $^2/_3$ of its length in softwoods and ½ its length in hardwoods. (For calculated loads, see Appendix J.) Where side piece and main member have different densities, the lighter density controls. When the spike penetrates in the main member a lesser distance, the allowable load shall be determined by straight-line interpolation between zero load at a zero penetration and full load at standard penetration, but the minimum penetration in the main member shall be ½ of the spike length in softwoods and $^2/_5$ of the spike length in hardwoods.

801–E–2. For spikes driven in side grain of unseasoned wood which will remain wet or will be loaded before seasoning, the allowable load per common wire spike in lateral resistance shall be ¾ of that given in par. 801-E-1.

801–F. LATERAL RESISTANCE OF SPIKES DRIVEN IN END GRAIN OF WOOD

801–F–1. The allowable *load per spike* in lateral resistance of a common wire spike driven in end grain (parallel to fibers) shall be $^2/_3$ of that for spikes driven in side grain given in par. 801-E.

801–G. SPACING OF SPIKES

801–G–1. The end distance, edge distances, and spacings of spikes shall be such as to avoid unusual splitting of wood.

802—DRIFT-BOLT JOINTS

802–A. WITHDRAWAL OF DRIFT-PINS OR DRIFT BOLTS FROM SIDE GRAIN

802–A–1. The *ultimate* withdrawal load per linear inch of penetration of a round drift bolt or pin from side grain when driven into a prebored hole having a diameter $^1/_8$ in. less than that of the bolt diameter shall be determined from the formula:

$$p = 6{,}000\, G^2 D$$

in which:

p = *ultimate* withdrawal load per linear inch of penetration
G = specific gravity of oven-dry wood (see NDS Appendix G)
D = diameter of drift bolt, in inches

802–A–2. The allowable load per linear inch of penetration shall be determined by dividing the ultimate withdrawal load given in par. 802-A-1 by a factor of safety which is consistent with the character of the work. A factor of 5 is suggested for general use.

802–B. LATERAL RESISTANCE OF DRIFT BOLTS

802–B–1. The allowable load in lateral resistance for a drift bolt or pin driven in the side grain of wood shall not exceed, and ordinarily shall be taken as less than, that for a common bolt of the same diameter. When possible, additional penetration of pin into members shall be provided in lieu of the washers, head, and nut on a common bolt.

803—WOOD-SCREW JOINTS

For wood screw joints with stress-grade lumber and the wood screws defined herein, the provisions of par. 803 and the tabulated values herein apply.

803–A. TYPE OF LOAD

803–A–1. Allowable loads for wood screws given in par. 803 are the maximum for normal loading. Pertinent adjustments of stresses and provisions of par. 200, 201, 202, 203, and 204 for lumber except as otherwise provided in par. 803 apply likewise to loads for wood screws given in par. 803.

803–B. NUMBER OF WOOD SCREWS

803–B–1. Loads given are for *one* wood screw either in withdrawal or in lateral resistance in a *two*-member joint.

803–B–2. Loads for more than one wood screw each of the same or miscellaneous sizes are the sum of the loads permitted for each wood screw, provided that spacings, end distances, and edge distances are sufficient to develop the full strength of each wood screw.

803–C. QUALITY OF WOOD SCREWS

803–C–1. The allowable loads herein are for any wood screw of sufficient strength to cause failure in the wood rather than the metal.

803–D. SPECIES OF LUMBER

803–D–1. The method of determining allowable loads for wood screws in the various species is indicated by formulas and provisions and tabulated values herein.

803–E. GRADE OF LUMBER

803–E–1. The allowable loads for wood screws in a given species apply to all grades of that species.

803–F. CONDITION OF LUMBER

803–F–1. The allowable loads determined by the provisions in par. 803 are for wood screws in seasoned lumber except as otherwise specifically provided.

803–G. SERVICE CONDITIONS

803–G–1. Allowable loads apply for joints used indoors or in a location "always dry."

803–G–2. When joints are to be exposed to weather, 75 per cent, and when always wet, 67 per cent of the otherwise allowable loads apply.

803–H. LEAD HOLES

803–H–1. Lead holes shall be prebored as follows:

(a) For withdrawal resistance:

(1) For hardwoods, the lead hole shall have a diameter of about 90 per cent the root diameter of the wood screw.

(2) For conifers, the lead hole shall have a diameter of about 70 per cent of the root diameter of the wood screw.

(b) For lateral resistance:

(1) For hardwoods, such as oak, the part of the lead hole receiving the shank shall have about the same diameter as the shank, and that receiving the threaded portion shall have about the same diameter as the root of the thread.

(2) For conifers such as southern pine and Douglas fir, the part of the hole receiving the shank shall be about $7/8$ the diameter of the shank and that for the threaded portion shall be about $7/8$ the diameter of the screw at the root of the thread.

803–I. INSERTION

803–I–1. The screw shall be inserted in its lead hole by turning with a screw driver or other tool, not by driving with a hammer.

803–I–2. Soap or other lubricant may be used on the screws to facilitate insertion and to prevent damage to screw.

803–J. PENETRATION OF WOOD SCREWS IN MAIN MEMBER

803–J–1. For withdrawal resistance:

(a) The effective length used to determine the total load capacity in withdrawal shall be the depth of penetration of the threaded portion of the wood screw into the member receiving the point.

803–J–2. For lateral resistance:

(a) The length of screw in main member shall be approximately 7 times the shank diameter.

(b) If the depth of penetration is less than 7 times the diameter of the shank, the allowable load for lateral resistance shall be reduced in proportion to the length of penetration, but a length of penetration of less than 4 times the shank diameter shall not be used.

803–K. WITHDRAWAL RESISTANCE OF WOOD SCREWS

803–K–1. If possible, the structural design shall be such that wood screws are not loaded in withdrawal. When this condition cannot be avoided, the following provisions shall apply:

(a) Tensile strength of wood screw:

(1) In determining the allowable withdrawal resistance from par. 803-K-1-(b), the allowable tensile strength of wood screw at net (root) section shall not be exceeded.

(b) Withdrawal from side grain:

(1) The allowable load in withdrawal from side grain with axis of the wood

screw perpendicular to the fibers shall be determined from the formula:

$$p = 2{,}850\ G^2D$$

in which:

p = the allowable load per inch of penetration by threaded portion of screw into member receiving point

G = specific gravity of oven-dry wood (see NDS Appendix G)

D = diameter of the screw, in inches (see NDS Appendix K)

(For calculated screw loads, see NDS Appendix K.)

(2) The preceding equation is applicable to the wood screw lengths and gauges given in NDS Table 18.

NDS TABLE 18 Screw lengths and gauge limits

Screw length	Gauge limits	Screw length	Gauge limits
½	1– 6	2	7–16
¾	2–11	2½	9–18
1	3–12	3	12–20
1½	5–14		

(3) Allowable loads for other wood-screw lengths and gauges may be adjusted proportionately to those herein in accordance with ref. 2, NDS Appendix R.

(c) Withdrawal from end grain:

(1) The structural design shall be such that wood screws are not loaded in withdrawal from end grain of wood.

803–L. LATERAL RESISTANCE OF WOOD SCREWS

803–L–1. Thickness of wood side piece.
(a) See par. 803-J-2.

803–L–2. Steel side piece.
(a) Where steel side plates rather than wood side pieces are used, the allowable load for wood screws in lateral resistance of any angle of load to grain may be increased by 25 per cent.

NDS TABLE 19 Allowable loads in lateral resistance for wood sc ews in side grain

Species	Equation
Ash, commercial white Ash, Oregon Beech Birch, sweet and yellow Cherry, black Elm, rock Hickory, true and pecan Locust, black Locust, honey Maple (hard), black and sugar Oak, commercial red and white Walnut, black	$P = 4{,}800\ D^2$
Douglas fir (coast region) Larch, western Pine, southern yellow	$P = 3{,}960\ D^2$
Alder, red Ash, black Birch, paper Elm, American and slippery Gum, black, red and tupelo Hackberry Magnolia, cucumber Magnolia, evergreen Maple, bigleaf Maple (soft), red and silver Sugarberry Sycamore	$P = 3{,}480\ D^2$
Cedar, Alaska, incense, Port Orford and western red Cedar, eastern red Cypress, southern Douglas fir (Rocky Mountain region) Hemlock, West Coast Pine, Norway Redwood Tamarack	$P = 3{,}240\ D^2$
Aspen and largetooth aspen Basswood Butternut Cedar, northern and southern white Chestnut Cottonwood, black and eastern Fir, balsam and white Hemlock, eastern Pine, lodgepole, ponderosa, sugar, northern white, and western white Poplar, yellow Spruce, Engelmann, red, Sitka and white	$P = 2{,}520\ D^2$

P = allowable load per screw, in pounds
D = shank diameter of screw, in inches

803–L–3. Depth of penetration of threaded portion in main member.

(a) See par. 803-J-2.

803–L–4. Penetration of shank in side and main members.

(a) See par. 803-J-2.

803–L–5. Allowable loads for lateral resistance with wood screws in side grain.

(a) The allowable loads for lateral resistance to any angle of load to grain when the wood screw is inserted perpendicular to the fibers (i.e., in side grain of main member) and a wood side piece is used, shall be determined from the formula in NDS Table 19 for the species under consideration. (For calculated screw loads, see NDS Appendix K.)

803–L–6. Allowable loads for lateral resistance when loads act perpendicular to the grain and the wood screw is inserted in end grain.

(a) The allowable loads for lateral resistance when the loads act perpendicular to grain and the wood screw is inserted parallel to the fibers (i.e., in the end grain of the main member) shall be two-thirds of those for lateral resistance given in par. 803-L-5.

803–M. PLACEMENT OF WOOD SCREWS IN JOINTS

803–M–1. Spacings, end distances, and edge distances for wood-screw joints shall be such as to prevent unusual splitting.

NDS Part IX. Glued-Laminated Structural Members

For structural glued-laminated lumber as defined herein, the provisions of NDS Part IX and the tabulated values herein shall apply.

900—GENERAL PROVISIONS

900–A. The term "structural glued-laminated lumber" as used herein refers only to those glued-laminated structural members in which the grain of all laminations of a member is approximately parallel.

900–B. Except as otherwise provided in NDS Part IX, pertinent provisions of NDS Parts I, II, III, and IV shall apply to structural glued-laminated lumber members.

900–C The pertinent provisions and allowable loads for fastenings given in NDS Parts V, VI, VII, and VIII shall apply to structural glued-laminated lumber members.

900–D. The allowable unit stresses for normal loading given in NDS Table 20 or obtained from multiplication of factors from NDS Table 21, Part A, by stress modules from NDS Table 21, Part B, apply when the structural glued-laminated lumber conforms to all pertinent provisions of the applicable specification. See notes in tables.

900–E. Allowable unit stresses for species and grades of structural glued-laminated lumber not given in NDS Table 20 or obtained from NDS Table 21 shall be established in accordance with the principles set forth in "Fabrication and Design of Glued-Laminated Wood Structural Members," Technical Bulletin No. 1069, Forest Products Laboratory, U. S. Department of Agriculture. (The structural glued-laminated lumber specifications for the species and grades noted on NDS Tables 20 and 21 are based on these principles.)

901—STANDARD SIZES

901–A. Standard sizes of structural glued-laminated lumber shall be as follows:

NDS TABLE 20 Allowable unit stresses for structural glued-laminated lumber

(For normal loading conditions. See other provisions of NDS Part IX for adjustments.)

SPECIES AND COMBINATIONS OF LUMBER GRADES				ALLOWABLE UNIT STRESSES IN POUNDS PER SQUARE INCH							
Combination Number	Outer Laminations		Inner Laminations	Extreme Fiber in Bending "f"[7-8]		Tension Parallel to Grain "t"[7]		Compression Parallel to Grain "c"[7]		Horizontal Shear "H"	Compression Perpendicular to Grain "c⊥"
	Grade	Number, Each Side	Grade	From 4 to 14 Laminations	15 or More Laminations	From 4 to 14 Laminations	15 or More Laminations	From 4 to 14 Laminations	15 or More Laminations		
TABLE NO. 20a—*Dry Conditions of Use* [3]											
DOUGLAS FIR, COAST REGION[1]											
1	Clear (Dense)*	One	Dense Select Structural	3,000	3,000	3,000	3,000	2,400	2,500	165	455
2	Clear (Dense)*	One	Dense Construction	3,000	3,000	2,600	3,000	2,200	2,300	165	455
3	Dense Select Structural	All	Dense Select Structural	2,800	3,000	3,000	3,000	2,400	2,500	165	455
4	Clear (Close-Grain)*	One	Select Structural	2,800	2,800	2,800	2,800	2,200	2,200	165	415
5	Select Structural	All	Select Structural	2,600	2,800	2,800	2,800	2,200	2,200	165	415
6	Select Structural	1/5 of total	Construction	2,600	2,800	2,400	2,600	2,000	2,000	165	415
7	Clear (Medium Grain)*	One	Construction	2,600	2,600	2,200	2,400	1,900	2,000	165	390
8	Dense Construction	All	Dense Construction	2,400	2,600	2,600	3,000	2,200	2,300	165	455
9	Dense Construction	1/14 of total	Construction	2,400	2,600	2,200	2,400	1,900	2,000	165	455
10	Select Structural	One	Construction	2,400	2,600	2,200	2,400	1,900	2,000	165	415
11	Select Structural	1/5 of total	Standard	2,200	2,600	2,400	2,600	1,900	2,000	165	415
12	Clear (Medium Grain)*	One	Standard	2,200	2,200	2,000	2,400	1,800	1,900	165	390
13	Select Structural	One	Standard	2,200	2,200	2,000	2,400	1,800	1,900	165	415
14	Construction	All	Construction	2,000	2,200	2,200	2,400	1,900	2,000	165	390
15	Construction	One	Standard	2,000	2,200	2,000	2,400	1,800	1,900	165	390
16	Standard	All	Standard	1,600	2,000	2,000	2,400	1,800	1,900	165	390
PINE, SOUTHERN[2]											
1-1	No. 1 Dense	All	No. 1 Dense	3,000	3,000	3,000	3,000	2,400	2,500	200	450
1-2	B & B Dense	One	No. 1	3,000	3,000	2,600	2,600	2,100	2,100	200	450
1-3	No. 1 Dense	1/14 of total	No. 1	3,000	3,000	2,600	2,600	2,100	2,100	200	450
1-4	B & B Dense	One	No. 2 Dense	2,800	2,800	3,000	3,000	2,400	2,400	200	450
1-5	No. 1 Dense	1/5 of total	No. 2 Dense	2,800	3,000	2,800	3,000	2,300	2,400	200	450
1-6	No. 1	All	No. 1	2,600	2,600	2,600	2,600	2,100	2,100	200	385
1-7	B & B Dense	1/14 of total	No. 2	2,400	2,800	2,600	2,600	2,000	2,000	200	450
1-8	B & B	One	No. 2	2,400	2,400	2,600	2,600	2,000	2,000	200	385
1-9	No. 1	1/5 of total	No. 2	2,400	2,600	2,400	2,600	2,000	2,000	200	385
1-10	No. 2 Dense	All	No. 2 Dense	2,000	2,600	2,600	3,000	2,200	2,300	200	450
1-11	No. 2 Dense	1/14 of total	No. 2	2,000	2,600	2,200	2,600	1,900	2,000	200	450
1-12	No. 2	All	No. 2	1,800	2,200	2,200	2,600	1,900	2,000	200	385

TABLE No. 20b—*Wet Conditions of Use* [4]

DOUGLAS FIR, COAST REGION [1]											
1	Clear (Dense)*	One	Dense Select Structural	2,400	2,400	2,400	2,400	1,700	1,800	145	305
2	Clear (Dense)*	One	Dense Construction	2,400	2,400	2,000	2,400	1,600	1,700	145	305
3	Dense Select Structural	All	Dense Select Structural	2,200	2,400	2,400	2,400	1,700	1,800	145	305
4	Clear (Close-Grain)*	One	Select Structural	2,200	2,200	2,200	2,200	1,600	1,600	145	275
5	Select Structural	All	Select Structural	2,000	2,200	2,200	2,200	1,600	1,600	145	275
6	Select Structural	1/5 of total	Construction	2,000	2,200	2,000	2,000	1,400	1,500	145	275
7	Clear (Medium Grain)*	One	Construction	2,000	2,000	1,800	2,000	1,400	1,400	145	260
8	Dense Construction	All	Dense Construction	2,000	2,200	2,000	2,400	1,600	1,700	145	305
9	Dense Construction	1/14 of total	Construction	2,000	2,200	1,800	2,000	1,400	1,400	145	305
10	Select Structural	One	Construction	2,000	2,000	1,800	2,000	1,400	1,400	145	275
11	Select Structural	1/5 of total	Standard	1,800	2,200	1,800	2,000	1,400	1,400	145	275
12	Clear (Medium Grain)*	One	Standard	1,800	1,800	1,600	1,800	1,300	1,400	145	260
13	Select Structural	One	Standard	1,800	1,800	1,600	1,800	1,300	1,400	145	275
14	Construction	All	Construction	1,600	1,800	1,800	2,000	1,400	1,400	145	260
15	Construction	One	Standard	1,600	1,800	1,600	1,800	1,300	1,400	145	260
16	Standard	All	Standard	1,200	1,600	1,600	1,800	1,300	1,400	145	260
PINE, SOUTHERN [2]											
2-1	No. 1 Dense	All	No. 1 Dense	2,400	2,400	2,400	2,400	1,800	1,800	175	300
2-2	B & B Dense	One	No. 1	2,400	2,400	2,000	2,000	1,500	1,500	175	300
2-3	No. 1 Dense	1/14 of total	No. 1	2,400	2,400	2,000	2,000	1,500	1,500	175	300
2-4	B & B Dense	One	No. 2 Dense	2,200	2,200	2,400	2,400	1,700	1,700	175	300
2-5	No. 1 Dense	1/5 of total	No. 2 Dense	2,200	2,400	2,200	2,400	1,700	1,700	175	300
2-6	No. 1	All	No. 1	2,000	2,000	2,000	2,000	1,500	1,500	175	260
2-7	B & B Dense	1/14 of total	No. 2	1,800	2,200	2,000	2,000	1,500	1,500	175	300
2-8	B & B	One	No. 2	1,800	2,000	2,000	2,000	1,500	1,500	175	260
2-9	No. 1	1/5 of tota	No. 2	2,000	2,000	2,000	2,000	1,400	1,500	175	260
2-10	No. 2 Dense	All	No. 2 Dense	1,600	2,000	2,000	2,400	1,600	1,700	175	300
2-11	No. 2 Dense	1/14 of total	No. 2	1,600	2,000	1,800	2,000	1,400	1,400	175	300
2-12	No. 2	All	No. 2	1,400	1,800	1,800	2,000	1,400	1,400	175	260

1. "Standard Specifications for Design and Fabrication of Structural Glued Laminated Lumber," by West Coast Lumbermen's Association, applies.
2. "Standard Specifications for Structural Glued Laminated Southern Pine," by Southern Pine Inspection Bureau, applies.
3. The Modulus of Elasticity (E) is 1,800,000 pounds per square inch for dry conditions of use.
4. The Modulus of Elasticity (E) is 1,600,000 pounds per square inch for wet conditions of use.
5. The rate of growth and density requirements of inner laminations shall apply to clear outer laminations.
6. In grade combinations 1-1, 1-6, 2-1, and 2-6 no provision has been made for use of B & B grade in outermost laminations because higher stress rating would not be justified. If, in these combinations, B & B quality is desired for one or both faces of a member to improve appearance, it should be particularly specified.
7. For special slope of grain requirements see applicable specifications listed in Notes Nos. 1 and 2.
8. The allowable unit stresses in bending in Table No. 20 apply only when the wide faces of the laminations are placed normal to the direction of the load. For allowable stresses in bending when the loading is applied parallel to the planes of the laminations, see the applicable specification indicated in Notes Nos. 1 and 2.

NOTE: Members with intermediate working stresses will satisfy most design requirements. Members with the highest working stresses are available when special strength requirements are needed. Where larger sizes are lesired, those combinations with lower stresses should be used.

NDS TABLE 21 Allowable unit stresses for glued hardwood laminated lumber[1-2] for normal loading duration and dry condition of use[4]

Part A

SPECIES	Multiply the appropriate stress module in part B by the factors below to determine allowable stress for		Allowable unit stress in pounds per square inch for		
	Extreme fiber in bending "f" or tension parallel to grain "t"	Compression parallel to grain "c"	Horizontal shear "H"	Compression perpendicular to grain "c_1"	Modulus of elasticity "E"
Hickory, true and pecan	3.90	3.05	260	730	2,000,000
Beech, American	3.05	2.45	230	610	1,800,000
Birch, sweet and yellow	3.05	2.45	230	610	1,800,000
Elm, rock	3.05	2.45	230	610	1,400,000
Maple, black and sugar (hard maple)	3.05	2.45	230	610	1,800,000
Ash, commercial white	2.85	2.20	230	610	1,600,000
Oak, commercial red and white	2.85	2.05	230	610	1,600,000
Elm, American and slippery (white or soft elm)	2.20	1.60	190	310	1,300,000
Sweetgum (red or sap gum)	2.20	1.60	190	370	1,300,000
Tupelo, black (blackgum)	2.20	1.60	190	370	1,300,000
Tupelo, water	2.20	1.60	190	370	1,300,000
Ash, black	2.00	1.30	170	370	1,200,000
Yellow-poplar	1.80	1.45	150	270	1,200,000
Cottonwood, Eastern	1.55	1.20	110	180	1,100,000

Part B Values for use in computing working stresses with the factors of Part A together with limitations required to permit the use of such stresses

Ratio of size of maximum permitted knot to finished width of lamination [3]	Number of laminations	Extreme fiber in bending			Tension parallel to grain			Compression parallel to grain	
		Stress module	Steepest grain slope	Steepest scarf slope	Stress module	Steepest grain slope	Steepest scarf slope	Stress module	Steepest grain slope
0.1	4 to 14	800	1:16	1:10	800	1:16	1:10	970	1:15
.1	15 or more	800	1:16	1:10	800	1:16	1:10	980	1:15
.2	4 to 14	800	1:16	1:10	800	1:16	1:10	930	1:15
.2	15 or more	800	1:16	1:10	800	1:16	1:10	950	1:15
.3	4 to 14	670	1:12	1:8	800	1:16	1:10	870	1:15
.3	15 or more	770	1:16	1:10	800	1:16	1:10	900	1:15
.4	4 to 14	520	1:8	1:5	640	1:12	1:8	810	1:12
.4	15 or more	660	1:12	1:8	750	1:15	1:8	860	1:14
.5	4 to 14	390	1:8	1:5	480	1:8	1:5	730	1:10
.5	15 or more	550	1:10	1:15	630	1:12	1:8	800	1:12

1. "Standard Specifications for the Design and Fabrication of Hardwood Glued Laminated Lumber for Structural, Marine, and Vehicular Uses", by Southern Hardwood Producers, Inc., Appalachian Hardwood Manufacturers, Inc., Northern Hemlock & Hardwood Manufacturers Association, applies.
2. The allowable unit stresses in bending obtained from Table 21 apply when the wide faces of the laminations are normal to the direction of the load. They also apply when the loading is parallel to the planes of the laminations provided certain additional restrictions, given in the applicable specification indicated in Note No. 1, are applied.
3. Factors for knot sizes of 0.1 and 0.2 are identical in case of extreme fiber in bending and in tension parallel to grain because a slope of grain of 1 16 is a greater limitation than knot size. The smaller knot size may be specified for reasons other than strength.
4. Allowable stresses for dry conditions of use shall be applicable when the moisture content in service is less than 15 percent, as in most covered structures. For wet conditions of use the following maximum percentage of the dry use stresses shall be permitted:

    "f" (bending) and "t" (tension) 80%
    "H" (horizontal shear) and "E" (modulus of elasticity) 90%
    "c" (compression parallel to grain) 70%
    "c_1" (compression perpendicular to grain) 67%

901–A–1. Width. Standard finished widths [1] of laminated members shall be as follows:

Nominal width 3 in., 4 in., 5 in., 6 in.
Net finished width 2¼ in., 3¼ in., 4¼ in., 5 in. (or 5¼ in.)
Nominal width 8 in., 10 in., 12 in., 14 in., 16 in.
Net finished width 7 in., 9 in., 11 in., 12½ in., 14½ in.

901–A–2. Depth. Straight and curved members shall be specified to the depth dimensions required.

901–A–3. Length. All members shall be specified to the length required.

901–A–4. Specification of dimensions. Net dimensions shall be specified.

902—SPECIFICATIONS

902–A. For structural glued-laminated lumber, the following shall be specified:

1. Whether for dry or wet condition of use
2. Species and applicable structural glued-laminated lumber specifications
3. Stress requirements
4. If the temperatures of the timber exceeds 150° F in service

903—DESIGN STRESSES

903–A. DRY CONDITIONS OF USE

903–A–1. Allowable stress values for dry conditions of use (NDS Tables 20a and 21) shall be applicable for normal loading when the moisture content in service is less than 15 per cent, as in most covered structures.

903–B. WET CONDITIONS OF USE

903–B–1. Allowable stress values for wet conditions of use (NDS Tables 20b and 21) shall be applicable for normal loading when the moisture content in service is 15 per cent or more, as may occur in exterior and submerged construction.

[1] Standard widths as shown constitute recommended practice and are based on the widths of lumber that can be used to best advantage for laminations.

903–C. MODIFICATION OF STRESSES

903–C–1. Curvature factor.

(a) For the curved portion of members, the allowable unit stress in bending shall be modified by multiplication by the following curvature factor:

$$1 - 2{,}000\left(\frac{t}{R}\right)^2$$

in which:

t = thickness of lamination, in inches
R = radius of curvature of a lamination, in inches

and t/R shall not exceed $^1/_{125}$ for softwoods or $^1/_{100}$ for hardwoods.

(b) No curvature factor shall be applied to stress in the straight portion of an assembly, regardless of curvature elsewhere.

903–C–2. Radial tension or compression.

(a) The maximum radial stress induced in a curved member of rectangular cross-section by a bending moment is:

$$S_R = \frac{3M}{2Rbh}$$

in which:

S_R = Radial stress, in pounds per square inch
M = bending moment, in inch-pounds
R = radius of curvature at centerline of member, in inches
b = width of cross section, in inches
h = depth of cross section, in inches

(b) When M is in the direction tending to decrease curvature (increase the radius), the radial stress is in tension and shall be limited to an allowable stress equal to one-third the allowable stress in horizontal shear.

(c) When M is in the direction tending to increase curvature (decrease the radius), the radial stress is in compression and shall be limited to the allowable stress in compression perpendicular to the grain.

NDS Appendix A

Lateral Distribution of a Concentrated Load

A. LATERAL DISTRIBUTION OF A CONCENTRATED LOAD FOR MOMENT

The lateral distribution of a concentrated load for computing bending moment may be determined by the following method (see ref. 19, NDS Appendix R):

When a concentrated load at the center of the beam span is distributed to adjacent parallel beams by a wood (plank or laminated strip) or concrete floor slab, the load on the beam nearest the point of application shall be determined by multiplying the load by the following factors:

KIND OF FLOOR:	LOAD ON CRITICAL BEAM
2-in. wood	$S/4.0$
4-in. wood	$S/4.5$
6-in. wood	$S/5.0$
Concrete, structurally designed	$S/6.0$

S = average spacing of beams in feet. In case S exceeds the denominator of the factor, the load on the two adjacent beams shall be the reactions of the load, with the assumption that the floor slab between the beams acts as a simple beam. For more than one traffic lane, see additional data in ref. 19, NDS Appendix *R*.

B. LATERAL DISTRIBUTION OF A CONCENTRATED LOAD FOR SHEAR

When the load distribution for moment at the center of a beam is known or assumed to correspond to specific values in the first two columns of NDS Table A.1, the distribution to adjacent parallel beams when loaded at or near the quarter point, i.e., the approximate point of maximum shear [see par. 400–D–2-(c)-(3)], shall be assumed to be the corresponding values in the last two columns of NDS Table A.1.

NDS TABLE A.1 Distribution in terms of proportion of total load

Load applied at center of span		Load applied at one-quarter point of span	
Center beam	Distribution to side beams	Center beam	Distribution to side beams
1.00	0.00	1.00	0.00
.90	.10	.94	.06
.80	.20	.87	.13
.70	.30	.79	.21
.60	.40	.69	.31
.50	.50	.58	.42
.40	.60	.44	.56
.33	.67	.33	.67

NDS Appendix B

Formulas for Wood Columns with Side Loads and Eccentricity

A. GENERAL

The following information is provided for use when more accurate calculation of the maxim ım direct compression load that can be put upon an eccentrically loaded column or one with a side load is desired.

The most accurate of all the column formulas for the critical load on a long, originally straight, centrally loaded column of uniform cross section is the Euler formula, and for long columns with an eccentric application of load is the secant formula.

The inaccuracies of these formulas are too small to be detected by the ordinary methods of testing such columns and are much smaller than the inaccuracy of calculating the stiffness of wooden beams neglecting the distortions due to shear.

The formulas here presented can be made to have an accuracy fairly comparable to that for the Euler column, but in their simplified form they do not pretend to such accuracy; however, they do have an accuracy well within an acceptable range for most engineering purposes (ref. 18, NDS Appendix R).

B. ASSUMPTIONS

The following assumptions have been made in arriving at the following simplified equations, but normally they change the results but little:

1. The stresses which cause a given deflection as a sinusoidal curve are the same as those for a beam with a uniform side load.

2. For a single concentrated side load the stress under the load can be used, regardless of the position of the load with reference to the length of the column.

3. The stress to use with a system of side loads is the maximum stress due to the system. (With large side loads near each end some slight error on the side of overload will occur.)

4. The equations can be used for solving for P/A with rectangular wood columns with an l/d ratio of 20 or more.

5. For columns with an l/d ratio of 11 or less, the stress due to deflection of the column may be neglected.

6. Between l/d ratios of 11 and 20 the stress may be assumed to vary as a straight line.

C. NOTATION

P/A = direct compressive stress in pounds per square inch induced by axial load

M/S = flexural stress in pounds per square inch induced by side loads

c = the allowable unit stress in compression parallel to the grain in pounds per square inch that would be permitted for the column if axial compressive stress only existed; that is, the allowable unit stress for the l/d of the column under consideration

= the allowable unit stress in flexure in pounds per square inch that would be permitted if flexural stress only existed

e = eccentricity, in inches

l = length of column, in inches

d = side in inches of a rectangular column, measured in the direction of the side loads

z = ratio of flexural stress induced by side loads to compressive stress induced by axial end load, i.e.,

$$\frac{M/S}{P/A}$$

D. FORMULAS

The following formulas, which are for pin-end columns of rectangular cross sections, apply when a member is subjected to both axial compression and moment (from eccentricity or side loads). (For design data on columns loaded axially only, see par. 401.) The formulas given are for determining the maximum permissible unit load or stress, P/A or M/S, which is permissible under the conditions of combined loading, i.e., the P/A and M/S induced by loading shall not exceed the values therefor obtained from the formulas. The two or three formulas in any one of the following groups are identical except for the arrangement of the terms and, therefore, any one within the group may be used for the specific condition indicated. The formula to be used is selected on the basis of the ease with which the values desired can be computed from the formula through insertion therein of known or assumed values.

1. Columns having an l/d ratio of 11 or less:

(a) End and side loads:

$$\frac{M/S}{f} + \frac{P/A}{c} = 1$$

or:

$$P/A = \frac{c(f - M/S)}{f}$$

or:

$$M/S = \frac{f(c - P/A)}{c}$$

(b) Eccentric load:

$$\frac{c\left(\frac{6e}{d}\right)}{f + c\left(\frac{6e}{d}\right)} + \frac{P/A}{c} = 1$$

or:

$$P/A = \frac{cf}{f + c\left(\frac{6e}{d}\right)}$$

(c) Side load proportional to end load: (A load carried by a chord member of a truss causes an end load in the member which has a proportional relation to the side load causing it.)

$$\frac{z(P/A)}{f} + \frac{P/A}{c} = 1$$

or:

$$P/A = \frac{cf}{(f + zc)}$$

or:

$$M/S = z(P/A)$$

(d) Combined end load, side loads, and eccentricity:

$$\frac{M/S + (P/A)\left(\frac{6e}{d}\right) + z(P/A)}{f} + \frac{P/A}{c} = 1$$

or:

$$P/A = \frac{c\,(f - M/S)}{f + c\left(\frac{6e}{d} + z\right)}$$

2. Columns having an l/d ratio between $l/d = 11$ and $l/d = 20$:

Assume that the stress induced by loads varies as a straight line between that for a column having an l/d ratio of 11 and for one having an l/d ratio of 20.

3. Columns having an l/d ratio of 20 or more:

(a) End and side loads:

$$\frac{M/S}{f - P/A} + \frac{P/A}{c} = 1$$

or:

$$P/A = \frac{f + c}{2} - \sqrt{\left(\frac{f + c}{2}\right)^2 - c(f - M/S)}$$

or:

$$M/S = \frac{(f - P/A)(c - P/A)}{c}$$

(b) Eccentric load:

$$\frac{c\left(\frac{15e}{2d}\right)}{f - P/A + c\left(\frac{15e}{2d}\right)} + \frac{P/A}{c} = 1$$

or:

$$P/A = \frac{f + c\left(1 + \frac{15e}{2d}\right)}{2} - \sqrt{\left[\frac{f + c\left(1 + \frac{15e}{2d}\right)}{2}\right]^2 - cf}$$

(c) Side load proportional to end load:

$$\frac{z(P/A)}{f - P/A} + \frac{P/A}{c} = 1$$

or:

$$P/A = \frac{f+c\,(1+z)}{2} - \sqrt{\left(\frac{f+c\,(1+z)}{2}\right)^2 - cf}$$

or:

$$M/S = z(P/A)$$

(d) Combined end load, side loads, and eccentricity:

$$\frac{M/S + (P/A)\left(\frac{15e}{2d}\right) + z(P/A)}{f - P/A} + \frac{P/A}{c} = 1$$

or:

$$P/A = \frac{f + c\left(1 + \frac{15e}{2d} + z\right)}{2} - \sqrt{\left[\frac{f + c\left(1 + \frac{15e}{2d} + z\right)}{2}\right]^2 - c(f - M/S)}$$

E. COLUMNS WITH SIDE BRACKETS

An exact solution of the stresses in a column with end and bracket loads is difficult. The following simple rule for determining loads to be used in the combined loading formulas is safe, and for brackets in the upper quarter of the height of a column is sufficiently accurate.

Instead of using the bracket load P in its actual position, add to the end load on the column an axial end load P equal to the load on the bracket and calculate the bending stress from an assumed side load P', concentrated at the center of the length of the column and determined as follows (see NDS Fig. B.1):

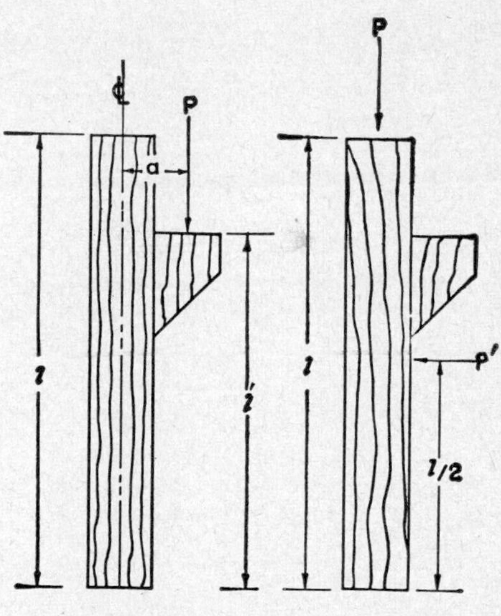

NDS Fig. B.1

$$P' = 3 \times \frac{l'}{l} \times \frac{a}{l}\, P = \frac{3a\, l'\, P}{l^2}$$

in which:

P = actual load, in pounds, on bracket
P' = assumed horizontal side load, in pounds, assumed to be placed at center of height of column

a = horizontal distance, in inches, from load on bracket to center of column
l = total length of column, in inches
l' = distance, in inches, measured vertically from point of application of load on bracket to farther end of column

Use P' to determine the induced unit flexural stress M/S, as if the column were a beam with a concentrated load P' at midlength. Then combine these stresses with those from other loads and apply the appropriate combined stress formulas previously given under par. D of this Appendix.

NDS Appendix C

Solution of Hankinson Formula

A. The allowable unit stresses in compression for lumber and allowable loads for connectors, bolts, and lag screws at an angle of load to grain between 0 deg and 90 deg are obtained from the Hankinson formula given in NDS Fig. C.1.

B. The Hankinson formula is for the condition where the loaded surface is perpendicular to the direction of the load. (See NDS Fig. 7, par. 405.)

C. Where the resultant force is at an angle other than 90 deg with the surface under consideration, the angle θ is the angle between the direction of grain and the direction of the force component which is perpendicular to the surface.

D. The bearing surface for a connector, bolt, or lag screw is assumed perpendicular to the force. (See NDS Fig. 23, par. 600–N)

E. For specific applications of the formula, see par. 211–A, 212, 405, 500–N, 600–N, and 702–G.

F. NDS TABLE C.1 lists $\sin^2\theta$ and $\cos^2\theta$ for various angles of θ.

NDS TABLE C.1 Values of $\sin^2\theta$ and $\cos^2\theta$

$\sin^2\theta$	θ	$\cos^2\theta$	$\sin^2\theta$	θ	$\cos^2\theta$
0.00000	0	1.00000	0.58682	50	0.41318
0.00760	5	0.99240	0.67101	55	0.32899
0.03015	10	0.96985	0.75000	60	0.25000
0.06698	15	0.93302	0.82140	65	0.17860
0.11698	20	0.88302	0.88302	70	0.11698
0.17860	25	0.82140	0.93302	75	0.06698
0.25000	30	0.75000	0.96985	80	0.03015
0.32899	35	0.67101	0.99240	85	0.00760
0.41318	40	0.58682	1.00000	90	0.00000
0.50000	45	0.50000			

G. The Hankinson formula may be solved graphically through use of the charts in NDS Fig. C.1.

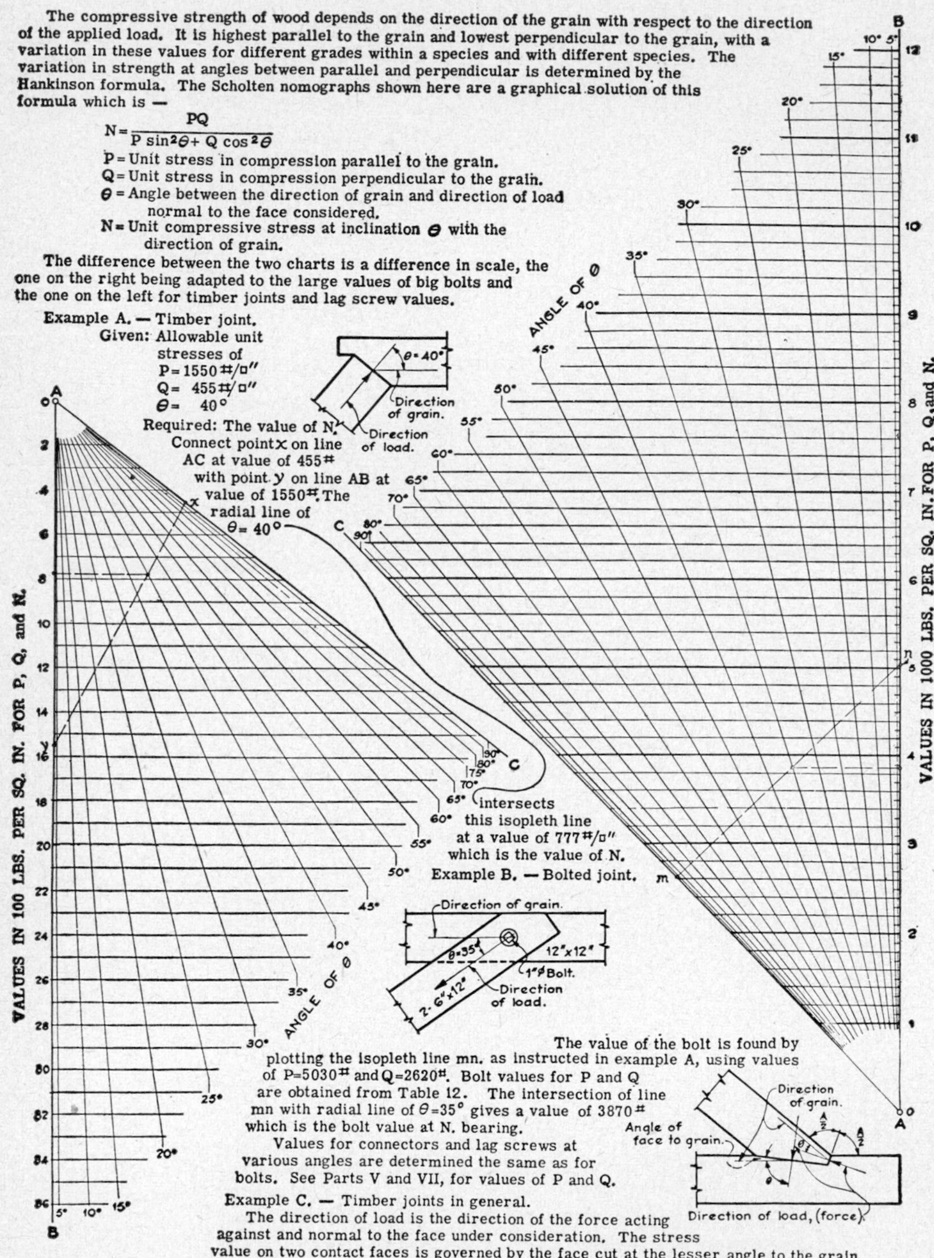

NDS Fig. C.1 Bearing strength of wood at angles to the grain (Hankinson formula)

NDS Appendix D

Depth, Form Factors, and Sections Other Than Rectangular

A. DEPTH-EFFECT FACTOR FOR RECTANGULAR BEAMS

Design procedure for timber beams of rectangular cross section does not require the application of a depth-effect factor when the depth of the beam does not exceed 16 in. In arriving at the basic stresses, from which the allowable unit stresses in bending for stress-grades of lumber are developed, a depth-effect factor was applied that corresponds approximately to a 12-in. depth of beam to take into account the slightly lower unit strength developed in deep beams as compared to shallow beams. If, however, the depth of a beam exceeds 16 in., a depth factor therefor should be calculated and introduced in the basic design formula for flexure. An empirical formula for determining the depth-effect factor is:

$$F = 0.81\left(\frac{h^2 + 143}{h^2 + 88}\right)$$

in which:

h = depth of the beam
F = the depth-effect factor

This formula gives a depth-effect factor, F, of unity when the beam depth, h, equals 12-in.

The depth-effect factor, F, is inserted in the usual beam formula as follows:

$$M = \frac{FfI}{n}$$

B. FORM FACTOR FOR BEAMS OF CIRCULAR SECTION

The form factor of a circular section is 1.18 and the formula for a beam of circular cross section is written:

$$M = \frac{1.18fI}{n}$$

From this it is found that a beam of circular section without appreciable taper has the same strength as a square beam of the same cross-sectional area.

C. FORM FACTOR FOR BEAMS OF SQUARE SECTION PLACED WITH DIAGONAL VERTICALLY

The form factor of a square section, so placed that a diagonal of the section is vertical, is 1.414, and the beam formula is written:

$$M = \frac{1.414\,fI}{n}$$

Hence, a timber beam of square section has the same bending strength whether placed in the usual manner or with a diagonal vertically.

D. FORM FACTOR FOR "I" AND BOX BEAMS

Recent investigations by the Forest Products Laboratory resulted in the development of the following formula for the form factor of "I" and box beams:

$$F = 0.81\left[1 + \left(\frac{h^2 + 143}{h^2 + 88} - 1\right)S\right]$$

in which:

F = the form factor
h = depth of beam, in inches
S = support factor obtained from the formula:

$$S = p^2(6 - 8p + 3p^2)(1 - q) + q$$

in which:

p = ratio of depth of compression flange to the full depth of the beam
q = ratio of thickness of web or webs to the full width of the beam

(For further information on depth and form factors and lateral stability of "I" beams and box beams, see ref. 2 and 61, NDS Appendix R.)

E. OTHER BENDING MEMBERS

(1) The form factor for the section should be determined (ref. 2 and 61).

(2) The section should be investigated for lateral buckling (ref. 2 and 61).

F. COMPRESSION MEMBERS

(1) For compression members use the formulas, par. 401 herein.

(2) Investigate the section in question for wrinkling or twisting if formed with outstanding flanges (see ref. 2 and 61, NDS Appendix R, also for box columns).

G. COMBINED BENDING AND COMPRESSION

Having determined the allowable working stresses in bending and compression, the allowable stress in combination may be determined by the formulas for wood columns with side loads and eccentricity given in NDS Appendix B.

NDS Appendix E

Horizontal Shear in Checked Beams

A. Shearing strength in a beam is a function of the shearing strength of the species and the extent of shake or checks. In a checked beam, however, there is a greater uniformity of distribution of shearing strength over the unchecked portion than in an unchecked beam, which explains why a checked beam will carry a load for which it would appear to be entirely inadequate from the standpoint of shear.

B. In addition to this, the Forest Products Laboratory of the United States Forest Service, located at Madison, Wisconsin, has determined that in a checked beam the upper and lower halves of the beam carry a large portion of the shear independently of that at the neutral axis, the proportion depending on the distance of the load from a support, varying inversely with the square of the distance, until, with a load close to the support almost the entire shear is carried by the upper and lower halves of the beam. The result is that with a concentrated or moving load the maximum end shear is not attained except when the load is at a distance of usually three or four times the depth of the beam from the support, and at this point, approximately one-fifth still is carried by the upper and lower halves of the beam—"two-beam shear action" it is called by the Laboratory.

C. For design formulas, see par. 400-D herein.

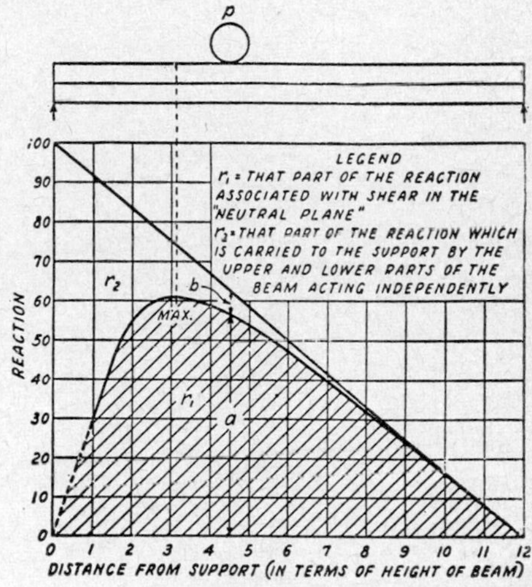

NDS Fig. E.1

A graphical representation of the total, single-beam, and two-beam reaction for a beam with a span-height ratio of 12. For a single concentrated load the ordinates to the straight line represent the total reaction; *a*, the ordinate in the cross-hatched portion, is the single-beam reaction, associated with shear in the neutral plane. The two-beam reaction is represented by *b*, that part of the ordinate in the unshaded area. Placing the load at 3.1 times the height of the beam from the support gives the maximum single-beam reaction and is the point at which to place the load for greatest likelihood of failure by shear. For a uniform load over the entire span, the area under the straight line represents the total reaction, the cross-hatched area, the single-beam reaction, and the unshaded area that portion of the reaction which is carried to the support by two-beam action and is not associated with shear in the neutral plane.

NDS Appendix F

Recommended Construction Practices

A. CARE OF MATERIAL

1. Lumber shall be so handled and covered as to prevent marring, and moisture absorption from snow or rain.

B. FOUNDATIONS

1. Foundations shall be adequate to support the building or structure and any required loads, without excessive or unequal settlement or uplift.

2. For permanent structures it is desirable:

(a) That foundations or piers be of concrete, masonry, wood with an approved preservative treatment, or the heartwood of a durable species;

(b) That where conditions within the crawl space are conducive to excessive moisture in the construction:

(1) The space under the floors of buildings without basements or cellars be ventilated through foundation walls, providing cross ventilation where practicable, by openings for a net area of not less than 2 sq ft for each 100 lin ft of exterior wall plus $^1/_3$ sq ft for each 100 sq ft of crawl space area, or

(2) As an alternative, that the soil be covered by asphalt-saturated and coated roll roofing weighing at least 55 lb for a roll of 108 sq ft, or by a material of equal vapor-barrier efficiency, and vents be provided which have an area equal to $^1/_{10}$ of that specified in par. B-2-(b)-(1) above.

(c) That a ventilating space of at least ½ in., preferably more, be provided on sides, tops, and ends of wood members such as girders, beams, or other structural members where surrounded by masonry, or concrete;

(d) That basement and exterior posts of materials other than provided in par. B-2-(a) be placed on concrete, masonry or cast-iron base blocks or piers extending at least 2 in. above floor levels or 6 in. above the finished ground level.

(e) That, wherever there is need to take precautions against entry of termites from the ground into the structure, all debris, whether above or below the ground, shall be removed from around foundations and under the structure, and one or more of the following construction practices shall be followed:

(1) Extend foundations at least 12 in. and preferably 18 in. above ground under the building and provide a solid reinforced cement mortar cap 2 in. thick over foundations of unit or hollow block construction. If foundations can be readily inspected for termite shelter tubes, the exterior grade line may be a minimum of 6 in. from the sills or siding.

(2) Place metal termite shields of an approved design at the upper edges of all unit or block foundation walls and piers, and, if not on top, in the sides of all monolithic foundation walls and piers, and around all pipes entering buildings, except that the overhanging portion of the shield may be omitted on exterior surfaces and basement or cellar interiors, which are open to easy occasional inspection. Foundations not easily inspected shall have termite shields set at least 12 in. and preferably 18 in. above the ground.

(3) Where structural lumber is in contact with the soil, or is less than 12 in. from the ground and not protected by termite shields, except for the exterior 6-in. minimum clearance as noted in recommendation in par. B-2-(e)-(1), it shall be impregnated with an approved preservative or be the heartwood of a termite resistant species.

(4) Insulate outside steps from the soil by

masonry foundations; also insulate steps from buildings or porches by metal shields.

C. STRUCTURAL DESIGN

1. Consideration shall be given in design to the possible effect of cross-grain dimensional changes which may occur in lumber fabricated or erected in a green condition, i.e., provisions shall be made in the design so that if dimensional changes caused by seasoning to moisture equilibrium occur, the structure will move as a whole, and the differential movement of similar parts and members meeting at joints will be a minimum.

2. When lumber is fabricated green and used in a dry location, application of end sealers to exposed end grain of material while wet is recommended. (See ref. 42 and 72, NDS Appendix R.)

D. DRAINAGE

1. In exterior structures the design shall be such as to minimize pockets in which moisture can accumulate, or adequate caps, drainage, and drips shall be provided. (See ref. 72, NDS Appendix R.)

E. CAMBER

1. Adequate camber in trusses to give proper appearance and to counteract any deflection from loading should be provided and for connector construction may be estimated from the formula:

$$\Delta = K_1 \frac{L^3}{H} + K_2 \frac{L^2}{H}$$

in which:

$\triangle$ = recommended camber in inches at center of truss
L = span of truss in feet
H = height of truss in feet at center
K_1 = 0.000032 for any type of truss
K_2 = 0.0028 for flat and pitched trusses, or 0.00063 for bowstring trusses, i.e., trusses without splices in upper chord

(See ref. 72, NDS Appendix R.)

F. ERECTION

1. Provision shall be made to prevent the overstressing of members or joints during erection.

2. Bolted connections shall be snugged-up but not to the extent of crushing wood under washers. (See ref. 72, NDS Appendix R.)

G. INSPECTION

1. Provisions shall be made for competent inspection of materials and workmanship. (See ref. 72, NDS Appendix R.)

H. MAINTENANCE

1. There shall be competent inspection and tightening of bolts (see par. F.2) in joints of trusses and structural frames. (See ref. 72, NDS Appendix R.)

I. WOOD COLUMN BRACING

1. In buildings, for forces acting in a direction parallel to the truss or beam, column bracing may be provided by knee braces or, in the case of trusses, by extending the column to the top chord of the truss where the bottom and top chords are separated sufficiently to provide adequate bracing action. In a direction perpendicular to the truss or beam, bracing may be provided by wall construction, knee braces, or bracing between columns. Such bracing between columns should be installed preferably in the same bays as the bracing between trusses. (See par. 407.)

J. TRUSS BRACING

In buildings, truss bracing to resist lateral forces may be provided as follows:

1. Diagonal lateral bracing between top chords of trusses may be omitted when the provisions of par. 400-F-4 are followed or when the roof joists rest on and are securely fastened to the top chords of the trusses and are covered with wood sheathing.

Where sheathing other than wood is applied, top-chord diagonal lateral bracing should be installed.

2. In all cases, vertical sway bracing

should be installed in each third or fourth bay at intervals not greater than 35 ft measured parallel to trusses.

Also, bottom chord lateral bracing should be installed in the same bays where practical as the vertical sway bracing and extend from side wall to side wall.

In addition, struts should be installed between bottom chords at the same truss panels as vertical sway bracing and should extend continuously from end wall to end wall. If the roof construction does not provide proper top-chord strut action, separate additional members should be provided.

NDS Appendix G

Specific Gravity (G), G^2, $G^{3/2}$, and $G^{5/2}$ of Commercially Important Species of Wood Based on Oven-Dry Weight and Oven-Dry Volume

Species of wood	Specific Gravity (G)	G^2	$G^{3/2}$	$G^{5/2}$	Species of wood	Specific Gravity (G)	G^2	$G^{3/2}$	$G^{5/2}$
Alder, red	0.43	0.1849	0.283	0.122	Hackberry	0.56	0.3136	0.419	0.235
Ash, black	.53	.2809	.386	.205	Hemlock, eastern	.43	.1849	.283	.122
Ash, Oregon	.58	.3364	.443	.256	Hemlock, west coast	.44	.1936	.292	.128
Ash, white	.64	.4096	.512	.327	Hickory	.80	.6400	.716	.572
Aspen	.41	.1681	.262	.108	Larch, western	.59	.3481	.453	.267
Basswood	.40	.1600	.252	.101	Locust, black	.71	.5041	.598	.425
Beech	.67	.4489	.548	.367	Locust, honey	.67	.4489	.548	.367
Birch, paper	.60	.3600	.465	.279	Madrone	.69	.4761	.573	.395
Birch, sweet	.71	.5041	.598	.425	Magnolia, cucumber	.52	.2704	.375	.196
Birch, yellow	.66	.4356	.536	.354	Magnolia, evergreen	.53	.2809	.386	.205
Buckeye, yellow	.38	.1444	.234	.089	Maple, big leaf	.51	.2601	.364	.186
Butternut	.40	.1600	.252	.101	Maple, hard (black)	.62	.3844	.488	.302
Cedar, Alaska	.46	.2116	.312	.144	Maple, hard (sugar)	.68	.4624	.561	.381
Cedar, eastern red	.49	.2401	.343	.168	Maple, soft (red)	.55	.3025	.409	.225
Cedar, incense	.37	.1369	.225	.084	Maple, soft (silver)	.51	.2601	.364	.186
Cedar, northern white	.32	.1024	.181	.058	Oak, commercial red	.66	.4356	.536	.354
Cedar, Port Orford	.44	.1936	.292	.128	Oak, commercial white	.71	.5041	.598	.425
Cedar, southern white	.35	.1225	.207	.073	Pecan	.69	.4761	.573	.395
Cedar, western red	.34	.1156	.198	.067	Pine, lodgepole	.43	.1849	.283	.122
Cherry, black	.53	.2809	.386	.205	Pine, northern white	.37	.1369	.225	.084
Chestnut	.45	.2025	.302	.136	Pine, Norway	.47	.2209	.322	.151
Cottonwood, black	.37	.1369	.225	.084	Pine, ponderosa	.42	.1764	.272	.114
Cottonwood, eastern	.43	.1849	.238	.122	Pine, southern	.59	.3481	.453	.267
Cypress, southern	.48	.2304	.333	.160	Pine, southern longleaf	.64	.4096	.512	.327
Douglas, fir	.51	.2601	.364	.186	Pine, sugar	.38	.1444	.234	.089
Douglas fir, dense	.54	.2916	.397	.214	Pine, western white	.42	.1764	.272	.114
Douglas fir, Rocky Mountain	.45	.2025	.292	.136	Poplar, yellow	.43	.1849	.283	.122
Elm, American	.55	.3025	.409	.225	Redwood	.42	.1764	.272	.114
Elm, rock	.66	.4356	.536	.354	Spruce, Engelmann	.36	.1296	.216	.078
Elm, slippery	.57	.3249	.431	.245	Spruce, red	.41	.1681	.262	.108
Fir, balsam	.41	.1681	.262	.108	Spruce, sitka	.42	.1764	.272	.114
Fir, commercial white	.42	.1764	.272	.114	Spruce, white	.45	.2025	.302	.136
Gum, black	.55	.3025	.409	.225	Sugarberry	.54	.2916	.397	.214
Gum, red	.53	.2809	.386	.205	Sycamore	.54	.2916	.397	.214
Gum, tupelo	.52	.2704	.375	.196	Tamarack	.56	.3136	.419	.235
					Walnut, black	.56	.3136	.419	.235
					Willow, black	.42	.1764	.272	.114

NDS Appendix H

Various Durations of Loading and Allowable Stresses Therefor

A. ADJUSTMENT OF ALLOWABLE STRESSES FOR DURATION OF LOADING

1. Normal duration of loading:

(a) The allowable unit stresses listed in NDS Tables 1 and 20 and obtained from NDS Table 21 and the various commercial grading rules for stress grades of lumber are for normal duration of loading. (See par. 201, 900-B, and 900-D.) *Normal load* duration contemplates fully stressing a member to the allowable stress by the application of the full maximum normal design load for a duration of approximately ten years (either continuously or cumulatively) and/or the application of 90 per cent of this full maximum normal load continuously throughout the remainder of the life of the structure, without encroaching on the factor of safety.

2. Adjustments for other durations of loading:

Since tests have shown that wood has the property of carrying substantially greater maximum loads for short durations than for long durations of loading (see NDS Fig. H.1, Load-duration stress relationship chart), the allowable unit stresses for normal loading are adjusted as follows for other durations of loads:

(a) When the member is fully stressed to the allowable stress by application of the full maximum load permanently or for many years, either continuously or cumulatively, use 90 per cent of the allowable stress (these adjustments apply to modulus of elasticity when used to determine allowable unit loads for columns, otherwise they do not apply thereto) given for normal loading conditions. (See par. 204 and 900-B and NDS Tables 1, 20, and 21.)

(b) Likewise, when the duration of the full maximum load does not exceed the following durations, adjust the allowable unit stresses (these adjustments apply to modulus of elasticity when used to determine allowable unit loads for columns, otherwise they do not apply thereto) for normal loading durations (see par. 203 and 900-B and NDS Tables 1, 20, and 21) to a new stress level by increasing them by:

15 per cent for two months' duration, as for snow
25 per cent for seven days' duration
$33^1/_3$ per cent for wind or earthquake
100 per cent for impact

Allowable unit stresses for normal loading conditions may be used without regard for impact if the stress induced by impact does not exceed the allowable unit stress for normal loading. (The allowable percentage increase for wheel loading on structures such as bridges is under current study. This impact provision contemplates only occasional impact loadings such as in buildings.)

(c) When adjustments for other durations of loading are applied to the allowable unit stresses for full load permanently applied (90 per cent of the allowable stresses in NDS Tables 1 and 20 and obtained from NDS Table 21. See par. 204 and 900-B), the preceding percentage increases for shorter durations of maximum loading become 10 per cent for ten years' duration as for normal loading, 30 per cent for two months' duration as for snow, 40 per cent for seven days' duration, and 50 per cent for wind and earthquake.

B. COMBINATIONS OF LOADS OF DIFFERENT DURATIONS

1. The preceding adjustments are not cumulative in the sense that the required

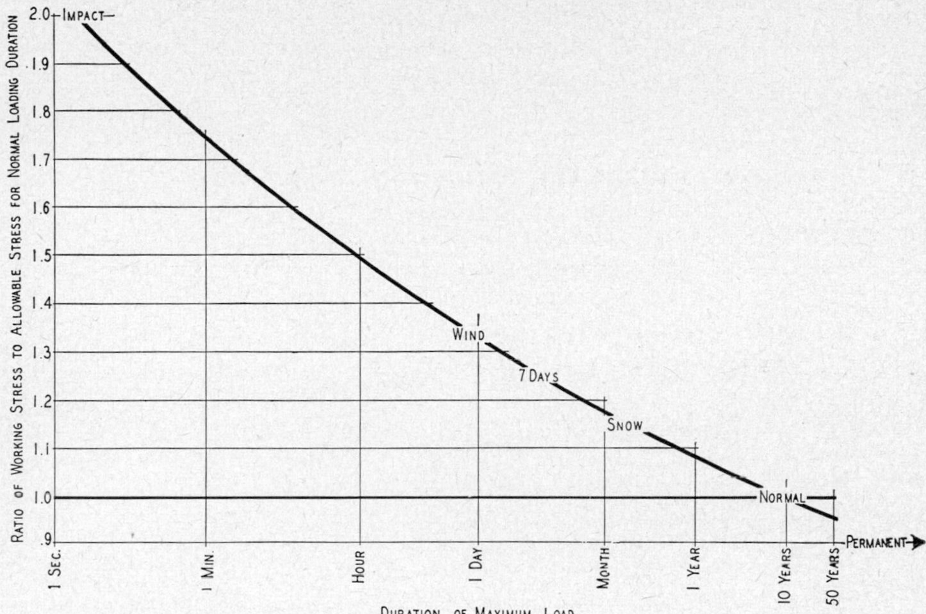

NDS Fig. H.1 Adjustment of working stresses for various durations of load

Derived from Forest Products Laboratory report No. R 1916.

size of a member can be determined for a load of particular duration without consideration of the total load resulting from that load together with the other loads of longer durations when applied simultaneously. (See par. 203 and 900-B.) In cases of a combination of loads of different durations applied simultaneously, the size of member is determined for the total of all loads applied simultaneously and the adjusted allowable stress level for that load which has the shortest duration in the combination of loads. In like manner, totally neglecting this load of shortest duration, the size of member required to support the total of the remaining loads at the allowable stress level for the load having the next shortest duration should be checked to insure that loads of longer duration do not control the size of member required. This should be repeated for remaining applied combinations of loads or single load of longer duration. However, when the permanently applied load equals or is less than 90 per cent of the total normal load (including permanently applied load), the permanent load need not be checked, because then the normal loading condition will control the size of member required. Actually, the controlling calculation is normally detected by inspection of the relative size of applied loads and the percentage stress adjustments for the various durations of loading.

C. MECHANICAL FASTENINGS

1. These percentage adjustments for duration of load apply to allowable loads for mechanical fastenings when the wood (i.e., not the strength of the metal fastening) determines the load capacity. (See par. 203, 204, and 900-C).

NDS Appendix I

Dimensions of Standard Lag Bolts or Lag Screws for Wood—Cut Thread, Gimlet, and Cone Point

[All dimensions in inches]

D = Nominal diameter.
$D_S = D$ = Diameter of shank.
D_R = Diameter at root of thread.
W = Width of bolt head across flats.
H = Height of bolt head.
L = Nominal length of bolt.
S = Length of shank.
T = Length of thread.
E = Length of tapered tip
N = Number of threads per inch.

Nominal length of bolt (L) in inches*	Item	Dimensions of lag bolt with nominal diameter (D) of— 3/16	1/4	5/16	3/8	7/16	1/2	9/16	5/8	3/4	7/8	1	1 1/8	1 1/4
All lengths	$D_S = D$	0.190	0.250	0.3125	0.375	0.4375	0.500	0.5625	0.625	0.750	0.875	1.000	1.125	1.250
	D_R	.120	.173	.227	.265	.328	.371	.435	.471	.579	.683	.780	.887	1.012
	E	5/32	3/16	1/4	1/4	9/32	5/16	3/8	3/8	7/16	1/2	9/16	5/8	3/4
	H	9/64	11/64	13/64	1/4	19/64	21/64	3/8	27/64	1/2	19/32	21/32	3/4	27/32
	W	9/32	3/8	1/2	9/16	5/8	3/4	7/8	15/16	1 1/8	1 5/16	1 1/2	1 11/16	1 7/8
	N	11	10	9	7	7	6	6	5	4 1/2	4	3 1/2	3 1/4	3 1/4
	D^2	.0361	.0625	.0975	.1406	.2256	.2500	.3164	.3906	.5625	.7656	1.0000	1.2660	1.5625
	$D^{3/4}$	.298	.354	.418	.479	.572	.594	.649	.703	.806	.905	1.000	1.103	1.184
1	S	1/4	1/4	1/4	1/4	1/4	1/4							
	T	3/4	3/4	3/4	3/4	3/4	3/4							
	$T-E$	19/32	9/16	1/2	1/2	15/32	7/16							
1 1/2	S	3/8	3/8	3/8	3/8	3/8	3/8							
	T	1 1/8	1 1/8	1 1/8	1 1/8	1 1/8	1 1/8							
	$T-E$	31/32	15/16	7/8	7/8	27/32	13/16							
2	S	1/2	1/2	1/2	1/2	1/2	1/2	1/2	1/2					
	T	1 1/2	1 1/2	1 1/2	1 1/2	1 1/2	1 1/2	1 1/2	1 1/2					
	$T-E$	1 11/32	1 5/16	1 1/4	1 1/4	1 7/32	1 3/16	1 1/8	1 1/8					
2 1/2	S	1	1	7/8	7/8	3/4	3/4	3/4	3/4					
	T	1 1/2	1 1/2	1 5/8	1 5/8	1 3/4	1 3/4	1 3/4	1 3/4					
	$T-E$	1 11/16	1 5/16	1 3/8	1 3/8	1 15/32	1 7/16	1 3/8	1 3/8					
3	S	1	1	1	1	1	1	1	1	1	1	1		
	T	2	2	2	2	2	2	2	2	2	2	2		
	$T-E$	1 27/32	1 13/16	1 3/4	1 3/4	1 23/32	1 11/16	1 5/8	1 5/8	1 9/16	1 1/2	1 7/16		
4	S	1 1/2	1 1/2	1 1/2	1 1/2	1 1/2	1 1/2	1 1/2	1 1/2	1 1/2	1 1/2	1 1/2	1 1/2	1 1/2
	T	2 1/2	2 1/2	2 1/2	2 1/2	2 1/2	2 1/2	2 1/2	2 1/2	2 1/2	2 1/2	2 1/2	2 1/2	2 1/2
	$T-E$	2 11/32	2 5/16	2 1/4	2 1/4	2 7/32	2 3/16	2 1/8	2 1/8	2 1/16	2	1 15/16	1 7/8	1 3/4
5	S	2	2	2	2	2	2	2	2	2	2	2	2	2
	T	3	3	3	3	3	3	3	3	3	3	3	3	3
	$T-E$	2 27/32	2 13/16	2 3/4	2 3/4	2 23/32	2 11/16	2 5/8	2 5/8	2 9/16	2 1/2	2 7/16	2 3/8	2 1/4

NDS Appendix I (Cont.)

Nominal length of bolt (L) in inches*	Item	Dimensions of lag bolt with nominal diameter (D) of— 3/16	1/4	5/16	3/8	7/16	1/2	9/16	5/8	3/4	7/8	1	1 1/8	1 1/4
All lengths	$D_S = D$	0.190	0.250	0.3125	0.375	0.4375	0.500	0.5625	0.625	0.750	0.875	1.000	1.125	1.250
	D_R	.120	.173	.227	.265	.328	.371	.435	.471	.579	.683	.780	.887	1.012
	E	5/32	3/16	1/4	1/4	9/32	5/16	3/8	3/8	7/16	1/2	9/16	5/8	3/4
	H	9/64	11/64	13/64	1/4	19/64	21/64	3/8	27/64	1/2	19/32	21/32	3/4	27/32
	W	9/32	3/8	1/2	9/16	5/8	3/4	7/8	15/16	1 1/8	1 5/16	1 1/2	1 11/16	1 7/8
	N	11	10	9	7	7	6	6	5	4 1/2	4	3 1/2	3 1/4	3 1/4
	D^2	.0361	.0625	.0975	.1406	.2256	.2500	.3164	.3906	.5625	.7656	1.0000	1.2660	1.5625
	$D^{3/4}$	.298	.354	.418	.479	.572	.594	.649	.703	.806	.905	1.000	1.103	1.184
6	S	2 1/2	2 1/2	2 1/2	2 1/2	2 1/2	2 1/2	2 1/2	2 1/2	2 1/2	2 1/2	2 1/2	2 1/2	2 1/2
	T	3 1/2	3 1/2	3 1/2	3 1/2	3 1/2	3 1/2	3 1/2	3 1/2	3 1/2	3 1/2	3 1/2	3 1/2	3 1/2
	$T-E$	3 11/32	3 5/16	3 1/4	3 1/4	3 7/32	3 3/16	3 1/8	3 1/8	3 1/16	3	2 15/16	2 7/8	2 3/4
7	S	3	3	3	3	3	3	3	3	3	3	3	3	3
	T	4	4	4	4	4	4	4	4	4	4	4	4	4
	$T-E$	3 27/32	3 13/16	3 3/4	3 3/4	3 23/32	3 11/16	3 5/8	3 5/8	3 9/16	3 1/2	3 7/16	3 3/8	3 1/4
8	S	3 1/2	3 1/2	3 1/2	3 1/2	3 1/2	3 1/2	3 1/2	3 1/2	3 1/2	3 1/2	3 1/2	3 1/2	3 1/2
	T	4 1/2	4 1/2	4 1/2	4 1/2	4 1/2	4 1/2	4 1/2	4 1/2	4 1/2	4 1/2	4 1/2	4 1/2	4 1/2
	$T-E$	4 11/16	4 5/16	4 1/4	4 1/4	4 7/32	4 3/16	4 1/8	4 1/8	4 1/16	4	3 15/16	3 7/8	3 3/4
9	S	4	4	4	4	4	4	4	4	4	4	4	4	4
	T	5	5	5	5	5	5	5	5	5	5	5	5	5
	$T-E$	4 27/32	4 13/16	4 3/4	4 3/4	4 23/32	4 11/16	4 5/8	4 5/8	4 9/16	4 1/2	4 7/16	4 3/8	4 1/4
10	S	4 3/4	4 3/4	4 3/4	4 3/4	4 3/4	4 3/4	4 3/4	4 3/4	4 3/4	4 3/4	4 3/4	4 3/4	4 3/4
	T	5 1/4	5 1/4	5 1/4	5 1/4	5 1/4	5 1/4	5 1/4	5 1/4	5 1/4	5 1/4	5 1/4	5 1/4	5 1/4
	$T-E$	5 3/32	5 1/16	5	5	4 31/32	4 15/16	4 7/8	4 7/8	4 13/16	4 3/4	4 11/16	4 5/8	4 1/2
11	S	5 1/2	5 1/2	5 1/2	5 1/2	5 1/2	5 1/2	5 1/2	5 1/2	5 1/2	5 1/2	5 1/2	5 1/2	5 1/2
	T	5 1/2	5 1/2	5 1/2	5 1/2	5 1/2	5 1/2	5 1/2	5 1/2	5 1/2	5 1/2	5 1/2	5 1/2	5 1/2
	$T-E$	5 11/32	5 9/32	5 1/4	5 1/4	5 7/32	5 3/16	5 1/8	5 1/8	5 1/16	5	4 15/16	4 7/8	4 3/4
12	S	6	6	6	6	6	6	6	6	6	6	6	6	6
	T	6	6	6	6	6	6	6	6	6	6	6	6	6
	$T-E$	5 27/32	5 13/16	5 3/4	5 3/4	5 23/32	5 11/16	5 5/8	5 5/8	5 9/16	5 1/2	5 7/16	5 3/8	5 1/4

*Length of thread (T) on intervening bolt lengths is the same as that of the next shorter bolt length listed. The length of thread (T) on standard bolt lengths (L) in excess of 12 inches is equal to 1/2 the bolt length (L/2).

NDS Appendix J

Common Nails and Spikes, Allowable Withdrawal Loads, Normal Duration

(Inserted perpendicular to grain in wood. Key: d = pennyweight; l = length, in inches; D = diameter, in inches.)

Allowable load in **WITHDRAWAL,** in pounds per inch of penetration ($p = 1380G^{5/2}D$) of nail or spike into the member receiving the point. (See Part VIII)

When specific gravity (G) (see Appendix G) of wood is		SIZE OF NAIL											SIZE OF SPIKE									
	d=	6	8	10	12	16	20	30	40	50	60	d=	10	12	16	20	30	40	50	60	5/16"	3/8"
	l=	2	2½	3	3¼	3½	4	4½	5	5½	6	l=	3	3¼	3½	4	4½	5	5½	6	7	8–12
	D=	0.113	0.131	0.148	0.148	0.162	0.192	0.207	0.225	0.244	0.263	D=	0.192	0.192	0.207	0.225	0.244	0.263	0.283	0.283	0.312	0.375
0.31	p=	8	10	11	11	12	14	15	16	18	19	p=	14	14	15	16	18	19	21	21	23	27
.32		9	10	12	12	13	15	16	18	20	21		15	15	16	18	20	21	23	23	25	30
.33		10	11	13	13	14	17	18	20	21	23		17	17	18	20	21	23	25	25	27	33
.34		10	12	14	14	15	18	19	21	23	24		18	18	19	21	23	24	26	26	29	35
.35		11	13	15	15	16	19	21	23	25	26		19	19	21	23	25	26	28	28	31	38
.36		12	14	16	16	17	21	22	24	26	28		21	21	22	24	26	28	30	30	34	40
.37		13	15	17	17	19	22	24	26	28	30		22	22	24	26	28	30	33	33	36	43
.38		14	16	18	18	20	24	25	28	30	32		24	24	25	28	30	32	35	35	38	46
.39		15	17	19	19	21	25	27	30	32	34		25	25	27	30	32	34	37	37	41	49
.40		16	18	21	21	23	27	29	31	34	37		27	27	29	31	34	37	39	39	43	52
.41		17	20	22	22	24	29	31	33	36	39		29	29	31	33	36	39	42	42	46	56
.42		18	21	23	23	25	30	33	35	38	41		30	30	33	35	38	41	45	45	49	59
.43		19	22	25	25	27	32	35	38	41	44		32	32	35	38	41	44	48	48	52	63
.44		20	23	26	26	29	34	37	40	43	46		34	34	37	40	43	47	50	50	55	66
.45		21	25	28	28	30	36	39	42	46	49		36	36	39	42	46	49	53	53	59	70
.46		22	26	29	29	32	38	41	45	48	52		38	38	41	45	48	52	56	56	62	74
.47		24	27	31	31	34	40	43	47	51	55		40	40	43	47	51	55	59	59	65	78
.48		25	29	33	33	36	42	46	50	54	58		42	42	46	50	54	58	62	62	69	83
.49		26	30	34	34	38	45	48	52	57	61		45	45	48	52	57	61	66	66	72	87
.50		28	32	36	36	40	47	51	55	60	64		47	47	51	55	60	64	69	69	76	92
.51		29	34	38	38	42	49	53	58	63	68		49	49	53	58	63	68	73	73	80	96
.52		31	35	40	40	44	52	56	61	66	71		52	52	56	61	66	71	77	77	84	101
.53		32	37	42	42	46	54	59	64	69	74		54	54	59	64	69	74	80	80	88	106
.54		33	39	44	44	48	57	61	67	72	78		57	57	61	67	72	78	84	84	92	111
.55		35	41	46	46	50	60	64	70	76	82		60	60	64	70	76	82	88	88	97	116
.56		37	43	48	48	53	62	67	73	79	85		62	62	67	73	79	85	92	92	101	122
.57		38	44	50	50	55	65	70	76	82	89		65	65	70	76	82	89	96	96	105	127
.58		40	46	52	52	57	68	73	79	86	93		68	68	73	79	86	93	100	100	110	132
.59		42	48	55	55	60	71	76	83	90	97		71	71	76	83	90	97	104	104	115	138
.60		44	50	57	57	62	74	80	87	94	101		74	74	80	87	94	101	109	109	120	144

NDS Appendix K

Wood Screws, Allowable Withdrawal Loads, Normal Duration

(Inserted perpendicular to grain in wood. Key: g = gauge of screw; D = diameter of screw, in inches)

Allowable load in **WITHDRAWAL**, in pounds per inch of penetration ($p = 2850G^2D$) of threaded portion of screw into the member receiving the point (see Part VIII)

When specific gravity (G) (See Appendix G) of wood is	Size of Screw											
	g =	6	7	8	9	10	12	14	16	18	20	24
	D =	0.138	0.151	0.164	0.177	0.190	0.216	0.242	0.268	0.294	0.320	0.372
.31	p =	38	41	45	48	52	59	66	74	81	88	102
.32		40	44	48	52	55	63	71	78	86	93	108
.33		43	47	51	55	59	67	75	83	91	99	115
.34		46	50	54	58	63	71	80	88	97	105	123
.35		48	53	57	62	66	75	84	93	103	112	130
.36		51	56	60	65	70	80	89	99	109	118	137
.37		54	59	64	69	74	84	94	104	115	125	145
.38		57	62	67	73	78	89	99	110	121	132	153
.39		60	66	71	77	82	94	105	116	127	139	161
.40		63	69	75	81	87	98	110	122	134	146	170
.41		66	72	79	85	91	103	116	128	141	153	178
.42		69	76	82	89	95	109	121	135	148	161	187
.43		73	80	86	93	100	114	127	141	155	169	196
.44		76	83	91	97	105	119	133	148	162	177	205
.45		80	87	95	102	110	125	140	155	170	185	215
.46		83	91	99	107	115	130	146	162	177	193	224
.47		87	95	103	111	120	136	152	169	185	201	234
.48		91	99	108	116	125	142	159	176	193	210	244
.49		94	103	112	121	130	148	166	184	201	219	254
.50		98	108	117	126	135	154	172	191	209	228	265
.51		102	112	121	131	141	160	179	199	218	237	276
.52		106	116	126	136	146	166	186	207	226	246	287
.53		111	121	131	142	152	173	194	215	235	256	298
.54		115	125	136	147	158	180	201	223	244	266	309
.55		119	130	141	152	164	186	209	231	253	276	321
.56		123	135	146	158	170	193	216	239	263	286	332
.57		128	140	152	164	176	200	224	248	272	296	344
.58		132	145	157	170	182	207	232	257	282	307	357
.59		137	150	163	176	189	214	240	266	292	317	369
.60		142	155	168	182	195	222	249	275	302	328	381

When specific gravity (G) (see Appendix G) of wood is	SIZE OF NAIL											SIZE OF SPIKE										
	$d=$	6	8	10	12	16	20	30	40	50	60	$d=$	10	12	16	20	30	40	50	60	5/16"	3/8"
	$l=$	2	2½	3	3¼	3½	4	4½	5	5½	6	$l=$	3	3¼	3½	4	4½	5	5½	6	7	8–12
	$D=$	0.113	0.131	0.148	0.148	0.162	0.192	0.207	0.225	0.244	0.263	$D=$	0.192	0.192	0.207	0.225	0.244	0.263	0.283	0.283	0.312	0.375
.61		45	53	59	59	65	77	83	90	98	106		77	77	83	90	98	106	114	114	125	150
.62		47	55	62	62	68	80	86	94	102	110		80	80	86	94	102	110	118	118	130	156
.63		49	57	65	65	71	84	90	98	106	115		84	84	90	98	106	115	123	123	136	163
.64		51	59	67	67	73	87	93	102	110	119		87	87	93	102	110	119	128	128	141	169
.65		53	62	70	70	76	91	97	106	115	124		91	91	97	106	115	124	134	134	147	177
.66		55	64	72	72	79	94	101	110	119	128		94	94	101	110	119	128	138	138	152	183
.67		57	66	75	75	82	97	105	114	124	133		97	97	105	114	124	133	143	143	158	190
.68		60	69	78	78	85	101	109	119	128	138		101	101	109	119	128	138	149	149	164	198
.69		62	71	81	81	88	105	113	123	133	143		105	105	113	123	133	143	154	154	170	204
.70		64	74	84	84	92	109	117	128	138	149		109	109	117	128	138	149	160	160	177	213
.75		76	88	99	99	109	129	139	151	164	177		129	129	139	151	164	177	190	190	210	252
.80		89	103	117	117	128	152	163	178	193	208		152	152	163	178	193	208	223	223	246	296

Common Nails and Spikes, Allowable Lateral Loads, Normal Duration

Allowable lateral loads (**SHEAR**) in pounds (p) for nails and spikes penetrating for 2/3 their length in softwoods and 1/2 their length in hardwoods into the member receiving their points. (See Part VIII.)

For woods to which following formulas apply (see Table 17)	SIZE OF NAIL											SIZE OF SPIKE										
	$d=$	6	8	10	12	16	20	30	40	50	60	$d=$	10	12	16	20	30	40	50	60	5/16"	3/8"
	$l=$	2	2½	3	3¼	3½	4	4½	5	5½	6	$l=$	3	3¼	3½	4	4½	5	5½	6	7	8–12
	$D=$	0.113	0.131	0.148	0.148	0.162	0.192	0.207	0.225	0.244	0.263	$D=$	0.192	0.192	0.207	0.225	0.244	0.263	0.283	0.283	0.312	0.375
	$D^{3/2}=$	0.038	0.0475	0.057	0.057	0.065	0.084	0.094	0.107	0.122	0.135	$D^{3/2}=$	0.084	0.084	0.094	0.107	0.122	0.135	0.150	0.150	0.175	0.230
$p=1080D^{3/2}$		41	51	62	62	70	91	101	116	132	146		91	91	101	116	132	146	162	162	189	248
$p=1350D^{3/2}$		51	64	77	77	88	113	126	144	165	182		113	113	126	144	165	182	202	202	236	310
$p=1500D^{3/2}$		57	71	85	85	97	126	140	160	183	202		126	126	140	160	183	202	225	225	262	345
$p=1650D^{3/2}$		63	78	94	94	107	139	154	176	202	223		139	139	155	176	202	223	248	248	289	380
$p=2040D^{3/2}$		78	97	116	116	132	171	191	218	249	276		171	171	191	218	249	276	306	306	357	469

NDS Appendix K (Cont.)

When specific gravity (G) (See Appendix G) of wood is	Size of Screw											
	$g =$	6	7	8	9	10	12	14	16	18	20	24
	$D =$	0.138	0.151	0.164	0.177	0.190	0.216	0.242	0.268	0.294	0.320	0.372
.61		146	160	174	188	201	229	257	284	312	340	394
.62		151	166	180	194	208	237	265	294	322	351	407
.63		156	171	186	200	215	244	274	303	333	362	420
.64		161	176	192	207	222	252	282	312	343	374	434
.65		166	182	198	214	229	260	291	323	354	385	447
.66		171	188	204	220	236	268	300	333	365	397	461
.67		177	193	210	227	243	276	310	343	376	410	476
.68		182	199	216	233	251	285	319	353	387	422	490
.69		187	205	223	240	258	293	328	363	399	434	505
.70		193	211	229	247	265	301	338	374	411	447	520
.75		221	242	263	284	305	346	388	430	471	513	596
.80		252	275	299	323	347	394	441	489	536	584	679

Approximately two-thirds of the length of a standard wood screw is threaded.

Wood Screws, Allowable Lateral Loads, Normal Duration

Allowable lateral loads (**SHEAR**) in pounds (p) for screws embedded to approximately 7 times the shank diameter into the member receiving the point. For less penetration reduce loads in proportion. Penetration should not be less than 4 times the shank diameter. (See Part VIII.)

For woods to which following formulas apply (see Table 19)	Size of Screw											
	$g =$	6	7	8	9	10	12	14	16	18	20	24
	$D =$	0.138	0.151	0.164	0.177	0.190	0.216	0.242	0.268	0.294	0.320	0.372
	$7D =$	.966	1.057	1.148	1.239	1.330	1.512	1.694	1.876	2.058	2.240	2.604
	$4D =$	.552	.604	.656	.708	.760	.864	.968	1.072	1.176	1.280	1.488
	$D^2 =$	.0190	.0228	.0269	.0313	.0361	.0467	.0586	.0718	.0864	.1024	.1384
$p = 4800D^2$	=	91	109	129	150	173	224	281	345	415	492	664
$p = 3960D^2$	=	75	90	106	124	143	185	232	284	342	406	548
$p = 3480D^2$	=	66	79	94	109	126	162	204	250	301	356	482
$p = 3240D^2$	=	62	74	87	101	117	151	190	233	280	332	448
$p = 2520D^2$	=	48	58	68	79	91	118	148	181	218	258	349

NDS Appendix R

References

1. "American Lumber Standards for Softwood Lumber—Simplified Practice Recommendation R16–53," by Bureau of Standards, U. S. Department of Commerce[1] (1953).

2. "Wood Handbook—Basic Information on Wood as a Material of Construction with Data for Its Use in Design and Specifications," by Forest Products Laboratory, U. S. Department of Agriculture[1] (1955).

3. "Miscellaneous Publication No. 185, Guide to the Grading of Structural Timbers and Determination of Working Stresses," 1934[2] and 1940 Supplement by T. R. C. Wilson, Forest Products Laboratory, U. S. Department of Agriculture, and 1948 Supplement.

4. "Technical Bulletin No. 479, Strength and Related Properties of Woods Grown in the United States," by L. J. Markwardt and T. R. C. Wilson, Forest Products Laboratory, U. S. Department of Agriculture[1] (1935).

5. "Grading Rules for Lumber." See column 2 of NDS Table 1 in Part II.

6. "Anchorage for Factory Roofs—Principles and Design Data," by Associated Factory Mutual Fire Insurance Companies, Boston, Mass. (1940).

7. "Factory Roofs Need Anchorage—Various Studies of Wind Forces and Their Effects Upon Buildings," by Associated Factory Mutual Fire Insurance Companies, Boston, Mass. (1940).

8. "Technical Bulletin No. 597, Lag Screw Joints: Their Behavior and Design," by J. A. Newlin and J. M. Gahagan, Forest Products Laboratory, U. S. Department of Agriculture[1] (1938).

9. "Technical Bulletin No. 332, The Bearing of Wood Under Bolts," by G. W. Trayer, Forest Products Laboratory, U. S. Department of Agriculture[1] (1932).

10. "Technical Bulletin No. 691, The Glued Laminated Wooden Arch," by T. R. C. Wilson, Forest Products Laboratory, U. S. Department of Agriculture[1] (1939).

11. "Department Bulletin No. 1500, The Gluing of Wood," by T. R. Truax, Forest Products Laboratory, U. S. Department of Agriculture[1] (1929).

12. "Wood Structural Design Data, Volume I and Supplements," by National Lumber Manufacturers Association, Washington, D. C.

13. "Douglas Fir Use Book with Supplements," by West Coast Lumbermen's Association, Portland, Ore.

14. "Southern Pine Manual of Standard Wood Construction," by Southern Pine Association, New Orleans, La.

15. "Timber Concrete Composite Decks —for Bridges, Piers, Docks, Ramps, Buildings, and other Structures Requiring Heavy Duty Floors," by Service Bureau, American Wood Preservers' Association, Chicago, Ill. (1941).

16. "Highway Technical Bulletin No. 1, Loading Tests on a New Composite Type Short Span Highway Bridge Combining Concrete and Timber in Flexure," by R. H. Bladock and C. B. McCullough, Oregon State Highway Commission (1934).

17. "Designing for Strength of Flat Panels with Stressed Coverings," by J. A. Newlin, Forest Products Laboratory, Madison, Wis., Mimeograph R-1220 (1946).

18. "Formulas for Wood Columns with Side Loads and Eccentricity," by J. A. Newlin, Building Standards Monthly (Dec. 1940).

19. "Standard Specifications for Highway Bridges," by American Association of State Highway Officials, Washington, D. C.

20. "Trouble-Shooter for Joint-Gluing,"

[1] Available from Superintendent of Documents, Government Printing Office, Washington, D. C.

[2] Out of print by Superintendent of Documents, but copy available from National Lumber Manufacturers Association.

by Casein Company of America, New York, N. Y. (1942).

21. "Exposing the Termite," by National Lumber Manufacturers Association, Washington, D. C.

22. "Wood as a Structural Material," by F. J. Hanrahan, Roads and Streets (Nov. and Dec. 1940).

23. "Built-Up Wood Columns Conserve Lumber," by J. A. Scholten, Engineering News-Record (Aug. 27, 1931).

24. "Teco Design Manual for Timber Connector Construction," by Timber Engineering Company, Washington, D. C.

25. "Modern Wood Adhesives," by Thomas D. Perry, Pitman Publishing Company (1944).

26. "Approximate Methods of Calculating the Strength of Plywood," Forest Products Laboratory, Madison, Wisc., Mimeograph R-1630.

27. "Designing Truss Joints with Timber Connectors," by West Coast Lumbermen's Assn., Portland, Ore.

28. "Technical Data on Plywood," Douglas Fir Plywood Association, Tacoma, Wash.

29. "Typical Designs of Timber Structures," by Timber Engineering Company, Washington, D. C.

30. "Blue Ox Series of Typical Designs," by West Coast Lumbermen's Association, Portland, Ore.

31. "Modern Timber Engineering," by W. F. Schofield and W. H. O'Brien, Southern Pine Association, New Orleans, La.

32. "Modern Timber Highway Bridges," by Timber Engineering Company, Washington, D. C.

33. "Highway Structures of Douglas Fir," by West Coast Lumbermen's Association, Portland, Ore.

34. "Typical Highway-Bridges of Pressure-Treated Timber," by The Wood Preserving Corporation, Pittsburgh, Pa. (about 1940).

35. "Acceptable Bridge Plans and Standard Lookout Structure Plans," by Division of Engineering, Forest Service, U. S. Department of Agriculture (about 1940).

36. "Reports of Committee 7 on Wood Bridges and Trestles," American Railway Engineering Association, Chicago, Ill.

37. "Heavy Timber Construction Details," by National Lumber Manufacturers Association, Washington, D. C.

38. "Lumber Grade-Use Guide for Softwood and Hardwood Lumber in Building and General Construction," by National Lumber Manufacturers Association, Washington, D. C.

39. "Lumber Literature" (a bibliography of literature available from various lumber manufacturers associations), by National Lumber Manufacturers Association, Washington, D. C.

40. "Redwood Technical Data Series," California Redwood Association, San Francisco, Calif. (current).

41. "Experience in Maintenance of Large Timber Structures," by John J. Gould, Engineering News-Record (Aug. 15, 1940).

42. "End Seals for West Coast Lumber," by West Coast Lumbermen's Association, Portland, Ore.

43. "Fabrication of Laminated Timber Members," by Verne Ketchum, Civil Engineering (Feb. 1943).

44. "Timber Structures," by L. P. Keith, Civil Engineering (Oct. 1942).

45. "Shear in Checked Beams," by J. A. Newlin, Bulletin 364, American Railway Engineering Association (1934).

46. "Timber - Connector Joints, Their Strength and Design," by J. A. Scholten, Forest Products Laboratory, U. S. Dept. of Agriculture[1] (1944).

47. "Servicing of Wartime Timber Structures," by C. J. Hogue, Civil Engineering, Vol. 14, No. 7, p. 299 (July 1944).

48. "Are Timber Checks and Splits Serious?" by V. Ketchum, T. K. May and F. J. Hanrahan, Engineering News-Record (July 27, 1944).

48A. "Timber Maintenance Methods," by Verne Ketchum.

49. "Modern Timber Roof Trusses," by Timber Engineering Company, Washington, D. C.

50. "Airplane Hangar Construction," by National Lumber Manufacturers Association, Washington, D. C.

51. "Timber Highway Bridges in Oregon," by C. B. McCullough and G. S. Paxson, Proceedings of Twenty-Third Annual Meeting of the Highway Research Board (Nov. 1943).

52. "Results of Accelerated Tests and Long-term Exposures on Glue Joints in Laminated Beams," by Forest Products Laboratory, Madison, Wisc., Mimeograph D-1729.

53. "Laminating Lumber for Extreme Service Conditions," by C. D. Dosker and A. C. Knauss, Mechanical Engineering, (Dec. 1944).

54. "Glued-Laminated Lumber Construction," by F. J. Hanrahan, Mechanical Engineering (Dec. 1943).

55. "Wood As An Engineering Material" (Eighteenth Edgar Marburg Lecture) by L. K. Markwardt, Proceedings of the American Society for Testing Materials, Vol. 43 (1943).

56. "Classified Bibliography on the Physical and Mechanical Properties of Wood and the Design and Construction of Timber Structures" (Progress Report of the Committee of the Structural Division on Timber Structures), Proceedings of American Society of Civil Engineers, Vol. 70, No. 3, pp. 321–339 (Mar. 1944).

57. "Composite Timber-Concrete Construction," by T. K. May, AREA Proceedings, Vol. 56, pp. 642–648 (1955).

58. "Timber Engineers Handbook," by H. J. Hanson, John Wiley & Sons.

59. "Modern Timber Design," by H. J. Hanson, John Wiley & Sons.

60. "Engineering Laminates," by A. G. H. Dietz, John Wiley & Sons.

61. "Fabrication and Design of Glued-Laminated Wood Structural Members," by A. D. Freas and M. L. Selbo, Forest Products Laboratory, U. S. Department of Agriculture, Technical Bulletin No. 1069.

62. "Strength of Nailed Joints in Frame Walls," by John A. Scholten and E. G. Molander, Agriculture Engineering, Vol. 31, No. 11, pp. 551–555 (Nov. 1950).

63. "Standard Specification for Structural Glued-Laminated Southern Pine," by Southern Pine Inspection Bureau.

64. "Standard Specification for the Design and Fabrication of Structural Glued-Laminated Lumber," by West Coast Lumbermen's Association.

65. "Timber Beams Reinforced with Spiral-Drive Dowels," by G. P. Boomsliter, West Virginia University Experiment Station Bulletin No. 23.

66. "Distribution of Wheel Loads on a Timber Bridge Floor," by G. P. Boomsliter, C. H. Cather, and D. T. Worrell, West Virginia University Experiment Station Bulletin No. 24.

67. "Laminating of Structural Wood Products by Gluing," by Forest Products Laboratory, Madison, Wisc., Mimeograph D-1635.

68. "Tests of Glued-Laminated Wood Beams and Columns and Development of Principles of Design," by Forest Products Laboratory, Madison, Wisc., Mimeograph R-1687.

69. "Relation of Strength of Wood to Duration of Load," by Forest Products Laboratory, Madison, Wisc., Mimeograph R-1916.

70. "Standard Specifications for the Design and Fabrication of Hardwood Glued-Laminated Lumber for Structural, Marine and Vehicular Uses," by Southern Hardwood Producers, Inc., Memphis, Tenn.; Appalachian Hardwood Manufacturers, Inc., Cincinnati, O.; and Northern Hemlock and Hardwood Manufacturers Association, Oshkosh, Wisc.

71. "Tentative Method of Testing for Integrity of Glued Joints and Laminated Wood Products for Exterior Service," ASTM Designation D-1101, American Society for Testing Materials, Philadelphia, Pa.

72. "AITC Standards," American Institute of Timber Construction, Washington, D. C.

73. "Manual of Recommended Practices for Wood Preservation," American Wood Preservers Association.

74. "Pressure Treated Foundation Piles. Economy, Advantage," American Wood Preservers Institute, Chicago, Ill. (Price $1.00.)

DESIGN MANUAL
FOR
TECO TIMBER-CONNECTOR
CONSTRUCTION

1943 EDITION

Revised 1955

DESIGN MANUAL FOR TECO TIMBER-CONNECTOR CONSTRUCTION

Use of Data and Charts

GENERAL. This book has been arranged with two facing pages devoted to each size of each type of the major connectors. On the left-hand page are the load chart and size data as well as required increases or decreases for various conditions, and on the right-hand page are the spacing, end-distance, and edge-distance charts. One page is given to the spike grids and one page to the clamping plates. The concluding pages have information on camber, truss weights, galvanizing, and net section.

LOAD CHARTS. The load charts show the allowable normal loads for one connector unit and bolt in single shear. The connector unit consists of one split ring or toothed ring, a pair of shear plates, or a single shear plate used with a steel sideplate.

The charts are broken vertically into the three species groups. Select the group from DM Table 1 according to the species of lumber specified and use the portion of the chart applying to this group. Within each group there are several curves, each representing a thickness of lumber and the number of loaded faces. Use the curve conforming to the condition existing in the joint. Each curve is plotted according to the Hankinson Formula, with load (in pounds) and angle of load to grain as the variables. Select the proper angle at bottom or top of chart, proceed vertically to the selected curve, and then horizontally to read the allowable normal load. Lumber thicknesses less than those shown on the load data charts for the corresponding number of loaded faces are not recommended.

For more than one connector unit, multiply the connector load by the number of units.

ANGLE OF LOAD TO GRAIN. The angle of load to grain is the angle between the resultant load exerted by the connector acting on the member and the longitudinal axis of the member. (See DM Fig. 1.)

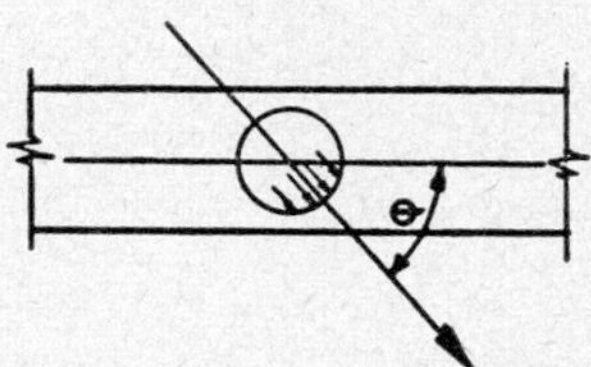

DM Fig. 1 Angle of load to grain

ANGLE OF AXIS TO GRAIN. The angle of axis to grain is the angle of connector axis formed by a line joining the centers of two adjacent connectors located in the same face of a member in a joint and the longitudinal axis of the member. (See DM Fig. 2.)

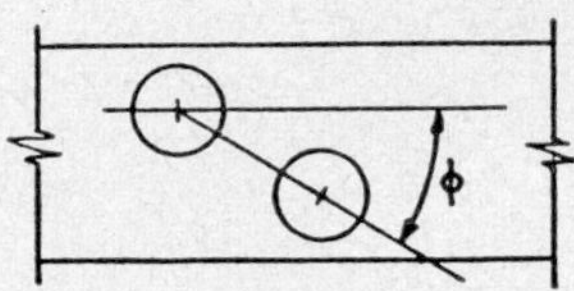

DM Fig. 2 Angle of axis to grain

CONNECTOR DATA. The data given cover dimensions of the connectors, minimum lumber sizes, recommended bolt and bolt hole diameters, recommended washer sizes, and similar self-explanatory information.

Lag screws of the same diameter as the recommended bolt sizes may be used instead of bolts in accordance with provisions set forth in the "National Design Specification for Stress-Grade Lumber and Its Fastenings." (See Chap. 13, NDS.)

CONNECTOR SPECIFICATIONS. The design data and other information in the publication are based on the use of standard TECO connectors and tools. It is recommended that the specifications be closely followed to insure the use of products for which the data were prepared.

ADJUSTMENTS FOR LOADING DURATIONS. The allowable connector loads given on the charts are for loadings of normal duration. Normal duration of loading contemplates that the joint will be fully loaded for approximately ten years, either continuously or cumulatively, by the maximum allowable normal design load shown on the charts or that 90 per cent of this load is applied throughout the remainder of the life of the structure. When the factors given with the data on each connector are applied to the load values in the charts, they give the allowable loads for other durations of loading, from those of impact character to those applied permanenttly.

Permanent loading, for which a factor of 90 per cent is given, contemplates that the connector will be fully loaded to that percentage of the normal design values on the chart either permanently or for many years.

Information on design with combinations of loads of different durations is given in the National Design Specification (see Chap. 13, NDS).

DECREASES FOR MOISTURE-CONTENT CONDITION. The expected condition of lumber when fabricated and used should be determined and the required decreases made, if necessary, in accordance with the tabulated data for each connector.

DESIGN OF ECCENTRIC JOINTS AND OF BEAMS SUPPORTED BY FASTENINGS Eccentric connector joints and beams supported by connectors shall be designed so that H in the following formula does not exceed the allowable unit stresses in horizontal shear:

$$H = \frac{V}{bh_e}$$

in which h_e (with connectors) equals the depth of the member less the distance from the unloaded edge of the member to the nearest edge of the nearest connector.

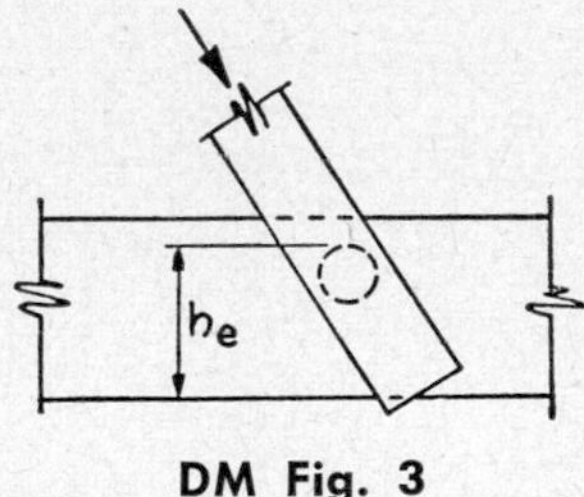

DM Fig. 3

MAXIMUM PERMISSIBLE LOADS ON SHEAR PLATES. Test failures have shown that there are limits beyond which shear plates should not be loaded. These limits vary with the bolt size and are given with the shear-plate data.

SPACING CHARTS. Spacing is the distance between centers of connectors measured along a line joining their centers. The distance, R, in DM Fig. 4 is the spacing between the rings shown.

Each spacing chart has five parabolic curves representing recommended spacing for full load at the particular angle of load to grain noted on the curve. For intermediate angles of load, straight-line interpolation may be used. If the spacing for full load is desired, select the proper angle-of-load-to-grain curve and find where it intersects the radial lines representing the angle of axis to grain. The distance from that point to the lower left-hand corner is the spacing. It is probably more convenient, however, in laying out this spacing to use the parallel-to-grain and perpendicular-to-grain components or measurements of the spacing. The parallel-to-grain component may be read at the bottom of the chart by projecting downward from the point on the curve. The perpendicular component of the spacing may be read at the left-hand side of the chart by projecting horizontally from the point on the curve.

The sixth curve on the chart is a quarter-circle. This curve represents the spacing for 75 per cent of full load for any angle of load to grain and also the minimum spacing permissible. For percentages between 75 per cent and 100 per cent of full load for an angle of load to grain, interpolate radially on a straight line between the 75 per cent curve and the curve corresponding to the proper angle of load to grain.

Reductions in load for edge distance and end distance are not additive to spacing reductions but rather coincident.

END-DISTANCE CHARTS. End distance is the distance measured parallel to grain from the center of a connector to the square-cut end of the member. If the end of the member is not square-cut, the end distance shall be taken as the distance from any point on the center half of the connector diameter, drawn perpendicular to the centerline of the piece, to the nearest point on the end of the member measured parallel to grain. The distance measured perpendicular to the end cut to the center of the connector shall never be less than the required edge distance. DM Fig. 5 demonstrates end-distance measurement, *A*.

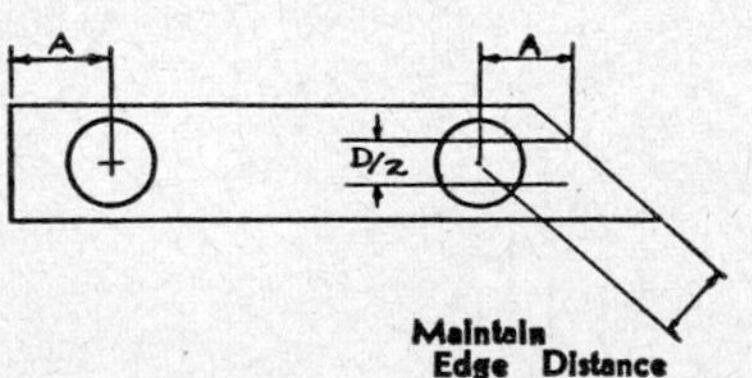

DM Fig. 5 End distance

On the same page with the spacing chart, the end-distance chart will be found. This chart is divided into two sections, for the member in tension and in compression. If it is in tension, project vertically on the chart from the end distance to the curve, then horizontally to get the percentage of full load allowable. This process can be reversed, of course, by going from percentage of full load required to spacing required. In compression, there is an additional variable of angle of load to grain. The operation is the same except the curve for the proper angle of load to grain should be used. For intermediate angles, interpolate between the curves on a straight line. On some of the charts, the curves are cut off at the right-hand side of the chart. The end-distance dimension marking this cut-off is the minimum permissible and gives full load for an angle of load to grain of 0 deg.

Reductions in load for edge distance or spacing are not additive to end distance reductions but rather coincident.

EDGE-DISTANCE CHARTS. Edge distance is the distance from the edge of the member to the center of the connector closest to the edge of the member measured perpendicular to the edge. The loaded edge distance is the edge distance measured from the edge toward which the load induced by the connector acts. The unloaded-edge distance is the edge distance measured from the edge away from which the load induced by the connector acts. DM Fig. 4 shows a typical measurement of edge distance, with *B* being the unloaded-edge distance and *C* the loaded-edge distance.

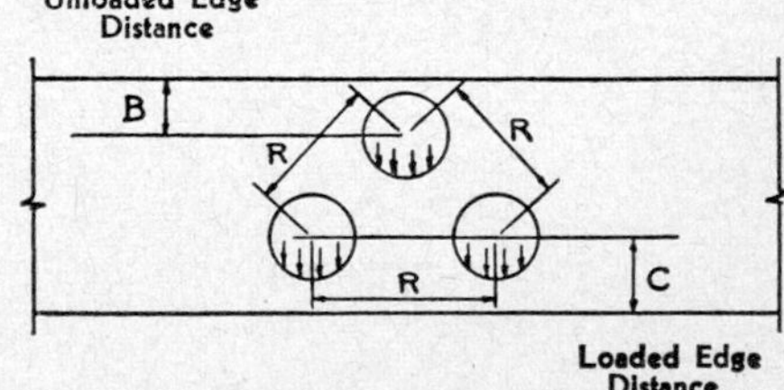

DM Fig. 4 Edge distance and spacing

On the same page with the spacing and end-distance charts, the edge-distance chart will be found. For unloaded-edge distance, the standard and minimum edge distance is the dimension at the right-hand edge of the chart. For loaded-edge distance, there is a variation according to angle of load to grain. Select the proper curve for the desired angle, and a given edge distance projected vertically to the curve and then horizontally to the side will give the percentage of full load allowable. The upper right-hand corner represents the standard and minimum loaded-edge distance for 0-deg angle of load to grain. For intermediate angles, interpolate on a straight line.

INTERRELATIONSHIP OF THICKNESS, DISTANCE, AND SPACING. Loads reduced because of thickness (see tabulated loads) do not permit any reduction of edge distance, end distance, or spacing without further reduction of load, and conversely, loads reduced for edge distance, end distance, or spacing do not permit reduction of thickness.

If allowable load is reduced because of reduced edge distance, end distance or spacing, the reduced allowable load for each shall be determined separately and the lowest allowable load so determined for any one connector shall apply to this and all other connectors resisting a common force in a joint. Such load reductions are not cumulative. Conversely, if the allowable load is reduced because of a reduced distance or spacing, the other distances or spacings may be reduced to dimensions resulting in the same reduced allowable load.

CAMBER CHART. The camber chart of this manual will give an empirical value for recommended camber for the average truss. The bowstring truss using a glued-laminated upper chord requires less camber than other types because of the absence of splices. The value for camber read from the chart is the amount the lower chord should be raised at the center of the span.

To use the chart, determine the values for L (span) and H (depth of truss at center) and multiply to get L^3/H. Then using this value at the left-hand side, proceed horizontally to the proper curve. Then project vertically to the bottom of the chart, and read the camber. For special cases for which detailed deformation data is required, write the Timber Engineering Company stating the conditions involved, and special recommendations will be made.

EFFECT ON CONNECTOR LOADS OF GRADE OF LUMBER AND SPECIES. The various commercial stress grades of lumber are affected by characteristics that have no effect on the strength values of connectors. Therefore, no variation in connector loads is permissible for variations in stresses assigned to lumber.

Connector loads vary according to the species of lumber with which they are used. The species have been classified in groups A, B, and C. Loads for species not listed may be obtained on request from the Timber Engineering Company.

DM TABLE 1 Connector-load grouping of species when structurally graded

Group A species	Group B species	Group C species
Douglas fir (dense) Oak, red and white Pine, southern (dense)	Douglas fir (coast region) Larch, western Pine, southern	Cypress, southern and tidewater red Hemlock, West Coast Pine, Norway Redwood

2½-in. Split Rings

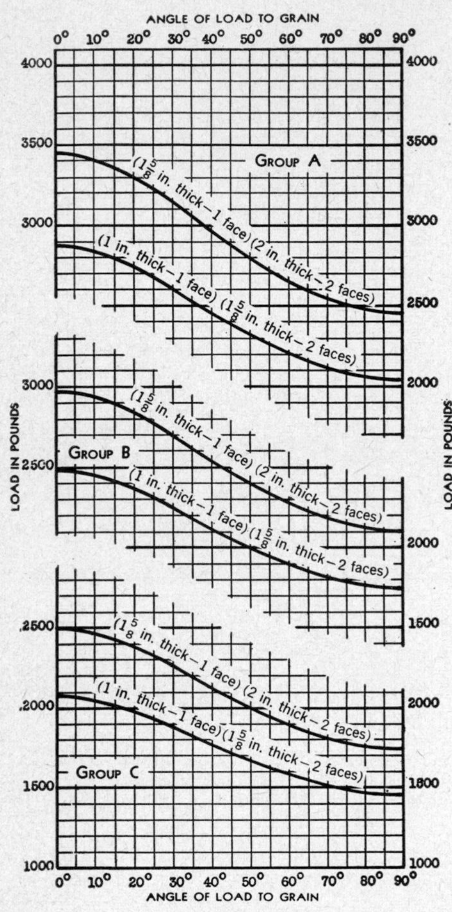

LOAD CHART
FOR NORMAL LOADING
ONE 2½" SPLIT RING AND BOLT IN SINGLE SHEAR

2½-IN. SPLIT-RING DATA

	in.
Split ring—Dimensions	
Inside diameter at center when closed	2½
Inside diameter at center when installed	2.54
Thickness of ring at center	0.163
Thickness of ring at edge	0.123
Depth	¾
Weight, per 100 rings (lb)	28
Lumber—Minimum dimensions	
Width	3⅝
Thickness, rings in one face	1
Thickness, rings opposite in both faces	1⅝
Bolt, diameter	½
Bolt hole, diameter	9/16
Projected area for portion of one ring within a member (sq in.)	1.10
Washers—Minimum dimensions	
Round, cast of malleable iron, diameter	2⅛
Square plate	
Length of side	2
Thickness	⅛
(For trussed rafters and similar light construction, standard - wrought washers may be used.)	

SPLIT-RING SPECIFICATIONS

Split rings shall be manufactured from hot rolled S.A.E.—1010 carbon steel. Each ring shall form a closed true circle with the principal axis of the cross section of the ring metal parallel to the geometric axis of the ring. The ring shall fit snugly in the prepared groove. The metal section of each ring shall be beveled from the central portion toward the edges to a thickness less than that at mid-section. It shall be cut through in one place in its circumference to form a tongue and slot.

DECREASES FOR MOISTURE CONTENT CONDITIONS

Condition when fabricated:	Seasoned	Unseasoned	Unseasoned
Condition when used:	Seasoned	Seasoned	Unseasoned or Wet
Decrease (per cent):	0	20	33

PERCENTAGES FOR DURATION OF MAXIMUM LOAD

Two-months' loading, as for snow	115
Seven-days' loading	125
Wind or earthquake loading	133⅓
Impact loading	200
Permanent loading	90

2½-in. Split Rings

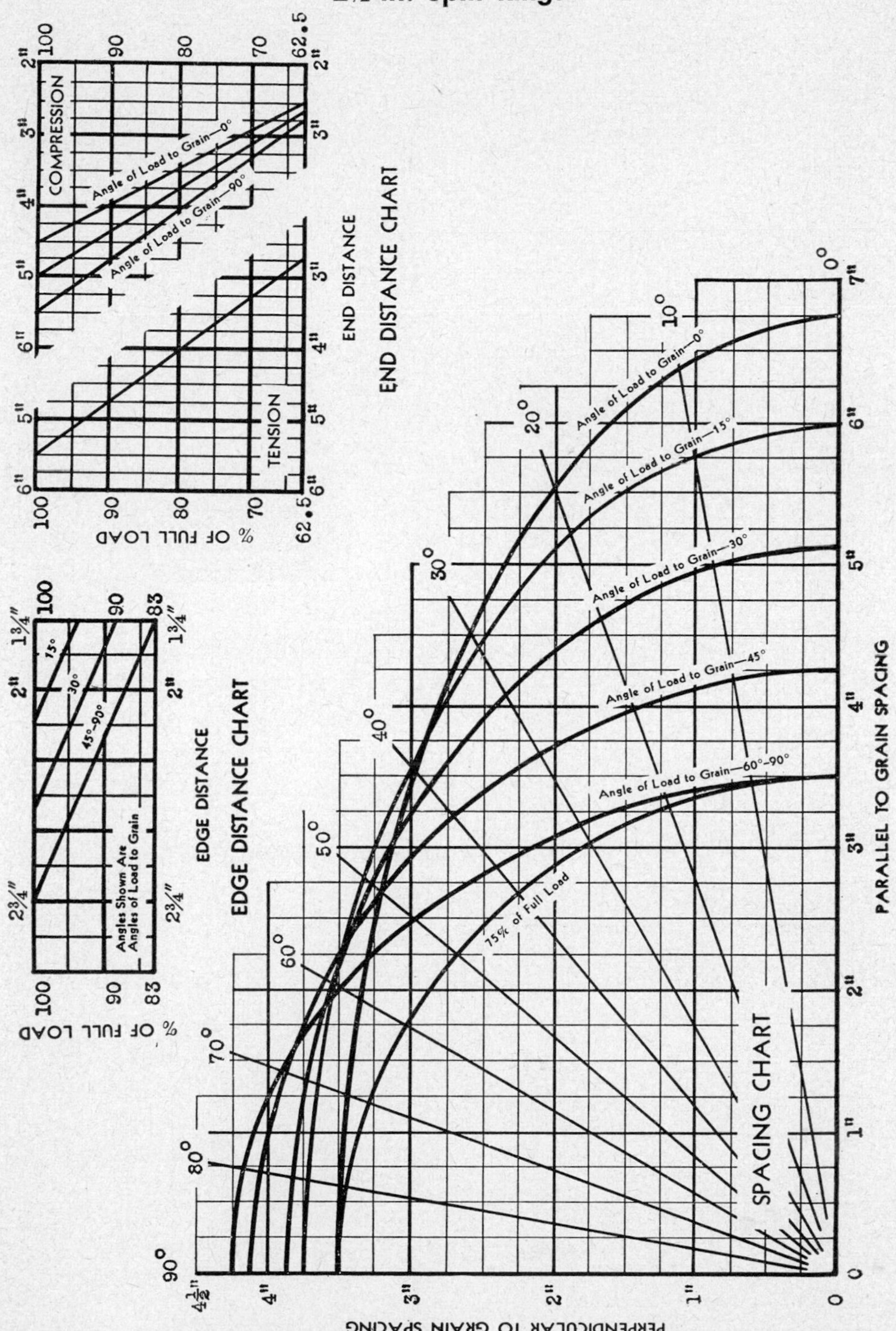

4-in. Split Rings

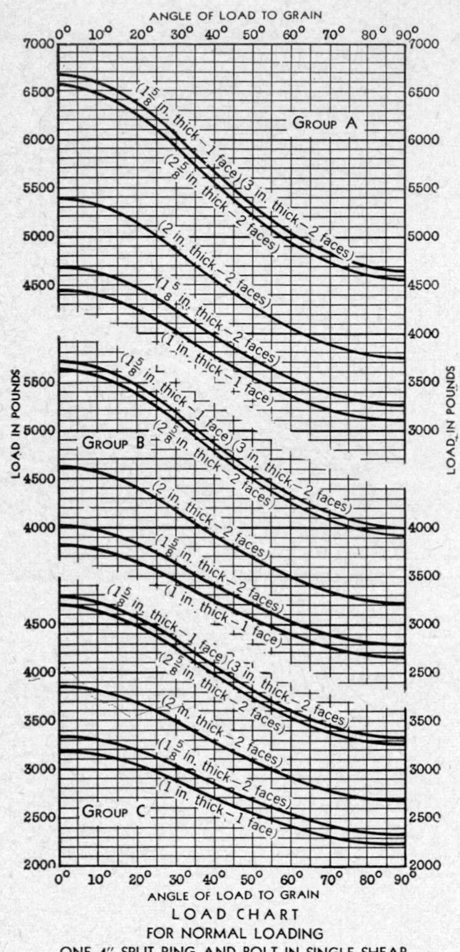

LOAD CHART
FOR NORMAL LOADING
ONE 4" SPLIT RING AND BOLT IN SINGLE SHEAR

4-IN. SPLIT-RING DATA

	in.
Split ring—Dimensions	
Inside diameter at center when closed	4
Inside diameter at center when installed	4.06
Thickness of ring at center	0.193
Thickness of ring at edge	0.133
Depth	1
Weight, per 100 rings (lb)	70
Lumber—Minimum dimensions allowed	
Width	5½
Thickness, rings in one face	1
Thickness, rings opposite in both faces	1⅝
Bolt, diameter	¾
Bolt hole, diameter	13/16
Projected area for portion of one ring within a member, sq in.	2.25
Washers—Minimum dimensions	
Round, cast of malleable iron, diameter	3
Square plate	
Length of side	3
Thickness	3/16
(For trussed rafters and similar light construction, standard - wrought washers may be used.)	

SPLIT-RING SPECIFICATIONS

Split rings shall be manufactured from hot rolled S.A.E.—1010 carbon steel. Each ring shall form a closed true circle with the principal axis of the cross section of the ring metal parallel to the geometric axis of the ring. The ring shall fit snugly in the prepared groove. The metal section of each ring shall be beveled from the central portion toward the edges to a thickness less than than at mid-section. It shall be cut through in one place in its circumference to form a tongue and slot.

DECREASES FOR MOISTURE-CONTENT CONDITIONS

Condition when fabricated:	Seasoned	Unseasoned	Unseasoned
Condition when used:	Seasoned	Seasoned	Unseasoned or Wet
Decrease (per cent):	0	20	33

PERCENTAGES FOR DURATION OF MAXIMUM LOAD

Two-months' loading, as for snow	115
Seven-days' loading	125
Wind or earthquake loading	133⅓
Impact loading	200
Permanent loading	90

4-in. Split Rings

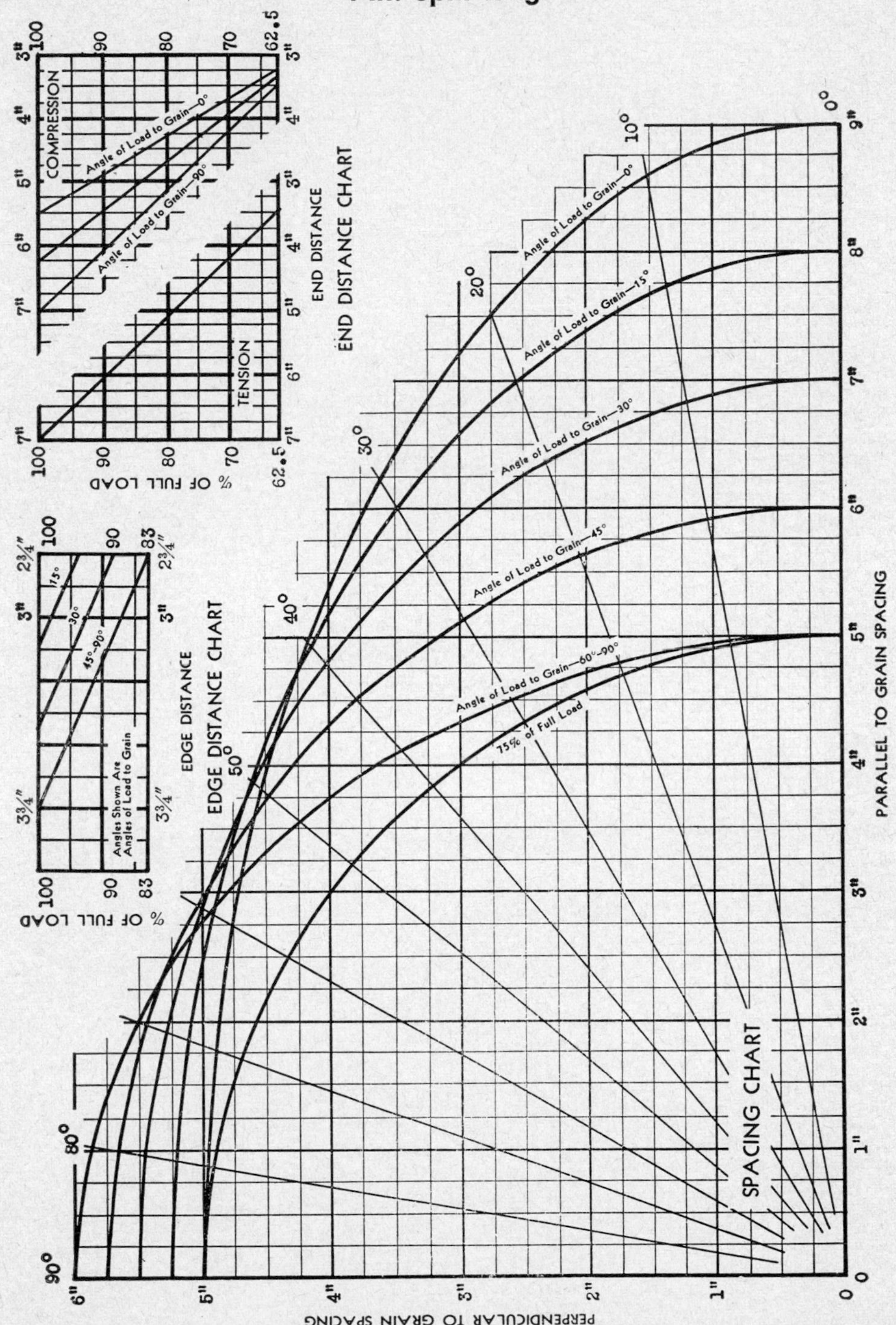

2⅝-in. Shear Plates

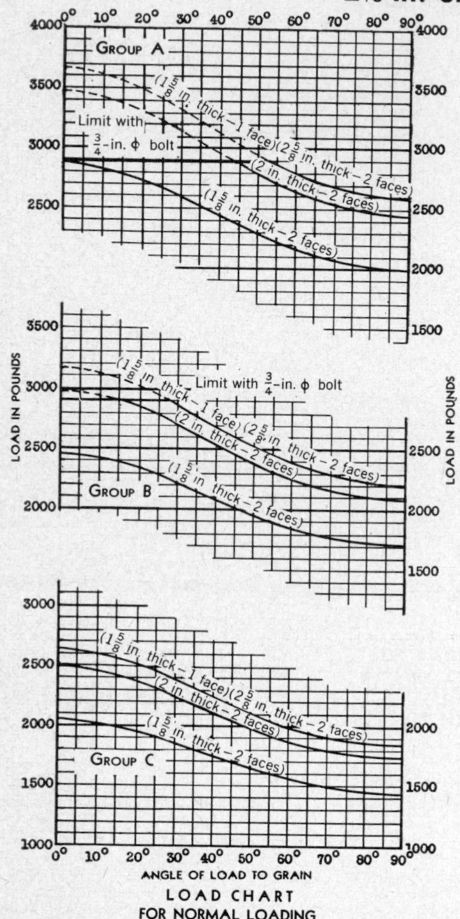

LOAD CHART
FOR NORMAL LOADING
ONE 2⅝" SHEAR-PLATE UNIT AND BOLT IN SINGLE SHEAR

DECREASES FOR MOISTURE-CONTENT CONDITIONS

Condition when fabricated:	Seasoned	Unseasoned	Unseasoned
Condition when used:	Seasoned	Seasoned	Unseasoned or Wet
Decrease (per cent):	0	20	33

MAXIMUM PERMISSIBLE LOADS ON SHEAR PLATES

The allowable loads for all loadings except wind shall not exceed 2,900 lb for $2^5/_8$-in. shear plates with ¾-in. bolts. The allowable wind load shall not exceed 3,870 lb. If bolt threads bear on the shear plate, reduce the preceding values by one-ninth.

2⅝-IN. SHEAR-PLATE DATA

	in.
Shear plates—Dimensions	
Material	Pressed steel
Diameter of plate	2.62
Diameter of bolt hole	0.81
Depth of plate	0.42
Weight, per 100 plates (lb)	35
Lumber—Minimum dimensions	
Face, width	3⅝
Thickness, plates in one face only	1⅝
Thickness, plates opposite in both faces	1⅝
Steel shapes or straps (thickness required when used with shear plates)	
Thickness of steel side plates shall be determined in accordance with AISC recommendations.	
Hole, diameter in steel straps or shapes	$^{13}/_{16}$
Bolt, diameter	¾
Bolt hole, diameter in timber	$^{13}/_{16}$
Washers, standard, timber-to-timber connections only	
Round, cast of malleable iron, diameter	3
Square plate	
Length of side	3
Thickness	¼
(For trussed rafters and other light structures, standard-wrought washers may be used.)	
Projected area, for one shear plate (sq in.)	0.98

SHEAR-PLATE SPECIFICATIONS

Pressed Steel Type—Pressed steel shear-plates shall be manufactured from hot-rolled S.A.E.—1010 carbon steel. Each plate shall be a true circle with a flange around the edge extending at right angles to the face of the plate and extending from one face only, the plate portion having a central bolt hole and two small perforations on opposite sides of the hole and midway from the center and circumference.

PERCENTAGES FOR DURATION OF MAXIMUM LOAD

Two-months' loading, as for snow	115[1]
Seven-days' loading	125[1]
Wind or earthquake loading	133⅓[1]
Impact loading	200[1]
Permanent loading	90

[1] Do not exceed limitations for maximum allowable loads for shear plates given elsewhere on this page.

2⅝-in. Shear Plates

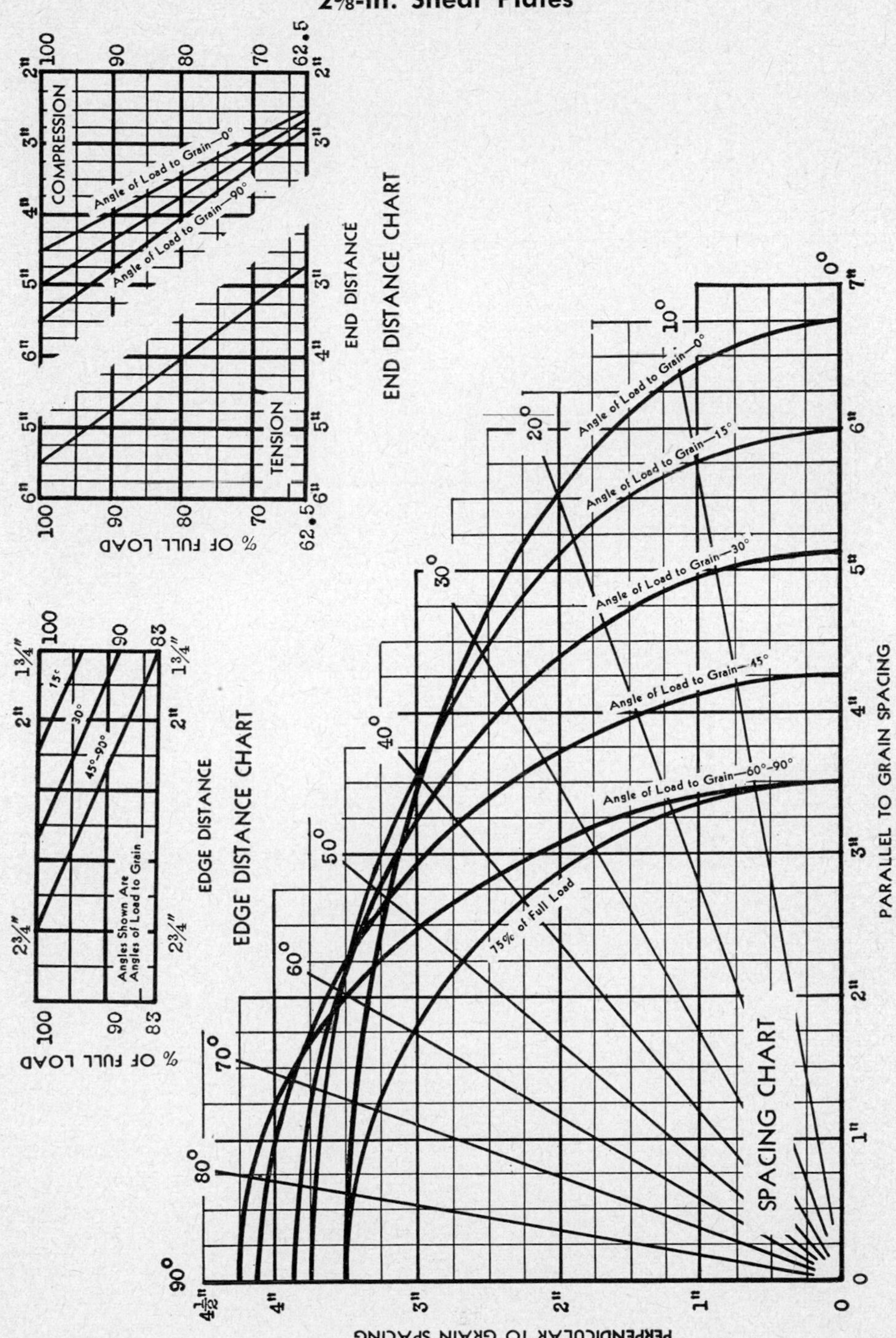

4-in. Shear Plates (Wood-to-Wood)

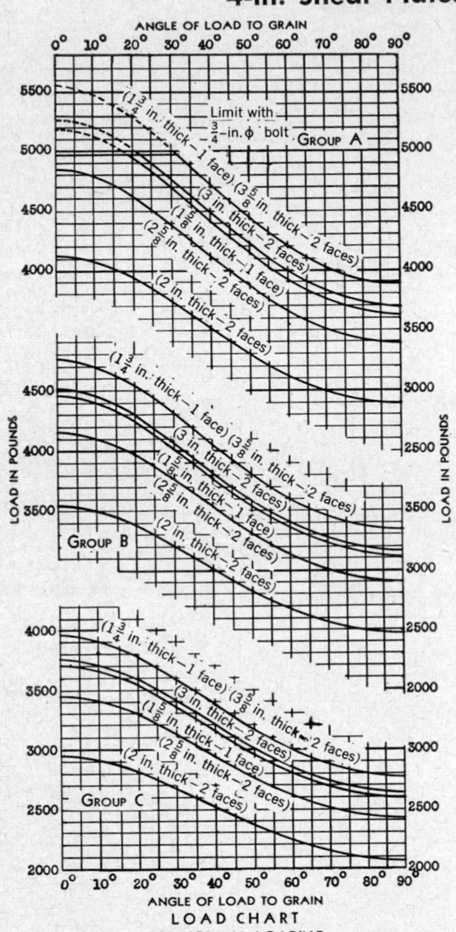

LOAD CHART
FOR NORMAL LOADING
ONE 4" SHEAR-PLATE UNIT AND BOLT IN SINGLE SHEAR

DECREASES FOR MOISTURE-CONTENT CONDITIONS

Decreases are same as for 2⅝-in. shear plates.

MAXIMUM PERMISSIBLE LOADS ON SHEAR PLATES

The allowable loads for all loadings except wind shall not exceed 4,970 lb for 4-in. shear plates with ¾-in. bolts and 6,760 lb for 4-in. shear plates with 7/8-in. bolts. The allowable wind loads shall not exceed 6,630 lb when used with a ¾-in. bolt and 9,020 lb when used with a 7/8-in. bolt. If bolt threads bear on the shear plate, reduce the preceding values by one-ninth.

4-IN. SHEAR-PLATE DATA

	in.	*in.*
Shear plates—Dimensions		
Material	Malleable iron	Malleable iron
Diameter of plate	4.02	4.02
Diameter of bolt hole	0.81	0.94
Depth of plate	0.62	0.62
Weight, per 100 plates (lb)	90	90
Lumber—Minimum dimensions		
Face, width	5½	5½
Thickness, plates in one face only	1⅝	1⅝
Thickness, plates opposite in both faces	1¾	1¾
Bolt, diameter	¾	⅞
Bolt hole, diam. in timber	13/16	15/16
Washers, standard, timber-to-timber connections only		
Round, cast of malleable iron, diameter	3	3½
Square plate		
Length of side	3	3
Thickness	¼	¼
(For trussed rafters and other light structures standard-wrought washers may be used.)		
Projected area, for one shear plate (sq in.)	2.48	2.48

SHEAR-PLATE SPECIFICATIONS

Malleable Iron Types—Malleable iron shear plates shall be manufactured according to ASTM Standard Specifications (A 47–33, Grade 35018) for malleable iron castings. Each casting shall consist of a perforated round plate with a flange around the edge extending at right angles to the face of the plate and projecting from one face only, the plate portion having a central bolt hole reamed to size with an integral hub concentric to the bolt hole and extending from the same face as the flange.

PERCENTAGES FOR DURATION OF MAXIMUM LOAD

Percentages are same as for 2⅝-in. shear plates.

4-in. Shear Plates (Wood-to-Wood)

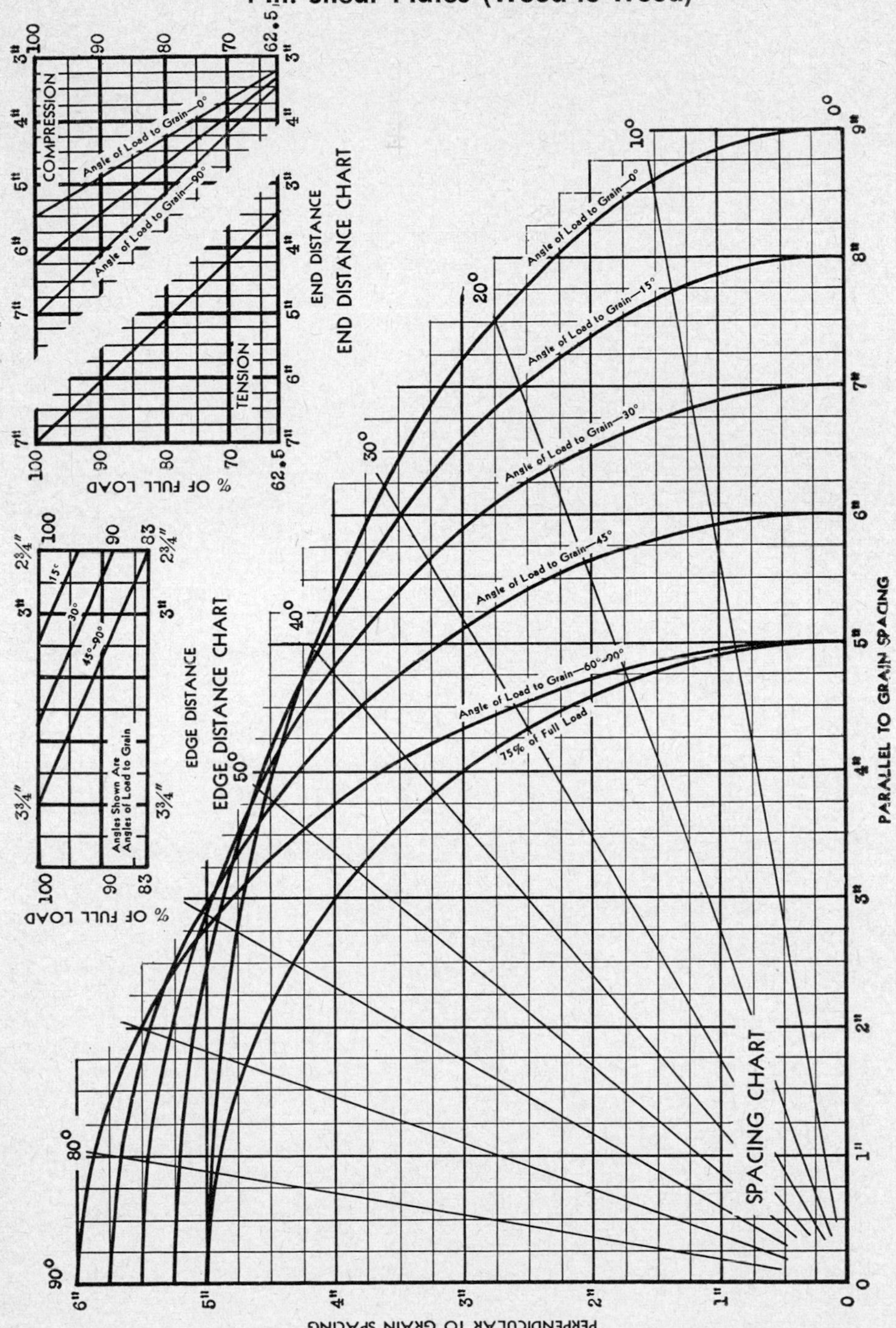

4-in. Shear Plates (Wood-to-Steel)

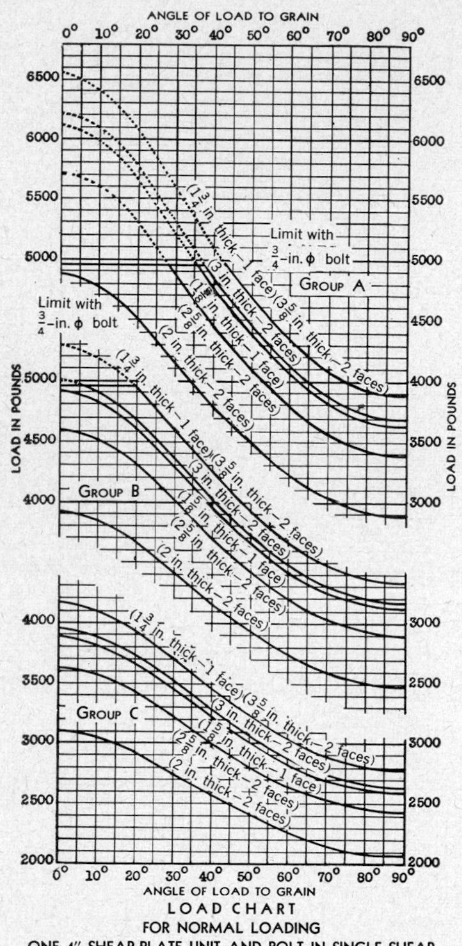

LOAD CHART
FOR NORMAL LOADING
ONE 4" SHEAR-PLATE UNIT AND BOLT IN SINGLE SHEAR

DECREASES FOR MOISTURE-CONTENT CONDITIONS

Decreases are same as for 2⅝-in. shear plates.

MAXIMUM PERMISSIBLE LOADS ON SHEAR PLATES.

The allowable loads for all loadings except wind shall not exceed 4,970 lb for 4-in. shear plates with ¾-in. bolts and 6,760 lb for 4-in. shear plates with 7/8-in. bolts. The allowable wind loads shall not exceed 6,630 lb when used with a ¾-in. bolt and 9,020 lb when used with a 7/8-in. bolt. If bolt threads bear on the shear plate, reduce the preceding values by one-ninth.

4-IN. SHEAR-PLATE DATA

	in.	*in.*
Shear plates—Dimensions		
Material	Malleable iron	Malleable iron
Diameter of plate	4.02	4.02
Diameter of bolt hole	0.81	0.94
Depth of plate	0.62	0.62
Weight per 100 plates (lb)	90	90
Lumber—Minimum dimensions		
Face, width	5½	5½
Thickness, plates in one face only	1⅝	1⅝
Thickness, plates opposite in both faces	1¾	1¾
Steel shapes or straps (Thickness required when used with shear plates, Thickness of steel side plates shall be determined in accordance with AISC recommendations.		
Hole, diameter in steel straps or shapes	13/16	15/16
Bolt, diameter	¾	⅞
Bolt hole, diameter in timber	13/16	15/16
Projected area, for one shear plate (sq in.)	2.48	2.48

SHEAR-PLATE SPECIFICATIONS

Malleable Iron Types—Malleable iron shear plates shall be manufactured according to ASTM Standard Specifications (A 47–33, Grade 35018) for malleable iron castings. Each casting shall consist of a perforated round plate with a flange around the edge extending at right angles to the face of the plate and projecting from one face only, the plate portion having a central bolt hole reamed to size with an integral hub concentric to the bolt hole and extending from the same face as the flange.

PERCENTAGES FOR DURATION OF MAXIMUM LOAD

Percentages are same as for 2⅝-in. shear plates.

4-in. Shear Plates (Wood-to-Steel)

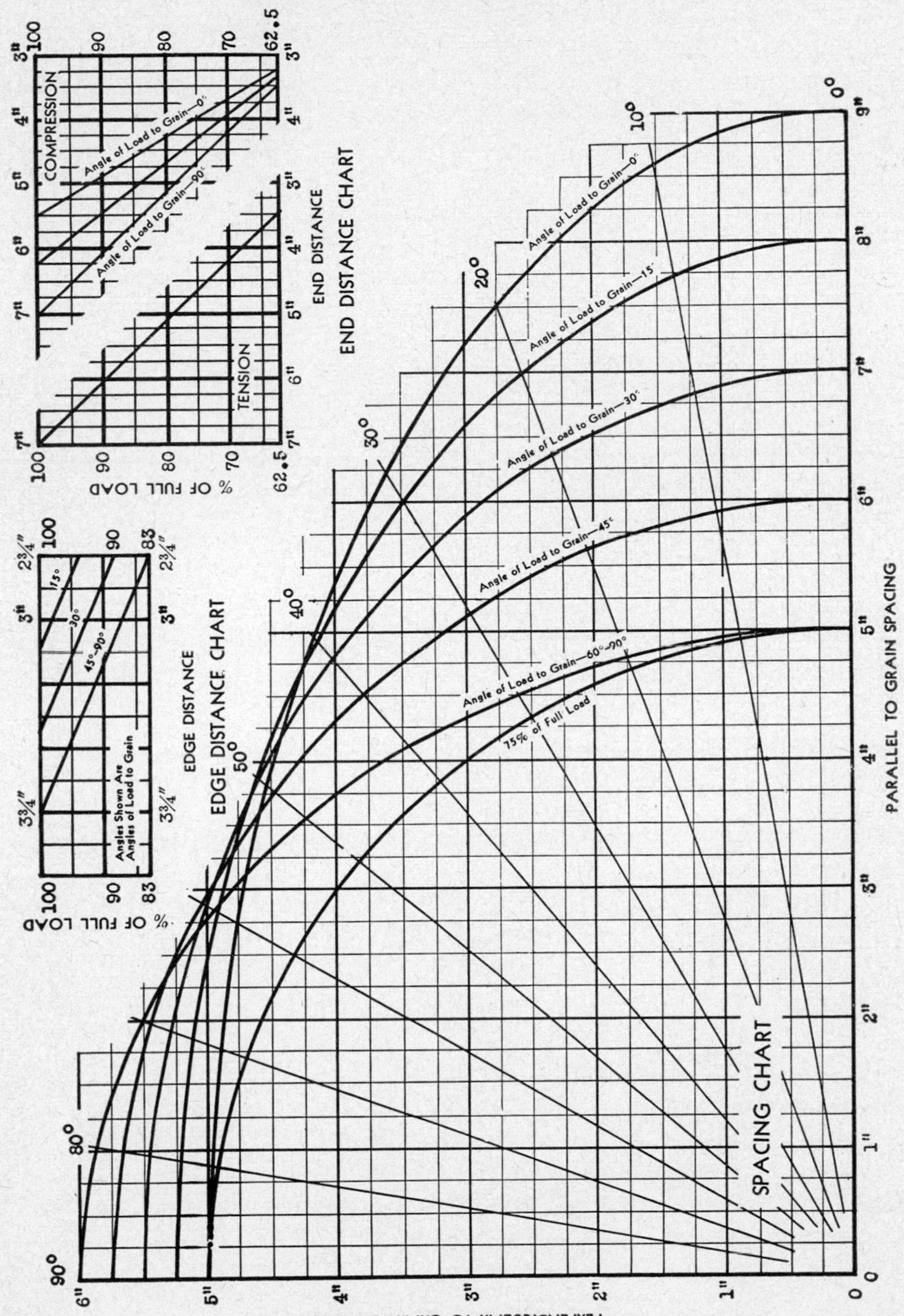

2-in. Toothed Rings

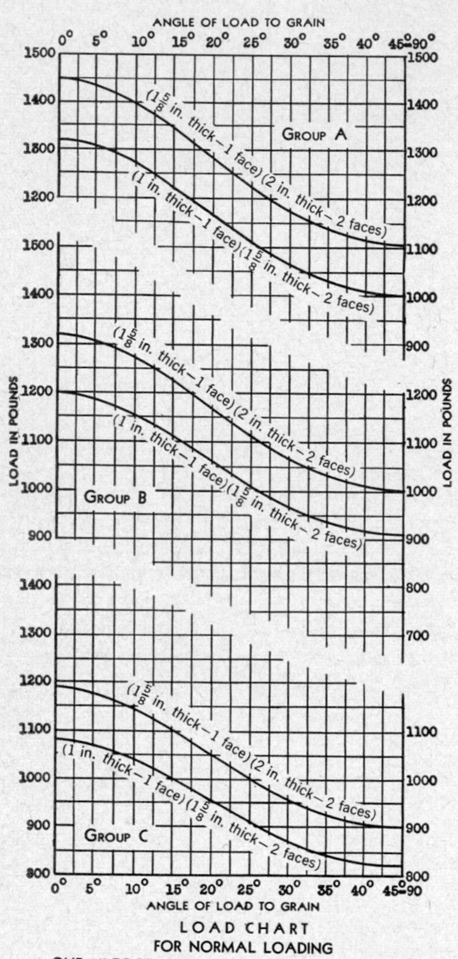

LOAD CHART
FOR NORMAL LOADING
ONE 2" TOOTHED RING AND BOLT IN SINGLE SHEAR

DECREASES FOR MOISTURE-CONTENT CONDITIONS

Condition when fabricated:	Seasoned	Unseasoned	Unseasoned
Condition when used:	Seasoned	Seasoned	Unseasoned or Wet
Decrease (per cent):	0	20	33

2-IN. TOOTHED-RING DATA

	in.
Toothed ring—Dimensions	
Diameter	2
Depth	0.94
Weight, per 100 rings (lb)	9
Lumber—Minimum dimensions	
Width	3
Thickness, rings in one face only	1
Thickness, rings opposite in both faces	1⅝
Bolt, diameter	½
Bolt hole, diameter	9/16
Washers—Minimum dimensions	
Round, cast of malleable iron, diameter	2
Square Plate	
Length of side	2
Thickness	3/16
Projected area for portion of one ring within member (sq in.)	0.94

TOOTHED-RING SPECIFICATIONS

Toothed-ring timber connectors shall be stamped cold from U. S. Standard 16 gauge hot-rolled sheet steel conforming to ASTM Standard Specifications for carbon steel (A 17–29, Type A, Grade 1) and shall be bent cold to form a circular, corrugated, sharp-toothed band and welded into a solid ring. The teeth on each ring shall be on a true circle and shall be parallel to the axis of the ring. The central band shall be welded to fully develop the strength of the band.

PERCENTAGES FOR DURATION OF MAXIMUM LOAD

Two-months' loading, as for snow	100
Seven-days' loading	100
Wind or earthquake loading	120
Impact loading	120
Permanent loading	90

2-in. Toothed Rings

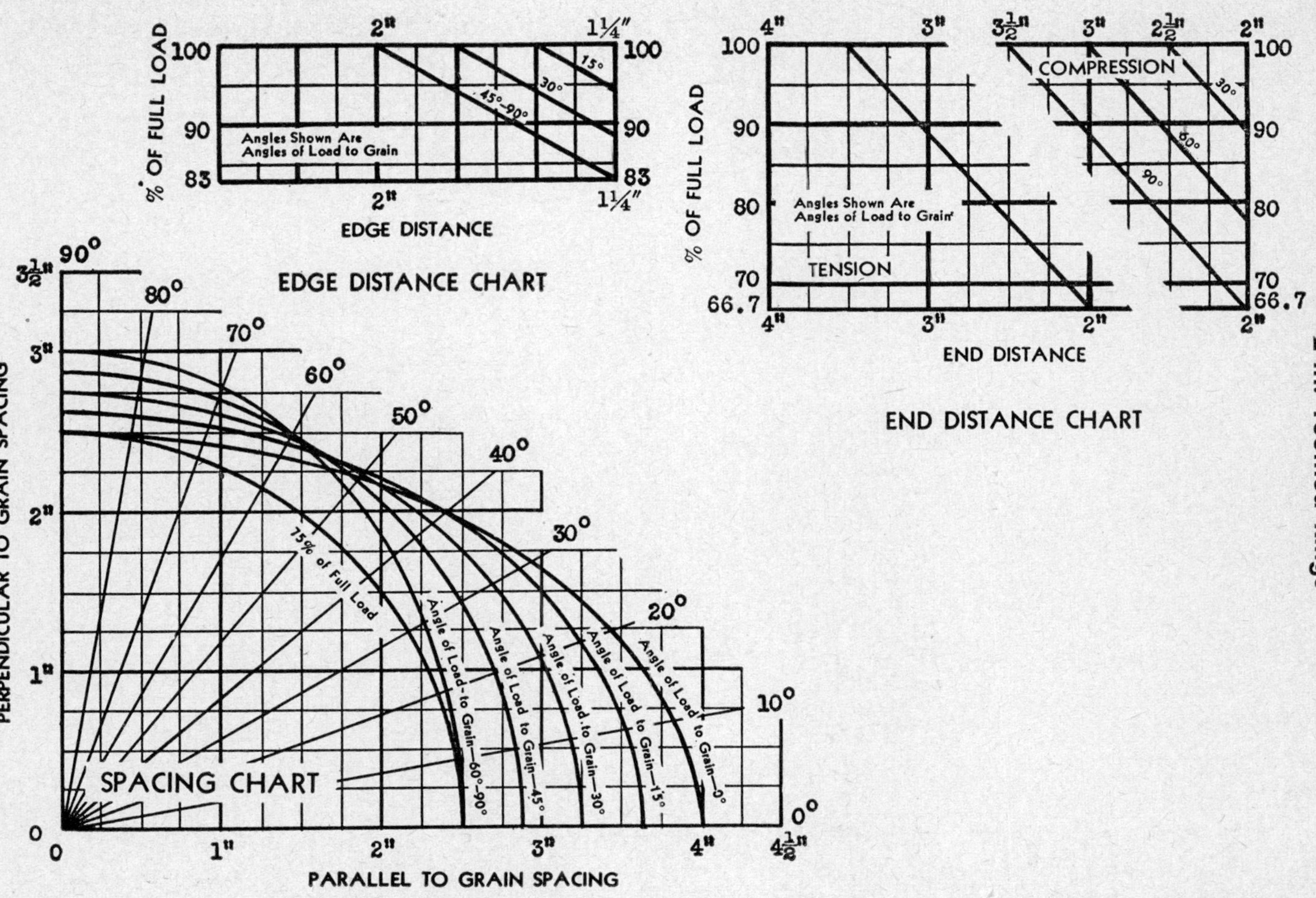

2⅝-in. Toothed Rings

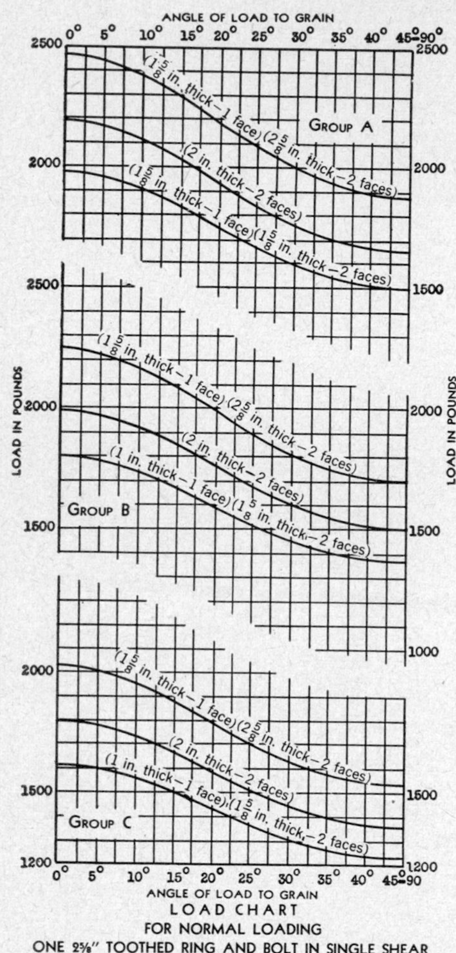

LOAD CHART
FOR NORMAL LOADING
ONE 2⅝" TOOTHED RING AND BOLT IN SINGLE SHEAR

2⅝-IN. TOOTHED-RING DATA

	in.
Toothed Ring—Dimensions	
Diameter	2⅝
Depth	.94
Weight, per 100 rings (lb)	12
Lumber—Minimum dimensions allowed	
Width	3⅝
Thickness, rings in one face only	1
Thickness, rings opposite in both faces	1⅝
Bolt, diameter	⅝
Bolt hole, diameter	11/16
Washers—Minimum dimensions	
Round, cast of malleable iron, diameter	2⅝
Square plate	
Length of side	2½
Thickness	¼
Projected area for portion of one ring within member (sq in.)	1.23

TOOTHED-RING SPECIFICATIONS

Toothed-ring timber connectors shall be stamped cold from U. S. Standard 16 gauge hot-rolled sheet steel conforming to ASTM Standard Specifications for carbon steel (A 17–29, Type A, Grade 1) and shall be bent cold to form a circular, corrugated, sharp-toothed band and welded into a solid ring. The teeth on each ring shall be on a true circle and shall be parallel to the axis of the ring. The central band shall be welded to fully develop the strength of the band.

DECREASES FOR MOISTURE-CONTENT CONDITIONS

Condition when fabricated:	Seasoned	Unseasoned	Unseasoned
Condition when used:	Seasoned	Seasoned	Unseasoned or Wet
Decrease (per cent):	0	20	33

PERCENTAGES FOR DURATION OF MAXIMUM LOAD

Two-months' loading, as for snow	100
Seven-days' loading	100
Wind or earthquake loading	120
Impact loading	120
Permanent loading	90

2⅝-in. Toothed Rings

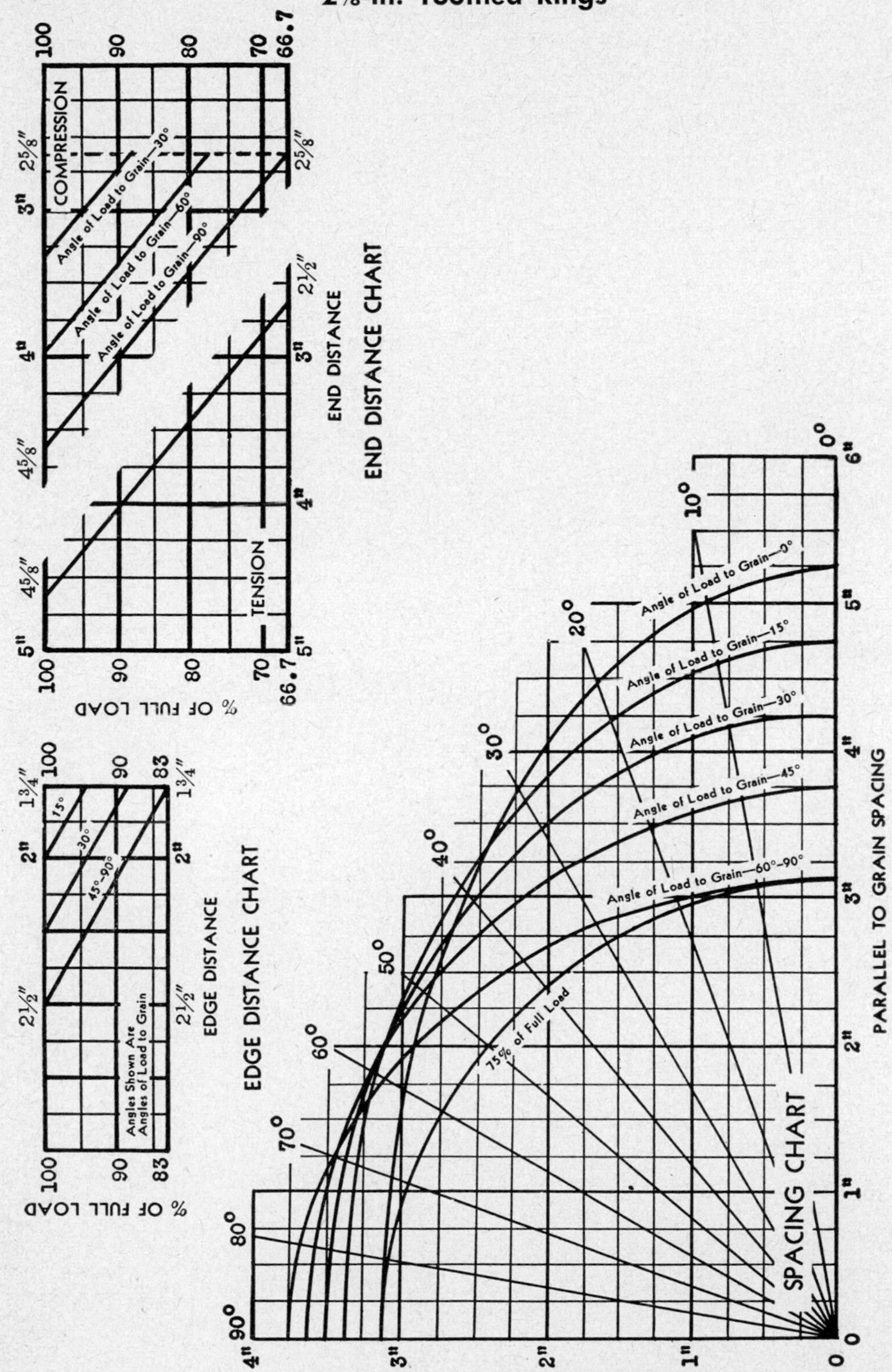

3⅜-in. Toothed Rings

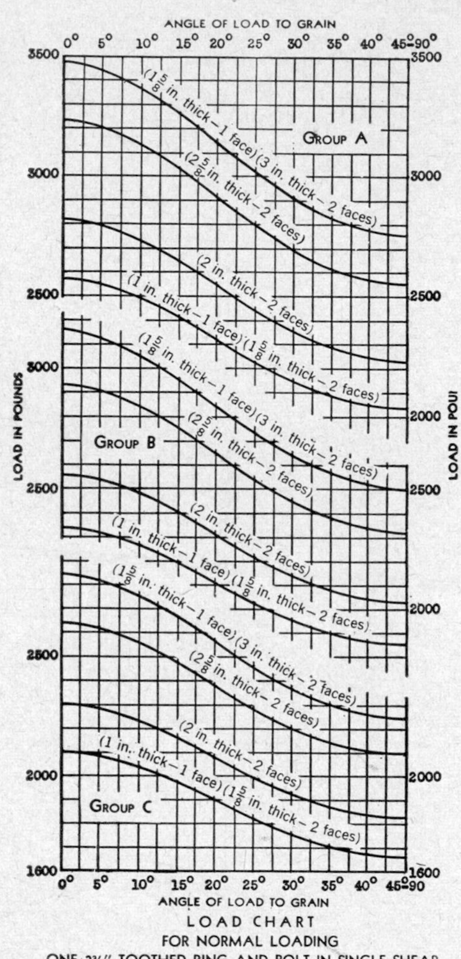

LOAD CHART
FOR NORMAL LOADING
ONE 3⅜" TOOTHED RING AND BOLT IN SINGLE SHEAR

DECREASES FOR MOISTURE-CONTENT CONDITIONS

Condition when fabricated:	Seasoned	Unseasoned	Unseasoned
Condition when used:	Seasoned	Seasoned	Unseasoned or Wet
Decrease (per cent):	0	20	33

3⅜-IN. TOOTHED-RING DATA

	in.
Toothed Ring—Dimensions	
Diameter	3⅜
Depth	0.94
Weight, per 100 rings (lb)	15
Lumber—Minimum dimensions allowed	
Width	4⅝
Thickness, rings in one face only	1
Thickness, rings opposite in both faces	1⅝
Bolt, diameter	¾
Bolt hole, diameter	13/16
Washers—Minimum dimensions	
Round, cast of malleable iron, diameter	3
Square plate	
Length of side	3
Thickness	¼
Projected area for portion of one ring within member (sq in.)	1.59

TOOTHED-RING SPECIFICATIONS

Toothed-ring timber connectors shall be stamped cold from U. S. Standard 16 gauge hot-rolled sheet steel conforming to ASTM Standard Specifications for carbon steel (A 17–29, Type A, Grade 1), and shall be bent cold to form a circular, corrugated, sharp-toothed band and welded into a solid ring. The teeth on each ring shall be on a true circle and shall be parallel to the axis of the ring. The central band shall be welded to fully develop the strength of the band.

PERCENTAGES FOR DURATION OF MAXIMUM LOAD

Two-months' loading, as for snow	100
Seven-days' loading	100
Wind or earthquake loading	120
Impact loading	120
Permanent loading	90

3⅜-in. Toothed Rings

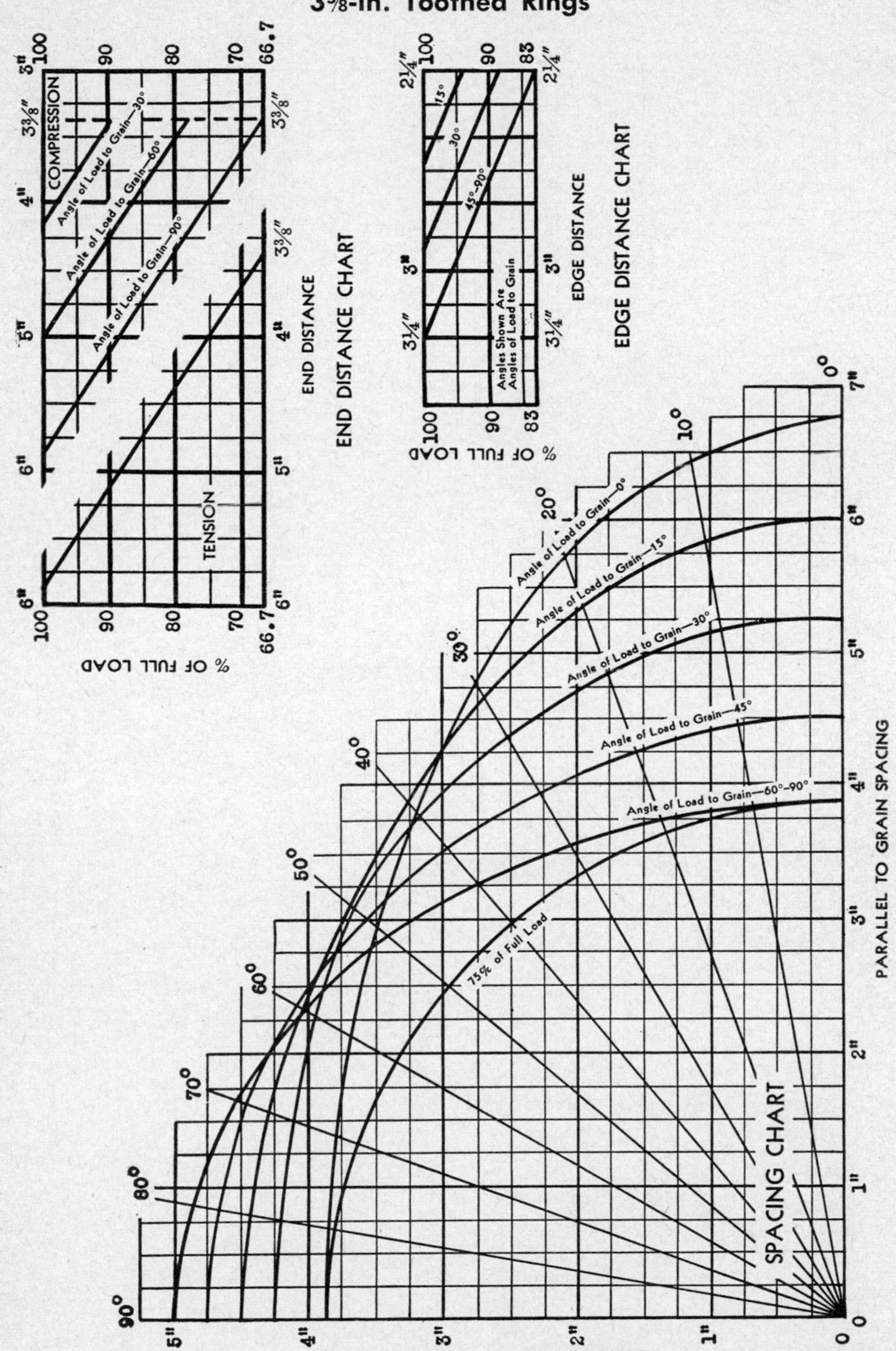

4-in. Toothed Rings

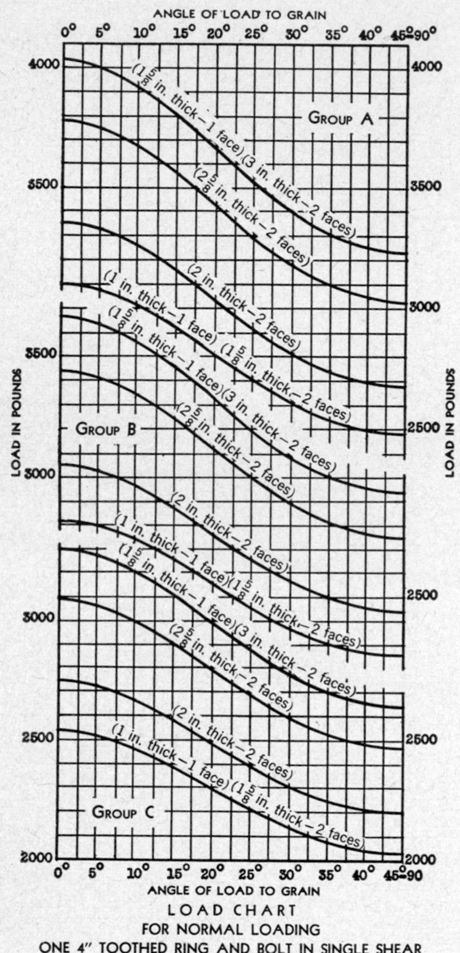

LOAD CHART
FOR NORMAL LOADING
ONE 4" TOOTHED RING AND BOLT IN SINGLE SHEAR

4-IN. TOOTHED-RING DATA

	in.
Toothed Ring—Dimensions	
Diameter	4
Depth	0.94
Weight, per 100 rings (lb)	18
Lumber—Minimum dimensions	
Width	5½
Thickness, rings in one face only	1
Thickness, rings opposite in both faces	1⅝
Bolt, diameter	¾
Bolt hole, diameter	13/16
Washers—Minimum dimensions	
Round, cast of malleable iron, diameter	3½
Square plate	
Length of side	3½
Thickness	⅜
Projected area for portion of one ring within member (sq in.)	1.88

TOOTHED-RING SPECIFICATIONS

Toothed-ring timber connectors shall be stamped cold from U. S. Standard 16 gauge hot-rolled sheet steel conforming to ASTM Standard Specifications for carbon steel (A 17–29, Type A, Grade 1) and shall be bent cold to form a circular, corrugated, sharp-toothed band and welded into a solid ring. The teeth on each ring shall be on a true circle and shall be parallel to the axis of the ring. The central band shall be welded to fully develop the strength of the band.

DECREASES FOR MOISTURE-CONTENT CONDITIONS

Condition when fabricated:	Seasoned	Unseasoned	Unseasoned
Condition when used:	Seasoned	Seasoned	Unseasoned or Wet
Decrease (per cent):	0	20	33

PERCENTAGES FOR DURATION OF MAXIMUM LOAD

Two-months' loading, as for snow	100
Seven-days' loading	100
Wind or earthquake loading	120
Impact loading	120
Permanent loading	90

4-in. Toothed Rings

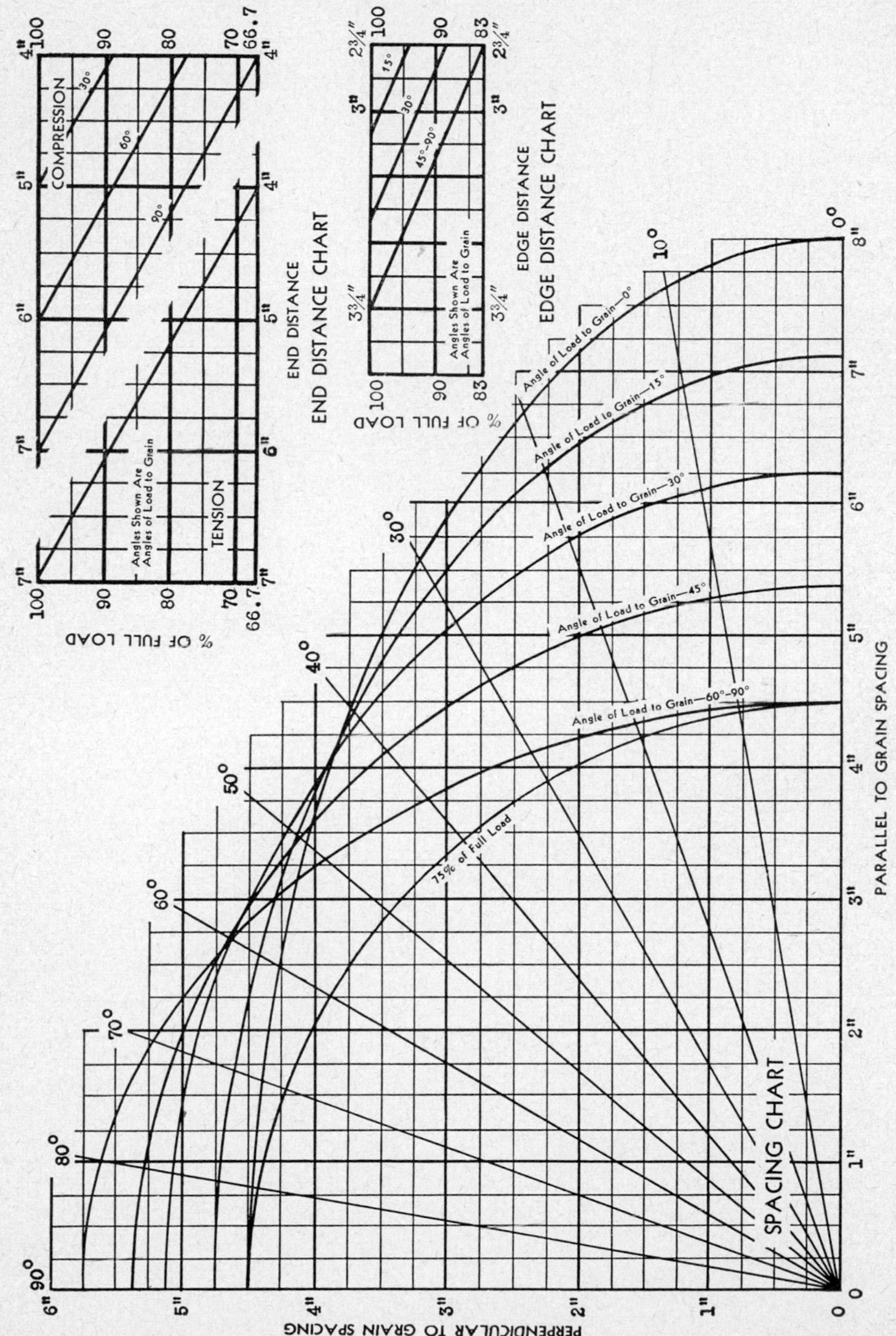

Spike Grids

Spike grid—Dimensions	*in.*	*in.*	*in.*
Type	Flat	Single curve	Circular
Size, square	4⅛	4⅛	3¼
Total depth of grids, maximum	1	1.38	1.20
Diameter of bolt hole	1.06	1.06	1.33
Weight, per 100 grids (lb)	50	75	26
Lumber—Minimum dimensions recommended for installation of flat grids			
Face width	5½	5½	5½
Thickness			
Grids one face only	1⅝	1⅝	1⅝
Grids opposite in both faces	2⅝		2⅝
Minimum diameter of pile for curved grids		10	
Bolt, diameter	¾ or 1	¾ or 1	¾ or 1
Bolt hole, diameter in timber	13/16 or 1 1/16	13/16 or 1 1/16	13/16 or 1 1/16
Washers			
Round, cast of malleable iron	Standard size for bolt diameter used		
Square plate	3 x 3 x ⅜ punched for bolt diameter used		
Spacing of grids, minimum, center-to-center			
0–30-deg angle of load to grain			
Spacing parallel to grain	7	7	7
Spacing perpendicular to grain	5½	5½	5½
30–90-deg angle of load to grain			
Spacing parallel or perpendicular to grain	5½	5½	5½
End distances, center of grid to end of piece (tension or compression members)			
Standard	7	7	7
Minimum (reduce loads 15 per cent)	5	5	5
Edge distances, center of grid to edge of piece			
Load applied at any angle to grain			
Standard	3¾	3¾	3¾
Minimum (reduce loads 15 per cent)	2¾	2¾	2¾
Projected area for portion of one grid within member (sq in.)	2.06	2.06	1.95

SPIKE-GRID SPECIFICATIONS

Spike-grid timber connectors shall be manufactured according to ASTM Standard Specifications A 47–33, Grade 35018, for malleable iron castings. They shall consist of four rows of opposing spikes forming a 4⅛-in. square grid with 16 teeth which are held in place by fillets. Fillets for the flat and circular grid in cross section shall be diamond shaped. Fillets for the single curve grids shall be increased in depth to allow for curvature.

WIND AND EARTHQUAKE LOADS

For wind or earthquake loads alone or a combination of wind or earthquake with dead or live loads or both, the safe loads on spike grids may be taken as 120 per cent of the Design Loads provided the resulting size and number of connectors is not less than required for the dead and live loads alone.

IMPACT

When using design loads, the load on a spike grid due to a force producing impact shall be taken as 115 per cent of the sum of the force as a static load and the load due to its impact.

LOADS IN RELATION TO DISTANCES AND SPACINGS

Standard Design Loads are for standard distances and spacings. Standard and minimum distances and spacings with load reduction factors are given in the table. Loads for end and edge distances and spacings intermediate of standard and minimum may be determined by interpolation.

Design loads for one spike grid and bolt in single shear[1]

Group A			Group B			Group C		
Type of grid	Bolt diam. *in.*	Allowable load *lb*	Type of grid	Bolt diam. *in.*	Allowable load *lb*	Type of grid	Bolt diam. *in*	Allowable load *lb*
Flat	¾	3900	Flat	¾	3500	Flat	¾	3000
	1	4200		1	3800		1	3300
Single curve	¾	4200	Single curve	¾	3800	Single curve	¾	3200
	1	4500		1	4100		1	3500
Circular	¾	3500	Circular	¾	3100	Circular	¾	2600
	1	3800		1	3400		1	2900

[1] Allowable loads on spike grids same for all angles of load to grain.

Clamping Plates

	in.	in.
Clamping plates—Dimensions		
Type	Plain	Flanged
Length of plate	5¼	8
Width of plate	5¼	5
Depth of flange		2
Length of teeth	0.68	0.72
Diameter of bolt hole	1.12	1.12
Weight per 100 pieces (lb)	65	200
Lumber—Minimum dimensions required for installation of plates		
Face width	6½	6½
Thickness, plates in one face only	1⅝	2⅝
Thickness, plates opposite on both faces	2⅝	5½
Bolt diameter, minimum	¾	¾
Bolt hole, diameter in timber	13/16	13/16
Washers		
Round, cast of malleable iron, diameter	3	3
Square plate		
Length of side	3	3
Thickness	¼	¼
Spacing of clamping plates		
Minimum center-to-center		
Parallel to grain	6	8½
Perpendicular to grain	6	5½
End distances		
Center of plate to end of piece		
Plain type	5	
Flanged type		
Toothed side		5
Flanged side		2½
Edge distances		
Center of plate to edge of piece		
Plain type	3¼	
Flanged type		
Toothed side		3¼
Flanged side		4

CLAMPING-PLATE SPECIFICATIONS

Clamping-plate timber connectors shall be stamped cold from mild steel conforming to ASTM Standard Specifications for carbon steel A 17–29, Type A, Grade 1.

Plain Clamping Plate—Plain clamping plates shall consist of a square steel plate with a central bolt hole and 12 teeth projecting from each face. The flat sides of the teeth on each face shall be parallel to each other and arranged with the flat sides of the teeth on opposite faces of the plate at right angles to each other.

Flanged Clamping Plate—Flanged clamping plates shall consist of a rectangular steel plate with a central bolt hole around which 14 teeth shall project from one face with their flat sides parallel to the long edges of the plate. The metal near the two narrow ends of the plate shall be bent at right angles to the plate and in a direction opposite to the teeth to form flanges.

WIND AND EARTHQUAKE LOADS

For wind or earthquake loads alone or a combination of wind or earthquake with dead or live loads or both, the safe loads on clamping plates may be taken as 116 per cent of the design loads, provided the resulting number of connectors is not less than that required for the dead and live loads alone.

IMPACT

If design loads are used, the load on a clamping plate due to a force producing impact shall be taken as 115 per cent of the sum of the force as a static load and the load due to its impact.

LOADS IN RELATION TO DISTANCES AND SPACINGS

Design Loads are for standard distances and spacings. Spacings of plates and end and edge distances less than the minimum specified are not recommended.

CONDITION OF LUMBER

Tabulated loads apply to the plain clamping plate (in which the teeth rather than the flange determine the load capacity) used in seasoned lumber. Loads for the plain clamping plates in green lumber should not exceed 60 per cent of those shown. Tabulated loads apply to the flanged clamping plate in either seasoned or green lumber.

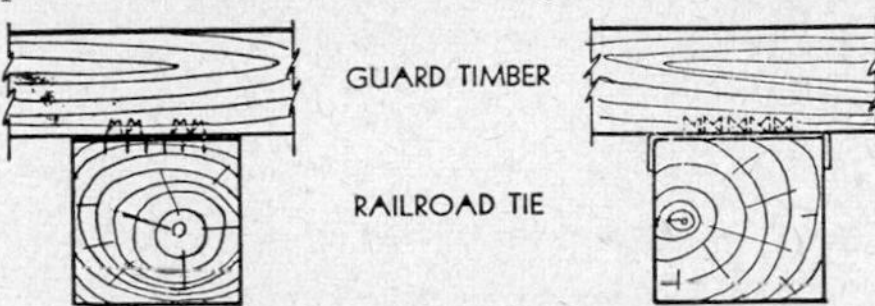

DM FIG. 6 Clamping plates used between railroad ties and guard timbers

Plates may be used with a bolt through each joint or at every third or fourth joint.

Design loads per clamping plate [1]

Species	Clamping-plate size *in.*	Type of joint connection	Load per clamping plate *lb*
Group A	5¼ x 5¼	¾-in. through bolt	3,400
		No through bolt [2]	2,460
	5 x 8	Teeth only (no through bolt)	2,920
		One flange only (no through bolt)	1,610
Group B	5¼ x 5¼	¾-in. through bolt	3,080
		No through bolt	2,230
	5 x 8	Teeth only (no through bolt)	2,660
		One flange only (no through bolt)	1,610
Group C	5¼ x 5¼	¾-in. through bolt	2,770
		No through bolt	2,010
	5 x 8	Teeth only (no through bolt)	2,390
		One flange only (no through bolt)	1,610

[1] Angle of load to grain of 90 deg.

[2] Joint members held in contact by bolts outside joint area.

Camber for Full-Load Deflection

FORMULA: $\Delta = K_1 \frac{L^3}{H} + K_2 \frac{L^2}{H}$

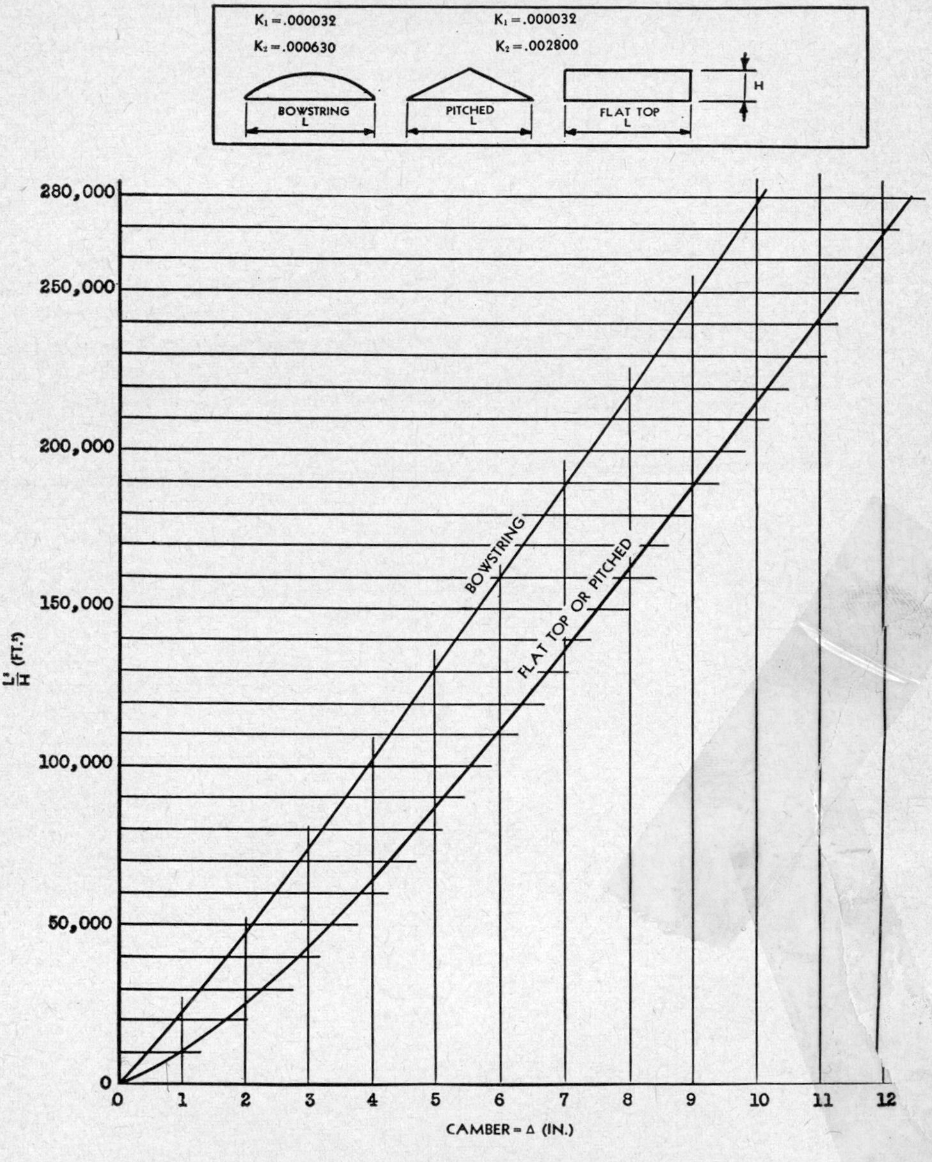

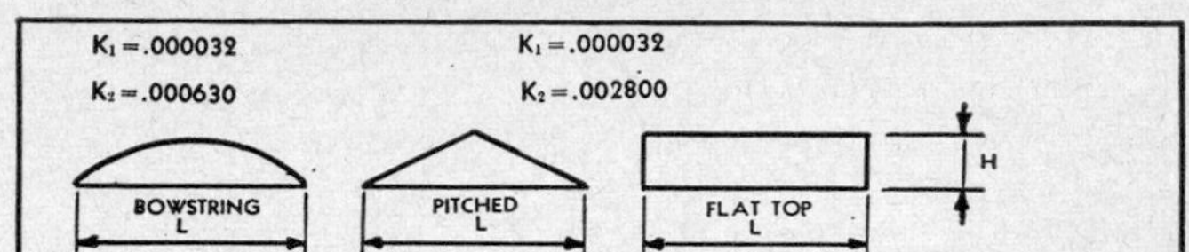

Net Section—Tension or Compression

The net section of a timber in a connector joint is usually adequate to transmit the full strength of the timber that can be developed outside of the joint when the lower grades of lumber are used. However, it may be desirable to check the strength of the net section of timbers when they are of the minimum size recommended herein for a given connector, particularly if a high stress-grade of lumber is used.

The critical or "net" section of a timber in a joint, which will generally pass through the centerline of a bolt and connector, occurs at the plane of maximum stress. The net cross section at this plane is equal to the full cross-sectional area of the timber minus the projected area of that portion of the connectors within the member and that portion

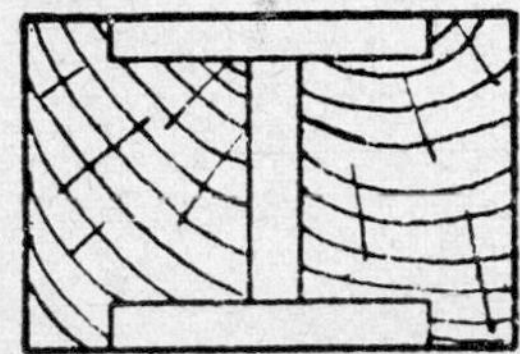

DM FIG. 7 Net cross section of timber (shaded area)

of the bolt hole, not within the connector projected area, located at this plane.

Because wood is able to support loads of short-time duration greatly in excess of permanently applied loads, computation of the required net section involves consideration of the different types and amounts of loadings.

The net cross-sectional area in square inches required at the critical section may be determined by multiplying the total load in pounds that is transferred through the critical section of the member, by the appropriate constant given in the table. Conversely, the total working load capacity in pounds of a given net area may be determined by dividing the net area in square inches by the appropriate constant.

The above recommendations assume that a knot approaching the maximum size allowed for the grade will not occur at, or within one-half the connector diameter of, the plane of the critical section. Unless the specifications and fabrication control provide that knots will not occur at the joint, stresses in the net section shall not exceed 87.5 per cent of the allowable extreme fiber in bending stress for the grade used.

Constants for use in determining required net section in square inches[1]

Type of loading	Thickness of wood member *in.*	Constants for each connector load group		
		Group A	Group B	Group C
Normal	4 or less	0.00043	0.00050	0.00061
	Over 4	0.00054	0.00063	0.00077
Permanent	4 or less	0.00048	0.00055	0.00067
	Over 4	0.00059	0.00069	0.00083
Snow	4 or less	0.00037	0.00044	0.00053
	Over 4	0.00047	0.00054	0.00067
Wind or Earthquake	4 or less	0.00032	0.00038	0.00045
	Over 4	0.00040	0.00047	0.00057

[1] The above constants, computed from basic recommendations of the Forest Products Laboratory, are based on a permissible stress at the net section equal to the basic stress for clear wood in compression parallel to grain.

Specification When Galvanizing Is Required

The galvanizing specifications for all types of timber connectors shall conform to ASTM Standard Specifications A 123–33 for galvanizing.

1. Zinc used in the bath shall be at least equal to "Prime Western."

2. The weight of the zinc coating per square foot of actual surface shall average

not less than 2.0 oz and no individual specimen shall show less than 1.8 oz, weight to be determined by stripping an entire piece by ASTM Standard Method A 90–39.

3. The zinc coating shall be adherent, smooth, continuous, and thorough, except that uncoated spots on the tongue and groove surfaces in contact will not be cause for rejection. It shall be free from imperfections such as bumps, blisters, gritty areas, uncoated spots, acid and black spots, dross, and flux.

4. When visual inspection and testing with ½-lb hammer is not conclusive, tests shall be made by the Preece method, in which case the minimum thickness of coating shall withstand at least 7 1-minute dips.

5. Test samples may be selected from deliveries at random and will be tested by the purchaser and at purchaser's expense.

Projected area of connectors and bolts

(For use in determining net sections)

Connector No.	Connector Size	Bolt diam. *in.*	Placement of connectors	Total projected area in square inches of connectors and bolts in lumber thickness of 1⅝ in.	2 in.	2⅝ in.	3 in.	3⅝ in.	4 in.	5½ in.	6 in.	7½ in.	8 in.
Split rings													
1	2½	½	One face	1.73	1.92	2.23	2.42	2.73	2.92	3.67	3.92	4.67	4.92
		½	Two faces	2.64	2.83	3.14	3.34	3.64	3.83	4.58	4.83	5.58	5.83
2	4	¾	One face	3.09	3.37	3.84	4.12	4.59	4.87	6.00	6.37	7.50	7.87
		¾	Two faces	4.97	5.25	5.72	6.00	6.47	6.75	7.16	8.25	9.38	9.75
Toothed rings													
1	2	½	One face	1.52	1.71	2.02	2.21	2.52	2.71	3.46	3.71	4.46	4.71
		½	Two faces	2.22	2.41	2.72	2.91	3.22	3.41	4.16	4.41	5.16	5.41
2	2⅝	⅝	One face	1.95	2.18	2.58	2.81	3.20	3.44	4.37	4.69	5.62	5.94
		⅝	Two faces	2.89	3.12	3.52	3.75	4.14	4.38	5.31	5.63	6.56	6.88
3	3⅜	¾	One face	2.46	2.74	3.21	3.49	3.96	4.24	5.37	5.74	6.87	7.24
		¾	Two faces	3.70	3.98	4.45	4.73	5.20	5.48	6.61	6.98	8.11	8.48
4	4	¾	One face	2.75	3.03	3.50	3.78	4.25	4.53	5.66	6.03	7.16	7.53
		¾	Two faces	4.28	4.56	5.03	5.31	5.78	6.06	7.19	7.56	8.69	9.06
Shear plates													
1	2⅝	¾	One face	1.92	2.20	2.67	2.95	3.42	3.70	4.83	5.20	6.33	6.70
		¾	Two faces	2.62	2.90	3.37	3.65	4.12	4.40	5.53	5.90	7.03	7.40
2	4	¾	One face	3.23	3.51	3.98	4.26	4.73	5.01	6.14	6.51	7.64	8.01
		¾	Two faces		5.52	5.99	6.27	6.74	7.02	8.15	8.52	9.65	10.02
2-A	4	⅞	One face	3.36	3.69	4.24	4.56	5.11	5.44	6.75	7.19	8.50	8.94
		⅞	Two faces		5.62	6.17	6.49	7.04	7.37	8.68	8.12	10.43	10.87
Spike grids													
1, 2	4⅛ x 4⅛	¾	One face	2.90	3.18	3.65	3.93	4.40	4.68	5.81	6.18	7.31	7.68
		¾	Two faces			5.34	5.62	6.09	6.37	7.50	7.87	9.00	9.37
		1	One face	3.18	3.56	4.18	4.56	5.18	5.56	7.06	7.56	9.06	9.56
		1	Two faces			5.75	6.13	6.75	7.13	8.63	9.13	10.63	11.

ASA SPECIFICATIONS FOR WOOD POLES

Standard values of ultimate fiber stress in bending for the 11 species of timber approved for poles by the American Standards Association have been established by that body and adopted by the National Electric Safety Code. The six values are shown below, with their applicable species of timber:

Group I: Fiber stress 3,600 psi
(See ASA Table 1)
Northern white (eastern) cedar

Group II: Fiber stress 5,600 psi
(See ASA Table 2)
Western red cedar

Group III: Fiber stress 6,000 psi
(See ASA Table 3)
Ponderosa pine

Group IV: Fiber stress 6,600 psi
(See ASA Table 4)
Western firs (true firs)
California red
Grand
Noble
Pacific silver
White
Lodgepole pine
Northern pine
Jack pine
Red (Norway) pine

Group V: Fiber stress 7,400 psi
(See ASA Table 5)
Douglas fir (all types)
Western hemlock
Southern pines
Longleaf Slash
Shortleaf Pond
Loblolly

Group VI: Fiber stress 8,400 psi
(See ASA Table 6)
Western larch

Ten classes of poles have been provided for each species to meet the requirements of utilities and other pole users. The first seven classes have ground-line dimensions computed for the following breaking loads applied 2 ft from the top of the pole:

Class	Load	Class	Load
Class 1	4,500	Class 5	1,900
Class 2	3,700	Class 6	1,500
Class 3	3,000	Class 7	1,200
Class 4	2,400		

In computing the accompanying tables, the required circumference at the ground line for the various species was calculated by the formula:

$$M_r = 0.000264 f C^3$$

in which:

M_r = the moment of resistance, in foot-pounds
f = the standard fiber stress, in pounds per square inch
C = the circumference, in inches

The ground-line circumferences thus obtained were converted to circumferences at distances of 6 ft from the butt by means of average taper values for the respective species. In arriving at the figures for 6-ft-from-butt circumference that appear in the dimension tables, the calculated figures were rounded up to the nearest ½ in.

The breaking load ratings given above are based on the minimum size pole for any given length and class. The ratings are conservative. Experience over a number of years has shown that the average size pole for a class, based on its 6-ft-from-butt circumference, is approximately midway between the minimum circumference permitted for the class and the minimum of the next higher class. In general, therefore, the excess size of the average pole of a given class will make it considerably stronger than its class rating, which is based on the minimum size permitted in the class.

No butt dimensions are specified for three classes—8, 9, and 10. These poles, bought on top sizes only, are used in lightly loaded lines for which high strengths are not required. Tops are such, however, that adequate ground circumferences for unimportant lines are obtained.

ASA TABLE 1 Dimensions of northern white cedar poles

(Fiber stress of 3,600 psi)

Class		1	2	3	4	5	6	7	8[2]	9[2]	10[2]
Min. circumference at top, *in.*		27	25	23	21	19	17	15	18	15	12
Length of pole *ft*	Ground-line dist. from butt[1] *ft*	Min. circumference 6 ft from butt *in.*									
16	3½					26.0	24.0	22.0			
18	3½			32.5	30.0	28.0	25.5	23.5			
20	4	39.5	37.0	34.0	31.5	29.0	27.0	25.0			
22	4	41.0	38.5	36.0	33.0	30.5	28.0	26.0			
25	5	43.5	41.0	38.0	35.5	32.5	30.0	28.0			
30	5½	47.5	44.5	41.5	38.5	35.5	33.0	30.5			
35	6	50.5	47.5	44.0	41.0	38.0	35.0	32.5			
40	6	53.5	50.0	46.5	43.5	40.0	37.0				
45	6½	56.0	52.5	49.0	45.5	42.0					
50	7	58.5	55.0	51.5	47.5	44.0					
55	7½	61.0	57.5	53.5	49.5	46.0					
60	8	63.5	59.5	55.5	51.5						

[1] The figures in this column are intended for use only if a definition of ground line is necessary in order to apply specification requirements relating to scars, straightness, etc.

[2] No butt requirements below horizontal line, which indicates length limits.

ASA TABLE 2 Dimensions of western red cedar poles

(Fiber stress of 5,600 psi)

Class		1	2	3	4	5	6	7	8[2]	9[2]	10[2]
Min. circumference at top, *in.*		27	25	23	21	19	17	15	18	15	12
Length of pole *ft*	Ground-line dist. from butt[1] *ft*	Min. circumference 6 ft from butt *in.*									
16	3½					23.0	21.5	19.5			
18	3½			28.5	26.5	24.5	22.5	21.0			
20	4	34.5	32.0	30.0	28.0	25.5	23.5	22.0			
22	4	36.0	33.5	31.5	29.0	27.0	25.0	23.0			
25	5	38.0	35.5	33.0	30.5	28.5	26.0	24.5			
30	5½	41.0	38.5	35.5	33.0	30.5	28.5	26.5			
35	6	43.5	41.0	38.0	35.5	32.5	30.5	28.0			
40	6	46.0	43.5	40.5	37.5	34.5	32.0				
45	6½	48.5	45.5	42.5	39.5	36.5					
50	7	50.5	47.5	44.5	41.0	38.0					
55	7½	52.5	49.5	46.0	42.5	39.5					
60	8	54.5	51.0	47.5	44.0						
65	8½	56.0	52.5	49.0	45.5						
70	9	57.5	54.0	50.5	47.0						
75	9½	59.5	55.5	52.0	48.5						
80	10	61.0	57.0	53.5	49.5						
85	10½	62.5	58.5	54.5							
90	11	63.5	60.0	56.0							
95	11	65.0	61.0	57.0							
100	11	66.0	62.0	58.0							

[1] The figures in this column are intended for use only if a definition of ground line is necessary in order to apply specification requirements relating to scars, straightness, etc.
[2] No butt requirements below horizontal line, which indicates length limits.

ASA TABLE 3 Dimensions of ponderosa pine poles

(Fiber stress of 6,000 psi)

Class		1	2	3	4	5	6	7	8[2]	9[2]	10[2]
Min. circumference at top, *in.*		27	25	23	21	19	17	15	18	15	12
Length of pole *ft*	Ground-line dist. from butt[1] *ft*	Min. circumference 6 ft from butt *in.*									
16	3½					22.5	21.0	19.5			
18	3½			28.0	26.0	24.0	22.0	20.5			
20	4	33.5	31.5	29.5	27.0	25.0	23.0	21.5			
22	4	35.0	33.0	30.5	28.5	26.5	24.5	22.5			
25	5	37.0	34.5	32.5	30.0	28.0	25.5	24.0			
30	5½	40.0	37.5	35.0	32.5	30.0	28.0	26.0			
35	6	42.5	40.0	37.5	34.5	32.0	30.0	27.5			
40	6	45.0	42.5	39.5	36.5	34.0	31.5	29.5			
45	6½	47.5	44.5	41.5	38.5	36.0	33.0	31.0			
50	7	49.5	46.5	43.5	40.0	37.5	34.5	32.0			
55	7½	51.5	48.5	45.0	42.0	39.0	36.0				
60	8	53.5	50.0	46.5	43.5						
65	8½	55.0	51.5	48.0	45.0						
70	9	56.5	53.0								

[1] The figures in this column are intended for use only if a definition of ground line is necessary in order to apply specification requirements relating to scars, straightness, etc.

[2] No butt requirements below horizontal line, which indicates length limits.

ASA TABLE 4 Dimensions of jack pine, lodgepole pine, red pine, and western fir poles

(Fiber stress of 6,600 psi)

Class		1	2	3	4	5	6	7	8[2]	9[2]	10[2]
Min. circumference at top, *in.*		27	25	23	21	19	17	15	18	15	12
Length of pole *ft*	Ground-line dist. from butt[1] *ft*	Min. circumference 6 ft from butt *in.*									
16	3½					22.0	20.5	19.0			
18	3½			27.5	25.5	23.5	21.5	20.0			
20	4	32.5	30.5	28.5	26.5	24.5	22.5	21.0			
22	4	34.0	32.0	30.0	27.5	25.5	23.5	22.0			
25	5	36.0	33.5	31.0	29.0	27.0	25.0	23.0			
30	5½	39.0	36.5	34.0	31.5	29.0	27.0	25.0			
35	6	41.5	38.5	36.0	33.5	31.0	28.5	26.5			
40	6	44.0	41.0	38.0	35.5	33.0	30.5	28.0			
45	6½	46.0	43.0	40.0	37.0	34.5	32.0	29.5			
50	7	48.0	45.0	42.0	39.0	36.0	33.5	31.0			
55	7½	49.5	46.5	43.5	40.5	37.5	34.5				
60	8	51.5	48.0	45.0	42.0	38.5					
65	8½	53.0	49.5	46.0	43.0						
70	9	54.5	51.0	47.5							
75	9½	56.0	52.5								

[1] The figures in this column are intended for use only if a definition of ground line is necessary in order to apply specification requirements relating to scars, straightness, etc.

[2] No butt requirements below horizontal line, which indicates length limits.

ASA TABLE 5 Dimensions of Douglas fir (all types), western hemlock, and southern pine poles

(Fiber stress of 7,400 psi)

Class		1	2	3	4	5	6	7	8[2]	9[2]	10[2]
Min. circumference at top, *in.*		27	25	23	21	19	17	15	18	15	12
Length of pole *ft*	Ground-line dist. from butt[1] *ft*	Min. circumference 6 ft from butt *in.*									
16	3½					21.5	19.5	18.0			
18	3½			26.5	24.5	22.5	21.0	19.0			
20	4	31.5	29.5	27.5	25.5	23.5	22.0	20.0			
22	4	33.0	31.0	29.0	26.5	24.5	23.0	21.0			
25	5	34.5	32.5	30.0	28.0	26.0	24.0	22.0			
30	5½	37.5	35.0	32.5	30.0	28.0	26.0	24.0			
35	6	40.0	37.5	35.0	32.0	30.0	27.5	25.5			
40	6	42.0	39.5	37.0	34.0	31.5	29.0	27.0			
45	6½	44.0	41.5	38.5	36.0	33.0	30.5	28.5			
50	7	46.0	43.0	40.0	37.5	34.5	32.0	29.5			
55	7½	47.5	44.5	41.5	39.0	36.0	33.5				
60	8	49.5	46.0	43.0	40.0	37.0	34.5				
65	8½	51.0	47.5	44.5	41.5	38.5					
70	9	52.5	49.0	46.0	42.5	39.5					
75	9½	54.0	50.5	47.0	44.0						
80	10	55.0	51.5	48.5	45.0						
85	10½	56.5	53.0	49.5							
90	11	57.5	54.0	50.5							
95	11	58.5	55.0	51.5							
100	11	60.0	56.0	52.5							

[1] The figures in this column are intended for use only if a definition of ground line is necessary in order to apply specification requirements relating to scars, straightness, etc.
[2] No butt requirements below horizontal line, which indicates length limits.

ASA TABLE 6 Dimensions of western larch poles

(Fiber stress of 8,400 psi)

Class		1	2	3	4	5	6	7	8[2]	9[2]	10[2]
Min. circumference at top, *in.*		27	25	23	21	19	17	15	18	15	12
Length of pole *ft*	Ground-line dist. from butt[1] *ft*	Min. circumference 6 ft from butt *in.*									
16	3½					20.5	18.5	17.5			
18	3½			25.0	23.5	21.5	20.0	18.5			
20	4	30.0	28.5	26.5	24.5	22.5	21.0	19.0			
22	4	31.5	29.5	27.5	25.5	23.5	21.5	20.0			
25	5	33.0	31.0	29.0	26.5	24.5	23.0	21.0			
30	5½	35.5	33.5	31.0	29.0	26.5	24.5	23.0			
35	6	38.0	35.5	33.0	31.0	28.5	26.5	24.5			
40	6	40.0	37.5	35.0	32.5	30.0	28.0	26.0			
45	6½	42.0	39.5	37.0	34.0	31.5	29.0	27.0			
50	7	44.0	41.0	38.5	35.5	33.0	30.5	28.5			
55	7½	45.5	42.5	40.0	37.0	34.5	31.5				
60	8	47.0	44.0	41.0	38.5	35.5	33.0				
65	8½	48.5	46.0	42.5	39.5	36.5					
70	9	50.0	47.0	44.0	41.0	38.0					
75	9½	51.5	48.0	45.0	42.0						
80	10	52.5	49.5	46.0	43.0						
85	10½	54.0	50.5	47.0							
90	11	55.0	51.5	48.5							
95	11	56.5	53.0	49.5							
100	11	57.5	54.0	50.5							

[1] The figures in this column are intended for use only if a definition of ground line is necessary in order to apply specification requirements relating to scars, straightness, etc.

[2] No butt requirements below horizontal line, which indicates length limits.

ASTM SPECIFICATIONS FOR ROUND TIMBER PILES

Any species of timber that will stand driving satisfactorily is suitable for piles, as the strains to which piles are subjected during driving are more severe than those resulting from permissible design loads.

Most piles are produced and ordered under the standard specification of the American Society for Testing Materials, which provides for three classes of piles. Classes A and B have identical physical specifications except for size. Class B piles provide a 12-in. diameter at cut-off and are suitable for all general construction. For extra heavy loads, however, and for developing full bearing for a 14-in. caps, such as those generally employed by the railroads on their trestles, Class A is usually specified.

Class C permits a lower quality of timber. This class is intended for falsework, for foundations that will be permanently submerged, and for such load support as can be developed with moderate driving.

The ASTM specification covers round timber piles to be used either untreated or treated with standard preservatives. Orders are construed as requiring treatment unless the contrary is directly specified.

The dimensions of ASTM Table 1 are from the "American Society for Testing Materials Specification for Round Timber Piles D25-55." Other specifications often used for timber piles are those of the American Railway Engineering Association and the American Association of State Highway Officials.

ASTM TABLE 1 Circumferences and diameters of timber piles

Length, ft	Class A						Class B						Class C					
	3 Ft from Butt				At Tip, min		3 Ft from Butt				At Tip, min		3 Ft from Butt				At Tip, min	
	Min		Max				Min		Max				Min		Max			
	Circumference, in.	Diameter (approx), in.	Circumference, in.	Diameter (approx), in.	Circumference, in.	Diameter (approx), in.	Circumference, in.	Diameter (approx), in.	Circumference, in.	Diameter (approx), in.	Circumference, in.	Diameter (approx), in.	Circumference, in.	Diameter (approx), in.	Circumference, in.	Diameter (approx), in.	Circumference, in.	Diameter (approx), in.
DOUGLAS-FIR, HEMLOCK, LARCH, PINE, SPRUCE, OR TAMARACK																		
Under 40	44	14	57	18	28	9	38	12	63	20	25	8	38[a]	12[a]	63	20	25	8
40 to 50 incl.	44	14	57	18	28	9	38	12	63	20	22	7	38	12	63	20	19	6
51 to 70 incl.	44	14	57	18	25	8	41	13	63	20	22	7	38	12	63	20	19	6
71 to 90 incl.	44	14	63	20	22	7	41	13	63	20	19	6	38	12	63	20	19	6
Over 90	44	14	63	20	19	6	41	13	63	20	16	5	38	12	63	20	16	5
OAK AND OTHER HARDWOODS, CYPRESS																		
Under 30	44	14	57	18	28	9	38	12	57	18	25	8	38[a]	12[a]	63	20	25	8
30 to 40 incl.	44	14	57	18	28	9	41	13	63	20	22	7	38	12	63	20	22	7
Over 40	44	14	57	18	25	8	41	13	63	20	19	6	38	12	63	20	19	6
CEDAR																		
Under 30	44	14	69	22	28	9	38	12	69	22	25	8	38[a]	12[a]	69	22	25	8
30 to 40 incl.	44	14	69	22	28	9	41	13	69	22	25	8	38	12	69	22	25	8
Over 40	44	14	69	22	25	8	41	13	69	22	22	7	38	12	69	22	22	7

[a] In Class C piles, a minimum circumference of 31 in. or diameter of 10 in. at cut-off may be specified for lengths of 20 ft and under.

Glossary

Air-dried (see *Seasoning*)

Annual growth ring (see *Ring*)

Bark The outside layer of a tree, composed of a living, inner bark called "phloem" and an outer bark of dead tissue.

Bastard-sawed Hardwood lumber in which the annual rings make angles of 30 to 60 deg with the surface of the piece.

Beams and stringers Lumber of rectangular cross section, 5 in. or more thick and 8 in. or more wide, graded with respect to its strength when loaded on the narrow face.

Bird's-eye A small spot with the wood fibers arranged around it in the form of an ellipse so as to give the appearance of an eye.

Boards (see *Lumber*)

Board-foot A measure of quantity, based on nominal dimensions, equal to 144 cu in., or a board 1 in. thick and 1 ft square. Also known as 1 foot board measure, or 1 fbm.

Bow A deforming curve in a piece along its length. It is measured at the point of greatest deviation from a straight line drawn from end to end of the piece.

Boxed pith Pith between the four faces on an end of a piece.

Brashness A condition of wood characterized by low resistance to shock and by abrupt failure across the grain without normal splintering.

Broad-leaved trees (see *Hardwoods*)

Burl A large wart-like excrescence on a tree trunk containing the dark piths of a large number of buds, which rarely develop.

Cambium The layer of tissue just beneath the bark from which the new wood and bark cells of each year's growth develop.

Cell A general term for the minute units of wood structure, including fibers, vessels, and other elements of diverse structure and functions.

Cellulose The carbohydrate that is the principal constituent of wood and forms the framework of the cells.

Check A lengthwise separation of the wood, which usually occurs across the rings of annual growth. When it extends from one surface of the piece to another, it is called a "through check," or "split."

Clear wood A wood member free from splits, checks, shakes, knots, etc.

Close grain (see *Grain*)

Coarse grain (see *Grain*)

Conifer (see *Softwoods*)

Connectors (see *Timber connectors*)

Crook A deforming curve along the edge of a piece. It is measured at the point of greatest deviation from a straight line drawn from end to end of the piece.

Cross break A separation of the wood cells across the grain, such as that caused by tension resulting from unequal shrinkage or mechanical stress.

Cross grain (see *Grain*)

Cup A deforming curve in a piece across its grain or width. It is measured at the point of greatest deviation from a straight line drawn from edge to edge of the piece.

Decay Disintegration of wood substance due to the action of wood-destroying fungi.

incipient decay The early stage of decay in which the disintegration has not proceeded far enough to soften or otherwise impair the hardness of the wood perceptibly.

typical or advanced decay The stage of decay in which the disintegration is readily recognized because the wood has become punky, soft, spongy, stringy, pitted, or crumbly.

Density rule Rules for estimating the density (mass per unit volume) of wood based on the proportion of summerwood and rate of growth.

Diagonal grain (see *Grain*)

Diffuse-porous woods Hardwoods in which the pores are practically uniform in size throughout each annual ring, or decrease slightly in size toward the outer border of the ring.

Dimension (see *Lumber*)

Dimension stock Square or flat stock—usually in pieces smaller than the minimum sizes admitted by standard lumber grades—that is rough, dressed, green, or dry, and cut to the approximate dimension required for the various products of woodworking factories.

Dote "Dote," "doze," and "rot" are synonymous with decay.

Dry rot A term loosely applied to many types of decay but especially to that which, when in an advanced stage, permits the wood to be crushed easily to a dry powder. The term is actually a misnomer for any decay, because all fungi require considerable moisture for growth, and the wood must have been moist at the time the "dry" rot occurred.

Durability A general term for permanence or lastingness, frequently used to refer to the degree of resistance of a species or of an individual piece of wood to decay. In this connection, "resistance to decay" is a more specific term.

Edge grain (see *Grain*)

Empty-cell process Any process for impregnating wood with preservatives or chemicals, in which air is imprisoned in the wood under the pressure of the entering preservative; the air expands when the pressure is released and drives out part of the injected preservative.

Encased knot (see *Knot*)

Extractives Substances in wood, not an integral part of the cellular structure, that can be dissolved out with inert solvents.

Equilibrium moisture content The moisture content at which wood neither gains nor loses moisture when surrounded by air at a given relative humidity and temperature.

Face width The width of the face of a piece of dressed and matched or shiplapped lumber, excluding the width of the tongue or lap. The amount of flooring, ceiling, siding, or other matched items required to cover a given area should be computed on the basis of the face width of the pieces (see *Over-all width*).

Factory and shop lumber (see *Lumber*)

Fiber A comparatively long (from $^1/_{25}$ in., or less, to ⅓ in.), narrow, tapering cell closed at both ends.

Fiber-saturation point The stage in the drying or in the wetting of wood at which the cell walls are saturated but the cell cavities are free from water.

Figure The pattern produced in a wood surface by irregular coloration and by annual growth rings, rays, knots, and such deviations from regular grain as interlocking and wavy grain.

Fireproofing The process of making wood resistant to fire to a degree that it is difficult to ignite and will not support its own combustion.

Flat grain (see *Grain*)

Flitch A thick piece of lumber with wane (bark) on one or more edges.

Full-cell process Any process for impregnating wood with preservatives or chemicals in which a vacuum is drawn to remove air from the wood so that the cells may be filled with the preservative.

Girder A large sized beam used as a main structural member, normally for the support of other beams.

Glued-laminated wood (see *Laminated wood*)

Grade Any of the quality classes into which lumber products are segregated.

Grain The direction, size, arrangement, appearance, or quality of the fibers in wood.

- **close grain** Wood with narrow and inconspicuous annual rings. The term is sometimes used to designate wood having small and closely spaced pores, but in this sense the term "fine-textured" is more often used.
- **coarse grain** Wood with wide and conspicuous annual rings in which there is considerable difference between springwood and summerwood. The term is also used to designate wood with large pores, but in this sense the term "coarse-textured" is more often used.
- **cross grain** Wood in which the cells or fibers do not run parallel with the axis or sides of a piece.
- **diagonal grain** Wood in which the annual rings are at an angle with the axis of a piece as a result of sawing at an angle with the axis of the tree.
- **edge grain** Wood in which the rings (so-called grain) form an angle of 45 deg or more with the surface of the piece; also called "vertical grain" and "quartersawed."
- **flat grain** Wood in which the rings form an angle of less than 45 deg with the surface of the piece; also called "plain-sawed."
- **interlocking grain** Wood in which the fibers are inclined in one direction in a number of rings of annual growth, then gradually reverse and are inclined in an opposite direction in succeeding growth rings, then reverse again.
- **open grain** Common classification of painters for wood with large pores; also called "coarse-textured."
- **plain-sawed** Another term for flat grain, used generally in hardwoods.
- **quartersawed** Another term for edge grain, used generally in hardwoods.
- **spiral grain** A type of growth in which the fibers take a spiral course about the bole of a tree instead of the normal vertical course. The spiral may extend right-handed or left-handed around the tree trunk.
- **vertical grain** Another term for edge grain.
- **wavy grain** Wood in which the fibers collectively take the form of waves or undulations.

Green Unseasoned, wet.

Growth rate (see *Rate of growth*)

Growth ring (see *Ring*)

Hardwoods The botanical group of

trees that are broadleaved. The term has no reference to the actual hardness of the wood.

Heart, Heartwood The wood extending from the pith to the sapwood, the cells of which no longer participate in the life processes of the tree. Heartwood is usually darker in color than sapwood.

Heavy Timber Construction Construction composed of planks or laminated floors supported by beams or girders. Exterior walls may be frame, masonry, or metal. For "Mill Construction," they must be of masonry.

Horizontal lamination (see *Laminated wood*)

Imperfect manufacture A term including all defects or blemishes that are produced in manufacturing, such as chipped grain, loosened grain, raised grain, torn grain, skips in dressing, variation in sawing, miscutting, machine burn, machine gouge, mismatching, and insufficient tongue or groove.

Interlocking grain (see *Grain*)

Joists and planks Lumber of rectangular cross section, from 2 in. up to, but not including, 5 in. thick, and 4 in. or more wide, graded with respect to its strength in bending when loaded either on the narrow face (joist) or on the wide face (plank). If 5 in. or more thick, the lumber is known as beams and stringers.

Kiln-dried (see *Seasoning*)

Knot The cross section in lumber of a branch or limb that was originally embedded in the tree but was cut through in the process of lumber manufacture. Knots are classified according to size, form, quality, and occurrence. Knot size is determined by averaging maximum length and maximum width, unless otherwise specified.

encased knot A knot whose rings of annual growth are not intergrown and homogeneous with those of the surrounding wood. The encasement may be partial or complete and may be of pitch or bark.

intergrown knot A knot whose rings of annual growth are completely intergrown with those of the surrounding wood.

Lamella A short piece of lumber used in the construction of the network arches that form a lamella roof.

Laminated wood An assembly of wood built up of plies or laminations that have been joined either with glue or with mechanical fastenings. The term is most frequently applied if the plies are too thick to be classified as veneer and if the grain of all plies is parallel.

horizontal lamination A method of lamination in which the wider dimension of each lamina, or layer, is approximately perpendicular to the direction of load.

vertical lamination A method of lamination in which the wider dimension of each lamina is approximately parallel to the direction of load.

Lignin A principal constituent of wood, second only to cellulose. It incrusts the cell walls and cements the cells together.

Lumber Lumber is the product of the saw and planing mill that is not further manufactured than by the processes of sawing, resawing, passing lengthwise through a standard planing mill, cross-cutting to length, and working. Lumber of thickness not in excess of ¼ in. to be used for veneering is classified as veneer.

factory and shop lumber Lumber intended to be cut up for further manufacture. It is graded on the basis of the percentage of its area that will produce a limited number of cuttings of a specified, or a given minimum, size and quality.

yard lumber Lumber of all sizes and patterns that is intended for general building purposes. The grading of yard lumber is based on the intended use of the particular grade and is applied to each piece with reference to its size and length if further manufacture is not considered.

strips Yard lumber less than 2 in. thick and less than 8 in. wide.

boards Yard lumber less than 2 in. thick, and 8 in. or more wide.

timbers Yard lumber 5 in. or more in least dimension.

dimension All yard lumber except boards, strips, and timbers; that is, yard lumber from 2 in. to, but not including, 5 in. thick, and of any width.

Matched lumber Lumber edge dressed and shaped for a tongue-and-groove joint when pieces are laid edge to edge or end to end.

center matched Matched lumber that is tongued and grooved in the exact center of the material on opposite edges.

standard matched Matched lumber that is tongued and grooved to correspond with a specification provided by the grading rules other than for the center of the thickness of the material.

Millwork Generally all building materials made of finished wood and manufactured in millwork plants and planing mills: doors, window and door frames, sashes, blinds, porch work, mantels, panel work, stairways, and special woodwork. Excluded are finished-dressed four sides, siding, or partition, which are items of yard lumber.

Moisture content Weight of the water contained in wood, usually expressed in percentage of the weight of the oven-dry wood.

Moisture gradient A condition of graduated moisture content between the inner and outer portions of the wood, caused by the loss or absorption of moisture.

Moistureproofing The process of making wood resistant to change in moisture content, especially to entrance of moisture.

Nominal dimension The dimension of lumber corresponding approximately to the size before dressing to actual size, and used for convenience in defining size and in computing quantities.

Open grain (see *Grain*)

Over-all width The total width of a piece of dressed and matched or shiplapped lumber, including the width of the tongue or lap. The amount of such lumber required to cover a given area should not be computed on the basis of the over-all width, because the tongue or lap is the means of joining the pieces and does not "cover" any surface (see *Face width*).

Peck Channeled or pitted areas or pockets of localized decay found in cedar and cypress.

Pile A round timber driven into the ground to be used as part of a foundation.

Pitch The resin of certain coniferous trees.

Pitch pocket A well defined opening between rings of annual growth, usually containing or once having contained pitch, either solid or liquid. Bark also may be present in the pocket.

Pith The small, soft core occurring in the structural center of a log. The wood immediately surrounding the pith often contains small checks, shakes, or numerous pin knots, and is discolored; any such combination of characteristics is called "heart center."

Plank (see *Joists and planks*)

Plywood A piece of wood made of three or more layers of veneer joined with glue and usually laid with the grain of adjoining plies at right angles. Almost always an odd number of plies is used to secure balanced construction.

Plain-sawed (see *Grain*)

Planing-mill products Products worked to pattern, usually in strip form, such as flooring, ceiling, and siding.

Pocket rot Typical decay that appears in the form of a hole, pocket, or area of soft rot usually surrounded by apparently sound wood.

Pole A round timber used upright for the purpose of support, primarily for nonstructural applications such as telephone poles.

Pore (see *Vessel*)

Posts and timbers Lumber of square or approximately square cross section, 5 x 5 and larger, graded primarily for use as posts or columns carrying longitudinal load but adapted for miscellaneous uses in which strength in bending is not especially important.

Preservative Any substance applied to or injected into wood to protect it from attack of fungi, insects, or marine borers.

Quartersawed (see *Grain*)

Radial Coincident with a radius from the axis of the tree or log to the circumference.

Rate of growth The rate at which a tree has laid on wood, measured radially in the trunk or in lumber cut from the trunk. The unit of measure in use is the number of annual growth rings per inch.

Rays Strips of cells extending radially within a tree and varying in height from a few cells in some species to 4 in. or more in oak. The rays serve primarily to store food and transport it horizontally in the tree.

Ring, annual growth The growth layer put on in a single growth year.

Ring-porous woods A group of hardwoods in which the pores are comparatively large at the beginning of each annual ring and decrease in size more or less abruptly toward the outer portion of the ring, thus forming a distinct inner zone of pores called "springwood" and an outer zone with smaller pores called "summerwood."

Rot (see *Decay*)

Sap The fluids in a tree except special secretions and excretions, such as oleoresin.

Sapwood The outer layers of growth in a tree, exclusive of bark, that contain its living elements. It is usually lighter in color than heartwood. Under most conditions, sapwood is more susceptible to decay than heartwood, and as a rule, more permeable to liquids. It is not, however, essentially weaker or stronger than heartwood of the same species.

Seasoning The evaporation or extraction of moisture from green or partially dried wood.

- **air-dried or air-seasoned** Dried by exposure to the atmosphere, usually in a yard, without artificial heat.
- **kiln-dried** Dried in a kiln with the use of artificial heat.

Second growth Timber that has grown after the removal by any means of all or a large portion of the previous stand.

Shake A separation along the grain, most of which occurs between the rings of annual growth.

Shiplapped lumber Lumber that is edge dressed to make a lapped joint.

Shop lumber (see *Lumber*)

Side-cut A cut eliminating pith in a piece.

Softwoods The botanical group of trees with needle-like or scale-like leaves, often referred to as conifers. The term softwood has no reference to the softness of the wood.

Spiral grain (see *Grain*)

Split A check or lengthwise separation of wood, usually across the rings of annual growth, that extends through a piece from one surface to the opposite surface, or to an adjoining surface; also called "through check."

Springwood The more or less open and porous tissue marking the inner part of each annual ring, formed early in the period of growth. It is usually less dense and weaker mechanically than summerwood.

Stain, blue A bluish or grayish discoloration of the sapwood caused by the growth of certain mold-like fungi on the surface and in the interior of the piece.

Strength The properties of wood that enable it to resist different forces or loads. Strength may apply to any one of the mechanical properties, such as strength in bending, hardness, strength in compression, etc.

Stringers (see *Beams and stringers*)

Strips (see *Lumber*)

Structural lumber Lumber that is 2 in. or more thick and 4 in. or more wide, intended for use where working stresses are required. The grading of structural lumber is based on both the strength of the piece and the use of the entire piece.

Summerwood The dense, fibrous outer portion of each annual ring, usually without conspicuous pores, formed late in the growing period, not necessarily in summer. It is usually more dense and stronger mechanically than springwood.

Tangential Coincident with a tangent at the circumference of a tree or log, or parallel to such a tangent. In common parlance, however, "tangential" often means roughly coincident with a growth ring.

Texture A term often used interchangeably with "grain."

Timber A broad term including standing trees and certain products cut from them, including lumber 5 in. or larger in least nominal dimension (see *Posts and timbers*).

round timber Timber used in the original round form, such as poles, piling, and mine timbers.

standing timber Timber still on the stump.

Timber connectors Rings, grids, plates, or dowels of metal or wood set in adjoining members, usually in pre-cut grooves or holes, to fasten the members together in conjunction with bolts.

Twist A form of warp caused by the twisting or winding of the edges of a board.

Veneer Thin sheets of wood (see *Plywood*).

Vertical grain (see *Grain*)

Vertical lamination (see *Laminated wood*)

Vessel Wood cells of comparatively large diameter that have open ends and that are set one above the other, forming continuous tubes. The openings of the vessels on the surface of a piece of wood are usually referred to as pores.

Virgin growth The original growth of mature trees.

Wane Bark on the edge or corner of a piece, or the absence of wood in a piece from any cause.

Wavy grain (see *Grain*)

Weathering The mechanical and chemical disintegration and discoloration of the surface of wood caused both by exposure to light and by the alternate shrinking and swelling of the surface fibers from continual weather-induced changes in moisture content. Weathering does not include decay.

Workability The degree of ease and smoothness of cut obtainable in a material.

Working Shrinkage or swelling of a piece of wood with change in moisture content.

Yard lumber (see *Lumber*)

Abbreviations of Terms

A.D.	Air-dried
a.l.	All lengths
B&S	Beam and stringer
bd ft	Board foot
bm	Board (foot) measure
btr.	Better
clr.	Clear
CM	Center matched—that is, the tongue and groove
com.	Common
cu ft	Cubic foot
D&H	Dressed and headed—that is, dressed one or two sides and worked to tongue and groove joints on both the edge and the ends.
D&M	Dressed and matched—that is, dressed one or two sides and tongued and grooved on the edges. The match may be center or standard.
D&SM	Dressed one or two sides and standard matched
D2S&CM	Dressed two sides and center matched
D2S&M	Dressed two sides and center or standard matched
D2S&SM	Dressed two sides and standard matched
dim.	Dimension
ECM	Ends center matched
E.G.	Edge grain
EM	Ends matched, either center or standard
ESM	Ends standard matched
fbm	Feet board measure
F.G.	Flat grain
ft	Foot or feet
Hdwd.	Hardwood
Hrtwd.	Heartwood
in.	Inch or inches
J&P	Joist and plank
k.d.	Knocked-down
K.D.	Kiln-dried
kip	Kilo-pound (1,000 pounds)
lb	Pound or pounds
lbr.	Lumber
l.c.l.	Less carload lots
lgth.	Length
lin ft	Linear foot; that is, 12 in.
Mbm	Thousand (feet) board measure
No.	Number
o.c.	On centers
P&T	Post and timber
res.	Resawed
rip.	Ripped
r.l.	Random lengths
Sap.	Sapwood
Sftwd.	Softwood
SM	Standard matched
Sq.E.	Square edge
S1E	Surfaced one edge
S2E	Surfaced two edges
S1S	Surfaced one side
S2S	Surfaced two sides
S1S1E	Surfaced one side and one edge
S2S1E	Surfaced two sides and one edge
S1S2E	Surfaced one side and two edges
S4S	Surfaced four sides

S4SCS	Surfaced four sides with a calking seam on each edge
S&CM	Surfaced one or two sides and center matched
S&M	Surfaced and matched—that is, surfaced on one or two sides and tongued and grooved on the edges—with the match either center or standard.
S&SM	Surfaced one or two sides and standard matched
S2S&CM	Surfaced two sides and center matched
S2S&M	Surfaced two sides and (center or standard) matched
S2S&SM	Surfaced two sides and standard matched
T&G	Tongued and grooved
Tbrs.	Timbers
V.G.	Vertical grain
wt	Weight
yd	Yard or yards

Index

C

G

H

I

T

U

V

W

Y